READING THE RIGHT TEXT

READING

AN ANTHOLOGY OF CONTEMPORARY

THE RIGHT TEXT

HINESE DRAMA

Edited and with an Introduction by

Xiaomei Chen

University of Hawai'i Press | Honolulu

© 2003 University of Hawai'i Press
All rights reserved
Printed in the United States of America
08 07 06 05 04 03   6 5 4 3 2 1

Library of Congress Cataloging-in-Publication Data
Reading the right text : an anthology of contemporary
Chinese drama / edited and with an introduction by
Xiaomei Chen.
    p. cm.
ISBN 0-8248-2505-5 (alk. paper)—
ISBN 0-8248-2689-2 (pbk. : alk. paper)
1. Chinese drama—20th century—Translations into
English. I. Title: Anthology of contemporary Chinese
drama. II. Chen, Xiaomei.

PL2658.E5 R43 2003
895.1'2508—dc21

                           2002155363

University of Hawai'i Press books are printed on acid-free
paper and meet the guidelines for permanence and
durability of the Council on Library Resources.

Designed by Santos Barbasa, Jr.
Printed by Maple-Vail Book Manufacturing Group

CONTENTS

PREFACE

Due to the complicated history of Western sinology, modern Chinese spoken drama *(huaju)*, from its inception to contemporary times, has received little attention in scholarly research, let alone in terms of important texts translated into the English language. From the Republican period to the post-Maoist period, Edward Gunn's *Twentieth-Century Chinese Drama: An Anthology* (1983) was the only work that, in a single volume, introduced translated texts. Martha P. Y. Cheung and Jane C. C. Lai's *Oxford Anthology of Contemporary Chinese Drama* (1997) contributed to our appreciation of Chinese drama by presenting five new plays, including works from Taiwan and Hong Kong. This pan-Chinese anthology would have been more helpful, however, had it contained a more substantial introduction that explained the historical background and critical issues of these three geopolitical locales, as well as the differences that characterized their diverse, and often opposing, ideological positions and histories. Similarly, Shiao-Ling S. Yu's *Chinese Drama after the Cultural Revolution* (1996) could also have provided readers with a more extensive introduction both to the plays and to their dramatic traditions. The critical introduction to theater of the post-Maoist period that precedes the four plays and one film script in Haiping Yan's *Theater and Society: An Anthology of Contemporary Chinese Drama* (1998) situates Chinese plays in their cultural and regional contexts in post-Maoist China so that teachers and students of drama may understand how these works emerged. Nevertheless, the majority of the plays in these anthologies are those better known for their artistic innovations.

This anthology seeks to engage scholars and students who have little or no background in Chinese culture but are eager to include modern Chinese culture in their comparative and cross-cultural curriculum. To this end the work presents here six plays, five of which are translated into English for the first time by established literary scholars. My introduction weaves together a history of twentieth-century Chinese culture and theater, highlighting the origin and development of different dramatic subgenres. I delineate six critical approaches for a comparative audience to situate each of the six plays in a particular theoretical context within their indigenous historical and cultural contexts. They include (a) the quarrels between form and content in experimental theater; (b) the paradox of the local and the global in regional drama; (c) the politics of representation of the masses in worker plays; (d) the reconstruction of revolutionary memory and popular culture in history plays; (e) gender, sexuality, and body politics in soldier plays; and (f) the negotiating space between the urban and the rural in peasant plays. Focusing on a particular play as an example of one approach by no means excludes the play from interpretation through other approaches. Indeed, it is possible to examine each play with a combination of different approaches, or to see some, if not all, of the approaches at work in different moments of one play. Similarily, seeing a play as a recent development of one particular subgenre does not, I believe, preclude it from being read as relating to other subgenres. In fact, examining the continuities and discontinuities among various subgenres and the connections between different approaches in order to flesh out these elements helps us greatly to appreciate the richness and complexities of both modern Chinese culture and its product, the texts of spoken drama.

This anthology is also meant as a companion volume to *Acting the Right Part: Political Theater and Popular Drama in Contemporary China*, my critical study of Chinese plays from the 1960s to early 1990s in the historical and ideological contexts of the People's Republic of China. While investigating the problematic relationship of self, subject, agent, state-building, and "national others" in the production and reception of drama in Maoist and post-Maoist China, it treats Chinese drama as an extended form of political drama, in which everyone acts the "right" part, both onstage and offstage, for his or her own survival. It also reflects the wide range of critical issues regarding cultural performance, gender studies, comparative theater, and the rethinking of the postcolonial paradigm in the representation of China in the post–cold war and post-socialist era. Since model revolutionary plays performed during the Cultural Revolution (1966–1976) have been extensively translated (see Appendix in *Acting the Right Part* for a list of plays in English translation), this anthology focuses on several important plays of the post-Maoist period that continued to address some of the fundamental concerns of Maoist China. In selecting the plays for this volume, I tried to balance representation of the social significance of the plays with artistic innovations recognized by the drama critics and the audiences of the time.

While working on *Acting the Right Part* and this volume, I constantly reflected on my teaching experience at Ohio State University, where I taught modern Chinese drama at the undergraduate and graduate levels, both to students with no knowledge of Chinese history and culture who needed to fulfill a general-education category in the non-Western contexts, and to students pursuing undergraduate and graduate degrees in Chinese literature and culture. I had long hoped to write scholarly works such as this for classroom use not just to better address students' needs in understanding Chinese theater and culture, but to provide them with the critical and analytical skills to access a non-Western culture beyond their limited experience in the classroom. This anthology is therefore dedicated to all the students I taught at Ohio State University, and to those students and scholars who may find a detour to Chinese theater study an exhilarating and rewarding adventure.

I am indebted to the six Chinese playwrights who granted me permission for English translations of their works and provided me with information for their biographical sketches. I want to express my deep gratitude to the six translators for their willingness to undertake this project, their excellent skills, and their patience with me to see this project through. I owe much to the enduring friendship of Kirk A. Denton, who remains an inspiration for solid and careful scholarship, and of Patricia Sieber, whose stimulating conversations about the Introduction encouraged its completion. I thank my colleagues and friends at Ohio State University, in the Department of East Asian Languages and Literatures and the Department of Comparative Studies, for their nurturing and supportive environment and for their belief in my work.

I am deeply grateful to Patricia Crosby, executive editor of the University of Hawai'i Press, for her unwavering belief in this project and for her cheerful spirit in steering through this project from beginning to end; to Cheri Dunn, managing editor, for her patience, understanding, and timely help; and to Karen Weller-Watson, copy editor, for her tireless effort and professional skills. This book could not have come about without their support and wisdom.

Mark Halperin remains the most patient reader of my work. I am grateful for his humor, inspiration, and encouragement.

Introduction

Xiaomei Chen

In Rodgers and Hammerstein's *The King and I,* the protagonist Anna comes across as both an Orientalist and a feminist. A nineteenth-century British widow, she will not stay home waiting for a chaperon or a second husband; instead she travels to Siam (as Thailand was known until 1939) to instruct in the English language and in Western culture the seven dozen children of King Mongkut. During her five years at the Siamese court, she has an ambiguous relationship with the Orient. King Mongkut's unique qualities fascinate her, but she becomes indignant at the brutal oppression in his royal harem, where thousands of women and children are confined as wives, concubines, captives, and slaves. As in Anna Leonowens' 1870s memoirs, on which *The King and I* is based, Anna exhibits the European imperialist's feeling that the natives of the Orient must be turned into a civilized and enlightened people. At the same time, she empathizes with the Siamese women, identifying with them as a woman and as a member of Victorian England's lower classes.[1] Thus an American dramatic representation of the Orient can be seen through the windows of race (white/colored), nation (Britain/Siam), gender (patriarchal king/Siamese woman), and class (poor British woman/establishment).

All these issues, as we shall find, can serve as points of comparison for a critical study of modern Chinese spoken drama. For example, in the third scene, the king's singers and dancers perform a play adapted from Harriet Beecher Stowe's *Uncle Tom's Cabin,* to demonstrate to the British royal visitors that the Siamese are already sufficiently civilized and require no British instruction. While playing Eliza, an escaped slave from Kentucky searching for the lover who has been sold to "Oheeo," Tuptim, one of King Mongkut's captive women, steps out of character to condemn "any King who pursues a slave who is unhappy" and tries to join her lover.[2]

The basis for this Siamese play within an American play is nowhere to be found in Anna Leonowens' memoirs, although Leonowens does write about the Siamese people's love of traditional drama and the anguish that women endured as slaves. These two themes, however, possibly inspired the creation of the Siamese woman in Margaret Landon's 1944 bestseller, *Anna and the King of Siam,* based on the author's research into Leonowens' life and writing. Landon's novel portrays a Siamese woman so moved by the courageous spirit expressed in *Uncle Tom's Cabin* that she turned "the beloved story into Siamese."[3] As a token of respect for the American woman, she adopted the name Harriet Beecher Stowe as the first part of her Siamese name. After her experience in Siam, Leonowens befriended Stowe while in America and shared her antislavery stand, which led to the Siamese staging of *Uncle Tom's Cabin* in *The King and I.* The combination of distinctive cultures rooted in history and drama is a hallmark of the long Orientalist tradition of Broadway (and Hollywood) flirting with exotic "others" (women in particular), as exemplified by such other theatrical creations as *Madame Butterfly* and *Miss Saigon.* The 1999 movie *Anna and the King* further testifies to the continuing fascination with crosscultural romance.

The Siamese staging of *Uncle Tom's Cabin* might strike us as an ingenious dramatic device for linking British, Siamese, and American experiences. The historical connection between *Uncle Tom's Cabin* and the origin of modern Chinese drama, however, does not require any comparable stroke of imagination. Despite early contacts with Western drama through missionary schools and foreign residents, modern Chinese drama did not really begin until the 1907 premiere of *The Black Slave Cries Out to Heaven (Heinu yutianlu)*.[4] This full-fledged dramatic adaptation of *Uncle Tom's Cabin*, by Spring Willow Society, formed by a group of overseas Chinese students in Tokyo, embodies a paradox in the development of modern Chinese drama. Using the American founding fathers' vision of equality to oppose the Confucian tradition, the first generation of Chinese dramatists was nevertheless attracted to *Uncle Tom's Cabin* for its denunciation of the slavery system, and its critique of the hypocrisy in the founding principles of the United States. Both Chinese and American writers saw in *Uncle Tom's Cabin* a springboard from which to challenge their own cultures. Indeed, Lin Shu's Chinese translation of Stowe's novel, in 1901, on which the dramatic adaptation was based, was triggered by a fury over reports of the brutal treatment of Chinese coolies overseas by the American "white race," who oppressed both the "black race" and the "yellow race." At its inception, therefore, modern Chinese drama took seriously the issues of racial conflict, national identity, and resistance to domestic and foreign oppressors, and developed these issues in subsequent plays during the War of Resistance to Japan, when the Japanese—that same "yellow race," and yet an ethnic "other"—became the arch enemy of the Chinese nation.

Indeed, even before the war against foreign aggressors broke out, *Uncle Tom's Cabin* was also successfully staged as a class-conflict play in the Jiangxi Communist Soviet areas in 1931. Li Bozhao, a female playwright in the Red Army, adapted her *Peasant Slaves (Nongnu)* from a dramatic version of Stowe's work she saw in the USSR. Unlike the performance by the Spring Willow Society in 1907, Li's production contained four acts, ending with the oppressed black slaves defeating white slave owners. Although racial conflict did not figure in the Chinese dramatic scene of the 1930s, local peasant audiences responded enthusiastically to the theme of class oppression against local landowners. The performances often ended to audiences' applause and slogans such as "down with slave owners" and "down with landowners."[5] A 1961 adaptation of *Uncle Tom's Cabin (Heinu hen)*, however, strikes a different tone. Although class conflict remained a major part of communist ideology, Sun Weishi, a female director who had received formal training in theater in the USSR for six years, attempted to break the "fourth wall" of illusionary theater and expanded dramatic actions to other space such as that of the orchestra.[6] In modern China, where female playwrights and directors were few, significantly both Li and Sun were drawn to this Western drama for its political and artistic appeal.

In terms of formalist innovations, modern Chinese dramatists drew inspiration from Western drama for their own theater reform. Modern Chinese drama, like its Western counterpart, consists mostly of speaking and acting; it challenges the conventions of the operatic theater, known as *xiqu*, which combines singing, speaking, acting, and acrobatics. As a seminal form of a new culture, modern drama developed around the beginning of the Republican period (1911–1949), which saw the fall of the last imperial dynasty and the establishment of the Republic of China, under the leadership of the Nationalist Party (hereafter referred to as KMT). At that time, "civilized drama" *(wenmingxi)*, characterized by improvised dialogues and spontaneous speeches addressing current political events, responded to the social concerns surrounding the Republican revolution. In the May Fourth movement, modern drama was explored as an alternative to operatic theater, viewed then as too "dehumanized" *(feiren)* to express the concerns of an increasingly problematic world. During the War of Resistance to Japan (1937–1945), it played an important role in the cultural construction of the concepts of knowledge, power, identity, nation/state, gender politics, and twentieth-century Chinese national characteristics.

In the Maoist period (1949–1976), theater in the People's Republic of China (hereafter referred to as PRC) mostly followed the Maoist ideology of literature and art, which viewed serving the interests of the proletariat cause—that is, the cause of workers, peasants, and soldiers—as its main function. As we shall see shortly, the politics of representing the proletariat raises intriguing questions about the relationship between dramatists and their objects of representation, many of whom were deprived of real power to express themselves at the same time as the state dubbed them masters of socialist China.

The post-Maoist era began in 1976 with the death of Mao and the end of the Cultural Revolution. Initiated in 1966, the Cultural Revolution had promoted "revolutionary-model plays" *(geming yangbanxi)* as the exemplary art of the proletariat in order to eliminate other forms of literature and art. Perhaps at no other time did theater exert such a powerful impact on the nation. As a radical reaction to this period, post-Maoist theater launched a popular political agenda against Maoist ideology and initiated artistic experiments in the production of Western and Chinese plays.

This anthology introduces six plays drawn from Chinese indigenous theater, proletarian theater, women's theater, history plays, and experimental theater in contemporary China. They are introduced with several different audiences in mind. For the general reader, I present and situate six contemporary plays, five of which had not previously been translated into English, in the political and cultural history of modern China in order to demonstrate the interrelationship between theater and history, society, and our everyday experiences. For students of literature and culture, I focus on one set of critical issues in each play to suggest its intercultural and theoretical implications for studies of other genres and other cultures, to introduce modern Chinese drama to Western classrooms as part of a curriculum on multiculturalism and non-Western literary and cultural studies. Such an enterprise requires an introduction that would portray the reception of each play while tracing its historical and critical connections between past and present, text and intertexts, and Chinese traditions and their counterparts in other cultures.

In terms of methodology, I attempt to analyze Chinese culture in different ways from those found in contemporary Western literature. Some critics in the United States consider challenging the canon their central task. They ask, for instance, whether authors who were not upper-class, white, or male were indeed excluded from the Western canon. These issues become complicated and problematic in the Chinese context. One might note that in the United States the issue of class in cultural studies receives far less attention than issues of race and gender politics. In the Chinese context, however, it would be difficult to talk about literature and culture without at least referring to class politics, which has significantly affected millions of people. Mao's championing of the Chinese revolution as fundamentally a peasant's revolution—and hence the principle that literature and art should serve the interests of the proletariat politics—largely determined literary production, canon formation, and literary reception. By the same token, the "nonwhite" issue in China became a question of perspective: to the predominantly white United States, China is yellow and colored; to other ethnic minority groups within China, "non-white," as a category, may indicate non-Han minority groups and/or non-Mandarin-speaking peoples within the Han majority. Furthermore, in contrast to the United States, where race became an issue of sustained scholarly concern only with the civil rights movement, attention to ethnicity was part of Maoist state ideology from the beginning. The PRC granted ethnic groups financial support and special rights, such as exemptions from the one-child policy to allow increases in the minority population. Similarly, as to the issue of gender, Chinese scholars in various disciplines have already pointed out that official feminism, despite its radical promotion of women's rights and equality, illustrated by Mao's adage that "women can hold up half of the sky," merely validated the existing socialist ideology. Simply put, the representation of women as key players in socialist China was always part of the Maoist official culture. Thus what constitutes "opening the canon" for some Western critics would in China mean returning to the Maoist canon, or to the Maoist principle of creating and preserving literary texts. Ultimately, then, what is politically correct in the West may be politically incorrect in post-Maoist China, which rejected many aspects of Maoist ideology years ago. Bearing such distinctions in mind, the reader may learn from the following discussion of theatrical representations in contemporary Chinese drama, which shed light on the social and institutional histories of canon formation in cross-cultural contexts.

The Dead Visiting the Living:
The Dynamics of Form and Content

Although the post-Maoist play *The Dead Visiting the Living (Yige sizhe dui shengzhe de fangwen)* premiered as late as 1985, it belongs to a well-established repertory in modern drama that sometimes skillfully combines such seemingly opposing elements as East and West, modern and traditional, and Brechtian and illusionist theater. Indeed, it crystallizes the century-old effort by the Chinese dramatists to seek an equilibrium between artistic form and political content.

The first such attempt can be detected in Hu Shi's 1919 play *The Main Event of One's Life (Zhongshen dashi)*, which used Ibsen (for the first time) as the quintessential Western model for writing about individualism and free love, against the expected Confucian content and traditional form of old theater.[7] Although primitive in terms of dramaturgy, Hu's play depicts a brave young woman rejecting her parents' wishes that she submit to an arranged marriage and instead eloping with her Japan-educated lover. With this play, Hu Shi pioneered a subsequently long tradition of exploring Western dramatic forms as a way of giving expression to the antitraditional agenda of the May Fourth intellectuals to further political and social reforms. The father in Hu's play, an apparently modern, educated man who lives in a house decorated in Chinese and Western styles and yet adheres to clan-centered old values, seems to symbolize the desire of Chinese intellectuals to borrow from the West while simultaneously preserving Chinese traditions. This ambiguous attachment to Western theater found its most telling example in Wang Zhongxian's expensive yet unsuccessful Shanghai performance, in October 1920, of Bernard Shaw's *Mrs. Warren's Profession (Hualun Furen zhi zhiye)*, which had been endorsed in the radical periodical *New Youth* as a laudable realistic drama from the West. The indifferent reception convinced Wang that he had no choice but to adapt to the popular taste of Chinese audiences, many of whom were still accustomed to the familiar features of operatic theater.

The ensuing development of "amateur theater" *(aimeiju)* in Beijing illustrates the dual-fold emphasis of theater as both an educational and an artistic experience. Whereas "amateur," the English term, refers to noncommercial performances by unpaid actors, the Chinese translation, *"aimei,"* which literally means "love of beauty," emphasizes art for art's sake. The best achievement of amateur theater was the 1924 production by Hong Shen of Oscar Wilde's *Lady Windermere's Fan (Shaonainai de shanzi)*, an event that drama historians now view as the beginning of a tradition of realistic performing art on the Chinese stage. It highlighted stage design, the role of the director, and the use of local flavor drawn from Shanghai life, while still adhering to the spirit of the foreign original.

Only with the creation of Cao Yu's watershed play *Thunderstorm (Leiyu)*, in 1933, did Chinese theater encounter a more vibrant combination of Western Aristotelian form with May Fourth content.[8] Indeed, *Thunderstorm* perfected an Aristotelian theater (characterized by a closed form, or the so-called three unities of time, plot, and place) as opposed to Shakespearean theater (characterized by an open form, with several places, multiple plots, and various time frames). Echoing

Western traditions such as Greek theater and the plays of Shakespeare, Ibsen, O'Neill, and Chekhov, as well as Chinese classics, *Thunderstorm* is a well-structured play of four acts and two scenes that center around the dramatic conflicts of two families with a secret, sordid thirty-year history, which unfolds and finds resolution within a twenty-four-hour period. Deviating, however, from the purely Aristotelian "three unities," the play's setting shifts between the two families of Lu and Zhou. When Lu Ma arrives at the Zhou household, where her daughter works as a maid, it is revealed (to Lu Ma's horror) that her daughter is in love with the first young master, who is her own son whom she had left behind with the Zhou family thirty years before. Thus Lu Ma sees her daughter reenacting the tragic history when Lu Ma herself was a maid and fell in love with the old master, who rejected her and drove her from his house after she had given birth to his two children. Complicating this tale of incest is another misalliance. The first young master earlier had an affair with Zhou Fanyi, his stepmother, who married the old master after Lu Ma's departure but was nevertheless alienated by her husband's indifference and cruelty. By the play's end, Lu Ma's daughter and the two young masters are dead, Zhou Fanyi is mentally ill, and a grief-stricken Lu Ma feels she has nothing left to live for. Like Ibsen's *A Doll's House*, the play concludes with the lonely patriarch on an empty stage, signifying the emptiness of a broken home, which was in fact never a "home." However, the two plays differ in a vital respect: where Ibsen's play celebrates Nora's leaving home as a courageous act, Cao Yu's play illustrates that for Chinese women, the lure of leaving home is only a trap. Lu Ma's departure from home thirty years before and her determination "never to see the Zhous again" merely ends with the dreadful realization that, despite her best efforts, her daughter has succumbed to the same pitfalls and has become trapped in the same home. As for Zhou Fanyi, leaving her parents' home thirty years earlier in quest of true love only delivered her back into a prisonlike house, with no opportunities for further escape.

Cao Yu's *Thunderstorm* was among the most frequently performed plays in the Chinese theater, especially in the Maoist period, when it was canonized as one of the works that best depicts the evils of a "big family" in the "old society" before 1949. On various occasions, Cao Yu echoed this official interpretation, despite his earlier statement about being motivated by a Greek-like emotional force, a longing for an explanation of the many mysterious forces in the universe that had captivated him. In the PRC revision of the play, moreover, Cao Yu changed Lu Ma and her second son, Lu Dahai, to oppressed characters with class consciousness, thereby highlighting the theme of class struggle.[9] Thus a work that had begun life as a well-made play was later rewritten and its political content changed to accord with prevailing ideologies.[10] Cao Yu, who as president of the Beijing People's Art Theater represented the party's policies on literature, typifies the predicament of Chinese dramatists. Theater could never be an art-for-art's-sake enterprise for them, despite their original artistic orientations.

Developed simultaneously in China with the Aristotelian form of theater, Shakespearean theater found its example in Hong Shen's *Yama Zhao (Zhao Yanwang)*. In imitation of Eugene O'Neill's *Emperor Jones*, the play revolves around a military deserter lost in a forest, where he addresses imagined ghosts of enemies and friends and vents his grievances over past tragedies.[11] Although some criticized Hong Shen's adaptation of the open form as a superficial imitation of Western masterpieces, the play deserves mention for its expression of early dramatists' concern with such social problems as corruption, poverty, and a weak national government confronted by foreign aggression. This direction reached its apex with Xia Yan's *Under Shanghai Eaves (Shanghai wuyan xia)*, a play whose innovative structure has only one setting: a cross section of a typical house in Shanghai, occupied by five poor families struggling to survive, with one family in each of the five distinct spaces on stage enacting different story lines concurrently.[12] The open structure proves ideal for a narrative about the discontent of these ordinary people—an unwilling prostitute, an impoverished primary school teacher, an eccentric old newspaper vendor with dreams about the homecoming of his son, who has already been killed in the war. All these subplots seem to hinge on the return of Kuang Fu, a revolutionary who, after a brief reunion, leaves his family again upon realizing that his wife and daughter lived with his best friend during the eight years of his imprisonment.

Both the Aristotelian close form and the Shakespearean open form found their fullest expression in the subsequent texts of "defense drama" during the War of Resistance to Japan, the Civil War period, and the PRC period, in plays reflecting on contemporary realities and on historical myth and figures. This tension between artistic innovation and political orientation peaked during the Cultural Revolution, when all "undesirable" forms of literature and art were denounced as harmful to the socialist state, and the model revolutionary theater, touted as the only proper proletariat genre, explored artistic forms from traditions that deliberately excluded all feudal and bourgeois influences. Of the eight model works promoted at the beginning of the Cultural Revolution, five are Peking operas and three draw from Western forms of ballet and symphonic music. Modern Chinese drama, as well as many other forms of literature and art, did not really exist during the Cultural Revolution, although some of the model operatic pieces such as *The Red Lantern (Hongdeng ji)* and *Azalea Mountain (Dujuanshan)* were earlier performed as modern Chinese drama.[13] In reaction to such neglect, post-Maoist theater revived artistic traditions from East and West alike, and modern as well as traditional plays. Both artistically and politically oriented plays (or a combination of the two) flourished in the dramatic renaissance of the late 1970s and early 1980s.

One example is Liu Shugang's *The Dead Visiting the Living,* which blends Brechtian theater with the socialist-realist tradition. Based on the real lives of two national heroes extolled by the post-Maoist regime, the play recounts the aftermath of Ye Xiaoxiao's murder by two thieves on a bus as other passengers look on passively. Throughout the rest of the play, the dead Ye comes back to visit the living, to confront the indifferent passengers, and to reconnect with his two best childhood friends: Tang Tiantian, the woman he loved, and Liu Feng, his rival in work and love.

The play relies on the illusionist-theater techniques of presenting realistic slices of life and highlighting social problems via the actions of the uninvolved passengers. As a visitor come back from the dead, Ye gradually understands and forgives onlookers whose preoccupation with their own problems inhibited them from aiding him. For example, a father was eager to get to the hospital to see his wife and their new baby; a party official was trying to think of ways to earn a promotion to provide better care for his blind daughter. After all, life was difficult for everyone after the Cultural Revolution. Ye's acceptance of people indirectly responsible for his death lends him the aura of a socialist hero, who gives without expecting anything in return. In this respect, *The Dead* could please both the authorities and the public: the crime scene in a crowded bus full of worrying people could be seen as a timely critique against the old regime of Cultural Revolutionary

China. The unrewarded hero, Ye, who rises above everyone in moral stature, points up the emptiness of adhering to the socialist spirit and the need to overcome past difficulties, a spirit promoted by the post-Maoist ideology of the 1980s.

Celebrated by many critics as an apt combination of socialist-realist, Western absurdist, stream-of-consciousness, and symbolist techniques, *The Dead* experimented with the Brechtian "alienation effect," along with the echoes of Greek tragedy obtained by the use of masks and a chorus. Drawing on Brecht's concept of an episodic plot with epic overtones that can effectively address social concerns, *The Dead* consistently "alienates" its audiences from the immediate events by connecting the past with the present, the dead with the living, and the actors with the audience who, as observers, are supposed to offer rational alternatives to the dramatic action. Most of these dramatic effects are achieved through the ingenious use of the chorus, whose members greet the audience at the beginning of the play, to help them realize that they are watching the play along with them. Besides commenting on the action and becoming part of the setting, with their symbolic costumes and props, the chorus members also use masks to step in and out of other dramatic roles, such as those of the passengers and the criminals on the bus, the detective, the corrupt party official, Ye's employer, and the doorman at the funeral home.

These dramatic techniques are meant to prompt audiences to reflect upon the dramatic action while Ye reflects on his journey through life. For example, Tang Tiantian, in her belated effort to demonstrate her love for Ye, kisses and embraces the ghost of Ye in front of a bewildered, jealous Liu Feng. The sight tortures Liu, because he is uncertain whether Tang and Ye were intimate before his death, as Tang now claims, despite the adamant denial of the ghost Ye. In the middle of this confusion of sense, vision, and experience, the audience is encouraged to continue to mull over the question Tang has posed for Liu: "As the living, can't you tolerate my feelings for and intimate acts with the dead Ye?"[14] This question forces the audiences to consider the lingering influence in socialist China of the Confucian moral code of chastity and virginity, which demands that women remain faithful to their husbands or betrothed, whatever the circumstances. The kissing onstage and the dramatic conflict surrounding it also reflected the new vogue of early post-Maoist theater, which highlighted love stories after years of their absence during the Cultural Revolutionary period. At the end of the play, when Ye is about to be cremated, Liu surprises every-one by confessing that he is the person Ye has been seeking—the pas-senger with a sense of justice to insist that the bus be immediately driven to the police station, so the criminals might be apprehended, but who remains too intimidated to incriminate them. Liu's additional admission that he wrote the play to allay his guilt turns the audiences' attention to the meaning of theater and of this play.

By presenting himself as one of the indifferent onlookers partially to blame for Ye's death, Liu actually situates himself above this other-wise undifferentiated crowd. His dramatic skills allow him, in a way denied to the others, to argue his own case in a privileged theatrical space. In this sense, the play is a meta-commentary on the problematic relationship between drama and life, between Chinese intellectuals and the people they claim to represent, and between what one aspires to be and what one is capable of being. This surprising ending dissolves the idealistic image of the dramatist as embodied in the stage charac-ter of Liu, a successful director who sought to communicate the spiri-tual, inner beauty of "one's heart" in his play. However, his alter ego, Ye, laments his failure as an actor early in his career and his subse-quent struggle to succeed as a costume designer, when he was entirely devoted to creating "the outward appearance" of human beings.[15] Members of the audience are prompted to ask: Who is the truthful man? The one who claims to be "spiritual," and whom society views as successful, but was too intimidated by the criminals to act? Or the one who admits to failing to be "spiritual" and yet was committed by a sense of justice to act when it mattered? In a similar juxtaposition, the dead (or the unsuccessful one when he was alive) is the one to be honored rather than the living (the successful one whose spirit is nearly dead). This image of the self-conscious dramatist, however, can also be read as symbolizing the ambiguities surrounding the position of Chinese playwrights. They are accustomed to learning from and serving the interests of the ordinary people, as Mao demanded, while being aware that it is they who hold the power to write and represent reality onstage.

The World's Top Restaurant:
The Paradox of the Local and the Global

While acknowledging its Western inspiration, PRC literary historians have also argued that modern Chinese drama sinicized Western dramaturgy. They maintain that Xia Yan and Cao Yu employed appropriate formalist features from the Chinese and Western traditions to best convey a sense of the daily lives of Chinese people in specific locales. Any given local culture of China was influenced by people's changing perceptions of the global context, but "local" in one particular play may embrace another dynamic, which casts the urban as the central and the rural as the marginal. Xia Yan's *Under Shanghai Eaves* represents the rural folk, such as the Huang family, who were victimized by the urban decadence after migrating to Shanghai. Xia Yan's Shanghai-flavored drama contrasts with Beijing-flavored plays in the PRC. These two schools helped shape the unique, indigenous genre known as local-flavored plays. In Lao She's plays, for instance, Beijing people act out their identities as either urban residents with rural roots or as longtime city dwellers from different classes confronting the challenges of life in a modern city. On the PRC stage, moreover, Beijing was depicted, in local terms, as the site of distressed people who were casualties of the old society. At the same time, the city was proclaimed, in global terms, as the center for world revolution, to be waged by suffering people who were invited to look to China for inspiration in their own national and regional movements for freedom and independence.

Usually cited as one of the earliest successful productions of Beijing-flavored plays, Lao She's 1951 *Dragon Beard Ditch (Longxugou)* capitalized on local dialects and expressions of the old Beijing culture to portray poor Beijing citizens who lived around Dragon Beard Ditch, such as the storyteller, the rickshaw driver, and the bricklayer. The play also depicted their living conditions, such as the stinking slum that for generations had trapped poor people, and the government efforts to rebuild the neighborhood after liberation.[16] The play earned Lao She the title of "people's artist," awarded by the Beijing People's Government. It was the only time any artist received such an honor in China throughout the entire Maoist period.

In 1958 Lao She's second Beijing-flavored play, *Teahouse (Chaguan)*, premiered to equal acclaim.[17] This time the drama presents more than sixty vivid characters, old Beijing citizens, including an imperial wrestler, a eunuch, a prostitute, a pimp, a bird lover, a fortune-teller, two KMT secret agents, two deserters, an industrialist, and a property owner. Characters meet at a teahouse during the time span following the failure of a political reform under the Qing dynasty in 1898 through 1945, after the defeat of the Japanese under the rule of the KMT. Despite its allusions to many historical events, the play focuses on the rise and fall of the teahouse and the struggles of the shopkeeper's family and friends. Lao She intended to commend the "new society" by satirizing the three declining political regimes and their failure to bring about a decent life for Beijing citizens. *Teahouse*, written and published at the height of the anti-rightist movement (1957), was still deemed controversial because it was interpreted as conveying sympathy for the property owner of the old society, rather than focusing on the "heroic deeds" of the common people as they worked to build the socialist state. Deeply rooted in the old culture of Beijing, however, one could also detect a resistance to change, no matter how frequently political regimes changed hands and claimed victory.

Consequently, the Cultural Revolution condemned Lao She and his well-received Beijing-flavored plays. However, his legacy was dramatized on Beijing's stage during the post-Maoist period, in Su Shuyang's *Taiping Lake (Taipinghu)*, published in 1986 to commemorate the twentieth anniversary of Lao She's death and premiered in 1988 after numerous revisions. The play depicts the day, August 24, 1966, when Lao She drowned himself to protest the brutal beating and humiliation he suffered at the hands of the Red Guards. Before the suicide, Lao She wanders around Taiping Lake for a day and night, meditating on the paradox of his past devotion to the party and the charges of antiparty activities it has now pressed against him. Heartbroken and confused, he engages in conversations with the living (Beijing citizens who still fondly remember his plays) and also with the dead (dramatic characters of his who committed suicide to decry the miserable pre-1949 society). Beijing-flavored plays, which had followed Lao She's lead and criticized the old society for marginalizing local people, now offered up a much harsher judgment of Maoist China's unfair treatment of dramatists.

The watershed 1979 revival of *Teahouse* by the Beijing People's Art Theater epitomized the entire history of modern Chinese drama for how it pitted "real-life" theater against the status quo in a national arena, in which scene after scene of political drama was being rehearsed and reinvented on the smaller stage of the theater. *Teahouse*'s successful tours in Germany, France, Switzerland, Japan, Canada, and Hong Kong in the 1980s proved to be the culminating act of this theater in the broader sense and marked the first time that modern Chinese spoken drama was exported to the global stage, thereby gaining an entry to the world repertory. This voyage by *Teahouse* simultaneously completes the "journey back home," which was undertaken at the very beginning of the twentieth century when the first generation of Chinese dramatists traveled to Japan and to the West. Thus the most indigenous and most local of plays, as some critics have happily pointed out, became the most universal and global, by virtue of its artistic appeal and its faithful reflection of the spectrum of the Chinese people's experience. The further development of Beijing-flavored plays in post-Maoist China, as represented by Guo Shixing's *Birdman (Niaoren)*,[18] dramatized events and characters in the quiet lanes and neglected corners of 1990s Beijing, where the citizens struggled to cope with the commercialized economy and transnational capital.

To provide another glimpse of the Beijing-flavored play, this anthology includes *The World's Top Restaurant (Tianxia diyilou)*, written by the woman playwright He Jiping and performed for the first time by Beijing People's Art Theater, in May 1988. Set in Beijing between 1917 and 1928, the play deals with the rise and fall of a legendary Beijing roast-duck restaurant, brought to greatness by hardworking managers, waiters, and chefs, only to be ruined later by the two young owners, who for years lived off the restaurant without learning how to run it. The play depicted a Lu Mengshi, a manager hired by the previous owner of the restaurant at his deathbed to continue the latter's wish to revive the restaurant. Three years later, in a period of great financial hardship, Lu Mengshi fends off interference by creditors and troublemakers as he expands his business by constructing a new building. Lu then tricks the two young owners into giving up their remaining interest in the business's management so that he might, by dint of his efficient management and creative abilities, restore the restaurant to its former greatness. Between Act II and Act III, eight years elapse, in the course of which the restaurant, while enjoying its golden age, becomes known as "the best one under heaven." To audiences' great dismay, however, the two heartless young masters suddenly return to reclaim the fruits of Lu's hard work. In the epilogue, after his departure, Lu has a couplet sent to the restaurant. Asking "who is the owner and who is the guest?" the couplet concludes the play in a suspenseful climax that has both characters and audience pondering the meaning of this message, which proves central to the thematic concerns of the play.[19] It is the guests, the outsiders of the family, who have shown themselves to be the genuine owners of the restaurant; those who were the owners in name were actually the outsiders.

The reception of *The World's Top Restaurant* centered around the performing aspects of the play as perfected by Beijing People's Art Theater, known as the only institution capable of producing real Beijing-flavored plays. Much credit was given to the directors and actors for their "second creation," which turned the script into a theatrical event, bursting with vivid and diverse Beijing characters of more than seventy years before. Without the older generation of directors and actors, who had spent years learning the dialect, mannerisms, customs, body movements, and lifestyles of the old Beijing people, one critic pointed out, we would never have been able to enjoy a first-rate Beijing-flavored play.[20] Reportedly, the directors attended every performance, to test the "authenticity" of the play in front of the Beijing audience and, depending on its effect, to modify the next performance.[21] All these factors contributed to making *The World's Top Restaurant* an unusually popular play, as demonstrated by the continuing strong ticket sales after more than fifty-eight performances in only two months,[22] a record high during the lean years of Chinese theater when critics were discussing how to solve "the drama crisis."

Other critics, however, criticized *The World's Top Restaurant* as being inferior to *Teahouse*, because the former's time span of 1917 to 1928 was not regarded as being as instructive as that for *Teahouse*. With the first act set in 1898 (the end of the reform movement), and the second act around 1918 (the transitional period between Qing dynasty and Republican mores), and the third act in 1945 (following the defeat of the Japanese), *Teahouse* was perceived as indicating the historical necessity of the decline of the previous political regimes. In *The World's Top Restaurant*, however, the rise and fall of a particular business seems irrelevant to the direction of historical events;[23] it could even be associated with an unhealthy nostalgic longing for the past at a time of economic and political reform, in 1980s China.[24] Such views were rebutted by other critics, who insisted that precisely because of its historical neutrality, *The World's Top Restaurant* surpassed the earlier play. Its appeal, they claimed, was attributable to its own internal conflicts and logic, thus avoiding the danger of contamination by political and ideological contingencies and interpretations.[25] In effect, the play was accorded the typical treatment meted out to contemporary Chinese drama: no matter how salient the aesthetic values of a particular play in the eyes of one group of critics, it was bound to be looked at as a forum for political texts by other critics, whose educational and personal experiences dictated a different approach.

He Jiping, the playwright, however, provided her own explanation for what she called the "universal appeal" of the play. While spending two and a half years "delving into life" in a Beijing roast-duck restaurant, she had been deeply touched by the intelligence and dedication of the managers, chefs, and waiters, who had been looked down on as belonging to the lowest rung in the social strata. Part of her intention had been to demonstrate that the rich, the leisured, and the so-called "cultivated" elite class excelled only at eating, drinking, and playing around, whereas the hardworking laboring people were the creators of Chinese culinary art, which should be deemed a form of high art on a par with classical music, poetry, and painting. By asking at the end of the play "who is the owner and who is the guest?" she felt she was restoring the status of the "guests" as equivalent to that of the "owners," or "the makers of history."[26]

One also needs to be aware of the complex, paradoxical problems entailed in ethnic representation: while Beijing-flavored plays can be seen as a means for local natives to challenge the mainstream tradition inherited from the Western dramatic canon, they also, for the most part, represent the theater of the Han people. In this capacity they stress the history, culture, customs, and lifestyle of the Mandarin-speaking Chinese majority and of the officials in the state and party apparatus, based in the national capital of Beijing. As for the fifty-some minority nationalities and traditions that are not visible in Beijing-flavored plays, they are indeed the real locals in their geographical areas, whose regional and cultural traditions need to be taken seriously in terms of their relationship with the mainstream culture. Indeed, the dramatic world of *Teahouse* itself provided a glimpse of the complexity of multi-ethnic China. As a Manchu who grew up in Beijing, Lao She expressed his ambivalence toward his own identities by dramatizing a eunuch and an imperial wrestler as diehards from the Manchu court that had conquered and ruled the Han people. On the other hand, Lao She also created another upright Manchu man who would rather sell vegetables to make his own living than depend on the stipends awarded only to the Manchus. Although class struggle and the inevitable victory of communist ideology as implicit themes remained the focus of its reception, *Teahouse* nevertheless offered us a valuable text imbedded with complex issues of personal, ethnic, and national identities.

Jiang Qing and Her Husbands: History, Revolution, and Political Theater

In *Acting the Right Part* I discuss the relationship between street theater in Tiananmen Square, such as state parades and student demonstrations, and the "theater of the street" that represented street theater in real life onstage. Indeed, theater of the street in early post-Maoist China comprised one of the three golden periods in modern spoken drama. It first rose as one of the most popular genres during the War of Resistance to Japan, when spoken drama raised the morale of the Chinese people. The second boom stretched from the late 1950s to mid-1960s in the PRC, when a strong socialist state promoted realist theater that educated mass audiences with collective values and common goals. The third boom arrived soon after the arrest of the Gang of Four, in 1976, when dramatists were among the first to respond to the post-Maoist regime's call to narrate "bitter stories" of the Cultural Revolution. The so-called anti–Gang of Four plays attracted many people to the theater, where audiences watched the downfall of traitors of the nation onstage while celebrating the nation's "second liberation." Some of them even reenacted onstage the Tiananmen protest of April 5, 1976, against Chinese authorities during the Cultural Revolution. Rarely before had "one play shocked the entire city," as seen in the simultaneous staging of forty performances of *In a Land of Silence* (*Yu wusheng chu*) in Beijing alone in 1978.[27]

Jiang Qing and Her Husbands (*Jiang Qing he tade zhangfumen*) was written in 1990, when drama had lost considerable ground to film and television. It is nevertheless one of the best political plays. As I have pointed out elsewhere, *Jiang Qing and Her Husbands* can be read as a "trial drama," in which a former "First Lady," after having been imprisoned in Mao's "doll's house" for forty years, presents her side of the story.[28] That story showcases a frustrated Nora in Ibsen's *A Doll's House*, which Jiang Qing performed in 1935; she spent the rest of her years imitating Nora's spirit of an independent woman. The trial drama reenacts the 1980 public trial of the Gang of Four, in which Jiang Qing was sentenced to death but received a two-year stay of execution. In the process it points up the differences in the judicial approaches of

China and of the United States. In the latter case, the trial is governed by the element of suspense, as the defense lawyer and prosecution vie for the jury's favorable verdict. The trial of the Gang of Four, however, was mostly a show, with the prosecution enumerating forty-eight counts of indictment for Jiang Qing, and the accused either refusing to cooperate or totally admitting guilt without submitting an effective defense. The Chinese people's denunciation of Jiang Qing for her destructive role during the Cultural Revolution can also be seen as one of the few options available, because Mao could not be directly challenged. On another level, it illustrates the formation of a political discourse on Jiang Qing, which draws from traditional culture's misogynist view of the seductive woman. For centuries this view scapegoated Yang Guifei, the beautiful concubine in the Tang dynasty, for having presumably brought down an emperor. The resentment against Jiang Qing also obscures the issue of Chinese official feminism, which was manipulated and abused by Jiang Qing when promoting her image as a public woman with an acting career while claiming to be the "banner woman" for all oppressed classes.

Jiang Qing and Her Husbands offers diverse interpretations that cut across the problematic relationship of gender (embodied in Jiang Qing as a strongwilled, independent woman) and nation/state (embodied in an even stronger male counterpart who was patriarch of both family and state). The play was written in 1990 at the request of a Hong Kong actress interested in playing Jiang Qing, and the playwright, Sha Yexin, seized the unusual opportunity of writing a play that would not be subjected to official Chinese censorship. He did his utmost, however, to follow closely the official and nonofficial documents at his disposal. At the same time, he exercised his playwright's prerogative of selecting the episodes that would best suit his construction of Jiang Qing. In terms of formalistic features, Sha Yexin smoothly combined a Brechtian structure (which distances audiences from the dramatic action, thereby reminding them that what they are watching is only a play) with illusionist theater (which draws audiences in, convincing them that they are watching real-life events). Originally intended as a movie script, the play also adapted a fluidity of time and space in which Jiang Qing travels between the past and the present, and between her inner world and the outer reality.

The illusionist dimension was adapted by the socialist-realist tradition to evoke the "revolutionary-history play," that is, the theatrical dramatization of historical events according to official history. On the other hand, the Brechtian structure highlighted Jiang Qing's self-reflections, which had been buried in post-Maoist official history, providing a subversive version of the "revolutionary-history play," if not the revolutionary history itself. Thus *Jiang Qing and Her Husbands* could be appreciated both as imitating and reacting to its precursor texts. Although the revolutionary-history play decisively shaped other subgenres during the early post-Maoist period, this subgenre has received scant scholarly attention, and no translations in English of the plays or critical studies are available. As a consequence, I discuss some of the popular revolutionary-history plays and their reception in order to provide readers with a clear sense of their roles in constructing a new nation/state in the late 1970s and early 1980s. *Jiang Qing and Her Husbands* provides the best example of this subgenre, albeit a belated and seditious one.

Revolutionary-history plays can be traced back at least to history plays in the May Fourth period. Guo Moruo's *A Trilogy of Rebellious Women (Sange panni de nüxing)*, written in the 1920s, reinterpreted the legend of three ancient women rebelling against the three-fold Confucian obligations that bound women to their fathers, husbands, and sons. During the War of Resistance to Japan, the history play became the most popular theater form. At that time many plays, such as Yang Hansheng's 1937 *The Death of Li Xiucheng (Li Xiucheng zhi si)*[29] and Guo Moruo's 1942 *Qu Yuan*,[30] depicted patriotic historical figures who perished in the battle against corruption and treason—clear allusions, according to PRC literary history, to the KMT government, which was described as resisting the Japanese invaders only reluctantly. After the anti-rightist movement of 1957, the history play saw a resurgence in popularity. For some playwrights, the history play served as an escape from the demanding task of depicting the contemporary life; it could thus be easily criticized as commentating on the status quo. Even the presumably politically safe "masterpieces" among the history plays, such as Guo Moruo's work *Cai Wenji*[31] and Tian Han's drama *Guan Hanqing*,[32] were criticized during the Cultural Revolution for using ancient, dramatic characters to voice a discontent with socialist China. They were reprimanded for having been obsessed by stories from the "old culture," about feudal "emperors, princes, generals, and ministers" *(di wang jiang xiang)* or about "talented scholars and beautiful women" *(caizi jiaren)*.

The significance of the history play on the Chinese stage resided in its dual temporal position, between the past and the present. While characters from the past could be lauded on their own terms according to their place in history, they were also inevitably judged by an audience that could see them as resembling familiar figures in contemporary times. The defense of history against excessive fictionality or innovative contemporary interpretations became a discursive strategy in the critical debate on the history play. Dramatists and critics could sometimes explain away questionable events by claiming that they were merely reenacted history, without reference to the politics of the present day. Their opponents, in turn, could argue against what they saw as excessive fictionality—or a disregard for historical fact—which pointed to evidence of deliberate allusions to and, hence, subversive activities against the ruling ideology. All these elements could prove to create serious political problems for dramatists. The best known case is Wu Han's "historically accurate" Peking opera *Hai Rui Dismissed from Office* (*Hai Rui baguan*).[33] Responding to Mao's call to write about Hai Rui, a legendary official of the Ming Dynasty (in order to encourage Chinese people to speak out), Wu Han, the deputy mayor of Beijing and a reputable historian, portrayed an incorruptible Hai Rui dismissed from his official post for having challenged the authority. Wu's Peking opera was absurdly interpreted as having used the drama to challenge Mao's dismissal of General Peng Dehuai, who questioned Mao's radical economic policies of the late 1950s. Wu's history play, which was based on thorough research and designed to address a contemporary issue in socialist China was first publicly criticized on November 10, 1965, in *Wenhui bao* (Wenhui newspaper), in Shanghai. It became the first shot in the Cultural Revolution.

Well versed in the complex navigation of past and present in relation to the history play, Chinese dramatists by the late seventies seemed to know exactly how to play the game. They answered the official call against the Gang of Four, and many playwrights explored to the hilt a thriving new genre known as the "revolutionary-historical drama" or "revolutionary-leader play," which reenacted episodes in the lives of communist leaders. Both *Newspaper Boys* (*Baotong*)[34] and *Turning Point* (*Zhuanzhe*),[35] for example, depict Zhou Enlai's revolutionary career during the war period, while *A Generation of Heroes* (*Yidai yinghao*) recounts Zhou's heroic leadership during three Shanghai workers' uprisings and the August 1 Nanchang uprisings in 1927, which were celebrated events in early Chinese Communist Party (CCP) history.[36] Similarly, *Eastward March (Dongjin! Dongjin!)*[37] and *Chen Yi Leaves the Mountains (Chen Yi chushan)*[38] describe the war legends surrounding the generals and vice premiers such as He Long and Chen Yi, both of whom were persecuted to death during the Cultural Revolution.

At first sight, the central theme of these "leader plays" might seem comparable to that of the Elizabethan history play, which Northrop Frye links to "the unifying of the nation and the binding of the audiences into the myth as the inheritors of that unity, set over against the disasters of civil war and weak leadership."[39] The great difference of the leader play, however, is that by depicting past glories, it highlights the leader's tragic death during the Cultural Revolution, thus ensuring "the simultaneous presence of irony" through questioning of the very myth of Chinese revolution.[40] Leader plays were particularly popular from 1978 to 1981 because they functioned as effective weapons for exposing the Gang of Four's crimes and for voicing Chinese dramatists' challenge to communist historiography, which had victimized not only its people, but its own leaders, the "pillars of Chinese revolution."

A typical example is *Morning Light (Shuguang)*, one of the first leader plays to be performed after the death of Mao.[41] Premiered in 1977 this six-act play relates Marshal He Long's early military career in developing the Honghu rural Soviet area, from 1931 to 1934, at the low ebb of Chinese revolution when the Central Committee of the CCP was said "to be dominated by Wang Ming's leftist opportunism."[42] Foregrounding the "two-lines struggle" within the central leadership of the CCP, the play gives an account of how the followers of Wang Ming's leftist line persecuted, arrested, and even executed faithful defenders of Mao's "correct revolutionary line." For example, Feng Dajian, the director of the Soviet Security Bureau, awed and terrified his enemies by frequently venturing into their headquarters in disguise to collect intelligence, and defeating them in numerous battles with his invincible troops. Yet, however heroic, he still could not survive the purge within his own party, which executed him as an enemy spy.

Thus *Morning Light* actually comes off as a conspiracy play, another subgenre of the history play, which, according to Herbert Linderberger, provides "the central fable shaping the vast majority of historical dramas."[43] As a conspiracy play concerned with "the transfer of power from one force to another," *Morning Light* suggests at least four different conspiracies within and outside the party's hierarchy.[44] The first conspiracy against Feng Dajian is followed by the second conspiracy, against Yue Minghua, a division commander in the Red Army who had been wrongfully accused of having protected Feng. Yue is condemned to death by Lin Han, the party representative of the CCP Central Committee whose main task is to put into effect Wang Ming's leftist line. In the nick of time, however, Yue is rescued by He Long, then Army Commander of the Second Army Corps of the Red Army, which had already lost 90 percent of its territory and its troops owing to Wang Ming's "incorrect policies."[45] Because of He Long's challenge to Lin Han, He Long's party loyalty was naturally questioned. His ensuing persecution and death during the Cultural Revolution undoubtedly touched a chord among some audience members, who might have been victims of conspiracies in their own lives, lending the play a sense of urgency and realism. When Yue Minghua onstage warned the Chinese audiences in 1977 to be on the lookout against conspirators within the party especially when victory would have been won for the Chinese revolution, many audience members (myself included) would have understood its allusions to the Gang of Four. This message led to a fourth conspiracy: the Gang of Four itself had fallen prey to a coup d'état, without which the post-Maoist regime would never have taken power.

Party history was one conspiracy after another. The subversive theme of the play was so blatant that it alienated some conservatives. After *Morning Light* was published, in 1977, several readers wrote to the editor to express their concern: it was depressing to see so many negative characters, who necessarily overshadowed the positive communist heroes. If the incorrect party line prevailed so easily, they argued, how could one sufficiently account for the inevitable victory of the Chinese revolution?[46] Others, however, seemed eager to connect conspiracies onstage with real stories, in order to validate the historical "truth," which, in their view, was reflected in the play. Tao Hanzhang, a Red Army veteran, testified that the character of Yue Minghua was based on the true story of Duan Dechang, a division commander in the Red Army who was executed by the leftist opportunists within the party.[47] Xue Baokun went further, suggesting that the play be revised so that Yue will have just been executed at the point when He Long arrives on horseback. Although Xue admitted that some audiences would find this bleak outcome too hard to swallow, he maintained that the deaths of both Yue and Feng would arouse a more profound sense of pathos suitable to tragic theater.[48] Furthermore, the audiences would be provided with a more vivid lesson of the price of revolution when it pursues incorrect party lines; they were, in fact, familiar with the most costly example, as had been seen in the recent struggle between Mao's revolutionary line and that of the counterrevolutionary Gang of Four.[49] These reactions indicated that 1977 was a historic moment, when a subversive discourse against the party apparatus, including that of the new post-Maoist regime, overlapped with the official call to discredit the regime's predecessors. A leader play could help vent one's resentment against the Gang of Four. Alternatively, it could disturb, by presenting the past heroic narrative as an illusion.

The leader plays that dealt with Mao understandably aroused the most debate. The first such play, *Autumn Thunder (Qiushou pili)*, was questioned for its hagiographic treatment of Mao, which ran counter to the Marxist view that the people, and not individual leaders, were the driving force of history. One critic pointed out that the character of Mao appeared only twice in the play's 1977 premiere: first, to declare the start of the autumn harvest uprisings; second, to announce the beginning of the peasant army's march toward the Jinggang Mountains, where the first rural soviet was to be established, in 1927. This insufficient dramatization of Mao, which was said to have turned him into an isolated idol, was addressed in the 1979 script, which portrayed Mao as "one of us"—that is, participating in and organizing peasant uprisings and even coming to the assistance of a poor peasant grandmother, carrying her hay for her on a shoulder pole.[50] Although at the cost of the fictionalization of some plot details, the creation of the "typical and beautiful" characters brought the revolutionary-leader play closer to the "essence of historical truth"; now, one critic stressed, Mao was accurately sketched as a real flesh-and-blood human being, not a godlike figure with a halo.[51]

Other critics believed that the leader play must simply function as another form of party history. They argued that it should be presented as factually as possible to provide proper education in cultural and revolutionary history through a theater experience. This view was most tellingly illustrated in the controversy over the production of *Yang Kaihui*, which dramatized Mao's loving relationship with his first wife. While received warmly by critics and audience, *Yang Kaihui* was nevertheless criticized for having "lost its power of conviction" by presenting Yang Kaihui as a guerrilla warrior. According to historical fact, Lu Bai argued, Yang was a gentle wife and true comrade who had always been supportive of Mao's career and had never participated in any warfare.[52] Over-fictionalization and exaggeration, Lu concluded, revealed an unhealthy trend in the leader play toward creating the kind of "tall, grand, and perfect" characters that had been favored in the Cultural Revolutionary–model theater. Because of this controversy, post-Maoist dramatists were thrown into a situation of irresoluble tension: they were called on to memorialize an epoch-making history and its leaders in order to justify CCP events. At the same time they were asked to take down from his pedestal the individual leader so that he could become "one of us." "His" history was to be appreciated as "our history," but, in another twist, the masses had to overlook their history to honor "his" history.

Owing to this dilemma, some commended *Yang Kaihui* in 1978 as a breakthrough for its focus on Mao's private life—his love, emotions, and sorrows as a husband and father. Presented as a gentle and supportive wife and mother, Yang Kaihui was extremely popular among many early post-Maoist audiences, who saw in her Mao's ideal wife, never to be replaced by Jiang Qing, his third wife.[53] Such sentiments brought about a flourishing subgenre known as "Yang Kaihui plays," which included the folk opera *Proud Yang (Jiaoyang)* and the Peking opera *Ode to My Beloved (Dielianhua)*.[54] The spoken drama *Yang Kaihui* was especially lauded for its romantic ending, when Mao and Yang, dressed as students, stride hand in hand toward the audiences from backstage among plum blossoms, white clouds, fresh evergreen, and red flags. By this finish, the directors intended to convey that Yang and Mao would "always live in the hearts of the millions of people"—that in real life, Mao, in his heart of hearts, had reserved his love for his first wife.[55] Audiences might then let this more personal message infuse Mao's poetic lines, as Yang imagines them in the last scene before her execution: "Kaihui, your life is pure because you have given it up selflessly for your people. Your life is heroic because you have fearlessly confronted your enemy. Your life is magnificent because it is combined with the ideals of Communism."[56] Speaking passionately from backstage, Mao declared that Yang did not just belong to him; above all, she was identified with the glorious course of the Chinese revolution. With one final, dramatic stroke, Yang's sexual love was thus transformed into a greater love put at the disposal of a great leader for the creation of his new nation/state.

To audience members aware of the historical facts, however, these episodes could deconstruct the very spirit of Yang's myth. When Yang was being tortured in prison (from October to November 1930) and refusing to yield to the authorities' demand that she renounce her legal status as Mao's wife, Mao had already married He Zizhen, "the most beautiful woman" in the Soviet area of the Jinggang Mountains, to quote from *Jiang Qing and Her Husbands* and various biographies. Thus the portrayal of Mao's imperishable love for Yang, as she imagined it in her prison cell before her execution, was far-fetched, and one wonders, would Yang still have refused the authorities' offer of freedom in exchange for denunciation had she been aware of Mao's infidelity? It is in this regard that the reception of Yang Kaihui seems particularly ironic. Yang's ennobling selflessness in prison—originally viewed as a means of softening the overly heroic image of Mao—can now be seen as a thoroughly meaningless sacrifice for a man she imagined to be faithful. A so-called true representation of a past love story in a leader play could, on the other hand, become an archaeological search for knowledge, in the Foucauldian sense of that term, with the object of recovering an episode buried in official history.

The issue of motherhood in the first family was tackled head-on in a 1985 leader play entitled *The Son of the World (Shijie zhi zi)*, which depicts the life of Mao Anying, the Chairman's firstborn son by Yang Kaihui. The play focuses on the war years in the Soviet Union when Mao Anying fought valiantly as a Red Army soldier, and on his heroic death as a volunteer soldier in the Korean War in 1950. An important subplot details the hardships endured by He Zizhen after she left China in 1938. During her brief appearance onstage, she is characterized as a caring and loving stepmother who tends to the needs of Mao Anying and his ailing brothers. In the years of famine, He Zizhen struggled to obtain medical treatment for Jiaojiao, the only daughter to survive of the six children she bore Mao during the war; for her pains she was "rewarded" with confinement in a Soviet asylum for almost five years. In the first act when news of her unfair treatment is conveyed to Moscow, Stalin refuses to help, since she is not Mao's current spouse. By refusing to rescue He Zizhen, Stalin believed he was helping Mao consolidate his absolute power at home as "a helmsman" for the army, the party, and the country.[57] Unlike the earlier *Yang Kaihui*, this play questions Mao's unfair treatment of his former spouse and contrasts it with the privileges given his firstborn son. He Zizhen half jokingly tells Mao Anying that as the "crown prince," he must never neglect to meet his father's great expectations. The son, however, is less concerned with power than with his search for a mother and father. Having lost his biological mother, he vainly urges his father to come to the aid of his stepmother. After exhibiting great valor in the war, Anying is warmly congratulated by Stalin, whom he worships both as a world leader and as a surrogate father. This father of the revolutionary world, we nevertheless learn, dispatches his own son to the battlefield and orders the arrest of his daughter-in-law as soon as he hears of his son's capture by the German army. Stalin asserts that his rule of punishing prisoners of war (and thus possible traitors) as well as their relations should be enforced even if it means imprisoning a family member.

Mao Anying probably ended his search for a father by seeing in his surrogate father something of his own father, whose indifference might be justified on the basis of the noble course he was steering for the country. Upon Mao Anying's return to China, Mao Zedong flatly rejects his son's request for a command position in the army and orders him to go down to the countryside to be reeducated by the local peasants. Mao Anying pleads with Mao as a son eager to live his own life, not as an imperial heir waiting for his royal orders; he tells his father of the heartbreaking farewell in prison with his mother, whose last wish was that he grow up to equal his father on the battlefield. "I am your father," Mao still insists in *The Son of the World*. "Although there is much that you learned in the Soviet Union, you have no idea how drastically different are the social realities of our two countries!" Dispirited, Mao Anying continues to plead that Mao make it possible for his stepmother to return home: "Aunt He has been shut up in an asylum for almost five years. Isn't it about time we get her back home?" Regarded from this vantage point, the play might be characterized as falling between what Herbert Linderberger defined as a "tyrant play" and a "martyr play," because it depicts Mao Anying and his stepmother as two martyrs who sacrificed their lives for Mao, the father figure, and were victimized by him in the process.[58] The characterization of He Zizhen as an angry Nora who slammed the door in the face of a helpless Mao in *Jiang Qing and Her Husbands* perhaps presented as well the perspective of Jiang Qing, who had cast herself as yet another Nora, most recently imprisoned in Mao's dollhouse.

Never staged, *Jiang Qing and Her Husbands* did not have to brave scrutiny for its possible effect on a culture's reception of its revolutionary leaders. This was probably fortunate, for Mao in this play is more "human" than in any other leader play before and after it. Mao is shown in his private life as a rustic peasant leader who craves unhealthy fatty pork, dances awkwardly, does not enjoy kissing women on the lips, and cannot even say the words "I love you." In fact, the stark contrast between a peasantlike Mao and a "sophisticated" Westernized Jiang Qing can be construed as the symbolic, unceasing power struggle between Chinese intellectuals and the laboring people they tried to please, only to be rejected by the latter for not really being one of them. The dichotomies between countryside and city, man and woman, society and individual, tradition and modernity, and East and West constantly shift positions and ultimately propel the development of the dramatic conflicts in the play. The characterization of Mao as a patriarch who was cut from the same cloth as his Chinese and Western forefathers, and the display of his helplessness and frustration in dealing with Jiang Qing, also present a dynamic interplay between revolutionary history, disruptive drama, and rebellious women, which might be resorted to as strategies for cultural suppression and cultural liberation. Thus the playwright's world can be studied as a crucial arena for political theater, in which history was written and rewritten according to the latest transmission of knowledge and power. It is in this sense that we can truly redeem early post-Maoist revolutionary-leader plays, which were later deemed as too political to be worth studying. Indeed, one could read them as precursor texts to *Jiang Qing and Her Husbands*. The Yang Kaihui plays, for instance, can be seen as earlier acts in a sequence of the revolutionary-history plays of the first family in the PRC. When one woman replaces another in Mao's dollhouse, she brings upon herself merely the invitation to stand trial for her man's past.

Black Stones: The Politics of Representing the Proletariat

As seen in the preceding discussion, Chinese spoken drama, especially in the PRC period, has often been characterized as too politically laden to warrant serious study. The politics of representation on the Chinese stage, however, evokes ideological critiques in other cultures, such as Plato's politically centered criticism of theater. According to Plato, the proper battle for theater is the ancient debate between the philosophical king, devoted to serving the interests and values of the ideal state, and the immoral poet, whose appeal to and expression of unhealthy emotions supposedly invalidate it. As did ancient Athens, the Chinese socialist state has punished questionable dramatists who were considered dangerous for conducting an anti-official discourse against the moral values of the ideal state.

Derived from Marx's sociopolitical theories, "ideal drama" is understood to depict the inevitable historical process in which the proletarian heroes, as George Lukács later saw it, express typical class struggle contradictions that are apparent in the typical circumstances of their time.[59] Drama's most important verisimilitude draws from the social reality as seen from the perspective of the proletariat, while exposing the evils of contemporary society and expressing the oppressed classes' lofty ideals. If the proletariat's cause is to be advanced, the language and artistic style of drama must not cater to the pleasures and tastes of the elite but be fashioned so as to be comprehensible and accessible to the multitude. Ideally, the representational triangular relationship should be such that it always favors the representation *of* the proletariat, *by* artists who understand them, and *for* the additional benefit of readers who uphold and appreciate their values.

In becoming one of the most important categories of Chinese drama, proletariat theater was further subdivided into the "worker play," the "peasant play," and the "soldier play," or together known as "worker-peasant-soldier play" (*gong-nong-bing xiju*). Because it both illustrated the Maoist theory of socialist realism and a continuous theatrical tradition, PRC literary historians interpreted Tian Han's one-act play *The Raining Season (Meiyu)*, 1931, as one of the earliest plays in Republican China.[60] In depicting the woes of a poor worker's family, Tian was said to have represented the darkness of the old society and the workers' inevitable insurrection against those in power.[61] Such stories became popular in the early years of the PRC, as demonstrated in *Number Six Gate (Liuhaomen)*, written in 1950.[62] The play painted the miserable life of the porters in the Tianjin train station before 1949 and then showed their new life after liberation, when they became masters of their own lives and country under CCP leadership. The play appealed to audiences and was later adapted into a film and a Peking opera. A *Wish of Forty Years* (*Sishinian de yuanwang*), produced in 1952, departed the simple conflict between poor workers and their oppressors before liberation and presented the more complex confrontation between an engineer and workers in the PRC. Supported by the party and army representatives, workers criticized the engineer for being too conservative in his blueprints for building the Chengdu-Chongqing railroad. With the help of the experts from the Soviet Union, the workers succeeded in completing the railroad in two years, in time to present it as a gift to celebrate an anniversary of the CCP funding and to fulfill the long-held wishes of people in Sichuan.

This play reflects the new theme of reeducating intellectuals whose pre-liberation trainings became a liability in the new society. This theme found its best expression in another worker play, *Braving the Torrent* (*Jiliu yongjin*), in which a former worker became a steel factory vice president after having been trained as a new intellectual, at once politically trustworthy and technologically up-to-date. Despite its dogmatism, the play, directed by Huang Zuolin and premiered by Shanghai People's Art Theater in 1963, occupied a special place in the theater history as one of the very few Brechtian productions in the 1949–1966 period.[63] In addition to using a narrator to introduce the background of different characters, Huang employed multiple scenes onstage to dramatize various events occurring at the same time. The most memorable scenes include the one where the protagonist rushes home in a roaring train in the background while his fellow workers wait for his homecoming in the center stage. In another scene, the protagonist tested the probability of a new plan while positioned in front of a steel furnace as others discussed it in a meeting. Such a fluid use of theatrical space attempted to create a new image of a worker leader, at once practical and knowledgeable.

While *Braving the Torrent* experimented with dramatic techniques to represent new workers in socialist China, other worker plays reminded their audiences of the heroic pre-liberation history before 1949. *Red Storm* (*Hongse fengbao*), for instance, dramatized the famous 1923 Beijing-Hankou railroad strikes, organized by the workers' union with CCP underground party members and brutally suppressed by warlords and their foreign supporters.[64] The class conflict between haves and have-nots pointed to the anti-imperialist theme still found on the PRC stage. Premiered in 1958, *Red Storm* ran for 273 shows, as an unparalleled hit with record-breaking ticket sales. Nevertheless, the play was later attacked during the Cultural Revolution for failing to represent workers exclusively. Its characters included a lawyer who provided legal advice to workers, but he was still considered a member of the petite bourgeoisie. It also hindered a dramatization of the typical contradictions of the time through the class struggle between workers and their oppressors, with a typical hero of the proletariat to lead the masses in circumstances typifying the Republican China.

In the 1960s, on the eve of the Cultural Revolution, the focus in worker plays shifted to alert the younger generation of workers to "never forget" their revolutionary history. Specifically, this means "never to forget class struggle" in socialist China as expressed in the title of Cong Shen's play *Never Forget Class Struggle (Qianwan buyao wangji)*.[65] Performed by Harbin City Theater, in 1963, and frequently produced throughout the country, *Never Forget* concerns the dilemma of a young worker whose marriage to a beautiful woman introduced him to a "bourgeois lifestyle" under the influence of his mother-in-law. Such a "corrupt" lifestyle saw him purchase a new wool suit, which cost over 100 yuan, raised by hunting and selling wild ducks in his spare time. The class struggle between the proletariat and the bourgeoisie persisted even in a worker's family. The link between the revolutionary heritage and one's own family played an even larger role in *Three Generations (Sandai ren)*, performed by the China Youth Art Theater in 1963. During the Cultural Revolution in 1970, it became better known in its model Peking-opera version as *The Red Lantern (Hongdeng ji)*.[66] Set during the War of Resistance to Japan, *The Red Lantern* narrates the story of Li Yuhe, a poor railway worker who adopts a mother and an orphan girl whose family members had been murdered during the Beijing-Hankou railway workers' strikes. In contrast to *Red Storm*, with its masses of striking workers, *The Red Lantern* focuses on the fortunes of a single family. Li Yuhe and his adopted mother are captured, tortured, and finally executed by a Japanese police chief. Carrying out the last wishes of her father and grandmother, Li Tiemei, Li Yuhe's adopted daughter, succeeds in sending secret codes to the CCP guerrillas. With this simple story line, *The Red Lantern* ingeniously denied blood relationships—the basis of families in all cultures —while extending their hierarchical and cohesive structure to the creation of "one big revolutionary family," whose members share class interests as they struggle against their common enemies.

Using a similar strategy, other model plays constructed a global discourse of "world revolution." Peking opera *On the Docks (Haigang)* portrayed the working class in 1960s Shanghai, where the daily loading and unloading of rice seeds on ships to the outside world was said to have greatly aided the liberation of Third World peoples oppressed by Western imperialism and colonialism.[67] The opera claimed that Western imperialists had attempted to stop African peoples from experimenting with growing rice, thus making them dependent on Western foreign aid. The heroes and heroines in these model plays were held up as role models for the "revolutionary masses" during the height of the Cultural Revolution, which was said to have world revolution as its ultimate goal.

While Maoist theater presented a teleological view of history perpetrated by inevitable class struggle, post-Maoist theater challenged this paradigm. An important example is *Winter Jasmine (Baochunhua)*, an early and popular anti–Gang of Four play.[68] It recounts the class discrimination endured by Bai Jie, a young female textile-factory worker, because of her politically incorrect family origins. Her father had been declared a counterrevolutionary for having worked for the KMT government before 1949, and her mother was condemned as a rightist for having challenged in 1957 the CCP's radical policies. The introduction of a Bai Jie to the Chinese stage signaled a historic turn, for even before the Cultural Revolution, when the party's policies were less rigid and dogmatic, postrevolutionary plays seldom had protagonists from questionable class backgrounds. The ban had extended to all works of literature and art, in order, it was said, to best serve the interests of the party, the working people, and the proletarian revolutionary cause.

If *Winter Jasmine* redeems a model worker from a politically incorrect family to denounce the extreme class politics that peaked during the Cultural Revolution, *Fashionable Red Skirts in the Street (Jieshang liuxing hongqunzi)*, premiered in 1984, questions the very value of the model-worker system in the Mao era. Tao Xing'er, a model worker just like Bai Jie, is confused by her title. Although expected to love her factory as her own home, she spends her precious time preparing for a university entry examination. She also purchases a "fashionable" red skirt, which leads her boss to chastise her for displaying "bourgeois taste." When her father, after years of separation, finds her through a newspaper story on her model-worker's deeds, her image embarrasses her and she rejects his love. The play dramatizes a divided self who struggles to free herself from the "glorious" tradition of the working class to become a woman true to her own desires. The play exposes the hypocrisy of the class issues in Maoist and post-Maoist China. In a Maoist country where there was no significant gap between the wealthy and the poor, class issues seldom revolved around economic circumstances but centered on the discourse of power to promote the political agenda of the ruling class.

The problematic nature of the representation of the workers is best illustrated in Yang Limin's *Black Stones (Heise de shitou)*,[69] one of the best-received dramas of the late 1980s. Labeled as a neorealistic play, *Black Stones* reworks the Maoist claim of protecting the welfare of the workers. Premiered by Daqing City Theatre (Daqingshi huanjutuan), the play depicts the hardships and suffering of petroleum workers, no longer portrayed as proud masters of socialist China. In spite of the dark view of the workers' lives, however, *Black Stones* was unanimously applauded by cultural officials, drama critics, and the audiences of various backgrounds.

Black Stones is best appreciated when set against PRC literary tradition, which stressed the heroic spirit of the working class. Many Chinese people in the early 1960s were familiar with the stories of legendary petroleum workers who forged China's first proletarian industry in the wilderness known as Daqing. *Black Stones* astonished post-Maoist audiences with its bleak description of workers and their daily fatigue in the "most barbarous" wilderness.[70] Indeed, the very image of black color in the title of the play contrasts sharply with that of red color in *Red Storm* and *The Red Lantern*, allusions to revolutionary zeal and heroic heritage for a lofty course. Rarely could one find the familiar characters who had combated nature and class enemies. In a messy camp cabin, one hears the sad story of Veteran, an oil-rig builder who nine years before left behind his wife in his remote hometown because he had no idea how to manage the red tape that would have approved her transfer. It should be noted that although the play is set in contemporary times, Veteran is depicted as a typical model worker of the 1960s —disciplined, diligent, and uncomplaining.

Veteran's basic honesty is ironically pointed out when he spends the greater part of a day wandering fruitlessly around the administrative building, not knowing which door to enter to deliver his gifts. At a subsequent meeting called to criticize his unlawful act, he apologizes wholeheartedly for his "terribly shameful" behavior, whereby he failed to live up to the expectations the party had of him as a veteran. Although a victim of the system, he still is loyal to it, blaming himself for letting it down, and not even contemplating that it might have let *him* down. This story, of course, typifies that of many a nameless veteran who fought in the war for the CCP and was sent, after 1949, to reclaim the virgin land in the remote Northeast, far away from his hometown. Like Veteran in the play, many of these men volunteered to relocate to the wilderness without knowing what was in store for them and what they stood to lose.

To drive home what Maoist history meant for the workers, *Black Stones* has another character, a Captain Qin, who personifies the revolutionary heritage that Daqing workers helped to create in the 1960s. For him, opposing this heritage would discredit his lifelong sacrifices and his stories of a glorious past. Holding on to his heritage allows Captain Qin to make sense of his past. He is prepared to die, forever faithful, at his post—the drilling ground where he belongs—rather than ever violate his tradition. Belatedly identifying with him, they commemorate him most meaningfully, perhaps, by erecting a national monument to the veteran workers, who were victims of socialist history. For this play to be accepted on a still-socialist stage in the 1980s and to bypass censorship required the help of a character, Lin Jian, the new secretary of the Party Committee of the Exploration Corporation. He represents the party's new policy in post-Maoist China of seeing to workers' welfare, which the previous regime had neglected, and his ploy of living and working among the workers without revealing his identity until the end suggests what they might hope for from the next generation of leadership. This device of creating a new party secretary to protect a play from being branded harmful to the regime in power was employed in several post-Maoist plays.

It is fitting to recall here that in the 1960s, Chinese theatrical discourse denied any need for scripting tragedy, which was only required for plays depicting the deadly class struggle between workers and their oppressors in the pre-PRC period, when revolutionary setbacks could give temporary victory to the reactionaries and result in the tragic death of the proletarian heroes. During the post-Maoist theater debate, however, some critics rescued tragedy by pointing out that it was a legitimate form for current plays, which were now allowed to focus on the tragic flaws of individuals without referring to society as the cause of their fall.[71] To validate post-Maoist ideology, tragedy was also permitted to depict the Chinese people's struggles against the Gang of Four or other Maoist radicals, who, for a limited period of time, caused tragedy to overtake socialist China.

Black Stones seems to bestride this duality with great effectiveness. On the one hand, Captain Qin's death occasions tragic sublimity; on the other, it is blamed on the residual Gang of Four radical ideology, which ignored the workers' interests, a situation that Lin, as the new party leader, promises to redress. As we have seen, Lin does not reveal himself until very late in the play—when his official status is needed to authorize the order for a helicopter to save Captain Qin's life. This type of official character holds out the promise of a new, more responsive regime and revalidates the idea of the "savior of the people" embodied in the old socialist system. In this case, however, the "savior" might have materialized too late. Not only had the audience already been exposed to Veteran's and Captain Qin's disillusioning stories, but they were also likely to sympathize with Jubilee, another "little man," whose life exhibits even more marginalization than that of his peers. An orphan of a veteran roughneck killed in an accident in the 1960s, Jubilee thinks of the team as his home. Returning from a dangerous journey and in search of cigarettes and wine for his fellow workers, Jubilee cannot believe that Blackie, his master and trusted friend, has killed his pet—an injured wild goose Jubilee rescued. Blackie had gone after the animal in a fit of rage after being criticized by the authorities for loving Phoenix, a married woman from the nearby town. Knowing this does not console Jubilee, who cries out in desperation and anguish: "Why on earth can't you let live a little thing like this!" It is at this point that the meaning of "Jubilee" comes into full play: literally defined as "little celebration," the word pays tribute to numerous little men like Jubilee whose sacrifices and sorrow must be remembered. It also questions the image of "Daqing" (literally, "grand celebration"), which, after years of "painstaking and arduous effort," still is a godforsaken wilderness, as so depicted in the play.

The play does not end with Lin's revelation, nor with Captain's Qin's death. Rather, it concludes with a denouement that leaves one uncertain as to what will happen to Blackie and his lover, Phoenix, who has just joined him after having murdered the husband who brutally abused her. The team having departed on time for a new construction site with the new party secretary in the lead, Blackie and

Phoenix are left alone onstage. Their embracing bodies appear deserted and vulnerable, as an insignificant couple barely surviving at the margin of a culture. Although the invention of the Lin character prevented the play from being attacked as an unhealthy tragedy, many audience members might feel free to ask themselves: who is to blame for these tragic events that occur not just onstage, not just before the smashing of the Gang of Four, but now, right in front of us? Thus protected by ambiguities and a double discourse, this desolate play was received as one of the most successful works of the post-Maoist theater.

After *Black Stones*, the worker play in post-Maoist China almost disappeared. Indeed, the play could be seen as the worker theater's swan song, since this kind of drama no longer attracted much of an audience, as box office sales clearly showed. In a society that no longer cast class differences as the driving force for historical change, the stories of the working class had lost their power. The representation of workers in Maoist and post-Maoist theaters was problematic, despite its attempt to honor workers. Nevertheless, a price is paid when theater no longer addresses contemporary issues in the lives of ordinary people. One wonders what Chinese contemporary theater would look like if it turned its attention to the stories of the urban poor who recently lost their jobs in government factories. One wonders, also, what contributions post-socialist societies could make to cultural production, especially to the dramatic genres, which cannot survive in local communities without making strong conscious efforts to link with the mass audience.

Wild Grass:
The Space between the Country and the City

If *Black Stones* is noteworthy for rewriting workers' history, *Wild Grass* (*Yecao*) should be credited for taking up the fate of the peasants. Chinese theater's fascination with rural life has a different dimension from that in the West, where some writers glorify it as the images of romantic exile. Mao saw the countryside as the most important site of revolution, which would eventually surround and overwhelm the cities. In postrevolutionary days, Lin Biao, Mao's chosen successor during the Cultural Revolution, promoted the idea that the exploited and colonized nations of the Third World were the "countryside of the world." When they united, they could eventually surround and conquer the evil "cities of the world," the United States and the Soviet Union. By this construct, the economic poverty of the Third World was equated with the fate of the Chinese peasants and assigned the term "rural," if not "primitive," in the world arena. This concept imputed that the countries in question possessed enormous capacity, motivation, and desire for revolutionary changes to these nations when confronted by their highly industrialized "others."

This exploitation of the image of an impoverished rural life also served the May Fourth playwrights' agenda of constructing a suffering people in need of a new nation. A case in point is Tian Han's play *The Night a Tiger Was Captured (Huohu zhi ye)*, which depicts a peasant girl's entrapment by her patriarchal family wherein Confucian doctrines demand total obedience to parental will.[72] The peasant girl is told that if a tiger is captured that night, it will be claimed for her dowry so she can be married off to a well-to-do family. However, the seriously wounded "tiger" in the mountain trap is found to be the young girl's secret lover, who kills himself later in the play to protest her father's actions. The fierce tiger in the play, symbolizing wild territories apart from civilization, evokes the ghost-haunted house in *Breaking Out of Ghost Pagoda (Dachu youlingta)*, written in 1928 by the female playwright Bai Wei.[73] Bai's play suggests that the large home of a rich landlord is like an evil-filled pagoda, from which a brave, Nora-like concubine breaks out in search of freedom. It also relates to a much more devastating story: a mother returning "home" from afar, and a daughter trapped at home, wage a fierce battle against patriarchal society, represented by a domineering, lustful father in his country home and by a new-nationalist "father" already skeptical of the revolution that was intended to eliminate the Confucian father. The death of the daughter in her mother's arms at the conclusion of Bai Wei's play signifies how any escape from the traditions presiding over both the country and the city is practically impossible.

Critiqued as possibly countering the spirit of the May Fourth tradition, Ouyang Yuqian's *Homecoming (Huijia yihou)* expanded the binary oppositions between the country and the city to those between Chinese tradition and Western influence.[74] Upon returning home after years of education abroad, a Chinese student finds himself more attracted to the virtuous wife obtained through an arranged marriage than to the nagging mistress he met in America. This portrayal of a rural Hunan province as a haven of domestic happiness and spiritual replenishment marks a turning point for Chinese dramatists: they were reflecting on the negative impact of the Western experience while trying to come to terms with some of the traditional values in rural life. In *Homecoming*, China has been transformed into a sort of peaceful utopia with no sense of urgency about surrounding the evil cities of the world, as a radical Maoist would prescribe later on during the Cultural Revolution. It is a "peach blossom spring," an idyllic landscape free of warfare, worldly concerns, and unfulfilled missions.

Before and during the War of Resistance to Japan, the Chinese countryside also served as an essential backdrop for drama. It did so, in this case, for the wartime drama that was promoted and reached its peak in August 1937 when twelve National Salvation Drama Troupes traveled throughout the country to perform. Chen Liting and others' *Put Down Your Whip (Fangxia nide bianzi)*,[75] one of the best-known wartime plays, presents a starving daughter being whipped by her helpless, tearful father, while others urge him to put down his whip and join in the national effort against the Japanese invaders. The play then relates their miserable journey on foot from the city of Shenyang to the countryside of the Northeast to escape the brutal occupying troops. Some lines were meant to incite responses from the audience, and the play was frequently performed outdoors, which mark it as an important work in the tradition of Chinese street theater. The image of the country as an escape from the city, as well as the open space where dramatists and soldiers could unite to bolster resistance against foreign troops, became a familiar trope in subsequent plays. In this sense, Mao's conception of the countryside as the place for rallying revolutionary energies and the nationalist spirit at times of crisis found its best expression.

The idea of the country as an arena for revolution received further elaboration onstage in the "liberated area" occupied by the CCP, especially in Yan'an, the party headquarters. Here dramatists, influenced by Mao Zedong's famous "Talks at the Yan'an Forum on Literature and Art" (1942), attempted to create a "national form" of theater, drawing inspiration from the commoners' experiences and from folk dance and drama. This body of work culminated in the Yan'an drama *White-Haired Girl (Baimaonü)*, a folk opera that premiered in April 1945.[76] In the play, the poor peasant girl Xi'er has escaped from a vicious landlord who had had her father beaten to death for failing to repay his debts. She survives in a mountain cave as a wild person whose hair has turned white. Only with the arrival of the CCP can she be rescued from her ghostly existence and take her revenge. Demonstrating how the old society turned a human being into a ghost and the new society turned a ghost back into a human being, *White-Haired Girl* reportedly met with great enthusiasm in the liberated areas during the 1940s. Consequently, it was often performed at mass meetings in rural regions in order to raise the peasants' "class consciousness" and set them against class enemies such as the vicious landlord. Xi'er's past, her suffering, and her aspirations constituted a potent aid in constructing a new Chinese nation and socialist state, which held out the promise of equality and freedom for peasants.

The Chinese countryside as an essential part of the world-revolutionary scheme reached its climax with the revolutionary-model theater to promote proletariat arts during the Cultural Revolution, as in *Song of the Dragon River (Longjiang song)*.[77] Set in 1963, this Peking opera depicts the dilemma of peasants from the Dragon River Brigade who must abide by the county party committee's decision to dam the Dragon River in order to save a drought-ridden area. When the peasants are asked to flood their own land so as to channel water onto the area, a dramatic conflict develops around the collective interest of one peripheral local community, whose members have repeatedly been asked to relinquish their personal aspirations for the good of the nation. The opera uses the narrative of a "bitterness story" about the "old society" to contrast the latter with the "loving and caring government" of socialist China, whose demand that one local community sacrifice to save another is shown to be justified. By such measures, the opera shows that China can become a powerful nation capable of championing revolutionary movements in Third World countries, where the remote "brothers and sisters" that make up the oppressed classes may draw inspiration from the Chinese revolution. Thus in this work, the most isolated and rural part of China has direct links to the outside world by dint of the local ideals of the Cultural Revolution. The opera could be said to function as the ultimate blueprint for Mao's theory of the relationship between the Chinese countryside and city.

If the peasant plays of Maoist China romanticized the socialist countryside for the purpose of constructing a utopia, post-Maoist theater presented a primitive place not unlike the oppressive mountain village and ghost house in the May Fourth plays. This subversive rewriting of history appears in *Sangshuping Chronicles (Sangshuping jishi*), known for its successful experimentation with some of the conventions of Greek theater.[78] Set in Sangshuping, an isolated village in northwest China, it relates the tragic as well as commonplace, which have remained unchanged for centuries—poverty, ignorance, sexual suppression, and brutal patriarchal structure. Nowhere is there a trace of any liberated peasantry longing to participate in the world revolution in socialist China. The play exemplified a literary and dramatic trend known as "meditation on the historical and cultural past," which sought to discover the roots of political upheavals such as the Cultural Revolution. The play attempted, in the words of its directors, to display a "living fossil," embodying the cultural and historical sediments of the past five thousand years, in order to call for real changes in contemporary China. Thus once more, Chinese intellectuals' writing and performing on the city stage, seemingly in the voice of the peasants, created a rural China that badly needed the cultural reforms first advocated in May Fourth theater.

The conflict between city and countryside was revived, to great effect, in the production of *Wild Grass*, written by Zhang Mingyuan, a woman playwright from northeast China. In a turnabout of the old literary theme of "braving the journey to the Northeast" (*chuang Guandong*), which depicted the plight of countryside paupers before 1949 who traveled beyond the Shanhaiguan mountain pass to eke out a hardscrabble existence in the Northeast, the play presents woes endured during an era of economic reform, when greed in the modern city inevitably broke down traditional values. As a realist drama, it also depicts the radical changes occurring in the countryside in the 1980s, when, after having abolished the collective farming system, many peasants left their impoverished villages behind and migrated to the cities as temporary workers in search of a better life. The play can thus be read as a powerful critique against capitalism and globalization in post-socialist China, where many poor peasants indeed "experienced the bitter life of the old society for the second time" (*chi erbian ku*), as Mao had predicted before and during the Cultural Revolution. In this regard, post-Maoist peasant plays both repudiated and celebrated Maoist values.

One of Zhang Mingyuan's themes is the growing alienation of Fourth, a poor man from the countryside who subsequently becomes a rich man in the city. He made his fortune by abandoning in his home village the woman he loved and seeking out a loveless match with a crippled woman so he can trade favors with her uncle, who sets him up with important job opportunities, a permanent urban residence, and a comfortable housing arrangement. Addicted to making money, Fourth is also drawn to other social evils, such as womanizing, bribery, and corruption, which finally result in his criminal trial. By the end of the play, Erqin, the woman Fourth loves, marries another man, who ironically has taken over Fourth's job as overseer of a construction company. Furthermore, he will live in a bigger city and build a fancier hotel than did Fourth. Overcome with loneliness, Erqin perhaps senses that as her new man tries to enrich himself, he is bound to repeat the mistakes of Fourth, who sacrificed everything once meaningful to him in his determination to make a fortune. She might foresee another five years of waiting just to be victimized again by her second man and, thus, the end of her pointless journey from the country to the city in search of love.

The play shows how women's bodies are turned into commodities and men become alienated from their former selves. It also represents a dramatist's attempts to probe into the life and aspirations of the new millionaires while highlighting the marginalized status of art and artists in a commercialized society. The plaint of the artist comes through when Fourth, in his new role of famous "entrepreneur of peasant origin" (nongmin qiyejia), announces proudly at a press conference that his company has decided to earmark seventy thousand yuan for a television program to demonstrate his support of the arts.[79] In the process of depicting the nouveaux riches as art patrons, the dramatist avails herself of the opportunity to promote cultural projects.

Yet the same situation, from another angle, conveys hope that perhaps art can somehow be salvaged, not by the empty promises of the state government but by the good offices of wealthy people with aspirations for gaining prestige as benefactors of the arts. Their craving for recognition in the realm of the spiritual and the artistic, now that they have mastered the materialistic world, is yet another important facet of life that realist-oriented illusionist theater can skillfully represent. Furthermore, the fact that Fourth's donation goes to a television station, which can return the favor via TV commercials, rather than to a theater, where the ideal of "pure" art is still sometimes pursued, could also be seen as a commentary on the fragile attempts by entrepreneurs—whose materialism has often placed them in opposition to art —to save art.

With its contemporary setting in the Northeast and its linear plot covering a time span of several years, this piece of theater attempts to isolate certain dramatic events for audiences who are lured into believing that they are watching the lives of other people as if through a keyhole—that is, without the actors knowing they are being observed. Besides its strong ties to these precepts of illusionist theater, *Wild Grass* has also (to a lesser degree) inherited some peculiarities of indigenous theater, which draws on local dialects and idioms of northeastern China in order to vividly and faithfully portray the people from a particular geographical region. In this regard, *Wild Grass* presents itself as a "sister play" to *Black Stones*, sharing with it a local setting and the flavor of northeastern China, in addition to its "sisterhood" of a peasant play to its "relative" genre of the worker play *Black Stones*. Northeastern theater *(Dongbei xiju)* falls short when compared with the most influential indigenous theater, the Beijing-flavored plays. Nevertheless, *Wild Grass*'s urgent concern with the social problems that accompany the rapid industrialization of society has continued to be a magnet for contemporary audiences. Its converging space between city and countryside—and the inseparable fate of both workers and peasants as struggling victims—radically departs from Mao's theory of the Chinese countryside, Third World revolution, and their anticipated roles in the writing of human history.

Green Barracks: Androgyny, Cross-Dressing, and Masquerade in Contemporary Chinese Theater

Along with the worker and peasant plays, the modern Chinese stage features the soldier play, the earliest of which can be traced back to Hong Shen's *Yama Zhao,* an experimental play from the Shakespearean open form. Focus on the male leads had been called for during the war period, as illustrated in the theater productions of the Red Army's Soldier's Drama Troupe (Zhanshi jushe) in the Jiangxi Soviet. The plays from this source include *August Nanchang Uprising (Bayi Nanchang qiyi)* and *The Snow on Lu Mountain (Lushan zhi xue),* both performed in 1933. The latter play enlisted amateur actors and actresses to depict their own real-life roles of soldiers and commanders as a stratagem to raise the morale of their peers. Even more remarkably, high-ranking Red Army commanders participated in the performance of this play, with Luo Ruiqing, a top CCP commander, playing the part of Chiang Kai-shek, the generalissimo of the KMT and arch-villain of wartime drama. This tradition of male leads persisted in PRC theater with Hu Ke's *Growing Up in the Battlefield (Zhandou li chengzhang)*.[80] This play centers on a family reunion, brought about after son and father, who had been kept apart by a rich landlord's exploitation, discover each other while fighting side by side in the same army unit. The characters' hard-won happiness intended to elucidate the necessity of the Chinese Communist revolution, which had supposedly liberated poor families from miserable circumstances. Illuminating a different angle of the same proposition, Chen Qitong's *Rivers and Mountains (Wanshui qianshan)* dramatizes the epic Long March with its panoramic view of the hardships the Red Army had to overcome.[81] The Red Army unit becomes a symbolic family that exemplifies how one might take care of one's comrades as though they were dearer than one's own flesh and blood. Consisting of a preponderantly male cast, however, the revolutionary family—although newly constructed in contrast to the traditional family hierarchy—remains patriarchal, with the CCP party leader forming the head of the new "household."

In spite of its predominantly male cast, *Soldiers under Neon Light (Nihongdeng xia de shaobing)* represented a departure by virtue of its vivid female character.[82] Chunni is the loving spouse of a soldier from the People's Liberation Army (PLA) stationed in early post-liberation Shanghai, where imperialist and bourgeois influence is considered rampant. Chunni comes to the aid of her husband, who, faltering in his revolutionary ardor, doubts his rural identity and resents the simple lifestyle in which he once took pride. During a visit to his army unit in Shanghai, Chunni reminds her husband of their past before he threw his lot in with the revolution, and she recalls with him the great love they shared since they grew up in their home village and their wedding, after which she sent him to the battlefield. In one of the most celebrated scenes of any PRC soldier play, her tender voice is heard offstage reading the letter she has written his superior, in which she asks him to help her revive her husband's revolutionary spirit. Her concern for her husband's affection is seen as encompassing her unwavering faith in the revolutionary cause, thus rendering her at once a new, socialist woman with a broad vision and the "virtuous wife" mandated by the prerevolutionary Confucian tradition. Despite her revolutionary traits, a female character like Chunni serves to confirm the persistent patriarchal values of the society.

The female protagonist of this play was a domestic caretaker with class consciousness. However, the film version of *The Red Detachment of Women (Hongse niangzijun)*, which was the precursor for the "revolutionary-model ballet" of the same title, presented a different picture. Promoted during the Cultural Revolution as the quintessential proletariat art, unlike the bourgeois art said to have dominated the PRC stage even after 1949, *The Red Detachment of Women* became the most representative of the soldier plays, thanks to its combination of the themes of military mobilization and women's liberation. But before proceeding to a close reading of this ballet and its parody, *Green Barracks*, we should ask why female leads began to be seen in soldier plays. One could, of course, talk about the imperial roots in the traditional tale (and operatic repertoire) of the long-celebrated Hua Mulan, the story of a filial daughter cross-dressing as a male soldier to fulfill her father's military duty. Maxine Hong Kingston's *The Woman Warrior* and the Disney movie *Mu Lan* represented the story's contemporary appeals to transnational audiences. What issues, however, relating to gender relationships and nationalism within the context of modern Chinese culture could require the presence of women soldiers on the Chinese stage?

Among the many reasons is a clue perhaps relevant to our study of theater culture, found in Lu Xun's critique of Mei Lanfang's performance tour in America in 1930.[83] At a time when modern Chinese writers were seeking efficient means of crafting a strong nation, Lu Xun was troubled by the warm reception given Mei's performances, in which he displayed his uncanny skill at acting female roles. Mei Lanfang was promoted as the most illustrious actor from Peking opera, and his work in his Western debut was felt to represent the national art of China *(guoju)*. Mei's performance in America and Japan, Lu Xun believed, suggested not the spreading of Mei's fame, and by extension, of the "light" of Chinese tradition, but the ending of such a "glory."[84] As is well known, Mei won particular plaudits for *The Drunken Honored Consort (Guifei zuijiu)* and *Farewell My Concubine (Bawang bieji)*. In the former, Mei played the tearful Yang Guifei, reduced to drowning her sorrows in solitary drinking after learning that the emperor Tang Xuanzong (r. 712–756) was disporting himself with another concubine in the Western Palace. The latter depicted the concubine Yu, who, after dancing one last time for her defeated lord Xiang Yu, impaled herself on a sword to prove to him the depth of her love. Both works celebrate the Confucian ethics of *"zhongjun,"* or "loyalty to one's sovereign," while setting forth the stereotypical traits of courtly women: obedience, patience, selflessness, passivity, and, at times, a reflexive readiness to sacrifice for imperial father figures. *Farewell My Concubine* is also known for its misogynist view that women, the source of evil, lead men away from their proper duties.

Lu Xun's remark that Mei Lanfang's "fame" was redounding to the Chinese people's shame is best understood in this context. In an earlier essay published in 1924, Lu Xun had already criticized the androgynous and cross-dressing features of Mei's performance. What was it about a Chinese man playing an elegant woman that so entranced his audiences? How is it that "the most noble, most eternal, and most universal" art in China "is the art of men acting as women"?[85] Was it because Mei played a set of androgynous, hence, mediocre personages without firm principles, distinctive personalities, and even gender identities? Was it possible that Lu Xun viewed Mei's theater art as expressing one of the chronic ills of the Chinese national character?[86]

Anxious to see the emergence of a strong China, Lu Xun might not have considered a feminized man a fitting symbol for the nation. Surely China should not be imagined as a passive woman, an object of desire without her own agency to be penetrated. Lu Xun could not have known, however, that Mei's performance in Moscow in 1935 would inspire Brecht to form his theory of "alienation effect," which challenged and reinvigorated Western dramatic art. Nor could he have predicted the success on Broadway of David Hwang's *M. Butterfly*, in which an actor from Peking opera cross-dressed as a woman in life as well as onstage, thus reversing the stereotype of a passive Oriental (Japanese) woman submitting to a strong Western man, as so expressed in the familiar story of Puccini's *Madame Butterfly*. For Lu Xun, androgyny and cross-dressing were political acts evoking a nation without a will of its own. Most pertinently in the 1930s China, Lu Xun's critique against androgyny fit into his larger concerns of national salvation of China, endangered by foreign powers as well as by the Chinese people's own inability to break away from their traditional culture, represented in its most decadent guise by operatic theater.

Lu Xun's fear of a feminized China is echoed in the PRC soldier plays in which women warriors come to the fore. In these plays not only can China not be feminized but neither can women themselves. As demonstrated in *The Red Detachment of Women*, the total mobilization of the Chinese nation necessarily drew on the energy of women, and in this setting, androgyny and cross-dressing came into play. Based on an authentic account of a women's detachment that waged war against local despots, the model ballet highlighted the transformation of Wu Qinghua from ex-slave to woman warrior. It was in the film version, released before the Cultural Revolution, that the name Wu Qinghua (which means "pure and stainless China" and can apply to a man as well as a woman) replaced Wu Qionghua (the original, traditional woman's name meaning "fine jade flower"). More significantly, the implicit attraction one senses between Wu and Hong Changqing, the male party representative in this women's detachment in the earlier film version, was dropped in the ballet, thereby desexing Wu, the "model" woman warrior.

The name shift and plot change alone, however, could not bring about Chinese official feminism, which always subsumes women under the socialist agenda of Maoist China. Like many comparable revolutionary war stories, *The Red Detachment of Women* used the oppression of women before 1949 to symbolize exploitation of all other oppressed classes of both genders. The raising of Wu's class consciousness is accompanied by her quick acquisition of a soldier's skills, such as shooting targets and throwing grenades. But neither these skills nor physical strength can endow Wu with the same power as that of her male counterparts. The missing ingredient is supplied by Hong Changqing, whom the play portrays as an intellectual giant with political vision. He takes her under his wing when she is attempting to join the detachment, instructs her in revolutionary truth, and prepares her to succeed him as party secretary in the likely event of his death in battle. Most important, he convinces her to give up her obsession with wreaking revenge on the personal foe who had abused and imprisoned her. A woman warrior must first dedicate herself to liberating mankind before she can liberate herself, Hong tells Wu. Although Wu and Hong share the same proletariat background and thus presumably the same political status, it is the male central character, Hong, who is endowed with a discursive power that enables him to instruct the women soldiers in their duties in the public sphere. Consequently, he plays a pivotal (and patriarchal) role in their ideological transformation.

Although *The Red Detachment of Women* shows Wu taking on some male characteristics such as physical strength, it does not provide Hong with similar androgynous possibilities. Hong's pitching in to wash vegetables and fish with the cooks in the women's unit does not qualify, since, in the context of this soldier play, it would reflect the CCP directive that army officers integrate themselves in the ranks of ordinary soldiers by participating in the meanest of their chores. Thus Hong comes off as the ideal male model, a symbolic father figure who leads a women's detachment to victory.

What shall we make of this instance of one-sided androgyny in Chinese theater? At first sight, gender differences seem to disappear as women warriors take to the battlefield as ably and courageously as their male counterparts. But it then becomes evident—when we see that women are encouraged to be androgynous but that men's so-called male characteristics remain inviolate—that the unequal power relationship between genders will persist.

As a critical response to the version of female liberation represented by the Maoist tradition, women playwrights like Zhang Lili rewrote the canonical soldier play. Zhang Lili's script, entitled *Green Barracks (Lüse yingdi)*, is situated in post-Maoist China, when economic reforms and materialist pursuits adversely affected women's lives. It dramatizes the stories of new PLA recruits who had become disenchanted with such civilian occupations as fashion model, peasant wife, or college student. Earlier dramas by Zhang Lili and other women playwrights like Xu Yan had depicted women of a previous period of the Maoist era returning home after rejecting the public role of "liberated women" that had sometimes been imposed on them. But fulfillment tended to elude them in the materialistic climate of the 1980s and 1990s.[87] Like their Nora-like sisters who had left home during and after the May Fourth movement in search of new identities outside the domestic spheres, Zhang Lili's female protagonists chose to abandon the hearth in the 1990s, in order to recapture their power as women who could still "hold up half of the skies." *Green Barracks*, then, attempts to answer that same question of Lu Xun's when he had asked in 1924: "What happened after Nora left home?" Lu Xun wondered whether these Nora-like women who had courageously left patriarchal homes might not at some later point find themselves back home again, when they could not pursue a public career that brought economic independence.[88] However, although *The Red Detachment of Women* made the case for the collective soldier's career being more fulfilling than an individual's search for happiness, it was left to *Green Barracks*—with its post-Maoist cynicism, irony, and direct engagement with earlier traditions—to reconfirm the necessity of leaving home for Nora-like characters.

It must be said that Zhang's women warriors are no carbon copies of Bai Wei's Nora-like characters who left patriarchal homes for revolutionary careers in the 1920s.[89] Nor could they be mistaken for that collective of Maoist "liberated" and "masculinized" women who contributed to advancing a single ideology before and after 1949. The location of a women's company next to a booming commercial area that has been accorded special privileges to promote a fledgling market economy discloses another aspect of the playwright's subject: the predicament of contemporary Chinese culture. For socialist ideology to demand of women that they sacrifice personal fulfillment to defend the nation makes little sense when that nation simultaneously advocates individualism and materialism to develop a capitalist economy. In this ambiguous and paradoxical milieu, Zhang's women soldiers attempt to balance their private and public roles as women and as citizens of a modern state. Not surprisingly, the transformative process into qualified women soldiers is accompanied by some frustration and disappointment. Some new recruits, for example, are censured for a weekend recreational outing to a nearby town where they hoped to relax as civilians after their strenuous basic training. Despite the hardships, the women succeed in emulating their political instructor and company commander, both of whom sacrificed motherhood and married life for military careers they believed to be more fulfilling and meaningful.

In a similar vein, Fang Xiaoshi, the female central character in *Green Barracks*, ends by renouncing her love for Sima Changjiang, the only male character in the play, so that no womanly desires will mar her as a model soldier. On the one hand, *Green Barracks* inherited the official Chinese feminist tradition depicted in *The Red Detachment of Women*: we witness a similar lesson of a woman who can—and should —be androgynous in service to her motherland, even in a time of peace. On the other hand, the story of frustrated love recounted in *Green Barracks* foregrounds what is absent in *The Red Detachment of Women*. Moreover, Fang does not give Sima up without a fierce struggle. Her heated argument with her commander, in which she asserts her right to love and to publicly express that love, can be viewed as a critique of the politics implicit in the representation of women on the Maoist stage. Unlike Wu Qinghua, who blindly admires her CCP leader, Fang challenges army officials, questions their personal sacrifices, and insists on her prerogative to love a man, before finally accepting the values of her commanders.

Sima's rejection of Fang's love is an important factor in steering her away from a focus on personal happiness. In the end she is led to embrace a military career both by the example of her female superiors, who represent the demands of the culture and the public, and by the rejection of her love object, whose view of women is still very much determined by the patriarchal society he lives in. Consequently, the gender politics play out differently in the two works. In *The Red Detachment of Women*, Hong Changqing embodies both the CCP party ideal and—as the object of women's love—an implicit male ideal. In *Green Barracks*, Fang opts for a kind of heroic, patriotic love only after Sima has given her passionate love the cold shoulder. Perhaps disappointment in personal love left the female lead in the latter play no choice but to substitute a love for the collective experience, which may compensate, to some extent, for a less fulfilling private life. Thus *Green Barracks* complicates women warriors' choices and circumstances while at the same time affirming some aspects of the gender politics it inherits from *The Red Detachment of Women*.

In Zhang's play the theme of blurring gender roles can be traced in Sima Changjiang's character. At first glance Sima seems to be made of the same cloth as Hong Changqing. Like Hong he is respected and trusted by new female recruits; he acknowledges their frustrations, recognizes their potential, and is there to encourage them when they are beset by difficulties. At the play's outset Sima is the only character who can approach and talk with Fang when she runs away from the barracks into the forest in protest over her company commander's harsh treatment. However, Sima, unlike Hong, is more than an inspirational mentor. He is also different from the two "manly" women commanders, for he is a "womanly" man—tender, soft, sensitive, and extremely skillful in communicating with his female colleagues. He is the proverbial "earth mother," but in an updated incarnation of technology instructor and modern man of science and reason, who brings the fresh air of knowledge to the otherwise stale and old-fashioned environment of the barracks. In the sense of exhibiting some androgynous (or cross-sex) traits, Sima represents a progression from Hong in *The Red Detachment of Women*, and to that extent makes gender equality seem more plausible.

On the whole, however, it is the unequal gender relationship that prevails. A charming and charismatic man, Sima longs for Bai Yu, the platoon leader who is described as the most beautiful woman in the army unit. According to Sima, she possesses "the abundance and richness of a woman" as well as "the brilliance and the spiritedness of a man." In this description are contained the essentialist binary oppositions of gender relations, which attribute to woman the beauty of the body and to man qualities of the mind. This reduction of Bai Yu to "ideal woman" preserves her traditional gender role of exemplifying female beauty while at the same time allowing her to continue the Maoist legacy of enacting the role of brilliant revolutionary man, such as Hong personified. In an ironic fashion, Bai Yu revives and replaces the Hong of Maoist theater, adding to that figure a feminine mystique and creating the illusion that this unlikely composite represents a more well-rounded post-Maoist woman than her predecessor. When Bai Yu ends up rejecting Sima for the sake of her warrior career, we see members of both genders (Fang and Sima) left with no choice but to compensate for failed attempts at personal happiness and meaningful relationships by rededicating themselves to their motherland. If neither man nor woman can be feminized while defending the nation—as we have seen in the Maoist-era *The Red Detachment of Women* and the post-Maoist-era *Green Barracks*—a man like Sima can only be "feminized" to the extent of being anguished by the loss of a woman who chose the defense of the country over the pursuit of personal happiness.

It would nevertheless be a mistake to equate femininity with lack of ambition; it is rather a case of lack of opportunity. As with the *caizi* (gifted scholar) of traditional romance who studied to pass a civil examination so that he would be in a position to win the best *jiaren* (beautiful lady), Sima in his role of technician has a more privileged position than is attainable by any woman. Thus Sima is actually a latter-day Hong: whereas Hong's power came from his elite party status, Sima derives his power from his command of privileged knowledge. His rejection by Bai Yu—the modern, "masculinized" version of a *jiaren* who retains her bodily beauty but without female agency—testifies to the futility, even in a post-Maoist era, of seeking happiness outside the collective. As a final analysis of the play, we might observe that science, technology, and modernity, with which the May Fourth writers had hoped to construct a strong China, did not entirely alter gender politics or the ways of thinking of the nation. Lu Xun's espousal of improved conditions, which he considered essential to increasing career choices for women, paradoxically placed post-Maoist women like Bai Yu in service to a new nationalist agenda, at the expense of their own subjectivity.

Additional factors point to the continuities and discontinuities between Maoist and post-Maoist drama. For example, the color green of *Green Barracks* evokes and plays against the quintessential Maoist color red, highlighted in the precursor text: Wu Qinghua's red shirt and pants in that earlier text symbolize her proletariat status as a slave girl eager to join the Red Army. On arriving at the revolutionary base, Wu is immediately drawn to the red flag, which, as the much-photographed scene during the Cultural Revolution attests, she had held in her hands while tears streamed down her face, which was registering her strong emotions. By contrast, the green color suggests a neutral space between a commercial culture that is no longer "red" and a marginalized army camp that still demands utter loyalty from women warriors in times of war. Furthermore, green could suggest the proverbial "gray area," that is, a perspective that can no longer be classified as either "black or white." Post-Maoist women no longer experienced their situation as a "life-and-death struggle" against evil landlords always dressed in black; in *The Red Detachment of Women*, the women these landlords oppressed had no recourse but a warrior's career if they wanted to survive. The green light that bathes the set of *Green Barracks* could be interpreted freely, according to the stage directions, as either "green barracks," "green daughters" who wear green army uniforms, or "green life," suggesting youth, vitality, and life itself.[90]

It is important to point out that after the mid-1980s, theater productions declined drastically, losing out to television, film, and other mass media. Gone were the days of early post-Maoist China when a play could draw large audiences with its pointed critique of contemporary society. Several influential plays raised the concern of the censors, who saw them as challenges to the ruling ideology and feared the negative impact they might have on the audience. Gone also were the "golden" times of the Cultural Revolution, when dramas of model theater like *The Red Detachment of Women* were familiar to the majority of the people—the elite and the masses, the rural and the urban, the young and the old. But by the time *Green Barracks* was published, in 1992, much had changed and no theater could be found to mount the production, in spite of the favorable comments the text had garnered from some distinguished drama critics. Critics viewed the play as especially precious for having come into being in a commercial climate that made theater an unprofitable commodity. One critic, Yu Qiuyu, fretted that Zhang Lili could not afford to continue writing dramas. One could not blame her, should she stop writing in the near future, Yu maintained, for she had already provided a valuable historic record of a woman playwright dreaming and working at a time when the theater had become one of the least popular media for mass consumption.[91] However, Chen Baichen, another well-known drama historian, characterized Zhang as a "foolish woman" for persevering in efforts that were profitless and not appreciated. Under such circumstances, it was a wonder, Chen claimed, that she had gotten three of her plays performed—plays that were well received by the limited audience still attracted to theater. For Chen the significance of these theatrical events was heightened by the fact that women playwrights appeared so rarely in the history of modern Chinese theater.[92] And indeed, it is this rare representation of the woman's viewpoint in theater that makes *Green Barracks*, despite its restricted outlook on gender politics, an invaluable preservation of women's experience in contemporary China. The inclusion of this text in our anthology also befits the long tradition in modern Chinese drama of regarding the reading of the text as important, if not more so, as seeing it enacted onstage. Moreover, on occasions when censorship caused the suspension of certain productions, curious readers lost no time in seeking out the published texts. In this respect, too, *Green Barracks* represented a departure from its most-watched precursor text, whose point of view it both inherited and rebelled against.

NOTES

1. Susan Morgan, "Introduction," in Anna Leonowens, *The Romance of the Harem*, ed. Susan Morgan (Charlottesville: University Press of Virginia, 1991), ix–xxxix. This paragraph presents a brief summary of some of the key points of Morgan's Introduction.

2. Richard Rodgers, *The King and I* (Winona, Minn.: H. Leonard Pub. Corp., 1951), 159.

3. Margaret Landon, *Anna and the King of Siam* (New York: John Day Co., 1944), 182.

4. Ge Yihong and others cited the staging of *Chahua nü* (La Dame aux Camélias) by Dumas fils as the first spoken drama produced by Chunliu she (Spring Willow

Society) in Japan, in February 1907. See Ge Yihong et al., *Zhongguo huaju tongshi* (A history of modern Chinese drama) (Beijing: Wenhua yishu chubanshe, 1990), 12. Since only two acts of *La Dame aux Camélias* were performed, other drama historians took the production of *Heinu yutianlu* (The black slave cries out to heaven) in its entirety as the first Chinese spoken drama, premiered in June 1907 by Spring Willow Society. More importantly, *The Black Slave Cries Out to Heaven*, although based on the translated text of Harriet Beecher Stowe's novel *Uncle Tom's Cabin*, was recreated as a spoken drama by Zeng Xiaogu. It was thus regarded as the first *"chuangzuo juben"* (original script). See Chen Baichen and Dong Jian, *Zhongguo xiandai xiju shigao* (A draft history of modern Chinese drama) (Beijing: Zhongguo xiju chubanshe, 1989), 8. For an English-language overview of modern Chinese theater, see Colin Mackerras, *The Chinese Theatre in Modern Times: From 1840 to the Present Day* (Amherst: University of Massachusetts Press, 1975). For English-language surveys of twentieth-century Chinese literature and spoken drama, see Bonnie S. McDougall and Kam Louie, eds., *The Literature of China in the Twentieth Century* (New York: Columbia University Press, 1997), and Xiaomei Chen, "Twentieth-Century Spoken Drama," in Victor H. Mair, ed., *The Columbia History of Chinese Literature* (New York: Columbia University Press, 2001), 848–877.

5. Bai Shurong and Liang Huaqun, "Lixiang zhihuo yongbu ximie" (An idealist spirit will never die), in Zhongguo yishu yanjiuyuan huaju yanjiusuo (The Research Institute of Modern Chinese Drama in the Chinese Academy of Art), ed., *Zhongguo huaju yishujia zhuan* (Biographies of modern Chinese dramatists) (Beijing: Wenhua yishu chubanshe, 1984), 1:104–123; see p. 111.

6. Zuo Lai and Liang Huaqun, "Sun Weishi zhuanlüe" (A biography of Sun Weishi), in Zhongguo yishu yanjiuyuan huaju yanjiusuo, ed., *Zhongguo huaju yishujia zhuan* (Beijing: Wenhua yishu chubanshe, 1986), 3:71–104; see p. 100.

7. *Zhongshen dashi* (The main event of one's life), by Hu Shi, was first published in *Xin qingnian* (New youth) 6, 3 (March 1919): 311–319 and later collected in Hong Shen, ed., *Zhongguo xin wenxue daxi: xiju ji* (Compendium of new Chinese literature, drama volume) (Shanghai: Liangyou, 1935), 1–8. For an English translation, see Hu Shih (Hu Shi), *The Greatest Event in Life*, trans. Edward Gunn, in Edward Gunn, ed., *Twentieth-Century Chinese Drama* (Bloomington: Indiana University Press, 1983), 1–9.

8. *Leiyu* (Thunderstorm), by Cao Yu, was first published in *Wenxue jikan* (Literature quarterly) 1, 3 (July 1934): 161–244. It was later published as a book by Shanghai wenhua shenghuo chubanshe in 1936. For an English translation, see Ts'ao Yü (Cao Yu), *Thunderstorm*, trans. Wang Tso-liang and A. C. Barnes (Beijing: Foreign Languages Press, 1978). *Thunderstorm* was premiered in April 1935, in Tokyo, by Zhonghua huaju tonghao hui (Chinese Modern Drama Friendship Association), organized by Chinese students in Japan.

9. Tian Benxiang, *Cao Yu zhuan* (A biography of Cao Yu) (Beijing: Beijing shiyue wenyi chubanshe, 1988), 370.

10. The PRC staging of Cao Yu's plays written before 1949 started in 1954, when Beijing renmin yishu juyuan (Beijing People's Art Theater) performed *Thunderstorm*.

The performances of Cao Yu's plays reached a peak around 1957, which witnessed the productions of *Thunderstorm*, *Richu* (Sunrise), *Beijing ren* (Peking man), and *Jia* (Family). See Tian Benxiang, *Cao Yu zhuan*, 398.

11. *Zhao Yanwang* (Yama Zhao), by Hong Shen, was first published in *Dongfang zazhi* (Eastern miscellany) 20, 1 (10 January 1923): 117–130 and 20, 2 (25 January 1923): 93–106. It was later collected in *Hong Shen xiqu ji* (Selected operas of Hong Shen) (Shanghai: Xiandai shuju, 1933), and in Hong Shen, ed., *Zhongguo xin wenxue daxi: xiju ji* (Compendium of new Chinese literature: drama volume) (Shanghai: Liangyou, 1935), 137–163. For an English translation, see Hong Shen, *Yama Chao*, trans. Carolyn T. Brown, in Edward Gunn, ed., *Twentieth-Century Chinese Drama*, 10–40.

12. *Shanghai wuyan xia* (Under Shanghai eaves) by Xia Yan was published by Xiju shidai chubanshe, Shanghai, in 1937, and later collected in Yu Ling, ed., *Zhongguo xin wenxue daxi: xiju ji 2, 1927–1937* (Compendium of new Chinese literature: drama volume 2, 1927–1937) (Shanghai: Shanghai wenyi chubanshe, 1985), 839–903. Hsia Yen (Xia Yan), *Under Shanghai Eaves*, trans. George Hayden, in Edward Gunn, ed., *Twentieth-Century Chinese Drama*, 76–125.

13. Zhongguo qingnian yishi juyuan (China Youth Art Theater) staged *Sandai ren* (Three generations) in 1963, with a similar story line as that in the Peking opera *Hong-deng ji* (The red lantern). The same theater also premiered *Dujuanshan* (Azalea Mountain), in July 1963, scripted by Wang Shuyuan.

14. *Yige sizhe dui shengzhe de fangwen* (The dead visiting the living), by Liu Shu-gang, was premiered by Zhongyang shiyan huajuyuan (Central Experimental Theater) 27 June 1985. Originally published in *Juben* (Drama script) 5 (1985): 8–37, it was and later collected in *Tansuo xiju ji* (An anthology of experimental plays) (Shanghai: Shanghai wenyi chubanshe, 1986), 365–445; see p. 423.

15. Ibid., 395.

16. *Longxugou* (Dragon Beard Ditch), by Lao She, first appeared in the supplemental issue (*zengkan*) of *Renmin xiju* (People's drama) 3, 1 (1951), which cited Lao She as the original scriptwriter and Jiao Juyin as the writer who revised it for stage performance. The play was published as a book by Renmin wenxue chubanshe, Beijing, 1958. It was premiered in 1951, by the Beijing People's Art Theater. For an English translation, see Lao She, *Dragon Beard Ditch*, trans. Liao Hung-ying (Beijing: Foreign Languages Press, 1956).

17. *Chaguan* (Teahouse), by Lao She, was first published in *Shouhuo* (Harvest) 7 (1957): 119–141 and later published as a book by Zhongguo xiju chubanshe in Beijing, 1958. It was premiered on March 29, 1958, by the Beijing People's Art Theater. For an English translation, see Lao She, *Teahouse*, *Chinese Literature* 12 (1979): 16–96.

18. *Niaoren* (Birdman), by Guo Shixing, appeared in *Xin juzuo* (New drama script) 3 (1993): 3–21. For an English translation, see Guo Shixing, *Birdmen*, trans. Jane C. C. Lai, in Martha P. Y. Cheung and Jane C. C. Lai, eds., *An Oxford Anthology of Contemporary Chinese Drama* (Hong Kong: Oxford University Press, 1997), 295–350.

19. He Jiping's *Tianxia diyilou* (The world's top restaurant) appeared in *Shiyue* (October) 3 (1988): 47–75. For a more detailed reading of the play, see Xiaomei Chen, *Acting the Right Part: Political Theater and Popular Drama in Contemporary China*

(Honolulu: University of Hawai'i Press, 2002), 319–323. Another English translation, entitled *The First House of Beijing Duck*, by Shiao-Ling S. Yu, can be found in *Chinese Drama after the Cultural Revolution, 1979–1989*, ed. Shiao-Ling S. Yu (Lewiston, N.Y.: The Edwin Mellon Press, 1996), 423–484.

20. Zhang Ziyang, "*Tianxia diyilou* bian" (Debate on *The World's Top Restaurant*), *Zhongguo xiju* (Chinese drama) 11 (1988): 10–12; see p. 12.

21. Gu Wei, "*Tianxia diyilou* de qian he hou" (Before and after the production of *The World's Top Restaurant*), *Xiju yanjiu* (Drama studies) 2 (1989): 53–54; see p. 53.

22. Ibid., 54.

23. Dou Xiaohong's speech was recorded by a reporter and included in Zhang Ziyang, "*Tianxia diyilou* bian," 11.

24. Qu Liuyi, "*Tianxia diyilou* de lishi wenhua yishi" (Historical-cultural consciousness in *The World's Top Restaurant*), *Xiju pinglun (jing)* (Drama review [Beijing]) 5 (1988): 4–5; see p. 4.

25. Zhang Ziyang, "*Tianxia diyilou* bian," 10. See also Tian Geng and Wu Linghua, "Shuishi zhuren shuishi ke" (Who is the guest and who is the owner?), *Xiju pinglun (jing)* 5 (1988): 7–8.

26. He Jiping, "*Tianxia diyilou* xiezuo zhaji" (Afterthoughts on writing *The World's Top Restaurant*), *Zhongguo xiju* 9 (1988): 42–43.

27. *Yu wusheng chu* (In a land of silence), by Zong Fuxian, was published in *Wenhui bao* (Wenhui newspaper) 28 October 1978, and later published as a book, by Renmin wenxue chubanshe, Beijing, 1978. It was collected in Li Moran, et al., eds., *Zhongguo huaju wushi nian juzuo xuan, 1949.10–1999.10* (Selected plays of modern Chinese drama in fifty years, 1949.10–1999.10), 8 vols., comp. Zhongguo huaju yishu yanjiuhui (Research Association of the Dramatic Art of Modern Chinese Drama), (Beijing: Zhongguo xiju chubanshe, 2000), 4: 369–425. For an English translation, see Tsung Fu-hsien (Zong Fuxian), *In a Land of Silence*, trans. Shu-ying Tsau, in Edward Gunn, *Twentieth-Century Chinese Drama*, 409–447. The play was premiered by the Shanghaishi gongren wenhuagong yeyu huajudui (Shanghai Worker's Cultural Club Amateur Drama Team), in 1978.

28. For historical contexts and a close reading of *Jiang Qing and Her Husbands*, see Xiaomei Chen, *Acting the Right Part*, 215–229.

29. *Li Xiucheng zhi si* (The death of Li Xiucheng), by Yang Hansheng, was published by Huazhong tushu gongsi, Hankou, in 1938, and later collected in Yang Hansheng, *Yang Hansheng juzuo ji* (Selected plays of Yang Hansheng) (Beijing: Zhongguo xiju chubanshe, 1982), 1:105–205. The play was premiered by Shanghai juyishe (Shanghai Dramatic Art Society) under the title of *Li Xiucheng xunguo* (Li Xiucheng dies for the country), in 1938, and performed by China Youth Art Theater in 1963 under the title of *Li Xiucheng*.

30. *Qu Yuan*, by Guo Muoruo, was premiered by Zhonghua juyishe (China Dramatic Society) and published by Wenlin chubanshe, Chongqing, in 1942. It was later collected in Chen Baichen, ed., *Zhongguo xin wenxue daxi, xiju juan 2, 1937–1949* (Compendium of new Chinese literature, drama volume 2) (Shanghai: Shanghai wenyi chubanshe, 1990), 3–77.

31. *Cai Wenji*, by Guo Moruo, was first published in *Shouhuo* 3 (1959): 4–30, and

as a book, by Wenwu chubanshe, Beijing, in 1959. It was premiered by Beijing People's Art Theater in 1959. For an English translation, see Guo Moruo, *Cai Wenji*, trans. Peng Fumin and Bonnie S. McDougall, in Guo Moruo, *Selected Works of Guo Moruo: Five Historical Plays* (Beijing: Foreign Languages Press, 1984), 315–406.

32. *Guan Hanqing*, by Tian Han, was premiered by Beijing People's Art Theater and first published in *Juben* 5 (1958): 2–33. An expanded version was later published as a book, by Zhongguo xiju chubanshe, Beijing, in 1958. For an English translation, see T'ien Han (Tian Han), *Kuan Han-ch'ing (Guan Hanqing)*, trans. Foreign Languages Press, in Edward Gunn, ed., *Twentieth-Century Chinese Drama*, 324–380.

33. The public criticism of Wu Han's *Hai Rui baguan* (Hai Rui dismissed from office) as a quintessential example of using drama to attack Mao Zedong and the party marked the beginning of the Cultural Revolution, during which Wu Han was persecuted to death. For accounts of this episode and other similar plays popular in the early 1960s, see Rudolf G. Wagner, "The Politics of the Historical Drama," in his *The Contemporary Chinese Historical Drama* (Berkeley: University of California Press, 1990), 236–323. For an English translation, see Wu Han, *Hai Jui Dismissed from Office*, trans. C. C. Huang (Honolulu: Asian Studies Program, University of Hawai'i, 1972).

34. Shao Chongfei, Zhu Yi, Wang Zheng, and Lin Kehuan's *Baotong* (Newspaper boys) was first published in *Renmin xiju* 6 (1978): 8–44 and as a book, by Henan renmin chubanshe, Zhengzhou, in 1978. It was premiered by Zhongguo ertong yishu juyuan (China Children's Art Theater) in March 1978, and the script was later collected in Li Moran, et al., eds., *Zhongguo huaju wushi nian juzuo xuan, 1949.10–1999.10*, 4:533–607.

35. Written by Zhou Lai, Wang Bing, Lin Kehuan, and Zhao Yunsheng, *Zhuanzhe* (Turning point) was premiered by Zhongguo huajutuan (China Drama Troupe) in August 1977. China Drama Troupe was established, during the later part of the Cultural Revolution, by combining three theaters into one: China Youth Art Theater, China Children's Art Theater, and Central Experimental Theater. After the Cultural Revolution, these three theaters resumed their separate status.

36. Gao Wensheng, *Zhongguo dangdai xiju wenxue shi* (A history of the dramatic literature of contemporary China) (Nanning: Guangxi renmin chubanshe, 1990), 255.

37. Written by Suo Yunping and Shi Chao, *Dongjin! Dongjin!* (Eastward march!) was first published in *Renmin xiju* 4 (1978): 55–95, and was later collected in *Qingzhu Zhonghua Renmin Gongheguo chengli sanshi zhounian xianli yanchu huo chuangzuo yidengjiang juben xuanji* (Selected first-prize plays from the PRC thirtieth anniversary drama festival), 3 vols. (Chengdu: Sichuan renmin chubanshe, 1980), 1: 275–379. It was premiered by Wuhan budui zhengzhibu huajutuan (Wuhan Garrison Political Bureau Drama Troupe), whose Beijing performances in April 1978 were warmly received.

38. *Chen Yi chushan* (Chen Yi leaves the mountains), by Ding Yishan, was first published in *Juben* 3 (1979): 2–33, and later collected in Li Moran, et al., eds., *Zhongguo huaju wushi nian juzuo xuan, 1949.10–1999.10*, 4:299–367. It was premiered by Zhongguo renmin jiefangjun kongjun zhengzhibu huajutuan (The PLA Air Force Political Bureau Drama Troupe) in Beijing, 1979.

39. Northrop Frye, *Anatomy of Criticism: Four Essays* (Princeton, N.J.: Princeton University Press, 1957), 283–284.

40. Ibid., 284.

41. *Shuguang* (Morning light), by Bai Hua, was first published in *Renmin xiju* 9 (1977): 27–65, and later collected in Li Moran, et al., eds., *Zhongguo huaju wushi nian juzuo xuan, 1949.10–1999.10*, 4:141–217. It was premiered in August 1977 by Wuhan Garrison Political Bureau Drama Troupe and China Drama Troupe.

42. Chong Long, "Geming douzheng de zhenshi fanying" (Faithful representations of revolutionary struggle), *Renmin xiju* 9 (1978): 54–57; see p. 55.

43. Herbert Linderberger, *Historical Drama: The Relation of Literature and Reality* (Chicago: The University of Chicago Press, 1975), 30.

44. Ibid., 31.

45. Chong Long, "Geming douzheng de zhenshi fanying," 55.

46. Yuan Huawen, in his letter to the editor, selected in "Xiju chuangzuo fanying liangtiao luxian douzheng de tantao" (Discussion on the representation of the two-lines struggle within the party in dramatic literature), *Renmin xiju* 1 (1978): 33–36; see p. 35.

47. Tao Hanzhang, "Yige xie luxian douzheng de haoxi" (An exemplary play on two-lines struggle), *Renmin xiju* 10 (1977): 73–74.

48. Xue Baokun, "Beiju de liliang—kan *Shuguang* xiangdao de" (The power of tragedy—afterthoughts on *Morning Light*), *Renmin xiju* 3 (1978): 35–37; see pp. 36–37.

49. Ibid., 35.

50. Shu Yuan, "Kaijue lishi de baozang" (Exploring the gold mines of history), *Xiju xuexi* (Dramatic studies) 4 (1983): 22–33. The revised version of *Qiushou pili* (Autumn thunder), by Zhao Huan and Pang Jiaxing, appeared in *Juben* 1 (1979): 3–35.

51. Shu Yuan, "Kaijue lishi de baozang," 26.

52. Lu Bai, "Dui huaju suozao lingxiu xingxiang de yidian yijian" (Suggestions on the creation of revolutionary leaders in modern drama), *Shanghai xiju* (Shanghai drama) 6 (1980): 60–61; see p. 61.

53. Nominally, Yang Kaihui was Mao's second wife. The first arranged marriage imposed by his parents was never consummated.

54. An Kui, "Bawo tedian tanqiu xinyi" (Grasping the individual characteristics in order to explore new aspects), *Renmin xiju* 3 (1978): 31–34; see p. 31.

55. Zhang Qihong, Li Zibo, and Ma Huitian, "Changshi yu tansuo" (Experiments and explorations), *Renmin xiju* 10 (1978): 17–20; see p. 20.

56. Written by Qiao Yu, Shu Yuan, and Li Zibo, *Yang Kaihui* was premiered by Zhongyang xiju xueyuan jiaoshi yanchutuan (The Teacher's Theatre of Central Drama College), in 1978. The script was published in *Renmin xiju* 7 (1978): 49–89. Quotations are from 88–89. The English translations are mine.

57. Zhang Guichi, *Shijie zhi zi* (The son of the world), *Juben* 11 (1985): 3–33; see pp. 8–9.

58. Herbert Linderberger, *Historical Drama: The Relation of Literature and Reality*, 38–53.

59. Marvin Carlson, *Theories of the Theatre* (Ithaca: Cornell University Press, 984), 424.

60. *Meiyu* (The raining season), by Tian Han, was first published in *Dushu zazhi* (Reader's magazine) 2, 1 (1931): 1–50, and was later collected in his *Tian Han juzuo xuan* (Selected plays of Tian Han), (Beijing: Renmin wenxue chubanshe, 1955), 169–204.

61. Chen Baichen and Dong Jian, *Zhongguo xiandai xiju shigao*, 260.

62. *Liuhaomen* (Number Six Gate) was created collectively and premiered by Tianjinshi banyun gongren wengongtuan (Tianjin City Porters Performing Troupe), with scripts by Wang Xuebo and Zhang Xuexin, in 1950. It was published as a book, by Beijing gongren chubanshe, 1953.

63. *Jiliu yongjin* (Braving the torrent) was written by Hu Wanchun, Huang Zuolin, and Tong Luo and premiered by Shanghai renmin yishu juyuan huaju yituan (Shanghai People's Art Theater, Number One Drama Troupe). The play was published as a book, by Shanghai wenhua chubanshe, in 1964.

64. Jin Shan, *Hongse fengbao* (Red storm) was first published in *Juben* 6 (1958): 10–52, and as a book, by Zhongguo xiju chubanshe, Beijing, 1959.

65. *Qianwan buyao wangji* (Never forget), by Cong Shen, was first published under the title of *Zhuni jiankang* (Wish you good health) in *Juben* 10 and 11 (1963): 2–43, and as a book under the title of *Qianwan buyao wangji*, by Zhongguo xiju chubanshe, Beijing, 1964. It was premiered by Harbin huajutuan (Harbin City Theater), in 1963, with the title of *Zhuni jiankang*.

66. The 1970 model-play version of the Peking opera *Hongdeng ji* (The red lantern) was published in *Hongqi* (Red flag) 5 (1970): 23–46. For an English translation, see *The Red Lantern, Chinese Literature* 8 (1970): 8–52.

67. The 1972 model-play version of the Peking opera *Haigang* (On the docks) was published in *Hongqi* 2 (1972): 22–48. For an English translation, see *On the Docks, Chinese Literature* 5 (1972): 52–98.

68. Cui Dezhi's *Baochunhua* (Winter jasmine) was first published in *Juben* 4 (1979): 2–40, and as a book, by Zhongguo xiju chubanshe, Beijing, 1980. It was premiered by Liaoning renmin yishu juyuan (Liaoning People's Art Theater), in March 1979.

69. Yang Limin's *Heise de shitou* (Black stones) was first published in *Juben* 2 (1988): 4–25, 36.

70. Ibid., 4.

71. Gao Wensheng, *Zhongguo dangdai xiju wenxue shi*, 334–339.

72. *Huohu zhi ye* (The night a tiger was captured), by Tian Han, was written in 1922, and published partially in *Nanguo Banyuekan* (Nanguo biweekly) 2 (January 1924), and was collected in Hong Shen, ed., *Zhongguo xin wenxue daxi: xiju ji*, 9–26. For an English translation, see *The Night a Tiger Was Captured*, trans. Randy Barbara Kaplan, *Asian Theatre Journal* 2, 1 (1994): 1–34.

73. *Dachu Youlingta* (Breaking out of Ghost Pagoda) by Bai Wei was published in *Benliu* (Running torrent) 1, 1 (79–113); 1, 2 (251–283); 1, 4 (673–734), 1928. It was later collected in Yu Ling, ed., *Zhongguo xin wenxue daxi: xiju ji 2, 1927–1937*, 3–77.

74. *Huijia yihou* (Homecoming), by Ouyang Yuqian, was first published in *Dongfang zazhi* (Eastern miscellany) 21, 20 (25 October 1924): 109–128 and later collected in Hong Shen, ed., *Zhongguo xin wenxue daxi: xiju ji*, 197–216.

75. After going through many changes, *Fangxia nide bianzi* (Put down your whip), by Chen Liting et al., was first published in *Shenghuo zhishi* (Guide to everyday life) 2, 9 (1936): 520–526. It was later collected in Shen Xiling, ed., *Jietou ju* (Street theater), vol. 1 (Hankou: Xingxing chubanshe, 1938).

76. The folk opera *Baimaonü* (White-haired girl) was collectively written by Yan'an Lu Xun yishu wenxueyuan (Yan'an Lu Xun Literature and Art Academy) with He Jingzhi, Ding Yi, and Wang Bin as scriptwriters, and Ma Ke, Zhang Lu, and Huo Wei as composers. It premiered, in 1945, in Yan'an. The first edition of the opera was published by Yan'an xinhua shudian in 1946, and a revised edition was later published by Beijing renmin wenxue chubanshe, 1952. For an English translation, see *White-Haired Girl*, trans. Gladys Yang and Yang Hsien-yi (Beijing: Beijing waiwen chubanshe, 1954).

77. The model-play version of *Longjiang song* (Song of the Dragon River) was first published in *Hongqi* 3:(1971): 36–62. For an English translation, see *Song of the Dragon River, Chinese Literature* 7 (1972): 3–52.

78. Chen Zidu, Yang Jian, and Zhu Xiaoping, *Sangshuping jishi* (Sangshuping chronicles), *Juben* 4 (1988): 4–28. For an English translation, see *Sangshuping Chronicles*, trans. Cai Rong, in Haiping Yan, ed., *Literature and Society: An Anthology of Contemporary Chinese Drama* (Armonk, N.Y.: M. E. Sharpe, 1998), 189–261.

79. *Yecao* (Wild grass), by Zhang Mingyuan, premiered in Harbin, in 1989, by Qiqiharshi huajutuan (Qiqihar City Drama Troupe). It was published under the title of *Duoyu de xiatian* (A rainy summer), *Juzuo jia* (Playwrights) 3 (1989): 4–27; see p. 20.

80. Hu Peng et al., revised by Hu Ke, *Zhandou li chengzhang* (Growing up in the battlefield) (Beijing: Xinhua shudian), 1950.

81. Chen Qitong, *Wanshui qianshan* (Rivers and mountains), *Juben* 11 (1954): 9–104.

82. *Nihongdeng xia de shaobing* (Soldiers under neon light), by Shen Ximeng et al., was first published in *Juben* 2 (1963): 2–41, and later as a book, by Zhongguo xiju chubanshe, Beijing, 1964.

83. Mei Lanfang visited Seattle; New York; Chicago; Washington, D.C.; San Francisco; Los Angeles; San Diego; and Honolulu during six months in 1930.

84. Lu Xun, "Lüe lun Mei Lanfang ji qita, shang" (On Mei Lanfang and other matters, part one), in his *Lu Xun quanji* (Complete works of Lu Xun) (Beijing: Renmin wenxue chubanshe, 1989), 5:579–581.

85. Lu Xun, "Lun zhaoxiang zhi lei" (On photography), in his *Lu Xun quanji*, 1:181–190. Quotation cited from Kirk A. Denton's translation of "On Photography," in his ed., *Modern Chinese Literary Thought: Writings on Literature, 1893–1945* (Stanford: Stanford University Press, 1996), 196–203; see p. 203.

86. Chen Mingshu, "Shenmei de rentong yu yiqu" (Similarity and differences in aesthetic views), *Xiju yishu* (Dramatic art) 2 (1986): 31–36; see p. 32.

87. See chapter 6 of Xiaomei Chen's *Acting the Right Part* for background on these texts.

88. Lu Xun, "Nuola zou hou zengyang" (What happened after Nora left home), *Funü zazhi* (Women's journal) 10, 8 (1924): 1218–1222.

89. In Bai Wei's *Breaking Out of Ghost Pagoda*, Zheng Shaomei, a concubine in

the household of Hu Rongsheng, left her patriarchal home with the help of Xiao Sen, Director of Women's Federation. Xiao herself had left Hu's house when she was only seventeen years old, after having been raped by Hu. The play ends in a tearful reunion of Xiao Sen and her daughter, who protected her mother from the gunshot of her evil father. Bai's revolutionary women can be seen as one of the earliest examples of Nora-like characters on the Chinese stage.

90. Zhang Lili, *Lüse yingdi* (Green barracks), in her *Zhang Lili juzuo xuan* (Selected plays of Zhang Lili) (Beijing: Zhongguo xiju chubanshe, 1992), 263–267.

91. Yu Qiuyu, "Xu" (Preface), in Zhang Lili, *Zhang Lili juzuo xuan*, 3–7; see p. 7.

92. Chen Baichen, "Dai xu" (Preface on behalf of the author), in Zhang Lili, *Zhang Lili juzuo xuan*, 1–2; see p. 2.

GLOSSARY

aimeiju　爱美剧

An Kui　安葵

Bai Hua　白桦

Bai Jie　白洁

Bai Shurong　白舒容

Bai Wei　白薇

Bai Yu　白羽

Baimaonü　白毛女

Baochunhua　报春花

Baotong　报童

Bawang bieji　霸王别姬

Bayi Nanchang qiyi　八一南昌起义

Beijing ren　北京人

Beijing renmin yishu juyuan　北京人民艺术剧院

Cai Wenji　蔡文姬

caizi jiaren　才子佳人

Cao Yu　曹禺

Chaguan　茶馆

Chahua nü　茶花女

Chen Baichen　陈白尘

Chen Liting　陈鲤庭

Chen Mingshu　陈鸣树

Chen Qitong　陈其通

Chen Yi chushan　陈毅出山

Chen Zidu　陈子度

chi erban ku　吃二遍苦

Chong Long　崇龙

chuang Guandong　闯关东

chuangzuo juben　创作剧本

Chunliu she　春柳社

Chunni　春妮

Cong Shen　丛深

Cui Dezhi　崔得志

Dachu youlingta　打出幽灵塔

Daqing　大庆

Daqingshi huanjutuan　大庆市话剧团

di wang jiang xiang　帝王将相

Dielianhua　蝶恋花

Ding Yi　丁毅

Ding Yishan　丁一山

Dong Jian　董健

Dongbei xiju　东北戏剧

Dongjin! Dongjin!　东进! 东进!

Dou Xiaohong　窦晓红

Duan Dechang　段德昌

Dujuanshan　杜鹃山

Duoyu de xiatian　多雨的夏天

Erqin　二芹

Fang Xiaoshi　方小诗

Fangxia nide bianzi　放下你的鞭子

feiren　非人

Feng Dajian　冯大坚

Gao Wensheng　高文升

Ge Yihong　葛一虹

geming yangbanxi　革命样板戏

gong-nong-bing xiju　工农兵戏剧

Gu Wei　顾威

Guan Hanqing　关汉卿

Guifei zuijiu 贵妃醉酒
Guo Moruo 郭沫若
Guo Shixing 过士行
guoju 国剧
Hai Rui baguan 海瑞罢官
Haigang 海港
Harbin huajutuan 哈尔滨话剧团
He Jingzhi 贺敬之
He Jiping 何冀平
He Long 贺龙
He Zizhen 贺子珍
Heinu hen 黑奴恨
Heinu yutianlu 黑奴吁天录
Heise de shitou 黑色的石头
Hong Changqing 洪常青
Hong Shen 洪深
Hongdeng ji 红灯记
Honghu 洪湖
Hongse fengbao 红色风暴
Hongse niangzijun 红色娘子军
Hu Ke 胡可
Hu Peng 胡朋
Hu Rongsheng 胡荣生
Hu Shi 胡适
Hu Wanchun 胡万春
Hua Mulan 花木兰
huaju 话剧
Hualun Furen zhi zhiye 华伦夫人之
　职业
Huang Zuolin 黄佐临
Huijia yihou 回家以后
Huo Wei 霍维
Huohu zhi ye 获虎之夜
Jia 家
Jiang Qing he tade zhangfumen 江青和她
　的丈夫们
Jiao Juyin 焦菊隐
Jiaojiao 娇娇
Jiaoyang 骄杨
Jieshang liuxing hongqunzi 街上流行
　红裙子
Jiliu yongjin 激流勇进
Jin Shan 金山
Kuang Fu 匡复
Lao She 老舍

Lao Si 老四
Leiyu 雷雨
Li Bozhao 李伯钊
Li Moran 李默然
Li Tiemei 李铁梅
Li Xiucheng xunguo 李秀成殉国
Li Xiucheng zhi si 李秀成之死
Li Yuhe 李玉和
Li Zibo 郦子柏
Liang Huaqun 梁化群
Liaoning renmin yishu juyuan 辽宁
　人民艺术剧院
Lin Biao 林彪
Lin Han 林寒
Lin Jian 林坚
Lin Kehuan 林克欢
Lin Shu 林纾
Liu Feng 柳风
Liu Shugang 刘树纲
Liuhaomen 六号门
Longjiang song 龙江颂
Longxugou 龙须沟
Lu Bai 鲁白
Lu Dahai 鲁大海
Lu Ma 鲁妈
Lu Mengshi 卢孟实
Lu Xiaoyun 卢晓云
Lu Xun 鲁迅
Luo Ruiqing 罗瑞卿
Lushan zhi xue 庐山之雪
Lüse yingdi 绿色营地
Ma Huitian 马慧田
Ma Ke 马可
Mao Anying 毛岸英
Mei Lanfang 梅兰芳
Meiyu 梅雨
Niaoren 鸟人
Nihongdeng xia de shaobing 霓虹灯
　下的哨兵
nongmin qiyejia 农民企业家
Nongnu 农奴
Ouyang Yuqian 欧阳予倩
Pang Jiaxing 庞加兴
Peng Dehuai 彭德怀
Qianwan buyao wangji 千万不要忘记

Qiao Yu　乔羽
Qiushou pili　秋收霹雳
Qu Liuyi　曲六乙
Qu Yuan　屈原
Richu　日出
Sandai ren　三代人
Sange panni de nüxing　三个叛逆的
　　女性
Sangshuping jishi　桑树坪纪事
Shanghai gongren wenhuagong yeyu
　　huajudui　上海工人文化宫业余
　　话剧队
Shanghai juyishe　上海剧艺社
Shanghai wuyan xia　上海屋檐下
Shanhaiguan　山海关
Shao Chongfei　邵冲飞
Shaonainai de shanzi　少奶奶的扇子
Shen Ximeng　沈西蒙
Shi Chao　史超
Shijie zhi zi　世界之子
Shu Yuan　树元
Shuguang　曙光
Sima Changjiang　司马长江
Sishinian de yuanwang　四十年的
　　愿望
Su Shuyang　苏叔阳
Sun Weishi　孙维世
Suo Yunping　所云平
Taipinghu　太平湖
Tang Tiantian　唐恬恬
Tang Xuanzong　唐玄宗
Tao Hanzhang　陶汉章
Tao Xing'er　陶星儿
Tian Benxiang　田本相
Tian Geng　田耕
Tian Han　田汉
Tian Xuxiu　田旭修
Tianjinshi banyun gongren
　　wengongtuan　天津市搬运工人
　　文工团
Tianxia diyilou　天下第一楼
Tong Luo　仝洛
Wang Bin　王滨
Wang Bing　王冰

Wang Ming　王明
Wang Shuyuan　王树元
Wang Xuebo　王血波
Wang Zheng　王正
Wang Zhongxian　汪仲贤
Wanshui qianshan　万水千山
Wei Yi　魏易
wenmingxi　文明戏
Wu Han　吴晗
Wu Linghua　吴令华
Wu Qinghua　吴清华
Wu Qionghua　吴琼花
Wuhan budui zhengzhibu huajutuan
　　武汉部队政治部话剧团
Xi'er　喜儿
Xia Yan　夏衍
Xiang Yu　项羽
Xiao Sen　萧森
Xiao Yuelin　萧月林
xiqu　戏曲
Xu Yan　许雁
Xue Baokun　薛宝琨
Yan'an Lu Xun yishu wenxueyuan
　　延安鲁迅艺术文学院
Yang Guifei　杨贵妃
Yang Hansheng　杨翰笙
Yang Jian　杨健
Yang Kaihui　杨开慧
Yang Limin　杨利民
Ye Xiaoxiao　叶肖肖
Yecao　野草
Yidai yinghao　一代英豪
Yige sizhe dui shengzhe de fangwen
　　一个死者对生者的访问
Yu Ling　于伶
Yu Qiuyu　余秋雨
Yu wusheng chu　于无声处
Yuan Huawen　袁华文
Yuchu'r　玉雏儿
Yue Minghua　岳明华
Zeng Xiaogu　曾孝谷
Zhandou li chengzhang　战斗里
　　成长
Zhang Guichi　张贵驰

Zhang Lili 张莉莉

Zhang Lu 张鲁

Zhang Mingyuan 张明媛

Zhang Qihong 张奇虹

Zhang Xuexin 张学新

Zhang Ziyang 张子扬

Zhanshi jushe 战士剧社

Zhao Huan 赵寰

Zhao Yanwang 赵阎王

Zhao Yunsheng 赵云声

Zheng Shaomei 郑少梅

Zhongguo ertong yishu juyuan 中国
儿童艺术剧院

Zhongguo huajutuan 中国话剧团

Zhongguo qingnian yishu juyuan
中国青年艺术剧院

Zhongguo renmin jiefangjun kongjun

zhengzhibu huajutuan 中国人民
解放军空军政治部话剧团

Zhonghua huaju tonghao hui 中华
话剧同好会

Zhonghua juyishe 中华剧艺社

zhongjun 忠君

Zhongshen dashi 终身大事

Zhongyang shiyan huanjuyuan 中央实
验话剧院

Zhou Fanyi 周繁漪

Zhou Lai 周来

Zhu Xiaoping 朱晓平

Zhu Yi 朱漪

Zhuanzhe 转折

Zhuni jiankang 祝你健康

Zong Fuxian 宗福先

Zuo Lai 左莱

The Dead Visiting the Living

Liu Shugang

TRANSLATED BY CHARLES QIANZHI WU

Characters

YE XIAOXIAO[1]   male, dead, amateur fashion designer

TANG TIANTIAN   female, private fashion dealer,[2] musical
show hostess

LIU FENG   male, theater director, YE XIAOXIAO's and
TANG TIANTIAN's chum since childhood

DRUMMER   male, white-haired, ruddy-cheeked, stern-
looking, somewhat neurotic

CHORUS   four males and four females; they sing, dance, and
play the roles of various pieces of scenery as well as
characters

(As soon as spectators enter the theater, they see their own images in large mirrors propped up on the stage. They also see in these mirrors a theater interior that is more mysterious and illusory than the real one. Driven by curiosity, some start gathering around the stage and upon closer examination discover a couple of distorting mirrors. Naturally, they laugh at their own bloated figures and those of others. Interest is keyed up, and in this livened-up atmosphere, the play begins.

The lighting changes. What appears on the stage looks like a music hall, or perhaps just a rehearsal studio, the drum set for the band placed in a prominent position. Enter DRUMMER. *He tunes up the drums and starts off with a round of hot beats.*

Enter CHORUS, *straggling to the front, dressed in uniform, unisex tights, and holding masks in their hands.)*

CHORUS: *(One by one striking an entry pose and calling out warmly to the audience)* Good evening, friends!

(The CHORUS *members go to their seats in the choir, hanging up their exquisitely made masks as they sit down. These masks, together with others with beards already up on the screen behind their seats, make up part of the stage decor. Each* CHORUS *member has a large shawl of a different color to be used as symbolic costume or stage prop.*

Enter musical show hostess TANG TIANTIAN *with a cordless mike in her hand. She is wearing jeans, high-heeled boots, bat-wing sleeves, and flowing long hair, with earrings and necklace that match. She carries herself with natural ease and a dash of mischief, smiles sweetly, and greets each and every member of the* CHORUS.

The CHORUS *members now put on their rainbow-colored shawls: red, orange, yellow, green, indigo, blue, and purple. They liven up, some cheer in amazement, some applaud.)*

CHORUS: Wow! Beautiful, boss!

Oh, just gorgeous!

Any VIP attending our dress rehearsal today?

Where's our fashion designer, Xiaoxiao? Why isn't he here yet?

Is Maestro Liu Feng coming, too?

TANG TIANTIAN: *(Makes a sharp and witty fillip at her stage partners)*

Oh, shut up! Time is money, let's not wait for anyone, okay?

(With a flourish of her arm, authoritatively) Get ready! *(She dances slowly to center stage, makes a deep bow to the audience.)*

The dress rehearsal of the Tiantian Fashion Musical Show now begins!
(*The band and the* DRUMMER *strike up a cheerful but lyrical overture.* TANG TIANTIAN *starts moving her hips and limbs and dances to a light rhythm. The* CHORUS *members leave their seats to harmonize with* TANG TIANTIAN *as she sings.*)
TANG TIANTIAN: When I was a little girl
I lived in a misty world
Mom gave me a bright mirror
And said it was her tender eyes
For the first time I got to know myself
And saw my own flowerlike face
I liked it, I really liked it—
Oh, my wondrous mirror . . .
(*The* DRUMMER *beats out an unhurried rhythm during a musical interlude.* TANG TIANTIAN *and the* CHORUS *dance.*

Enter a man, staggering and shuffling with visible difficulty, his left hand on his heart, his right arm hanging limp, dragging a beige jacket. He pushes open the two-paneled door formed by two CHORUS *members and enters the music hall. Barely keeping himself on his feet, he leans against the post of the stage entrance as he watches* TANG TIANTIAN *sing. Oh, what burning, yearning eyes! His name is* YE XIAOXIAO.

Step-by-step YE XIAOXIAO *struggles toward* TANG TIANTIAN. *She sees him, moves toward him while singing, and glides around him in a graceful dancing step. She and the* CHORUS *continue to sing.*)
TANG TIANTIAN: I don't remember since when it was
That your shadow came into my mirror
Like entering a brightly lit stage
Together we began knitting a colorful dream
The mirror reflected a dazzling world
The mirror refracted the complexity of life
In it we saw your love and my affection
I liked it, I really liked it—
Oh, my wondrous mirror . . .
(*During the singing,* YE XIAOXIAO, *enduring great pain, tries to dance a few difficult steps. His lips quiver, as if wanting to tell something, but he can't utter a sound. The singing continues.*

Enter a man in a fashionable windbreaker. In a hurry, he pushes open the music hall door and steps in, then leans quietly against the post of that stage entrance. He watches YE XIAOXIAO *and* TANG TIAN-TIAN *closely, as if pondering problems of a rehearsal, with a professional eye. But there seems to be something more in those eyes. This is* LIU FENG. *Nobody notices his presence, as if he is an outsider.*

By now YE XIAOXIAO *has come to a standstill. Longingly he gazes into* TANG TIANTIAN's *eyes. A tranquil but sad smile ripples across his face.)*

TANG TIANTIAN: *(Eyeing him quizzically)* Xiaoxiao . . .

YE XIAOXIAO: *(Forces a smile, haltingly)* Tiantian, I've always been . . . lousy . . . insignificant actor. . . . Never can play a good guy . . . just can't help giggling . . . can't even play dead . . . on the stage . . . always get an earful from the director . . .

TANG TIANTIAN: *(Laughs)* Oh, that's funny! The show of your designs starts tomorrow, and you still want to dabble with playacting as a downsized actor? What role are you playing now? Uh-uh, no good! No good . . .

YE XIAOXIAO: This time . . . it's not playacting . . . This time it's for real. . . . I won't gig . . . giggle anymore. . . . It's for real. . . . Still no good? I think I'm doing great. . . . *(Slowly he releases the hand that clutches his heart. Crimson blood wells up. A scarlet gauze handkerchief floats down from his chest.)*

CHORUS: *(In alarm)* Oh no?! Blood? Blood!

TANG TIANTIAN: *(Stupefied)* Xiaoxiao! What's happened?!

*(*LIU FENG, *in his own niche, covers his face with both hands, in great agony. With a last mischievous smile at* TANG TIANTIAN *and the* CHORUS, YE XIAOXIAO *falls.)*

CHORUS: *(Crying out)* Xiaoxiao!

Ye Xiaoxiao!

Oh, blood! Look at all the blood you shed!

TANG TIANTIAN: *(Shocked)* Xiaoxiao! Xiaoxiao! *(She kneels at* YE XIAO-XIAO's *side and holds up the upper part of his body. His head droops on her warm and supple chest, tranquil, like a statue.)*

*(*LIU FENG *dashes across in a fluster and throws himself down at* YE XIAOXIAO's *feet.)*

LIU FENG: *(Tears of agony in his eyes)* Tiantian, he— Xiaoxiao . . . is gone.

(Sounds of people chattering, sirens screaming, police cars and an

ambulance approaching. CHORUS *members strike different poses, and become still as sculptures. Only the* DRUMMER *is still playing, his beats as powerful as ever.*

YE XIAOXIAO *rises from the arms of* TANG TIANTIAN *and* LIU FENG, *and, like the wisp of a wandering ghost, floats past the* CHORUS *members, and disappears. . . . As if still holding* YE XIAOXIAO, LIU FENG *and* TANG TIANTIAN *exit, trailing the scarlet gauze handkerchief. . . . The* CHORUS *members start humming a tune and, in a slow step, dance back to their seats in the choir. Only the* DRUMMER *continues playing beneath a kaleidoscopic spotlight.*

Enter TANG TIANTIAN, *slowly, with a guitar on her back and a bunch of flowers in her hands. Two* CHORUS *members form a one-panel door. She pushes it open, enters, looks around, and goes up to the seated* CHORUS.)

TANG TIANTIAN: *(In a low voice)* Excuse me, grandpa![3] Excuse me! Are you there, grandpa?

(One of the CHORUS *members answers, "Yes!" and puts on the mask of an* OLD MAN *with a flowing beard, picks up a large bunch of keys, and steps down from the choir, doddering.)*

OLD MAN: I'm the custodian here. Can I help you, young lady?

TANG TIANTIAN: *(Looking sad)* Gee, it's so quiet here! You just can't hear a sound . . .

OLD MAN: This place I look after here—the mortuary—has a pretty nice name: it's called Hall of Peace.[4] No wind, no waves—it's all so peaceful.

TANG TIANTIAN: I know. I want to see someone.

OLD MAN: Who is it?

TANG TIANTIAN: Ye Xiaoxiao. Just moved down here from the emergency room.

OLD MAN: *(Babbling)* So it's he! I know, I know, it's all in the papers. *(Fishing out a newspaper from his pocket)* A scuffle on the bus. Got stabbed. The two hooligans ran off, still at large, and the guy who got stabbed seven times just reported to me here today.

TANG TIANTIAN: I know.

OLD MAN: Then why come? The case's still open. Besides, it's a pretty sorry sight.

TANG TIANTIAN: I'm not afraid. I saw everything in those years.

OLD MAN: Those years?—How old are you?

TANG TIANTIAN: A year older than last year.

OLD MAN: No kidding, a year older than last year! When you get to my age, you would say "a year younger than next year."

TANG TIANTIAN: Please, let me in.

OLD MAN: Any letter of introduction? An ID will do.

(TANG TIANTIAN *shakes her head.*)

OLD MAN: Unemployed?

TANG TIANTIAN: They all call me boss now.

OLD MAN: Boss? That's interesting.

TANG TIANTIAN: You see, I'm a fashion dealer, a private entrepreneur, a vendor. Just let me in, please. I brought him a garment.

OLD MAN: Are you his . . . wife?

TANG TIANTIAN: N-nope.

OLD MAN: Then you are his? . . .

TANG TIANTIAN: Grandpa, are you taking census, or what?

OLD MAN: Taking census? I only take names *off* the census here. Listen, young lady, the police have orders: No visitors for him whatsoever.

TANG TIANTIAN: That was when he was in the emergency room. Now the curfew should be over. Let me take a look at him.

OLD MAN: *(Sighs)* Just now a man came and I didn't let *him* in.

TANG TIANTIAN: That must be Liu Feng, the theater director. We're both good friends with Xiaoxiao.

OLD MAN: Friends, friends—Do you have to see him?

TANG TIANTIAN: Well, I owe him something—just like a debt, you know.

OLD MAN: A debt?

TANG TIANTIAN: I want to sing him a song.

OLD MAN: Look, miss, he can no longer hear!

TANG TIANTIAN: Then, I'll just sing it to myself.

OLD MAN: *(Babbling again)* Oh, it must've been tough for you, must've been tough. I'm really touched. I've been here all my life, and my heart's quite callused. I don't mind seeing dead people, but I am afraid of seeing living people. You wait here . . . *(Exits)*

(*Enter* LIU FENG, *who has been waiting at the other end.*)

LIU FENG: *(With a heavy heart)* Tiantian.

TANG TIANTIAN: Is that Liu Feng? I knew you'd been here before. . . . Look at your eyes. Have you been crying?

LIU FENG: I haven't slept at all the past few days. Kept writing. Just felt it wasn't fair for Xiaoxiao . . . I feel kind of responsible.

TANG TIANTIAN: You, responsible?

LIU FENG: *(Agonizing)* What I mean is . . . Xiaoxiao and I have been competitors— We took college exams together, and he flunked. Then we both wanted to do something in art, but he was downsized by the theater. And we've also been competitors in love. Now . . . he's died this horrible death.

TANG TIANTIAN: *(Painfully)* Liu Feng, let's not talk about this.

(Enter OLD MAN pushing a wheeled bed. Underneath a white shroud lies the dead YE XIAOXIAO.)

OLD MAN: *(Babbling)* Okay—here we are. Don't be afraid. When a person dies, it's just like a light's gone out. There's no such thing as ghosts and spirits—it's all superstition, all crap. I never ran into any. . . . Miss, would you need my company?

(TANG TIANTIAN shakes her head.)

OLD MAN: *(Nods to LIU FENG. Keeps babbling)* Must be tough, must be tough. People can't do without friends!

(OLD MAN returns to his seat and takes off his mask and beard. CHORUS hums a melody as the DRUMMER beats out his measured, fantastic rhythm. TANG TIANTIAN and LIU FENG lay their flowers respectively on the chest and at the foot of the deceased. The CHORUS members flash props symbolizing raindrops, and rattle thunder sheets and rain fans. It's raining.)

TANG TIANTIAN: It's all so sudden. Who would've thought you would leave us so quickly. I don't want to use that word—*death*. Liu Feng and I came here to see you. . . . Can you hear me sing?

(TANG TIANTIAN strums her guitar. The CHORUS harmonizes with her.)

LIU FENG: It's raining. . . . Xiaoxiao! The sky—it's also weeping.

TANG TIANTIAN: *(Singing to her own accompaniment)*

I dreamed about stars scattered on the ground
Like flowers, like gold in bloom
I wondered: in the season when petals fall
Would they clink and clank all over the fields?

(Thunder and rain are created by the CHORUS, and the symbolic raindrops. . . . TANG TIANTIAN stares at the wheeled bed, strumming her guitar. LIU FENG stands with his head drooping. Their thoughts hover around.

The deceased YE XIAOXIAO *under the white shroud stirs. By and by he turns down the shroud from his face and begins to slowly sit up. He looks around with bewilderment, as if waking from a deep dream and trying to remember something.*

TANG TIANTIAN *and* LIU FENG *don't seem surprised. Serenity prevails. Only the* DRUMMER *is playing his measured beats.)*

YE XIAOXIAO: *(Breathes a long sigh)* Whew! It's cold! Tiantian, Liu Feng, who placed these ice cubes around my body? What's this all about? I'm frozen stiff.

TANG TIANTIAN: This is the hospital mortuary.

YE XIAOXIAO: Mortuary? Why am I here?

TANG TIANTIAN: Your heart has stopped beating. Xiaoxiao, you are . . . dead.

YE XIAOXIAO: Dead? *(Feels his own pulse)* I see, the heart's no longer beating. Dead? *(Thinks)* Right, right, now I remember, yes, I *am* dead! They unplugged all the tubes. . . . *(Chuckles)* How funny! I remember reading in an evening paper, or somewhere, that there's a law in a foreign country that says a person cannot be pronounced dead if only his heart stops, that only when his brain cells stop working can he be considered dead.

TANG TIANTIAN: Why talk about foreign countries? You lost all your blood.

LIU FENG: Your heart . . . was pierced through and through.

YE XIAOXIAO: My heart pierced? My blood all gone? What happened? Let me see . . .

TANG TIANTIAN: The newspaper says that there was a scuffle on the bus and someone got stabbed, but it says that the case is still not closed and that we still don't know who's good and who's bad.

YE XIAOXIAO: Hey, listen. This is the worst case of injustice!

LIU FENG: No, no! Everything will be cleared up. I'm . . . I'm writing a-about you.

YE XIAOXIAO: Wait, wait; give me a second. That day, I got on a number thirteen bus—many countries don't have number thirteen; it's an unlucky number— Foreign countries again; never mind! Stream of consciousness, which shows that my brain cells are still quite active. Anyways, I got on a number thirteen bus . . . *(Recalls)* As soon as I got on the bus, I noticed a girl . . .
(Two of the CHORUS *members put on their masks—one, the girl, in a fashionable dress; the other, her father, a middle-aged man with a*

gift pack in his hand. Hand in hand, they get on the bus and stand close together, a spotlight focused on them.)

YE XIAOXIAO: *(Stares at and admires the girl)* Oh, she's so beautiful! Just like a colorful cloud in the sky, like a flower with dewdrops— Oh, I just adore her.

TANG TIANTIAN: *(The corner of her mouth twitches)* Oh, you idiot; why did you have to keep staring at beautiful girls?

YE XIAOXIAO: *(Turns to face* TANG TIANTIAN*)* I was talking about that dress she was wearing—it was so in harmony, so elegant. It's just, just . . . indescribable.

TANG TIANTIAN: But you were saying you were adoring *her*.

YE XIAOXIAO: Forget it! I knew at first sight it was the kind of dress you sell—that young-sailor model that I designed. I even thought about inviting her to our fashion musical show. *(The girl on the bus starts moving, displaying her dress, while* YE XIAOXIAO *gazes at her, spellbound.)* Just because I kept staring at her, something went wrong.

TANG TIANTIAN: People thought you were a *womanizer*?!

YE XIAOXIAO: No, it's not that! Look, what are the other two guys doing?

(Two more CHORUS *members put on their masks. They are the two* PICKPOCKETS *on the bus, closing in on the* GIRL *and her* FATHER, *covering each other while getting down to business.* PICKPOCKET A *fishes out the father's wallet;* PICKPOCKET B *cuts a slit in the girl's dress with a razor blade.*

YE XIAOXIAO goes up and grabs A's *hand.* A *hurriedly throws the wallet on the floor.* YE XIAOXIAO *puts his foot on it. The two engage in a staring bluff.)*

PICKPOCKET A: *(Flustered)* What d'you want? What d'you want, huh?

YE XIAOXIAO: *(To the father)* Sir, your wallet's been stolen. *(Turns to* B*)* And you! You made a slit on the girl's dress with your blade— Oh gosh, what a beautiful dress!

(The passengers on the bus are in an uproar: "Knife?!" "A Knife!" "Dagger?" They all back off, leaving in the center the GIRL, *the* FATHER, *and the* PICKPOCKETS, *whom* YE XIAOXIAO *grabs. As the spotlights focus on them, the rest fall into shadow.)*

PICKPOCKET A: *(Protesting)* Who's stealing? Who's slitting? You slander!

YE XIAOXIAO: (*Picks up the wallet from under his foot and holds it up to the father*) Is this yours?

PICKPOCKET A: (*Threateningly*) Are you trying to set me up?! Want to die?!

YE XIAOXIAO: (*Offers the wallet to its owner*) It's yours, sir.

FATHER: (*Glances uneasily at the ferocious* PICKPOCKET) Wallet? . . . Doesn't seem like mine. . . . Is it mine? . . . There's no money in it, anyways. . . .

(*The* GIRL *stares blankly and fumbles at the slit in her dress—she's obviously blind.*)

GIRL: (*Cries out*) Dad! Dad! Someone slit my dress! My dress! . . .

(*Hurriedly the* FATHER *pulls his daughter to one side, covers her mouth with his hand, urging her to be quiet.*

YE XIAOXIAO *makes a wry smile and quietly puts the wallet in his own pocket, keeping his eyes on the two* PICKPOCKETS *the while.*)

PICKPOCKET A: (*Sweeps his eyes across the passengers and trumps up a countercharge*) So that's what it is! You stole someone's wallet and tried to plant it on us. It won't be all that easy!

PICKPOCKET B: (*Viciously*) He needs a lesson so he can see better who we are!

(*In the shadows a youth among the passengers yells: "Hey, guys! It's show time! You want to see some workout on a bus?!"*

YE XIAOXIAO *stiffens.* PICKPOCKET A *gives him a slap in the face;* PICKPOCKET B *gives him a kick in the belly. He puts his hand on his stomach and doubles up.*)

TANG TIANTIAN: (*Almost breaks down, and cries out*) Xiaoxiao! Xiaoxiao!

YE XIAOXIAO: (*Slowly straightens up and cocks his head to listen*) I hear a cry. It sounds somewhat anxious, somewhat nervous, somewhat trembling . . .

(*The* PICKPOCKETS *continue to attack* YE XIAOXIAO, *who resists. The passengers are in pandemonium. They all crowd to a corner near the front door. In the meantime a male voice is heard shouting, "Mr. Driver! Take us to the nearest police station!"*

YE XIAOXIAO *retreats to the door and leans on it, holding back his pain and fury.*)

PICKPOCKETS A and B: (*Rushing at* YE XIAOXIAO) Get out of my way! You! Get up!

(*They hit and kick* YE XIAOXIAO, *who defends himself and hits back.*

The youth's voice from the dark shadows: "Oh, stupid ass! Give him the Iron Threshold! Black Tiger Gouges Out the Heart! Heart Licking Elbow![5] Yeah, Heart Licking Elbow!"

YE XIAOXIAO *knocks down one of the* PICKPOCKETS *and grabs hold of him. The other pounces on him. They are all in a scramble.*

The youth's voice from the dark shadows: "How come there's no Lei Feng[6] here today? And no Master Huo Yuanjia,[7] either? Hey, it's time to take credits. Who wants to be a hero? Come on!"

With a snap PICKPOCKET B *whips out a pocketknife. The passengers, gasping in alarm, all pack into a corner, holding their breath —a silhouetted group sculpture of shock, apathy, and woodenness.*

The stern and neurotic DRUMMER *is still playing his quaint beats. The blind* GIRL *suddenly cries,* "Dad! Dad! Quick! Quick!" *She reaches forward but is gagged by her* FATHER *and held tight in his arms.*

YE XIAOXIAO *fights a lone battle.* PICKPOCKET B *closes in with his knife—)*

TANG TIANTIAN: *(In alarm)* Xiaoxiao! Knife! Knife! Watch out!

(YE XIAOXIAO *receives a stab by* B *from the back.*)

TANG TIANTIAN: *(Covers her face)* Oh no! Xiaoxiao! Xiaoxiao!

(YE XIAOXIAO *stands up to his full height with open arms and his back against the door.*)

TANG TIANTIAN: *(Breaks down)* Look at all these people on the bus! Look at all these people!

YE XIAOXIAO: *(His hand on his wound, straining)* H-help, help me, everyone! Grab these thugs! G-give me a hand!

(*The* PICKPOCKETS *try to reach the door, and get into another scuffle with* XIAOXIAO. *The passengers hold their sculpturelike, immobile postures.* YE XIAOXIAO *receives more stabs. The bus pulls over at the next stop. The pneumatic door pops open. The* PICKPOCKETS *dash off and run away.*

YE XIAOXIAO, *with his hand on his wounded heart, staggers off the bus to chase them but falls on his stomach.*

The DRUMMER *sways his body and strikes up a fanatic round of wild beats. The* CHORUS *members doff their masks and return to the choir. They hum their wordless song.* TANG TIANTIAN *strums her guitar softly, quite forlorn.* LIU FENG *looks disturbed and is lost in deep thought.*)

YE XIAOXIAO: *(Approaching them)* . . . That was how it happened.

I chased for less than thirty yards and collapsed . . . just outside your music hall. I heard Tiantian singing—

TANG TIANTIAN: You've been foolish, Xiaoxiao, really foolish! You wanted to be a hero?

YE XIAOXIAO: Hero? *(Sneers)* No.

TANG TIANTIAN: It was foolish of you, Xiaoxiao, very foolish! All these people on the bus just watched; no one offered to help you.

LIU FENG: *(Somewhat agitated)* Xiaoxiao, don't you hate them? No one, *no* one on the bus helped you.

YE XIAOXIAO: *Hate?* Who should I hate? I thought about it. . . . I just felt a bit lonely. At that time, I just felt like . . . deserted. It was— Don't you think it was an unworthy death?

LIU FENG: *(Deploringly)* No, no, Xiaoxiao! You shouldn't say that.

YE XIAOXIAO: I just thought at the time: If only Tiantian and Liu Feng were on this bus, then I wouldn't be all by myself.

LIU FENG: *(With tears in his eyes)* Xiaoxiao, you will always be remembered! *(Turns around in agony)*

YE XIAOXIAO: What's there to remember about me? I'm nobody.

TANG TIANTIAN: You're an optimist.

(YE XIAOXIAO *grows pensive.* TANG TIANTIAN *and* LIU FENG *look on.*)

YE XIAOXIAO: *(Gloomily)* Tell me honestly; what did people say about my death?

(*Silence.* TANG TIANTIAN *strums a few trembling notes on the guitar.*)

YE XIAOXIAO: Did the police crack the case yet? Did they think it was just a bunch of hooligans fighting among themselves?

LIU FENG: *(Comfortingly)* No, no. Maybe there's been some speculation . . .

YE XIAOXIAO: Then, why do they say they can't tell who's good and who's bad?

TANG TIANTIAN: The murderers are still at large. You were in a coma and didn't say a word about the case—

YE XIAOXIAO: But— There were a lot of people on the bus. Didn't they see? Where are they?

TANG TIANTIAN: They all dispersed.

YE XIAOXIAO: I can recognize them. I'll go look them up and ask them some questions . . .

LIU FENG: *(Anxiously)* Xiaoxiao, did you see everyone on the bus clearly?

YE XIAOXIAO: Oh, it was quite chaotic. I couldn't tell the ones in back, but those in front, I can still remember. *(Recalling)* Let me think . . . What did they look like? Give me a second . . . *(The* DRUMMER *strikes up his fantastic beats.)*

LIU FENG: *(Pressing)* Who did you see, Xiaoxiao?

YE XIAOXIAO: *(Shaking his head)* Didn't see clearly . . . just can't recall.

LIU FENG: *(Thinking aloud)* Couldn't see clearly . . . can't recall.

TANG TIANTIAN: Doesn't matter. The police are looking for the passengers, anyway; they need some eyewitnesses . . .

YE XIAOXIAO: *(To himself)* I'd better check them out, ask them what they were thinking at the time. . . . Gee, I'm so lonely. I just feel claustrophobic.

TANG TIANTIAN: *(With a flick that spreads out a fashionable snow cape)* Xiaoxiao, I brought you this to put it on you—

YE XIAOXIAO: It's gorgeous! Wouldn't it be a waste to put it on a dead man?

TANG TIANTIAN: This was your last design. I just trial-made one. Also the last; I'm not gonna make any more. This is for you and you alone.

YE XIAOXIAO: *(Smiles teasingly)* So I designed it for myself—for the dead Xiaoxiao alone. *(His eyes fill with tears.)* Thank you, Tiantian! *(Turns to* LIU FENG*)* Liu Feng, our competition is over. I withdraw. . . . If you really love Tiantian, you should be good to her. She's a wonderful girl.

LIU FENG: *(Touched)* Xiaoxiao, I, I—

TANG TIANTIAN: *(To* YE XIAOXIAO*)* Xiaoxiao! What are you talking about? I'm not your property to be bequeathed in your will, am I?!

YE XIAOXIAO: That's not what I meant, Tiantian. . . . I know lots of men are after you, all for your money. But Liu Feng's different. We three grew up together—

TANG TIANTIAN: *(Explosively)* Oh, shut up! Shut up! I love you, I love you! I'm already your wife. I'll announce it right away.

LIU FENG: *(Astonished. Doubtfully)* Xiaoxiao, Tiantian, is that true? Are you really already. . . ?

YE XIAOXIAO: *(Agitated)* Tiantian! What's all this crap? Calm yourself down—

LIU FENG: Tiantian, maybe you're stressed out—

TANG TIANTIAN: No, this is true. Otherwise . . . Xiaoxiao, your life would've been incomplete.

YE XIAOXIAO: (*Even more uneasy*) But I'm dead, dead, Tiantian! Is it because I'm dead that you are saying all this? Before, none of us knew what to do; we just didn't want to let anyone feel hurt. Now it's all over! Liu Feng's still living. He lives! Love him! I won't be jealous; I'll just envy you— Tiantian, and Liu Feng, I love you both. All I want to do now is to look up those people. I've got to go. (*Backing off*) I want to visit those living people . . .

(*The* DRUMMER *beats out a bouncing rhythm. The* CHORUS *members surround* YE XIAOXIAO *and slowly drift away with him . . .* TANG TIANTIAN *emotionally dashes after him, but she's unable to cross the life-and-death boundary formed by the* CHORUS *members . . .*

With the snow cape on his shoulders, YE XIAOXIAO *disappears amidst the dancing* CHORUS. *Only the white-haired, ruddy-cheeked* DRUMMER *is still playing, beneath a kaleidoscopic light.*)

(*The drumming continues from the previous scene. This looks like an office in the criminal investigation section of the city police department. One of the* CHORUS *members puts on the insignia of a police officer. She steps down from the choir with a portfolio under her arm. She is* HAN YING. *Another* CHORUS *member puts on a mask and steps down carrying a briefcase. He is* DIRECTOR FAN.)

DIRECTOR FAN: (*Goes up to* HAN YING) You must be Comrade Han Ying of the police?

HAN YING: You must be Director Fan from Ye Xiaoxiao's unit.[8] I'm the officer in charge of his case.

DIRECTOR FAN: I've brought Ye's file for your investigation.

HAN YING: (*Takes the folder*) What was his overall behavior like—this Ye Xiaoxiao?

DIRECTOR FAN: So-so. He was an actor for some time, had worked as stage staff, nothing much. In no respect was he a candidate for promotion. If there was anything outstanding, it was his passion for tailoring, making clothes, you know. Quite an obsession! (*Laughs*) Ha! especially clothes for women, I mean, young girls. (*Using both hands to delineate human contours*) See?

HAN YING: (*Gives a noncommittal smile*) Could you please write a comprehensive report on Ye Xiaoxiao?

DIRECTOR FAN: Well, since the case is still under investigation, do you think it would be appropriate for us to get involved? It would be hard for us in the leadership to take a stand one way or the other. Besides, Ye's no longer on our payroll. He just submitted a job transfer report.

HAN YING: *(Thinking)* I see. But isn't he still a member of your staff?

DIRECTOR FAN: We can't take responsibility for what he did outside our unit. . . .

HAN YING: Sure, sure. I know there's a competition going on in the city right now for the Best Ethics Unit Award—

DIRECTOR FAN: Oh, no-no-no, that's not what I mean. Of course we'd be happy to supply information. As a matter of fact I was going to bring you some clues. They say Ye Xiaoxiao had an intimate relationship with a woman named Tang Tiantian, who belongs nowhere. Perhaps you should look into this and see if there's any problem.

HAN YING: Thanks very much. If anything comes up, we'll get in touch. *(Shakes hands with DIRECTOR FAN)*

(HAN YING walks her guest to the door. DIRECTOR FAN returns to his seat in the choir and takes off his mask.

HAN YING starts pondering. Solemnly, she walks to the choir and takes a sweeping glance.)

HAN YING: *(With professional confidence, opening her portfolio and announcing to the choir)* Comrades, please be prepared. We'll start the meeting in a minute.

(Four CHORUS members put on police insignia and sit straight. The meeting for case analysis and reports begins.)

HAN YING: Our superiors have requested an early solution to case thirteen-oh-three, i.e., a thorough investigation of the three people involved in the incident on bus number thirteen and solve the case as soon as possible. Will each subgroup of the task force please give a progress report?

OFFICER A: My group went to the neighborhood near the music hall stop to find passengers from that bus but had no result.

OFFICER B: My group found one passenger. He's here.

HAN YING: *(Recalls something and interjects)* Right, didn't you have a breakthrough?

OFFICER C: According to grassroots reports, after case thirteen-oh-three happened, two young men were seen riding one bike, with blood on their bodies, and scurrying off from east to west along North Street near the music hall. . . .

HAN YING: Did you find them?

OFFICER C: Yes sir. They are in custody and have gone through preliminary interrogation.

HAN YING: *(Thinks for a moment)* Bring them in.

(OFFICER D *goes to the door to call: "Zhang Sanli! Li Sihai!" Two*
CHORUS *members answer, "Here!" They put on their masks, step
down from the choir, and follow* OFFICER C *into the office.)*

OFFICER C: *(To the two)* Now come clean and fess up everything as it
happened. Okay?

LI SIHAI: *(Nervously)* Y-yes, s-sir! That day, we tried a hit-and-run but
didn't know things would turn out that bad. We'll confess everything—spill all the beans!

ZHANG SANLI: It was like this: I took him on my bike to see the movie
Hot Pursuit. I was afraid we were running late, so I was speeding
and hit an old man. We also fell over—two or three yards from
the collision. There was blood all over my face, and a big cut on
his thigh, also bleeding. We looked around and found the old
man quite motionless. We were afraid he would rip us off for his
medical expenses. So we hopped on the bike and fled. Didn't
even get to see the movie . . .

HAN YING: Is that true?

LI SIHAI: Oh yes, sir, every bit of it! Just look—*(pulling up his pant
leg)*—see, the gash's still not quite closed. See that scab on his
face? Also, here's the slip from the bike shop. The bike's being
fixed there.

ZHANG SANLI: *(Taking out the movie tickets)* Look, here's the two
movie tickets from that day. We were thinking of going to see
that movie *Hot Pursuit* today with these tickets. Who'd have
thought we'd end up here as objects of *your* hot pursuit?

(HAN YING *and the other officers exchange glances.)*

LI SIHAI: We've been really mean; we hit the old man and tried to
run.

ZHANG SANLI: We thought the matter would blow over. Didn't know
it would be such a big mess.

HAN YING: Were you on bus number thirteen that day?

LI SIHAI: Oh, my gosh! For god's sake don't tie us to that case—

ZHANG SANLI: Actually, we should've taken the old man to the hospital . . . what a heck of a mess . . .

HAN YING: *(To* OFFICER C, *with a deadpan face)* Please bring in that
comrade.[9]

(OFFICER C *goes to the door and calls: "Comrade Zhao Tiesheng!"*
A CHORUS *member answers "Here!" He dons the mask of the youth*
on the bus and follows C *into the room.*

ZHANG SANLI *and* LI SIHAI *have no idea what's coming. They just*
watch ZHAO TIESHENG.

ZHAO TIESHENG *greets* HAN YING *and the other officers. Inno-*
cently, he also greets the unidentified ZHANG SANLI *and* LI SIHAI.

HAN YING *and the other officers, who have been watching them*
all along, don't appear to find anything abnormal.)

HAN YING: *(Expressionless)* Comrade Zhao Tiesheng? Take a seat.
(Pointing to ZHANG SANLI *and* LI SIHAI*)* Did you ever meet?

ZHAO TIESHENG: *(Takes a close look at* ZHANG SANLI *and* LI SIHAI,
and shakes his head in bewilderment) Never. Don't know them.
Hey, who are you two?

*(*HAN YING *motions to* OFFICER D *to take* ZHANG SANLI *and* LI SIHAI
away. The three return to the choir and take off their masks.)

HAN YING: Comrade Zhao, you were on that bus number thirteen
that day, weren't you?

ZHAO TIESHENG: Oh yes! Gee, how did you know? That's weird!

HAN YING: *(Smiles)* Weren't you bragging to so many of your friends
that you almost became a hero? And lots of vivid details, too!

ZHAO TIESHENG: True; I am a bit of a big mouth.

HAN YING: Could you tell us what you saw on the bus?

ZHAO TIESHENG: *(A little nervous)* Actually, I didn't see clearly. No,
not at all. It's not because of anything except that my wife had
been in labor those few days and I had been waiting in the hospital all those nights without a wink of sleep and I was just so tired
I could've dropped dead walking. *(Acting out as he tells his story,*
as if in a flashback) I wobbled along on the street *(staggering)*,
and possibly got on a bus number thirteen. As soon as I got on the
bus, I grabbed a seat *(rushing for a seat)*, and without having time
to yawn, I fell asleep *(covering his eyes with his cap)* and didn't
wake up till the bus stopped, and then the three guys were already
fighting their way off the bus. *(Looking out the bus window)* I
pressed my nose to the window and watched—but they were all
gone. You see what a hopeless sleeper I was!

HAN YING: So you didn't see anything?

ZHAO TIESHENG: That's right! Tell you the truth, nowadays nobody's
afraid of anybody. And I know martial arts, and I make it my

business to fight injustice when I see one. At least I could have gone up to offer help and save a life, and to prevent the suspects from escaping, too. But, come to think of it, who knows what those three guys were fighting for. If you have no idea who was right and who was wrong, who were you supposed to help? And how? It was hard to get involved. You just didn't know where to begin. I just sat there and watched and watched. It was like being on pins and needles, but just no way—

HAN YING: So, you *watched*? Just now you said you were asleep and didn't see anything.

ZHAO TIESHENG: *(Lost for words)* Y-yes, you're right; I was asleep . . . then, how did I see, right? Right . . . well, I got it from all the rumors afterwards, that's how.

HAN YING: I see. Remember what the two suspects looked like?

ZHAO TIESHENG: Looked like? *(Recalls)* Well . . . anyways, one's big and the other's small and dark-skinned, too! Didn't see their faces clearly.

HAN YING: What about the third one?

ZHAO TIESHENG: The guy who was stabbed to death? That one I remember clearly. His picture always stays in my mind: not tall, not terribly handsome, but not bad-looking, either. Fair complexion, fashionably dressed—had on a Western-style beige jacket, quite cool. Couldn't tell what he did—an intellectual or something . . .

(As ZHAO TIESHENG *carries on with his descriptions,* YE XIAOXIAO, *wearing his snow cape, enters, walks slowly across the stage, and stands in front of* ZHAO TIESHENG.*)*

YE XIAOXIAO: *(All smiles)* So, you still remember me?

ZHAO TIESHENG: Just can't forget. Honestly, I quite admired you, brother! You did fine. Those hooligans were mean and cruel, but they don't have the real thing. If you had learned martial arts and had a few tricks up your sleeve, you wouldn't have suffered so miserably.

YE XIAOXIAO: You've practiced martial arts?

ZHAO TIESHENG: You bet. I was quite fond of martial arts when I was a kid. Learned *xingyi, shaolin, baguazhang* . . . [10]

HAN YING: *(Doesn't see* YE XIAOXIAO*)* Comrade Zhao, are you okay? Who are you talking to? What have you been saying? Could you speak a bit louder, please?

(As if in a trance, ZHAO TIESHENG looks at HAN YING and then at YE XIAOXIAO perplexedly.)

YE XIAOXIAO: Why didn't you give me a hand? . . . Ah yes, you said you were asleep.

ZHAO TIESHENG: (Shaken, heart and soul) No no, that wasn't true. I was just pretending—pretending I was asleep. Actually I was quite excited that day, wasn't sleepy at all. Hadn't been staying up late the previous nights, either. On the contrary, I was just feeling great— That morning I went and made a phone call in a telephone booth . . .

(As ZHAO TIESHENG narrates his experience, a CHORUS member comes up and stands still to one side. She plays the role of the phone booth, with a coin-operated telephone in her left hand and her right hand stretched forward to make the door. ZHAO TIESHENG opens the door and enters the booth. He dials a number. The phone on the other end rings. Another CHORUS member, in her choir seat, picks up the receiver— She's a hospital NURSE.)

ZHAO TIESHENG: Hello! Is this Maternity Hospital? Could you check for me if bed number thirty-six has delivered?

NURSE: (Checking the roster) Yes. Delivered. A boy. Nine pounds.

ZHAO TIESHENG: (Elated. Pushes open the booth door and yells) Mom! Mom! Extra good news! My son gave me a big wife!

NURSE: (Into the receiver) What? What did you say?

ZHAO TIESHENG: My son gave me . . . no, no! I mean, my wife gave me a big son. Make sure you made no mistake!

NURSE: What a jerk! (Hangs up)

(ZHAO TIESHENG throws open the booth door, which winces as if hurt and rebounds on the bouncing young father.)

ZHAO TIESHENG: (Hit by the door) Ouch! (Waves to the booth, apologizes) Sorry!

(The CHORUS member playing the booth takes the phone back to her seat. YE XIAOXIAO chuckles.)

ZHAO TIESHENG: (Excitedly) My head was reeling with joy. I just can't tell you how happy I was. I rushed out to the stores to buy gifts for my son . . .

(As ZHAO TIESHENG speaks, he runs over to the choir, buys a pack of things here and a pack there, paying out of his wallet and adding to his armful of packages as he goes from place to place.)

ZHAO TIESHENG: *(Pointing and paying)* Give me that set of comics—
Huo Yuanjia, knight-errant of Tianjin.
(As the sales clerk hands him a stack of comics)
ZHAO TIESHENG: That's for my son, so he won't cry.
YE XIAOXIAO: Would your son be able to read? I guess he hasn't
opened his eyes yet!
ZHAO TIESHENG: That's true, come to think of it. I'll let my wife read
them first while she's on maternity leave. Master Huo's absolutely
my idol. That day, on my way to the maternity hospital *(walks in
a hurry)*, as soon as I hopped on a number thirteen bus and
grabbed a seat, I started reading about him right away. *(Pretends
he's browsing a comic book on the bus)*
YE XIAOXIAO: You like reading, don't you?
ZHAO TIESHENG: Tell you the truth, what I really wanted was to keep
my eyes on the book so I didn't have to yield my seat to senior
citizens or women with children when I saw them. I must confess
I do have a weakness: I can't hold back anything I'm crazy about.
I just have to get it out of my lungs and make some noise. . . .
What happened that day, well, I saw everything from the very
beginning. But just because I was so pumped up, I had to make
all those loud remarks. . . .
YE XIAOXIAO: I heard you, I heard your shouts.
(The stern and neurotic DRUMMER *strikes up a fantastic round. The
large distorting mirror starts turning—*ZHAO TIESHENG *has been
seated in front of it. Now he seems to have resumed his posture on
the bus.*

> YE XIAOXIAO *paces back and forth, thinking. He, too, appears to
be back on the bus.)*
ZHAO TIESHENG: *(Shouts with gusto)* Hey, time for fun! You brothers
want a workout on the bus?
(Noise of the scuffle)
YE XIAOXIAO: *(Thinking painfully; heart aching)* Maybe his life is just
too mundane, too boring, so he has to look for something to stim-
ulate his nerves, no matter what—he wants to have fun!
(The noise of the scuffle grows louder.)
ZHAO TIESHENG: *(At the top of his lungs again)* C'mon, stupid ass!
Give him the Iron Threshold! Black Tiger Gouges Out the
Heart! Heart Licking Elbow! Yeah, Heart Licking Elbow!
YE XIAOXIAO: *(Tormented)* At that point I had already knocked down

and subdued one of them. How I wished someone would give me a hand!

ZHAO TIESHENG: *(Hyperactive)* How come there's no Lei Feng here today? And no Master Huo Yuanjia, either? Hey, it's time to take credits. Who wants to be a hero? Come on!

YE XIAOXIAO: Not only didn't you help me, but you jeered and taunted. You not only scoffed at Lei Feng, but you also made fun of your idol Huo Yuanjia! *(A wry smile)* It was just at that moment that the murderer flashed open his knife! *(Clutching at his chest in pain)* That was a challenge to human conscience! You understand?

ZHAO TIESHENG: *(Shamefaced)* Knife? Knife? I . . . no one was ready to put himself on the line. I . . . *(looking around)* I wasn't, either. Just didn't want to get hurt . . . Too dangerous, you see . . . So, I didn't try.

YE XIAOXIAO: But from the beginning you took this for entertainment, not a matter of life and death! What kind of role did you play?

ZHAO TIESHENG: I know. It was a rotten case of cold-blooded apathy! *(Sorrowful)* Then I read in the papers later that you'd received seven stabs and died in the emergency room. *(Suddenly realizing)* Eh? Aren't you . . . d-dead?

YE XIAOXIAO: *(Nodding)* Yes, I'm dead. No one helped me, so I bled to death.

ZHAO TIESHENG: *(Neurotically)* Dead? Bled to death?! You're really dead? Dead?! . . . *(He clasps his head and withdraws.)* Just because no one helped you . . . Oh, what a bastard I was! . . . Actually, when the fighting first began, I did want to get up to pull you apart but . . . I always like to have a seat on the bus. I was afraid I might lose my seat getting up . . .

YE XIAOXIAO: "Have a seat"? Just for that petty desire of yours?

ZHAO TIESHENG: *(Mumbling)* Just for a seat . . .

HAN YING: *(Not knowing what's going on)* Comrade Zhao, are you all right? Who are you talking to?

ZHAO TIESHENG: *(Dazed, pointing at* YE XIAOXIAO*)* Him—don't you see? He's standing right in front of me, as if he's not dead. . . .

HAN YING: *(Goes up to* ZHAO TIESHENG *and sits him down. Comfortingly)* There's nothing out there. Maybe it's an illusion. Don't be nervous. We're just taking eyewitness accounts. We need to verify what actually happened and find clues that will lead to the early arrest of the suspects.

ZHAO TIESHENG: (*Mumbling to himself*) He's dead. . . . Why . . . why didn't I go up to help? I knew how to do acupoints.[11]

(YE XIAOXIAO *paces up and down, lost in thought.*)

HAN YING: (*To* ZHAO TIESHENG) According to your colleagues, you're quite good at martial arts.

ZHAO TIESHENG: (*Emotionally to* YE XIAOXIAO) To be honest with you, we martial arts practitioners should be early risers. We're not supposed to stay in bed late and cuddle with our wives. But I love my wife, and I especially love kids. That's why that morning, I was in a hurry to go to the hospital to see my wife and son. I didn't want to get involved in anything and miss the hours . . . you see how I love them!

YE XIAOXIAO: I know. You were quite right wanting to make it to the hospital. You were going to welcome a newborn life!

ZHAO TIESHENG: I'm going there again today to pick them up.

HAN YING: (*To* ZHAO) That's all for today! We'll keep in touch.

(HAN YING *and the other officers see off* ZHAO TIESHENG, *who looks back at* YE XIAOXIAO *from time to time as he departs. Then they all return to the choir and doff their masks and insignia.*

YE XIAOXIAO *stands where he was, lost in deep thought.*)

YE XIAOXIAO: He sure loves his wife and child. Who doesn't have beloved ones? Who doesn't have his own wishes? (*A wry smile*) How can I blame him?

(YE XIAOXIAO *paces up and down while the* DRUMMER *is again playing his fantastic beats.* YE XIAOXIAO *sings to himself:* "Smile, smile, on the past I smile . . . " *He seems to find himself on familiar ground again once back inside the music hall, where the* CHORUS *dances gracefully and display their fashion garments.* TANG TIANTIAN *is wearing a young-sailor dress just like the one the blind girl had on. Playing her guitar, she sings a song dedicated to* YE XIAOXIAO, *who drifts to and fro dreamily amongst the dancing* CHORUS.)

TANG TIANTIAN: Life's like the boisterously receding tide
Leaving behind on the beach that colorful shell

(YE XIAOXIAO *stands still, thinking. The* CHORUS *harmonizes with* TANG TIANTIAN.)

CHORUS: Never mind the pearl is lost and gone
Take my smile and loving embrace

(YE XIAOXIAO *starts pacing again, looking up to give free rein to his thoughts. He seems to be holding that colorful shell.*)

TANG TIANTIAN: With that shell I scoop a cup of the blue sea
In that shell I see the splendid morning glow
In my hand the waves of the sea dance

YE XIAOXIAO: Smile, smile, on the past I smile . . .

(*Fondly he gazes at* TANG TIANTIAN *and admires her beauty.* TANG TIANTIAN *returns his gaze, lovingly displaying to him all the best angles of her garmented contour, as if inviting him to feast his eyes to his heart's content.* CHORUS *dance around them, gracefully.* TANG TIANTIAN *lifts her head, closes her eyes, and waits for* YE XIAOXIAO *to approach, like a bride waiting for her groom's nuptial kiss.* YE XIAO-XIAO *approaches, bends over till the two feel each other's breath. But abruptly he restrains himself and retreats slowly. He stands in a corner, gazes at her silently for another second, and disappears.*

TANG TIANTIAN *opens her eyes with a start.* YE XIAOXIAO's *no longer there. She looks frantically around and feels utterly forlorn. She then produces two sheets of red paper from her pocket, overcome with emotion.*

Enter LIU FENG, *in a hurry. He's been looking for* TANG TIAN-TIAN.)

LIU FENG: (*Wiping sweat from his face*) Tiantian, I've been looking for you. I'm desperate!

TANG TIANTIAN: What happened, Liu Feng?

LIU FENG: (*Not knowing what to make of it*) And you're in this beautiful dress?

TANG TIANTIAN: Xiaoxiao likes it. He likes the young-sailor model that he designed. I put this on and accomplished something really important.

LIU FENG: (*Anxiously*) What could be more important? Listen, notice has come from some office: no memorial service for Xiaoxiao; cremation without delay![12] Look at this . . .

TANG TIANTIAN: (*Shocked*) Why? Why all this? It's injustice!

LIU FENG: Injustice? Don't you know your fashion musical show and all the sales activities have been canceled? There's even a ban on loaning the place to you.

TANG TIANTIAN: (*Outraged*) What's all this about?

LIU FENG: (*Dejected*) It's all because of Xiaoxiao. The main excuse is the case is not cleared. Anyways, there are all kinds of rumors . . .

TANG TIANTIAN: *(Agitated)* I don't care. Just because these garments are designed by Xiaoxiao, I've got to have the musical show.

LIU FENG: I was told there are objections to these fashions and musical shows as well. Who knows which way the latest political wind is blowing![13]

TANG TIANTIAN: I don't get it. Xiaoxiao used to say that as a director your job is to sculpt the character's inner beauty while his is to sculpt people's outer beauty. Only when these two are put together is the picture complete. Liu Feng, you should know him well enough. Why don't you give him a helping hand—help him fulfill his wish . . .

LIU FENG: *(Starts, as if stung)* Give him a hand? You say why didn't I help him? . . . *(Sighs and changes the subject)* You don't under-stand—I've been writing, writing every day. I want to help him, to have people see his worth.

TANG TIANTIAN: See his worth? I know Xiaoxiao deserves a monument—

LIU FENG: Right now the number one thing is to restore to him the basic right to a memorial service.

TANG TIANTIAN: I'll go and talk to the leaders. Why don't they allow a memorial service? Is it because they want to save the family pen-sion for the deceased?

LIU FENG: Come on, don't get confused. Xiaoxiao was a loner. There's no family pension to speak of. Who would they give it to?

TANG TIANTIAN: Me! *(Produces the two sheets of red paper)* Here's the marriage certificate. I'm Xiaoxiao's wife. I'm entitled to make the claim.

LIU FENG: *(Astonished)* How could that be possible? How could they possibly issue you a marriage certificate? It's all bullshit!

TANG TIANTIAN: Sounds absurd? Don't forget, I'm a millionaire![14] I've got both money and buddies.[15] The most you have to do is take them out to dinner. That's not so hard. *(Smiles bitterly, almost in tears)*

LIU FENG: Of course. I understand you absolutely. But what would other people think? Because you wanted the pension?

TANG TIANTIAN: I don't care what other people say. I need that money.

LIU FENG: They all say you're worth more than a million. Are you still short of money?

TANG TIANTIAN: Money can also be a pain in the neck. Can't tell whether people love me for myself or for my purse.

LIU FENG: (*Somewhat displeased*) Am I one of those? Don't be so harsh on people, Tiantian. I don't care about that money at all! On the contrary, I've always wanted you to call it quits. You should go to school, or I could find you another job.

TANG TIANTIAN: I'm thinking of quitting, but not because people look down on this profession. There's just no way that they can stop my fashion musical show and sales expo! I'll go right now to look up the head of the managerial office in the Department of Commerce. . . . (*Leaving*)

LIU FENG: (*Anxiously*) What about Xiaoxiao? What should we do?

TANG TIANTIAN: I'll go and tell them I have all the rights and privileges! I've got to go. (*She walks a few steps and returns, picking up* LIU FENG's *hand, sincerely*) Forgive me, Liu Feng, I didn't mean to hurt you. I'm very confused, very confused . . .

LIU FENG: (*Emotionally*) Okay, Tiantian, I understand . . . The three of us grew up together. I understand you.

TANG TIANTIAN: Thanks . . . Finish your writing, for Xiaoxiao's sake, for my sake . . .

LIU FENG: Also for my own heart. I feel kind of responsible.

(*She kisses him impulsively on the cheek, stands back, and hurries off.* LIU FENG *stands still, disquieted. The hoary-haired, ruddy-cheeked* DRUMMER *beats out a soul-stirring rhythm. Exit* LIU FENG, *slowly. The* CHORUS *hums a tune.*)

(*The measured drumming continues.* LIU FENG *comes to a street corner. He wants to light a cigarette. A* CHORUS *member puts on a red scarf and a young girl's mask and steps down from her seat in the choir.*[16]

RED SCARF *hides herself here and there as if shadowing someone. She's tense but serious. It seems she confirms a situation and so emerges from her secret lookout. She looks anxiously around.*

Another CHORUS *member, holding a telephone, goes to one side to play the phone booth.*

RED SCARF *quickly goes into the booth but as quickly zips out. She catches up with the passing* LIU FENG.)

RED SCARF: (*Imploring*) Uncle![17] Dear uncle! I beg you, could you please exchange a dime for my ten-cent bill?[18] I've got to make an urgent phone call! (Holding up a ten-cent bill)

LIU FENG: (Smiles and fishes out a few coins) Here, just take these.

RED SCARF: (Gives a Young Pioneers' salute) Thank you, uncle! I'll pay you back later, on Young Pioneers' honor. (Scrutinizing LIU FENG) Gee, I seem to have seen you before somewhere.

LIU FENG: Is that right? You don't have to pay me back. Never mind. (He moves on. She watches him recede into the distance, then goes back into the booth. But once again she pushes open the door to look out, and makes sure there's no one around. Then she quickly puts the coin in the slot and dials a number. The telephone rings on the other end of the line. HAN YING, now in her CHORUS seat, picks up the phone.)

RED SCARF: (Nervous but serious) Police department? I got something important to report . . .

HAN YING: (Into the receiver) Hi, you must be a young girl! Calm down, don't rush.

RED SCARF: (Anxiously) The two murder suspects on bus number thirteen . . .

HAN YING: (Alert) What? Suspects thirteen-oh-three? Don't rush! Speak clearly!

(CHORUS members come close around HAN YING to listen.)

RED SCARF: (Out of breath) They, the two of them, turned into Xianglai Street, entered number fifteen compound . . . Come! Come quick!

HAN YING: (Professionally) Where are you right now? Give me your exact location.

RED SCARF: I . . . I'm at the Dongsheng Road intersection, the telephone booth . . .

HAN YING: We'll be there shortly! Stay on the watch. Make sure you don't reveal yourself!

RED SCARF: (Solemnly) Yes, ma'am! (Hangs up)

HAN YING: (Giving orders to CHORUS members) C'mon! Let's get out there quick!

CHORUS: Yes, ma'am!

(RED SCARF walks out of the booth, retreats into a corner, and looks out vigilantly into the distance. She waits for the police to arrive, feeling a strong sense of sacred mission.

The hoary-haired, ruddy-cheeked DRUMMER *strikes up the beats of the "Young Pioneers' March."*)

RED SCARF: *(Fantasizing)* . . . Uncle! Uncle . . . the criminals—they are trapped! . . .

(The drumming goes on. The CHORUS *members march in a light dancing step. Enter* YE XIAOXIAO, *with his winged snow cape on. He stands quietly next to* RED SCARF, *for fear of disturbing her.)*

RED SCARF: *(Lifts up her head and sees* YE XIAOXIAO. *Showing no surprise, she walks up to him.)* Uncle! You must know that I was on the bus the other day . . .

YE XIAOXIAO: I saw you. You must be scared, kid.

RED SCARF: *(Almost in tears)* I wasn't able to help you. . . . I felt so bad; I really hate myself! Uncle, would you forgive me?

YE XIAOXIAO: *(Touched)* Don't think that way, kid; you did nothing wrong at all. You are too young; you wouldn't have the strength. You deserve protection from the adults.

RED SCARF: Uncle, I don't understand why all those adults on the bus who had the strength didn't help you. You were doing something good. Why didn't they help you?

YE XIAOXIAO: Don't know. That's what I'm going to ask them.

RED SCARF: Those two pickpockets were real vicious. They were evil! Did it hurt, uncle?

YE XIAOXIAO: Not anymore.

RED SCARF: The paper says you're dead. How sad! Uncle, you must have been a hero or model worker or something, often helping people out and that kind of thing.

YE XIAOXIAO: No, no.

RED SCARF: Uncle, you must be a Communist Party member. That's what you are!

YE XIAOXIAO: *(Blushing)* No-no-no, really, I'm nothing. . . . Oh yes, I was like you—had a red scarf, was a Young Pioneer.

RED SCARF: How modest you are, uncle . . .

YE XIAOXIAO: *(Scratching his head, embarrassed)* Yes, I did send in an application for party membership, but . . . I . . . I wasn't good enough—

(Sound effect of police cars and motorcycles arriving at a screeching halt. HAN YING *steps down from her seat among the* CHORUS.)

HAN YING: (*Commanding*) Block off Xianglai Street! Keep close watch on number fifteen compound!

CHORUS: Yes, ma'am!

RED SCARF: (*Running up to* HAN YING) Auntie!

HAN YING: You're the little girl who called? Give me the details.

RED SCARF: (*As she recalls and narrates, she seems to be reliving the whole incident*) That day, on the bus, I was really scared. . . . I wasn't able to help uncle catch the thieves. I'm so sorry. . . . As soon as the bus stopped, the suspects ran off. I thought as a Young Pioneer I should learn from the good example of the uncle fighting the bad guys. So I followed them secretly all the way to Dongsheng Road, where they disappeared. (*Walks around, disappointed, looking in different directions from time to time*) Since then I've been back here every day after school. I remember what they look like, those two bad guys. (*Bracing herself up*) Just now I suddenly spotted them. So I shadowed them quietly and saw them enter the compound. . . .

HAN YING: (*Moved*) What a courageous and clever child! Thank you so much!

RED SCARF: (*Ingenuously*) Don't thank me; thank him!

HAN YING: (*Puzzled*) Who?

RED SCARF: (*Pointing at* YE XIAOXIAO) Him! He taught me to do what I did.

HAN YING: (*Looking around*) Who taught you?

RED SCARF: The uncle who caught the thieves . . . No one helped him . . . so he was killed!

HAN YING: I'll claim credit for you when the criminals are caught.

RED SCARF: No, no! It was this wonderful uncle who taught me. It was his heroic struggle with the criminals that inspired me. You should claim credit for him.

YE XIAOXIAO: (*Very uneasy*) No, kid, please don't say that anymore; I can't stand it. You see, I'm almost in tears. I should thank *you*.

HAN YING: Child! What did you see? What did you see? (*Looks around and finds nothing abnormal*) Maybe you've been too keyed up. Don't be afraid, child! It's the bad guys who are afraid of the good ones. We're here with you.

RED SCARF: I'm not afraid anymore. (*Looks up at* YE XIAOXIAO) Uncle, the police will catch the criminals and you will be revenged. You will be revenged, I'm positive!

YE XIAOXIAO: *(His eyes fill with tears)* Thank you, kid!

(YE XIAOXIAO breaks down sobbing, covering his face with both hands. A beeper calls HAN YING, who talks into her radio.)

HAN YING: *(Calls out)* This is oh-one, this is oh-one. Please speak.

(Voice from the radio says, "Thirteen-oh-three escaped over the wall. Thirteen-oh-three escaped over the wall!")

HAN YING: *(Calls)* Don't shoot! Just apprehend! Pursue! Notify all precincts!

(Exit HAN YING in a rush, taking RED SCARF with her. They return to their seats in the choir. YE XIAOXIAO reins in his gushing emotion, wipes off his tears, and begins pacing again, singing softly to himself, "Smile, smile, on the past I smile . . . " He feels something in his pocket, takes it out, and finds it to be the wallet he picked up from the thief. He studies it for a long time. The DRUMMER strikes up a fantastic rhythm. The CHORUS hums a wordless song.)

(Only the DRUMMER is playing his measured beats. This looks like the managerial office of the Commerce Department. A meeting is in progress. A CHORUS member puts on the mask of the head of the office, MR. HAO. He is the one whose wallet was stolen on the bus. Right now he is concluding his speech. He steps down from the choir and addresses the CHORUS peripatetically.)

MR. HAO: . . . Therefore, my dear comrades, in our daily routine to enforce market regulations, we should abide by the rules and have the courage to confront head-on all illegal activities, especially criminal persons and activities. We have to understand that courage, even sacrifice, is sometimes required in combating the enemies of law and order.

(The bell rings for offices to close. MR. HAO looks at his watch.)

MR. HAO: Okay. Tell everybody in your sections: no more overtime. We all have families, lots of chores at home, and the crowded bus rides. All section chiefs should care for the staff's well-being. Meeting is adjourned.

(People start putting their things together for the day. MR. HAO picks up his briefcase and is ready to leave when one of the staff members catches him up and starts reporting something to him. He listens and nods from time to time.)

MR. HAO: Uh-huh, mm-hm. Good. That'll be fine. *(The staff member is about to go.)* Wait a minute. Look. *(Brushes away a speck of dust on the staff member's jacket)* Okay, you can go now. Get home early!

(The staff member returns to the choir. MR. HAO *hurries on, and then he enters a store. He walks back and forth in front of the choir, examining the products in the glass counter. He buys a big birthday cake. He moves on. Two* CHORUS *members form a door.* MR. HAO *walks up to this door to his apartment and reaches into his pocket for the key. It's not there.)*

MR. HAO: *(Knocks and calls)* Liangliang! Liangliang!

(A CHORUS *member puts on the mask of the blind girl and fumbles her way from the choir to the door.)*

LIANGLIANG: Who's that? Is it Dad? *(Opens the door. Chiding affectionately)* Daddy, you forgot your key again!

*(*MR. HAO *enters the apartment, closes the door behind him, takes off his jacket together with his mask, and places them on one side.)*

FATHER: Daddy's been busy, very busy. Too many things. My head's stuffed with all those endless tasks. *(He touches the girl's hair.)*

LIANGLIANG: *(Playing the naughty child)* Absentminded! One of these days I'm going to be away for a whole day. See if you don't get locked out!

FATHER: *(Smiling, dismissively)* That's impossible. What would you go out for?

LIANGLIANG: *(Sensitively)* I can't stay home all day. I want to go out to work, sooner or later. . . .

FATHER: But your eyes . . . *(lovingly)* You think Daddy can't support you?

*(*LIANGLIANG *is speechless.)*

FATHER: *(Comfortingly)* Oh, take it easy, child. I'll see what I can do as soon as the leadership reshuffle is completed and everything gets settled down.

LIANGLIANG: *(After a long pause)* Daddy, it's going to be my birthday again.

FATHER: Daddy may forget everything else, but he can't forget what day is today! Look, I've bought you a big birthday cake, and candles, too. Come, let's put the candles on . . . *(They stick the candles in the cake.)*

LIANGLIANG: Thank you, Daddy. What I want to say is, I'm twenty now . . .

FATHER: *(Emotionally)* Twenty years old . . . Yes, my daughter is

twenty years old now. I know, I know. Daddy has not remarried—
it's because of you . . .

LIANGLIANG: *(Tears welling)* I wasn't thinking of that kind of thing.
. . . I'm blind! Daddy, I've been a burden to you. . . .
(Silence.

Enter TANG TIANTIAN. *She's carrying a bag of food. She looks
from door to door for the right number, finds it, and presses the door-
bell button.* LIANGLIANG *feels her way toward the door.)*

LIANGLIANG: *(Reaching the door)* Who is it?

TANG TIANTIAN: *(Standing outside the door. Loudly)* I'm looking for
Mr. Hao!

LIANGLIANG: *(Opens the door a crack)* What is it?

TANG TIANTIAN: *(From outside)* Business.

LIANGLIANG: *(From inside)* Business? Why don't you see him in his
office tomorrow?

FATHER: No, Liangliang; that won't do. Let her in. It wouldn't look
good if the word got around that your dad is a bureaucrat.

LIANGLIANG: It's a bit much for you—to even have to work at
home. . . .
*(*FATHER *puts on his jacket and mask.)*

MR. HAO: *(To* TANG TIANTIAN *outside the door)* Come on in! Come
on in!
*(*TANG TIANTIAN *comes in and* LIANGLIANG *closes the door.)*

TANG TIANTIAN: It's real hard to get an audience from Your Excel-
lency. I won't disturb you for long; just ten minutes.

MR. HAO: *(Apologetically)* Please forgive us. My daughter hasn't been
too well and she's just feeling a little depressed. Take a seat.
Please sit.

TANG TIANTIAN: *(Looking around the room)* Birthday cake! Quite a
celebration going on!
*(*TANG TIANTIAN *checks out* LIANGLIANG, *who's sitting quietly to one
side. They are both wearing exactly the same young-sailor dress.)*

MR. HAO: *(Trying to place her)* So you are . . .
*(*TANG TIANTIAN *hands over a business card.)*

MR. HAO: Ah, Tang Tiantian . . . We've met before.

TANG TIANTIAN: You have an excellent memory, sir.

MR. HAO: It's because your name's easy to remember. Tang, like
sugar, and Tiantian, like sweet, sweet![19] Ha-ha! Tang Tiantian,
a memorable name! Only it's kind of . . .

TANG TIANTIAN: Kind of namby-pamby—like sentimental music, or the name of a Hong Kong or Taiwan pop singer? If that's what you mean, just say it. It doesn't matter.

MR. HAO: (*Chuckles*) No, no, it's not that bad! Ha-ha! (*Suddenly notices something*) Don't move, don't move (*Picks a bit of thread from* TANG TIANTIAN's *dress*) Ah, here's some thread . . .

TANG TIANTIAN: (*Smiles*) We garment dealers are never short of thread. Wouldn't be a surprise if you found a needle on us.

MR. HAO: (*Not knowing what to make of this, as if stung*) Is there anything I can do for you?

TANG TIANTIAN: Oh sure, or I wouldn't have come to visit Your Majesty. I heard you've canceled my fashion musical show and the sales expo. You also told the music hall not to loan their place to us.

MR. HAO: Number one, the Commerce Department leadership feels that you're stealing the business of the state-owned store across the street. That's a big embarrassment for their manager.

TANG TIANTIAN: Well, in a competition, only the big fish eat the small fish, never the other way round. The state-owned store has all the big guns on its side. They just haven't realized yet. What about number two?

MR. HAO: (*Choosing his words*) Number two . . . the kinds of fashions you display and put on sale, aren't they . . . somewhat . . .

TANG TIANTIAN: Punky? Inappropriate?

MR. HAO: That's not what I mean, nor did the leaders say that.

(TANG TIANTIAN *goes up to* LIANGLIANG, *pulls her up from her seat, and admires her from different angles.*)

TANG TIANTIAN: Look at this young-sailor dress on her. How beautiful! How splendid! It's like a colorful cloud in the sky, a petal with dewdrops on a flower tree . . . that's how someone described it. (*Knowingly quoting from* YE XIAOXIAO, *she is filled with sadness*)

LIANGLIANG: (*Delighted*) Who said that? I know I can't see, but every time I go out I can hear what the girls are saying on the streets, as if I could feel all their eyes fixed on me. . . . Often people ask where I bought it. It fills my heart with joy. I always answer, "Sorry I don't know. My dad bought it for me."

(TANG TIANTIAN *smiles and goes over to* MR. HAO.)

TANG TIANTIAN: (*Softly*) Mr. Hao, you are really something. You bought this? Didn't you tell your daughter the truth, that it was a tribute to Your Majesty from me?

MR. HAO: *(Feeling a little awkward)* Because it's truly beautiful, it's gorgeous . . . *(Clears his throat and changes the subject)* Well, as for your fashion show and expo, it's mainly to do with the designer. He was involved in that gang fight on bus number thirteen that's become the talk of the whole town.

TANG TIANTIAN: *(Agitated)* Gang fight?

LIANGLIANG: What are you talking about, Dad? Was it a gang fight on the number thirteen bus? I don't think so, no! That person was a good guy! A good guy he was!

(The DRUMMER *strikes out a round of mysterious beats.*

Enter YE XIAOXIAO *with his snow cape. He paces back and forth outside the door and then drifts in.)*

TANG TIANTIAN: *(Excited)* How did you know, dear girl? How did you know Xiaoxiao was a good guy? Tell me!

LIANGLIANG: Dad and I were on that bus at the time.

MR. HAO: What would she know? She couldn't see.

LIANGLIANG: *(With tears in her eyes)* Yes, I'm blind, but I have a beautiful name, which means "bright bright." [20]

YE XIAOXIAO: *(Gazing at* LIANGLIANG) Thank you, young lady. You haven't forgotten me. . . . I also remember your lovely features.

LIANGLIANG: *(Her searching eyes suddenly brighten up.)* Oh, where are you? Where? You—are you Ye Xiaoxiao? *(She stares at her with her big, bright eyes)* Oh, you're not as handsome as I imagined, or as big and tall. *(She runs to him on tiptoe and makes a circle around him.)* Oh, I know, a girl should not stare at a strange man like that. You won't laugh at me, will you?

YE XIAOXIAO: *(Smiles between tears)* No, Liangliang. People should be friends with one another.

LIANGLIANG: Forgive me, Tiantian! It seems like I've known him for a long time. He's actually a friend in my heart. Hope you don't hate me for that?

TANG TIANTIAN: No no, Liangliang. I feel so happy I could cry.

LIANGLIANG: *(To* YE XIAOXIAO, *sadly)* I wasn't able to help you that day! How I hate myself . . . My eyes! Why am I blind?!

YE XIAOXIAO: Don't be upset, Liangliang. I heard you cry and saw your heart.

MR. HAO: *(Puzzled)* Liangliang, what are you doing? Why do you keep mumbling to yourself?

LIANGLIANG: *(Turns around to face her father, a blind girl again)* Dad! Where are you? *(Reaches out her hands to feel her way)* Look, Dad, look! It's Xiaoxiao! Xiaoxiao's there!

MR. HAO: *(Looking around, seeing nothing)* What Xiaoxiao? I don't see anything!

LIANGLIANG: *(Feeling hurt)* Dad, you forgot him—you have no place for him in your heart. Don't you see? *(Again like a person with normal vision, she runs back to* YE XIAOXIAO *and grabs him)* Don't feel bad. I know you must be quite upset. *(Puts her cheek on his shoulder)*

*(*YE XIAOXIAO *fixes his eyes on* MR. HAO *and remains silent.)*

TANG TIANTIAN: I think I know. *(Goes up to* MR. HAO*)* Mr. Hao, please be fair and tell everyone what actually happened. Think about it!

MR. HAO: Look at the young people these days, bad-tempered, would use knives and daggers for the most trivial excuse. That's what society's like today! Must be an infight among those three. Maybe because they didn't get equal shares of their booties? Maybe out of jealousy, or something. So there goes the knife.

LIANGLIANG: *(Shrieks)* Daddy!

TANG TIANTIAN: So you didn't do anything about it that day?

MR. HAO: *(Sneers)* Do anything? What can you do about gang fights? It's a case of bad guys fighting bad guys.

TANG TIANTIAN: *(Agitated)* But someone was being killed! Murdered! A human being—

MR. HAO: There's no such thing as an abstract human being!

TANG TIANTIAN: So, you're saying, when bad guys fight bad guys, it serves them right, eh?[21]

MR. HAO: *(Shaken. Thinks for a second)* Well, I wouldn't exactly put it that way. . . . So you, young lady, you're trying to set me up, that's what it is!

TANG TIANTIAN: *(Not giving up)* So what happened that day had nothing to do with you?

MR. HAO: With *me?* What did it have to do with me? *(Visibly disturbed)*

(Emotionally YE XIAOXIAO *produces the wallet and step-by-step goes up to* MR. HAO*.)*

MR. HAO: *(Drooping his head, as he sits)* Oh, my gosh! My wallet?

(YE XIAOXIAO *holds up the wallet in front of* MR. HAO, *who lifts his head to see the wallet, and raising his eyes further, sees* YE XIAOXIAO *facing him.*)

YE XIAOXIAO: I can endure truth, no matter how cruel and painful, but I can't tolerate lies. I want to live like an open book, and die like an open book. (*Asking* MR. HAO) Is this your wallet?

MR. HAO: Yes, it is.

YE XIAOXIAO: Then, why didn't you admit it at the time it got stolen?

MR. HAO: Those thieves had their vicious eyes on me.

LIANGLIANG: You also told me my dress was slit, and I did find a slit this long.

YE XIAOXIAO: Why didn't you help me? We could've easily caught the thieves. If you had taken action, many people on the bus would've pitched in.

MR. HAO: I, I . . .

YE XIAOXIAO: If only you had said a few words to denounce them! They would've felt the power of justice. But you went and got scared. Was that how it was?

MR. HAO: (*Stuttering*) I . . . wasn't exactly scared, only my legs were trembling.

LIANGLIANG: I cried out. I wanted Dad to help.

MR. HAO: Yes, that's right! All I was thinking was how to protect Liangliang. She's blind, and a motherless child!

LIANGLIANG: (*Starts crying*) But the criminals were hitting him; they were killing him! Not only didn't you report the case to the police afterward, but you didn't let me report, either. . . . Oh, why am I blind! Why am I blind!

YE XIAOXIAO: (*Softens*) Just to protect your daughter? Yes, Liangliang deserves protection . . . and you love your daughter. You are a good father, aren't you?

MR. HAO: Yes, I love Liangliang. I spent all I had to get her eyesight back. I was willing to pay for the most expensive medicine.

YE XIAOXIAO: That's quite true. You really didn't have a lot of money in your wallet, but I did find a receipt for some very expensive ginseng.

MR. HAO: (*Touched to the quick, as if some secret was revealed. Keeping his eyes on* YE XIAOXIAO) . . . It was all because of that damn ginseng! I was feeling real lousy that day—
(*The* DRUMMER *strikes up a fantastic round of beats.*)

MR. HAO: *(Reminiscing)* That morning, I took Liangliang with me and left home real early—

LIANGLIANG: *(Reminiscing)* Dad wanted me to put on my best dress—

(FATHER, *all dressed up, picks up the exquisitely packaged box of ginseng and walks out onto the street with his daughter.* LIANGLIANG *clings to his arm.* YE XIAOXIAO *and* TANG TIANTIAN *watch the two acting it out.*)

LIANGLIANG: Daddy, where are we going?

MR. HAO: To see our venerable chairman of the department. He's sick and has been in the hospital for quite a few days now. I just didn't get to find the time to see him.

LIANGLIANG: Is this expensive ginseng for him?

MR. HAO: Oh yes, child. This is no ordinary ginseng, but American ginseng. The old man needs a potent tonic but is not supposed to take anything too powerful. Chinese ginseng won't do. American ginseng is imported, not available on the market. I got it through a friend of mine. Wasn't easy.

LIANGLIANG: *(Giggles)* Daddy, you are an officer of the Commerce Department. You also use the back door?[22]

MR. HAO: You're still too young to understand. In this upcoming leadership reshuffle, Daddy is a candidate for deputy chairman. The chairman holds the decisive vote.

LIANGLIANG: *(Bewildered)* Dad, you . . . ?

MR. HAO: Oh, you silly girl! It's all for your sake! You'll understand by and by.

LIANGLIANG: *(Comes to a halt)* Dad, why must you take me there? I'm blind; I can't see a thing. I don't like people always asking me this and that. I hate older people showing me pity.

MR. HAO: That's quite okay. I never remarried. I'm both Dad and Mom. I support my daughter, and we depend on each other. There are lots of able candidates for leading positions, but what the chairman sees as most important are personal conduct and moral integrity.

(MR. HAO *leads the daughter on.*)

MR. HAO: Here we are at last at the hospital.

(MR. HAO *leads his daughter to the choir to inquire.*)

MR. HAO: Excuse me, miss. We need two visitors' cards for Senior Cadres' Ward.

NURSE: Who are you visiting?

MR. HAO: Chairman Shen, room five.

NURSE: Sorry, you can't see him now. He's in emergency.

MR. HAO: *(Shocked)* Wasn't the surgery quite successful? The doctor even said he was not in serious condition.

NURSE: That was for the family to hear. Actually it's a late-stage liver cancer, already widely spread.

MR. HAO: *(Astounded)* Then, Mr. Shen, he . . .

NURSE: Too late. At most twenty days . . .

(MR. HAO *is at a loss what to do, fumbling the exquisitely packaged box of ginseng.)*

NURSE: We can pass on what you've brought. His family is in there.

MR. HAO: *(Thinks for a second)* No, thanks.

NURSE: You can talk to his wife in the lounge. Shall I bring her over?

MR. HAO: *(Quickly stops her)* No, no, it's not necessary, thanks. *(He walks out slowly with* LIANGLIANG.)

LIANGLIANG: Dad, why didn't you leave behind the ginseng for the patient? Didn't you say it's good for the disease?

MR. HAO: *(Morosely)* It may be good for the disease, but it's not going to save his life. . . . He's useless now.

LIANGLIANG: Useless? Who's useless?

MR. HAO: *(Equivocates)* Oh, oh, I was talking about the ginseng . . . useless now. Such expensive products should be used where they can be useful. Oh, you don't understand, child.

YE XIAOXIAO: So, you didn't know you were actually coming to pay your last respects to a dying man. He was no longer useful to you. So, with disappointment, you left and got on the bus. Right? I saw it all. . . .

(The DRUMMER *strikes up a rousing rhythm, intense, frantic.)*

LIANGLIANG: *(Tears in her eyes, throwing herself on* YE XIAOXIAO) Xiaoxiao, you're dead. Do you hate? Do you hate my dad?

YE XIAOXIAO: *(Evasively)* Liangliang, you are a good girl—

LIANGLIANG: Do you resent him? Will you forgive him?

YE XIAOXIAO: *(Shakes his head slightly)* I can't talk about resentment or forgiveness; it's up to the living. I guess everyone has his or her wishes and aspirations. Some are beautiful; some not so beautiful.

LIANGLIANG: Look! Dad never forgets my birthday. He always buys me birthday cakes and candles. The red candle is a symbol of life. Once lit, it sheds tears.

YE XIAOXIAO: (*Shedding tears*) He's a good father to you. You should thank him.

LIANGLIANG: Today's my birthday. Xiaoxiao, if I call you brother, will you light twenty candles for me and bless me?

YE XIAOXIAO: (*Cheering up*) Of course, I'd be most happy to bless my little sister.

LIANGLIANG: (*Handing him matches*) Please light the flame of life for me! I thank you!

(YE XIAOXIAO *strikes a match. It's not lit, but still he uses the match stick to "light" the candles on the cake. None of the candles are lit.*

Everyone watches YE XIAOXIAO *with wonder; he's not aware what's going on.*)

YE XIAOXIAO: (*Discovers that the candles are not lit. Dejectedly*) No flame, no, not a single one is lit. . . . I'm dead. All my blood is drained. Cold as ice. Can't light up anymore. I can't light those candles anymore. . . . I'm so sorry, little sister! I disappointed you. Please forgive me.

(LIANGLIANG *cries her heart out in* YE XIAOXIAO'*s arms.*

TANG TIANTIAN *takes the box of matches, lights one, and with it lights the candles on the cake. In the dim light, the* CHORUS *members hold up lighted red candles like torches, making a total of twenty. The room seems to warm up in an orange red glow.*

The Torch Dance: with YE XIAOXIAO *in the lead and* LIANGLIANG *and* TANG TIANTIAN *following, the three of them zigzag among the burning torches like wandering ghosts. The* CHORUS *members fade out slowly as they whirl around with torches in hand.* LIANGLIANG *holds up her birthday cake and counts the candles in it: ". . . four, five, six, seven, eight, . . . " With* TANG TIANTIAN *as her companion, she also whirls her way out.*

YE XIAOXIAO *stands still, thinking.* MR. HAO *approaches him gingerly.*)

YE XIAOXIAO: (*Forcing a smile*) I want you to take off your mask.

(MR. HAO *is stunned. Finally, he painfully doffs his mask and hands it over to* YE XIAOXIAO. . . . *Suddenly he seems to feel myriad eyes trained on his unmasked face. He covers it with both hands and flees the stage.*)

YE XIAOXIAO: (*Examining the mask in his hand, thinking aloud with emotion*) Right. Who doesn't have his or her own wish and aspiration, be it ever so small, so petty. . . . (*He hurls the mask back to its place in the choir.)* How wonderful it is to live in an age of aspiration! I love them—Red Scarf, Liangliang, and that man on the bus who shouted, "Drive us to the police station!" His voice was a bit taut and trembling, but after all, it was the voice of justice! I've always wanted to find him. What's he like? It's a pity he stood in the back, I couldn't see . . .

(The DRUMMER *strikes up those wonderful beats. The* CHORUS *hums a wordless song.)*

YE XIAOXIAO: *(Thinking)* I've got to find him. . . . *(He starts humming and singing the "Song of the Fledgling.")*

I'm a happy fledgling
On spring's keyboard I jump and sing
Let my enchanting melodies
Tell the secrets of spring—
Hello, early spring! Hello, early spring!

I'm a pure fountain
Forever joyful forever bubbling
I keep strumming Life's strings
Let the music strike the fountain
From which a rainbow springs

Follow my song, oh soul of love
Leave behind the spirits of beauty
But carry my heartfelt joy on your wings
Ah . . .

(Exit YE XIAOXIAO *on his winged walk. The* CHORUS's *wordless song lingers in the air . . .)*

(The DRUMMER *strikes up an impassioned rhythm.*

Somewhere on the street. A CHORUS *member puts on a red scarf and mask and steps down from the choir. She holds a big stack of newspapers in her arms and cries out her wares.)*

RED SCARF: *(Calling out)* Paper! Newspaper!

(Enter LIU FENG, *hurrying along with a book bag slung across his shoulder. He hears* RED SCARF's *cries and comes up to her.)*

LIU FENG: *(Fishing for money, then buying a newspaper)* Hi! Are you a student worker?

RED SCARF: No, I just like this. There's some news I want everyone to know!

LIU FENG: *(Turning the pages)* What news? Where is it?

RED SCARF: *(Pointing it out to him)* Here!

LIU FENG: I see. Just this tiny square? *(Reads carefully)* Oh, "Thirteen-oh-three suspects arrested"?

RED SCARF: *(Recognizing him)* Hey, uncle, I've been looking for you! I owe you four cents.

LIU FENG: Four cents?

RED SCARF: I wanted to make an emergency phone call, so I borrowed four cents from you, remember? I said I would give it back to you.

LIU FENG: You've got a good memory. You recognized me right away?

RED SCARF: I was sure I had met you before somewhere. You look so familiar!

LIU FENG: *(Smiles)* Is that right? Forget the four cents. Bye-bye, Red Scarf.

(LIU FENG walks away, reading the paper. He looks around from time to time, apparently expecting someone.

RED SCARF holds up the four cents as if dazed. She retreats slowly, back to the choir.

Enter TANG TIANTIAN with her guitar on her back, shouting, "Liu Feng! Liu Feng!" as she runs up to him.)

TANG TIANTIAN: Liu Feng! Sorry to have kept you waiting.

LIU FENG: I also just got here. *(Pointing at the paper)* Look, the suspects were nabbed.

TANG TIANTIAN: *(Reading)* Just a little blurb like that—is that all? Didn't even mention Xiaoxiao!

LIU FENG: As long as the case is solved, Xiaoxiao will be able to rest in peace.

TANG TIANTIAN: I doubt it. The suspects' arrest was a matter of time. What really upset him is the way those passengers behaved.

LIU FENG: *(Falls silent for what seems an eternity)* Let's go, Tiantian. If I were you, I wouldn't mention the pension issue at the police office.

TANG TIANTIAN: Why not?

LIU FENG: Nothing. Better not mention it, okay?

(They walk side-by-side up to the choir.)

LIU FENG: *(Inquiring)* Excuse me, is this the criminal investigation office?

CHORUS MEMBER: Yes, can I help you?

LIU FENG: *(Shows his ID)* We have an appointment with Comrade Han Ying.

(Another CHORUS *member puts on her police insignia and responds, "I'm Han Ying.")*

HAN YING: *(Checks the ID, steps down from the choir, and shakes hands with* LIU FENG *and* TANG TIANTIAN*)* So you are Theater Director Liu Feng? You must be Tang Tiantian. Please sit down. You were both good friends with Xiaoxiao?

LIU FENG: Yes. We all grew up together.

HAN YING: The news of the suspects' arrest is already in the papers. You must have seen it. . . .

TANG TIANTIAN: Just a few lines in small print at the bottom of the page. Who would've noticed it?

LIU FENG: *(Hushing her up)* Tiantian!

HAN YING: *(Smiles)* This is only local news. The suspects have gone through preliminary interrogation. These are tough guys—slippery, too—but the case is by and large clear now. The gang-fight hypothesis can be dropped.

TANG TIANTIAN: We never doubted Xiaoxiao's character.

LIU FENG: *(Afraid she might shoot off her mouth)* Tiantian! *(To* HAN YING*)* What we want to say is Xiaoxiao should be posthumously honored as a martyr.[23]

TANG TIANTIAN: Xiaoxiao should be recognized as a hero.

HAN YING: Of course, but a comprehensive check of his personal history is required. I've also invited a leading comrade from his unit to join us.

(A CHORUS *member dons the mask of* DIRECTOR FAN, *who hurries down from the choir with a briefcase under his arm.)*

DIRECTOR FAN: *(Shakes hands with* HAN YING*)* I'm terribly sorry, Comrade Han. I was tied up with other business. Sorry, sorry. *(Greets* LIU FENG*)*

HAN YING: That's okay. Well, I've asked you all to come out here to see if you can help me put together a life story of Xiaoxiao and compile something in writing—

DIRECTOR FAN: Life story? In writing? Is that a directive from the higher authorities?

HAN YING: No, no, I'm just thinking of submitting something. It was my idea. I dropped a hint to the news reporters who came for the story. They also want to have something in hand.

TANG TIANTIAN: *(Sneering)* Hmm, they seem to have made an about-face. The initial news reports lumped all three together. All a mishmash; no distinction between good and bad. Could be anybody's guess.

HAN YING: You know how reporters all want to get the scoop. Of course, we have our share of responsibility.

DIRECTOR FAN: You're absolutely right. It seems we should view the whole thing in a new perspective. As for the life story and the related data, well, we need to talk about it at the leadership level. We need to set some limits and boundaries, you know. *(To LIU FENG and TANG TIANTIAN)* Now, you two know Xiaoxiao the best; you were his best friends. Could you say something?

LIU FENG: I've been writing about Xiaoxiao. I feel a sense of responsibility. I want to make him look great, a man of stature—

DIRECTOR FAN: A man of stature?

HAN YING: *(Regretfully)* Ye Xiaoxiao died fighting against criminals. How cruel these criminals were needs no belaboring. But from what we know, there were quite a lot of passengers on the bus, yet no one stepped forward to lend him a hand. Even the owner of the wallet was cold and apathetic! That's something that has also drawn the attention of the higher authorities.

TANG TIANTIAN: Shouldn't you then look up these passengers? Don't they deserve to be criticized and penalized?

HAN YING: *(Thinking)* Uh-huh, but that's beyond the purview of the police and the court of justice. . . . Shouldn't you writers look into this?

LIU FENG: Yes, yes, deep down in every soul is a court of ethical justice. Along with it is also a monument to the worthy. . . .

TANG TIANTIAN: A monument to the worthy? *(Thinks and suddenly remembers)* May I ask, then, what about Xiaoxiao's family pension?

DIRECTOR FAN: Family pension?

HAN YING: If he has any immediate relative, such as parents, spouse, or children, he sure should qualify.

DIRECTOR FAN: Ye Xiaoxiao had no immediate relative. He was single all these years.

TANG TIANTIAN: I'm his wife.

DIRECTOR FAN: *(Surprised)* What? You?!

TANG TIANTIAN: Yes, me!

LIU FENG: *(Anxiously pulls her to one side and whispers)* Tiantian, don't say anything about the pension.

TANG TIANTIAN: Why not? You think I've been too vulgar? *(Eyes fill with tears)*

(LIU FENG is silent.)

TANG TIANTIAN: Or is it because you don't want to admit I'm his wife?

LIU FENG: No! No! You've never been his wife!

TANG TIANTIAN: Can't I even fight for the right to be his pallbearer?

LIU FENG: *(Anxiously)* I understand how you feel, but surely there's some other way! If you need money, I can find something for you.

TANG TIANTIAN: *(Sneers)* Wouldn't be enough! How much money can you come up with? Can writing a play bring you more than a couple hundred bucks? What I need is a large sum, a *huge* sum of money. I've got to make the fashion musical show and the sales expo work!

LIU FENG: *(Baffled, growing impatient)* Tiantian! How could you?!

TANG TIANTIAN: *(Handing DIRECTOR FAN the two pieces of red paper)* I'm Xiaoxiao's wife. Here's the marriage certificate!

DIRECTOR FAN: *(Examines the certificate, looks at TANG TIANTIAN, and chuckles)* Ye Xiaoxiao's wife? . . . That's very interesting . . . I don't think Xiaoxiao has bequeathed any legacy.

TANG TIANTIAN: *(To HAN YING)* In the event Xiaoxiao is posthumously recognized as a martyr, a hero, then the family pension . . . ?

HAN YING: Would be quite a sum.

DIRECTOR FAN: *(Equivocates)* Mmm . . . we'll think about it carefully.

TANG TIANTIAN: I'll do all I can for Xiaoxiao!

(DIRECTOR FAN says something to HAN YING as they walk upstage, back to the choir.)

LIU FENG: *(Displeased)* This is really stupid, Tiantian! You're doing Xiaoxiao a disservice. Also think of your own future.

TANG TIANTIAN: *(With a toss of her head)* Hmm, Xiaoxiao died without enjoying a woman's love. That's what I call imperfect! Let people say what they want; I'm not afraid. I've got a lot of things to do.

(The stern and neurotic DRUMMER beats out an impassioned and disorderly round. The CHORUS hums an emotional melody and gets up to do a graceful dance. TANG TIANTIAN and LIU FENG walk slowly ahead.)

(*The* DRUMMER *plays a florid round. This looks like* TANG TIANTIAN's *bedroom. She sits slouching on the side of her bed, steeped in senti-mentality.*)

TANG TIANTIAN: (*Rhythmically intoning*) When I was a little girl, Mom gave me a bright mirror and said it was her tender eyes . . . Oh, I liked it, I really liked it—Oh, my wondrous mirror . . .
(*Sings softly*)
I don't remember from when it was
That your shadow came into my mirror
Like entering a brightly lit stage
Together we began knitting a colorful dream
(*Almost like in the opening scene, enter the snow-caped* YE XIAO-XIAO, *drifting to his original position at the stage entrance. Leaning against the post, he watches with admiration, his eyes burning with desire. Then he walks up to* TANG TIANTIAN, *who gazes lovingly at him with big, shining eyes. Only the* DRUMMER *is playing, his beats resembling the throbs of the heart.*)

TANG TIANTIAN: (*Filled with yearning for love*) Xiaoxiao, it seems like a long time.

YE XIAOXIAO: Really? I live in the heart of anyone who thinks of me—in your songs, on your guitar strings, I'm a tremor of thought . . .

TANG TIANTIAN: The murderers are under arrest. The truth is all clear now. You must be happy to hear that! The newspapers are full of your story, calling you a role model.

YE XIAOXIAO: (*Smiles faintly*) I know . . .

TANG TIANTIAN: The papers are also criticizing those who didn't help you!

YE XIAOXIAO: (*A little uneasy*) I know. Made them all terribly nerv-ous. When I visited them, I noticed—they all looked at me with strange eyes, and talked to me in a strange voice. . . . I felt rather uneasy. Is this all quite necessary? I can't wait to see that other person. . . . I have to say there was at least one person on the bus who wanted to help me. I want to see him real bad.

TANG TIANTIAN: Did you ever think of me all these days?

YE XIAOXIAO: You've been busy running around. I just couldn't find you.

TANG TIANTIAN: I'm really tired, completely washed out— Oh, I almost can't take it anymore.

YE XIAOXIAO: What've you been doing?

TANG TIANTIAN: I won't tell you now. You might want to stop me. I'm really exhausted—

YE XIAOXIAO: Stop it, then, call it quits. Now I'm dead, there's no one to help you. I can't make new designs for you anymore. Without the creations of beauty, all that's left is just business.

TANG TIANTIAN: I am thinking of quitting. It's always buying and selling and inventory taking and bookkeeping . . . Now you get something hot and sell well. Now you get something cold and lose a big amount. Even after you go to bed, you have to lose sleep thinking how to beat the next guy.

YE XIAOXIAO: Quit then. It's been too hard for you.

TANG TIANTIAN: But this is addictive! Just like gambling. I can be quite ruthless sometimes. I can even keep the source of my goods secret and look the other way when people lose.

YE XIAOXIAO: I know. You may have lots of money, but you are not happy. Your life is not fulfilling.

TANG TIANTIAN: (With tears welling up in her eyes) It's kind of strange—I make a lot more money than you all, but I don't find my life as substantial and meaningful as yours. . . .

YE XIAOXIAO: I didn't do as well as Liu Feng. He's an accomplished director, but there were so many things I didn't accomplish. I achieved so little in my career. So many of my wishes ended like a blank.

TANG TIANTIAN: No-no. Ever since you died, I felt as if my heart was a total blank. Why does Liu Feng always look at me with a kind of sympathy or pity? It seems he wants to be a hero, one who saves me and redeems me.

YE XIAOXIAO: No. Liu Feng loves you. We three grew up together . . . I know you also like him, only you haven't made up your mind.

TANG TIANTIAN: (Smiles wryly) If I wasn't good-looking, what would I have to show for it to be his equal? Just my money? (Shakes her head) I suddenly felt recently that I'm like those passengers on your bus . . . I've been real cold.

YE XIAOXIAO: No, Tiantian. Why belittle yourself? It's all because you've been thinking too much about what happened on that bus—

TANG TIANTIAN: Yes, you're dead, dead . . . I'm different from them. I have to finish the business on hand and make enough money . . . all for your sake.

YE XIAOXIAO: For my sake? (*Chuckles mischievously*) Then you don't have to go to all that trouble! All you have to do is buy some yellow straw paper, make a square hole in each piece to make sacrificial money, and burn it. These days people even burn paper cars, paper villas, and paper refrigerators for their departed.

TANG TIANTIAN: (*Fakes scolding*) You naughty child! How can you have the heart to joke? I've grieved so much over your death! You don't know a thing about what's been going on in my mind.

YE XIAOXIAO: (*Muttering to himself*) Death? Yes, I'm dead. I am dead! I know there are people grieving for me . . . (*Thinking, he steps to one side and stands still there.*)

(*Enter* LIU FENG, *in a rush, sweating profusely.*)

LIU FENG: (*Panting*) Tiantian!

TANG TIANTIAN: What's up? Weren't you writing for Xiaoxiao?

LIU FENG: (*Anxiously*) Precisely! I finished the article, took it to the editors' office, but . . . some new problem came up!

TANG TIANTIAN: What problem?

LIU FENG: They told me at the office that the titles of martyr and hero are being considered for Xiaoxiao. . . .

TANG TIANTIAN: Isn't that good news?

LIU FENG: Good! Just at this critical moment, the press and the authorities have received several letters of objection.

TANG TIANTIAN: What did they say?

LIU FENG: (*Acting hesitant to talk*) Hmm . . .

TANG TIANTIAN: (*Anxiously*) Go on! What did they say about Xiaoxiao?

LIU FENG: (*Complainingly*) What did they say? It was all because of that marriage certificate of yours and that pension.

TANG TIANTIAN: What has that to do with Xiaoxiao being a martyr or hero?

LIU FENG: Okay, I'll tell you the truth. People are asking if Xiaoxiao led a moral life. Someone raised the suggestion to investigate the possibility of illegal cohabitation. See?

TANG TIANTIAN: (*Roars with laughter*) Ha-ha-ha! (*Bitterly*) These people just have nothing better to do! Good for nothing except an extremely potent imagination in those matters—as soon as they see a man and a woman shaking hands, they begin to think of fondling, and then bedroom scenes, and then babies out of wedlock! (*She sounds wronged and almost tearful.*)

LIU FENG: *(Doesn't like it)* Tiantian! Look, this is no time for tantrums!

TANG TIANTIAN: *(Stops her sardonic laughter)* Liu Feng, be honest with yourself; don't you have the same suspicion? Don't you? *(*LIU FENG *lowers his head in silence.)*

TANG TIANTIAN: *(Pressing)* You also feel something that makes you uncomfortable, right?

LIU FENG: No! I don't believe such rumors. I know Xiaoxiao. Besides, Xiaoxiao knew I liked you.

TANG TIANTIAN: *(Painfully)* Do you mean to say that if the rumors were true, then he would not qualify as a hero? That he would no longer be a hero?

LIU FENG: That's why the authorities want to make an investigation. The commendation is still pending; so is the publication of my article.

TANG TIANTIAN: I'll go find them. I'll go and declare—

LIU FENG: Right! You're the only one who can clarify the matter. As they say, it takes the one who ties the knot to untie it.

TANG TIANTIAN: I'll declare to them I've long been Xiaoxiao's wife.

LIU FENG: *(Stunned)* What? You and Xiaoxiao . . . were you really? *(*TANG TIANTIAN *becomes contemplative.* YE XIAOXIAO *hastens over.)*

YE XIAOXIAO: Tiantian! Don't do that! Why say such things? Liu Feng, never mind what she said! Maybe it was just because she couldn't stand the shock of seeing a childhood friend die. You know people sometimes have illusions. . . . Everything in the haze looks real, but it's all a mirage.

TANG TIANTIAN: *(In tears)* How come, Xiaoxiao, you also talk like this? You want to be a saint?

YE XIAOXIAO: Never thought of that. D'you think I look like a saint in any remote way? My thoughts aren't always that clean. Remember the time I was over at your place, from dusk till dawn, just the two of us . . . Now I think I should fess up to you—you know what, I *was* thinking along those lines that night. My heart was topsy-turvy, and my head kept reeling like mad—

TANG TIANTIAN: I know. I was particularly sorry for that, sorry that I didn't even let you kiss me . . . and now you're dead.

LIU FENG: *(Comes over. Comfortingly)* Tiantian, you should think for the living, not the dead. Think for yourself. Suppose you make that kind of declaration; what would you do as a woman for the rest of your life? What would I do? We are still living. . . .

TANG TIANTIAN: *(Pondering)* Living? Do you mean as one living, you, too, can't tolerate what I felt for and did with the dead? Is that what you mean?

*(*LIU FENG *is silent.)*

YE XIAOXIAO: Don't believe all those things that can never be proved. Tiantian's a good girl. Don't just look at the appearance of things. She may sound like she has a sharp tongue, but she has a good heart. Love her.

LIU FENG: Tiantian, I'll explain to people that there was no such thing between you and Xiaoxiao.

TANG TIANTIAN: *(Stubbornly)* What if there was "such a thing"? Wouldn't you love me anymore?

*(*LIU FENG *is tongue-tied, silent.)*

TANG TIANTIAN: Then there was such a thing. That snowy night, Xiaoxiao and I were studying a tailoring method from Japan called prototypical cut, when time slipped by deep into the night . . .

(The hoary-haired, ruddy-cheeked DRUMMER *strikes up an unhurried, dreamy round.*

The CHORUS *hums a romantic tune. They throw bits of white paper into the air—it's snowing.*

TANG TIANTIAN *acts as if she's trying on a beautiful, newly designed dress, in front of a large mirror.* YE XIAOXIAO *gazes at her in a trance, his eyes burning with desire.*

TANG TIANTIAN *detects in the mirror that* YE XIAOXIAO *is admiring her. She turns around to look at* YE XIAOXIAO, *her eyes filled with yearning love.*

YE XIAOXIAO *withdraws his enchanted gaze and walks away shyly to push open the door. The snow keeps falling. The* CHORUS *members skim across the stage, hurling up more paper flakes of all colors into the air—the snowflakes become a kaleidoscopic display.)*

YE XIAOXIAO: Gee! What heavy snow!

TANG TIANTIAN: *(Putting her finger to her lips)* Shhh! Be quiet! It's late, and there's no more bus.

YE XIAOXIAO: What shall I do? The snow was so quiet I didn't realize . . .

TANG TIANTIAN: Then, don't go. Just stay here.

YE XIAOXIAO: But, eh . . . mmm . . . okay, let's sit and talk till daybreak.

TANG TIANTIAN: Why sit till daybreak? And talk, too! I'd die of fatigue.

(YE XIAOXIAO, *at a loss what to do, looks at* TANG TIANTIAN *uneasily.*)

TANG TIANTIAN: Remember the song we used to sing together as kids?
Little toddler
Sitting on the threshold
Crying for a young wife
A young wife for what?
Be his mate when the light's on
Chat with him when the light's off
(*She giggles.*)

YE XIAOXIAO: (*Also giggles. Walks up to her*) Tiantian, Tiantian! I, I . . . (*Controlling himself*) Am I acting like a fool? Tiantian, I can never tell if you really . . . care for me.

TANG TIANTIAN: Why?

YE XIAOXIAO: I'm kind of good-for-nothing—I have many wishes, but have accomplished very little and haven't been up to much, either. Not like Liu Feng. He's doing much better.

TANG TIANTIAN: Somehow each of you seems to lack something. If only you two could be put together to make one!

YE XIAOXIAO: (*Gazes at her. After prolonged silence*) Tiantian, I've got to go . . . (*About to push open the door*)

TANG TIANTIAN: (*Pulling him back*) Are you crazy? How can you go in such heavy snow? Just stay here tonight. What're you afraid of?
(*The two stand at the door, gazing at each other in silence.*)

LIU FENG: (*Concerned*) So you did live together?
(TANG TIANTIAN *and* YE XIAOXIAO *remain standing at the door, gazing at each other in silence.*)

LIU FENG: Tiantian! This just isn't true; it's not true! Right? There's nothing of the kind whatsoever! It's all your own fabrication because you feel guilty for Xiaoxiao. Right?

TANG TIANTIAN: No! It's true! It's true!! (*She goes up to* YE XIAOXIAO *and cuddles against his chest*) I said to Xiaoxiao: "Kiss me! Hold me tight! Kiss me like a man! I'm yours. We've both long reached the marriageable age. What's there to be afraid of? I'll give you everything. Take me—now, right now . . . Oh, how beautiful—that snow!"

(*Transfixed and amazed,* YE XIAOXIAO *looks at her—motionless as a statue completely immune to all her hugs and kisses—as if totally insentient.*

LIU FENG *covers his eyes in agony and bows his head.*)

TANG TIANTIAN: Liu Feng, you write all this down. Write it out! It's all true, all real! Only when you write about all this can Xiaoxiao appear like a real man. How wonderful would that be! (*Her eyes fill with tears.*)

LIU FENG: (*Painfully*) Then his image would no longer be perfect—flawed, you understand? And there's you, Tiantian, and me, too—what would become of us? . . . I've tried to help him, create a good image of him. I tried hard to patch him up in other respects as I wrote.

YE XIAOXIAO: (*Walks up to* LIU FENG) What she said was all her imagination—what she thinks up now—to make me feel better. Actually, I spent that whole night huddled up on her living-room sofa.

LIU FENG: Xiaoxiao, you deserve to be a hero. I've been trying to help you. I've put in a lot of efforts to collect all your stories.

(*The* DRUMMER *plays an unhurried rhythm. A* CHORUS *member puts on his mask and steps down from the choir. Enter* DIRECTOR FAN *in a rush, with his briefcase. He pushes open the door, enters, and looks around.*)

DIRECTOR FAN: There you are, Liu Feng! I've been looking for you all over the place.

LIU FENG: For me? For what?

DIRECTOR FAN: The leaders are considering a memorial meeting in honor of Xiaoxiao. Please write up a memorial speech or something . . . (*Exit, talking with* LIU FENG)

TANG TIANTIAN: Did you hear, Xiaoxiao? They are going to have a memorial meeting for you.

YE XIAOXIAO: Memorial meeting? Do I have to attend, too?

TANG TIANTIAN: Of course, you are the lead character.

YE XIAOXIAO: The lead? No, I'm a lousy actor and good for the least important roles only. I never played a lead role in my life.

TANG TIANTIAN: This time you'll be the lead, and a hero at that.

YE XIAOXIAO: No, no, that won't do. What if I couldn't hold back my giggle?

TANG TIANTIAN: Don't be nervous. It's only once in a lifetime. (*She walks across to the other side of the stage.*)

YE XIAOXIAO: (*Standing there lost in thought*) Memorial meeting? Lead character? How funny! Don't you ever giggle when the time comes! (*Suddenly realizing*) Oh, my gosh! Aren't they going to cremate me first before the memorial meeting? Does it hurt? Oh, forget it! I've got to use the remaining time to finish my visits. Where's that guy—the guy who shouted, "Drive the bus to the police station"?

(*The* CHORUS *members walk about the stage in criss-cross lines, with masks in hand and completely expressionless.* YE XIAOXIAO *searches amidst this dizzying crowd, examining the postures of the pedestrians, trying hard to think and recall . . .*)

YE XIAOXIAO: (*Remembering something*) That's right—there was a young couple on the bus that day. . . .

(*The* CHORUS *members return to their seats in the choir.* YE XIAOXIAO *walks on and fades out.*

The DRUMMER *strikes up a spirited and bouncing rhythm. Two* CHORUS *members put on their masks and descend from the choir to enter as the young couple. Gingerly they push open the door and walk into the music hall, as if looking for something.*)

WIFE: (*Looking around*) Gee, there's no one around. . . . They say that Ye Xiaoxiao finally collapsed right here, with seven wounds in his body! (*A bit nervous*) Let's go!

HUSBAND: No! For all these days I've been wanting to come out here to pay him my last respects. Every time I see the story in the papers, it breaks my heart. I just get choked up—

WIFE: Of course, he's a hero now, but you have to keep on condemning yourself in public. . . . Oh, forget it! Anyways, the papers have not singled you out. Besides, who's there to blame?

HUSBAND: Who? You! (*Sits down on his haunches, puffing with fury*)

WIFE: (*Sarcastically*) All right! A big hunky guy like you didn't go up to help, and you have to find a woman like me to be your scapegoat.

HUSBAND: If you hadn't pulled me back, I would've stepped forward. Ever since I was a child I wanted to be a hero but never got a chance. It was disgusting! Now I'm dreaming every night how I charged up—*bang! bang!*—and helped him bring those rotten eggs to their knees!

WIFE: *(Exasperated and amused at the same time)* I see. That's why you box and kick in bed in the middle of night. All out of remorse!

HUSBAND: *(Still reveling in his imaginary victory)* I step out from the crowd, and with a big shout, the murderers are in my hands! How macho! What triumph!

WIFE: Hey, what's the story? Yelling and screaming—what's that all about?

(Enter YE XIAOXIAO, *to the beating of drums. While the drumming goes on, the couple looks around in panic and sees* YE XIAOXIAO.*)*

YE XIAOXIAO: *(Interested)* Was it you who yelled those words on the bus?

HUSBAND: *(Paranoid)* What words? What yelling?

WIFE: *(Tries to explain)* Yes, there was someone on the bus who made a lot of noise and tried to pour oil on the fire. But that wasn't him.

YE XIAOXIAO: I'm talking about the one who shouted, "Drive the bus to the police station." Those were words of justice!

WIFE: So, that's what you mean! Yes, yes, I heard it. I would've clean forgotten if you hadn't reminded me. *(To her husband)* Was it you? Yes, it was you, can't be wrong. You shouldn't feel depressed anymore. Tell everyone and your boss about it.

HUSBAND: *(Puzzled)* "Drive the bus to the police station!" Sure enough! Words of justice! No kidding! I actually thought of this . . . *(Asking his wife)* Hey, did I say it out loud?

WIFE: Of course you did. I heard with my own ears!

HUSBAND: Right! I heard it, too! Maybe it was me? . . . Wait; how come it didn't quite sound like my voice?

YE XIAOXIAO: *(Curious)* Not you?

WIFE: *(Not giving up)* How come it sounded like you to me? If it was you, just say so. Didn't you hear him say it was the words of justice? It was a good deed performed.

HUSBAND: I felt it in my guts. It must be that I thought about it but never uttered it out loud.

WIFE: This is no time to be modest!

YE XIAOXIAO: Those were the words of justice after all—even though the voice sounded a bit nervous and trembling.

WIFE: A bit nervous and trembling? That—that's not too good.

HUSBAND: To be frank with you, I was feeling a little nervous and trembling. Anyways, my mind was like a hell that day. *(To his wife)* It was all because you'd been arguing with me before we got on the bus. I was trembling all over with fury.

WIFE: *(To* YE XIAOXIAO*)* Please don't blame him. We did have a squabble before we got on the bus. Please don't ever think badly of him. He's usually a righteous person. That day it was all my fault . . . we were on our way to see my parents.
(The couple are both dressed up, walking on the street, acting out the story as they tell it.)

WIFE: That was the third day after our wedding, and we were supposed to visit my parents.[24] On our way I said to him—*(To her husband)* "Hey, why don't you go and get two boxes of pastries? Make sure it's not all cheap almond cookies! Nowadays people all look for deluxe products. All my sisters will be going home to see the groom. We'd better not lose face! Go on, now! I'll be waiting for you here."

HUSBAND: *(Feeling set up)* Sure, sure. *(To* YE XIAOXIAO*)* How would she understand? For the sake of all the deluxe material culture she desires—color TV, sound system, refrigerator, plus the wedding gifts—I spent all my savings and still went into the red! My pockets are empty, but I have to brace up and put up a bold front in the store. . . .
(He approaches the choir and browses in front of the display counter. A CHORUS *member playing the salesclerk greets him and introduces him to different commodities. The husband shakes his head and moves on. He empties all his pockets to find only four dimes. He scratches his head for ideas.)*

HUSBAND: *(Awkwardly goes up to a display case, points, and hands over the coins)* Two of these!
(The clerk hands him two strings of hawberry candies.[25] He comes out of the store and hands the candies to his wife.)

WIFE: *(Taken aback)* What? Just these two strings of hawberries?!

HUSBAND: *(All apologetic smiles)* I found only four dimes on me—

WIFE: *(Fit to burst)* You . . . what nerve!

YE XIAOXIAO: *(Intercedes)* Easy, easy! Hawberries are good for hypertension—soften the blood vessels. Good for both old and young.

HUSBAND: Exactly! Special products of China. Bet you can't find this stuff abroad!

WIFE: *(Blowing up)* Are you kidding? You want my old man to break his teeth on those? Oh, you mean, unconscionable rat!

HUSBAND: Don't you call me unconscionable! Better watch your language!

WIFE: Unconscionable—that's what you are. You don't like it? Okay, let's break up! Divorce!

HUSBAND: *(Pretty worked up)* Divorce! You said *divorce?* Fine! If you want divorce, so be it! Who cares!

YE XIAOXIAO: No, don't! Don't! You know it's not easy for a couple to stay together and perfectly understand each other.

WIFE: *(Tearfully to her husband)* So that's what you want! We've been married only three days and you go so heartless! Tell you what— Don't you think you can bluff me with divorce!

HUSBAND: Now you're putting your own words in my mouth! As far as I can see, you only married me organizationally but not ideologically![26]

WIFE: What did I do to you? What did I want this marriage for? For your salary? All the money you make can only buy two roast chickens! For your ability? You don't even have a college diploma! Oh, what am I doing all this for?

YE XIAOXIAO: Actually, you know he's a good guy. That's why you should care for and love each other. That's what love is all about. Even for other people, for strangers, you should have a loving heart—

WIFE: Love him? How could I love such a guy? I bet I made a mistake—I fell in love with a shit bug!

HUSBAND: *(To YE XIAOXIAO)* That's exactly what she said that day. Yelling and screaming, she dashed onto a number thirteen bus. Said she wanted to go home by herself. I got on right after her . . . *(The couple are now on the bus.)* When that incident happened on the bus, I was still steaming with anger. I felt a big lump in my chest! What's more, I couldn't very well go up to break up the fight with a stick of hawberries in each hand. I wouldn't want to spoil the hawberries.

YE XIAOXIAO: Yep, everyone has his bad moments. Those hawberries!

HUSBAND: Ever since we heard you were dead, we haven't had the heart to fight one another anymore. I just felt as if my heart was overgrown with weeds. It just felt strange. Oh, those two sticks of haw candies!

WIFE: To tell you the truth, he did try to intervene. It was I who pulled him back. True, I quarrel with him, I raise hell with him,

but at crucial moments I always fear for him, afraid something
might happen to him.

YE XIAOXIAO: Just for those two strings of haw candies . . . you didn't
give me a helping hand . . . So, it wasn't you who shouted,
"Drive the bus to the police station"?

HUSBAND: *(Remorsefully)* No, wasn't me. Where I work, we've been
discussing case thirteen-oh-three over and over, and I keep
making self-criticisms.[27] I was torn to pieces by regret. That's
why I came to pay you respects . . . you were a true hero.

YE XIAOXIAO: *(Thinking aloud as he walks away)* Who could it be?
The memorial meeting's right around the corner and I still
haven't found him. . . .
(The couple watch YE XIAOXIAO *as they back off slowly to return to
their seats in the choir.)*

YE XIAOXIAO: *(Suddenly remembers something and looks for the couple.
Not seeing them around, he shouts in the direction of the choir)*
Don't quarrel anymore, you two! Remember: people should all
have a heart of love! *(Muttering to himself)* Why should people
keep fighting? . . .
(As YE XIAOXIAO *thinks, he moves on and fades away. . . . Once
again the* DRUMMER *plays a jubilant round.)*

(This looks like somewhere in the theater office. CHORUS *members
play the parts of file cabinets and archive shelves. In a great rush*
DIRECTOR FAN *pulls open and pushes back drawers and thumbs
through the files, working himself into a frenzy.* LIU FENG *rushes in
with a newspaper galley proof.)*

LIU FENG: *(Holding up the galley proof)* Director Fan, here's the
galley proof. It'll be in the papers in a day or two. Would you
please take another look for final approval?

DIRECTOR FAN: *(Hastily waves his hand)* No need, no need! On this
matter we leaders of Xiaoxiao's unit are already on the defensive.
The police department and the municipal party committee have
both acknowledged him as martyr and awarded him the title of
Class A Hero. It's all in the official document with red letterheads.
That managerial officer Hao has been disciplined, removed from
all his posts, even from the party roster. We, Xiaoxiao's leaders,
have also been cited for tardiness in response.

LIU FENG: *(Smiles)* Yeah, a bit too slow. Still, better late than never.

DIRECTOR FAN: (*Mysteriously*) We'll make it up in some other way. Look, the party committee is considering granting him posthumous membership before the memorial meeting. It'll have to be done real quick.

LIU FENG: That's as it should be.

DIRECTOR FAN: (*Thumbing through the file in his hand*) The municipal party leaders will come to inspect the way we implement the relevant directives and will personally attend the memorial meeting. You'll have to help me remember when it was that Xiaoxiao turned in his party membership application. How come I can't find it?

LIU FENG: About the same time I submitted mine.

DIRECTOR FAN: Yes, yes, it's been quite a few years now since you joined up. . . . Let me look again.

(*The two of them fumble through the cabinets and shelves.*

Enter TANG TIANTIAN *with her guitar on her back. She looks worn out. She looks around, appearing to be too tired for anything. She watches* DIRECTOR FAN *and* LIU FENG *in silence.*)

DIRECTOR FAN: (*To* LIU FENG) Did he really submit an application? I didn't see that it had made any difference in him—

TANG TIANTIAN: (*Blurting out*) He did. I can testify!

DIRECTOR FAN: Comrade Tiantian? You can testify?

TANG TIANTIAN: (*Sadly*) I laughed at him for that. I said, "You better wait for posthumous admission!" Who would've thought it would come true. When Liu Feng got admitted, I jeered at Xiaoxiao . . .

(*All three fall silent, each lost in his or her own thought. The* DRUMMER *plays a mysterious series.*

Enter YE XIAOXIAO *in his flowing snow cape, appearing to be in a good mood.*)

TANG TIANTIAN: Xiaoxiao! A memorial meeting will soon be held in your honor. The papers are filled with articles praising you as martyr and hero. You will also be admitted into the party. Aren't you happy?

YE XIAOXIAO: (*Uneasily*) I've been feeling rather uneasy these days. Some of the newspaper articles are just too far-fetched. That heroic figure is no longer your good friend Ye Xiaoxiao. How come all of a sudden I've become distanced from you people? It seems as if I'm no longer myself. Do you call this alienation, or what? I'm really nervous.

LIU FENG: *(Laughs)* C'mon, Xiaoxiao, what are you talking about? People are trying to recreate your image! That article of mine will appear in the press in a day or two.

YE XIAOXIAO: What've you written, Liu Feng? How did you write it? Tell me, quick! I've been under inspection all my life. This time I'll be the inspector and look at your manuscript.

LIU FENG: *(Turning pages of the galley proof)* I start with your childhood—

YE XIAOXIAO: In my childhood I wore open-seat pants like every other kid, and I was terribly naughty, too. Did you write about all that?

TANG TIANTIAN: *(Laughs)* Xiaoxiao! Don't interrupt!

(DIRECTOR FAN sits on one side, busy with his files.)

LIU FENG: *(Reading from his galley proof)* "When Xiaoxiao was a child, he had a strong sense of justice and the character of a rebel against tyranny—"

YE XIAOXIAO: Is that so? *(Walks up to LIU FENG to look at the manuscript)* Let me take a look! *(Laughs)* Liu Feng, what's all this rubbish? Is there any truth in this?

TANG TIANTIAN: What's wrong? What's the matter?

YE XIAOXIAO: That was when we three were in kindergarten. Liu Feng was taller and stronger than the rest of us. He often bullied us smaller ones—took away our toys, and even beat you once and brought you to tears. . . . You may have forgotten, but to take it out on him, I did something real bad, and you kept watch for me.

TANG TIANTIAN: What was it? I kept watch?

YE XIAOXIAO: *(Embarrassed)* Hee-hee-hee . . . I poured out all the orange juice from his bottle and took out my dick and peed into it.

TANG TIANTIAN: *(Breaks into a fit of laughter)* Yes, yes, I remember! You were bad, Xiaoxiao. . . . Liu Feng! You've got to write this down. What a wonderful story!

YE XIAOXIAO: *(Seriously)* No, that won't do! That would make a fool of me.

LIU FENG: *(Seriously)* You were trying to punish someone who bullied young kids.

YE XIAOXIAO: You only write about "sense of justice" and "fighting injustice" in the abstract and never dare to touch on the concrete. That won't do. Just delete it, delete it!

LIU FENG: *(Giving in)* Okay, okay. I also say you were an excellent actor and played dozens of roles. That can't be wrong, can it?

YE XIAOXIAO: *(A little embarrassed)* If you brag about me like that, will people let you get away with it? Actually I never played a single character with a name. Neither did my own name, Ye Xiaoxiao, ever appear in the programs. I was always listed as "staff."

LIU FENG: And you never complained about it. You never argued for roles. Oh yes! Once you did play the lead. Remember?

YE XIAOXIAO: No, I didn't forget. That was when the lead actor was sick one day and I was asked to stand in. *(Reminiscing and acting the role)* I played the hero walking to his death, step-by-step up the platform. All of a sudden a shot went off—Oh! *(Puts his hand on his chest and staggers)* More shots. Somehow I never believed I was a hero. I just felt awkward. *(Can't control his giggles)* So I giggled. Too bad! *(To* LIU FENG*)* So you, the director, gave me quite an earful! Did you forget?

LIU FENG: Later you were transferred to the stage staff to take care of lights and props. And you did a good job.

YE XIAOXIAO: But then I became infatuated with fashion designs. I liked cutting and making clothing for members of the theater, especially women.

LIU FENG: That I wrote. I did. Look, a whole long paragraph!

YE XIAOXIAO: But people said I was moonlighting at the expense of my duties.

LIU FENG: Nowadays people have to wait up to six months to get their clothes made at the tailor's. Everybody's saying, "If only Xiaoxiao were still living!"

YE XIAOXIAO: *(Getting emotional)* So, they still think of me! Yes, it was my mission to make people look prettier.

LIU FENG: *(Getting emotional)* I've described your love for fashion designing and your fervent pursuit of a dream, a tenacious pursuit!

YE XIAOXIAO: *(Somewhat excited)* Yes, a pursuit . . . a tenacious pursuit . . . I even thought about starting a fashion design company and competing in the global market . . . *(struck by a wave of sadness)* but nothing happened, nothing was accomplished. . . . Oh, stop writing! Don't write anymore! Don't write about anything. . . .

LIU FENG: *(Finding himself in an awkward position)* Xiaoxiao, you don't want me to write about this, you don't want me to write about that; what am I supposed to do? I sincerely want to write well about you, to create an image of you. You know, this piece will be used at the memorial meeting as the main speech.

YE XIAOXIAO: Really?

LIU FENG: Really. Only when I write this way can I feel at peace, can I do you justice . . . and feel I've done what I should.

YE XIAOXIAO: No, no, don't! Suppose you read that piece at the meeting and I start giggling. What bad taste that would be!

LIU FENG: Perhaps you're not aware yet, but this piece may very well become part of your dossier as a substitute for your autobiography. That's why I've got to write it this way.

(DIRECTOR FAN, *who has been looking through the files, is sweating with anxiety.*)

DIRECTOR FAN: *(Muttering to himself)* No, I don't think I can find it at all. . . . If only Xiaoxiao could write a new one! Oh my dear Xiaoxiao, you've given us all a real tough time. . . .

YE XIAOXIAO: *(Walks up to DIRECTOR FAN)* You want me to write a new one of what?

DIRECTOR FAN: *(Looks up and sees YE XIAOXIAO. A vague hope dawns)* Oh, my gosh! Xiaoxiao! Is that you? This thing's been driving me crazy. I just can't find your party membership application. Really don't know where I placed it. Glad you're here. Now you can rush a new application. There's still time. Without that we wouldn't be able to complete the formalities. Our superiors would hold us accountable for it. We've already gotten citations. Please do help us!

YE XIAOXIAO: *(Moved)* Yes, yes, I should apply—I should reapply . . . I've dreamed about . . . After all, I'm not a total void.

DIRECTOR FAN: Right, right, you are now the honor and pride of our unit! Come on, quick, here's your pen and paper, and here's a desk—

(Two CHORUS *members kneel on the floor, holding a tablecloth between them to serve as the desk.* YE XIAOXIAO *bends over at the desk, thinks for a moment, and dashes off something on the paper.* TANG TIANTIAN, LIU FENG, *and* DIRECTOR FAN *stand around him, watching with amazement.* YE XIAOXIAO *finishes writing, holds up the paper solemnly to go over it once, and makes a few changes.*)

YE XIAOXIAO: *(Solemnly hands the application to DIRECTOR FAN, not without a feeling of sacredness)* This is what I've written.

(DIRECTOR FAN *solemnly receives the application. Exit the "desk."*)

DIRECTOR FAN: (*Looks at the application, flabbergasted*) How come, Xiaoxiao, this is a blank sheet of paper! Xiaoxiao, how come there's nothing there?

YE XIAOXIAO: (*Puzzled*) Don't tease me. I did write. I did.
(TANG TIANTIAN *and* LIU FENG *pass around the unwritten application, staring at each other in bewilderment.*)

YE XIAOXIAO: (*Distressed*) Oh no, I can't write anymore. I can't put words on paper anymore. . . . I'm dead, dead!

TANG TIANTIAN: (*Weeping over* YE XIAOXIAO's *shoulder*) . . . I shouldn't have laughed at you last time when you submitted your application! Forgive me, Xiaoxiao! Now they're going to build a statue of you.

YE XIAOXIAO: Statue? Don't do that. I'm not good-looking. In fact, I'm quite ugly, not tall and big and all that—

LIU FENG: But you're a hero. You fought the hooligans completely without fear.

YE XIAOXIAO: (*Sincerely*) Did you actually see? You never saw what actually happened. I was very nervous . . . with no one on my side . . . had to face a killer with his knife . . .

LIU FENG: Then what was going on in your mind? How did you feel? I have to describe that. I . . . didn't see . . . but I'd like to know.

YE XIAOXIAO: You mean when I was facing two armed killers? (*Somewhat resentfully*) Even Napoleon said he felt only one thing the first time he was on the battlefield: a desire to go to the loo.

TANG TIANTIAN: (*Hugging him*) Xiaoxiao, you are wonderful! Just great! I worship you from the bottom of my heart!

YE XIAOXIAO: I only felt they shouldn't steal, shouldn't cut up people's dresses and destroy beauty. I felt I should stop them. I didn't think much else . . . that's about it.
(A CHORUS *member puts on a mask. A staff member carries a big wooden frame down from the choir and rests it on a shelf represented by two* CHORUS *members.*)

STAFFER: (*Showing the frame to* DIRECTOR FAN) Director Fan, the frame's done. I think we should find a photo of Xiaoxiao and have it enlarged immediately, before it's too late for the memorial meeting.

DIRECTOR FAN: (*Rushes through a stack of stage photos*) I've gone through all the pictures in the archives. None of them seem suitable.

YE XIAOXIAO: I don't look good, not photogenic. Never liked picture taking.

LIU FENG: *(Anxiously)* Find a stage photo. A stage photo will do.

DIRECTOR FAN: *(Finds one. Cheerfully)* Here's one that has Xiaoxiao in it!

(LIU FENG *and* TANG TIANTIAN *pass around the photo and look at each other blankly.)*

LIU FENG: No, this one won't do! He's playing Enemy Spy A . . .

DIRECTOR FAN: *(Finds another)* Here's another with Xiaoxiao.

LIU FENG: No, no! In this one he plays Bandit B—

YE XIAOXIAO: Don't worry, don't worry! In that adaptation from one of the model operas I played a positive character—a militia man.[28]

DIRECTOR FAN: *(Quickly produces a large stage photo)* Here it is! Here we go!

LIU FENG: *(Looks at the photo. Sadly)* Xiaoxiao is standing sentry with a rifle at the corner of the stage. But all we see here is the back of his head! . . . It was my fault not to have assigned him a better role.

TANG TIANTIAN: *(Tears twinkling in her eyes)* Don't be upset, Xiao-xiao. You will have a statue, a big, big statue, gilded . . . standing where you fell. *(She buries her face in her hands and walks away, crying.)* Xiaoxiao, do you believe me?

(YE XIAOXIAO *feels a bit sad. His eyes wet, he walks slowly behind the large picture frame held by the two* CHORUS *members, and stands there contemplating.)*

DIRECTOR FAN: *(Suddenly discovering* YE XIAOXIAO *standing silently behind the frame like a perfect portrait)* Wait, wait! Look!

(TANG TIANTIAN *and* LIU FENG *look and see* YE XIAOXIAO *smiling in the frame.)*

DIRECTOR FAN: Oh, my dear Xiaoxiao! Do us a favor and help me one more time! Come to the memorial meeting just like this . . .

YE XIAOXIAO: No problem! . . . Do I look okay? Am I going to play the lead role this time? . . .

DIRECTOR FAN: *(Smirking)* Xiaoxiao, when the time comes, brace up a little! Look a little more spirited. Let people see at first glance you are a hero!

YE XIAOXIAO: But don't you make me laugh! I don't pose well on the stage. I tend to giggle.

(*Enter a* CHORUS *member to report.*)

CHORUS MEMBER: R-reporting! Mr. Director! Just received a phone call. The motorcade of the municipal leadership is on its way!

DIRECTOR FAN: (*Hurriedly*) Good, good! (*To the choir*) Comrades, get ready! Get ready at once. . . .

(*Everyone gets busy. Directed by* DIRECTOR FAN, *the* CHORUS *members place in order the elegiac couplets on scrolls and line up for the march. Amidst all the tumult* LIU FENG *and* TANG TIANTIAN *fade away.*

Four CHORUS *members, each carrying a funeral scroll, stand ready around* YE XIAOXIAO *in the frame, in the formation of a funeral procession.*)

DIRECTOR FAN: (*Ordering*) Now comrades! Let's go!

(*The* DRUMMER *strikes up a march. The procession, with the scroll bearers in the lead, and with* YE XIAOXIAO *in the frame in its midst, marches off briskly toward the crematorium.* DIRECTOR FAN *busies himself going back and forth around the procession.*

YE XIAOXIAO *looks around longingly at the beautiful scenes of everyday life along the way. He often departs from the frame and the procession but is again and again shoved back in his place by* DIRECTOR FAN. *He seems to be still looking for someone, or still bothered by unfulfilled wishes hovering in his mind . . .*)

DIRECTOR FAN: (*Begging* YE XIAOXIAO *as he proceeds*) Xiaoxiao! For heaven's sake, when you see the leaders of the municipal government, please don't ever mention the missing party-membership application!

YE XIAOXIAO: Why's that?

DIRECTOR FAN: The head of our unit already got a reprimand. Don't you worry. We can definitely solve the problem—I'll be your recommender.[29] How's that? You may not be aware, but actually the gate of the party has always been open to you!

YE XIAOXIAO: (*Smiles*) Yes, only the gatekeeper in our unit was a little too severe. Never mind. I guarantee I'm not going to mention the matter.

(*The march continues. Two* CHORUS *members, wearing the masks of* BROTHER *and* SISTER, *stand facing the approaching procession and bow deeply to the "portrait" of* YE XIAOXIAO *in the frame.*)

DIRECTOR FAN: *(Waving to the marchers)* Stop! Stop for a second! *(To the* BROTHER *and* SISTER*)* You two are . . . ?

BROTHER: *(Holding up a black briefcase)* Here's our donation of five thousand yuan . . .

DIRECTOR FAN: *(Bewildered)* What's this? Giving away five thousand yuan just like that?

SISTER: *(Carrying a big basket on her arm)* We heard a young woman donated fifty thousand yuan to an arts and crafts shop as deposit for a statue of the hero. We also want to express our good wishes.

DIRECTOR FAN: We appreciate your good wishes, but we can't take your money.

BROTHER and SISTER: *(Sincerely)* Please take it!

*(*YE XIAOXIAO *steps out of the frame and walks up to the two.)*

YE XIAOXIAO: *(Trying to recall)* Who are you? You look quite familiar.

SISTER: *(Almost breaks down in tears)* Do you still remember us, brother and sister?

BROTHER: We felt so bad that day getting off the bus.

YE XIAOXIAO: *(It dawns on him suddenly)* Oh yes, now I remember. You must be the ones who cried, "Drive the bus to the police station." Right?

BROTHER: *(Shaking his head, ashamed)* No, I didn't. I had five thousand yuan in my bag and was going downtown to buy my sister her dowry.

YE XIAOXIAO: *(Understandingly)* It's a good thing peasants are getting rich now.

BROTHER: *(Recalling, narrating, and acting)* As soon as I heard all the noise about thieves, my hair stood up on end and I quickly checked my bag. . . . When the fighting began, I just hung on to my bag and forgot about everything else. All I knew was to protect my five thousand yuan! I couldn't, and didn't have the guts to, go up and give you help. . . . I just watched you. . . .

YE XIAOXIAO: That money must be hard earned. I understand.

SISTER: *(With tears in her eyes)* None of us on the bus were able to help you . . .

YE XIAOXIAO: I seem to recall you had tripped and fallen on the floor, but you covered that big basket with your body to protect whatever was inside. . . . You just didn't have a spare hand to help.

SISTER: *(As if still protecting the basket)* There were twenty little rabbits, all just one month old . . . twenty young lives!

YE XIAOXIAO: (*Interested and squatting down next to the basket*) Little rabbits? Fascinating!

SISTER: The Number One Kindergarten in town wanted the kids to raise some small animals. They wanted the kids to learn to feed the animals with grass and leaves and learn to care for them. Look at these furry young lives. . . .

YE XIAOXIAO: (*Thrilled*) Oh, that's a great idea! Teaching kids to care for small animals—that's wonderful!

BROTHER: We two have started a pet store. We have puppies, kittens, rabbits, birds. . . . They're all extremely popular.

YE XIAOXIAO: That's really fascinating! How did you get the idea?

BROTHER: My sister always loved pets. She used to have a lovely kitten, but it was hanged by some kids. . . .

YE XIAOXIAO: (*Somberly*) Oh . . . I see, I see.

DIRECTOR FAN: (*Urging*) Xiaoxiao, get back to your place, please!
(*Once again puts* YE XIAOXIAO *behind the picture frame*)
Comrades! On the march!
(*The drumming starts. The procession continues.*)

BROTHER and SISTER: (*Catching up with the procession*) Please let us attend the meeting!
(*The procession reaches its destination. The funeral scrolls and the picture frame are set up in their proper places and the* CHORUS *members return to their seats.* YE XIAOXIAO *stands behind the frame, looking a bit fatigued.*

A pause. Enter TANG TIANTIAN *in a white dress. She rushes in and sweeps her eyes around the meeting place.*)

TANG TIANTIAN: (*Walking slowly up to the picture frame*) Sorry, I'm late, Xiaoxiao. Hope you're not angry with me?
(*Enter* DIRECTOR FAN *in a rush, sweating all over, frantically looking around.*)

DIRECTOR FAN: (*Anxiously*) Ah, Tiantian! Did you see Liu Feng? Wasn't he with you? Too bad! The leaders are all here but the meeting can't begin.

TANG TIANTIAN: What's wrong?

DIRECTOR FAN: Oh, boy, the memorial speech! The memorial speech's in Liu Feng's hands—the piece approved by Xiaoxiao himself—it's still in Liu Feng's hands!

YE XIAOXIAO: (*Thrusting through the frame*) That's okay. That's okay! It's much better without it. Saves me from giggling.

DIRECTOR FAN: *(Alarmed)* Oh, my gosh! Xiaoxiao, please don't give me more trouble! *(To* TANG TIANTIAN*)* Comrade Tiantian, I'll do my best about your pension!
(He dashes off crying "Liu Feng!" Exit.)

YE XIAOXIAO: *(Trying to dissuade her)* Tiantian, forget about the pension—

TANG TIANTIAN: No! I need five thousand yuan—

YE XIAOXIAO: Forget it, really. This is a bad time for drama, and the theater's in financial straits because of low box-office returns. If you save this money for them, they can produce another play.

TANG TIANTIAN: Xiaoxiao, you're trying to be generous to them, but did they think about you?! I've paid fifty thousand yuan for deposit. I staked my last penny! The statue has to be in bronze. . . . It's still ten thousand yuan short.

YE XIAOXIAO: *(Doesn't know what to say)* What for? It's not necessary! Tiantian . . . what are you going to do from now on?

TANG TIANTIAN: Anyways, I'm quitting the garment business.

YE XIAOXIAO: *(Sincerely)* Liu Feng has always loved you.

TANG TIANTIAN: Maybe, maybe I'll just marry him. Is it okay with you?

YE XIAOXIAO: . . . In a little while I'll just become a wisp of blue smoke. . . . I'll be shoved into that big furnace. I'll be set on fire for the last time. It must be quite painful, right?

TANG TIANTIAN: *(Her eyes wet with tears)* No, Xiaoxiao, you won't feel any pain. It's those who live and love you—their hearts will ache. Xiaoxiao, you have any regrets?

YE XIAOXIAO: *(Thinking deeply)* Regrets? For what? Only a slight sense of loss . . .
(A moment of silent passion. The drifting thoughts and emotions of the two intertwine to transform into song flowing forth from their trembling hearts— TANG TIANTIAN*'s "Song of the Colorful Shells" and* YE XIAOXIAO*'s "Song of the Fledgling" blend and intermingle to transcend into infinite space.)*

TANG TIANTIAN: *(Sings)*
Life's like the boisterously receding tide
Leaving behind on the beach that colorful shell . . .

YE XIAOXIAO: *(Sings)*
I am that wounded fledgling
That gave people warmth with his feathers . . .

TANG TIANTIAN: *(Sings)*
> With that shell I scoop a cup of the blue sea . . .

YE XIAOXIAO: *(Sings)*
> Smile, smile, on the past I smile . . .

TANG TIANTIAN: *(Sings)*
> In that shell I see the splendid morning glow
> In my hand the waves of the sea dance . . .

YE XIAOXIAO: *(Sings)*
> I am a withering blade of grass
> That prays silently for the green spring . . .
> *(When they finish singing, the two of them hold hands and look into each other's eyes for a long time.)*

TANG TIANTIAN: What a pity! I wanted the arts and crafts shop to make the statue the way I wanted, but they wouldn't do it.

YE XIAOXIAO: Like what?

TANG TIANTIAN: *(Carried away)* I once saw a photo—Rodin's sculpture *Kiss*. It's just beautiful! Like this—
> *(The* CHORUS *members play different sculptural forms.*
>
> TANG TIANTIAN *takes away the picture frame, cuddles against* YE XIAOXIAO, *kisses him—forming the sculpture* Kiss. *The mirrors on the stage reflect from different angles the image of the* Kiss *formed by* YE XIAOXIAO *and* TANG TIANTIAN.
>
> YE XIAOXIAO *floats away from* TANG TIANTIAN, *leaving behind, however, the multicolored spotlight in the curve of her arm.)*

YE XIAOXIAO: *(Looking around at the people as if bidding them a reluctant farewell)* That huge furnace is already roaring with fire. In a minute I will plunge into it, to evaporate into a wisp of blue smoke. Many years from now, the air will still be filled with numerous indestructible particles, floating around you, softly calling you . . .

CHORUS: *(Searching around and calling)* Xiaoxiao! Xiao— Xiao—!

YE XIAOXIAO: *(Tearfully, with deep emotion)* Folks! I'll be with you for ever and ever—
> *(*YE XIAOXIAO *meanders among the people who are searching for him . . .*
>
> CHORUS *members hold high the empty picture frame—only an orange red spotlight is cast on it.* TANG TIANTIAN, *forlorn, pitches forward to cling to the frame.*

Enter LIU FENG *in a hurry. He captures the whole scene at a glance, stands on one side, watches* TANG TIANTIAN *clinging to the empty frame, and* YE XIAOXIAO *retreating slowly into the deep rear. His thoughts are in turmoil. In the meantime the* CHORUS *members metamorphose to become once again the frozen postures of the passengers at the time of the fatal fight.*)

LIU FENG: Xiaoxiao! Tiantian! You may have guessed already. I was on that number thirteen bus that day. Xiaoxiao didn't see me. I was the one who shouted, "Drive the bus to the police station!" It was with this sentiment that I wrote this play afterward. No, no, maybe all this was just an afterthought following Xiaoxiao's death —an idea that kept hovering in my head, in my soul: If I were on that bus, what would I be like?

(*Meandering slowly through the crowd,* YE XIAOXIAO *recedes into the deep rear and finally disappears. . . .*

The stern and neurotic DRUMMER, *who may have been moved to tears, strikes up round after round of resounding beats.*

People stand listening with uplifted heads—as if the air is charged with the eternal sound of drumming!

Only an orange red spotlight is shed upon that empty, empty wooden frame. . . .)

NOTES

The translator wishes to thank Beverly Linens for reading the draft and correcting the English.

The Dead Visiting the Living (Yige sizhe dui shengzhe de fangwen) was first published in *Juben* (Drama script) 5 (1985): 8–37. This English translation was based on a revised text in Tian Xuxiu, ed., *Duoshengbu de juchang* (Multi-voiced theater) (Shijiazhuang: Huashan wenyi chubanshe, 1988), 249–329.

1. Chinese surnames precede given names.

2. Private enterpreneurship is the most vibrant component of the Chinese economy thanks to the economic reform that began toward the end of the 1970s.

3. In China, "grandpa" is a respectful way of addressing an elderly man.

4. This is the actual euphemistic word in Chinese (*taipingjian*) for "mortuary."

5. These are all street gang lingo, referring to different techniques in martial arts.

6. A role model set up by the Communist Party in the sixties.

7. A folk hero and martial arts master of the early Republican era, popularized by Hong Kong kungfu movies.

8. Most people in urban China have to be affiliated with an institution or community, be it a school, a factory, a government office, or a neighborhood. They call this their unit, where all their personal dossiers are kept and from where all their rations of housing and food come. The burgeoning market economy of the last two decades has freed an increasing number of the population from such bondage.

9. "Comrade" is a form of address still used in the People's Republic but chiefly among and by Communist Party members and government officials. It may also be used to address any ordinary citizen of presumed good political standing, but such usage is being superseded by more traditional terms, such as Mr., Miss, and Ms.

10. Different styles of martial arts.

11. A trick in martial arts whereby one can incapacitate the adversary by touching or pointing at his vital acupoints.

12. Despite the thriving market economy, the Chinese government still maintains a high level of political and ideological control over its citizens. Memorial services and funeral ceremonies are denied those with allegedly questionable political standing.

13. Bans on such Western influences as fashion shows and pop music concerts are alternately imposed and lifted depending on the political wind and whim of the moment from the top.

14. The Chinese original is *wanyuanhu* or, literally, a ten-thousand-yuan-aire. Given the economic boom and inflation rate, that symbol of opulence is already out of date. In its place are literal millionaires and multimillionaires.

15. These are actually the two most important lubricants in China's booming economy.

16. The red scarf is the insignia of the Young Pioneers, a nationwide organization for school children, corresponding in some ways to the Boy Scouts and Girl Scouts.

17. It is quite customary for Chinese children to address adult strangers by kinship terms such as "uncle," "aunt," "grandpa," and "granny."

18. The basic denominations of the Chinese currency are the *yuan* (or *kuai* in everyday speech), which corresponds to the dollar; the *jiao* (or *mao* in everyday speech), corresponding to a dime or ten cents; and the *fen*, corresponding to a cent. Both coins and paper notes are in currency for each denomination.

19. The surname "Tang" is homonymous with *"tang"* meaning "sugar" or "candy," just as the character *"tian"* in the given name "Tiantian" is homonymous with the *"tian"* meaning "sweet."

20. The character *"liang"* in her name means "bright" or "light."

21. This is a hidden allusion to a statement made by Jiang Qing, Mao's wife, to the Red Guards at the beginning of the Cultural Revolution (1966–1976). Since both Jiang and the CR have been thoroughly discredited, still quoting her, consciously or unconsciously, may easily be perceived as a sign of political anachronism.

22. *Zou houmen* or "going through the back door" is an umbrella term for such under-the-table practices as influence-pedaling, nepotism, cronyism, etc. that people commonly resort to for jobs, products, and services that are in short supply.

23. A title inherited from the years of revolution, conferred posthumously, after political clearance, on anyone who dies in action for the cause of the revolution or in

service of the public. The martyr's family receives a permanent pension and enjoys a whole range of privileges.

24. Traditionally, the bride is supposed to pay a return visit to her parents accompanied by her groom three days after the wedding.

25. An inexpensive street food, very popular in Beijing, with about a dozen sugar-coated berries strung together on a bamboo stick, like shish kebab.

26. This is a parody of the kind of language used about Communist Party membership, which requires both organizational allegiance and ideological conformity. Tongue-in-cheek parody of party jargon is quite characteristic of post-Maoist literature of the eighties and nineties.

27. Recommended by Mao and enforced by the Communist Party, criticism and self-criticism are widely practiced in political-study sessions in all institutions.

28. During the Cultural Revolution (1966–1976) when virtually all forms of artistic creation were banned, only a handful of stage productions sponsored by the top party leaders were shown to the public. These were known as revolutionary-model operas or *yangbanxi*. In these operas, characters are classified strictly along political lines into positive and negative characters.

29. An applicant for party membership is required to have two members as his/her recommenders.

3

The World's Top Restaurant

He Jiping

TRANSLATED BY EDWARD M. GUNN

Translator's note

Following the collapse of the Qing dynasty, in 1911, China took the name of a republic but was in fact dominated by a set of competing warlord generals. During the years in which this play is set, 1917–1928, what remained of the imperial family that had governed the Qing empire continued to live in the imperial palace with a portion of their former retinue. The imperial family were members of an ethnic minority known as Manchus, who, together with their closest allies, the Mongols, still lived in large numbers in the former imperial city of Beijing. Manchus and Mongols were known as "banner people," after their distinctive form of social organization. During the Qing dynasty, the aristocrats and well-to-do Manchus and Mongols were entitled to living stipends from the imperial government and enjoined to avoid employing themselves in commerce and trade. The result was that, apart from those Manchus and Mongols active in government, the remainder formed a leisure class of unusual size. A large service-and-leisure industry developed in Beijing, catering to this leisure class, including the sort of restaurant depicted in this play. Even after the end of the Qing and its social and political order, this distinctive culture remained in Beijing.

The restaurants of Beijing were of several types. The most prestigious were known as *fanzhuang*, catering to aristocrats on the occasions of births, weddings, and funerals. Next were the *fengwei'r fanguan*, or "special flavor restaurants," like the one offering roast duck in this play, each specializing in dishes from a particular province. Extending beyond these classes were ordinary restaurants, teahouses, and taverns. Brothels, also, as this play indicates, could serve exquisite fare, just as their prostitutes were expected to provide cultivated companionship to their customers and their parties. A great many of the chefs, managers, and other employees in Beijing restaurants were ethnic Han Chinese from the nearby coastal province of Shandong and therefore excelled in seafood dishes, as well as the poultry recipes celebrated in this play. While Manchus and Mongols were not supposed to operate businesses, they frequently invested their capital in restaurants and other leisure enterprises. The sons of the Shandong proprietor of the restaurant in this play imitate the young Manchus in devoting themselves to being amateur theater buffs, martial arts devotees, and the like, living off the profits of the restaurant while avoiding working in it.

Characters

LU MENGSHI   manager of the Fujude Restaurant (Restaurant of Fortune of Accumulated Virtue)

TANG DEYUAN   former manager and proprietor of the Fujude

TANG MAOCHANG   older son of Tang Deyuan

TANG MAOSHENG   younger son of Tang Deyuan

CHANG GUI   the headwaiter of the Fujude

LUO DATOU   the first chef in charge of duck dishes in the Fujude

WANG ZIXI   assistant manager of the Fujude

YUCHU'R   Lu Mengshi's lover, a prostitute

LI XIAOBIAN'R   the first chef (apart from duck dishes) in the
        Fujude
XIU DINGXIN   Maître d'hôtel, cashier, and accountant of the
        Fujude; Ke Wu's gourmet companion
KE WU   descendant of a prince, a customer
CHENG SHUN   apprentice in the Fujude
FU SHUN   apprentice in the Fujude
FU ZI   Tang Maochang's attendant
Police; staff members of the imperial palace roast duck
        and pork kitchen (baohaju); Mr. Qian, a legal
        and business agent; attendants and officials from
        the presidential palace; fourth son-and-heir from
        the Ruifuxiang Fabric Store; prostitutes; servant
        delivering flowers; customers, et al.

ACT I

Time: summer of 1917
*Place: Fujude Restaurant in the meat market outside Qianmen, or
Front Palace Gate, also known as the Zhengyangmen, or Gate Fac-
ing the Sun*

*(Zhengyangmenwai, or Southern Palace Gate District [also called
the Qianmen District] is worthy of the sobriquet "At the feet of the
Son of Heaven." It is his front yard, so to speak, the site of a dense
population, thriving markets, and the elite of the capital. Shops, teahouses, and theaters are packed like the scales of a fish or teeth on a
comb. During the day crowds stream through in commotion, and at
night lanterns blaze in splendor, a prosperity undiminished for five
hundred years.*
    *Just behind the building of the Eastside Market, outside South-
ern Palace Gate, popularly called Qianmen, there's a street called
Meat Market Lane. Every morning when it's still barely light, the
meat market comes alive. Poles of sha wood are sunk into the narrow
lane as hitching posts for horses, while awnings cover it, crowded to
overflowing with counters for selling meat. On these counters is a
great selection of fresh pork brought in from the Dongsi and Xisi
slaughter pens. Buyers for the restaurants come here to buy their
meat, as do the cooks for the wealthy mansions, the housewives of*

ordinary homes, and even the occasional eunuch from the imperial kitchens within the palace. Bargaining up and down, buying and selling, clamorous waves of sound swell chaotically. By about ten o'clock, when the meat has been sold off and the buyers have dispersed, business in the taverns and teahouses begins to pick up. Bringing with them their caged birds and their servants, arm in arm with their friends, the Manchu banner men of the inner city who have just arisen, come to drink tea and jaw and listen to storytellers, installing themselves there for the day. In a wink it's supper time, and once again Meat Market Lane changes appearance. Now it is time for the distinctive delicacies served in each of those restaurants packed together one after the other along each side of the lane: the mutton and the crab at Zhengyanglou; the carp in soy sauce at the Dongxinglou; the hang-fried pancakes at the Shaobingwang; the millet gruel at the Tiantaiguan[1]—and what must be counted as most representative of all, so celebrated in the capital, the Peking duck, also once known as shaoyazi [and which only around the time of liberation, in 1949, acquired the current name kaoya].

In 1838 a young man named Tang, with an accent he brought from Rongcheng in Shandong Province, laid a plank for a counter across two rocks and thereby established a stall selling raw chicken and duck next to the stone pavement of the imperial walkway reserved for the emperor. His personality was amiable and his dealings honest, so that business grew until, with his hard-earned savings, he was able to buy a store beside the main thoroughfare, among the forest of shops in the Qianmen neighborhood, and founded the enterprise that would extend into the next century.

Now, the family business of the Tangs, the Fujude, has been passed down to its third generation. Three carved wood signs run above the frame of the front door at the shop front: the middle one reads "Fujude," the right-hand one reads "Chicken and duck," and the left one, "Peking duck restaurant." Currently the Fujude operates three enterprises: Peking duck, raw chicken and duck, and southern-style assortment boxes [suhezi, the name for the specially made boxes in which varieties of cooked meat used in spring rolls are packed after being diced]. Two large wooden tubs flank the left side of the front hall, used for boiling off duck feathers. During the busiest seasons the tubs are kept filled with steaming hot water and surrounded by busy employees, sitting and nimbly plucking duck feathers. Along the *walls plucked, uncooked ducks hang from racks, already inflated with air and basted with sugar, looking pale, plump, and tender, a delicious sight. To the right of the front hall is the century-old duck oven of the Fujude, red brick from top to bottom, its fire always glowing. A couplet is written on two vertical scrolls flanking the oven door, "May this oven burn for a thousand years. May its silver hooks hold a hundred flavors forever fresh." A horizontal phrase reads, "Master oven." This is the spot with the most mysterious atmosphere in the Fujude. The craft of this oven and how to cook duck are the topmost secrets of the establishment. Besides managing the business of the counter itself, it is the job of the cashier and assistant manager, seated behind the counter shaped like a carpenter's square, to watch over the oven and prevent anyone from going near it.*

To the rear of the main hall is a wide room, divided on each side into storage and cupboard rooms and the room used to prepare the ducks to be hung out in the main hall, as well as two private dining rooms, which have recently been added. A paneled partition screen illustrated with golden peonies occupies the center of the hall, in front of which is a large basin for keeping live fish, and behind which is the door to the kitchen where frying is done. [During the first act nothing else is present except the partition.]

As the curtain rises it is supper time. Meat Market Lane is extraordinarily busy, as the stoves of every restaurant are baking, steaming, pan-frying, or deep-frying; waiters call out greetings to customers entering; seated customers toast each other, clinking cups of tea or wine. Business has been particularly good for the taverns and restaurants the past few days. The last emperor of the Qing dynasty has ascended the throne, to the cries by "loyal subjects" that "the imperial system must be restored; the common people want their former lord," escorted by the warlord Zhang Xun. Restorationists and other enthusiasts of nostalgia living inside and outside the Forbidden City have dug out court clothes from the bottoms of trunks, displayed braided queues, whether genuine or false, and filled the streets with a flood of campy-looking "ancestors." According to the traditions of our Chinese nation, the one and only form for expressing joy is eating, and so Meat Market Lane has erupted with this momentary revival like the last glow of the setting sun or of a dying man.

The Fujude Restaurant's assistant manager, Wang Zixi, stands at the entrance, gesturing with his hands toward the Yuanxinglou pan-

cake house opposite. At this point in time there is no cake or noodle counter in the Fujude, and all cakes and pancakes are bought from the outside.)

WANG ZIXI: Two hundred lotus leaf pancakes! Send somebody over to the west side to get ten sesame seed cakes, and make sure they're good and warm.

(The apprentice FU SHUN *acknowledges* WANG ZIXI's *orders, takes two bamboo slips indicating the order, and exits at a jog. A uniformed policeman calls out as he enters, holding a bundle of wrinkled cotton crepe flags.)*

POLICEMAN: Hang out the imperial flag! Hang up the imperial flag! Manager Wang, how come you haven't hung up the flag yet?[2]

WANG ZIXI: Hey, I was out looking for one all last night, and I planned to tell someone today to go over to the secondhand clothes shop to order one, but everybody's too busy to go so far.

POLICEMAN: Forget it. I'll sell you one. *(Takes out a flag)* Be careful with it. It's made of toilet paper. *(Studying* WANG*)* Where'd you get such a fake-looking queue? *(Yanks the braid with his hand)*

WANG ZIXI: *(Cries out)* Ow! Okay, take it easy. Take home some of these baked meatballs to go with your cabbage for supper.

(The policeman takes the meat and walks on, resuming his cry.)

WANG ZIXI: *(Testing his braid with a firm tug)* After all, it was a horse-tail to begin with.

*(*KE WU *and* XIU DINGXIN *enter, coming out of a private dining room.* KE WU *is a rich man's son who is tired of eating in his father's house and spends all day restaurant hopping, by now a celebrated customer in the capital.* XIU DINGXIN, *behind* KE WU, *is a "companion," a high-class servant whose duty is to accompany his master dining out. As a discerning gourmet and gourmand, he knows how to criticize, and all restaurants are aware that when hosting aristocrats young or old, the crucial people are these "companions."* KE WU *and his companion are both dressed in Qing dynasty robes, their hair braided in large queues, looking totally incongruous with their surroundings, as if they've just popped out of a couple of coffins.*

CHANG GUI *attentively escorts them, leading the way, and* WANG ZIXI *greets them from below.)*

KE WU: *(Delighted with his meal, his face flushed)* Say Chang, my good man, what were you saying before while I was going upstairs to eat?

CHANG GUI: *(Thinking on his feet)* I said, "You are rising to eminence, step-by-step."

KE WU: Eh, as soon as the emperor was on the throne he bestowed upon our father both the privilege of wearing the official peacock-feathered hat, and the sedan chairs covered in green wool.

CHANG GUI: It was my way of offering felicitations to you for him; now that his lordship's meritorious service to the emperor has been recognized, he must also surely ascend to a high promotion.

KE WU: And now that I'm going downstairs?

CHANG GUI: *(Relying on his own quick wit)* This just shows that the younger generation always rises to greater prominence than the elder generation. In the future, you, sir, must surely excel over his lordship.

KE WU: *(Laughing)* Well said, Chang, my good man. With a mouth like yours, you could talk a cooked duck back to life again.

CHANG GUI: I'm just concerned whether our service to Mr. Ke was adequate. Mr. Xiu, did you find the food to your taste?

KE WU: It topped braising, didn't it Mr. Xiu?

XIU DINGXIN: *(Reserved)* It was good.

WANG ZIXI: It was a favor of you to come.

KE WU: *(Handing CHANG GUI a sum of money)* Share this among the waiters.

CHANG GUI: *(Stepping quickly to the counter, he pours the cash, with a ringing sound, down into the bamboo tube used to keep tip money.)* Let's hear it for Mr. Ke's generosity. *(From behind the curtain, voices in unison shouting)* "Thank you, Mr. Ke, sir!"

KE WU: My pleasure. *(Studying the imperial dragon flag hanging up)* You do know that the emperor has ascended the throne, don't you?

CHANG GUI: Certainly! Just look how busy things are on the streets.

KE WU: *(Stern as an important court official)* On the very first day, the emperor in one breath issued nine decrees, ordering Li Yuanhong to resign his position, but Li had the nerve to refuse the order. My father sent up a memorial to intervene, requesting the emperor to have Li Yuanhong take his own life.[3]

CHANG GUI: That's it, let him hang himself.

KE WU: But our emperor has a kind heart, said he didn't want to see blood spilled just after he'd ascended the throne. Still, in consideration of my father's loyalty, he awarded him a purple python robe and peacock feather.

XIU DINGXIN: His lordship will offer his thanks for heaven's blessings tomorrow with twenty ducks and a roast pig.

WANG ZIXI: Yes, of course, we'll definitely have them delivered to you on time! We do look forward to you gentlemen gracing us with your presence often and adding luster to our humble establishment.

KE WU: *(With a wave of his hand)* Mr. Xiu, is our carriage here?

XIU DINGXIN: It's been waiting for us some time.

KE WU: Then, what's our next stop?

XIU DINGXIN: The Xinshengchang is opening tomorrow morning, and they've invited you to try the first bowl of eel noodles.

KE WU: *(Impatiently) Another* noodle dish; I'm sick of them.

XIU DINGXIN: This eel noodles is a light dish that the eldest son of Emperor Wu of Liang, the Crown Prince Zhaoming, learned in Yangzhou. They steam a live eel until it's tender enough to debone, and blend it into the noodle flour, then add clear chicken broth and knead it, then roll it out until it's thin as paper, slice it with a small knife into strips about as wide as chives, cook them until they're about four-fifths done, add chicken extract, ham extract, mushroom extract, then bring to a boil. They're served in lots of soup, plenty of green garlic, and spice. They make the noodles nice and long, and add diced vegetables. Savor them in your mouth; the soup is clear, the noodles smooth.

KE WU: *(Stirred by the description)* From what you say, we should put in an appearance over there and give them a bit of face. *(Suddenly belches)* I don't think I have much space left for anything more just yet.

XIU DINGXIN: Over at the Huaqing Baths they've just put in brand-new steam baths, totally western equipment, gold faucets, and everything. Their manager keeps inviting you over. So let's first go take a steam, let you relax and digest your dinner, and then after that go over to Xinshengchang for a midnight snack. How's that?

KE WU: Just as you say.

CHANG GUI: A pleasant evening to you, gentlemen.

KE WU: *(Looking back over his shoulder)* Chang old boy, next time I come I'll have to test you on something new and different, see how much progress you've made.

CHANG GUI: Your humble servant, sir, would never ignore your kind favor.

(KE WU *and* XIU DINGXIN *exit.*)

WANG ZIXI: From the way he looked, Ke Wu was pleased as he could be. He didn't complain about anything, did he?

(CHANG GUI *merely shakes his head, his mouth too dry to speak. The young apprentice* CHENG SHUN *smartly hands him a cup of tea cooled to just the proper temperature to drink.*)

CHANG GUI: (*Draining the cup in one gulp*) He said the way we roasted our duck hanging in the oven was better than braising it.

WANG ZIXI: Thank god!

CHENG SHUN: I was scared the minute I laid eyes on Ke Wu's face. I heard that once when he took Xiu Dingxin to the Zhengyanglou to eat crab, they forgot the bed of purple perilla leaves, and he kicked the table over. Scared them so bad, they didn't reopen for two days.

CHANG GUI: Everyone knows what a gourmet he is. Actually, it's his sidekick Mr. Xiu who's the gourmet. He started out as dinner companion to Ke Wu's father, and now he does it for Ke Wu. That's his specialty. That's all he does, be a gourmet dinner companion. Once when Ke Wu's father was eating duck at the Bian-yifang, he said the napkin was too stiff to wipe his mouth on, so this Mr. Xiu showed how smart he was: he thought of having him wipe his mouth on baker's bread with leavening in it. So from then on, all the places serving duck—we've always got to have six pieces of lotus leaf pancake on hand for our important customers to wipe their mouths with.

WANG ZIXI: Is he a banner man?

CHANG GUI: He's from Zhejiang, Jinhua, where they turn out nothing but ham. He said the reason Jinhua ham is so good is because each ham they cook has to have a dog's leg inserted into it.

WANG ZIXI: That sounds pretty weird.

CHANG GUI: He says no matter what you cook, it works. It's called "dogleg—"

(*The voice of* LUO DATOU *in a bellowing Shandong accent comes from behind the curtain: "Cheng Shun! It's ready!"* CHENG SHUN *is so startled, he jumps and runs toward the oven.*)

CHANG GUI: Sounds like something's bothering him.

WANG ZIXI: He's out of cash and he's got the habit. Go deal with him and make sure the old manager doesn't hear him. (*He purses his lips in the direction of the cupboard room behind curtains.*) (CHENG SHUN *enters holding a glistening, date-red roast duck.* CHANG GUI *takes it from him carefully and slips it into a clean metal tube.*)

WANG ZIXI: This duck is for the Liu family over at the east entrance to the Donkey Market. Mr. Chang won't be going over that way today, so you'll be taking it to them.

CHENG SHUN: Can I slice it?

(CHANG GUI *nods.*)

WANG ZIXI: Keep in mind, now, each slice includes a piece of skin, altogether one hundred and three slices—

CHENG SHUN: (*Continuing*)—the size of lilac leaves, if there's a bone in so much as one piece, I lose my job on the spot! (*About to exit*)

CHANG GUI: Take two lotus leaf pancakes to snack on, in case they haven't finished their mahjong game by the time you get there; otherwise, you'll be hungry.

CHENG SHUN: Yes sir!

WANG ZIXI: When you drive the cart past the entrance of the Quanyingde opposite us, give the cart bells an extra shake, let them know we're alive.

CHENG SHUN: Aye! (*Exits running*)

(*The chief chef for duck,* LUO DATOU, *a large man from Shandong Province, enters. He is rotund, head shaved bald, with a sandalwood roasting pole in one hand, and a duck in the other.*)

LUO DATOU: (*Slings the duck away*) I'm not cooking!

WANG ZIXI: Not cooking again? When we say roast duck, the most important thing is roasting, and we're looking to you to do the roasting. If you don't cook, we'll have to close down.

LUO DATOU: I haven't worked in a restaurant as pissy as this one since I started out as an apprentice. Mr. Assistant Manager, what day is it today?

WANG ZIXI: The fifteenth.

LUO DATOU: Payday! And since this morning, neither one of our managers has shown his face around here. One's over at the martial arts studio; the other's at that theater. Neither one of them wants to have anything to do with their own restaurant. And I don't want to waste my talents on them.

CHANG GUI: We don't do it for them; we do it for their father.

LUO DATOU: I've done well for them. Back in 1900, when the Allied Army burned out Qianmen after the Boxer Rebellion, if I hadn't snatched this sign from the flames, there wouldn't be the Fujude there is today! As long as I've worked here I, Big Luo, have never had so much as one extra silver dollar. But I'm telling you this: if I get one cent less than what's coming to me today, I walk!

WANG ZIXI: Mr. Luo, please, not so loud.

LUO DATOU: (*Louder and louder*) And there's just one place I'll be headed: right over there across the street to the Quanyingde Peking Duck Shop.

CHANG GUI: Big Luo! Our old manager is sick enough; do you have your mind set on killing him off?

LUO DATOU: Boss, this is no way to run a business!

(*The door curtain is raised, and* MR. QIAN *enters.*)

MR. QIAN: Chef Luo is right. They have two vacancies for duck chefs across the street right now. If you want to switch jobs, I'll get word to them for you.

LUO DATOU: Are you here to collect on a debt? Whatever you're doing here, whatever you've got to say for yourself, what's between me and the guys here is none of your business.

MR. QIAN: You've got spunk! We're all alike; we all have to make a living off these streets, and who doesn't need somebody some-times?

LUO DATOU: I don't need you! An agent like you is a punk making a living taking bribes for people, a pimp, a go-between—nothing an honest man would do.

WANG ZIXI: Big Luo has been pretty worked up these past few days, Mr. Qian. Don't take it personally. Mr. Luo, it's just about time for those ducks in the oven to start to sweat, so why don't you look after them.

(WANG *nudges* LUO *offstage.*)

MR. QIAN: Doesn't know what's good for him.

CHANG GUI: (*Offering tea*) Try a warm cup.

MR. QIAN: (*His face set*) No, thanks. (*Picking up the abacus on the counter*) Wheat flour from Tongdinghe, one hundred silver dollars; sweet sauce from Liubiju, fifty; repairs to the duck store-room—that's three hundred, plus the latest shipment of wild ducks, altogether six hundred and twenty.

WANG ZIXI: We go way back. As a friend, try it one more time and give us a break.

MR. QIAN: Spare me the bullshit.

CHANG GUI: Don't be down on us. Seriously, I'm talking to you man to man—with the old manager sick and his two sons taking turns running the place, nobody can keep the management decisions straight or figure out who's in charge of what. Just bear with us a little and tell these folks things will be all right, to just let it ride for a few days, and I'll do you the honor of a bow myself!

MR. QIAN: (*Glaring*) Skip it! I take bows from managers, not waiters like you! Settle it in full today or don't; it's all the same to me. Let's see your money!

WANG ZIXI: I've tried to be nice about this, but no matter what, you should help us out.

MR. QIAN: Do you have the money or don't you? If you don't, then don't be surprised if I'm not nice about it!

(MR. QIAN *waves his hand and four or five men crowd in and stalk around preparing to trash the restaurant.*)

WANG ZIXI: (*Frightened*) Hey!

(*The old manager,* TANG DEYUAN, *enters.*)

TANG DEYUAN: (*Calling them to a halt*) Why, it's "Fifty Percent" Qian!

MR. QIAN: (*Relenting*) Ah, elder manager, been doing okay recently?

TANG DEYUAN: You're here to collect on some bills?

MR. QIAN: (*Gesturing to his thugs to retire*) Not at all. I stopped in to congratulate you. Your business has been excellent recently, not like it was when your dad bought this place.

TANG DEYUAN: Back then you were just starting to get your feet wet over at the Xianyukou Labor Market.

MR. QIAN: (*Nonplussed*) There isn't anybody in the whole city of Beijing who doesn't know about the Peking duck at the Fujude. So, if you could provide this sum, then I'll take care of everything for you.

TANG DEYUAN: Go back and tell these gentlemen that Fujude has a big account to settle today and I can't get away from business, but first thing tomorrow morning my assistant manager will be around to each of them and settle each bill in full. Chang Gui, wrap up a couple of ducks and tell Fu Shun to go with Mr. Qian and carry them for him.

MR. QIAN: *(Not daring to offend, backs down)* Thank you so much. I don't need to take any ducks away, but I would appreciate a ticket for one at another time.

TANG DEYUAN: Give Mr. Qian a ticket for a duck, in addition to his two ducks.

MR. QIAN: *(Overcome by such generosity, he smiles)* I'm much obliged. Mr. Tang, do take care of yourself, sir. And Wang Zixi, we'll see you tomorrow, then. *(Exits)*

(TANG DEYUAN sits, panting. Several customers enter together, one dressed as a clerk, through the front entrance.)

CLERK: *(To CHANG GUI)* One southern-assortment-box order.

CHANG GUI: One southern assortment coming up. *(Exits)*

WANG ZIXI: You're from the secondhand clothes shop, aren't you? How's business; pretty good?

CLERK: Fantastic! All the old clothes we took in last year when the Revolutionary Party was up in arms, we sold off completely in two days.[4] It was getting so my boss was ready to strip them out of coffins.

WANG ZIXI: Hey, I remember when you cut your braid off.

CLERK: *(Whispering)* I coiled it up inside my cap. When the revolution is on, I keep it coiled up; when the emperor comes back, I let it down again.

WANG ZIXI: I get it, like a well rope.

(CHANG GUI enters carrying a round lacquer box, six inches in diameter by four inches high, and opens the lid.)

CHANG GUI: Here they are; sixteen kinds. We've substituted pig's tongue for chicken in soy.

CLERK: *(Sniffing)* Did you use thick soy sauce?

CHANG GUI: Relax. "Seven measures of salt to eight measures of soy." And if it's short so much as one grain of *huajiao* spice, we don't sell it. Enjoy.

WANG ZIXI: *(Cautiously to TANG DEYUAN)* It's getting late now, shall we lower the signs for the evening?

TANG DEYUAN: Has the Guanghe Theater let out yet?[5]

WANG ZIXI: They're staging *Happy Auguries of Dragon and Phoenix* in its entirety this evening, so they'll go on past midnight.

TANG DEYUAN: Wait a while. Did you ask the geomancer to come by?

WANG ZIXI: I did. He said he'd be by between eleven and one for sure.

TANG DEYUAN: (*Picking up the cylinder of commonly used house tea and sniffing it*) How come we're down to using tea-leaf dust for the customers?

WANG ZIXI: (*Covering up*) The dust in the batch of tea leaves from the Zhang Yiyuan shop is unusually flavorful.

TANG DEYUAN: (*Not pursuing the question further*) How's business been the past few days?

WANG ZIXI: Great. Ke Wu was here this evening with Mr. Xiu.

TANG DEYUAN: Oh? He didn't find fault with anything?

WANG ZIXI: Not a thing. In fact, he put in an order for twenty ducks and left a big tip.

TANG DEYUAN: Did Chang Gui look after them?

WANG ZIXI: Yes sir.

TANG DEYUAN: Tell the cashier to give Chang Gui twenty percent of Ke Wu's tip.

CHANG GUI: Oh, sir, there's no need—

TANG DEYUAN: I know things are tight at home; you don't have to pretend on my account. Zixi, are our accounts all taken care of?

WANG ZIXI: They are, and ready for you to look over.

TANG DEYUAN: That's all right, as long as my sons have a look at them.

WANG ZIXI: Well, they . . .

TANG DEYUAN: Neither one of them has been in? Again?

CHANG GUI: Eh, I'm sure they've been held up by some other important matters. They've been very conscientious about management recently. Why, now that the Quanyingde is getting set to open across the street, your youngest bought a thousand good-sized firecrackers and told us to set them off the day they're to open, before they set theirs off, to get rid of any bad luck. And your eldest was pretty worked up, too; said we'd show them who'll come out on top! So you see, your sons have a lot of drive and determination.

TANG DEYUAN: (*Ignoring this*) Zixi, figure up everything we owe and draw the money out in advance tonight. As if we're going to compete with them across the street still owing a mountain of debt! (*Sees that* WANG ZIXI *remains expressionless*) Hmm?

WANG ZIXI: *(Mumbling)* Ah.

TANG DEYUAN: Zixi, did you hear me?

(LUO DATOU enters holding a raw duck.)

LUO DATOU: *(Shouting as he walks)* Who accepted these ducks? Do they want to ruin us?

CHANG GUI: *(With a wink)* Just pick another, Big Luo. There are always one or two rotten apples in every barrel.

LUO DATOU: *(Ignoring his expression)* They're all like this! These are sick ducks somebody's brought in because they're trying to buy cheap. I can't roast ducks like these. I, Luo Datou, practice an art that's been served to the empress in the imperial palace. Anybody who knows this will know that it's the duck that's no good. But if they don't know, they'll think that I don't know what I'm doing!

TANG DEYUAN: *(Taking the duck and feeling it with practiced fingers)* Zixi, sell this lot off for soup tomorrow morning. We can't use them. The reputation of Fujude depends entirely on quality, like the old saying, "It's the food that does the talking."

LUO DATOU: I'm glad to hear you say that. I don't feel angry anymore. It's a nice night out. I think I'll go out and take a walk around.

CHANG GUI: Don't be too long, or we won't be able to find you when pay is distributed.

(LUO DATOU exits.)

TANG DEYUAN: Has Luo Datou kicked the habit or not?

CHANG GUI: He can't. He lost his wife over opium.

WANG ZIXI: I hear the person he sold her to isn't bad at all. Last year she gave birth to a daughter. She's better off with that guy than Luo.

TANG DEYUAN: No matter what, he is her first husband. Like the old saying goes, "A decent woman doesn't marry twice; decent goods never switch owners." *(Remembering the previous topic)* Zixi, did you sign for those ducks?

WANG ZIXI: It was your youngest who signed.

TANG DEYUAN: He spends all day playing with swords and poles; how is he going to take the time to look over ducks? You should stay with him a bit more.

WANG ZIXI: I did go with him, and I said—

TANG DEYUAN: Zixi, you didn't start working with me yesterday. As the management of this place stands now, everything depends on you, and you have to be firm if you're going to bring it off. Now,

they're going to open across the street in three days. So if our
duck, or our scallions, or our pancakes aren't any better by then,
just invite our best customers to try theirs across the street.

WANG ZIXI: Manager, I'll never forget how well you and your father
have always treated me. It's just that now, I don't know what's
happening; I've got this headache sickness—*(with affectation)*
such pain, it feels like the sky is going black and the ground
cracking open—

TANG DEYUAN: A few days ago you said you saw a classmate.

WANG ZIXI: Ah, Lu Mengshi—studied business management; the
accountant over at the Yushenglou now.

TANG DEYUAN: And he grew up in our town?

WANG ZIXI: Rongcheng, Daluying. We've been together since we
were kids. Someday I'm going to bring him by to meet you—a
square face with heavy brows, really lucky-looking. I hear when
his mother gave birth to him, she had visions of people blowing
horns and beating drums and a sedan chair carried by eight men,
with a boy inside, nice and fat.

TANG DEYUAN: *(Unwilling to listen to this)* Will he come here?

WANG ZIXI: As ambitious as he is now, who doesn't want to move up?
Besides, he's got it in for the manager at the Yushenglou, and he
doesn't want to work there anymore. If he comes, I'll retire and
you can make him assistant manager.

TANG DEYUAN: I need to think it over some more.

CHANG GUI: You're tired out. You should lie down in back for a while
and stretch out.

TANG DEYUAN: Close out the accounts once those two sons of mine
get back. I don't know what sins I committed in a former life to
deserve those two in this one. *(Exits)*

CHANG GUI: Zixi, a word of advice. Ever since he took over management, it's always been a "family-owned, family-managed" business. With you as assistant manager, he's always felt at ease, since
you're a distant cousin of his. But Lu Mengshi's no relation to
him or to you.

WANG ZIXI: But I can't take it if things go on like this. The worst is
that he told me to go out tomorrow and pay off what we owe
today. What am I supposed to pay them with?

CHANG GUI: We work like crazy. Don't we have some income?

WANG ZIXI: *(Opening the ledger)* Elder son withdraws five hundred to entertain a famous performer; younger son withdraws one thousand to pay what he owes to some Superior Martial Arts Society. I don't have the nerve to say no when they want money. Our manager says I'm not firm enough; I have to listen to him. Didn't you see how he invited a geomancer in? Our luck is running out! If Fujude closes up some day, people will say it was my fault.

CHANG GUI: The old man likes public respect. Let him save face. Just fudge a little here and there.

WANG ZIXI: I can fudge things for a day but not a month.

(*Suddenly there is the sound of a commotion: carriage bells, horse hooves, people's voices, and shouts. The Guanghe Theater has let out.*)

WANG ZIXI: Fu Shun, they're coming out! (*Seeing* FU SHUN *is asleep, he gives him a kick.*) Sleeping again! Get on out there!

FU SHUN: (*So startled, he leaps up and runs to the door*) Duck here! (*Yawns*) Roast duck here! Drip-roasted, crispy skin—
(*Three people enter.*)

CHANG GUI: (*Greeting them*) Gentlemen. Show's over? Care for something to eat? Something to drink? (*He shows them to a private room.*)
(LU MENGSHI *enters. He is some thirty years old, clean and neat, with a spring in his step and an energetic manner.*)

LU MENGSHI: Zixi, brother!

WANG ZIXI: No sooner do we mention you than you arrive on the spot. Chang Gui, this is the Lu Mengshi I was just telling you about.

LU MENGSHI: Mr. Chang, I've heard of your reputation often but never had a chance to meet you, so this is my lucky day.

CHANG GUI: (*Sizing up this straightforward young man*) There's no need for ceremony with me; I just take orders around here, and I don't give them.

LU MENGSHI: I wouldn't put it that way. Whatever the skill, there's always someone who's best at it: for writers there's Sima Qian; for painters, Tang Yin; for shoeing horses there's Blacksmith Liu. I've always heard how you have a loyal clientele who'll follow you wherever you go. For a restaurant to get you amounts to getting a set of permanent customers.

CHANG GUI: It would be flattering to think so. (*Serves tea, then attends to customers*)

WANG ZIXI: How are you doing; been to the theater with Miss Yuchu'r?

LU MENGSHI: *(With a smile)* As it happens, I have some business to attend to.

WANG ZIXI: No need to pretend. There's nothing wrong with having a mistress, as long as she's not married. Just don't take her too seriously.

LU MENGSHI: I actually did look her up on a matter. I've heard there's a book they keep secret in the Neiliansheng Shoe Store called *Notes on Celebrities' Shoes*. Do you know about it?

WANG ZIXI: Never heard of it.

LU MENGSHI: It's a record of the shoe sizes for all the royalty in Beijing, plus what styles they each like.

WANG ZIXI: What for?

LU MENGSHI: Say Gentleman Jia wants to get in the good graces of Lord Li by sending him a pair of official, embroidered thousand-layer-sole boots. All he has to do is tell Neiliansheng and they'll guarantee to make him a pair of boots that will fit Lord Li perfectly. A gift like that is discrete, elegant, and just the right gift, too.

CHANG GUI: So what you have in mind . . .

LU MENGSHI: So what I have in mind is for our restaurants to set up a record of all the important dates for everyone in all the important households in Beijing. Then, when we get to some particular date, our people can deliver gifts. If somebody reserves tables for a banquet, we're all ready to go. If they're not certain, then we can deliver a box of longevity peaches or noodles, something to make them feel good, let them know we've thought of everything to keep them in mind. Then they'll give us more business.

WANG ZIXI: You just love these gimmicks. You're really wasting good ideas working for a manager like the one you've got.

(LU MENGSHI heaves a long sigh.)

WANG ZIXI: He doesn't know how to treat people. Otherwise your father wouldn't have—

LU MENGSHI: *(Unwilling to discuss a painful subject)* Oh, but he was too trusting. If I had—

(The GEOMANCER enters.)

WANG ZIXI: Here you are, sir. Our manager has been expecting you for some time.

GEOMANCER: I'm earlier than I said I'd be.

(TANG DEYUAN *enters.*)

TANG DEYUAN: When I asked you over, what I had in mind—

GEOMANCER: *(Interrupting him)* No need to explain; just show me your blissful abode.

TANG DEYUAN: This way, please.

GEOMANCER: Best for you to remain in place.

TANG DEYUAN: Zixi, show the gentlemen the premises, and I'll keep Mr. Lu company.

WANG ZIXI: Mengshi, this is our manager.

(WANG ZIXI *accompanies* GEOMANCER *offstage.*)

LU MENGSHI: Sir, here's to your health.

TANG DEYUAN: I'm embarrassed by a toast; please, have a seat. I heard what you were just talking about.

LU MENGSHI: Zixi and I were just shooting the breeze—give you something to laugh over.

TANG DEYUAN: You gave me something to think about. Aren't you afraid if you tell us all this, we'll steal your business away from the Yushenglou?

LU MENGSHI: The river can hold more than one boat. Things improve only when you have competition.

TANG DEYUAN: Well said. There is something I wanted to tell you about to see if you have any ideas.

LU MENGSHI: Tell me.

TANG DEYUAN: There's a roast duck restaurant that's going to open right across from us, fixed up to look exactly like we do, down to the tables and chairs. Even the door curtain looks like ours. Their manager was our accountant; their chef is one I let go. They're calling themselves the Quanyingde, meaning they plan to beat us out of business. Now, what would you do about it if this were your problem?

LU MENGSHI: Go over to Ruifuxiang and get seven or eight yards of red silk, make it into a huge banner, and write across it, "With best wishes, from all your colleagues at the Fujude on Meat Market Lane." When the day comes for the Quanyingde to open, I'd march everyone over there, with the manager in the lead and a band of drums and cymbals, to congratulate them on their opening, and I'd wish them every success.

TANG DEYUAN: Why?

LU MENGSHI: We all take our chances living by what we can sell, not by bullying or cheating. Whether we succeed at business depends on our abilities.

(*The* GEOMANCER *enters, speaking.*)

GEOMANCER: It's a good location, very good, a truly precious spot! It fronts on a thoroughfare, with a high wall in the rear, and there's even a small alley on one side. What's it called?

TANG DEYUAN: Well Alley.

GEOMANCER: "Well." You see, things too low will fall into the well.

TANG DEYUAN: You're saying—

GEOMANCER: Your building's too low, not high enough to be auspicious. You need to build up here. If you build up, then you've got two lanes on each side as carrying poles, to make your edifice into a sedan chair, an eight-man sedan chair. Then nothing can stop you. You'll have all the luck in the world!

TANG DEYUAN: You mean build another story up? (*Seeing there are too many people around*) Please, have some tea with me where it's quieter in back. (TANG DEYUAN *and* GEOMANCER *exit.*)

LU MENGSHI: (*Half mulling it over, half talking to himself*) He says this is a sedan chair . . .

WANG ZIXI: He could say it's the throne room, for all the good it'll do.

LU MENGSHI: Business still off?

WANG ZIXI: There's no one who really cares about the place. Oh, that's right, there's something I wanted to talk over with you—

(TANG MAOCHANG, *the elder son designated manager, enters, followed close behind by his attendant,* FU ZI.)

TANG MAOCHANG: (*Studiously perfecting his singing while he walks*) "Liu Bei was a descendant of the Prince of Jing, great-great-grandson in the bloodline of the emperor himself—"

(FU ZI *passes through the entrance, imitating cymbals and drums with his voice, playing the musical bridge to the next singing line.*)

TANG MAOCHANG: It's that word "in." You know, Tan Xinpei, Maestro Tan, had the best style for that word.

FU ZI: You do your "in" with a different touch—it's the touch of the Yu School, the style of Yu Zhenting.

TANG MAOCHANG: Is that so? (*Sings*) "In the bloodline—" Fu Zi, I want to invite those performers tonight to join us. What do you think? Will they accept my invitation?

FU ZI: Accept an invitation from the young manager of the Fujude? They'll come for sure!

TANG MAOCHANG: I need someone to teach me.

FU ZI: Are you going to turn pro?

TANG MAOCHANG: I can't go on like this; I need some professionals to give me some recognition.

FU ZI: Who knows, maybe they'll join you for a performance on stage.

TANG MAOCHANG: *(Warming to the thought)* Fu Zi, if you can do that for me, you can have the run of this restaurant!

FU ZI: *(Brows raised, eyes smiling)* Thank you, sir!

TANG MAOCHANG: *(Taking a small teapot* CHANG GUI *hands him)* My brother?

CHANG GUI: He hasn't returned yet.

TANG MAOCHANG: *(Discovering* LU MENGSHI*)* Who might this fellow be?

WANG ZIXI: My schoolmate Lu Mengshi, from the Yushenglou.

LU MENGSHI: *(Advancing)* Manager Tang, I was one of the audience for your rendition of "The Black Pot."

TANG MAOCHANG: *(Suddenly showing interest)* Oh?

LU MENGSHI: At the Tiansheng. Your aria had real style, and you looked the part, too.

TANG MAOCHANG: My eyebrows were uneven that day, one higher than the other. Could you see it from the audience?

LU MENGSHI: *(Tactfully)* Why, no, it didn't show at all.

TANG MAOCHANG: And my throat was scratchy, I couldn't get the high notes, only "rasp" it out.

LU MENGSHI: It's the kind of throat they call "clouds covering the moon."[6] The lower pitch sounds good.

TANG MAOCHANG: Wow! That's exactly what Maestro Yu said! *(In a tone of deep friendship)* Next week I'm doing a scene from *Si Lang Visits His Mother*. I'll reserve a seat for you.

LU MENGSHI: That's splendid; *(offhandedly)* I love listening to you perform.

TANG MAOCHANG: *(Holding him back)* Don't leave. Have some dinner with me, and offer some more of your constructive criticism.

LU MENGSHI: What time is it? Eat dinner?

TANG MAOCHANG: Whenever I watch theater or perform, I go without dinner. Chang Gui, give this fine gentleman a duck to take out.

LU MENGSHI: Thank you, but I won't be taking the duck, just please don't forget my seat.

(Exits)

TANG MAOCHANG: Hey, let my rickshaw take you home. *(Puzzling)* He looks so familiar, who is he?

WANG ZIXI: He's the Yu—

TANG MAOCHANG: *(Suddenly recalling)* Oh! Will you look at what's happened to my memory? He's Yu Liancheng, sings young-scholar roles!

WANG ZIXI: *(In helpless frustration)* Hopeless.

TANG MAOCHANG: *(To himself)* Came especially to attend my performance. . . . *(Growing excited)* That's what I'll do; Fu Zi, tomorrow send them all written invitations. Don't miss a one.

FU ZI: I guarantee they'll be here! Ah—*heh-heh*—sir, I haven't had dinner yet.

TANG MAOCHANG: Chang Gui, wrap up a duck for Fu Zi to take out.

WANG ZIXI: Sir, your father's here; he's in back, lying down.

TANG MAOCHANG: Oh. *(Straightens his clothes, and exits to see his father)*

(FU ZI exits ecstatically, carrying a large duck.)

WANG ZIXI: He'd make a better name for himself if he just opened a duck donation center as a charity.

CHANG GUI: *(Swatting flies) Ai*, not very businesslike!

(Suddenly the two men are startled by a rumbling noise from the rear courtyard.)

WANG ZIXI: That's Tang Maosheng! Jumping over the wall at this hour, as if the door weren't open.

(TANG MAOSHENG enters. He is dressed up in martial arts clothes: gray satin pants, a wide silk sash around his waist, with a green peony embroidered on the tassel.)

TANG MAOSHENG: Did you hear me enter?

WANG ZIXI: I heard you.

TANG MAOSHENG: *(Speaking to himself in dismay)* I have to practice silent movement more. Chang Gui, that's not the way to swat flies. Look. *(Inhales deeply)* Here we go! *(Picking up a pair of chopsticks from the table, he snatches two flies.)* That's the way to do it.

CHANG GUI: But, sir, I can't do that.

TANG MAOSHENG: Then, learn! I'm not very good at it, either. My
    master could just stand there, and the flies would go over to him.
CHANG GUI: He probably just finished eating fish.
TANG MAOSHENG: Come on, he uses energy, moves it from his lower
    abdomen to his head. Here, *ai*— *(Strikes a pose)*
    *(*TANG MAOCHANG *enters.)*
TANG MAOCHANG: *(Annoyed)* Go on back over to the west side if you
    want to practice.
TANG MAOSHENG: Mind your own business. I care about this, just like
    you have your pastime.
TANG MAOCHANG: Look at the way you're dressed up. If you want to
    learn from someone, then learn from Lin Chong. There's some-
    one who knows "Deep in the night / I hear the faint drops from
    the clepsydra." What's your Wang Huzi compared to that? Just a
    bandit.
TANG MAOSHENG: *(Excited)* You say Wang Huzi was a bandit? Let me
    tell you, last year, when they decapitated him in the marketplace,
    I saw it with my own eyes. When his head fell to the ground, his
    eyes were still wide open, staring, and he opened his mouth and
    gnawed at the dust. Now, there was a man!
TANG MAOCHANG: All right, all right, I won't argue with you. Papa
    wants to see you. If you take my advice, you'd better put a gown
    on over that stuff so he doesn't scold you.
CHANG GUI: *(Handing him a gown)* Just slip into this, sir.
    *(*TANG MAOSHENG *submits disdainfully to putting the gown on and*
    exits.)
TANG MAOCHANG: *(Without enthusiasm)* Bring in the table.
    (Several guests emerge from a private dining room. All are a bit
    drunk.)
A: *(Trying to grab the bill)* I'll take that. It's on me.
B: What's the matter? Can't show your elder a little respect? When
    we first came in, I said this is my invitation!
C: *(Taking out a handful of coins and giving them to* CHANG GUI*)* I'm
    paying.
B: *(Pushing his hand down to restrain him)* No, you're not.
CHANG GUI: True gentlemen; all for one and one for all! With the
    emperor back on the throne, the theaters are putting on good
    plays every day, so tomorrow when you gentlemen are done at

the theater, why not have some drinks here and you can take turns picking up the tab. How about that?

B: That makes sense. Okay, today it's my elder brother's turn, and tomorrow it's mine!

CHANG GUI: Well said! Altogether that'll be two and twenty-six. Settled! Thank you, gentlemen. Take care, now.

(*The men exit talking and laughing. Several apprentices bring a table into the front hall. The table is covered with account books, brush pens and inkstones, and an abacus. Behind the screen,* TANG DEYUAN *and* TANG MAOSHENG *argue.* TANG MAOSHENG *enters, full of exasperation.*)

TANG MAOSHENG: You don't want to see me? Well, I still don't want to come back! Don't force me to run away and do something you'll regret!

TANG DEYUAN: (*Enters following him*) Go as far away as you like. We've been in honest business for three generations. We won't miss the likes of you!

(*Bystanders seek to dissuade them from quarreling.*)

TANG DEYUAN: (*Exasperated*) Settle the pay accounts!

(*With his two sons seated behind the table,* TANG DEYUAN *sits, leaning back, in an armchair at one end of the table.*)

TANG MAOCHANG: (*To* WANG ZIXI) Start the roll call.

WANG ZIXI: (*Opening an account book*) Everybody wait in the second courtyard and don't enter until your name is called. Chang Gui!

(CHANG GUI *walks to the front of the table.*)

TANG MAOCHANG: (*Leafing through the account book*) You've done well these past six months, Chang Gui. For that, you deserve a larger share. However, just at the moment, cash on hand is a bit tight. You've been with us a long time, so you will have ten percent.[7]

CHANG GUI: (*His lips moving as if about to protest; he then restrains himself*) Sir.

TANG MAOCHANG: Chang Gui, you do have some outstanding loans. When your wife was sick in May, you borrowed thirty, then when your son was ill you borrowed another twenty. Altogether that's fifty. Subtracting your debt, you still owe the till twenty.

(WANG ZIXI *standing next to* TANG MAOCHANG *says something to him.*)

TANG MAOCHANG: I hear that you have a lot of dependents at home and you're short on cash. Still, the till is short, too. You have half a month. Next month settle up.

TANG DEYUAN: You can repay it in installments over three months.

CHANG GUI: Thank you, sir.

TANG MAOCHANG: (*With a glance at his father*) Next.

WANG ZIXI: Call in Cheng Shun next. Big Luo isn't back yet.

(CHENG SHUN *comes to stand before the table.*)

TANG MAOCHANG: You've done well these past six months, so you're receiving ten dollars in silver. (*Looks at* CHENG SHUN's *expression*) That's not bad, considering that apprentices at other restaurants don't receive any cash to spend on their own. You ought to be satisfied.

CHENG SHUN: I am satisfied.

TANG MAOCHANG: The money will stay in the till. Don't spend it recklessly. You can withdraw the amount you need when you want to spend it. Next.

(LUO DATOU *enters. He's finished smoking his opium, and his mood is changed.*)

LUO DATOU: Sir, it's my turn, isn't it?

TANG DEYUAN: (*Maintaining routine formality*) You've done well these past six months, and you deserve a raise. However, the till is short on account of debts, and there's no surplus to draw from, so we'll all have to share in the financial burden.

LUO DATOU: (*Detests euphemism*) In plain language, how much are you giving me?

TANG MAOCHANG: Fifteen percent.

LUO DATOU: (*Raising the pole for roasting ducks, together with a duck dangling from a hook at the top, he hurls them both out the window.*) Then you can find yourself another chef. (*Head hung low, he starts to walk off.*)

WANG ZIXI: Big Luo! Big Luo!

TANG MAOSHENG: (*Refusing to give in*) You think you can twist people's arms, acting like that, don't you? Well, not mine. If you want to quit, you just go right ahead and—

TANG DEYUAN: (*Raising his voice to silence his son*) Big Luo, come on back!

LUO DATOU: Sir, someday you'll destroy this business! (*Exits*)

TANG DEYUAN: We can settle all that later! *(To the employees)* You all leave us for a while.

(Only father and son are left onstage.)

TANG MAOSHENG: All just because he saved our sign once. As if he's rendered some great service! It's all because you and grandfather have spoiled him. Acting like that in front of his manager. That's too—

TANG DEYUAN: Be quiet! Give me the account book.

*(*TANG MAOCHANG *passes the account book to him.)*

TANG DEYUAN: Tell me, this past six months, how much has been overdrawn, how much paid out in bonuses, and how much is the cash surplus?

TANG MAOCHANG: Wang Zixi keeps the books. I've looked at them, but I don't recall. Probably around—

TANG DEYUAN: *(Interrupting, to* TANG MAOSHENG*)* You tell me.

TANG MAOSHENG: *(Simply)* My brother's looked them over, I haven't.

TANG DEYUAN: You've made a fine mess of the accounts! Is this how you've been managing things? You are deliberately ruining the enterprise handed down from our ancestors!

TANG MAOCHANG: Dad, you're ill. Don't get so upset. Actually, the two of us have our own interests. It's just that we don't like working for a bunch of ducks.

TANG DEYUAN: Despicable! I don't understand how you can say that. Where would you be today if it weren't for that bunch of ducks? Your grandfather came to Beijing when he was fourteen years old, set up this family by laying a chopping board across a couple of stools. The year we bought this property, you were born. Your grandfather named you Maochang for "prosperity," so that the Tang family would hold on to this restaurant as a family business for generations to come.

TANG MAOSHENG: Nobody said we ought to sell Fujude.

TANG DEYUAN: Be quiet! Look at you. Your ma died giving birth to you. Better if she hadn't bothered with a traitor like you.

TANG MAOSHENG: Hey, that's absurd, it's so unfair. You wouldn't be alive today without me.

TANG DEYUAN: You've failed as a filial son, and you're not fit to be called human. Get out.

TANG MAOSHENG: So I've failed as a filial son, have I? Look at this!

(He pulls up his sleeve) What is this? *(There is a scar on his arm.)* It's called "slicing off flesh to save a parent." It's in those operas you like to sing, brother. But they're not real. This is! The real thing! The last time you were sick, Papa, and didn't recover for a long time, I sliced off this piece of my arm and put the flesh in the pot to cook with your medicine. And that's when you got well.

(TANG DEYUAN glares, and he is unable to speak.)

TANG MAOSHENG: Do you understand? It was only after I put my own flesh into the soup for your medicine and you drank it that you were cured.

(TANG DEYUAN, overwhelmed by a wave of disgust, screams and vomits copiously.)

TANG MAOCHANG and TANG MAOSHENG: Papa!

(Employees enter, some pound his back, some pinch the dimple of his upper lip.[8] But TANG DEYUAN continues vomiting as before, and gradually the others give up, everyone anxiously at a loss for what to do.)

TANG DEYUAN: *(Panting, his voice weak)* Zixi . . .

WANG ZIXI: I'm here, sir. You must hold on; the doctor's on the way.

TANG DEYUAN: *(Struggling)* I . . . don't want a doctor. Go out, go out right away and get Lu . . . Meng . . . shi . . .

TANG MAOCHANG: *(Astonished)* Lu Mengshi? That guy who sings young-scholar roles?!

ACT II
SCENE I

Time: three years later (1920)
Place: Fujude Restaurant

(From the three facades of the Fujude at ground level rises a large building. The wide hall on the ground floor appears the same as before. But at stage left, a flight of stairs has been erected, with a row of arch-shaped private dining rooms at the top of the stairs. Each window lattice is decorated with carved flowers, and bare wood shows on some that have not yet been painted. The main hall has an air of quality, the door pillars have been newly lacquered, gaps in the brickwork filled with mortar, walls papered white from floor to ceiling, and the old signs dressed up in gold calligraphy.

The curtain rises. It is still morning, and the employees of the Fujude are still sleeping soundly. WANG ZIXI *enters.)*

WANG ZIXI: Up, everybody, up. It's daylight out.

(*The employees rouse themselves, crawling up from corners everywhere.* LUO DATOU *comes out of a dining room upstairs, stretching himself. Young* FU SHUN *has strapped himself onto the counter and can't free himself. He calls out anxiously.*)

FU SHUN: Cheng Shun, brother, help me get out of this.

WANG ZIXI: Hold on. Say, what have you been up to?

FU SHUN: The counter's too narrow; I fall off it when I go to sleep, so I—

WANG ZIXI: Aren't you full of clever ideas. If you'd just put that brain of yours to work learning a little business, you'd get rich. Untie him.

(FU SHUN *struggles awkwardly until he stands up properly.*)

WANG ZIXI: Now, let's get to work before second manager sees you like this. He'll turn you loose for good.

(*The employees busy themselves stowing away their bedding, sweeping, stoking fires, hanging out signs, et cetera.*)

WANG ZIXI: (*Continues giving instructions*) Today is the first day we'll be using the upstairs dining rooms, so keep that in mind. There's no reserved seating for lunch. But this evening first manager has invited his teachers over, and the tables from all fourteen dining rooms will be put together to serve a full banquet — (*Sees* CHENG SHUN *carrying a live duck in from the rear*) Be careful it doesn't start quacking. Second manager's not up yet.

LUO DATOU: Boy, if you interrupt Second Manager Lu's dreams of love, he'll fire your ass on the spot.

CHENG SHUN: Look! (*Holding the duck's head in his armpit, one hand clamping its beak shut*)

LUO DATOU: (*Peering toward the rear court, to* WANG ZIXI) That young woman hasn't left since last night.

WANG ZIXI: (*Smiling*) That's none of our business. (*Continues instructing*) Take forty of the best pick and get them plucked; tell them across the street at Yuanxinglou and Taifengguan that we will want four hundred lotus leaf cakes and two hundred hang-fried cakes nice and hot and ready to go when we ask for them this evening. Get over to Tianqiao right away and sell off last night's roast pork. See to cooking the rice gruel, slicing the scallions, and pounding the garlic. *(When he has finished giving assignments, he starts to go for his usual morning walk, to eat a snack.)*

LUO DATOU: Sir, I wanted to ask you about something.

WANG ZIXI: Go right ahead.

LUO DATOU: Li Xiaobian'r, the cook hired on a trial basis a few days ago, is he coming to work tonight?

WANG ZIXI: Yes, he'll be here. Second manager said now that we've added another floor, we're a full-fledged upscale restaurant and we can't go on with the same old four-ways-to-prepare-a-duck, so we need to add some new items to the menu.

LUO DATOU: I hear he's going to be promoted to oven chef.

WANG ZIXI: *(Quickly avoiding the topic)* I don't know anything about that. Hiring people is second manager's department. Fu Shun, keep your eye on the raffle box. Only our paying customers can draw in the raffle.

LUO DATOU: *(Losing his temper)* Putting a second-rate temporary hire into competition with me, you watch out I don't just let this place slide.

WANG ZIXI: These past two days the second manager's been really bothered with what's owed for the new construction, so just don't go looking for trouble.

LUO DATOU: I recommended Lu Erchun, one of the Rongcheng-school cooks through and through, apprenticed with Wang Yushan, king of the fast friers. Why wasn't he hired?

WANG ZIXI: He's always said, anyone named Lu related to his kin won't be hired.

LUO DATOU: That's just for show, to make himself look honest. Don't make me—

WANG ZIXI: Ah, all this time I've been talking with you, I almost missed my shredded turnip cake.

LUO DATOU: Turnip? What's so special about that?

WANG ZIXI: That's what you don't know. Ivory turnip, white refined sugar, some green and red decorator fruit strips, rose and cassia syrup, in a crust of flour blended with high-quality pork fat. Light, but substantial. Substantial, but melts in your mouth. Only you have to eat it hot out of the oven! *(He is already exiting with a smile as he finishes this description.)*

LUO DATOU: Slippery character. Fu Shun, go buy some fritters.

CHENG SHUN: (*Cleverly producing hot fried fritters*) Master, these are right out of the frier, crisp.

LUO DATOU: (*Mulling as he eats*) Li Xiaobian'r, Li the screwed-up man with the queue.

CHENG SHUN: (*Serving him a bowl of soy milk*) I hear that old fellow's stubborn, wouldn't cut his pigtail off to save his life.

LUO DATOU: I bet he was one of Zhang Xun's pigtailed soldiers they left behind on the streets when they ran off in 1917.[9] (*Laughs*)

FU SHUN: (*Plucking feathers from a duck*) They say he can do a full Manchu-Chinese banquet.

LUO DATOU: Shit, he's nothing but a temporary hire. He shows up anywhere somebody hires him with his vegetable cleaver in his armpit. Only he (*pointing to the rear*) would hire somebody like that to come in here as a master chef. I'm telling you, if you fall in with the likes of that, you won't amount to much in this life. Do you hear that? (*Gives* FU SHUN's *forehead a hard jab with his finger*)

FU SHUN: (*The jab almost knocks him off balance into the hot water vat.*) Hey!

CHANG GUI: (*Carrying in a pot of boiled water*) What are you hollering about? You know we don't do that around here!

FU SHUN: (*Aggrieved*) It wasn't me—

CHANG GUI: Always an excuse. Second manager hasn't asked you about what went on yesterday, eh.
(*A tidy, well-groomed young man enters, carrying an exquisite-looking bamboo basket filled with blooming tuberose.*)

YOUNG MAN: Sir, these are the flowers you ordered.

LUO DATOU: Except for the ducks, there's only a bunch of guys in this place. Now, who do you think would be ordering flowers?

YOUNG MAN: Fujude Restaurant, Meat Market Lane, right?

CHANG GUI: (*Realizing*) It's probably Yuchu'r. Hold on a minute, I'll go ask. (*Exits*)

YOUNG MAN: (*Studying the building*) This place isn't bad, huh, and you've got a raffle.
(*Reaches into the raffle box*)

FU SHUN: Hey, are you having something to eat?

YOUNG MAN: I bet the prizes are compacts and garters, right? So I don't have any place to put them.

(CHANG GUI *enters, followed by* YUCHU'R.)

YUCHU'R: Here you are.

(YUCHU'R is actually not pretty so much as her looks have a certain charm and intelligence, dressed smartly as she is in a quietly refined, pale blue short jacket and pants.)

YOUNG MAN: Your tuberose, ma'am. You can see: seven tassels, eight petals, and plenty of flowers.

YUCHU'R: *(Picking one to sniff)* Mmm.

YOUNG MAN: Our manager picked this pair of magnolias especially to give you to enjoy their scent.

YUCHU'R: *(Inserting it into the top of her jacket)* Please thank your manager for me. *(Taking out a red purse)* This is for you.

YOUNG MAN: You're always generous, ma'am, thank you. *(Exits)*

YUCHU'R: Fu Shun, put them in a bowl with water for now. This evening set out five per table, and remember to strip off any leaves that are faded or withering. *(Looking around)* The door curtain isn't up yet?

CHANG GUI: It's getting starched, as you told us to do. It will be here in a while.

(YUCHU'R starts to go upstairs.)

CHANG GUI: There's a letter here for Mr. Lu you might take to him. Fu Shun, Fu Shun, go upstairs with Miss Yuchu'r to see if there's anything that still needs to be done up there.

(YUCHU'R and FU SHUN exit up the stairs.)

LUO DATOU: Huh, so she's a manager now, too. Tuberose. She'll have this place looking and smelling like a whorehouse.

CHANG GUI: I wouldn't look down your nose at her if I were you. In Beijing the dishes they serve in the Eight Lanes can be pretty exquisite, too.[10]

LUO DATOU: Don't blow her horn for her. I wouldn't eat her cooking if it were free.

CHANG GUI: You're just too good for us. A prince in the imperial palace tried her cooking and said she was the best. That's why he gave her the name Yuchu'r [jade chick]; it's a pun in the imperial palace kitchen, Yuchu'r. He thought she's that good.

LUO DATOU: Fujude is a big success, with a whore as a manager and a temporary hire as a master chef. When that little-queue fellow, or whatever, shows up this evening, the guys here are going to show him a thing or two.

CHANG GUI: (*Pouring out hot water, his voice quiet but forceful*)
You've got money; you're doing okay, right?

LUO DATOU: I've been on good behavior ever since Lu Mengshi
started here as manager, haven't I. So why does he always look
down on me?

CHANG GUI: It's the eating and the drinking, the dope and the bragging. That's what he looks down on.

LUO DATOU: Hey! What chef with any reputation in this business is
any different?

CHANG GUI: That's the point, really. Manager Lu doesn't want other
people looking down on us in this business.

LUO DATOU: What difference would his respect make, anyway?
Didn't the manager at Yushenglou take his dad and—

CHANG GUI: Big Luo! What are you yelling for? You don't want your
own rice bowl! (*Takes off his apron*)

LUO DATOU: Where are you going?

CHANG GUI: My family's waiting for me outside for the money we got
last night selling off ducks' blood. Xiaowu'r is sick again.

LUO DATOU: You spend your whole life running around taking care
of those kids. What are they going to do for you when they grow
up?

CHANG GUI: Did I say I expect them to do anything for me? I just do
the best I can, that's all.
(*Exits*)

LUO DATOU: Cheng Shun, when that Li Xiaobian'r shows up, see he
gets put in his place.

CHENG SHUN: You bet, I'll tell him! My master is the pillar of the
Fujude, apprentice of Hunchback Liu, true successor of
Venerable Sun, oven chef for the imperial dining hall.

LUO DATOU: (*Satisfied*) Mmm, and if he asks which school?

CHENG SHUN: What do you mean "which school"?

LUO DATOU: Have you gone soft in the head?! Chefs are divided into
two schools. One is the emperor school, which is particular about
color, fragrance, flavor, appearance, slow cooking over low heat,
preserving natural juices and flavors. And one is the bodhisattva
school, which is particular about small servings, quick cooking
over high flame, heavy on oil and rich flavors, emphasizing
genuine benefit.

FU SHUN: And you?

CHENG SHUN: *(Cleverly)* No need to ask that. Of course, he's emperor school.

LUO DATOU: Yeah, Emperor Zhan the king.

FU SHUN: I don't understand.

LUO DATOU: The only damn thing you understand is how to eat! It was back in ancient times, when the Three Emperors and Five Rulers reigned, back then. One day the emperor got tired of all the things he had to eat from land and from sea, so he summoned the head chef Big Zhan, and he asked him what in this whole world has the most flavor. For a long time that stumped Big Zhan. So finally, he said it's salt that has the most flavor. Now, when the emperor heard that, he got upset and pounded his gavel: "Rubbish! That is contempt of this court. Take him out and cut off his head!"

FU SHUN: Did they execute him?

LUO DATOU: They executed Big Zhan. Then the three thousand chefs in the royal dining hall got together to figure out what to do. So from that day on, they all stopped using salt in their dishes. And before two days were out, the emperor said he had to admit that the thing with the most flavor in the world really is salt. Now the chefs were indignant, since Big Zhan had been wrongfully executed, and so they called on the emperor to step down for a week and pay homage to Big Zhan the Master as Emperor Zhan the king. Zhan the king is the ancestor we chefs worship. From then on—

(LU MENGSHI has entered unnoticed and seen everyone listening to LUO DATOU telling his tall tales, and dissatisfied with this, has coughed. The effect is instantaneous, as the employees spring to work, and even LUO DATOU picks up his roasting pole, casually looking him over and humming a tune.)

LU MENGSHI: *(Eyes sweeping the restaurant, he dips a hand into the wooden vat used to boil feathers off ducks.)* Are you using this water to boil off feathers? Let's get some hot water in here.

(CHENG SHUN adds a pot of boiling water, and steam rises from the vat.)

LU MENGSHI: *(To FU SHUN)* Put your hand in.

(FU SHUN puts his hand into the bubbling vat and immediately withdraws it, looks up at LU MENGSHI, and puts his hand in a second time.)

LU MENGSHI: *(Forcefully)* Again!

FU SHUN: *(Teeth clenched, puts his hand into the water again, where it is immediately scalded and he pulls it out)* I can't.

LU MENGSHI: How many times did you put your hand in?

FU SHUN: Three.

LU MENGSHI: Three times for ducks; two for chickens. Remember that! *(Taking a towel from* CHENG SHUN *and drying his hand)* Fu Shun, did you deliver ducks yesterday?

FU SHUN: *(Rapidly explaining)* I didn't make a mistake. Sixty-five West Zongbu Lane, Wu—

LU MENGSHI: Slowly, from the beginning, one thing at a time.

FU SHUN: Yesterday at noon, Wang Zixi sent me to deliver two ducks to sixty-five West Zongbu Lane. When I got there I saw it was a low-rent courtyard divided up into apartments, so poor they couldn't even afford corn muffins let alone duck. I went door to door asking for this Mr. Wu who'd ordered duck. The guys there just glared at me, and one young one said I was deliberately making fun of them. Said he was going to punch me.

LU MENGSHI: Is this true?

FU SHUN: May lightning strike me if I'm lying!

LU MENGSHI: Ask Wang Zixi to come here.

LUO DATOU: Right now, he's almost sure to have gone out to Zhimeizhai for those cakes of his.[11]

*(*WANG ZIXI *enters in a hurry, carrying a small rush bag.)*

WANG ZIXI: *(Smiling with embarrassment that he's late)* I had to wait for these shredded turnip cakes to come out of the oven. Mengshi, see this. They look like those hexagonal tiles in the kitchen over at Liuguo Hotel, all fit together. Try one *(passing one to him)*.

LU MENGSHI: *(Not amused by this attitude)* I had breakfast earlier.

WANG ZIXI: Take a couple for Miss Yuchu'r.

LU MENGSHI: *(Even less amused by this inappropriate pleasantry)* Did you take the call to deliver duck yesterday?

WANG ZIXI: Yes. It sounded genuine. A young voice, sounded cultured.

LU MENGSHI: There's a mystery for you. You got the order right; he got the delivery right. So how am I going to put this down in the accounts?

WANG ZIXI: Well, the meat's still in the pot, as they say. It wasn't wasted. We didn't lose anything, after all.

LU MENGSHI: (*Picks up the abacus*) Just the delivery fee, the labor for cooking, and the spoilage cost for loss of sale; altogether that's four sixty-seven. I'm not covering it up. We've run up a lot of debts on the new construction, so we have to be careful with the accounting.

WANG ZIXI: (*Silently withholding his speech, his face growing somber, muttering*) What bastard's stirring up trouble for us . . .

(YUCHU'R *enters, coming down the stairs.*)

YUCHU'R: Forget about it. I'll pay the bill, so just forget about it. Zixi, could you please take a look upstairs. A couple of the window frames haven't been nailed in securely.

(WANG ZIXI *exits. The other characters exit quietly.*)

LU MENGSHI: From now on, I'll charge all the additional expenses to you.

YUCHU'R: (*Smiling*) There's no one left now you haven't offended. If you had a sedan chair to ride in, no one would give you a lift. (*Opens a handkerchief, takes out a jade decoration, and hands it to* LU)

LU MENGSHI: How did you get it? (*Receiving it*)

YUCHU'R: You dropped it underneath the bed.

LU MENGSHI: (*Fondling the jade*) I couldn't sleep last night thinking about how my mother bought this little jade sedan chair for me when I was a child. When we were looking through the Lujiaying marketplace to buy it, I just kept tugging on my mother, to buy me elm pastries, instead.

YUCHU'R: I think you can say now that you haven't let her down. You've lived up to your parents' expectations.

LU MENGSHI: If only they could have lived long enough to know that. The way my father died, underneath the steel weights on a scale . . .

YUCHU'R: (*Trying to avoid stirring up his feelings, interrupts him*) Have you thought about those scrolls by the doorway?

LU MENGSHI: I sent someone to ask Xiu Dingxin to write them for us. Say, I know; I could hire Xiu Dingxin as our surveillance security, to keep an eye on what money goes into what hands.

YUCHU'R: (*Tidying up the counter*) I'm afraid he wouldn't condescend to that.

LU MENGSHI: He would now. Ke Wu's property's been confiscated by the law. He doesn't have enough to live on, let alone be choosy. Hey, I want to put up names for each of the private dining rooms upstairs, little adages with numbers in them—by the numbers, you know, like, "One for the road," "Five sons graduate," "Lucky double sixes," ah . . .

YUCHU'R: *(With mock indignation)* You haven't even paid off the construction bills, and already you have these funny ideas. Today's the day Mr. Qian is coming to be paid off.

(LU MENGSHI *looks around, whispering.*)

YUCHU'R: Be careful not to give it away.

LU MENGSHI: The coin wrappers I told you to roll up?

(YUCHU'R *purses her lips in the direction of the counter.*)

LU MENGSHI: They look like the real thing.

YUCHU'R: You've got nerve.

LU MENGSHI: If I didn't, would I dare try to win over the most captivating woman in the Eight Lanes? *(Taking her hand)* This gold ring isn't much to look at. I'll get a jade one for you tomorrow.

YUCHU'R: You can take it easy on the charm. Who knows whether you mean it or not?

LU MENGSHI: I promise—

YUCHU'R: Forget it. Aren't you afraid your wife will find out?

LU MENGSHI: I'm done with her.

YUCHU'R: And what if she has your children?

LU MENGSHI: You should see what she looks like. She's so ugly her children would be freaks. She can have them, I don't want them. *(Nuzzling up to* YUCHU'R's *ear)* I'm waiting for you. It's you who have to give me a boy—

YUCHU'R: Give up! *(Handing the letter to* LU*)* This just came for you.

LU MENGSHI: I don't want to read it.

YUCHU'R: It could be something important. You can't tell.

LU MENGSHI: *(Casually glances over the letter, gradually growing excited)* Why, that bag, she actually had . . . she actually had a son! I have a son. Look.

YUCHU'R: *(At once both jealous and envious)* Is that so!

LU MENGSHI: *(Excited)* Chang Gui! Tell the kitchen, cook up some extra dishes tonight. It's on me. I have a son!

CHANG GUI: This calls for a celebration! When Xiaowu'r was born,

I invited enough guests for three tables. Mr. Lu, you need to hold a banquet.

LU MENGSHI: You're invited, you're all invited to a full dress banquet, all you can eat. Yuchu'r— *(Only now discovers she's left)*

WANG ZIXI: She left.

(LU MENGSHI shakes his head, smiling.)

CHANG GUI: *(Entering)* Mr. Lu, the Quanyingde Restaurant knows about us opening a second floor today, so they've cut their prices twenty percent.

LU MENGSHI: Oh? Zixi, did you put the ad in the paper about our grand-opening raffle?

WANG ZIXI: No, I didn't. I've always felt having a raffle in the restaurant just wasn't right somehow.

LU MENGSHI: Well! Chang Gui, what do you say?

CHANG GUI: Last year the Taifenglou had one at their grand opening.

LU MENGSHI: Chang Gui, watch the entrance. If you see any important customers outside, be sure to intercept them and bring them in here.

CHANG GUI: Don't worry. Just now my family told me you sent someone with money over to our place yesterday, otherwise Xiaowu'r would have burned up with fever. I won't forget what you did as long as I live.

LU MENGSHI: Is your child better?

CHANG GUI: The fever's gone. I know the till isn't doing so well. I'll repay what I owe for sure.

LU MENGSHI: *(With a pat)* No matter what you owe, you have to spend what is necessary, Chang Gui. You've done a lot for the Fujude. Say, is Li Xiaobian'r here?

CHANG GUI: He's been waiting out in back for a long time.

LU MENGSHI: Cheng Shun, go to the kitchen and stand in for Master Luo so he can join us.

(LI XIAOBIAN'R enters. About fifty years old, he is thin and alert, with a small, thin queue hanging down the back of his neck. He meets LUO DATOU and starts to greet him, but LUO ignores him, seating himself center stage with exaggerated dignity.)

LU MENGSHI: This is our new chef, Master Li. As of this evening, he'll be starting with us. He'll be in charge of all kitchen preparations. Big Luo will be in charge of all oven preparations. Chang Gui, give us a rendition of tonight's menu, please.

CHANG GUI: (*Sings in a clear, sharp voice with a strong beat, like characters cut into a steel plate*) Cold duck webs on nine-inch plates, nine-inch plates of spicy marinated duck slices, pig's tongue on nine-inch plates, nine-inch plates of shredded chicken and cucumber, deep-fried yellow croaker on nine-inch plates, nine-inch plates of hot and sour marinated fish slices, soy fried shrimp on nine-inch plates, nine-inch plates of quick-fried stomach; braised chicken slices in medium bowls, medium bowls of braised *sixi* dumplings, braised diced meat and vegetables in medium bowls, medium bowls of braised "Office for the Management of the Business of All Foreign Countries" Zongli Yamen.

LI XIAOBIAN'R: Excuse me, could you sing that last one again?

CHANG GUI: Braised "Office for the Management of the Business of All Foreign Countries." It's a stylish name for chop suey.

LI XIAOBIAN'R: Oh, chop suey.

CHANG GUI: Mr. Wang, has the fish come in?

WANG ZIXI: They're in the vat in front of the partition.

CHANG GUI: (*Continues singing*) Dry-fried mandarin fish in pairs, paired three-pound platters of *pa* fish, large platters of sea cucumber in scallions by the pair, paired stewed leg of pork, stewed duck bones in cabbage, mixed vegetables in eight-treasures bean paste, three nonsticks, with fruits, nuts, and sweets. Canapés and dried fruits when they arrive.

LU MENGSHI: Two roast ducks per table. Lotus leaf pancakes— pancakes, and *zhou* gruel on demand. Set out hot tiger sauce for the gents and refined sugar for the ladies on each table. Tonight the senior manager is entertaining his teachers, all of them major performers from the theater. So look sharp, and I'll ask the owner for a bonus. Fu Shun, get me something to eat. (*Exits*)
(LI XIAOBIAN'R *fastens on a large apron and scoops a live fish out of the wooden vat.*)

LUO DATOU: (*With deliberate ambiguity*) The mandarin fish has twelve spines, one for each sign of the zodiac. If the spine with your sign sticks you in the year of your sign, you're done for.

LI XIAOBIAN'R: (*Hurling the fish onto the floor to kill it*) We'll just fix that so we can't get stuck by it.

LUO DATOU: My teacher was Venerable Sun, duck chef in the imperial palace. Did you know that?

LI XIAOBIAN'R: *(Unperturbed)* One of the guys I apprenticed with is the chef for the Xuantong emperor these days.

CHENG SHUN: *(Enters)* Sir, the ducks ought to be hung up now.

LUO DATOU: *(Calling out)* Bring me the roasting pole!

(Taking up the sandalwood roasting pole, LUO DATOU *lightly plucks an uncooked duck off the rack and raises it on his pole with its back to the oven; his front hand twists to the right, the hanging hook held slantwise. Deftly the duck is delivered to the oven chamber, swung through dancing flames, until it rests firmly on the front rack of the oven. Hearing an involuntary cry of admiration from his apprentices,* LUO DATOU's *face glows with satisfaction.*

With a "Shua," LI XIAOBIAN'R *pulls a piece of red silk from beneath his shirt, and with a "Hua" spreads it over a pile of raw chopped vegetables. From a cabinet, he produces a piece of soy-cooked meat. "Dang, dang, dang." His hand rises; the blade falls; the meat is thinly sliced into crescent shapes.* LI *arranges the meat slices on a saucer, then raises the red silk cloth. There is not even a shred of meat left on the unblemished fabric of the red silk.*

The onlookers gasp with admiration.)

LUO DATOU: *(With disdain)* Chopping meat on silk, that's the sort of amusement you get from street performers over at Tianqiao. Can you do a Manchu-Chinese banquet?

LI XIAOBIAN'R: I've amused myself with it a few times.

LUO DATOU: How many types of food in a Manchu-Chinese banquet?

LI XIAOBIAN'R: One hundred and eight.

LUO DATOU: Why is it one hundred and eight?

LI XIAOBIAN'R: The thirty-six star deities of heaven and seventy-two star deities of earth make one hundred and eight. It means that nothing in heaven or earth is left out.

LUO DATOU: And their special characteristics?

LI XIAOBIAN'R: Cold and hot, sweetness and saltiness, meat and vegetable. Omit the rice gruel on birthdays and the peach dumplings at weddings. *(Eyeing* LUO DATOU *with scorn)* Actually, these rules are just for show. There's nothing of substance to them.

*(*LUO DATOU *is about to display his temper, when a man dressed in court clothes of the imperial palace dashes in.)*

PALACE ATTENDANT: Who is the manager? The director of the palace roast duck and pork kitchen is here. Someone needs to greet him!

WANG ZIXI: Get Mr. Tang Maochang here, quickly!

CHANG GUI: He's gone to the carriage races at Pantaogong. Ask Mr. Lu to greet him!

WANG ZIXI: You all clear out now. *(Employees exit)*

(LU MENGSHI enters putting a formal magua *jacket on over his gown, and rushes forward to greet the director, who has just entered the restaurant.)*

LU MENGSHI: *(Presenting a Manchu salute)* Greetings and felicitations, Director.

DIRECTOR: Don't stand on ceremony. Say, when did you finish these renovations? And how is Tang Deyuan?

LU MENGSHI: Our manager Mr. Tang passed away. I'm the second manager of Fujude, Lu Mengshi.

DIRECTOR: The palace wants to order duck for tomorrow.

LU MENGSHI: Right.

DIRECTOR: Deliver twenty of them around noontime to the palace at the roast duck and pork kitchen for inspection first, then you can take them on into the imperial dining hall.

LU MENGSHI: Right.

DIRECTOR: Do you have permits to enter?

LU MENGSHI: We do.

DIRECTOR: Have the deliveryman bring a permit with the ducks. And whatever you do, don't be late.

LU MENGSHI: Rest assured, I guarantee we'll be on time. *(Offering a cup of tea with both hands)*

DIRECTOR: *(Sipping the tea and looking LU over)* Where are you from?

LU MENGSHI: Daluying in Rongcheng, Shandong.

DIRECTOR: How have things been in the countryside these past two years?

LU MENGSHI: They've done all right. Thinking of a vacation there?

DIRECTOR: Well, if by any chance that warlord Feng Yuxiang tries bombing the palace again, we'll need some place to go, eh? [12]

LU MENGSHI: I like your sense of humor.

DIRECTOR: Sense of humor? I'm not joking. The day I can't stay in the Forbidden City anymore I'll come running over to you all here. We're all in the same business, anyway. *(Takes a drink of tea)* Did you get a telephone call yesterday to deliver duck to West Zongbu Lane?

LU MENGSHI: We sent them right out but couldn't find anyone.

DIRECTOR: Sending you out there to look for someone was the emperor's little joke.

WANG ZIXI: So, it was the emperor! Whew, I though it was some jerk . . . (*Quickly slaps his own face*)

DIRECTOR: I have two silver ingots here from the Home Affairs Office to compensate you for that.

LU MENGSHI: Oh, we couldn't accept that. For a telephone call from the emperor, we'll set up a sacrificial altar and give thanks.

DIRECTOR: (*Resentfully*) We're a republic now, so it's not such a big deal. We'll be going now.

(*Several Republican Army soldiers stride into the restaurant, followed by an officer of the presidential guard, followed by* CHANG GUI.)

CHANG GUI: Adjutant Wang, you left us for the Quanyingde. Have we lost your favor, sir?

ADJUTANT: Expensive here?

CHANG GUI: Expensive people eat expensive things. Ours are good!

LU MENGSHI: Just for you I brought in a famous chef. He was the first meat chef over at the Tongheju.

ADJUTANT: I feel full just listening to you. (*Discovers the director*) This gentleman is . . .

LU MENGSHI: (*Quietly*) Director of the Palace Purchasing Office.

ADJUTANT: Oh?

(*The director is mulling over how to greet this government officer.*)

ADJUTANT: (*Saluting the director*) How do you do!

DIRECTOR: Oh, ah, how do you do! (*Still uncertain what gesture to make in response*)

ADJUTANT: Wait. That salute I just gave was from the Republic. But this is from me. (*He starts to offer a bowing Manchu salute of the Qing dynasty.*)

DIRECTOR: (*Reaching to catch him*) Please, don't stand on ceremony.

ADJUTANT: Is His Highness well?

DIRECTOR: He is, thank you. And President Xu?

ADJUTANT: He is, thank you. President Xu has the utmost respect for the Great Qing. He's always telling us we are acting as regents for the young monarch.

DIRECTOR: You are altogether too modest. Nowadays the emperor believes in the Republic. Why, just the other day he held an audience with the great philosopher of the foreign camp, Dr. Hu

Shih, and recited one of the professor's seven-word *jueju* poems. *(As if reciting a passage from the Four Classic Books)* "Picnicking on the banks of the Yangzi." That fellow's poem really is Manchu-Chinese with a foreign flavor. *(The two laugh uncomfortably.)*

DIRECTOR: You have business to attend to, I suppose, so we'll be on our way.

LU MENGSHI: Good day to you, sir.

(The director and his retinue exit.)

ADJUTANT: Do you know him well?

LU MENGSHI: The palace orders our ducks a lot.

ADJUTANT: Can you ask him, for me, for something from the palace?

LU MENGSHI: I don't have that kind of leverage.

ADJUTANT: I don't mean anything grand like what a president might want. Just something the emperor wrote and tossed away, or some snuff he's used, whatever. Once the imperial household is gone, things like that become antiques, collectibles.

LU MENGSHI: Now, that's thinking! Say, why don't you try your hand at our raffle again? *(To an employee)* Ask Miss Yuchu'r to come here!

ADJUTANT: That's just something you've rigged up with needle and thread to fool people. I won't be fooled into that.

LU MENGSHI: Just try it.

(YUCHU'R has changed clothes. All smiles, she holds up the raffle tickets for the adjutant to draw.)

ADJUTANT: *(Haphazardly drawing a ticket)* I know what you're up to.

LU MENGSHI: *(Receives the ticket, turns around, swiftly shuffles the ticket, then cries out with surprise)* Look at that!

ADJUTANT: What is it?

LU MENGSHI: That's amazing! You drew a gold ring!

(Everyone sounds amazed.)

ADJUTANT: *(Delighted)* Really?

LU MENGSHI: How could I cheat you! Yuchu'r, the prize, please.

(Signals YUCHU'R with a look. YUCHU'R understands and, turning around, with difficulty pulls the ring off her finger.)

ADJUTANT: I've got a lucky hand, all right. Last night I won at mahjong off my own draw.

LU MENGSHI: If you want some luck, take a look at this building now. It's in the shape of a sedan chair carried by eight bearers. Invite a few guests here and you're bound to receive important promotions.

ADJUTANT: All right! I'll just borrow some of your good fortune right now. Tonight, six tables for the presidential palace. Next Friday, reserve four tables for me and the bodyguards. Next month on the fourth, for the president's wife's birthday, we'll have a celebration with performers and everything. I'll turn all that over to you to cater, as well.

LU MENGSHI: *(Noting these down)* Fine!

ADJUTANT: The fellow I'm inviting tonight is the commander of General Duan Qirui's bodyguard, and we have some important matters to settle. So if the service here isn't good, he'll find an excuse to start fighting.

LU MENGSHI: Don't scare me.

ADJUTANT: Once fighting's started on the front, we'll be snapping up stuff on credit. Why, we'll be taking away loads of three-seven coagulant just from the Tongrentang pharmacy alone.

LU MENGSHI: Will the fighting reach Beijing?

ADJUTANT: Haven't you heard what they say? The worse it gets at the front, the more people eat in the rear. Even if the fighting reaches Beijing, it won't hurt your business. See you later. *(Exits)*

WANG ZIXI: *(Vexed)* With raffle prizes like that, we won't stay in business for more than three days.

LU MENGSHI: Where's Yuchu'r?

WANG ZIXI: She went back to Eight Lanes.

(MR. QIAN *enters, leading a group of creditors. Each of them holds a blue cloth tag for settling accounts.)*

MR. QIAN: Mr. Lu. Mr. Lu, we're back.

LU MENGSHI: Right on time. And these gentlemen? . . .

MR. QIAN: These gentlemen represent the Liubiju Pickle Company, the Taifenglou Restaurant, the Quanheng Bank . . .

LU MENGSHI: *(Without listening to the end)* Valued customers all! Cheng Shun, brew up some cups of our best tea.

MR. QIAN: Mr. Lu, we won't beat around the bush today. Let's be straightforward, shall we?

LU MENGSHI: How would you like to proceed?

(A *porter enters.)*

PORTER: Sir, your white flour's here.

WANG ZIXI: We didn't buy any—

(*Several police patrolmen enter.*)

POLICE: Here we are, sir.

LU MENGSHI: You came just at the right time. Could I trouble you to keep an eye on these fellows while they deliver our flour?

WANG ZIXI: (*Perplexed*) When did you buy white flour? You could have—

LU MENGSHI: (*Drawing* WANG ZIXI *over to him*) You all take care with this flour. I don't want you dropping any bags. If one of them splits open and the flour spills on the floor, I'm not giving you a thing for it.

(*The porters carry in sack after sack of flour. The police stand around making a great empty show of ordering people about.*)

LU MENGSHI: (*Taking hold of an abacus*) We still owe six hundred, plus one month's interest at seven-point-six percent, to the Kuixiang Carpentry Shop. That's . . .

(*The attention of the creditors is fixed on the flour.*)

MR. QIAN: How expensive is that flour?

LU MENGSHI: We don't use anything cheap here at Fujude. There's an officially fixed price at two dollars silver per sack.

CREDITOR: What are you going to do with all that?

LU MENGSHI: When you're broke, fix the door; when you're loaded, fix the oven, right? (*Continues calculating on the abacus, and carelessly knocks over a silver-coin roll, which rolls onto the floor*)

MR. QIAN: Business is booming, eh, Mr. Lu?

LU MENGSHI: We're getting by. Before noon the merchants show up; afternoons it's the sons and daughters of the official class. Then in the evening, well, tonight it's six tables for the presidential palace, next month the First Lady's birthday. We're so tired we can hardly move.

MR. QIAN: You've earned a lot for the Fujude.

LU MENGSHI: (*In a confiding tone*) The business belongs to the Tang family. I just do the buying and watch people eat. As for the loans you gentlemen have extended, if it were up to me, I'd pay them off entirely and be done with it. A sum like that wouldn't mean anything to the Fujude.

CREDITORS: Sure. Absolutely.

LU MENGSHI: It's the owners who won't do it! And after all, paying off in installments has its advantages, too. You all collect more interest, and it makes things easy for me, too. But then, you all have to make extra trips here. Mr. Qian, you've been our agent for a long time now. What do you say? You stop by every month. How have I treated you?

MR. QIAN: Honestly, you're a good man. But you know we have an old saying: "Inside your business the employees want loans; outside, the creditors want payment." If you'd just pay off the balance, you'd rest a lot easier, wouldn't you?

LU MENGSHI: If there's one thing I'd stake my reputation on in this business, it's trust. If you made me pay up everything today, I'd pay off those bills if I had to strip everything out of my own home to do it. But if it came to that, it would be the end of a good friendship. It would be the end of Fujude's ordering your products, and the end of your coming here to look for business. You're taking a short view of things. You ought to take a longer view. Think it over, gentlemen. (*Turning his attention away from them to direct activities; several creditors exchange glances*)

MR. QIAN: Mr. Lu, don't get upset. We have feelings, too. Whether we do business or not, we're all friends here, it's just that we have to work for others just like you.

(LU MENGSHI *is impassive.*)

MR. QIAN: Let's do it this way. Since Mr. Lu is busy today, why don't you all go back to your bosses and talk things over with them. We'll let you know after that.

LU MENGSHI: That's fine with me. Ducks-to-go for everyone. Make them big, now. (*Creditors exit*) Mr. Qian, wait a moment. The emperor just had these silver ingots delivered to us. Why don't you keep them as a souvenir.

MR. QIAN: (*Eyes growing big as he looks at the silver ingots*) Leave this problem to me. With the Fujude as successful as this, they're bound to treat you as someone they want to keep doing business with.

LU MENGSHI: I'm much obliged.

(MR. QIAN *exits.* LU MENGSHI *collapses in the armchair and heaves a long sigh.*)

WANG ZIXI: So, what happened. Take a high-interest loan?

LU MENGSHI: Come here. (*Whispers to* WANG ZIXI)

WANG ZIXI: (*Astonished*) *What?* Damn, my calf's got a cramp. (*Weak in the knees, he sits down.*)

LU MENGSHI: (*Laughing*) Didn't I tell you? When it floods, block the gate, not the drain sewer. Take care of things here while I make a trip over to Eight Lanes. (*Relaxed,* LU MENGSHI *exits.*)

WANG ZIXI: (*Now that the crisis has passed, he feels all the more nervous.*) Chang Gui.

(CHANG GUI *enters.*)

WANG ZIXI: Mind the door while I go back to lie down. (*Exits*)

(CHANG GUI *sits by the entrance, mending an apron. The quiet is broken by the sounds of peddlers hawking their wares, their voices growing louder or fainter.* KE WU *wanders in. He has lost his former imposing look, his silk robe is torn in several places, and the upper portions of his shoes are also worn.*)

CHANG GUI: (*Hearing* KE WU'*s shuffle*) May I help you?

KE WU: Chang, old man, do you still recognize me? Ke Wu. Wow, this is quite a building you have now. A sedan chair. You know, Tang Deyuan wanted to fix this place up like a sedan chair all along, but in the end he never did get to ride it.

CHANG GUI: So, it is you. But who are you looking for?

KE WU: I'm not looking for anyone. (*Scanning the restaurant, his eyes fix on the rack of ducks, and his mouth begins to water.*) I think I'll have something to eat.

CHANG GUI: You?

KE WU: What's the matter? Don't think much of Ke Wu? Never mind our family got into difficulties; a wrecked boat still has three thousand nails to it.

CHANG GUI: Otherwise, why would they say a scrawny camel is still bigger than a horse.

KE WU: In the old days you couldn't even get me to come here. Whenever I ate anywhere, I could host ten tables on the spot. The dishes in my home were decorated in the dragon pattern.

CHANG GUI: Certainly.

KE WU: The imperial dragon had five claws. Princes' dragons had four. The dragons of highest ranked officials had only three claws. Do you know how many claws the dragon for our family had?

CHANG GUI: It was five claws for certain. Otherwise, how could your family have offended the imperial countenance and had all your property confiscated?

KE WU: Chang, old man, you rascal; you're clever! Can you guess what I was looking around for yesterday?

CHANG GUI: Gold bars.

KE WU: Something more beneficial than that stuff. *(Carefully pulls a piece of paper out of his clothing)* A ticket for duck at the Fujude Restaurant!

CHANG GUI: We published notice that ever since the old manager died those tickets are no longer valid.

KE WU: *(Agitated)* What? It says here in black and white, "The bearer of this ticket is entitled to two ducks." And it has your seal on it.

CHANG GUI: No matter what it says, it's worthless.

KE WU: Hey! I spent good silver to buy this. Is silver worthless?

CHANG GUI: The silver you spent on that wouldn't buy more than a duck's thigh today.

KE WU: *(Pouting temperamentally)* That's not fair. I'm going to eat that duck today no matter what!

(TANG MAOCHANG enters.)

TANG MAOCHANG: Fu Zi, walk the donkey down to Xianyukou and let it out to sweat a while.

CHANG GUI: *(Quickly rising to his feet)* Good day, sir. Ah, where did all that dirt on your trousers come from! Fu Shun, go fetch a duster.

(CHENG SHUN and FU SHUN enter and busy themselves cleaning off TANG MAOCHANG.)

CHANG GUI: A big day for racing at Pantaogong today, sir?

TANG MAOCHANG: You bet. They were all experts: the Prince of Tao, the Prince of Su, the Fifth Master of Le. But it was Yu Zhenting who was really outstanding, Maestro Yu. Cheered him each time he finished a lap. What a sight. Black felt cap, sleeveless deerskin jacket, leather pants, brocade boots, and pleated socks with lace trim, and a cummerbund, not too tight and not too loose. Once he was in the saddle—*dadadada*—his horse's hooves sounded like a *kuaiban* tune: *tata, ta, ta, clang!* Awesome!

KE WU: You were in the carriage race, weren't you?

TANG MAOCHANG: Did you see it?

KE WU: You handled the whip, and the famous male lead, Jiaotian Junior, rode on the side.

TANG MAOCHANG: *(Suddenly showing interest)* Did it look okay?

KE WU: Except the way the donkey was dressed out could have used improvement.

TANG MAOCHANG: *(Thoroughly concerned)* Oh, tell me!

KE WU: Pay more attention to the tassels in front of the mule's head. There ought to be pearls through the tassels so that when it runs it has a *"tita"* sound. You know the way the saying goes, *"tita* tinkling jade."

TANG MAOCHANG: *(Respectfully)* What an expert! Please, do go on.

KE WU: In those days, my grandfather held the whip, Tan Xinpei rode on the side, the whip cracking and the pearls tinkling all the way—really had class.

TANG MAOCHANG: *(Thoroughly envious)* A gentleman of this caliber— (CHANG GUI *whispers to him.*)

TANG MAOCHANG: Oh, but of course, it's the son of His Lordship Ke; my humblest apologies.

KE WU: Fallen on evil times.

TANG MAOCHANG: Reminds me of *Qin Qiong Selling the Horse.* You're better off than he was! Think of him having to move out into the wilds— *(Sings from the opera* Selling the Horse*)* "Qin Shubao could not help himself; his tears course down like rows of hemp, for this horse you want has a special meaning. It was a gift to me from the Minister of War. Now that heaven has delivered us into such misfortunes, there is nothing we can do to pay you the rent we owe, but sell this horse—"

KE WU: The way you sing this old man's song really has a touch of Maestro Yu's style.

TANG MAOCHANG: *(Excited)* Do you think so? Mr. Ke Wu, sir, if you have no pressing engagement at the moment, come on back with me where we can continue our chat.

KE WU: There is one matter. This is a ticket for duck from your establishment, but Chang here says they won't give me anything for it.

TANG MAOCHANG: Why won't you honor the ticket?

CHANG GUI: Sir, we published an announcement a long time ago that these coupons were no longer valid.

TANG MAOCHANG: That's right, I forgot. Let's do it this way: just redeem Mr. Ke's ticket this once as an exception.

CHANG GUI: Sir, we can't establish that kind of precedent. (FU ZI *enters running.*)

FU ZI: Sir, the rickshaw is waiting to take you to see opera costumes. You need to hurry.

TANG MAOCHANG: Don't be in such a rush. I still have to take off this armor and change into a gown. *(Starts to exit)*

KE WU: Say, Mr. Tang, about those ducks—

TANG MAOCHANG: Oh yes! *(Continues where he left off singing the lines from the opera* Selling the Horse*)* "With a wave of my hands, I surrender my possession to you." *(Exits)*

KE WU: *(With satisfaction)* Did you hear that? Service, now! Chang, old man, I'll have one duck here, and take away the other. And I'll take the breastbone from the one here with me, too. *(He sits down, crossing his legs, and assumes the air of a man of privilege.)* *(*CHANG GUI *drags* WANG ZIXI *onstage.)*

WANG ZIXI: *(Loudly scolding)* Ke Wu!

KE WU: *(So startled he stands up, then sees it's* WANG ZIXI *and sits down again)* Chang, old man, go over to the Taixingguan and get me a bowl of millet gruel and buy a couple of peaches; make them crisp ones.

WANG ZIXI: Ke Wu, those coupons have been worthless for ages, so get on out of here!

KE WU: The owner said they were good! And for your information, after I'm done eating here today, I'll be back again to eat tomorrow. Because after I'm done with this coupon, I have a whole stack of them at home!

WANG ZIXI: *(Beside himself with exasperation)* Our gentleman Mr. Tang is gone all day, and no sooner does he return than he stirs up trouble.

CHANG GUI: No matter what, we can't let him have these ducks. If we give in to Ke Wu's coupon we'll have to deal with a thousand more out there.

WANG ZIXI: Mengshi isn't here, and you can't throw him out yourself. *(With sudden inspiration)* Got it! I'm going over to the martial arts studio to find Tang Maosheng. Ke Wu's gutless, so once we scare him he's sure to take off. *(Exits quickly)*

KE WU: Are they roasting yet? Here I've been eating duck since I was a kid and I still don't really know how they're cooked. *(Walks toward the oven)* Hey, how come it's that hot?

CHANG GUI: Ai, watch where you're going; you'll get yourself burned! *(*LUO DATOU*'s angry voice is heard:* "Get away from there! Move away!" *He enters.)*

LUO DATOU: Who the hell is getting in the way?!

KE WU: Why, if it isn't Luo Datou.

LUO DATOU: You still owe me two plugs of opium!

KE WU: I'll repay what I owe you. Why so excited? Say, Big Luo, have you tried out the technique I showed you?

LUO DATOU: It does have more of a kick than smoking it dry. You know some tricks, all right, you joker.

KE WU: I myself learned this through study with a master.

LUO DATOU: So, even to smoke opium you studied under a master teacher? Quit the bullshit.

KE WU: You don't believe me? When I was young my father didn't want me going out to fool around, so he looked around for something to keep me tied down at home. That's when he hired a master to teach me to smoke opium. He was paid a fee first, and was promised a bonus if he could hook me. Hey, I really fought it, but before a week was out, I was hooked. You knew old Ke Wu had an appetite for food and opium, but you never heard about Ke Wu fooling around in Eight Lanes. That's on account of my father's foresight.

CHANG GUI: His Lordship your father really knew how to handle you.

KE WU: That teacher said that smoking opium had three great advantages: "It prevents illness, dispels loneliness, promotes thought." Luo Datou, if you want to learn, I'll teach you for nothing. Just let me eat duck once every three days, and that will be payment in full.

(XIU DINGXIN *enters, dressed smartly.*)

XIU DINGXIN: Excuse me, I was wondering whether Mr. Lu Mengshi is in?

CHANG GUI: May I know your—

KE WU: (*With a shout*) Xiu Dingxin! (*Rushing forward to embrace him*)

XIU DINGXIN: (*Sighing all the while, but pushing* KE WU *away*) Fifth son and heir, let me take care of business first, then we can chat about old times. Mr. Qian said you were looking for a surveillance man here, is that so?

CHANG GUI: Yes, we are. But Mr. Lu is not here right now. Why don't you have a seat?

KE WU: That bronze skillet we used in the winter to cook *shuan-yangrou* was sold for the bronze by Her Ladyship. And those wood mallets and little picks we used for eating crab have all been burned, and the pot of Buddha-climbing-the-wall stew we buried in the rear garden was dug up and carried off by soldiers, in the Republican mutiny. I only got to smell it; I never got a chance to taste it. . . .

(WANG ZIXI *enters with* TANG MAOSHENG.)

TANG MAOSHENG: Where's Ke Wu? Ke Wu! Your old man joined up with Zhang Xun to restore the emperor. That makes him a criminal. As for you, spending all day in opium dens and making trouble in restaurants, you'd better reform or I'll teach you a lesson here and now!

KE WU: What are you doing?

TANG MAOSHENG: Give me that duck coupon!

(KE WU *is unwilling*.)

TANG MAOSHENG: (*Grabbing the coupon and tearing it up*) Get out!

KE WU: What do you think you're doing, treating me like this. Your father used to play up to me as "a parent to the people"; that's what he called me. I didn't pay any attention to him.

TANG MAOSHENG: (*Losing his temper*) Say that again!

XIU DINGXIN: (*Seeing the situation looks bad*) Ke Wu, you'd better go.

KE WU: (*Stubbornly*) I'm not afraid of him. Striking an important customer on the day he opens this new building for business— wouldn't that be unlucky?

TANG MAOSHENG: (*Roaring*) Close that door!

(*Several young apprentices call out loudly:* "Close the front door!")

CHANG GUI: (*Restraining* FU SHUN *et al.*) Mr. Tang, closing the entrance and striking a customer will bring us bad fortune!

WANG ZIXI: Frightening him is one thing; you can't really hit him.

TANG MAOSHENG: (*Pushing* CHANG *and* WANG *aside*) Stand aside, all of you! Ke Wu, don't run if you have any guts!

(CHENG SHUN *and* FU SHUN *take down the open shop sign and close the door.* WANG ZIXI *and* CHANG GUI *are so agitated that they run around in circles.* KE WU *has also panicked. Hearing the shouting,* TANG MAOCHANG *has also run onstage.*

LU MENGSHI *enters.*)

LU MENGSHI: What's going on here? Closing the entrance in broad daylight!

WANG ZIXI: You are back! (*Describes events to* LU)

LU MENGSHI: Enough of this! Mr. Tang, when they closed the door and beat a person at the Yihelou, the next year they went out of business. Besides, today of all days people are coming to see the new building. Aren't you afraid it will ruin business?

TANG MAOSHENG: Business be damned, then.

KE WU: *(Hiding behind* LU MENGSHI*)* Huh! Today you'll hit me, I'm telling you, or you're not a man! Look, everybody, look how a manager of the Fujude beat up an important customer— *(*TANG MAOSHENG *hurls a chair at him.)*

LU MENGSHI: *(Seizing* KE WU *with his hands)* Ke Wu, get going, fast. Xiu Dingxin, drag him out.

(Pulling and shoving, XIU *and others push* KE WU *offstage.)*

TANG MAOSHENG: Ke Wu! Don't let me lay eyes on you again! *(*TANG *is dragged off by employees).*

TANG MAOCHANG: What was that all about? Wasn't it just a coupon for duck? You could have given him one and been done with it.

LU MENGSHI: You can't change a policy once it's set.

TANG MAOCHANG: You always have an answer. Your position is second manager, and you're okay at routine business. But you make a big deal out of small things, and you make a disaster out of important things. I really don't know how you manage this business.

FU ZI: Mr. Tang, you'd best be going.

TANG MAOCHANG: If we'd had a scene like this tonight, who would be willing to be my teacher? *(Listens intently)* Where did that sound come from?

CHENG SHUN: The younger Mr. Tang is so angry he's in the back courtyard beating the flour sacks.

TANG MAOCHANG: Look at how angry you made him. If this were—

WANG ZIXI: *(Suddenly remembering)* Oh no; he can't beat those flour sacks!

TANG MAOCHANG: He's not beating a person, anyway, so what's wrong with beating a few sacks? Don't be so fussy. Let him be. *(Walks over to the counter, picks up a red paper coin roll and hands it to* FU ZI*)* Let's go.

LU MENGSHI: Sir, you can't take that money out.

TANG MAOCHANG: Now what are you up to? My father may have hired you on his deathbed, but he never said he was turning the business over to you. I am the manager of Fujude, not you! Fu Zi, take it.

*(*TANG MAOSHENG *enters running.)*

TANG MAOSHENG: Maochang, I can't believe it! Those flour sacks in the back courtyard are filled with dirt!

TANG MAOCHANG: *(Shocked)* Dirt?!

LU MENGSHI: Sir, I can explain—

TANG MAOCHANG: (*Shouting angrily*) So you've sold us out! Lu Mengshi, you're coming with me to the police! Maosheng, take all this money away!

WANG ZIXI: (*His face red with agitation*) Mr. Tang, sir, and you, sir, Mr. Tang, I didn't know anything about this dirt. It was all his—

LU MENGSHI: Those silver-coin wrappers are full of dirt also.

TANG MAOCHANG: (*Stunned into silence*) Wha——? (*The coin wrapper rolls from his hand onto the floor where, sure enough, dirt spills out of it.*)

(*The onlookers' stunned, frightened, and suspicious gazes all turn toward* LU MENGSHI.)

TANG MAOSHENG: (*Leaping up, with a thunderous roar*) Lu Mengshi—

LU MENGSHI: (*Anxiously*) Whatever you do, don't shout. Cheng Shun, bolt the door!

(*Curtain.*)

ACT II
SCENE II

(*It is evening and the Fujude is brightly lighted inside, where people are coming and going. The booths in the mezzanine are packed with customers, and the restaurant is filled with the sounds of cups clinking, dishes clattering, laughter, and conversation.*

Waiters scurry about upstairs and down. CHANG GUI *is presiding at this moment. Very dignified in appearance, he has the alert, composed, and thoughtful look of a general in command.*)

CHANG GUI: (*Hearing movement upstairs, he realizes that almost all the customers have arrived. Walking to the screening wall, facing sideways, he speaks toward the rear of the screen.*) Mr. Li, I have eight tables now; the customers are all in the house. Wait for word on the hot dishes; the cold ones can go on.

(FU SHUN *and other apprentices and waiters bearing platters of cold dishes file onstage, past the wide room, up the stairs, following* CHANG GUI's *directions, and deliver vegetable and meat dishes separately to each private dining booth.*

On the main floor a customer from a private dining room downstairs calls out to settle his bill.)

CHANG GUI: *(Rapidly comes forward, holding up the door curtain)*
All finished, gentlemen? The total is three dollars sixty-eight.
(To customers with formal politeness) It's my pleasure to pay,
gentlemen. *(Smoothly deposits the money at the counter, makes
change, and hands it to the customer)* It's dark outside, so take
your time. See you again. *(Tosses the customers' tips into the
bamboo tube, and takes advantage of the moment to have a drink
of tea)*

XIU DINGXIN: Those three didn't look at all familiar to me.

CHANG GUI: They were pretending to be high spenders. You could
tell from what they had on. They live in expensive hotels and eat
at expensive restaurants, and when they see something they like
at jewelry stores, they go on in and buy it up. But once they've
taken what they want, they disappear without a trace.

XIU DINGXIN: You don't miss much.

CHANG GUI: There's a knack to watching people. For instance, if you
see a bunch of people going after a ball, say, they're sure to be
Americans. Or a bunch of people taking a bath together, they're
Japanese. Now if you see a bunch of people fighting over who'll
pay the bill for dinner, they're bound to be Chinese. (XIU DINGXIN
laughs.)

FU SHUN: Sir, they've gone through one round of drinks.

CHANG GUI: *(To XIU)* I figured you wouldn't be used to standing up
so much at first, and could use a joke to take off the stress and
relax a bit. *(Stepping nimbly up the stairs, he stands at the head
of the stairs and calls out in a resounding voice)* Bring on the raw
ducks for inspection.
*(Waiters go to the racks and take down one plump, white, tender
uncooked duck after another and carry them into the private dining
rooms for their customers to see.*

*Showing customers the uncooked ducks is a time-honored rule in
roast duck restaurants.*

CHANG GUI *himself, with practiced hands, picks up an uncooked
duck, parts the curtain to the room of the guest of honor, and stands
sideways displaying the duck. Then he goes downstairs, not by tread-
ing on the steps themselves but sliding down along the edge of the
steps [where a railing would be expected], swiftly and silently.*

The waiters also one by one return downstairs, delivering their ducks to the oven. Only FU SHUN, *the last down the stairs, looks agitated.)*

FU SHUN: Sir! One of the customers wrote on this one— *(The character "longevity" appears in cursive writing on the duck's pale body.)*

CHANG GUI: Mr. Xiu, have a look at this. This is—

XIU DINGXIN: *(With a disapproving glance)* This is Fan Dongbo's writing. He's written on the duck so you can't switch this one with a smaller one. Secondly, he's testing the chef's skill, to see whether the character keeps its shape after it's been cooked.

CHANG GUI: Tell Luo Datou to be careful with this one. So, Mr. Xiu, you know our business.

XIU DINGXIN: *(Starting to feel satisfied)* Fan Dongbo doesn't amount to much of a gourmet, anyway. He ate chrysanthemum firepot with me once, and after that he never tried to impress me again.

CHANG GUI: *(Intrigued)* Oh?

XIU DINGXIN: Chang, old man, tell me: If you want your *shuanyangrou* boiled mutton to taste—

FU SHUN: Hold on, what did you call Chang *Shifu?*[13]

CHANG GUI: *(Generously)* Mr. Xiu's not used to things here. Go on.

XIU DINGXIN: If you want your boiled mutton *shuanyangrou* to taste fresh, what do you put in the broth?

CHANG GUI: Some *donggu* and *koumo* mushrooms, and prawns.

XIU DINGXIN: That's what Fan Dongbo said.

CHANG GUI: That's not right?

XIU DINGXIN: How do you write the character for "fresh"?

CHANG GUI: A "fish" and a "lamb."

XIU DINGXIN: In the north, "lamb" is what they think of as fresh; in the south, it's "fish." At the Guangheju they have a dish called Pan's fish, that's based on the scholar Pan Zuyin's theory of fish and lamb. It's fish quick-boiled in mutton broth. So, if you want the full flavor of "freshness," then buy some live carp to boil up in a broth and use that for your dipping broth for *shuanyangrou* mutton.

CHANG GUI: You are a first-class gourmet, all right. You said once that when you cook ham, you need to insert a dog's leg inside it. I wonder what you meant by that?

XIU DINGXIN: *(Smiling)* If you want sweetness, add a dash of salt. If you understand that when you're cooking, it's bound to taste great. And if you understand that about life, you'll get along fine.

(The sound of woks being knocked against pans comes from behind the curtain.)

CHANG GUI: *(Knowing this sound means the vegetables are being taken out of the cooking pans)* Prepare to send out the vegetables! *(Instructing the waiters)* Remember: deep-fried, stir-fried, boiled, shallow-fried, and braised, in that order. Don't mix them up. This is Mr. Li's first day in this kitchen, so don't try to get away with anything. Now go on.

(The waiters carry the vegetable dishes on, each platter inspected first by CHANG GUI.*)*

CHANG GUI: This is for the host's table. Some people in the theatrical profession do not eat coriander. Xiaoshengzi, roll down your sleeves. There are ladies present. . . .

(LI XIAOBIAN'R quietly goes upstairs, parts the curtains, and peeks in.)

CHANG GUI: *(Coming out of a dining room)* Looking for the manager?

LI XIAOBIAN'R: How did I do?

CHANG GUI: The presidential palace like their salty dishes; the actors like their bland ones. You did fine!

LI XIAOBIAN'R: I owe it all to your pointing things out to me. And I plan to show you my thanks.

XIU DINGXIN: Li San'r, don't you taste the leftovers when you cook?

LI XIAOBIAN'R: *(Looking over at* XIU*)* What did you call me?

(XIU DINGXIN does not respond.)

CHANG GUI: He just started here. He doesn't understand yet. You—

LI XIAOBIAN'R: *(Not letting up)* The manager calls me *shifu*, so what gives you the right to call me by my familiar name?

XIU DINGXIN: What are you so steamed up about?

LI XIAOBIAN'R: You aren't what you used to be anymore! Don't think you can push people around all the time!

CHANG GUI: Mr. Li, brother, please, for my sake, don't. You have some cooking to do.

(LI XIAOBIAN'R throws down his apron and exits.)

XIU DINGXIN: *(So angry he stomps about)* I'm leaving. I'm not going to put up with this. Where's Mr. Lu?

CHANG GUI: Mr. Xiu, in this business you need to learn tolerance.

XIU DINGXIN: I, Xiu Dingxin—I was a customer here, and now I work for the people who wait on them. Does some ninth-rate[14] plebian chef think he can talk like that to me?

CHANG GUI: Don't say that! The managers made that term "ninth-rate" taboo around here!

(*An army officer comes out of a dining room and orders cigarettes.*)

CHANG GUI: They've finished three rounds of drinks. Put the ducks in the ovens— (*Several prostitutes enter wearing eye-catching makeup and clothes.*)

(LU MENGSHI *comes downstairs and calls to the girls to go upstairs. Two girls stand around* LU, *chattering away.*)

LU MENGSHI: Two women are noisier than a hundred ducks.

A GIRL: (*Offended*) What was that? Who's a duck?

LU MENGSHI: The customers are all here, so go on up quickly! (*Pushes them upstairs*)

A GIRL: Manager, there's still "fifty ducks" at the door!

(LU MENGSHI, *not understanding, starts to go out, and runs into* YUCHU'R *as she enters.*

The girl laughs mischievously and exits.)

LU MENGSHI: (*With a smile*) Here you are. (*Looking at* YUCHU'R) I apologized to you all afternoon long. Are you still put out?

YUCHU'R: There's a rickshaw at the entrance that looks like Maestro Yu's.

LU MENGSHI: He's here.

YUCHU'R: Your gentleman owner is a capable man.

LU MENGSHI: After all, I arranged the invitation for him.

YUCHU'R: Shouldn't he reward you?

LU MENGSHI: Reward me? He practically turned me over to the police.

YUCHU'R: (*Laughs*) Over that dirt?

LU MENGSHI: You think that's funny.

YUCHU'R: I think it's funny that capable people order others around, so people who aren't capable get ordered around.

LU MENGSHI: So I'm not capable. (*Starts to exit*)

YUCHU'R: That's just like you, always getting worked up with me over something. See what I brought? (*Takes out a small delicatessen box*) Try some. (LU MENGSHI *selects a piece and puts it in his mouth.*)

YUCHU'R: There's an old woman in the lanes over where I live who peddles a basket of these things every afternoon, soy duck wings, duck liver in sauce, whatever. She has everything. All the sisters over there love her stuff. We serve them with wine.

LU MENGSHI: This is delicious.

YUCHU'R: That's all you think about, eating. It's all from your restaurant.

LU MENGSHI: But it's the parts we can't roast.

YUCHU'R: So you can't roast them. Does that mean you can't sell them? Didn't you say "four-ways-to-prepare-a-duck" was too dull? Why not make use of the liver and the other stuff you throw out and start five-ways-to-prepare-a-duck, or eight ways?

LU MENGSHI: *(Seized by excitement)* Get me a pen. *(YUCHU'R goes to the counter to get a pen and paper.)*

LU MENGSHI: *(Suddenly deflated)* What am I getting so excited for? With those two interfering managers I can't get anything done.

YUCHU'R: You're like some kite—a little wind and up you go, then crash.

LU MENGSHI: They're the ones who hold the strings. It's not up to me where I go.

YUCHU'R: What if I cut the string?

LU MENGSHI: What?

YUCHU'R: If you don't take control of management, you'll be taking orders the rest of your life.

LU MENGSHI: You're saying—

YUCHU'R: You've really never thought about it?

LU MENGSHI: Tang Deyuan told me on his deathbed, I wasn't being hired to steal this business away from his family.

YUCHU'R: Who said anything about stealing it away? Make it work. That is your purpose in this life, that is your contribution—to leave behind to the world a restaurant like the Fujude.

LU MENGSHI: *(Cannot help being impressed by* YUCHU'R's *distinctive vision)* Go on!

YUCHU'R: Tang Maochang loves opera so much, let him go sing and forget about the restaurant.

LU MENGSHI: And Tang Maosheng?

YUCHU'R: Leave him to me.

LU MENGSHI: *(Jealous)* No way!

YUCHU'R: *(Scolds* LU *with a smile)* Come on, now, I'll find him someone else good. So there you are. You have someone to bear you a son, and someone to show you the road to success, my manager in chief Lu Mengshi.

LU MENGSHI: *(As if rediscovering her)* Yuchu'r, the first thing I'm going to do when I become manager is buy you out of the brothel.

YUCHU'R: I've heard that before a hundred times. We'll see. (*Starts to exit*)

LU MENGSHI: (*With feeling*) I mean it!

(WANG ZIXI *enters in a rush.* YUCHU'R *frees her hand and runs upstairs.*)

WANG ZIXI: Mengshi, that lot of five hundred white-eyed ducks we wanted was bought out by the Quanyingde for a higher price.

LU MENGSHI: It's odd that we didn't know anything about it. How come?

WANG ZIXI: They paid him off secretly.

LU MENGSHI: Very well. If he's going to cheat at this, so can I. Aren't they trying to find out how we raised our ducks? Go find some people to spread the word that the fat on our ducks is from ventilation. Tell the old man at the storehouse to open up all the windows of the duck coops.

WANG ZIXI: As cold as it is today, won't the ducks catch cold?

LU MENGSHI: Exactly. So put all our ducks in my room!

WANG ZIXI: I see. I see. I'm on my way. (*Exits*)

LU MENGSHI: Fu Shun, go up and ask Mr. Tang Maochang to see me.

FU SHUN: Sir, right now . . .

LU MENGSHI: Right now.

(*Shortly,* TANG MAOCHANG *comes downstairs.*)

LU MENGSHI: There are some urgent matters I need to talk with you about.

TANG MAOCHANG: (*Annoyed*) Let's hear it.

LU MENGSHI: The place across the street snatched our duck order.

TANG MAOCHANG: So, if it was taken, then go find a way to buy some more.

LU MENGSHI: I will. Right now there are three kinds of duck in Beijing. The southern ducks from the Yun River, called "lake ducks," are small but tender. Chaobai River "White River rush ducks" are large and plump, but few in number. Finally, the "grease ducks" from Yuquan Mountain have small bones and a lot of fat, so they cook up too greasy. The snack shops use duck grease for—

TANG MAOCHANG: *(Patience exhausted)* Will you tell me the point of all this?

LU MENGSHI: I just can't make up my mind which kind to order in, so I thought—

TANG MAOCHANG: Get whatever the best are. Do you need to ask me that?

LU MENGSHI: It's something important that I couldn't act on without talking to you first. There is one other thing: recently we haven't been getting a decent price on our duck feathers in the small market, so I thought the woodcraft stores—

MAN UPSTAIRS: *(Leans down to call)* Mr. Duck, sir, Duck Maestro, why did you steal out? Did you hear your ducks calling you? *(He laughs.)*

TANG MAOCHANG: Maestro Yang, please explain to my master. I'll be right up. All right, what else? Get on with it!

LU MENGSHI: As of yesterday there are new restrictions closing the city gates. We can't take deliveries of ducks in the evening, and we can't ship out the blood, the intestines and innards, so I want—

TANG MAOCHANG: Fine. Do whatever you think best! *(Goes upstairs)* Ducks, ducks, they'll peck me to death yet! *(Exits)*

LU MENGSHI: *(Smiling to himself, he sees XIU)* Mr. Xiu, getting used to things?

XIU DINGXIN: Sir, I came to work here because I heard you've always treated everyone equally.

LU MENGSHI: We can't let people look down on restaurant staff like us; that's what I've always wanted.

XIU DINGXIN: And how will they respect us?

LU MENGSHI: We ourselves have to respect each other first, then they won't dare not to.

XIU DINGXIN: I don't think you can succeed in that.

LU MENGSHI: I want to try. Do you have the couplet I asked you to write?

XIU DINGXIN: Couplets need to be exquisite, something to cheer and delight, or to stir a sense of beauty and awe, or evoke nostalgia for distant times, or suggest the uncertainty of this world. What is your pleasure?

LU MENGSHI: You've spent your life as a gourmet, spent half your life in restaurants. What's your pleasure?

XIU DINGXIN: Well, when it comes to food, there's only one epigram I really like: "There's never been a banquet in this world that didn't come to an end."

LU MENGSHI: *(Giving* XIU *a look)* That's not very auspicious for a couplet.

XIU DINGXIN: But it's very true.

CHANG GUI: *(Enters)* Over at the presidential palace tables, they're all talking about fighting and killing and what all.

LU MENGSHI: They can go kill to their hearts' content, as long as they don't start killing in here. I'll go up and take a look. *(Goes upstairs)*

*(*CHENG SHUN *enters carrying a dish, pushed on by* LUO DATOU.*)*

LUO DATOU: Go on, dump it out.

CHENG SHUN: *Shifu,* this is what they ordered at the table where they're all carrying guns. Mr. Lu warned us not to get them angry—

LUO DATOU: No more back talk! Go on and dump it, someplace far off! *(*CHENG SHUN, *left with no choice, exits.)*

LUO DATOU: Li Xiaobian'r, we'll see just how capable you are.

(The sounds of pipes and strings from upstairs. Several people drag out TANG MAOCHANG.*)*

TANG MAOCHANG: You're all stars. How can you say it's my turn?

PEOPLE: The maestro won't take you as his student if you don't sing!

TANG MAOCHANG: Then I'll do a piece from *Temple of the Gate of Doctrine.*

PEOPLE: No! Not that! Do a female role. Do "Su San's Journey."

TANG MAOCHANG: How about a piece from *Red Maid. (Smoothly relieving a waiter of the plate in his hand)* Miss Wu, strum me an interlude.

(As she begins to play the shrill jinghu, *or Peking lute,* TANG MAO-CHANG *starts to sing and dance: "Hide Scholar Zhang under the chess board—")*

TANG MAOCHANG: I can't do this! I'm really too lousy! Everyone just have a seat and enjoy your dinner, please.

*(*CHANG GUI *and* XIU DINGXIN *enter carrying platters loaded with large and small packets.)*

CHANG GUI: Cheng Shun! Where is that scamp? Go give these to the rickshaw pullers, one packet of roast meat and one packet of money each. Make sure they understand this is from Mr. Tang Maochang.

(Two waiters acknowledge the instructions and exit.

LI XIAOBIAN'R enters in a state of extreme agitation, followed by WANG ZIXI.)

LI XIAOBIAN'R: Brother Chang, have you see a platter of red beans?

WANG ZIXI: Where did you put it? We're supposed to serve eight-treasures bean paste right now.

LUO DATOU: *(Emerging from the side of the oven, strolling past)* Could it be you forgot to cook it?

LI XIAOBIAN'R: I cooked them this afternoon.

WANG ZIXI: Let's change the order to hot candied yams.

XIU DINGXIN: But the order was from the presidential palace tables.

WANG ZIXI: *(Nervous)* That crowd is always looking for something to complain about. That's all we need, a disaster!

LI XIAOBIAN'R: *(Head bathed in nervous perspiration)* Send someone to buy mung bean cake, now!

WANG ZIXI: Cheng Shun, hurry, the Tianyishun on the south side.

(As CHENG SHUN starts to leave, LUO DATOU gives him a significant look. CHANG GUI exits, quietly slipping away.)

LUO DATOU: Eight courses of fish, fowl, vegetable and meat—that isn't something a first-rate chef can't handle.

LI XIAOBIAN'R: *(Suddenly realizing)* Luo Datou, we work together to make a success of this place. Don't go screwing things up.

LUO DATOU: *(Glaring and shouting)* Hey, it's you who screwed up. Don't go looking for someone else to pin it on.

WANG ZIXI: Back off, now; oh, my ancestors! There are still customers upstairs.

(CHENG SHUN returns empty-handed.)

CHENG SHUN: They're out of mung bean cake.

LUO DATOU: *(Delighted with this bad news)* Looks pretty bad.

XIU DINGXIN: If those folks don't eat well, somebody could lose their head.

LI XIAOBIAN'R: *(Resolutely)* Losing your head just means dying. Failing at my art means a lifetime's reputation.

WANG ZIXI: Let's change the order. I'll go talk to the manager.

LI XIAOBIAN'R: Don't change it! Today Li Xiaobian'r's failed. I'm finished, for good. *(Takes off his apron)* Good-bye!

(CHANG GUI *rushes on, holding a paper packet in his hands.*)

CHANG GUI: *(Panting)* Mr. Li, sir, mung . . . bean cake.

LI XIAOBIAN'R: *(Taking it, he breaks off a piece and sniffs it)* It's okay. *(Lunges for the kitchen, suddenly turning around)* You are my brother, Chang Gui. I won't forget what you've done for me, ever. *(Exits quickly)*

CHANG GUI: *(Wiping off perspiration)* Clear away the meat and fish, distribute the hand towels, and prepare to serve duck! *(Exits)*

LUO DATOU: *(Resentfully)* Damn. I never would have expected it! Cheng Shun, look after getting the ducks out of the oven, then shut down the fire. I'm going to bed. *(Exits)*

LU MENGSHI: *(Enters)* Where's Li Xiaobian'r? He did well today. Got some tips from the opera maestros. The day after tomorrow Maestro Yu is having a party and he's asked him to do the cooking.

LI XIAOBIAN'R: *(Speaking as he enters)* When they're steamed, then cut the flame and take out the wok.

LU MENGSHI: Li *Shifu!*

LI XIAOBIAN'R: *(Hiding his face)* Sir, I don't have the skill for this. I'd better try a fresh start someplace else.

LU MENGSHI: What's all this about?

LI XIAOBIAN'R: I've never before put up with places that go for back-stabbing.

LU MENGSHI: That's not the Fujude. We're fair to each other here. What makes you say that?

LI XIAOBIAN'R: Today was our first day working together, and I don't mind being tested, but I won't take being undermined.
(WANG ZIXI whispers in LU's ear.)

LU MENGSHI: *(Expression darkening as he listens to WANG)* He's always up to something ninth-rate like this. Li *Shifu,* why don't you go take a rest in the back rooms. *(LI XIAOBIAN'R exits.)*

LU MENGSHI: Call Luo Datou!

CHENG SHUN: He went to bed.

LU MENGSHI: Then roll down his covers.

WANG ZIXI: I really think you shouldn't disturb him right now. Mr. Tang Maochang is trying to win over a teacher, and this is a very important moment for him—

LU MENGSHI: Call him!
(LUO DATOU enters, looking unconcerned.)

LU MENGSHI: *(Point-blank)* Was it you who threw out the bean paste?

LUO DATOU: No.

LU MENGSHI: You ought to be man enough to own up to whatever you've done. You'll look like a coward if I find out on my own.

LUO DATOU: *(Glaring scornfully)* So what if it was me; what are you going to do about it?

LU MENGSHI: There are two things about people that matter, as far as I'm concerned. At home they should obey and care for their parents; outside they should treat their associates with respect. I don't like you, Luo Datou!

LUO DATOU: Like it or not, I work for the Tang family; not you!

LU MENGSHI: I'm the second manager here.

LUO DATOU: And I was hired by Mr. Tang Deyuan, your boss's father. So where does that leave you?

LU MENGSHI: Mr. Tang Maochang is upstairs. Go on up and bellow at him.

LUO DATOU: Don't think I won't—

*(*TANG MAOCHANG *comes downstairs with* MAESTRO YU.*)*

TANG MAOCHANG: *Shifu,* we're just about to serve the duck. There's no need to rush off.

MAESTRO YU: Not tonight, I'm afraid. I have a martial arts scene to do.

TANG MAOCHANG: I'll have someone send the duck over to your theater in a pot to keep it warm.

LU MENGSHI: *(Coming forward to meet* YU*)* Maestro, leaving so soon?

MAESTRO YU: The food wasn't bad. *(Taking out a red money packet)* Divide this among your staff. And add two more dishes to the presidential palace party. Say it's from me.

LU MENGSHI: It's an honor to have you, sir, and very generous of you to leave such a gift. *(To the staff)* Thank Maestro Yu!
(Voices of waiters on- and offstage resound with the cry: "Thank you, Maestro Yu.")

MAESTRO YU: Maochang, later this evening sit near stage left, where the orchestra plays.

TANG MAOCHANG: *(Overwhelmed by this show of favor)* Sir.

MAESTRO YU: When you hear me singing "Last night I drank so much, still in my clothes I went to sleep," pay attention to the turn I put in after "sleep." I sing: "sleep"—

LUO DATOU: *(Thunderously)* Mr. Tang, sir.

(TANG MAOCHANG and MAESTRO YU are startled.)

TANG MAOCHANG: *(Angry)* What do you think you're doing? *Shifu*, he didn't startle you, did he?

LUO DATOU: Lu Mengshi wants to fire me!

TANG MAOCHANG: If he's fired you, then go.

LUO DATOU: You'd let me go, too?! I laid the bricks for that oven. Maybe you think you can get along without me, but you can't get along without those ducks!

TANG MAOCHANG: Get him out of here, will you! *Shifu*, you were just saying—

MAESTRO YU: *(With a laugh)* No wonder they call you Maestro Duck. You're busy here, so I'll go along. *(Exits)*

TANG MAOCHANG: *(Pursuing him)* Maestro Yu, *Shifu!*

LUO DATOU: *(Oblivious to the consequences)* Mr. Tang!

TANG MAOCHANG: *(Freeing himself from LUO)* You're all to blame for ruining my plans. From now on none of you—not you, or you, or you *(pointing to LU, WANG, LUO)*—will ever again in my presence mention the word "duck"! Fu Zi, let's go!

LU MENGSHI: *(Expectations borne out, smiles to himself)* Chang Gui, prepare to serve duck!

(Curtain)

ACT III

Time: eight years later (1928)

Place: main hall of the Fujude

> *(At this time the Fujude is at the height of its prosperity. The building is resplendent with carved rafters and painted columns, and gleaming old signs with their gold characters incised in a black background. Now cars and horse-drawn carriages, as well as the prestigious sedan chairs decorated in green wool, pull up to the front door, through which walk powerful officials and wealthy merchants. The Fujude is now a famous spot, celebrated throughout the capital.*
>
> *Today is the sixth day of the Chinese New Year, the day businesses reopen from the holidays. Waiters crowd around WANG ZIXI as he hangs up the traditional signs "Open for Business," where they belong above the main door. Then assistants begin cutting at the chopping boards with loud whacks, cooks bang away with their spoons and ladles, abacuses clicking and clacking appear on the*

counter, and the hundred-year-old duck oven spews sparks as if doused with fuel oil. This is "clamor boards," what merchants in the old days insisted on as the right way to ask for prosperity in the new year.

The waiters are shaven and clean, wearing new shoes and new caps, their faces cheerful, their arms hanging slightly in front of their bodies in an attitude of deference. They greet the first customers of the new year.)

WANG ZIXI: Fu Shun, look after the entrance. If somebody important shows up at the mouth of the lane give us an early warning shout.

FU SHUN: *(Now a mature young man)* Don't worry, Second Manager, sir. *(Exits)*

WANG ZIXI: After the fifth it's back to work just like always. The holiday was over in no time.

CHANG GUI: A grand reopening for us, but a big closing out across the street.

WANG ZIXI: The manager at the Quanyingde didn't have the look of a successful businessman. He'd get put out if his staff ate half a steamed bun too many.

CHANG GUI: Yes, the waiters over there are bad off. They ought to talk with Mr. Lu about a way to make ends meet.

WANG ZIXI: Mr. Lu already thought of that. Don't forget, his father was a waiter, too.

CHANG GUI: I haven't even dared ask for these past ten years or so whether the manager at the Yushenglou really did do such a rotten thing.

WANG ZIXI: It was all over losing a few ounces of gold. He used a big scale like that one *(pointing to a large scale some five feet in length hanging on the wall)* to weigh the cashiers each time they came in and each time they went out.

CHANG GUI: And that's how his father died, treated like that?

WANG ZIXI: That's why he'd grind his teeth and stamp the floor, trying to swallow his anger.

CHANG GUI: Now that we're opening today, why haven't I seen him around?

WANG ZIXI: He was pretty busy at the start of the new year. He forgot to send a present to the police.

CHANG GUI: Not the sort of ancestors you can afford to annoy.

WANG ZIXI: So he's gone out again to send them a present. Here's the accounts blackboard for today. Chalk up on this whatever we serve. This afternoon the owner of the Ruifuxiang Fabric Store and the commander of the Beiping Garrison have reserved tables. I have to get over to the Zhimeizhai Restaurant today to catch some shredded turnip cake fresh out of the oven.

(CHANG GUI *exits.* WANG *starts to exit.* TANG MAOCHANG *enters with* FU ZI, *obviously upset.*)

WANG ZIXI: (*Seeing* TANG*'s expression is angry, speaks cautiously*) It's a day for you to relax, sir. Weren't you going to the theater?

TANG MAOCHANG: Where's Mr. Lu?

WANG ZIXI: He's gone out.

TANG MAOCHANG: Yesterday I told Fu Zi to draw five hundred from the till. Why wouldn't he give it to him?

WANG ZIXI: According to what's written in the agreement on division of income, sixty percent goes to the owner and forty percent to the enterprise. Your portion is to be delivered without fail at the first of each month. Amounts in excess of this—

FU ZI: (*Like an aggressive dog relying for backup on its master's status*) Amounts in excess? The whole place belongs to him! His purchase of costumes and accoutrements is a business expense for image. It's not as if he were spending money on a whore!

WANG ZIXI: Say, don't sound off like that. Yuchu'r is pretty much a half-time manager here now.

TANG MAOCHANG: (*All the angrier*) You tell them this business belongs to the Tang family. Now open the safe.

WANG ZIXI: (*In a predicament*) Sir, I—

TANG MAOCHANG: Open it.

(*Left with no choice,* WANG ZIXI *opens the cash drawer, and* FU ZI *takes out some money.*)

TANG MAOCHANG: Lu Mengshi has been buying up land in his hometown these past few years. Did you know that?

WANG ZIXI: No, I didn't know at all.

TANG MAOCHANG: Zixi, you're the senior employee here. These past few years I haven't paid much attention to the business, and with my brother off in Tianjin, it's up to you to look after the till.

WANG ZIXI: (*Timidly*) Yes, sir. I—

(*There is a commotion outside, and* FU SHUN *enters.*)

FU SHUN: Chang *Shifu*'s son, Xiaowu'r, says we have to let him in to look for his father.

WANG ZIXI: We can't have poor scamps coming in here on opening days like today. That's taboo. Have his father go outside. (YUCHU'R *enters.*)

YUCHU'R: What're they arguing about at the front door? Oh, Mr. Tang, how are you, sir?

TANG MAOCHANG: *(Coldly nodding his head)* Fu Zi, let's go!

YUCHU'R: Don't be in a rush. Relax a while and have some tea.

FU ZI: We're afraid we might sprain our tongues. *(Follows* TANG *off)*

YUCHU'R: What's wrong with Mr. Tang?

WANG ZIXI: I'm puzzled myself. People are saying Mengshi's been buying real estate in his hometown. Did you know that?

YUCHU'R: Who've you been listening to?

WANG ZIXI: I didn't really believe it, either.

YUCHU'R: Mengshi's put in ten years of hard work, and he's saved up a little, it's true. But he spent a lot of effort to fix up this restaurant when it was on the verge of closing down, and he's turned it into the famous place it is today. It's really unfair if he gets the sort of reputation you say.

WANG ZIXI: True, true. Oh, my shredded radish pie! *(Exits)* *(Several men enter, dressed more or less the same—by appearance not proper customers.)*

CHANG GUI: Happy New Year, gentlemen! We have seats available for dining upstairs.

MAN A: *(Checking out the main hall and then* YUCHU'R*)* I've always heard you've got someone here named Chu'r who's the best hand at brothel dishes.

CHANG GUI: *(Responding)* Our chef's name is Li Xiaobian'r, the best at "the three nonsticks"—won't stick to chopsticks, won't stick to teeth, won't stick to—

MAN B: *(Interrupting him)* The gentleman's come especially for brothel fare. Do you have it or don't you? Spit it out and stop wasting your breath!

CHANG GUI: *(Discovering the men have guns concealed under their gowns, signals to* YUCHU'R *to leave)* Don't get excited, gentlemen. I'll—

MAN B: *(Pushing him aside)* Get lost!

YUCHU'R: Take it easy. I'm Yuchu'r.

MAN A: *(Moving close to her)* You have quite a reputation. It costs gold just to meet you back at the brothels. Why don't you offer us fellows something today.

YUCHU'R: *(Calmly)* Why not? Gentlemen, what do you like to eat?

MAN B: *(Stunned)* What can you cook?

YUCHU'R: I'm from the countryside near Suzhou, so I cook ordinary country-style dishes. I'll recite some for you: Pearls and Jade Duck, Fame and Fortune Fish, Successful Sons Longans and Lotus Seeds, Happily Wed a Hundred Years Artichoke, Green Jade in Blue Fields Taro, Good Deeds and Wealth Moss, Gems in Snow Beancurd, Pearls Recovered Meatballs, Sprouts and Catkins Garlic Cloves, and Gold and Jade Fill the Hall. I don't know whether you gentlemen have in mind a wedding party, a plum party, a family reunion, a birthday celebration, a *qiang* feast, or a graduation party?

(The men are nonplussed.)

MAN B: *(Pretending expertise)* Never mind what the occasion is, we want a little excitement. Let's have a "Gold and Jade Fill the Hall."

(The others join in this proposal.)

MAN A: *(Skeptically)* We've been around, you know, tried every big-name restaurant in town. What I'd like to hear is what is this "Gold and Jade Fill the Hall."

YUCHU'R: *(Poised and relaxed)* Take three ounces of used swallow's nest that's been through a frost, soak in natural spring water, select the dark strands using a silver needle, add tender chicken broth, top ham, and *yuzhu* mushrooms, and cook soft to the color of jade; take Luzon green shark fin, leave the oily coating on, together with shoulder of pork, chicken broth, fresh bamboo shoots, sugar lumps, and stew two days to a golden color; marinate with short-spined sea cucumber in boiled pork broth three times over; cook with chicken juice, pork juice, and shrimp juice to a date-red color; add a half ounce of "Xi Shi Tongue" mollusk, seven snakehead fish eggs, ten gingko fruits, together with shredded bamboo shoots, carp stomach, dried mushrooms, auriculate wood-ear fungus, and sliced pheasant; boil, add cornstarch, and cover with hot oil. Serve it in a clay bowl with a gold base, gold cover, and four-clawed golden-dragon design. Name: "Gold and Jade Fill the Hall."

MAN B: *(Involuntarily spewing a breath)* I'll be damned. How much is a bowl of that stuff?

YUCHU'R: Not much, really. Four ounces gold is enough.

MAN A: That's something you'd serve the emperor.

YUCHU'R: Actually, I doubt whether the emperor has had the good fortune you gentlemen now have. *(Shaking out a smart-looking apron, she starts to exit toward the kitchen.)*

MAN A: *(Realizing* YUCHU'R *is not to be taken lightly)* We're not in the mood for any gold or jade today. We just want to try some of your home-style cooking.

YUCHU'R: Fine. I'll put together a bowl of hot-and-sour shredded duck soup. It'll help you sober up. How about that? Chang Gui, show them to a table upstairs.

(The men go upstairs. YUCHU'R *pulls* CHANG GUI *over to her.)*

YUCHU'R: You take care of yourself. Those guys are up to no good. *(Exits)*

*(*LUO DATOU *enters, followed by* KE WU.*)*

LUO DATOU: What are you doing following me around all the time?

KE WU: Please, let me see the ducks; I'll settle for duck bones. *(Voraciously looks around in all directions)*

*(*FU SHUN *enters in pursuit.)*

FU SHUN: Out! Get out! Who let you in here?

KE WU: Hold on, you. For your information, I'm now officially with the Scent Detection Unit.

LUO DATOU: No wonder you're always hanging around restaurant entrances! *(Onlookers laugh.)*

KE WU: You are looking at a member of the Criminal Investigation Unit, and what I smell is opium!

LUO DATOU: Huh! For once what your father taught you turned out to be useful.

KE WU: Luo Datou! You are in possession of opium on your person!

LUO DATOU: True, but it's just two plugs of smoking opium I got for cooking a duck, from the garrison commander's family just now.

KE WU: That's still a violation. Let's see them!

LUO DATOU: The commander's household has a whole chestful of them. Go smell out theirs if you're so great at it.

KE WU: I can't get the scent when there's too much of it. (*Laughing*)
Okay, give me two ducks' necks in exchange.

LUO DATOU: This punk's been giving me a hard time on purpose.
Don't forget, you've still got a punch coming from Mr. Lu, and I
may just take it for him first! (*Picks up his roasting pole*) Hey,
what's this?

CHENG SHUN: (*Nervously enters, running*) I was—I was wiping it off
for you.

LUO DATOU: (*Feeling it with his hand*) Bullshit! The tip's still warm.

CHENG SHUN: (*Realizing he can't prevaricate*) The manager let me
try—

LUO DATOU: Is the manager your ancestor? Kneel down.

(*A neatly dressed young waiter enters, running, and waves his thumb
horizontally. This gesture signals everyone that a manager is coming
back in. Everyone immediately resumes his proper position, standing
at attention.*

*LU MENGSHI enters. Now middle-aged, he is dressed elegantly,
his face has filled out, and he looks dignified. XIU DINGXIN enters
following him. LU MENGSHI looks around the establishment and sits
in TANG DEYUAN's old high-backed chair. When LU MENGSHI extends
his hand, immediately a waiter places a small blue-and-white pat-
terned porcelain bowl in it.*)

LU MENGSHI: (*Taking a sip*) Fire's not strong enough.

XIU DINGXIN: The fire isn't hot enough for the duck soup. Tell the
second oven chef to add some kindling and build up the fire.

LU MENGSHI: (*Drinking, not looking up*) Who let him in?

(*XIU DINGXIN silently signals KE WU with his eyes to leave.*)

KE WU: (*On the contrary, moves closer to LU*) Mr. Lu, I can go into
the household of the imperial prince if I want, let alone your
place here. I roam the lanes at will. And what I smelled in your
rear courtyard was opium!

LU MENGSHI: Get out!

KE WU: Give me a duck and the matter will be settled. Otherwise—

FU SHUN: Go!

XIU DINGXIN: (*Quietly*) Mr. Ke, be a gentleman and go.

KE WU: Here you eat to your heart's content all day long, and you
can say that to me. You're a man without a conscience, Xiu old
boy. Lu Mengshi, just you wait! (*Exits, dragged out by
employees*)

LU MENGSHI: *(Somberly)* Who went to the theater on the fourth day of New Year?

YOUNG WAITER: I did, sir.

LU MENGSHI: And what did you watch?

YOUNG WAITER: *(Mumbling)* The . . . the opera.

LU MENGSHI: Where's your ticket?

YOUNG WAITER: *(Fearfully)* I threw it away.

LU MENGSHI: Nonsense! The performance on the fourth was a lewd show. Now, smut lover, what is written in the house rules? Recite it!

YOUNG WAITER: Rule, rule nine: "Employees may not attend lewd performances or flower-drum songs, and may not—"

LU MENGSHI: Why is it people look down on our profession? We cannot permit base behavior among our own! You look well fed to me. Your family's well off. Get out!

YOUNG WAITER: *(Panicking)* Please don't fire me. I won't do it again, sir. *(He looks for support from the onlookers, but no one dares to speak.)*

LU MENGSHI: Someone has reported to the owners that I've been buying real estate in my hometown. True, I have. Can't people who work in restaurants invest in real estate? Are we just supposed to spend our money on eating and drinking, whoring and dope, and be degenerates? I have a mind to buy up all of Tianjin, and then I'll buy the Qianmen Arch! Cheng Shun!

CHENG SHUN: Sir.

LU MENGSHI: When is your wedding day?

CHENG SHUN: Second day of the second month.

LU MENGSHI: When the dragon raises its head! A perfect day![15] *(Taking a red packet from* XIU's *hand)* A contribution from the till for a silk scroll congratulating you on the occasion of your wedding.

CHENG SHUN: Thank you, sir!

LU MENGSHI: Let's make the decorations bright, let's have horses and sedan chairs, bands and all—whatever it takes to make this an occasion, let's have it. Let's show anyone out there who still won't recognize it that the people who work at the Fujude are also worthy of respect! All right, dismissed!

LUO DATOU: *(His pent-up anger to the point of exploding)* Hold on! Cheng Shun used my roasting pole.

LU MENGSHI: *(Calmly)* What of it?

LUO DATOU: It's violating the rules of the house! Apprentices don't replace oven chefs before they're seventy. Even the emperor has recognized that rule.

LU MENGSHI: *(Laughs)* The emperor's sitting in exile in a Japanese concession. And that rule should have been changed long ago.

LUO DATOU: Don't forget how you wound up asking me to come back to work here the last time. If I put down this pole, you're out of business.

WANG ZIXI: *(Mediating)* There's no need for this. Who doesn't know that when people think of the Fujude they think of Luo Datou and his roasting pole, right?

LUO DATOU: *(Deliberately baiting)* I'm not cooking today. You all can go find somebody better! *(Starts to exit, with a sweep of his hand)*

WANG ZIXI: Hey, there're still customers upstairs.

LU MENGSHI: If you leave, you're not coming back again.

LUO DATOU: *(Exploding)* Lu Mengshi! Don't put on airs around me, acting so self-important, as if I didn't know your little secret!

CHANG GUI: *(Hastily intervening)* Big Luo!

WANG ZIXI: What are you doing? Stop it!

LUO DATOU: *(Brushing off CHANG GUI)* How was it your papa died? Hooked to a scale, with his legs tucked up, so he could be weighed like a piece of meat—that's how he died, bullied to death. Don't think I don't know—

LU MENGSHI: *(His face turned white, he suddenly starts laughing, the sound of misery touched with defiance, sending shivers through the onlookers.)* You—get out of my sight.

LUO DATOU: Don't act so high-and-mighty with me. You and your superior ways—there hasn't been a manager in your family for generations, and you come in here like god almighty.

LU MENGSHI: *(At the top of his voice)* Get out!

(Onlookers start to intervene.)

LU MENGSHI: Anyone who wants to take his side in this can go with him!

(LUO DATOU exits, cursing.)

LU MENGSHI: Cheng Shun, pick up your pole. You'll cook for today's customers. I'm promoting you to first oven chef. That's all!

(Employees exit.)

WANG ZIXI: *(Worried)* This afternoon Mr. Meng the fourth of the Ruifuxiang Fabric Store has a reservation. He's a key customer.

LU MENGSHI: Who's waiting on him?

FU SHUN: I am.

CHANG GUI: I'll take care of it, sir.

(From upstairs MAN A *shouts: "Waiter, where's Yuchu'r's soup?"* MAN B: *"Need her to feed you more?" Laughs lewdly.)*

LU MENGSHI: *(Brows knit)* Who're they? Why are they talking about Yuchu'r?

WANG ZIXI: I don't know. Did you get the present to the police?

LU MENGSHI: They wouldn't take it. Looks like they want to hit us up for more.

XIU DINGXIN: Here's the deed and the account books for the Quanyingde Restaurant. Put your chop here and ownership is transferred.

LU MENGSHI: *(Sensing something isn't right)* Let me look them over this evening. Any of the employees at the Quanyingde who want to stay on can stay. On no account should they be left with no place to go. Also . . . *(He feels faint.)*

WANG ZIXI: *(Supporting him)* What is it? Go on back and lie down. *(*TANG MAOSHENG *enters.)*

TANG MAOSHENG: Say, the storm lanterns out front have all been changed to electric bulbs!

LU MENGSHI: *(Forcing himself to attend to* TANG*)* Mr. Tang Maosheng's here. Steep some tea. Business booming at the Fujude in Tianjin?

TANG MAOSHENG: Boom nothing!

LU MENGSHI: It's a great location. The Industrial Exposition's in front, the Xinming Theater's across the street. It's a busy place.

TANG MAOSHENG: The location doesn't make any difference; the staff is no good.

LU MENGSHI: You have that new Ernainai. Tianjin folks are tough customers, but even the gangsters there don't take her lightly. She doesn't fear anyone but you.

TANG MAOSHENG: *(Laughing)* Where'd you hear all that?

LU MENGSHI: I've got connections.

TANG MAOSHENG: Those girls aren't pushovers.

LU MENGSHI: Stay awhile and have something to eat. I'll tell Yuchu'r to cook you something.

TANG MAOSHENG: I came today to talk about a loan.

LU MENGSHI: Listen to you. This whole place is your family's.

TANG MAOSHENG: We want to spend some to redo the facade of the branch in Tianjin.

LU MENGSHI: Spend how much?

TANG MAOSHENG: However much my brother spent building that house of his at Fajia Gardens, that's how much.

LU MENGSHI: *(Realizing his ill intent)* Very well. After the Duanyang Festival I'll send it to you in Tianjin.

TANG MAOSHENG: Say, you're holding out on me.

LU MENGSHI: Look, the gold on that partition needs to be refinished, the storeroom needs a new roof—

TANG MAOSHENG: The Fujude takes in a hundred in gold every day. Why give me this old story?

LU MENGSHI: There are plenty of expenses that go with that income. Mr. Xiu, bring out the books.

TANG MAOSHENG: *(Ignoring them)* It's decided, so just do it. And there's one more thing. I want to borrow someone.

LU MENGSHI: Who?

TANG MAOSHENG: The branch needs a decent headwaiter. I want Chang Gui.

LU MENGSHI: I can't do that. A restaurant stands or falls on three things: its waiters, its cashier-accountants, and its cooks. Take one away and you might as well pull down one of these pillars, right? I'll find someone else for you. *(Signals to* WANG ZIXI *to support him)*

WANG ZIXI: *(Unwilling to make an issue of it)* If Mr. Tang wants him, then—

LU MENGSHI: It won't work. We have long-standing customers here who'll leave us if Chang Gui goes.

(CHANG GUI comes downstairs.)

TANG MAOSHENG: Chang Gui, you're coming with me to the branch in Tianjin.

CHANG GUI: Me? Well, I—*(looks at* LU MENGSHI, *who is so angry he can't speak)*—I'm needed at home a lot.

TANG MAOSHENG: Afraid your wife will run out on you? I've bought your ticket for the evening train already. *(To* LU*)* Remember, I want that check right away. I'm going now to see my brother. I'll

have dinner here this evening, take the money then, and Chang
Gui will go with me. (*Exits*)

CHANG GUI: (*Looks longingly at* LU) Well, then, sir . . . I'm off.

(LU MENGSHI *is unable either to swear or to weep. He smashes his
fist on the counter.*

   *Several men, who've eaten and drunk their fill, come down-
stairs.*)

MAN A: Of everything we ate, it was that last bowl of soup that was
delicious.

MAN B: Why don't you say who made it?

MAN A: (*To* LU) Manager, you really have an eye for business. Got
yourself a money tree planted right in your back courtyard. Hey,
what're you staring at me like that for? Jealous? Ha-ha . . .

CHANG GUI: (*Supporting the inebriated* MAN A) This way, sir.

MAN A: Are we leaving? I've got to come back tomorrow for a return
engagement. See you tomorrow, Yuchu'r. (*The men exit.*)

LU MENGSHI: (*Venting his suppressed resentment and anger on*
YUCHU'R) You come down here. Come down, you slut. (*He starts
to strike* YUCHU'R, *when he suddenly staggers from a fierce headache and collapses onto her.*)

WANG ZIXI: Help him into the rear so he can rest. I'll take care of
things here.

(YUCHU'R *supports* LU *and they exit.*)

WANG ZIXI: *Ai,* you never know where interference will come from.
You can plan everything all out perfectly, and still it will all fall
apart.

XIU DINGXIN: It's too much pressure to take. The place can't survive
with one man doing all the work while eight others tear it down.

WANG ZIXI: My head aches, too. I'm going out for a walk. (*Exits*)

CHENG SHUN: Mr. Xiu, it's done!

(CHENG SHUN *enters. On his roasting pole is a small chicken roasted
to a golden orange.*)

CHENG SHUN: Just smell that fragrance.

XIU DINGXIN: I've eaten roast duck all my life, but I've never had
roast chicken.

CHENG SHUN: This was something Luo Datou was a genius at. And
the managers never found out about it.

(XIU DINGXIN *reaches out to take the chicken.*)

CHENG SHUN: *(Pulling back quickly)* The last time you had me do a roast for you, the manager saw it and fined me half a day's wages.

XIU DINGXIN: *(Impatiently producing a dollar)* Take it. *(Holds the chicken under his nose to sniff its odor, half singing, with feeling)*
"Wok-wok" went your song in previous days;
Now that you're gone there's no place for your grave.
Oh, take for your coffin this stomach of mine,
And while I am mourning I'll have, please, some wine—*(Carried away by sadness)*
(LI XIAOBIAN'R enters quietly and imitates the sound of LU MENG-SHI's cough. Startled, XIU DINGXIN hides the chicken beneath his gown.)

LI XIAOBIAN'R: So, when the cat's away the mice will play.

CHENG SHUN: I don't know what's wrong with Mr. Xiu today.

XIU DINGXIN: Come, come, gentlemen. Here's our wine, and here's our food. Now I, Xiu Dingxin, will discourse with you on dining. The *Book of Changes* refers to cauldron cooking and the *Book of Documents* refers to salt and plum. This means that in our most esteemed, ancient classics, cooking was written about, and the blending of flavors was discussed, such as the mixing of sour plum and salt. My family has produced three generations of officials, but do you know whom I most admire?
(LI XIAOBIAN'R and CHENG SHUN shake their heads in bafflement.)

XIU DINGXIN: Cooks. *(Bows to LI and CHENG)*

LI XIAOBIAN'R: Don't amuse yourself at our expense.

XIU DINGXIN: I mean it! Even my name has something to do with cooks.
(LI XIAOBIAN'R laughs doubtfully.)

XIU DINGXIN: *(Earnestly)* Xiu Dingxin. The character "Ding" is the name of a utensil used for cooking, the cauldron. Think of it: it is the symbol of established power, the emblem of empire. And those who remove the old and establish the new, those who renovate, are illustrious cooks, the instruments of renewal.
(CHENG SHUN shakes his head, at a loss.)

XIU DINGXIN: That spatula in your hand is itself the cauldron. Before you are arrayed the ingredients: the sour, the sweet, the bitter, the pungent. You blend them into flavors that never existed before. Yours is the grace of genesis, the miracle of harmony, the accomplishment of renovation.

LI XIAOBIAN'R: That's idealizing us.

XIU DINGXIN: No-no. Prime ministers used to be called "the caul-dron's support." In other words, the cook who holds the spatula.

CHENG SHUN: He's had a lot to drink.

XIU DINGXIN: *(Taking another drink)* Whether a place is as big as a country or as small as a room, somebody has to be in charge. The ancients had a poem with the line "In the gold cauldron he blends beautifully the sour plum with salt,"[16] which likens the way a prime minister manages the court to cooking food with a spatula.

CHENG SHUN: *(Looking strangely at* XIU*)* He hasn't had that much to drink.

LI XIAOBIAN'R: Get him some soup to clear his head, quick. No matter what, we can't let Mr. Lu find out.

XIU DINGXIN: Managers wield spatulas, too. You and I, we're his ingredients. You're the salty one, I'm the bitter, and Luo Datou's the pungent. The Fujude's his spatula. I'm watching what kind of dish he can come up with. Not much . . .

LI XIAOBIAN'R: Quick, take him to the well out back and rinse his mouth. Wipe his face with cold water.

XIU DINGXIN: I'm not drunk— *(Exits, dragged off by* CHENG SHUN*)* *(*LI XIAOBIAN'R *is about to exit, when he suddenly hears the sound of sighing.* CHANG GUI *enters, his expression desolate.)*

LI XIAOBIAN'R: Chang Gui? *(Recalls* CHANG GUI *is about to leave the Fujude)* After all these decades, they say go, and off you go. It must be hard.

CHANG GUI: *(Shaking his head)* A place as hard to bear as this, I won't miss it. What I can't bear is having my boy, Xiaowu'r, despise his father.

LI XIAOBIAN'R: What's the matter?

CHANG GUI: All along I've scolded him: don't argue, don't fight, don't look for revenge. Even if you're crying inside, keep a smile on your face. Everything I've done has been for my family. . . .

LI XIAOBIAN'R: Chang, buddy, what's this all about?

CHANG GUI: My boy, Xiaowu'r, has his mind set on apprenticing at the Ruifuxiang Fabric Store.

LI XIAOBIAN'R: That's fine. Like they say, "The best in life is Suzhou and Hangzhou; the best in death is Ruifuxiang."

CHANG GUI: But—

(FU SHUN's *voice is heard greeting a customer:* "Good evening, Mr. Meng!" *This call is like a signal. Fujude employees enter, pouring onto the stage from all directions, each standing at his place.* XIU DINGXIN *enters to greet* MR. MENG.)

MR. MENG: Do you have our reservation?

CHANG GUI: (*Wiping away his tears and moving forward with total alertness*) Room six upstairs. See, over the door is carved "The Six Little Boys Worship Buddha." Today is the sixth day of the New Year. Lucky double sixes everywhere. Everything's going your way! Gentlemen, please!
(CHANG GUI *leads the gentlemen upstairs, shows them into a room, and steps out, standing sideways at the doorway.*)

CHANG GUI: Gentlemen, for your dinner this evening, I will sing today's menu for you: Duck hearts in soy sauce, webs in mustard, duck stomach, marinated duck gizzard, dry-fried duck intestines, fried duck tongue, braised duck kidneys, ground duck dumplings. This evening's duck is served ten ways, utilizing the duck's tongue, heart, liver, intestines, pancreas, breast, and webs, in the style of "Complete Duck Banquet." Gentlemen, what is your pleasure?

MR. MENG: Sounds delicious. We'll trust your judgment to choose for us.

CHANG GUI: Very good. I will be back. (*Going downstairs, he avoids the steps altogether, sliding down the side, until his leg gives at the level of the last step and he falters. Just at that moment,* WANG ZIXI *enters and catches him.*)

WANG ZIXI: (*Supporting him*) Chang Gui, what made you go limp?

CHANG GUI: (*Smiling*) It's nothing. (*Exits*)

WANG ZIXI: Fu Shun, why was Chang Gui's son Xiaowu'r looking for him this morning?

FU SHUN: (*Moving close to* WANG *and speaking softly*) The kid wants to apprentice at Ruifuxiang, but they wouldn't take him.

WANG ZIXI: Why not?

FU SHUN: Because his father's a waiter.

WANG ZIXI: But Chang Gui's not some ordinary waiter. Everyone knows who Chang Gui is, from the president on down to the man on the street.

CHANG GUI: (*Enters, carrying four appetizers*) I'm coming— (*Turns toward the kitchen*) Stretch the bean-starch noodles thin, cut them narrow, give them one slice across, and add lots of *huajiao* sauce. *(Goes upstairs)*

XIU DINGXIN: *(Observing* CHANG GUI, *wistfully)* Chang Gui is the bittersweet.

WANG ZIXI: What did you say?

*(*TANG MAOCHANG *enters, followed by* LUO DATOU.*)*

LUO DATOU: *(Talking nonstop)* Here I was, the roasting chef for your father, and when he got to be second manager, he had no respect for me. No respect for me, that means he had none for you, sir, or your father—

TANG MAOCHANG: *(Interrupting)* All right, you just leave this matter to me to handle.

LUO DATOU: You stay away from the accounting, so you don't know what's going on with the accounting. Where's he get all that money to buy houses and land? He still has a mind to buy Tianjin and the Qianmen Arch!

TANG MAOCHANG: You go on back now. *(*LUO *exits.)* Did Mr. Meng arrive?

WANG ZIXI: *(With solicitude)* They're upstairs now, sir, in room six.

*(*TANG *starts to go upstairs, when* CHANG GUI *gently holds him back.)*

CHANG GUI: Sir, I'll be leaving the Fujude today. It's been most of my life.

TANG MAOCHANG: Where are you going?

CHANG GUI: Your brother wants me to go to his branch in Tianjin.

TANG MAOCHANG: *(Unconcerned with these matters)* Off you go, then. Wherever, it's still the Fujude.

CHANG GUI: *(Circumspectly)* Sir, in the decades I've worked here, I've never asked you for anything, but today I must ask you a favor, sir.

TANG MAOCHANG: Then ask, ask away.

CHANG GUI: I have only one son, named Xiaowu'r. He wants to apprentice at the Ruifuxiang Fabric Store, and I was wondering if I could trouble you, sir, to put in a word for him with Mr. Meng.

TANG MAOCHANG: Just that? Very well. *(Goes upstairs)*

CHANG GUI: Thank you, sir. *(As though rejuvenated)* Fu Shun, clear off the meat dishes, pass out hand towels, and prepare to serve the hot dishes. *(As though he's remembered something, steps briskly to the door of room six)* Gentlemen, while you're enjoying your food and drink, I'll offer you a pleasant song to go with your wine.

*(*WANG ZIXI *looks up at* CHANG GUI *in surprise.)*

CHANG GUI: (Red-faced, his voice quivering slightly, he clears his throat)

We dress for success and dine on emoluments;
The capital has all the very best restaurants.
The Fujude there outshines any pearl,
Its roast duck famous throughout all the world.
With skin so crispy it's crunchy to eat,
No grease mars its plumpness, nor bones its lean meat.
Not ducks by the thousand could ever fulfill
Our craving for duck, ever more yet more still.
Thirty yuan buys a "Duck Banquet Complete."
When it goes down the hatch, you'll know such a rare treat
That nothing, not even a new house, can compete.
The sight of our rooms is such a sensation,
You'll think you've gone to Suzhou on vacation.
And now here's our wine, more sweet than sweet dew,
Here's to more sons, more wealth, and long life;
Drink to good fortune, may it all come to you.
(From the dining room comes the sound of applause and cheers, and a cup of wine is passed out the door to CHANG GUI.)

CHANG GUI: (Respectfully receiving the wine) Thank you, Mr. Meng, sir! I usually don't drink, but since this is coming from you, sir, I shall enjoy it. (Drains the cup in one swallow. The strong drink makes his face flush even more. He pulls himself together.) The first round of drinks is done; put the ducks into the oven. (Exits)

WANG ZIXI: He sang that song once, the year his son was born. Today was an exception.

FU SHUN: With the manager of the Ruifuxiang Fabric Store sitting inside, it ought to be pretty obvious why.

(TANG MAOCHANG and MR. MENG emerge from the dining room.)

TANG MAOCHANG: The ticket's for tomorrow evening at the Changle Theater; you have to come.

MR. MENG: I'll be there for certain, and I'll bring along some reporters from the Daily Times and tell them to write you up well.

TANG MAOCHANG: That would be great. Go on back in and enjoy yourself. Don't bother about me; I'll be off.

CHANG GUI: (Carrying a food platter, quietly reminding) Sir—

TANG MAOCHANG: (Remembering) Oh, yes, Mr. Meng, our headwaiter has a son who'd like to apprentice at your establishment, and we're hoping you'll put in a word for him.

MR. MENG: I don't want to cause you to lose any face, but I'm afraid I can't do that.

TANG MAOCHANG: But Chang Gui is someone you know.

MR. MENG: It's not a question of whether I know him; it's a rule of the house: sons and younger brothers of restaurant employees may not be employed as clerks at the Ruifuxiang.

TANG MAOCHANG: Why's that?

MR. MENG: On the spring equinox, the Dragon Boat Festival, the Mid-Autumn Festival and New Year's Eve, the management is supposed to put up a big awning and treat the employees to a banquet. Now, these banquets are always catered by one of the big restaurants, and the food is served by restaurant waiters. If one of our clerks had a father who was one of those waiters, how could he let himself be part of the banquet and be served by his father?

TANG MAOCHANG: That makes sense. Well, please do rejoin your guests. See you tomorrow.

(CHANG GUI *is so dismayed he sways for a moment.*)

WANG ZIXI: Watch yourself, food coming through!

(TANG MAOSHENG *enters.*)

TANG MAOCHANG: Maosheng, I was just going to look you up. (*He leads* MAOSHENG *off to one side.*)

(*Voices are heard from outside, including the sound of foreign languages and a dog's bark.* FU SHUN *enters in a state of anxiety.*)

FU SHUN: Mr. Wang, there are foreigners here!

WANG ZIXI: You've seen them before. What are you so upset about?

FU SHUN: They all look the same. How do I collect the bill from them?

WANG ZIXI: Let them in the front way. Show them out the back. Collect a dollar from each before they go. . . .

FU SHUN: But I don't speak their language.

WANG ZIXI: Get Chang Gui.

(*A group of foreigners pours in, calling, "Duck!"*)

CHANG GUI: (*Going to greet them*) Hello, please, up! Don't take the dog.

FOREIGNER: Why not?

CHANG GUI: It's a rule of the house. We have house rules here.

FOREIGNER: (*Looking scornfully at* CHANG GUI) So why is it Chinese dogs got in?

CHANG GUI: They haven't. The Fujude has always treated Chinese and foreigners alike.

FOREIGNER: But here you are, a Chinese dog, running around following people. (*Imitating* CHANG GUI *as he speaks, while the other foreigners burst out laughing*)

CHANG GUI: (*Suppressed feelings of humiliation suddenly breaking out*) I am a waiter, so I serve people. But I am a human, and you can't look down on a human!

FOREIGNER: (*Laughing*) Human dog! (*He strikes* CHANG GUI's *face.*)

(*The foreigners surge upstairs.* CHANG GUI *stands stiffly erect.*)

WANG ZIXI: Mr. Chang, are you okay?

CHANG GUI: I . . . I deserved it. I deserve to be despised, a stinking waiter . . .

WANG ZIXI: Fu Shun, you go look after them.

CHANG GUI: (*Forcefully pushing* FU SHUN *aside*) We'll see if they still want to use their fists!

(*Stomps up the stairs*)

TANG MAOSHENG: He wants to run the Fujude? No way. Get rid of him, and we'll take back the business.

TANG MAOCHANG: I want to take it back, but that means we'll have to find an excuse to get rid of him.

(CHANG GUI *comes back downstairs.*)

CHANG GUI: (*Face bloodless, voice strained*) Two ducks for upstairs, thirty pancakes, two *jin* of rice wine, top grade, and— (*Suddenly one hand reaches forward and he collapses on a table.*)

XIU DINGXIN: Mr. Chang, Chang Gui! Hurry, get the manager!

(LU MENGSHI *enters hastily and everyone stands in a commotion around* CHANG GUI.)

LU MENGSHI: It's a stroke. It's bad.

XIU DINGXIN: He was holding out five fingers. What did that mean?

WANG ZIXI: He wanted to say something, that's for certain. Hurry, call out! Call to him![17]

(*Onlookers call out, but because of customers, they don't dare call loudly.*)

CHANG GUI: (*Speaking with difficulty, breathing weakly*) Five, five ounces of *baijiu* liquor—(*Once he's spoken his head droops weakly onto the table.*)

FU SHUN: Chang—

LU MENGSHI: *(Covering* FU SHUN's *mouth)* Don't cry. Zixi, get a rickshaw to take him to the hospital.

TANG MAOSHENG: Forget Chang Gui; I'll take Fu Shun instead.

LU MENGSHI: Saving Chang Gui is what matters right now!
(People exit, carrying CHANG GUI *off.)*

TANG MAOCHANG: Mr. Lu, what do you plan to do for Chang Gui?

LU MENGSHI: Help him get well, or if he dies, give him a decent burial.

TANG MAOSHENG: Your concern for the employees is admirable, but the money you use is ours.

LU MENGSHI: As a manager I don't make decisions for them at their expense.

TANG MAOSHENG: Have you made some at ours?

LU MENGSHI: *(Archly)* What do you mean by that?

TANG MAOSHENG: The Fujude takes in a hundred in gold every day. Where does it all go? Don't think we don't know!

TANG MAOCHANG: Our father on his deathbed entrusted running the business to you, not us, and for that you should respect his wishes and his trust in you.

LU MENGSHI: I know that I have tried to do just that.

TANG MAOSHENG: Tell me, then, is it true you've said that this is your business and that all decisions here will be made by you?

LU MENGSHI: *(Calmly)* It is.

TANG MAOCHANG: And that we're not to be consulted about the money, the accounts, or the management. Did you say that?

LU MENGSHI: I did.

TANG MAOSHENG: So, you've never intended to consult us and you've run this place entirely according to your own decisions. Is that what you've done?

LU MENGSHI: That's exactly what I've done.

TANG MAOSHENG: Just what have you had in mind?

LU MENGSHI: I could see that you and your brother were not business-men, and I was afraid you'd get in the way of the enterprise left to you by your family.

TANG MAOSHENG: How dedicated of you. Whether or not we were in the way, what made you go to such great pains?

LU MENGSHI: I wanted to. It was I who saw to renovating this build-ing, I who gave it the reputation it has, I who set down house

rules. These people were all trained by me personally. Everything in here down to every abacus bead and every blade of grass
I brought in here. I wouldn't ruin it all!

TANG MAOCHANG: Mr. Lu, no matter what you say, don't forget that
this business bears the name Tang! Under no circumstances have
we stopped being managers also! And we're taking control of the
business back as of now.

(KE WU *enters at the head of a gang of men who surge into the restaurant aggressively. Among these are the men who ate dinner earlier
this afternoon.*)

KE WU: I'm back.

LU MENGSHI: What's all this?

KE WU: The Bureau of Investigation! People are hiding opium here.

LU MENGSHI: Ke Wu, you need evidence before you say something
like that.

KE WU: (*Tapping his nose*) Here it is.

BUREAU CHIEF: (*Waving his arms*) Search the place!

(*The men of the Bureau of Investigation trash the restaurant.* KE WU
and others drag on LUO DATOU.)

KE WU: (*Holding a bag of opium*) Look here, hidden in the wine jars.

LU MENGSHI: (*So furious he can hardly speak*) You—you don't care
about anything except your stomach!

LUO DATOU: It wasn't even three ounces! Ke Wu's doing this
deliberately!

BUREAU CHIEF: Huh, you ninth-rate scum. Tie him up and parade
him in the streets.

(KE WU *and others tie up* LUO's *hands and feet.*)

MAN: Hey, we'll borrow these scales of yours for a while.

LU MENGSHI: (*Dazed, as if seeing all over again the scene of his
father's humiliation, staggers backward*) Wait, wait! Luo Datou is
an oven chef, not a drug dealer. I'll testify. The Fujude will stand
guarantor!

BUREAU CHIEF: (*Looking scornfully*) Who'll guarantee you?

(*The employees look toward the* TANG BROTHERS, *but they remain
silent. Pause.*)

BUREAU CHIEF: Who's the manager?

TANG BROTHERS: (*Pointing to* LU) He is—

BUREAU CHIEF: Mr. Manager, shall we go down to the station for a
chat?

LUO DATOU: (*Loudly*) I've been fired from the Fujude. This doesn't have anything to do with them!

LU MENGSHI: (*Untying* LUO) I didn't fire you, Big Luo. Go on now and cook your ducks. Be a good man.

(LUO DATOU *is stunned.*)

YUCHU'R: (*Enters, running; throws herself on* LU) Mengshi!

LU MENGSHI: (*Smiles and pats* YUCHU'R's *shoulder*) I treated you badly today. (*Looking up at the building he has erected*) We got as far as building this place like a sedan chair; I just never got to ride it. (*Taking off the sedan-chair-shaped jade from his belt, he lightly tosses it outside and exits with dignity, walking off together with the police.*)

LUO DATOU: (*Voice choked with tears*) Mr. Lu . . . I've been so unfair to you!

KE WU: (*Leaping onto the armchair*) From today on, I'll be your regular guest once again. Chang Gui, service! I'll have one here and take one to go, and I'll want the bones to take home, too! (*Curtain.*)

EPILOGUE

(*The main hall of the Fujude.* TANG MAOCHANG *sits in the armchair.*)

TANG MAOCHANG: Lu Mengshi is gone, and we've taken back the business. From now on, my brother and I are the managers, and Zixi will continue as assistant manager. Zixi?

(WANG ZIXI *enters quickly, carrying a package.*)

WANG ZIXI: (*Knowing he is late, changing to suit the times*) Shredded turnip cakes just out of the oven. I went a bit early to buy some for you.

TANG MAOCHANG: For some years now Lu Mengshi has had his way at our expense. . . .

(FU ZI *enters.*)

FU ZI: Sir, I've brought the orchestra. They still haven't played the "Epilogue" right.

TANG MAOCHANG: Have them rehearse out back. (*Continuing*) As I was saying, we've been—

(*The policeman from Act I enters.*)

POLICEMAN: (*Calling as he enters*) Hang out the flag! Hang out the flag!

WANG ZIXI: Now what flag is it?

POLICEMAN: Managers come and go. Flags come and go. Let's pay up.

WANG ZIXI: *(Taking a flag and examining it)* Tell me, is there anything you guys stick with?

POLICEMAN: Hey, we're just like you. Never mind who's manager, you still have to cook duck. Never mind whether it's an emperor, or a president, or a rebel Taiping, or a generalissimo, they all have to eat duck. They say you can change mountains and rivers a lot easier than human nature. Wrap me up the usual to go. *(Takes his duck and exits, calling, "Hang out the flag")*
(YUCHU'R enters.)

YUCHU'R: *(As though others weren't present)* Fu Shun, the bags are on the carriage. See they don't fall off.

TANG MAOSHENG: Yuchu'r, why didn't Lu Mengshi take you with him when he went home?

YUCHU'R: *(Tranquilly)* He has a wife there. *(Toward the street outside)* Bring them in!
(Several porters carry on a vertical scroll couplet painted in gold on two wooden plaques.)

YUCHU'R: Mengshi said he's done everything he set out to do in this life, except this set of couplet plaques for the entrance. Just before he left, he had them finished. Would you mind putting them up now, please?

TANG MAOCHANG: *(Reading)* "Such a precarious building—who is the owner, who are the customers? Just a few old rooms—sometimes fit the moonlight, sometimes fit the wind."
(The porters hang up the couplet.)

XIU DINGXIN: *(Studying the meaning)* "Such a precarious building— who is the owner, who are the customers? Just a few old rooms— sometimes fit the moonlight, sometimes fit the wind. . . ." They still need a horizontal epigram to balance them out: "There's never been a banquet in this world that didn't come to an end."
(TANG MAOCHANG, sensing there's something wrong with this, is on the verge of saying something.

The "Epilogue" music from the opera, which the orchestra is rehearsing in the rear, is heard. This is a familiar tune for concluding Peking operas, and once it begins, the curtain begins to close.

The curtain falls slowly, covering everything onstage except for the couplet.)

NOTES

The English translation is based on the Chinese text *Tianxia diyilou* (The world's top restaurant), first published in *Shiyue* (October) 3 (1988): 47–75.

1. For the curious, the names of these restaurants are genuine. The Dongxinglou (Eastern prosperity house), the Zhengyanglou (Facing the sun house), and the model for the fictional Fujude, the Quanjude (Accumulated virtue), among others, receive brief notes in L. C. Arlington and William Lewishohn, *In Search of Old Beijing* (Beijing: Henri Vetch, 1935), 269–270. The Shaobingwang (Wang's pancakes), and the Tiantaiguan (House of celestial harmony), preparing humbler fare, were less celebrated. Various other details in this introductory passage, as well as many throughout the play, are taken from Xing Botao, *Quanjude shi hua* (Historical anecdotes of the Quanjude Restaurant) (Beijing: Zhongguo shangye chubanshe, 1983).

2. In June 1917 General Zhang Xun, although commissioned as an officer in the young Republic of China, seized Beijing in the name of restoring Emperor Puyi, last ruler of the Qing dynasty, overthrown by the Republic.

3. Li Yuanhong assumed the presidency of the Republic of China in June 1916. A year later he requested General Zhang Xun to enter the capital with his troops to support him in a dispute with other leaders of the Republic. Zhang Xun, however, promptly reinstated the erstwhile Qing dynasty emperor. Li Yuanhong survived this coup, which lasted only a month, only to be driven from office by rival Republican leaders after they defeated Zhang Xun's restoration.

4. The Revolutionary Party, or Nationalist Party, which established the Republic of China in 1912, rebelled in 1916 when General Yuan Shikai, who had assumed the presidency of the Republic, declared his intention to be emperor of a constitutional monarchy.

5. The Guanghe Theater, or "Tower of Extensive Harmony," was said to be the oldest theater in Beijing at that time, dating back to the Qianlong era in the eighteenth century, located in the Meat Market neighborhood. See Arlington and Lewishohn, *In Search of Old Beijing*, 274.

6. "Clouds covering the moon" was the phrase used to describe the voice of Tan Xinpei (1847–1917), the most famous Peking Opera performer of the era.

7. The percentages mentioned in this scene refer to the method of paying ranking employees a share of the profits after the percentage due the ownership was subtracted. Lower-ranking employees received a cash amount. The scene follows the description of how employees were paid in the Quanjude Restaurant, prior to 1949, in Xing Botao, *Quanjude shi hua*, 105.

8. Pounding the back is intended to facilitate breathing. Pinching the philtrum, or dimple of the upper lip, is used to prevent loss of consciousness or to restore it.

9. After General Zhang Xun staged a restoration of the Qing dynasty emperor in

1917, his soldiers fled the city when confronted by superior forces representing the Republic. The hair of Zhang's soldiers remained braided in conformity to Qing custom and in defiance of Republican reforms, which viewed the queue as a sign of Han ethnic submission to the Manchu minority ruling China during the Qing.

10. Eight Lanes (Bada hutong) was the most celebrated red-light district of Beijing. The brothels of such quarters served men as social meeting spots to conduct business, and the women employed in them were renowned for their various skills in the arts and social graces as much as for their sexual favors.

11. A house specialty of the Zhimeizhai Restaurant, or "House of Exquisite Beauty," was, indeed, turnip cake, according to Arlington and Lewishohn, *In Search of Old Beijing*, 269.

12. During the violent response of Republican loyalists to the proposal of Yuan Shikai that he govern as emperor in 1916, planes briefly bombed the imperial palace.

13. *Shifu*, or "master," has been the term of respect for addressing a teacher or master of a skill or craft, popularized for non-Chinese-speaking audiences in the dialogues of Hong Kong martial arts films.

14. "Ninth-rate" is a translation of *"xia-jiu-liu"* (lower ninth class), a reference to the mean social status of various occupations in late imperial China, including restaurant employees, and the prejudice shown them.

15. "The dragon sleeps during the winter, hidden deep in the ground, and he breaks the earth and ascends to heaven the second day of the second month, the day of the first thunderstorm, which is indeed produced by the awakening dragon. But this is what all dragons do every year." Wolfram Eberhard, *Chinese Festivals* (New York: Henry Schuman, 1952), 56.

16. The line quoted is from a poem by Guanxiu (Jiang Deyin, 832–912), noted chiefly for his career as a court poet.

17. Calling out is a shamanistic practice intended to bring back the soul departing the body of a person who is critically ill.

Black Stones

Yang Limin

TRANSLATED BY TIMOTHY C. WONG

> Weighty stones, fiery stones;
> Angry stones, joyful stones.
> —*Untitled verse*

Characters

LIU MING   geologist, twenty-two years old
VETERAN   oil rig builder, thirty-five years old
BIGGIE   roughneck, nineteen years old
BLACKIE   roughneck, twenty-six years old
SHI HAI   roughneck crew chief, twenty-four years old
JUBILEE   roughneck, eighteen years old

CAPTAIN QIN   captain, petroleum-exploration team, forty-six
    years old
LIN JIAN   secretary, Political Committee, Petroleum Explo-
    ration Corporation
QIN FANG   traveling nurse for frontline petroleum explora-
    tion teams; daughter of Captain Qin
PHOENIX   country woman, nicknamed "Li'l Red Jacket"
BLOSSOM   Veteran's wife
ZHAO FA   a greedy farmer
JIN PENG   son of a head cadre
PUDGY   an overweight cook and janitor
A youth playing a harmonica, THIRD-SHIFT LI, FOURTH-SHIFT
    WANG, BIG SHOT LIU, BROODER, and assorted police-
    men and workers

ACT I
SCENE 1

Time: the present, or perhaps it was yesterday
Place: on a most desolate area of the Sanjiang Plain[1]
(*A quiet summer's eve at the bend of a river, where more than ten rail-
car-style camp cabins sit on a high bluff, streams flowing off in every
direction. Behind them, a solitary derrick. Faraway streaks of light
stretch gradually out into the vast wilderness.*

*Inside one cabin are two sets of bunk beds, and a small window
inset on wood paneling like a railcar's.*

*The curtain rises on the cabin's interior, which is in utter chaos.
Large and small plates and food containers are stacked on toolboxes;
old playing cards and chess pieces are scattered about. The head of
each bed is a cluttered little world: one with a picture of a movie star
revealing a swatch of white flesh; another, a photograph of family, on
the flip side of a little framed mirror. In short, each occupant's tastes
differ, and his decor varies accordingly. Far to the right is a chest
piled with oil-stained work clothes and miscellaneous items. Outside
the cabin stretch a long bench and a clothesline, and in the distance,
with their little windows in a line, the exteriors of other such cabins
can be seen.*

As the curtain rises VETERAN *and* LIU MING *are asleep in the
upper bunks and* BIGGIE *is below, all in different postures. From out-*

side comes the occasional clash of metal from the construction of the oil rig. Now and then the headlights of a bulldozer pushing dirt around also sweep past. The monotonous sounds make the wilderness seem empty and forsaken.

A youth just learning the harmonica repeatedly plays tiresome notes from a familiar melody, making it seem unfamiliar. Each time he plays, he comes to an abrupt stop before finishing, which is highly irritating. Strange howls issue now and again from the swampy environs.

VETERAN *flips over, turns on his flashlight, and surreptitiously reads a letter.)*

LIU MING: Hey listen, Vet. What kind of noise is that?

VETERAN: From what the locals tell me, that's the call of the Big Black Fish.

LIU MING: Why haven't Shi Hai and his people come back? It's already midnight—

VETERAN: They're busy getting ready for tomorrow's drilling. I ask you, Mr. Geologist, how are prospects this time? Think we'll bring in a well?

LIU MING: From what we've gathered from our probes, we have the highest expectations for this one. It's in the best spot to hit the ancient fossil bed.

VETERAN: Then the bosses must think highly of our team.

LIU MING: I don't know. We've got to get to it quickly in any case. Otherwise, once the rainy season comes, we won't be able to pull out.

VETERAN: This place—What's it called? Halaba . . .

LIU MING: It's called Talaha. The Mongols and the Daurs moved here in Qing times. *(Sighs)* With the days so dark now, what can they do but go back to their camp? How far is that camp from here, anyway?

VETERAN: About seven miles—over two hours on foot. If you lost your way and fell into one of the swamps or a dark ditch, you'd drown. *(The harmonica starts up again.* BIGGIE *suddenly sits up and opens the small window.)*

BIGGIE: *(Hoarsely)* Don't fucking *blow* anymore! Like it's right on my heels. Irritating as hell. *(He leans on the window opening, ready to piss out.)*

LIU MING: Biggie! Can't you be a bit more civilized?

VETERAN: Shut the window quick, before mosquitoes get in! Go outside to take your pee.

BIGGIE: Outside? Lao Er tried that the other night and is still swollen from all the bites. (*He shuts the window, gropes for a small bottle from his bed, and begins to piss into it with his back turned.*)

VETERAN: You little—

LIU MING: That music doesn't sound as good as the pissing.

VETERAN: Now that you're done, throw it out.

BIGGIE: I'll do that on the way to my night shift; all right with you?

VETERAN: I was wondering, Biggie, why you ever chose to go through the pain of joining the roughnecks? Your dad was in the government.

BIGGIE: My dad? The old fart. When it came to increasing his political capital, he never gave a damn about his own flesh and blood.

VETERAN: How's that?

BIGGIE: How's that? Well, listen up. Once he could claim at a general meeting that his son had joined the petroleum workers, what could anyone say against him? But could I take it for long? My dad did level with me: if the chance came along for him to send me to school later on, no one could say anything, since I would have worked my way up from the bottom. It's not like you. Three years in the army without firing a shot, then came to the oil fields after demobilization to join us roughnecks. A real wife in the country, but she could not be sent here because she doesn't have her fucking city residency. What shit . . . (*Pauses*) Hmm. Listen here, Vet. You've been married all these years, how come you haven't got any kids?

LIU MING: (*Trying to stop it*) Biggie!

(VETERAN *very somberly lights up a cigarette.*)

BIGGIE: Don't trouble yourself. I'll help you out. Get your wife sent here, and I'll play farmer: plant her year in and year out without worrying about collecting any harvest!

VETERAN: (*Not unangered*) Biggie, it's time. Get up, eat something, and let's go work on the well.

BIGGIE: (*Depressed as he picks up his stained work clothes, unsure of which trouser leg to slip on first*) Damn. It's tough to put on these duds. All damp and sticky. My flesh begins to crawl even before I get 'em on me.

(BLACKIE *and* JUBILEE *return from the rig.*)

VETERAN: Blackie, are all the preparations done?

(BLACKIE *does not respond.*)

VETERAN: If we can begin drilling tomorrow, we can have regular shifts. That way you guys won't have to work the day after working half the night. (*Exits wearing the safety straps of derrick workers*)

BLACKIE: (*Panting*) Jubilee. Take off my shoes!

(*Subserviently,* JUBILEE *bends over and removes* BLACKIE*'s shoes.*)

BLACKIE: (*Kicking* JUBILEE *over*) Can't you go a bit easier? You're dainty as a kitten on the job, but so rough when you're taking off shoes.

BIGGIE: Hey, Blackie, aren't you afraid of getting hurt, fucking bullying a good man like that?

BLACKIE: If your skin's stretched on too tight, I'll go ahead and loosen it for you.

BIGGIE: Why would I be scared of you? I've yet to meet up with somebody I can't handle! If I hadn't been able to hold my own against anyone in the oil fields, my dad wouldn't have sent me to be on the team. Ask around. I'm not a lamp that skimps on oil.

(BLACKIE *picks up a shoe and is about to hurl it, when* JUBILEE *jumps in the way.*)

JUBILEE: Quit it, quit it. Just now on the job, the drill shaft went off line and Blackie pushed me away, but then his foot got caught in the machinery and we had a hard time getting it out. The foot's probably swollen now; he just got upset when it hurt to take his shoe off.

BLACKIE: Why waste your breath? Go fetch me some water.

JUBILEE: All right.

BLACKIE: Take along a plate and bring back some chow.

JUBILEE: Okay! (*Exits*)

BIGGIE: What a worm! How'd he manage to get fathered?

BLACKIE: (*Sneeringly*) His father wasn't like yours! When the oil fields were getting set up, he was crushed to death on a rig. Your father? He has people to boss around, no matter what. He's all-powerful.

BIGGIE: So what? He's what we call "a credit to the nation."

BLACKIE: Sure. How else could we "credit" him for sending his eldest son to slave in the oil fields?

BIGGIE: Bastard! You've got a warped mind.

BLACKIE: What're you worried about? Your dad may be worried

about getting demoted from being a boss to being someone's helper, but *I'm* not worried about being made a worker's assistant. (*JUBILEE enters, carrying hot water and food.*)

BLACKIE: We've got booze with us. Come, Jubilee, have a drink with your old buddy here.

BIGGIE: You're messing with me?

BLACKIE: (*Fetching a bottle from under his bed*) Not much left. Look around, Jubilee. See who else's still got some.

JUBILEE: There's a bottle under Biggie's bed.

BLACKIE: Well, then, bring it over here.

JUBILEE: But . . .

BLACKIE: He may argue with you, or he may fight with you. But Biggie's never been the petty sort. Right, Biggie?

BIGGIE: Go ahead and have it! Consider the stuff my peace offering to you. (*JUBILEE takes the "liquor."*)

BLACKIE: (*Grabbing it from JUBILEE and reading the label*) "General Thunder." Good stuff, good stuff.

BIGGIE: Of course. "Pleasant bouquet; refreshing tartness."

BLACKIE: Let me have some—
(*LIU MING throws his quilt over himself and doubles over laughing. BIGGIE heads for the door, ready to run away.*)

BLACKIE: (*Taking a sip to taste it*) How'd it get like this? Piss-putrid!

JUBILEE: (*Still without a clue*) Could be . . . could be it's turned bad? Let me try it. (*Takes a mouthful*) Mmm. Mmm. Could be all foreign liquors taste like this.

BLACKIE: Don't act like you're an expert. Foreign liquors!
(*LIU MING's bed shakes from his laughter. BIGGIE can no longer contain himself and bursts out laughing as he is about to escape.*)

BLACKIE: Ah! We've been screwed. It could be . . . (*Swings the bottle around and whacks BIGGIE on the buttocks*)
(*BIGGIE leaps out of the cabin.*)

BLACKIE: (*Has to laugh*) That devious son of a bitch. He got me good this time.

JUBILEE: I was wondering why he was so agreeable today.

LIU MING: *Ai.* Why isn't Shi Hai back?

JUBILEE: He said he thought he heard someone calling out something from one of the streams.

BLACKIE: That's all bullshit. Why didn't I hear anything?

JUBILEE: Earlier today, you got into that fight at the camp store. Very likely they're coming to look for you.

BLACKIE: So those "happy campers" are coming round to get whupped!

JUBILEE: I heard they're bad. They're upstarts with motorbikes and guns!

BLACKIE: They don't scare me, even if they've got guided missiles. What did the guy think he was doing, playing touchy-feely on the woman shopkeeper? He was about to get to her crotch. Just the son of some village cadre and he's as high-handed as all that? What would happen if the father got to be county boss? Then he'd be allowed to kidnap and rape! I tried to say something and he smashed a wine bowl on the floor. The woman got so upset, she was about to cry. So how could I let him go on, without taking a poke at him?

LIU MING: Blackie, what's happened to my briefcase?

BLACKIE: It was broken—and maybe got lost in the scuffle.

LIU MING: Darn it! Oh, darn it! I have geological surveys in the inside compartment. Those get lost and my job's kaput.

(From outside the cabin comes the voice of CAPTAIN QIN.*)*

BLACKIE: What cursed luck.

JUBILEE: The captain's here. Let's not talk about that for now.

*(*CAPTAIN QIN *enters, followed by* LIN JIAN.*)*

CAPTAIN QIN: This is Comrade Lin.

LIN JIAN: *(Putting down his luggage)* My name's Lin Jian.

CAPTAIN QIN: Orders have come down from company headquarters. Mr. Lin is to be a worker on the team, which means just that: he'll be a worker—no more, no less. There'll be no speculating about this, such as whether he's had problems in the organization, or that there is something wrong with him, or—

LIN JIAN: No problem by me if you want to speculate.

CAPTAIN QIN: Inform your crew chief, Shi Hai, about this. He's assigned to be a member of your team and will be bunking in Big Mao's bed.

BLACKIE: What happens when Big Mao comes back?

CAPTAIN QIN: Big Mao's been reassigned.

BLACKIE: Reassigned? But he's just been with us a few days.

LIU MING: Yet another one being sent away . . .

JUBILEE: Doesn't he even want his belongings?

BLACKIE: What for? They'd just clutter up his home. Hmm. So the team's getting the green light again?

CAPTAIN QIN: Stop your sarcasm! I'm just a low-level bureaucrat. How can I not follow orders from above? What are you bugging your eyes out about? I haven't been on your case yet. Who all will be going down to the camp with the cars today?

JUBILEE: The two of us. Also Big Li and Little Zhao from the third shift, and Delong and Big Zhu from the fourth.

CAPTAIN QIN: Who's been getting into fights?

BLACKIE: Me.

CAPTAIN QIN: Don't you guys care about the effects of your behavior? What do you think the people are saying? They're saying "the Oil Ogres" have invaded. Do you think that sounds good? When you guys get on a bus, you make a loud fuss whenever you see a female. How can you be so uncouth? Okay, so it's been months since you've seen someone of the other sex. You still don't have to carry on like that! You've all got sisters at home. What if they were the ones on that bus—?

BLACKIE: Everybody was just having fun. We didn't mean anything by it.

CAPTAIN QIN: Having fun? Aren't there other ways of doing that? The cafeteria bought over a hundred catties of salt cabbage at the camp. The load was down to just over thirty catties when it was weighed here. You jerks had thrown out over half of it along the way. Is that having fun?

BLACKIE: That's exactly "having fun." The last time *you* didn't see your wife for a half year, you shed tears when you finally did. Is that what being "couth" is to you?

CAPTAIN QIN: I . . . I'm just more of a romantic. Don't you laugh about it, Lin. The situation is just like that with the team. But it's gotten much better than when it was first set up.

BLACKIE: How can you compare like that? Why don't you compare us to primitive society? In those times, people didn't wear pants and ate grass roots and tree bark.

CAPTAIN QIN: This is known as our glorious legacy, unanimously affirmed by the Central Committee.

LIU MING: What they affirmed is the spirit, not the way things used to be done. Captain, I really don't want to hear you say that again.

CAPTAIN QIN: Say what again?

LIU MING: *(Mimicking* QIN's *voice)* "The situation is just like that with the team. It's much better than during wartime!" That way our situation can never be corrected, never be changed.

CAPTAIN QIN: How should it be changed?

LIU MING: I won't argue with you. Go ask Shi Hai, why don't you? The position paper he's been writing has gotten as thick as a half catty of dried bean curd.

CAPTAIN QIN: I've read it. Not one feasible suggestion in it.

LIU MING: How not feasible? Unit two forty-seven has already put it into effect: setting up changing rooms, a rec. room, an electronics shack; workers off shift have even had a dance party.

BLACKIE: Their dumplings are being made by machine.

JUBILEE: I heard there's no filling in them; nothing but dough.

CAPTAIN QIN: An electronics shack is over twenty thousand dollars! Where can the petroleum department come up with that kind of money, huh? You're saying—

BLACKIE: On their team, everyone has to talk about members with problems before having them sent away. Just on this point, I am with them! They're not like us here, treating every slip of paper from above like an imperial edict and every piece of bullshit like it was gold.

CAPTAIN QIN: Unit two forty-seven drills over twenty thousand meters in a year; it's the gold-medal team of the entire nation. How come you don't compare yourselves to that?

LIU MING: That's not beyond comparison with us. We're all still young.

CAPTAIN QIN: *(Hurt)* So, you think I'm too old. . . . Mr. Lin, go get yourself some sleep. *(Exits)*

LIN JIAN: The captain is angry, isn't he.

BLACKIE: Not to worry. He's a high-minded sort, thrown in with us workers to suffer the pains of trying to lead us. He's also been ill. . . .

LIU MING: Actually, *there* is an aspect of tradition itself that is obsolete. Philosophically speaking, the logic of life is nothing other than unceasing creation and unceasing destruction. Fundamentally, the job of science is to break down tradition.

LIN JIAN: This is Marx's view. Have you read much philosophy?

LIU MING: Shi Hai's brother is in the philosophy department at Peking University and often sends books to us. I've long urged the captain to read some philosophy as well. Hey, Mr. Lin, how is it that you've come to join our team?

LIN JIAN: *(Pulling out cigarettes)* Come. Have a smoke, have a smoke. It's a new brand, pretty strong.

(SHI HAI enters from the right with PHOENIX, who is obviously nervous and anxious, her trousers rolled up at the bottom, one hand clutching a briefcase. Her eyes are wide with curiosity, taking in everything, so strange and new. Still, the pink blouse she has on makes her very attractive.)

SHI HAI: You wait here.

(PHOENIX nods. SHI HAI enters the cabin.)

SHI HAI: Blackie, there's a woman to see you.

BLACKIE: Don't you be playing around with me.

SHI HAI: Pick up this place a bit and put away those smelly socks.

LIU MING: Really? A woman? Then I ought to—

SHI HAI: You just get to sleep. *(Seeing LIN JIAN)* This is . . .

LIN JIAN: My name's Lin Jian, and I've been assigned to your team as a worker. If there's anything I can do, just let me know.

SHI HAI: As a worker? . . . *(Looks LIN JIAN over)*

(JUBILEE hurries about picking up the cabin. He never questions anything SHI HAI says.

Outside, PUDGY the janitor sneaks weird glances toward PHOENIX, then slips stealthily off to the side.

THIRD-SHIFT LI, wearing a cloth belt on his pants, emerges from the rear, ready to relieve himself. The sight of PHOENIX there startles him and he scurries back like a mouse, to the row of cabins in the rear.

All this occurs simultaneously just after SHI HAI enters the cabin.)

SHI HAI: C'mon in.

PHOENIX: Mm. *(Enters the cabin)*

SHI HAI: *(Pointing at BLACKIE)* He's the one you're looking for.

BLACKIE: It's you? . . .

PHOENIX: Ah, this is the man I've been looking for.

BLACKIE: Looking . . . looking for me?

PHOENIX: Ah . . . yes. It's you.

(A pause. Everyone is extremely uneasy and embarrassed. PHOENIX, too, becomes disconcerted. She moves slowly toward BLACKIE.)

SHI HAI: Take a seat.

JUBILEE: *(Filling a cup with water)* Have a sip!

PHOENIX: Mm. The reason I've come looking for this gentleman is to bring the briefcase to him.

LIU MING: Briefcase?

PHOENIX: *(Quite startled to discover, on turning her head just then, that one of the top bunks holds yet another person)* Yes . . . it's a briefcase.

BLACKIE: Thank you very much. I was just worrying about it.

PHOENIX: Right after you all left, I found the case and ran after your car, shouting, for quite a while. But you never stopped. Then I thought I should just forget it. It's only a fake-leather briefcase; surely not worth your bother. But when I opened it after I got back to the store, I found a stack of maps in the inner compartment, all drawn up with squiggly lines. There were even circles here and there. I was frightened to death, thinking they could be secret documents.

(Several people chuckle at this.)

PHOENIX: Don't you laugh at me. It's the truth. I became so tense, every bit of noise made me jump. I had blisters in my mouth. Last evening I went up a ridge and looked out over the flatlands. Against the broad blue horizon stood the derrick, big and tall. I thought, you've all got to be there. But it was like running a dying horse toward distant mountains: You go on and on and never get there! It was already dark, but I couldn't reach the derrick. As I went forward toward it, the derrick seemed to be going forward, too. Weird . . . It got all dark and I couldn't get myself out of the stream once I was in it. I . . . I was ready to cry from desperation. . . . *(Laughs)* Then, I screamed—and if not for this gentleman here . . . well . . . You've just been listening to *me* go on and on . . . when, really . . .

LIU MING: No, we darn well have got to thank *you!*

PHOENIX: As long as we're giving out thank yous, I have to thank this nice man. He really helped me out in the store. Otherwise . . . well . . . I needn't say any more.

JUBILEE: Your camp is really in a large area.

PHOENIX: I heard if we strike oil, we can become a town.

BLACKIE: Then, you're not afraid of us "Oil Ogres" invading you?

PHOENIX: Don't put it like that! These desolate and isolated boondocks can sure use something to stir us up! It was awesome when you moved in, all that stuff on the camp road! So many trucks— and those tractors with the big broad wheels!

JUBILEE: They were the D-eighty imported models.

PHOENIX: With electronic boxes in front and in back—

JUBILEE: Those are radios.

PHOENIX: They just looked so grand. For a couple of days after you went through, the people in the camp seemed to be jumping with excitement, whispering back and forth to each other. *(Pausing)* I should also say that you fellas ought to be careful. Some people will be coming to you who want to get rich by getting hold of your things.

BLACKIE: What have we got that anyone would want?

PHOENIX: Stuff like oil, or steel, or rope. Anyway, they'll grab anything.

JUBILEE: You seem to be just like one of us oilers.

PHOENIX: Do you guys want me with you?

SHI HAI: Isn't it nice running a little store?

PHOENIX: *(Sighing)* I've not had good fortune in my life. . . .

JUBILEE: You still talking about fortune in this day and age?

PHOENIX: I know the idea is false. But some things . . .

BLACKIE: What are you afraid of? Just go ahead and be an open and straightforward person!

PHOENIX: You're a man. But I'm a woman, you know.

SHI HAI: What about your husband?

PHOENIX: Him? *(Suddenly in despair)* He went off just days after we were married. He wanted money, cheated, stole . . . Ha! Let's not talk about that—not talk about that anymore.

(PUDGY, having reported to CAPTAIN QIN, leads him to the cabin; the two mumble to each other as they walk along.)

CAPTAIN QIN: *(Pretending he was delivering the mail)* Shi Hai, mail for your crew. *Aiya!* This lady comrade is—

PHOENIX: I'm from the camp store. I've come—

CAPTAIN QIN: *(With a hollow laugh)* Heh-heh-heh. With just men here on the team, it's not quite convenient. It is now *(glancing at his watch)* past ten o'clock. Shi Hai, get a couple of people to escort her.

PHOENIX: Yes, I should leave.

SHI HAI: Blackie, you go with her.

CAPTAIN QIN: Let Jubilee do it.

JUBILEE: I . . . I'm scared.

PUDGY: Captain. If it's okay, I can go along with Jubilee. Hee-hee.
I'm already done fixing you your late-night snack.

CAPTAIN QIN: (Angrily) Haven't I said that you are not to fix me any?

PUDGY: You've got so much to concern yourself about all day, and
you've not been well. . . .

BLACKIE: (Glaring at PUDGY) Hm! Brown-nosing and squealing.
What're you up to, anyway?

PUDGY: What do you mean by that, Blackie?

BLACKIE: (To PHOENIX) Let's go. I'll escort you.

CAPTAIN QIN: You! . . .

BLACKIE: We lost something, and she came all this way to return it.
How can you be like that, Captain? . . . Let's go.
(PHOENIX exits with BLACKIE.)

CAPTAIN QIN: (Losing his temper) Let me tell you, Shi Hai! This
woman is also known as "Li'l Red Jacket." She's not on the straight
and narrow. If something smelly happens on this team because of
you, I'll kick you out so fast you won't have time to finish dinner!
(VETERAN and BIGGIE enter with ZHAO FA, who is carrying a plastic
bucket.)

VETERAN: Get in there!

ZHAO FA: Let me go this one time. Uncle, I'm begging you.

VETERAN: Move! We'll talk about it inside.
(VETERAN, BIGGIE, and ZHAO FA enter.)

CAPTAIN QIN: What's going on?

VETERAN: He's been stealing firewood and kerosene.

ZHAO FA: Captain, sir! I've gotten myself in trouble! I was just helping
myself to some kerosene when my uncle here nabbed me. I'm
just not a goddamn human being; I'm the son of a mule!

CAPTAIN QIN: Where're you from?

ZHAO FA: The big camp on the north side.

CAPTAIN QIN: The kerosene was brought here from several hundred
kilometers away. Don't you know you're breaking the law stealing
a whole bucketful like this?

ZHAO FA: I know it, I know it. I admit, yes, I deserve to be punished.

PUDGY: Do you know who "Li'l Red Jacket" is?

ZHAO FA: I know her. I know her. She's my nephew's wife, and I'm her uncle by marriage. When you go to her store from now on, I'll take care of the bill.

CAPTAIN QIN: Don't make such pointless offers. Let's continue this at the team's headquarters.

(CAPTAIN QIN, PUDGY, *and* ZHAO FA *exit.*)

SHI HAI: Letter for you, Veteran. (*Hands it over*)

VETERAN: Who's opened it?

SHI HAI: The envelope broke open.

LIN JIAN: That farmer kept calling you "uncle." How much over forty are you, anyway?

VETERAN: Me? I'm only thirty-five. I guess I look old.

(LIN JIAN *is obviously embarrassed.*

SHI HAI *changes clothes.* JUBILEE *gets him water to wash his face.*

VETERAN *reads the letter, trying very hard to hide the emotions welling up inside him.*)

SHI HAI: What's going on, Vet?

BIGGIE: Must be missing your wife. (*Grabbing the letter away*) Let's have a look-see. What's she been writing to you?

VETERAN: Don't . . . No, don't! . . . Don't you rip it.

LIU MING: (*Puts down the book he's been reading*) It's impolite, Biggie, to read someone else's personal mail.

BIGGIE: There're no secrets among us in this little world of ours.

VETERAN: (*Helplessly*) If you're going to read it, read it. Nothing much in it, really.

BIGGIE: That's the spirit. I'll read it to all of you. (*He reads out loud.*) "Veteran: I miss you. When I go to bed at night, I quietly place your pillow by my side. Even though you're not here, I feel that you are whenever I shut my eyes. I really want to become a mommy. A child can help take away quite a bit of the loneliness. Only, you come back just once a year and are always in a hurry. If I could joke about the whole thing, I'd say that it takes several waterings to grow even one little bean sprout. Other people in the village are doing better and better these days, but things have been harder for me. Whenever night falls, the village lights up and other people's houses are filled with husbands, kids, steamy soup and rice. Mine, however . . . *Ai!* I don't want to talk about it anymore. Who told me to go and marry an oiler! I really miss you. Sometimes, I cry when no one's around." (*He pauses as tears roll down his cheeks.)* Liu Ming, you read it. . . . I can't take this.

LIU MING: *(Continuing)* "Vet, if things are not too pressing, put in an official request for a vacation. Ask for a few more days, in order for me—for us—to have a child. Only don't say that when you're actually making the request, because it'll seem that we're not high-minded. If it gets rejected, then wait a while longer. Opening oil wells is an important job. Also, you've got to study hard. Without an education you'll always be put down. In addition, let's talk about the letters you write to me, always on a single page with overly large handwriting, but without even one punctuation mark from beginning to end. The opening salutation is followed right away with 'That's all for now.' *What's* all for now? You've not told me a thing! The kind of work you have to do, the clothing you have to put on—just breaks my heart to think of it. The people who ride in motor cars—who among them can imagine what it takes to provide them with gasoline!"
(Those in the cabin fall silent.

  VETERAN *washes with the water* JUBILEE *brought, shielding his face as he scrubs it with the washcloth.)*

JUBILEE: Mr. Veteran. Your wife's really fine. If I could find a wife like that in the future, wouldn't bother me if we couldn't be together all year. I'd be content just to get words like those.

LIN JIAN: Where are you from, Vet?

VETERAN: My home's in Henan.

LIN JIAN: How many years ago were you demobilized?

VETERAN: It's been nine years.

LIN JIAN: Why isn't your family with you?

VETERAN: Village residency.

LIN JIAN: Don't the regulations say residencies can be changed after eight years of service?

VETERAN: We don't have a house and can't be registered.
  (Another pause.

    LIN JIAN *takes the envelope and looks at it.*

    SHI HAI *brings out a tray holding a large cake with candles on it. Everyone is greatly surprised.)*

SHI HAI: Come, come. Let's get on another topic. It's the eighteenth of June today, Jubilee's birthday. *(Looks at his watch)* Another fifteen minutes and it'll be too late to celebrate.

JUBILEE: My birthday?

SHI HAI: Says so in the roster.

JUBILEE: Hey, that's right; it is today! I . . . I'd forgotten it myself.

(*Thoroughly moved and delighted, everyone congratulates* JUBILEE *on his birthday.*)

BIGGIE: Way to go, Shi Hai! Doing this kind of thing is exactly what's so rare among our leaders. In the future, you can be a pacesetter, a model worker, and be promoted to be with big-shot officials.

VETERAN: How can you be saying that, Biggie?

BIGGIE: Fine. I'll shut up. Tonight I'm going to have to get soused again.

SHI HAI: (*Lighting the candles*) Jubilee, come blow out the candles.

(JUBILEE *does so gently. The pale red light in the eastern sky fades bit by bit into darkness. The spasmodic music of the harmonica starts up once more.*)

ACT I

SCENE II

(*Lamps light up. It is a cool, fresh summer morning. Although the scenery is identical to that in scene one, the atmosphere is greatly changed. Larks chirp as they flit about, and the broad blueness of the azure sky is intoxicating. A pale mist floats above the river, dampening and sweetening the air. Straight graceful reeds partially shield the dark blue railcar cabins. In the distance, the river meanders in a series of bends, like a belt of golden brocade slowly twisting forward. The derrick, which seems to pierce the sky, is bathed in an afterglow that gives it majesty.*

From backstage come the roar of the drill and the clatter of the big earthmovers, now drilling the well.

SHI HAI's *crew is off work today, taking a twenty-four-hour break. Everyone has changed into stylish clothing, ready to go into town.*

Outside the cabin, LIN JIAN *is setting up a volleyball net with used rope. Roughnecks changing shifts come and go. A youngster whistles as he hangs laundry on the clothesline.*

SHI HAI *enters, walking gingerly. He carries in a clam scooper a tiny fish he has just caught.*)

SHI HAI: Hey, Lin. Come quick and look at this! See how pretty this little fish is. Golden fins and golden scales, jumping all over the place.

LIN JIAN: Where'd you get the little creature?

SHI HAI: The riverbank. You just stomp around hard on the sand and make an indentation, which'll fill with water as a wave washes over it. Before long the little fishies will swim over, one after another. Then it's easy to catch 'em.

LIN JIAN: Let's keep it as a pet.

SHI HAI: Yeah. There ought to be more color in life. Lin, ol' buddy, have you ever heard this before? "No matter how threatening life's situation may be, people will always seek out beauty in creating their lives." Whose famous statement is that?

LIN JIAN: Tagore's.[2]

SHI HAI: It'd be so good if the elders and the political cadres all had this quality of yours. (Sighs) How did you come to be here? Did you fall into the wrong political category? Or was it your lifestyle?

LIN JIAN: (Guffawing) I'm not qualified to get myself into political trouble. As to my lifestyle, that's a distinct possibility. Because, you see, whenever I encounter a pretty woman, I cannot help looking her over a few times.

SHI HAI: That's perfectly normal. People who are unmoved by beauty have no passion for living. Hey, what really brought you here?

LIN JIAN: I was incompetent. . . .

SHI HAI: There are lots of incompetents! Most cadres are lackeys, in my opinion. They mostly have a slave mentality. They're robots following orders.

LIN JIAN: But those with slave mentalities are ultimately obedient, don't you see?

SHI HAI: This is also our glorious tradition.

LIN JIAN: You can't say that.

SHI HAI: Oh no?

LIN JIAN: Cadres with a sense of creativity are not all that difficult to find.

SHI HAI: I'm pointing to the common ones, not the standouts. If you're talking about standouts, it's entirely possible to find millionaire peasants in old China. Then, of course, there were also the landlords.

LIN JIAN: Last night, Shi Hai, I was at team headquarters and saw a stack of requests for transfer. Why're so many people wanting to get out?

SHI HAI: How should I put it? Everybody is saying that deprivation and hard work don't bother them any. It's the joyless way of life that wears them down.

LIN JIAN: What do you mean by "joyless"?

SHI HAI: Around the big river, you're worried about drowning whenever you bathe in it. Get to town when your shift's done and you're worried about drinking too much and causing trouble. Watch movies and you're worried about poisoning your mind. Find a woman and you're worried about the condom breaking. So what's left? Just taking your meals, digging the well, going to sleep . . .

LIN JIAN: What if you were in charge?

SHI HAI: If I were in charge, requests for transfer could go down by ninety percent.

LIN JIAN: I thought you'd have more moxie than to claim that. Couldn't you make it so that there wouldn't be a single request?

SHI HAI: No, I can't.

LIN JIAN: Why's that?

SHI HAI: I've got to account for those who'll be sneaking out by the back door.

LIN JIAN: *(Laughing)* You rascal. *(Looks fondly at* SHI HAI*)* You're too much.

(From backstage, strange shouts: "Let's go! Let's go see some women!" "Let's get to town!"

THIRD-SHIFT LI, FOURTH-SHIFT WANG, LIU MING, *and* BIGGIE *prepare to take the service van. They talk things over outside the cabin.* LIU MING *sports a very Western look, with his long hair and tight jeans.* CAPTAIN QIN *enters in an angry huff.)*

CAPTAIN QIN: What're you guys shouting about at the top of your lungs? Don't all of you leave. I want one person from each shift to help take inventory of the stuff we should be moving out.

THIRD-SHIFT LI: Please, let us go.

FOURTH-SHIFT WANG: Captain, I beg you. We haven't been out on the town for over three months.

(Everyone gathers around the captain, imploring him to relent.)

WORKER A: I haven't even been smoking.

WORKER B: My razor blades can't cut it anymore.

CAPTAIN QIN: No! That town's so small, a whole street stinks up from one little fart. It's only about thirty-five miles from here. You guys raise holy hell there and it makes us look bad. Get back, all of you. Just get back. Soon we'll be receiving an official delegation and will have to welcome the head of the inspection team.

(They are hesitant to disperse.)

CAPTAIN QIN: If none of you are concerned about losing a month's bonus money, then go ahead; take off! *(Snapping an order)* Start up the van!

(The sound of the van driving off)

THIRD-SHIFT LI: *(Grumbling to himself)* Up your mother's!

CAPTAIN QIN: Who do you think you're cussing at? Watch your mouth, you son of a bitch.

THIRD-SHIFT LI: I was cussing at myself. Isn't that allowed?

CAPTAIN QIN: Cussing at yourself?

(PUDGY comes forward to break up the confrontation. CAPTAIN QIN exits.)

PUDGY: All right, all right. The captain was well-meaning. He was concerned that you'd get soused and not make it back. That would hurt production. Isn't this the time to "Sacrifice my one self, and gladden a billion others"?

THIRD-SHIFT LI: Don't give me your bullshit. Just start making the food decent in the cafeteria. We've been eating soggy chives everyday for two weeks. I taste it even when I talk.

(Heads hung in dejection, the group is about to break up. PHOENIX enters, a basket of dry goods on her back. The young workers rush up and surround her.)

WORKER A: You're really a sight for sore eyes!

PHOENIX: You don't need to say that. I'm doing this to make some money.

WORKER B: What all have you got?

PHOENIX: I've got cigarettes, wine, canned goods; also toothpaste, laundry soap, deodorant soap.

WORKER A: Terrific. Our shift will take them all.

(WORKER A picks up the whole basketful of stuff and is about to run off with it when THIRD-SHIFT LI blocks his way.)

THIRD-SHIFT LI: Hey, don't you guys be selfish about this.

PHOENIX: The stuff with me—it's all I can carry. Why don't you guys just divvy it up?

WORKER A: (*Thrusting a few large bills at* PHOENIX) Money. For you.

PHOENIX: *Aiya!* I've got to give you a couple dollars change.

WORKER A: What for? This piece here for eighty cents—

PHOENIX: Hey, friend. There's someone here called Blackie. Is he around? (*She looks about in anticipation.*)

WORKER A: I'll get him for you! (*Runs off*)

(BIGGIE *sees that* PHOENIX *is holding a bottle of hot sauce in her hand.*)

BIGGIE: How much is that?

PHOENIX: Oh, that's something I brought for someone.

(BLACKIE *comes over from the rig.*)

PHOENIX: Blackie—

BLACKIE: Phoenix, you're here.

PHOENIX: I brought some stuff for the team and sold it all just like that. This is for you. Fried meat and peppers.

(*The workers purchasing things do not leave. They stand at a distance, looking at* PHOENIX.)

BLACKIE: You've come so far, and the road is tricky.

PHOENIX: Then, why don't you walk me back.

BLACKIE: Let's go, then. (*Exits with* PHOENIX)

(JUBILEE *enters, running, carrying a small injured gray goose in his arms.*)

JUBILEE: Crew Chief, Crew Chief! A goose, a goose.

SHI HAI: Where did you come up with that?

JUBILEE: Big Shot Liu shot him with a small bore rifle. Got the wing. Look, he's trembling with pain. . . . What should I do, what should I do?

LIU MING: Get in the cabin, quick. Put some salt water on him so he won't get infected.

JUBILEE: You take him. I'll go look for some cloth to bandage him up. (*He rips a strip from his own bedsheet hanging on the clothesline.*)

(BIG SHOT LIU *and* THIRD-SHIFT LI *barge in.*)

BIG SHOT LIU: Jubilee, we're not going to let you have the goose.

JUBILEE: But you agreed!

THIRD-SHIFT LI: We want him back. We'll cook him up and have him with a bit of booze.

JUBILEE: Don't. Don't, don't. I'm begging you. This little gray goose is so helpless.

THIRD-SHIFT LI: No deal. (*Grabs for the goose*)

JUBILEE: (*About to break into tears*) I . . . I'll buy you ten bottles of good booze, ten cases of canned goods, all right? If I renege, you can just slaughter me and eat my flesh!

(*A pause.*)

BIG SHOT LIU: Ah, forget it! Let 'im keep it.

(THIRD-SHIFT LI *and* BIG SHOT LIU *exit.*

VETERAN *returns, with presents.*)

SHI HAI: You're back!

VETERAN: Yeah. I took the bus out yesterday and spent the night at the base.

SHI HAI: Get inside and relax.

VETERAN: This goose here . . .

SHI HAI: Belongs to our crew. (*Exits with* JUBILEE)

(VETERAN *and* LIU MING *enter the cabin.*)

BIGGIE: Gone and delivered stuff again, huh, Vet?

LIU MING: You're really something. All that stuff, why don't you just enjoy it yourself? Be good for your own health.

LIN JIAN: Deliver what stuff?

LIU MING: Because his wife's living in the countryside, you know.

VETERAN: (*Sighing*) I don't mind you making fun of me. But, hard as I try, I can't get the things sent to the right place. So, Biggie, you think it's easy to send gifts? If the address isn't clear, the person won't get it.

BIGGIE: That's right.

VETERAN: The big headquarters building where they handle things? I couldn't even find the front door. The sign seems to disappear just as soon as they hang it up. In the whole place, the cadres alone amount to several thousand. So madly busy day after day. I stood there for over an hour and no one paid any attention. It occurred to me that, with all the important matters everyone was taking care of, how would anyone find the time to take care of me? So, I shouldn't bother them; I should just leave. On the way back, I really wanted to slap my own face. In my heart, I was saying to myself: you're losing face for everyone who used to be in the service!

LIN JIAN: What else did you need to do?

VETERAN: I'm not sure. But there are already sixteen chops on the declaration form. (*Takes it out*)

LIN JIAN: *(Taking it)* Leave it with me here.

VETERAN: But it's—

LIN JIAN: I'll get somebody to try to take care of it for you.

VETERAN: *(Embarrassed)* Wouldn't that be too much trouble?

LIN JIAN: I've got friends in high places.

VETERAN: Then, what would you need? Just say. Money, whatever . . .

LIN JIAN: No, nothing . . . don't need anything.

VETERAN: I ran into Blackie on the road. There was even a woman with him. Looked like she's been to our place.

BIGGIE: That "Li'l Red Jacket" is such a sexy sort. Blackie's caught her eye.

VETERAN: Don't talk such nonsense.

BIGGIE: It's true. Haven't you seen the pointy boobs on her? Any man who looks at 'em and remains unmoved is nothing but a fucking castrated donkey!

LIU MING: You! You manage to dirty up anything good with that mouth of yours.

BIGGIE: That's fine! Blackie's got his heartthrob. Even the crew chief's little lady will be coming out here on her medical rounds. All you guys have something to look forward to!

LIN JIAN: And you?

BIGGIE: Me? I'm gonna be out of here! Just happened days ago. I've got confidential orders, written just for me.

LIN JIAN: Orders written just for you? Come. Let's all have a look, all right?

BIGGIE: No! Can't! It's top secret.

LIU MING: Why hadn't I heard anything about Shi Hai having a "little lady," Biggie?

BIGGIE: By the time *you* hear, she'd already be carrying a baby around.

LIU MING: Where's she from?

BIGGIE: Frontline Health Organization. She's the oldest daughter of our own Captain Qin.

LIU MING: Is that so?

BIGGIE: Right now, I still can't say for sure about their relationship. She's a real strange broad, damn bright and beautiful. The son of Section Chief Jin has also got his eye on her. There'll probably be some kind of fight for her.

VETERAN: That's all bullshit.

(JUBILEE *enters carrying the little gray goose, now bandaged up.* SHI HAI *follows.*)

SHI HAI: Just put 'im over there. He'll be fine.

JUBILEE: No. What'll I do if he dies?

SHI HAI: I've got a little fish here. Feed it to him. See if he'll take it.

(*A pause.* BIGGIE *is bored stiff.*)

BIGGIE: C'mon. C'mon, let's play some cards. C'mon down, Liu Ming.

LIU MING: I'm not playing.

(BLACKIE *enters the cabin, quite unable to hide the happiness in his heart. Returns to his bunk.*)

BIGGIE: (*Seeing* BLACKIE's *jubilation*) D'ya nail her good?

BLACKIE: Up your mother's! What kind of asinine question is that?

BIGGIE: How 'bout a hand of cards, Shi Hai?

SHI HAI: You guys go ahead.

BIGGIE: Okay! Blackie and Vet, let's play. And Lin, help us out and be a fourth.

LIN JIAN: I don't quite know the game.

BIGGIE: Oh, just sit in. You'll catch on after a few hands. Nothing else to do, anyway. Might as well while away the time before dinner. Let's all agree right now: both losing partners must crawl under the bed like dogs! Make or break twice, and the hand's over.

(*The foursome begin to play, with* BLACKIE *and* LIN JIAN *paired up against* VETERAN *and* BIGGIE.)

VETERAN: I hear a former leader is coming to take a look at our team.

BIGGIE: The hell with that. Whoever wants to come can come. It's like the wedding of somebody's maiden aunt: he gets to booze it up no matter who she's marrying. (*Glancing at his hand*) Say, Blackie, you can't throw down any more cards, can you? So it's my turn.

SHI HAI: Biggie, I really feel sorry for your father. With a precious son like you.

BIGGIE: But *your* father can't even hold a candle to him. Blackie, how many years is it gonna take you to throw down a card, huh?

VETERAN: Liu Ming, see if you can get me a book to read.

LIU MING: (*Tossing one over to him*) Here. "Pushy Kim's" love poems. Learn some. They'll help you sweet-talk your wife.

VETERAN: "Pushy Kim"? What nationality is he?

BIGGIE: Korean. All Koreans are named Kim. C'mon, put down a card!

SHI HAI: Don't pretend to know something when you don't. Pushkin[3] is a great Russian poet.

BIGGIE: *(Jumps up in his excitement)* No reneging! You guys start crawling!

BLACKIE: Me crawl? What for?

BIGGIE: *(Counting the points)* One, two, three, four, five, six, seven. Five seven and you're done for, right? Come, come, come. Give the man some room, some room here!

BLACKIE: *(Throwing down his cards)* Jubilee, do it for me this once.

BIGGIE: No sir, no sir. No substitutions!

BLACKIE: I'm too big, can't get under there.

JUBILEE: I'll be his substitute. I'll crawl a few more turns, all right?

BIGGIE: You goddamn . . . what the! . . . I said . . .

(JUBILEE crawls under the bed for BLACKIE.)

VETERAN: I think Mr. Lin should be exempted.

JUBILEE: Crawl! Crawl! Crawl! If you're older, you ought to take the lead even more. Come on. No pussyfooting around. You may be embarrassed the first time. Then you get used to it.

(LIN JIAN begins crawling with great difficulty. Everyone chuckles at the sight.)

BIGGIE: *(Pushing LIN on his buttocks)* You're dumber than a black bear's grannie!

(CAPTAIN QIN barges in.)

CAPTAIN QIN: Mr. Lin, what're you . . . what're you doing, horsing around with them like that at your age?

LIN JIAN: *(Smiling, embarrassed)* I was just joining in the fun.

CAPTAIN QIN: Quit it, quit it. Pick up this place. The old boss will be here presently. I've got the message that he's been on the road for over four hours. He'll be visiting team two seventeen, and then coming over here.

LIU MING: Which old boss?

CAPTAIN QIN: Higher up than I am, anyway. Be on your best behavior. Don't make things tough on me.

(The people in the cabin are a bit uptight. They bustle about, cleaning up the place while CAPTAIN QIN walks around inspecting.)

CAPTAIN QIN: Look at this place! What a mess. Full of useless trash.

Who's weaving this net with the large holes? Guess you're planning to catch some big fish.

LIN JIAN: I'm weaving it.

CAPTAIN QIN: You?

LIN JIAN: It's a volleyball net. For recreation after work.

CAPTAIN QIN: Who's keeping a fish in the clam scooper? And don't you try to hide, Jubilee. Good heavens, you guys are even raising a goose! Are you starting a zoo here? Shi Hai, you'll have to take care of these matters right away.

SHI HAI: There's no need to get all worked up like that.

CAPTAIN QIN: Also, you guys must watch yourselves. Don't always be thinking about such good-for-nothing distractions as families or women. During those years when we were starting up the industry, we went three years before visiting home, five years before having a girlfriend, eight years before getting married. We drilled for oil in daylight and fought battles at night. Even when our eyes clouded over from starvation, we maintained good discipline and order. The troops were also much easier to lead than you guys.

SHI HAI: All right. Let's do what the captain says. Snap to it!

CAPTAIN QIN: Pick up the broken bottles and old cans under your beds. Take down the picture of the woman in the shirt with no collars, and also, from your headboard, the one with the bare thighs.

LIU MING: This one's a woman doing gymnastics. And that one is of Miss Jade Zhang.

CAPTAIN QIN: I don't care if it's of Fish Zhang or Fowl Zhang. Stick it under the covers. (*He looks* LIU MING *up and down, quite displeased at what he sees.*)

(PUDGY *rushes in.*)

PUDGY: Captain! Captain! I've fixed eight dishes. Is that enough?

CAPTAIN QIN: Are you looking to get in trouble! Four dishes and a soup, as always.

PUDGY: (*In a softer voice*) That Zhao Fa who stole kerosene that time has brought us a goat. He wants a bit of—

CAPTAIN QIN: So give him some cash!

(THIRD-SHIFT LI *hurries in in his oily work clothes.*)

THIRD-SHIFT LI: Shi Hai, we need help.

SHI HAI: What happened?

THIRD-SHIFT LI: The drill's stuck. Blackie knows what to do. He's got experience—

BLACKIE: Quit all that damn flattery. Let's just get to it! (*Exits with* THIRD-SHIFT LI)

CAPTAIN QIN: Liu Ming, why don't you do something about your hair? It flops all over your face and it's hard to tell whether you're male or female. You look like an old lady! The old boss really dislikes this kind of appearance.

LIU MING: Captain, you ought to respect my character.

CAPTAIN QIN: Doing a good job—that's character.

BIGGIE: Does long hair mean nonrevolutionary to you, Captain? Karl Marx[4] had a bushy beard and long hair, and he was an architect of revolutions. Now, Lin Biao[5] was a baldy. But he was nevertheless a counterrevolutionary.

CAPTAIN QIN: All you can do is make jokes. Liu Ming, you're an intellectual and should carry yourself with simple dignity as a role model for the entire team. Look at yourself, with those skin-tight pants—a copper label in back and a bulge popping out like a codpiece in front. Your balls are all but visible. (*Sighing*) I feel strapped in just thinking about it.

(*A burst of laughter from everyone.*)

LIU MING: (*Agitated*) Captain, this is purely my own choice. I don't bother anyone else, and my work's not affected. You have no right to meddle in what is not your business.

CAPTAIN QIN: (*Insistently*) Since you're on my team, this *is* my business! You cut your hair right now, and change your clothes!

LIU MING: On this matter, I have the right to ignore your orders.

CAPTAIN QIN: (*Losing control*) You . . . (*He suddenly sees hanging on* LIU MING's *headboard the reproduction of* The Spring, *an oil painting of a nude woman. Severely*) What kind of picture is that, huh?

LIU MING: A picture I like.

CAPTAIN QIN: Take it down!

(LIU MING *does not respond.*)

CAPTAIN QIN: Take it down!

(LIU MING *has no choice but to do so. He hands it to* CAPTAIN QIN.)

CAPTAIN QIN: Mr. Lin and all of you, look at this. Can this . . . this kind of thing be tolerated here? It's basically a naked thing, isn't it?

JUBILEE: *(In a small voice)* Captain, that's called a nude.

CAPTAIN QIN: Oh, a nude. What do you think, Mr. Lin? Is this obscene or not?

LIN JIAN: It's a world-famous painting, Mr. Qin, the work of the great nineteenth-century French master Ingres.[6] It's called *The Spring*.

CAPTAIN QIN: Yeah, it sure springs out at you, leaves nothing hidden. If I ever reported something like this to the authorities, you'd surely be arrested for keeping pornographic material around. Liu Ming, I am trying to protect you. Destroy the picture at once!

LIU MING: I cannot destroy beautiful art!

LIN JIAN: There are artists who equate the beautiful human body with truth, because truth is also stark naked, with no concealment whatsoever.

CAPTAIN QIN: Now, Mr. Lin. How can you be saying such things at your age without blushing?

LIN JIAN: *(With a smile)* For my sake, just let him have the painting back.

CAPTAIN QIN: Let him have it back? *(He angrily tears up the painting.)* I simply cannot allow this kind of thing to exist in any nook or cranny! *(He is still boiling as he is about to exit.)*

LIU MING: Wait a minute!

CAPTAIN QIN: What now?

LIU MING: You must take responsibility for today's unpleasant matter!

CAPTAIN QIN: I'll take responsibility to the day I die. *(He paces back and forth in his anger.)*

LIU MING: *(Solemnly)* Captain, I have the obligation to give you, as our leader, due respect. But even though I'm a minor functionary, you likewise have the obligation to respect me. That's because we are both citizens. If I want to grow my hair out a little, or I enjoy putting on tight-fitting jeans, it's because I find doing so to be attractive. It's purely my personal preference. I don't at all get in the way of anyone or of our work, and I don't force my tastes on anyone. I think this little bit of freedom belongs to me. I hope, Captain, that you will apologize to me in front of everyone on the team. Secondly, this world-renowned painting was a gift from one of my classmates. Even though it's just a reproduction, it's worth some money. I hope you'll be making restitution for it to me. Otherwise, I will sue you in a court of law.

(CAPTAIN QIN *breaks into loud laughter. Right after the initial guf-faw, however, something suddenly dawns on him.*

THIRD-SHIFT LI *enters, supporting a mud-splattered* BLACKIE.)

SHI HAI: What's happened?

THIRD-SHIFT LI: A stuck piece of rock rolled out and smashed onto Blackie's foot.

(VETERAN, JUBILEE, *and* LIN JIAN *all surround* BLACKIE.)

SHI HAI: Does it hurt?

BLACKIE: Dumb question!

(JUBILEE *gently removes* BLACKIE*'s shoes.* BLACKIE *endures the intense pain.*)

CAPTAIN QIN: You just hold on for a little while. I'm giving a call to the frontline health clinic.

JUBILEE: *Aiya!* The shoe's filled with blood.

BLACKIE: What the shit! Losing a bit of blood never killed anyone. Go get me some spirits.

JUBILEE: Okay . . . uh!

BLACKIE: Hurry up!

(JUBILEE *hurries to get the liquor.* BLACKIE *quickly downs a mouthful.*

The harmonica starts up yet again.

Lights dim.)

ACT I
SCENE III

(*Lights up on a wondrous evening. Scenery is identical to that in scene two. A falling mist is the color of persimmons, and it reddens the alluring river bend in the distance. The tall derrick looks to be a gold-inlaid, silver-plated pyramid. The railcar cabins don't appear dark blue anymore; the persimmon red of the evening mist has blended with the color and changed it into a remarkable hue. Everything appears soft and serene.*

SHI HAI *and* LIU MING *are mulling over the latest core sample.* BLACKIE *is propped up in bed, nursing his injury, which has already become less painful.* JUBILEE *uses a small net to pick out recently captured tiny fish and shrimp, getting ready to feed the goose.*)

LIU MING: (*Staring at the core sample with a magnifying glass*) How odd!

SHI HAI: What?

LIU MING: Normally a core sample from this layer of rock would show the strong presence of petroleum.

SHI HAI: But what's been taken out is not oil-permeated sand but water-permeated rock.

LIU MING: *(Coming to a conclusion)* Gimme the hammer!

SHI HAI: *(Handing it over)* Here.

(LIU MING *breaks up the rock, then takes out another core sample and studies both with the magnifying glass.*)

LIU MING: *(Excitedly)* Look, Shi Hai! This rock here looks very much like that core sample with traces of natural gas! We don't encounter this very often.

SHI HAI: You must write an analytical report to Zhang Zong, the one in charge of this district.

LIU MING: I suppose they could also have discovered this.

SHI HAI: Then our evidence would corroborate theirs. Wouldn't that be even better? But if somehow they follow routine procedures and don't send down a probe, the loss would really be huge. You go write that report. I'll think of something. *Ai*. Mr. Lin, where in the world are you?

LIU MING: He had some kind of emergency. Took the bus out before the crack of dawn.

SHI HAI: Liu Ming, what do you think of Mr. Lin?

LIU MING: I suspect he's been sent here by the higher-ups.

SHI HAI: Not so. I've had someone look into that.

LIU MING: Person like that's got a lot more to him than we know.

SHI HAI: Maybe . . .

(A pause.)

JUBILEE: Blackie, my little gray goose has healed. I let him go today but he's flown back. On the way back, he even circled the rig a couple of times, honking as he did so. He acts like he knows the team.

BLACKIE: That little gray goose will become a beautiful woman in the future and will keep Jubilee company forever.

JUBILEE: Don't you tease me. Once autumn comes, that little goose will be flying away. I wonder if he'd fly back here next year?

BLACKIE: Even if he could, we don't know where all of us would have gone to by then.

JUBILEE: I've been thinking of buying a small chain, to put around the little fella's neck. Then, no matter where he flies to, he'll be able to remember us at the big rig.

LIU MING: He's a goose without a flock. When winter comes, he'll die of cold or starvation.

JUBILEE: I don't believe you, don't believe you!

(QIN FANG, *a medical bag slung over her shoulders, walks by behind* CAPTAIN QIN *and* JIN PENG, *who is wearing a motorcycle jacket.* QIN FANG *stops at the door of the cabin and knocks on it.*)

QIN FANG: Can I come in?

LIU MING: Please do!

(QIN FANG *enters the cabin and proceeds to change* BLACKIE's *bandages.*)

QIN FANG: Your injury is mostly healed, you brave man. In a few days, you can get back on the rig.

BLACKIE: Liu Ming, come take a walk with me outside.

LIU MING: Ah . . . sure, sure! What a gorgeous evening. Yes, we ought to get out in it.

JUBILEE: I'll be leaving also. Have to feed the little goose.

(*They all exit, chuckling to themselves. Only* SHI HAI *and* QIN FANG *remain in the cabin. Silence. Both seem rather uncomfortable.*

SHI HAI *stands up, about to leave.*)

QIN FANG: Wait, wait.

SHI HAI: Heard you're about to get married.

QIN FANG: Do you hate me?

SHI HAI: Why would I hate you?

(QIN FANG *picks up the pack of cigarettes from the table and lights one up.*)

SHI HAI: So, you've learned to smoke?

QIN FANG: (*Painfully*) Helps to calm my nerves—

SHI HAI: Don't talk about such things with me. Have you brought my pictures?

QIN FANG: (*Takes out a stack of photographs and tosses it on the table*) Take them! That way they won't mar your good reputation!

SHI HAI: (*Looking them over one by one*) There's one missing.

QIN FANG: Which one?

SHI HAI: When we were little . . .

(*A pause.*)

QIN FANG: (*Suppressing a sob*) It's lost. . . . (*Then loudly, sorrowfully*) It's lost!

SHI HAI: All right. If it's lost, then . . . it's lost.

QIN FANG: Let me keep that one! Don't be so hard-hearted as to take it away.

SHI HAI: Is he good to you?

QIN FANG: I only agreed to marry him after his father used his connections to get me into the university.

SHI HAI: Sounds like a good business deal to me.

QIN FANG: Don't make it so hard on me. The feelings you and I have for each other are more—

SHI HAI: What feelings? Had my father been a captain, then the "feelings" we had would not have depreciated.

QIN FANG: Then, run off with me. Leave the roughnecks.

SHI HAI: Why can't you run off with me? Come here to be in the midst of Mother Nature . . .

(Another pause.)

QIN FANG: I guess neither one of us could go with the other.

SHI HAI: That's right. Ultimately, life is a very practical matter. You were following your ideals, to become a doctor. But you don't yet have that diploma, so if he can help you realize your dreams, then just go with him! I wish you both happiness.

QIN FANG: (Sobbing) Happiness . . .

SHI HAI: I said some things out of anger. Please, forgive me. . . . I'm really—how should I put it? . . . When I saw butterflies in the grasslands, I could somehow only think of the ribbons tied to the ends of your braids. . . . But that was when we were little. . . . Me? I think it was meant for me to wander about to the ends of the earth.

QIN FANG: (Moved) Oh, Hai, I can never forget, can never . . . From the time we were kids . . . But I had no faith. (She tearfully falls into SHI HAI's arms.)

(CAPTAIN QIN rushes in, JIN PENG in tow. They are shaken on seeing the embrace.

QIN FANG and SHI HAI do not let go of each other immediately. This makes CAPTAIN QIN and JIN PENG extremely upset.)

JIN PENG: (Controlling himself) I'm sorry. . . . (Turns to leave)

QIN FANG: Wait. Let me introduce you. This is Shi Hai, the person I've often spoken to you about.

JIN PENG: (Lethargically) I've heard of you.

QIN FANG: And this is Jin Peng.

SHI HAI: Oh.

CAPTAIN QIN: This is outrageous. Fang, you come outside with me!
(QIN FANG *exits the cabin with* CAPTAIN QIN; JIN PENG *and* SHI HAI *also follow.*)

CAPTAIN QIN: You're way beyond proper bounds, a foot in each boat! Even . . . even introducing them to one another.

QIN FANG: Don't worry. I can marry only one of them. But I could keep the other one as a friend, couldn't I?

CAPTAIN QIN: Please, leave your father a bit of face. How did our family produce a hussy like you? Looking for a mate *and* a "friend" at the same time.
(PUDGY *goes over to* JIN PENG's *side, to ingratiate himself.* BLACKIE *and* LIU MING *finish their stroll and return.* THIRD-SHIFT LI, FOURTH-SHIFT WANG, *and* JUBILEE *look on from a distance. All these young people carry a basic grudge against any stranger who would come to their place to compete for a woman.*)

JIN PENG: Let's get out of here, Qin Fang! This isn't a civilized place.

BLACKIE: *(Glowering)* What did you say? Not a civilized place? What do you think your roughneck daddies do here?

PUDGY: Mr. Jin didn't really mean that. Don't jump to conclusions, Blackie.

JIN PENG: I didn't mean that. I was just concerned that it would be inconvenient for Qin Fang to be here after it gets dark.

BLACKIE: We can take good care of her. On the other hand, I'm concerned about you taking advantage of her on the way back.

JIN PENG: What do you mean by that?

PUDGY: *(Mad at* BLACKIE*)* They're engaged to be married. So how can you be saying that? Look, it's all a lot of—

BLACKIE: Mind your own business, and get the hell out of my sight! Now, Mr. Jin, I know all about your unsavory background. Didn't you buy your university diploma through your father, using public funds? And aren't you the one who got into the pants of several women by giving some people job transfers? Listen to me, you son of a bitch. Shi Hai and Qin Fang are childhood sweethearts. If you break them up by throwing your weight around, I'll break both your legs.

JIN PENG: Humph! Don't threaten me when you've got your people around. If you want to have it out, just say where! The one who fucking shows up late is a chicken!

BLACKIE: Are you itching to get whupped? You wanna go home on a stretcher?

SHI HAI: *(Stopping it)* Blackie, forget it—

BLACKIE: You scared of him, Shi Hai?

SHI HAI: It's not worth it—

LIU MING: Humph! You're even leaning on your big-shot father when you're courting a wife. Jerk! You better get the hell out of here!

PUDGY: This is getting out of hand. When Section Chief Jin gets wind of this, there'll be hell to pay.

JIN PENG: Let's go, Qin Fang. I'll take you on the motorbike.
(BIG SHOT LIU *enters in a huff.*)

BIG SHOT LIU: Nurse! Several on our crew have diarrhea and high fevers. Please, go and take a look at them.

QIN FANG: Ah . . . I've got medicine with me here. Take it to them.

CAPTAIN QIN: That won't do. If it's food poisoning, that won't take care of it. Go quickly and see them, Fang.

QIN FANG: What good would I do them by going over there?

JIN PENG: C'mon. Let's get out of here.

CAPTAIN QIN: Your dad also started out as a roughneck, Fang.

QIN FANG: That's why you've wasted a whole lifetime.

CAPTAIN QIN: Nonsense!

QIN FANG: *(Angered)* You . . . All you've wound up doing is playing leader to a bunch of ruffians!

CAPTAIN QIN: *(Cannot stop himself from slapping* QIN FANG *across the face)* Get out! I don't have a daughter like you!

QIN FANG: *(Startled and shaken)* You—

JIN PENG: Don't say any more. Just leave. *(He feels the stares of angry eyes from every direction, and is greatly disconcerted.)*
(A very long pause. Pair after pair of eyes emitting angry sparks.
JIN PENG *exits with* QIN FANG.)

PUDGY: C'mon, let's regroup. Let's wish Section Chief Jin well. Don't get upset—
(BLACKIE *gives* PUDGY *a swift kick.*)

PUDGY: Who was that? Captain, look what—

CAPTAIN QIN: You, too, are dismissed.
(There is the sound of a motorcycle leaving.)

CAPTAIN QIN: Shi Hai, prepare your crew to go to the well.
(Everyone disperses. SHI HAI, LIU MING, *and* JUBILEE *reenter the*

cabin. *They silently change into their work clothes.* CAPTAIN QIN
stands in the yard, lost in thought. VETERAN *and* BIGGIE *return.)*

BIGGIE: *(Appearing to be in great spirits, singing "Desert of Love")*
"My heart's fervent fire, ooh,
Like a raging pyre, aah."

CAPTAIN QIN: Are you goddamn in heat or something? *Ooh*ing and
*aah*ing like that.

BIGGIE: *(Taking out his orders)* Captain, here're my orders. I guess
you'll be letting me go!
(CAPTAIN QIN looks over the document.)

VETERAN: Captain, I . . . I sent in a transfer request. I was thinking
that as long as my wife cannot be sent here, I'll just transfer back
there. My old father has been ill in bed at home for quite a
while. It's really—

CAPTAIN QIN: *(Shaking with anger)* Go, then; get out of here. Go tell
the crew!
(The three enter the cabin.)

CAPTAIN QIN: Veteran is a member of the party. For him to take the
lead in writing a transfer request and to send out gifts everywhere,
do you think that's proper?

SHI HAI: But he ought to receive some consideration for his personal
problems.

BIGGIE: What about me, then?

SHI HAI: You haven't got a good excuse.

CAPTAIN QIN: Biggie has orders from the top. How can we not let
him go?

SHI HAI: Let me see the document.
(CAPTAIN QIN hands it over to SHI HAI.)

SHI HAI: Leave it here with me. I'll say what's unpleasant up front:
anyone here who gets such an order by using political connections, I'll personally tack the document up on the front door of
the disciplinary committee's office.

BIGGIE: *(Furious)* You're too fucking mean-spirited, Shi Hai! Why the
hell do you pick on Biggie? Why is it that I annoy you so? People
call me "the Kid with Nine Lives"—three times I was in the
detention center; four times I was cut, and I have the scars to
prove it. Since you're not going to be a brother to the likes of me,
don't blame me for turning on you! Get out of the way, guys. I'm

going to let him have it! (*He knocks* SHI HAI *down with one punch.*)

(CAPTAIN QIN *and* VETERAN *restrain him.*)

BIGGIE: (*Begins to bawl*) Fucker! . . . If you wanna show you're big stuff, cast your lot with the roughnecks—fine! Why stand in someone else's way? Damn it. I'll never get out now, never get out. I'll be dying in this place.

CAPTAIN QIN: Oh, what a screwed-up mess. (*Exits*)

(*A pause.*)

SHI HAI: (*Giving the document back to* BIGGIE) If you really want to leave, then leave. But I think it'd be in your own best interest if you worked here another couple of years.

(BIGGIE *calms down a bit.*

The sky gradually darkens.

SHI HAI *picks up* BIGGIE's *work clothes.*)

SHI HAI: Put these on. Get ready for your shift.

(ZHAO FA *enters, bowing and scraping, with a bag full of stuff slung over one shoulder.*)

ZHAO FA: *Aiya!* All you gentlemen here, getting set to go on night duty, I suppose?

SHI HAI: What do you want?

ZHAO FA: Nothing, nothing, really. I saw that you fellas are, you know, kind of deprived here. So I've brought you some goodies from the farm. Nothing special, really. Some bean-paste dumplings I steamed, a bit of fried fuzzy nuts, and also some dried fish—for you fellas to enjoy with your drinks.

(BLACKIE *enters as* ZHAO FA *is still speaking.*)

BLACKIE: What are you doing here?

JUBILEE: He's come to see how we are. Let's eat the stuff. Eat up. If you're not going to, it's your own tough luck.

ZHAO FA: This gentleman here's got the right idea. He knows what it's all about.

VETERAN: Just a minute, there. You can put everything back in your bag and take it away.

ZHAO FA: Whatever you may think, how can I bring any more trouble to you guys?

VETERAN: You just want to invest a little to gain a lot. Take the stuff away!

ZHAO FA: *Aiya!* This uncle here is really something, What have I done to look so bad to you? What would I want from you?

VETERAN: Kerosene! But it belongs to the nation. Don't even think about making off with a single drop.

ZHAO FA: You're really wound up too tight. Not a bit of fun about you.

BLACKIE: Zhao Fa!

ZHAO FA: *(Jumps)* Yeah!

BLACKIE: I won't stick my nose into anything else, but you people better be good to Phoenix from now on. Don't fucking start any bullshit rumors about her. If you don't let up on her, don't be surprised if I waste you!

ZHAO FA: This good man here has really got it bad for Phoenix. All things aside, if you fellas can make it easy for me, I'll shut one eye and pretend I'm not looking. I say, you fellas who work with entire fleets of cars, why should you concern yourselves over a few buckets of fuel? If you're good to me, I'll be good to you. Do me a favor or two and I'll set you up. Phoenix is my nephew's wife. I can make sure you lonely guys working here in the sticks will receive your share of favors and comforts.

BLACKIE: *(Angrily grabbing* ZHAO FA *by the collar)* Mother-fucking bullshit!

ZHAO FA: *(Begging for mercy)* Aiya, aiya, I'm sorry! I won't say that anymore.

(VETERAN *thrusts the bag into* ZHAO FA's *arms.)*

BLACKIE: Get the fuck out!

ZHAO FA: Isn't this ridiculous? Really . . . I've never seen . . . *(Exits)*

SHI HAI: Let's get going. Eat. Get to the well.

(SHI HAI, LIU MING, VETERAN, BIGGIE, *and* JUBILEE, *each holding a lunch box, leave the cabin one after the other.* BLACKIE *remains in bed, his foot still in bandages.*

Darkness has descended everywhere. Nearby, that harmonica again.

PHOENIX *tiptoes into the cabin, carrying a basket.)*

BLACKIE: You . . .

PHOENIX: Have they all gone to the well?

BLACKIE: I've told you never to come here to look for me.

PHOENIX: But I can't stop thinking about you.

BLACKIE: What's there about me to think about?

PHOENIX: Many, many nights, I've stood on a hill to look toward your place. I'd see the light on the top of the derrick. . . .

BLACKIE: Don't talk to me about that.

PHOENIX: You're injured. Can't I come here to visit you? I've cooked some chicken for you. It smells good. Try it. *(She takes it out of the basket.)*

BLACKIE: Why . . . why are you doing this?

PHOENIX: I have a fondness for you. In the cities, people would call it love.

BLACKIE: Love . . . what for?

PHOENIX: You're sturdy, and of good character. You're a mountain. I can lean on you.

BLACKIE: But we can't—

PHOENIX: You're in a major industry. Why're you still so backward?

BLACKIE: No, you've got a husband.

PHOENIX: I've already told you: he was arrested by the police the day after we married. He wanted money, conned people, stole things. He's been sentenced to six years in prison. I long ago started divorce proceedings.

BLACKIE: Keep your voice down. Don't let people hear this.

PHOENIX: I'll shut the door tight. *(She goes to do so.)*

BLACKIE: Just close it quietly. It's gotten dark. Aren't you afraid?

PHOENIX: When I'm with you, there is no day or night.
    (Pause.)

PHOENIX: Why are you always looking around?

BLACKIE: I heard people coming.

PHOENIX: It was the noise from the drilling.

BLACKIE: It's really quiet, isn't it? It's rare for the cabin to be so quiet.

PHOENIX: Look at you. You're sweating. Let me wipe you off—

BLACKIE: Don't touch me. . . .

PHOENIX: Why's that?

BLACKIE: Once I feel your touch, I . . . I lose all my strength.

PHOENIX: You don't like me?

BLACKIE: It's precisely because I do.

PHOENIX: It's pouring rain outside. I feel a little cold.

BLACKIE: Then, close the window.

PHOENIX: *(After doing that)* It's still chilly.

BLACKIE: What should we do, then?

PHOENIX: How can I feel cold when I'm with you?

BLACKIE: Just wait a while. After you're divorced, I'll marry you.

PHOENIX: Divorce . . .

BLACKIE: I'll help you with it. Be done in a month, at most.

PHOENIX: But how will I go on during the month? If only I could sleep for a month with my head on your chest, listening to your heartbeat, to each breath you take, then I could stand it.

BLACKIE: Sometimes, I'm afraid . . .

PHOENIX: Afraid of what?

BLACKIE: Afraid that you'd have a life of suffering if you hooked up with me.

PHOENIX: I'd be happy to suffer until I die. You just don't know how hard it is right now. *(She moves closer and closer to* BLACKIE.*)*

BLACKIE: Don't get so close to me.

PHOENIX: Hold me, like in the movies.

BLACKIE: Listen. There're noises. . . .

PHOENIX: That's just the wind.

BLACKIE: The rain's also pouring down.

PHOENIX: I'm a bit cold. Let me warm up.

BLACKIE: Don't do that.

PHOENIX: You're used to dealing with steel and metal, rocks and stones. Don't you ever think of—

BLACKIE: Never experienced it. I was afraid it would shatter me.

PHOENIX: No, it won't. It won't.

BLACKIE: *(Embracing* PHOENIX *tightly)* Phoenix, be honest with me. You're the first one I've—

PHOENIX: I'll be the last one . . . until we die . . .

(PHOENIX *douses the light. Conversation in the dark.)*

PHOENIX: Your hands are so strong.

BLACKIE: I don't want you to be cold.

PHOENIX: Go easy. Don't tear my jacket.

(PUDGY *and* ZHAO FA *enter, gesticulating to two local constables following behind.)*

PHOENIX: People are really coming this time.

BLACKIE: Then let them come.

(A *policeman enters the cabin. Lights go on.* CAPTAIN QIN *also hurries in.)*

POLICEMAN: You're the one called "Blackie"?

BLACKIE: Yes.

POLICEMAN: I've been sent here from the station in town. You are under arrest.

BLACKIE: I . . . I haven't broken any law!

POLICEMAN: You hurt someone in a fight in North Camp. Also, you're breaking up a happy family.

PHOENIX: No. That's not so! He's innocent. It was me. I am the perpetrator. I wanted a divorce. I have the right!

POLICEMAN: But the divorce has not yet been properly approved. Take him away!

CAPTAIN QIN: Just a minute. *(Pleading)* Comrade, please. We'll step up our worker education. We'll take disciplinary action against him. Please don't take him away! He . . . his foot is still injured.

POLICEMAN: *(Coldly)* No. Take him away!

PHOENIX: *(Getting down on her knees)* I'm begging you! Let him remain here. Arrest me instead.

CAPTAIN QIN: Comrade, please. Show us some consideration.

POLICEMAN: Can't do that. The family has pressed charges. Take him away! *(Exits)*

PHOENIX: *(With a heartrending cry)* Blackie!

(CAPTAIN QIN *glares angrily at* PHOENIX, *who is in great distress.*
That harmonica starts up again.
Curtain.)

ACT II

SCENE I

(The rainy season. Morning and evening have become indistinguishable. Scenery is identical to that of act one. The boundless wilderness is shrouded in mist. The leaden sky is nearly caressing the towering derrick, while the bend of the river in the distance emits a whitish light. Everything is drenched under the battering of wind and rain. Raindrops pitter-patter on the metal skin covering the top of the railcar cabin, keeping up a monotonous staccato that sears the souls of all who listen. As the curtain rises, inside the cabin, yellow in the twilight, SHI HAI, LIU MING, VETERAN, BIGGIE, *and* JUBILEE *are all in bed, reclining in every sort of position.)*

LIU MING: How many days has it been raining now?

SHI HAI: Dunno. Can't keep track anymore.

VETERAN: *(Reading a letter)* The road has become impassable, completely under water.

SHI HAI: Got another letter from home, Veteran?

VETERAN: Uh-huh. My wife's still rooting for me.

SHI HAI: *(Takes the letter and is moved as he reads it)* Don't you worry. She'll get her residency changed.

VETERAN: Never mind trying to make me feel good.

LIU MING: Get me a basin, Jubilee. It's leaking water over here.

(JUBILEE finds one and places it under the drip.)

VETERAN: *Ai,* this rain here . . .

(Now and again, someone rushes past the cabin toting a meal tray. Silence has again fallen inside the cabin. The only sound heard is the rumble from the drilling until BIGGIE throws down the cards in his hand and opens the small window to look outside.)

BIGGIE: *(Shouting loudly)* Don't—rain—already! Damn it. Maybe ol' Mother Goddess became diabetic or something: once she starts peeing, there's no end to it. Hey, Vet. You still got some loose tobacco? Roll me a smoke.

VETERAN: The tobacco pouch's been turned inside out.

BIGGIE: *(Crawling on the floor to look for butts)* Who the fuck smoked this one? What a chicken shit. Didn't even leave me a teeny tiny little bit. *(He throws away the charred filter tip he found and gets down to look again.)* Without a smoke, all energy leaves my body, and all taste leaves my mouth!

SHI HAI: Why don't you run over to another team and borrow a pack or two?

BIGGIE: Everything's smoked up. In this kind of stew, nobody can go out. A few more days of this, and we'll all be acting like turtles.

(He stays down on all fours, looking for butts on the floor.)

SHI HAI: Yeah, you're fast becoming a creepy animal.

BIGGIE: Geez.

(BIG SHOT LIU enters, drenched and mud-splattered, clutching a branch in his hand.)

BIG SHOT LIU: Got any water here? Gimme a drink.

BIGGIE: What else is there but water around here?

BIG SHOT LIU: Yeah. Dirty water. Even the river's looking like muddy soup. Logistics department can't get any water to us. We're soaked all day, and are goddamn thirsty at the same time.

LIU MING: How far in d'ya go?

BIG SHOT LIU: To the hard limestone. Worked on that a good long time without getting through.

BIGGIE: That's why they call it "virgin territory."

BIG SHOT LIU: You li'l . . . Never have anything proper to say. What have you been looking for, anyway, bugging your eyes out like that?

BIGGIE: Leftover smokes. *Aiya!* Here's a real long one, a major brand even! *(He lights up his find, more than half unsmoked.)*

BIG SHOT LIU: Lemme have a puff. Been dying for it.

BIGGIE: Okay, but just one.

*(*BIG SHOT LIU *takes a deep drag.)*

BIGGIE: Hey there. Go easy, will ya? You're getting to the end already! What an animal you are. But I gotta say you've got some lungs!

VETERAN: Let me take a turn.

BIGGIE: One more turn and I won't have any left.

VETERAN: Hey, we're one family when it comes to liquor or tobacco.

BIGGIE: One family, yes. But anyone brings in smokes here, I'll get down on my knees in front of him and call him Daddy.

SHI HAI: Why are you holding on to that branch, Big Shot?

BIG SHOT LIU: To shoo away the mosquitoes for the chief driller. You see, the guy's standing there holding on to the brake crank, his feet on the clutch. How can he be doing anything else? These huge mosquitoes with the spotted legs can just have a ball. They sting him all over his cheeks, his face, until he's covered with welts. Got so itchy he started hopping about and nearly bumping into the crown block.

SHI HAI: He's got to watch it. That brake crank controls the three vitals: human life, the well, the equipment.

BIG SHOT LIU: That's why I stand behind him, flicking away the mosquitoes for him with the branch.

LIU MING: Say, those mosquitoes ought to start practicing family planning.

BIGGIE: What they practice is called sexual liberation. Take us now . . . Damn it! My buddy down there's so stiff, you can hang a pair of hobnail boots on it! In another day, I'll just go and be a monk —shave six tonsure spots on my head bald.

BIG SHOT LIU: I'm out of here. *(Exits)*

BIGGIE: Hey, might as well go fight on the frontline. Die there and you're a martyr; stay alive and you're a hero.

LIU MING: Yeah, and you'll get letters from female college students, with turns of phrase that'll stir your blood when you read them out loud.

BIGGIE: We should be so lucky. If it flooded tonight and we got washed away, likely nobody would even know about it. *(Everyone falls silent inside the cabin.)*

JUBILEE: Biggie, will you feed the little goose for me in a while? Just take this plate of food out there.

BIGGIE: Where are you off to?

JUBILEE: I'm going to buy some tobacco for you guys.

BIGGIE: Where can you buy any?

JUBILEE: I've wandered past the area along the swamp. On the north side is a shelter for fishermen. I was thinking that they may have dried tobacco there. They're all locals.

BIGGIE: That's right, that's right! They're always prepared for the rainy season.

JUBILEE: I was thinking I'd get an extra supply and pass them out to all the crews. Let all the smoke fiends satisfy their cravings.

BIGGIE: *(Falls to his knees in front of* JUBILEE*)* Jubilee! You're my daddy, my living ancestor! Anybody bullies you from now on, just let me know. If the opportunity comes along, I'll get you the right connections to transfer out of this roughneck team.

JUBILEE: No, no. Don't be saying that. I feel great to be part of the crew. I'm not strong; can't do heavy work. But I can run errands for you guys, fetch you water, things like that. Besides, when we go out together, we're like real brothers.

SHI HAI: Jubilee . . .

VETERAN: The way there isn't far off, but you're not all that familiar with it. Don't get yourself into trouble.

LIU MING: Watch out for the dark ditches. Once you fall in, it'll be useless to call for help.

BIGGIE: That won't happen. Here's some money, Jubilee. *(Takes out a ten-dollar bill.)*

JUBILEE: I've got money.

BIGGIE: Take it! *(He stuffs the money into* JUBILEE*'s pocket. Then he takes out a couple of bottles.)* You've got to ask them. If they could spare us a bit of booze, that'll be even better.

JUBILEE: I'll check that out. Those fishermen, they all like to drink. But maybe I can humor them a little.

BIGGIE: That's right! That's right!

SHI HAI: Put on your raincoat.

VETERAN: If you get stuck in the mud, then leave your shoes there. Much easier just to pull your bare feet out.

JUBILEE: Nothing's going to happen. *(Exits)*

VETERAN: The rain's let up a bit—

SHI HAI: Let up? It'll be pouring again in a short while.

(CAPTAIN QIN *enters, with a disheveled and grimy* BLACKIE *right behind.)*

SHI HAI: So, you're back.

(BLACKIE *does not answer.)*

SHI HAI: Go get changed.

(BLACKIE *makes no move.)*

VETERAN: Nothing's the matter, is it?

CAPTAIN QIN: Nothing's the matter? We're calling an immediate meeting to settle a serious matter with you guys. Biggie, go tell another crew to send a representative here.

BIGGIE: My salary doesn't cover such duties.

CAPTAIN QIN: You, you son of a bitch—

SHI HAI: Let me go get somebody. *(Exits)*

CAPTAIN QIN: I'm giving special consideration to you guys today. Otherwise, I would be calling for a meeting of the entire team.

LIU MING: A meeting of the entire team? Is there room for that? It's raining outside, you know.

CAPTAIN QIN: I'm not done with you yet.

LIU MING: Even if *you* think we're done, *I* don't think so. I'm still waiting for an apology from you.

CAPTAIN QIN: Then you can keep on waiting!

(SHI HAI *returns dispiritedly with* THIRD-SHIFT LI *and* FOURTH-SHIFT WANG.)

SHI HAI: Let's start the meeting.

CAPTAIN QIN: I'll have my say, then you can have yours. The most important person in all this is Blackie. Then there's Veteran. Liu Ming, Biggie, and Shi Hai are all involved.

BIGGIE: Our crew doesn't have a single good guy, then?

CAPTAIN QIN: What? You're gonna jaw with me? Well, your crew is the one that's loaded with fuckheads.

LIU MING: Hey, let's be a bit more civilized in our speech.

CAPTAIN QIN: Is what you guys have done "civilized"? Huh? Shi Hai, you say.

SHI HAI: No, you go ahead and speak first.

CAPTAIN QIN: All the trouble has come from this crew, which has lost every bit of face the team's had.

THIRD-SHIFT LI: You can't say that. Shi Hai joined the crew with the highest qualifications; he is a person of outstanding character who's been pretty active on the job.

CAPTAIN QIN: So, *how* active has he been? He's activated the practice of bringing women into the cabins.

SHI HAI: This solves nothing. Just say what's true.

CAPTAIN QIN: I still must refer to tradition. When we were living in my hometown years ago, a worker was fired just for telling an off-color joke to the homeowner's wife. After that, the people took us to be out-of-uniform members of the People's Liberation Army. Those days, we had chrysanthemum stalks for our food, usually grown right on the platform of the rig—

BIGGIE: (*Singing out in mock grief the operatic lines*)
"Calling a big meeting in the production team
To speak out about the wrongs
Why, in that all-evil old society—"
(*Everyone lets out a burst of laughter.*)

SHI HAI: Biggie. What the heck are you doing?

BIGGIE: I'm being moved to tears.

CAPTAIN QIN: I . . . I'm going to fire you!

BIGGIE: I'll thank you for that.

CAPTAIN QIN: Shi Hai, I can't control your crew. Go get yourselves another leader!

SHI HAI: Captain—

CAPTAIN QIN: Ah, about this, this, this meeting . . . Let's just speak from the bottom of our hearts. Is what you're doing proper behavior? Veteran is a member of the party, but he's the first to apply for a transfer, all the time going about sending gifts to this place and to that. How do you think this looks? Liu Ming likes to buck authority, makes unreasonable arguments. He's seriously infected with petty bourgeoisie thought. And Biggie? He's an undisciplined and cunning piece of shit, complete with all the vices. Shi Hai is their group leader, who allows all this to go on, pretending not to see. Now, Shi Hai, your father was an old oiler. The glorious traditions he began have all been thrown away in your generation. How can you not feel bad about that in your heart?

SHI HAI: *(Angrily)* We have to *develop* our traditions, not stick to them.

CAPTAIN QIN: Let's not discuss this matter today. Blackie, I am giving you a chance. You've got to examine yourself deeply. Go ahead. Speak.

(Everyone remains silent. BLACKIE *says nothing.)*

CAPTAIN QIN: Speak up.

BLACKIE: There's nothing for me to say.

CAPTAIN QIN: Start by telling us what happened.

BLACKIE: *(Solemnly)* I got hurt, and she came to see me. Even brought me some chicken she'd cooked. We sat there, with nobody else in the room . . . She said she was cold, so I told her to shut the door and the window. She came very close, her breath blowing hot on my face, her eyes filled with tears. She said she really liked me, and so I hugged her. . . . Captain, I don't care if you put me in front of a firing squad. Just don't give her any grief. *(His tears flow.)* Phoenix lost her mom and dad when she was still little, and the Zhaos bought her with money. They made her work like a domesticated animal. That man she's married to is a no-good; wound up in prison just days after the wedding. Captain, Phoenix never had a single day of happiness. She deserves so much better.

(Many are moved to tears.)

CAPTAIN QIN: *(Not as stern as before)* But . . . but she still hasn't been divorced, and you know that. What you've just said is neither deep nor thorough. You haven't seen through your own bias.

LIU MING: As I see it, the matter is simple. Subjectively, Blackie is a man; objectively, she is a woman. This is a matter of consent between two parties, and there's nothing illegal about it. We should not interfere in the private lives of other people.

CAPTAIN QIN: You just stop with that modern-day drivel! Speak up, each of you.

FOURTH-SHIFT WANG: If we are to think about it, Blackie, we workers ought to follow the rules. That woman does have a husband, after all. Your action will bring about disharmony between workers and farmers, and that's very bad.

CAPTAIN QIN: Well said, Wang. Who's next?

BIGGIE: I just have a couple of things. I blame the woman in this matter. If she hadn't come to seduce Blackie, nothing would've happened. Just look at her, with her tits sticking up under that li'l red jacket, swaying this way and that when she walks . . . *(He does an imitation of a woman walking.)*

BLACKIE: *(Rushing over and grabbing* BIGGIE*)* I won't let you insult her!

BIGGIE: *(Appearing cowed)* I . . . I was only trying to help you out!

CAPTAIN QIN: *(Coming forward to break up the tussle)* Let him go! Are you out of your head? Let Biggie finish what he wants to say.

BIGGIE: Anyway, females are all no damn good. If I had the power, I'd put all of 'em to death. Ah, no. I'd spare one. I'd spare my mom. *(Another burst of laughter from everyone)*

CAPTAIN QIN: Vet, you say something.

VETERAN: I'll talk a bit about myself.

CAPTAIN QIN: Fine.

VETERAN: I felt terrible inside when I heard what the captain said. I joined the party while I was still in the army, and the party invested years of training on me. But now, because of personal needs, I've been going around passing out gifts. I have disgraced you all. This gift-giving business has been my own doing, Captain. You can discipline me as you see fit.

FOURTH-SHIFT WANG: This matter does call for strict discipline. The comrades on the team have long been disturbed about such practices. Now Veteran, who is a party member, has gone ahead and done them. What does this make us look like?

CAPTAIN QIN: It would be more excusable for most people. But you are a member of the party. Do you think doing that is proper for a party member? Huh?

VETERAN: *(About to break down in tears)* I'm not worthy, not worthy . . .

SHI HAI: *(Deeply moved)* No. I think Vet *is* worthy to be a member of the party. In fact, he is a pretty good member.

CAPTAIN QIN: You—

SHI HAI: Can I have my say?

CAPTAIN QIN: Speak up!

SHI HAI: This meeting should have been called. But while a part of what you have criticized us for is correct, Captain, another part is plain wrong.

CAPTAIN QIN: What nonsense!

SHI HAI: Let me finish. Take Blackie. He's impetuous, but his heart is in the right place. Phoenix likes him, and he likes her. What in the world is wrong with that? If it's a matter of following legal procedure, let's work on that. And Liu Ming. He asked you to respect his individual dignity by apologizing, and he is completely in the right! As for Veteran, I am profoundly moved by his plight. Yes, he did intend to hand out a gift as a kind of bribe. But each time he's taken it to the place, he's brought it back. People have seen him pacing back and forth in front of the official's door. Why? Why do you think he's had to resort to using a gift? He's had a problem at home; do you guys know about that? Most people would not be able to take what he's been going through.

VETERAN: Say no more, Shi Hai. I've written down everything on my transfer request.

SHI HAI: Have you read that over carefully, Captain? Soon as you see the words "Request for Transfer," you lose your temper.

(CAPTAIN QIN *says nothing.*)

LIU MING: Let me speak. I've thought for a long time about what I have to say, but I don't know whether I should say it.

CAPTAIN QIN: If you've got something to say, say it. Don't beat around the bush.

LIU MING: Captain, you ought to quit your job!

(*Everyone is speechless with surprise.*)

LIU MING: You have the ability to be a pretty decent factory hand/model worker. But to lead a roughneck team with an average age of twenty-one is beyond your capabilities. The longer you go on, the more difficulties you will have.

FOURTH-SHIFT WANG: This is going too far.

LIU MING: Think about it. What've you got to offer? Just your references to tradition, or getting mad, or lecturing people. We're going to be getting new imported equipment at the end of the year, and you probably will not be able to read the instruction manuals. You're always comparing everything to the past, talking about the old days every time you open your mouth. But if our hard work has not been able to change our lives, why go on talking about this "ism" and that "ism"? Nowadays the exploration workers of even small nations like Kuwait and Saudi Arabia are using helicopters to change shifts. So you can see what Shi Hai has been pointing out is not so wild or unreasonable. The crux of the matter is your unwillingness to criticize yourself and your lack of courage to emerge from your out-of-date views. That's all I've got to say.

BIGGIE: What he says is the truth. Captain, you should resign. If, like Marx, you wait until someone kicks you out, then it'll look bad.

CAPTAIN QIN: How "like Marx"? What are you talking about?

BIGGIE: Like Marx in the Philippines.

CAPTAIN QIN: When has Marx ever gone to the Philippines? What unfounded bullshit!

BIGGIE: Even if you won't resign, I would still urge you to get out of the Communist Party.

BROODER: Are you a goddamn human being, Biggie? What are you doing? What are you doing? You figure the captain is someone easy to kick around? (*He goes over to* CAPTAIN QIN *and pulls him up.*) Take a good look at the captain, all of you. Which little part of his body has not been injured? He gets up bright and early every day and gets home after dark. Any place in camp has problems, he's the one they look to for solutions. These last few years, has anyone seen him take off during a holiday? As human beings, we at least gotta have a bit of conscience! The people who started out with him in the oil fields are all riding around in cars now. But he has always remained with the roughnecks. When he does get home, his wife tells him he's a vagabond, his daughter calls him a good-for-nothing. On the team, anyone who wants to say anything against him will say it, anyone who feels like cussing him out will cuss him out. You are all his Big Daddies, and only he is a child. If you guys want to, go ahead and write to the secretary general! Just don't fucking use the captain as your punching bag. I want nothing to do with a meeting of this kind. (*He gets up to leave.*)

VETERAN: Hold it, Brooder.

BROODER: (*In tears*) We can't say that the captain is outstanding. But he—he's a good man, you know.
(*The younger people fall silent.* BROODER'*s words come from the heart, and they ring true.*
Suddenly, an unusual noise issues from the rig, spreading concern and fear among everyone.
BIG SHOT LIU *rushes in.*)

BIG SHOT LIU: Extraordinary, what's happening at the well.

LIU MING: Maybe they've gotten to the natural gas. Great! This clearly indicates tremendous pressure, and things look very good.

BIG SHOT LIU: The rig is unsteady. It's really wobbling around.

VETERAN: The cables have gotten loose. I'll get up there and tighten them. Captain, here's my self-criticism report. Don't worry; Ol' Vet won't be doing anything to bring criticism down on us ever again.

CAPTAIN QIN: *(Receiving the report)* Don't talk about it anymore . . . and take care getting up on the rig.

SHI HAI: Prepare to go!

CAPTAIN QIN: *(Touched)* Shi Hai, let me lead them up. We won't need this many people.

SHI HAI: Biggie can stay with Blackie. All the rest of you come along. *(Everyone rushes about. The young people's ready spirit of self-sacrifice is obvious and admirable. The unusual rumbling from the rig continues.*

LIN JIAN *enters with* BLOSSOM, *a basket of vegetables strapped on his back. Everyone is surprised.)*

VETERAN: Blossom! How'd you get here?

BLOSSOM: You sent me the telegram, and even had a car meet me.

VETERAN: I . . . I never sent any telegram.

LIN JIAN: This is your residency certificate, already approved. *(He hands it over.)*

VETERAN: This—

CAPTAIN QIN: *(Grabbing the tools from* VETERAN*)* Don't you go up; I'll do it. Take Blossom over to the hostel. You can stay there for the night.

BLACKIE: Captain, let me go up.

CAPTAIN QIN: You're not feeling well. Just stay here.

BIGGIE: Damn it; let me go up.

CAPTAIN QIN: Get out of here. You don't know how to get up there.

LIN JIAN: This well has great promise. We've got to save it.

CAPTAIN QIN: Let's go see what's happening.

*(*CAPTAIN QIN *rushes off, followed by* LIN JIAN *and the younger workers, except* BIGGIE.

VETERAN *introduces* BLOSSOM *to* BLACKIE *and* BIGGIE.)*

VETERAN: This is Blackie, and that's Biggie.

BIGGIE: How do you do, ma'am. Had you delayed your coming any longer, Ol' Vet would not have been able to go on, he's been missing you so badly.

(BLACKIE *says nothing, heavyhearted over his own problems.*)

BLOSSOM: It was hard finding my way to this place. The car is still over by the pasture. Is that all right?

VETERAN: No problem. Who was it who sent you the telegram?

BLOSSOM: Strange, really. It was so clearly written and all.

VETERAN: Let's get going to the hostel. I'll get you something to eat, and you can get changed.

(VETERAN *exits with* BLOSSOM.)

BIGGIE: (*To himself*) It'll probably not be gushing yet.

BLACKIE: Good if it will. Where's Jubilee?

BIGGIE: He's gone to get smokes and booze. (*He picks up the plate of food for the goose and is about to leave.*)

BLACKIE: What're you going off to do?

BIGGIE: Feed the goose for Jubilee.

BLACKIE: What fucking for? Let's butcher it and eat it.

BIGGIE: No-no-no. That's the creature Jubilee is most fond of.

BLACKIE: The creature he's fond of? Get out of here.

BIGGIE: Why have you gotten so barbaric, Blackie?

BLACKIE: Barbaric? Me? I was just feeling an urge to kill.

(BLACKIE *gropes under the bed and takes out a cleaver.* BIGGIE *jumps in his way.*)

BIGGIE: Don't you do it. You'll regret it when Jubilee gets back.

BLACKIE: (*Ruefully*) The weather's turned cold, and the geese have flown off . . . and they won't be back.

BIGGIE: Yes, that's so . . .

BLACKIE: I'm not cut out to deal with drippy sentiment. For me, what's truly worthwhile is booze to guzzle and meat to stuff into my mouth. Anyway, what I do is no concern of yours.

BIGGIE: Can . . . can you really be like that?

BLACKIE: All sentimental wimps, stand aside! (*He rushes off with the cleaver.*)

BIGGIE: You're right. What a damn shame if it were to just fly off.

(SHI HAI *and* LIU MING *return.*)

BIGGIE: How was it?

LIU MING: The proportion of muddy water is too great. We're still watching it carefully.

SHI HAI: Where'd Blackie go?

BIGGIE: He . . . he wants to butcher the goose and have it with his liquor.

SHI HAI: What? (*He starts to leave.*)

(BLACKIE *enters, carrying the goose dripping with blood.*)

BLACKIE: (*Tossing the goose on the ground*) I killed it! Let's drink! Let's have meat!

LIU MING: You're too uncivilized! You've killed it. You've killed it!

BLACKIE: We're not civilized here; I killed—

SHI HAI: You did that just to vent your frustration, you animal! (*He slaps* BLACKIE *across the face.*)

BLACKIE: So, I'm aching inside for poor, unhappy Phoenix. Is that illegal? You guys are so civilized, you tell me! I want a drink! A drink!

(*All are silent.* JUBILEE *staggers into the cabin, naked from the waist up and covered with mud from head to toe. Cradled in his arms is a tool bag wrapped with his clothing and his raincoat.*)

JUBILEE: I've brought it! Tobacco—and liquor, too. Everything's here. . . . When it rained, I took off my clothes and wrapped up the tobacco in them. Can't smoke the stuff if it's wet. I'm not late for my shift, am I, Chief? I was surrounded by mosquitoes all the way, my whole face and body . . .

(*All remain silent.*)

JUBILEE: What's the matter with you guys? Weren't you unhappy yesterday because you wanted smokes and booze? (*He finally sees the dead and bloody goose on the ground and becomes mute with shock. He nearly does not believe his own eyes.*) Who did it? Who? . . . Why, oh why? . . .

(*Silence. A silence like death.*)

JUBILEE: Say it. Say something. What has the little gray goose ever done to you guys?

(*Continued silence.*)

JUBILEE: (*Crying*) You guys wouldn't even spare such a little thing. (*He howls out his anger.*) Tell me! How did you look after the goose for me, Biggie?

BLACKIE: It was I who killed it.

(JUBILEE *moves toward the cleaver, wanting to have it out with* BLACKIE. *He is grabbed and restrained by* SHI HAI.)

BLACKIE: (*Picking up the cleaver from the floor and handing it to*

JUBILEE) If you need to let out all that steam, then just go ahead
and cut me up.

(JUBILEE *seems to go mad. He drops the cleaver to the floor.
Again, silence.*)

JUBILEE: (*Bawls as he picks up the little goose*) The little gray goose is
dead. He won't be flying anymore. He's really pitiable, isn't he?

LIU MING: How could you bear to do it?

JUBILEE: (*Clawing at his own chest*) I'm really itching! Scratch me.
Oh, scratch me.

SHI HAI: Quick. Get some lotion and rub it on him.

(*Everyone helps* JUBILEE *onto his bed.*)

BIGGIE: Oh, Mama. How'd he get bitten up like that? It's all swollen
and broken out. Blood everywhere.

LIU MING: His skin's bursting from all the bites.

JUBILEE: Scratch me, please. Harder! I said harder!

SHI HAI: (*Not daring to touch* JUBILEE'*s swollen face and back*)
This . . .

JUBILEE: (*Clawing at the skin on his own chest and tossing this way
and that on the bed*) It's so hard to stand—the pain in there—so
very hard, so hard. . . . I'm itching, itching. Get a knife quick and
cut me! I can't take it anymore.

BLACKIE: (*Holding* JUBILEE *in his arms*) Jubilee, don't . . . Quick,
pour some water into the basin.

(BIGGIE *pours the water;* BLACKIE *takes off* JUBILEE'*s shoes, washes
his feet, and rubs his body.*

Utter silence inside the cabin.)

BIGGIE: Let's all stop smoking. . . .

BLACKIE: I don't even feel like drinking anymore.

(*Silence again.*

PUDGY *enters, carrying a hot bowl of noodles.*)

PUDGY: Jubilee, have some hot noodles. I've been saving them for you
after I heard that you were going off to get smokes for everyone.
Aiya! How'd you get bitten up like that?

BLACKIE: (*Taking the noodles*) This, you son of a bitch, is the first
decent thing you've done. From now on, just don't kiss so much
ass.

PUDGY: Hell, don't you know you can offend anyone but a leader? If
I hadn't gotten on the wrong side of Director Zhang in Logistics
early on, do you think I would have wound up here with the

roughnecks? I would've been a fucking section chief by now! *(He stops momentarily.)* To go back to what I was trying to say, there are leaders and there are leaders. Take Captain Qin, now. I've never met up with such a fine person. If you guys go on treating him the way you have been, well, it's a sin to kick an honest man around.

(From far away comes a loud clashing of metal, followed by a frightened wail: "Caap—taain!")

SHI HAI: What was that?

LIU MING: An accident . . .

BIGGIE: Can't be. Hasn't the gushing been controlled?

(THIRD-SHIFT LI enters carrying CAPTAIN QIN on his back. LIN JIAN and a few workers rush up.)

SHI HAI: *(Shaken)* What's happened?

THIRD-SHIFT LI: The rig became unstable. The captain was climbing up to tighten the cables, but the big ladder was slippery from the heavy rain. He fell all the way down.

LIU MING: Captain . . .

THIRD-SHIFT LI: He wouldn't let anyone else go up.

JUBILEE: *(Jumping out of bed and hugging QIN)* Captain! What's happened to you? You wake up now. Wake up, please! I brought some tobacco back for you, your favorite kind.

BIGGIE: The leg is still bleeding.

LIU MING: Get some cloth and make a tourniquet. Hurry. Hurry, please.

(BLACKIE rips a strip from his bedsheet. He winds it tight around the captain's leg.)

SHI HAI: Call the dispatcher, on the double, and ask for a car! The man is about gone. Ask whether the nurse Qin Fang is at the front line.

(THIRD-SHIFT LI runs off.)

LIU MING: This won't do. Any car they dispatch won't get here for hours. Besides, the road isn't passable.

BLACKIE: I'll put him on my back, take him to the hospital!

JUBILEE: Let's all of us carry him.

LIU MING: It'll take until sunrise tomorrow before we can get him to the nearest hospital.

BIGGIE: We'll use the tractor!

LIN JIAN: The tractor is slower than walking.

SHI HAI: What'll we do, then? Wait for him to die?

BIGGIE: The blood! We can't stop it! It's still pouring out.

(*They pause.*)

JUBILEE: Is he dead?

BIGGIE: A man doesn't die that easily.

JUBILEE: Then why won't he have a smoke?

SHI HAI: He's fallen asleep,

BLACKIE: Asleep?

LIU MING: His face looks really serene.

(THIRD-SHIFT LI *rushes up.*)

THIRD-SHIFT LI: Crew Chief, the dispatcher is sending a vehicle right away! The military department commandeered a tank as escort. They're bringing along a doctor.

SHI HAI: How long will they take?

THIRD-SHIFT LI: Most optimistically about two hours and forty minutes. Also, Qin Fang is not working on the front line. I heard she is preparing for her college entrance exams.

SHI HAI: Damn it.

LIN JIAN: (*Giving an order*) Radio the general office for a helicopter!

SHI HAI: Nonsense. How do we have that much clout?

LIN JIAN: Just say that I am Lin Jian, the new secretary on the Party Committee of the Exploration Corporation!

(*Startled, everyone turns to stare at* LIN JIAN.

THIRD-SHIFT LI *hurries off again.*)

LIN JIAN: Qin, my good man. Please wake up. Wake up now.

ALL: Captain!

(CAPTAIN QIN *slowly opens his eyes. He doesn't seem to be suffering, his face extraordinarily tranquil. Perhaps this is the momentary calm experienced by those who are at death's door.*)

CAPTAIN QIN: (*Looking each person over*) Veteran, here's the key to the team's hostel. The place is too damp these days, so use the electric blanket there. Vet, I'm sorry about the way I've been to you and your wife.

VETERAN: (*Sobbing*) Captain, you went up there in my place!

CAPTAIN QIN: Don't be angry with me, Liu Ming. Perhaps you are right. Just take me to be your elderly big brother, and spare me the need to grovel and apologize.

LIU MING: Don't say any more about it, Captain. It's I who's been immature.

BIGGIE: Go ahead, Captain, and bawl me out some more. I've never been understanding, never cared to make you proud.

CAPTAIN QIN: *(With a quick smile)* Ah, human beings! Some things they can't get straight even after a lifetime. *(He gently closes his eyes.)*

BLACKIE: Can't wait any longer! Let's move—

(The young people pick up the army cot with CAPTAIN QIN *in it. One of* QIN*'s arms slips down limply and dangles from the cot.)*

LIN JIAN: *(Coming up to feel* QIN*'s pulse, then slowly shaking his head)* Remember him as a person who struggled his entire life for the petroleum industry, a person who came to us right out of history. *(The young people put down the cot, then get on their knees together around the captain and begin choking with sobs.*

The harmonica sounds again, from far off.

Lights dim.)

ACT II
SCENE II

(Several days later, before dawn. Lights up. Scenery identical. The night sky of autumn is deep and translucent. A few stars peek out from behind pale wandering clouds, twinkling like mysterious eyes. Crystalline wavelets shimmer in the distant bend of the river. Reeds by the shore release their catkins, which drift about in the wind. In the vast wilderness, the outlines of the derrick—now taken down— the railcar cabins, and the various accoutrements appear to be both magical and natural in the misty haze. All the earth is fast asleep.

The people in SHI HAI*'s crew are all lying down, each on his own cot. But one can see that, this night, they have all lost sleep. For young people like they are, the loss of proper rest grates on them.)*

LIU MING: What time is it?

SHI HAI: Still a ways from sunrise. Get back to sleep.

LIU MING: Where are we being sent to do the next well?

SHI HAI: Possibly to Hailar.

LIU MING: Hailar? It'll take two weeks just to get there. I heard there's basically no road to the place.

SHI HAI: Where the hell have we ever gone to where there was a road? *(*BIGGIE *sits on his bed, a quilt over his shoulders, smoking cigarette after cigarette.)*

BIGGIE: I'll have to be going, everybody. A car will be here to get me in a little while. (*He pauses.*)

SHI HAI: (*Sitting down at* BIGGIE's *side, a coat draped over himself*) Lemme have one of those.

(BIGGIE *hands over a cigarette, still lost in thought.*)

SHI HAI: What're you thinking about?

BIGGIE: Last night I had a dream. Captain Qin was standing in front of me. . . . (*Sighs*) While someone's still alive, you may think he's full of faults. But once he's gone, you feel that everything about him was just fine.

(*Both* SHI HAI *and* BIGGIE *are now lost in thought for a moment.*)

BIGGIE: Hey, Liu Ming. How'd it go with the first breakthrough on that well of ours yesterday?

LIU MING: It'll be turning out over eight hundred thousand cubic units of natural gas a day, with geological reserves of over three billion cubic units.

SHI HAI: A chemical plant can be set up here in the future. Soon as it becomes operational, it can be producing tens of millions of units the very first year.

BIGGIE: (*With a big sigh*) Ahh, me . . .

SHI HAI: Now, Biggie, you ought to take advantage of your opportunity and go get yourself an education!

BIGGIE: (*Seizing* SHI HAI's *hand, feeling tears coming on*) Shi Hai, forgive me.

(*All again fall silent. The sky gradually brightens.*)

SHI HAI: Let's get going. We've got to get ready early for today's move. (*He pauses.*) In a little while, we have to say good-bye to Biggie. Let's help him get his luggage together and put his belongings in order.

BIGGIE: Come, have a smoke with me.

(LIN JIAN *enters.*)

LIN JIAN: I'm here to announce a new directive. Shi Hai will be the captain of this team. Liu Ming will be the technician and cocaptain. The branch party secretary will be appointed later.

SHI HAI: Why don't you come see us some time and stay a few days, Secretary Lin? If you don't mind, we'd like you to play a few more hands of cards with us.

LIN JIAN: I will do that. I will be coming.

LIU MING: You were a pretty good actor, Secretary Lin.

LIN JIAN: I want to apologize to one and all today! I was dishonest with you that one time because I wanted to get to the bottom of what was really going on with your crew. Please forgive me. Ah, yes. The orders for your team have been approved. Take a look. *(He takes out the document from his briefcase and hands it to* SHI HAI.*)*

SHI HAI: *(Reading the orders)* "Change to imported hydraulic pressure drill number twenty. Set up entertainment center with video player and mobile library. . . ." This . . . is this genuine?

LIN JIAN: They're pretty generous provisions, aren't they? I was only concentrating on the small stuff, however.

LIU MING: You won't be sorry for doing this.

LIN JIAN: I'm heading out for team three twenty-nine now. So excuse me. See you in Hailar! *(Exits)*

*(*JUBILEE *helps* BIGGIE *pack his bags.* LIU MING *and* BLACKIE *join in, picking up scattered items.* BIGGIE, *however, just stands there, immobile.)*

SHI HAI: *(Patting* BIGGIE *on the shoulder)* The time you've spent here will probably prove to be useful to you the rest of your life. Whenever you can, come back and see us.

BLACKIE: Don't you forget your hard-luck brothers!

*(*BIGGIE *just stands there, without saying a word.)*

LIU MING: *(Taking out a core sample from his bed)* This is for you—a souvenir! This is no ordinary hunk of stone. It was formed over two thousand meters under the earth, and has endured countless eons of wind and rain and massive pressure. Yet it has remained so hard, so resiliently tough.

*(*BIGGIE *takes the stone core and hefts it in his hand. Outside, the sound of a car horn.)*

SHI HAI: Let's go; it's time.

LIU MING: So, good-bye. Perhaps we'll see you again.

JUBILEE: *(Breaking down in tears)* Biggie, my brother. Write to me. I'll come see you during winter break.

BIGGIE: *(Tearfully)* My brothers, I . . . I seem to have grown old all of a sudden . . . grown old.

*(*BIGGIE *looks all around the little cabin, throws his bags over his shoulders, and, as he goes outside, trains his gaze on the vast wilderness. Everyone follows him out.)*

BIGGIE: *(Suddenly hearing the sound of the harmonica drifting over from far off, he breaks into loud sobs and throws his arms around* SHI HAI.) I can never forget any of you. Not for the rest of my life. *(Getting on his knees, facing the audience)* Captain, Biggie is leaving now.

SHI HAI: Get going. *(Helping* BIGGIE *up)* The car's still waiting. (BIGGIE *leaves.*)

SHI HAI: Big Shot, see if the tow trucks and the trailers are accounted for.

BIG SHOT LIU: Yes sir! *(Goes off)*

(Those on SHI HAI's *crew enter the cabin to gather their luggage. From high up in the sky comes the honking of geese flying south. At that, the young people stop their work and lapse into silence. . . . They have finally matured. Like all grown-ups, they have come to understand what reality is, in all of human history, in grief and in joy.*

PHOENIX, stumbling and hobbling, enters, her hair disheveled, her clothing badly torn, her blood-splattered shoulder, thighs, and back exposed. Everyone is speechless with surprise.

Outside the cabin a circle of workers getting ready for their meal has gathered.)

BLACKIE: *(Embracing* PHOENIX) What happened? Phoenix, Phoenix!

PHOENIX: *(Speaking in stops and starts)* He's out of prison . . . not a bit changed! He beat me up, beat me all over, beat me with anything he got his hands on . . . kept at it all day and all night.

SHI HAI: What an animal! Why'd he do it?

PHOENIX: When I suggested that we get divorced . . . he wanted to kill me. *(Wailing)* I want a divorce! A divorce! A divorce!

BLACKIE: I'll kill him!

(Several others are ready to rush out with him.)

PHOENIX: No, don't! Don't go! He was choking me, till I couldn't breathe. . . . I picked up this pair of scissors . . . and stabbed them into his chest without thinking. Blood. Blood spurting everywhere.

BLACKIE: You killed him?

PHOENIX: Yes, killed him.

JUBILEE: Murder! He's dead?

PHOENIX: I don't know. . . . I'm done for also. . . . Blackie, I won't be seeing you anymore! *(Stifling a sob)* I'll be executed. Collect my remains and throw them out into the wilderness. Let the wild dogs tear me apart. Oh, dear Blackie, at least I've gotten to know you in this life. To die now will be worth it.

(Fire seems to leap out from BLACKIE's *glowering eyes. Many there are moved to tears.* BLOSSOM *goes over to prop up* PHOENIX.)

BLOSSOM: Don't be so down on yourself. Everyone here will vouch for you.

EVERYONE: Yes, we'll be your witnesses.

VETERAN: Wherever the trial is, I'll be there to speak for you.

*(*BIG SHOT LIU *enters.)*

BIG SHOT LIU: Captain, all the tow trucks, tractors, and bulldozers are present and accounted for.

SHI HAI: Blackie, you stay with Phoenix for now. The rest of you assemble in the field!

EVERYONE: Yes sir! *(All exit)*

BLACKIE: Phoenix . . .

*(*PHOENIX *and* BLACKIE *lock in a tight embrace.*

From backstage comes SHI HAI's *stirring cry: "Forrrrward marrrrch!" The loud rumble of the tow trucks, tractors, and bulldozers comes closer and closer, until it becomes a deafening roar, obliterating all other sounds and seeming to make the earth tremble.*

Lights dim. Curtain.)

NOTES

The English translation is based on the Chinese text *Heise de shitou* (Black stones), published in *Juben* (Drama script) 2 (1988): 4–25.

1. Located in northeast China, not far from the Siberian border.

2. Sir Rabindranath Tagore (1861–1941) has been admired in some Chinese intellectual circles since he received the 1913 Nobel Prize in literature.

3. Alexander Pushkin (1799–1837) is widely considered Russia's greatest poet.

4. In China, Karl Marx (1818–1883) remains officially revered as the founder of democratic socialism and revolutionary communism.

5. Lin Biao (1907–1971), once designated to succeed Chairman Mao Zedong as China's top leader, reportedly attempted to kill Mao and overthrow the government. He died in an airplane crash in Mongolia while attempting to escape.

6. Jean August Dominique Ingres (1780–1867), a French neoclassical painter, is known partly for his sensuous nudes. Most famous among these is *La Source*, here rendered as *The Spring*, painted in 1856. The original hangs in the Louvre, in Paris.

Jiang Qing and Her Husbands

Sha Yexin

TRANSLATED BY KIRK A. DENTON

Highest Directive

There is no love in this world that is without reason or cause,

no hatred in this world that is without reason or cause.

— *Mao Zedong*

Principal Characters

JIANG QING (LAN PING)	HE ZIZHEN
MAO ZEDONG	XIAO FENG
TANG NA	BODYGUARD

PROLOGUE

(The stage is empty, dark, still, and silent. After a short while, a ray of white light descends from above, then "walks" hurriedly, as if looking for something, onstage from the side curtain. Not finding it, the light becomes agitated and picks up its "steps," rushing around in all directions.)

VOICE: Here I am, over here!

(The white light stops and listens carefully so as to determine from which direction the voice is coming, then moves toward it, searching intently.)

VOICE: How fucking stupid can you get. I'm over here, here!

(The white light stops again and again and intently listens to determine from whence the noise has issued, and then gingerly proceeds to search left and right.)

VOICE: Are you blind? Why are you just looking in the corners? Am I someone who would hide in a corner?

(The white light once again stops and listens intently.)

VOICE: I am Jiang Qing, Mao Zedong's wife, standard-bearer of the Cultural Revolution, the most outstanding actress. In China I am the center of things, on center stage.

(With fear and trepidation, the white light immediately rushes to center stage and finally finds its target. Under its light can now be seen the face of the principal character of this play: JIANG QING. She is sixty or seventy years old, but she doesn't seem very old—much younger than her actual age.)

JIANG QING: *(Raising her head and looking at the white light with an attitude of haughty considerateness, she taps the spotlight with her hand.)* That's right; very good, thank you. Shine on me, shine on me forever, thank you. . . . *(Suddenly angry)* No, wait. Damn! White light? Do I want white light? White light is counterrevolutionary, revisionist. No white light!

(The white light changes immediately into a yellow light.)

JIANG QING: No, no!

(The yellow light changes into a blue light.)

JIANG QING: Ugly as sin, ugly as sin! No blue light!

(The blue light changes to red.)

JIANG QING: Make it green, make it green. Give me green light, green, apple green.

(The red light changes into a green light. Only then does JIANG QING *settle down.)*

JIANG QING: I like green, apple green. When I was young, I liked blue, so I was called Blue Apple, Lan Ping. *(She gently strokes the light.)* Ah, what a lovely spotlight! My whole life has been spent under the dazzling lights, on the resplendent stage, because I am an actress. Really, I am an actress, an outstanding actress. *(*JIANG QING *walks out of the circle of light, the performance area enlarges, and the entire stage lights up.* JIANG QING *plays* NORA *from Ibsen's* A Doll's House.)

NORA: *(Enters her home, humming a tune)* Helene, be sure to hide the Christmas tree well. We don't want the children to see it in the daylight. We'll light it in the evening. *(Gets her purse and asks the porter)* How much? Here's a kroner; keep the change. . . . *(To* HELMER*)* Torvald, come quickly, look at the things I bought, and so inexpensive! Look, this is a new outfit for Ivar, and a little sword. And this is Bob's little bird[1] and trumpet. And this doll and cradle are for Emmy. . . .

JIANG QING: *(Appreciating herself)* I was trained professionally. At fifteen I tested into the Shandong Provincial Experimental Theater Troupe, specializing in spoken drama. I can still perform Peking opera, you know. *(*JIANG QING *goes to the side curtain and dresses as* GUIYING *in the Peking opera* The Fisherman's Revenge; *sings the "Interjective Aria" from offstage: "Pulling the oars the boat shoots forward like a flying arrow . . ."* GUIYING *enters rowing a boat.)*

GUIYING *(Singing "Animated Aria")*:
"On and on rolls the river, spreading spray around.
Summer or winter, it's all the same for families of the poor.
Father and daughter fish for their livelihoods. *(Lowers her head in the crying position)*
        (At this time, the wooden railings one sees in a courtroom descend from above and encircle JIANG QING. *Behind the railing stands a sign on which is the word "Defendant.")*

JIANG QING: *(Raising her head and discovering she has been enclosed by the railing, she is taken aback.)* What are you doing? What are you doing? You— What is this? You're going to try me? Why? Huh? I can't hear you! *(Takes out a hearing aid and places the plug in her ear)* Say it again. What? I have committed four big crimes! Framing and persecuting leaders of the party and the country; persecuting and suppressing the party cadres and the broad masses, et cetera, et cetera. Humph, heinous crimes indeed! What? How many? *(Pushes the earplug further in and listens intently)* I have persecuted seven hundred thousand people? Thirty-seven thousand have died as a result? Implicated a total of one million people? *(Laughs loudly, raises her finger and points back, and says with a pouting expression)* Nonsense, fabricated rumors! How could I have persecuted Liu Shaoqi to death! Ha-ha-ha, that's fucking malicious slander. The dead cannot bear witness! No, I don't deny it—I was on the group deciding Liu Shaoqi's case, but I was only a helper. You have recorded proof? Okay, let's listen then. (JIANG QING *holds on to the railing and extends her head forward, listening attentively.)*

RECORDING: (JIANG QING's *voice)* . . . I am now taking responsibility for the nation's number-one special investigatory case . . . and I can now tell you, Liu Shaoqi is a big counterrevolutionary who embodies all evil, an informer within the ranks, an arch-traitor, a spy. He is odious! This traitor should be sliced to pieces with a thousand knives, ten thousand knives . . . *(The recording finishes.)*

JIANG QING: Mmm, seems like my voice—pretty nice—probably a talk I gave in September of 1968 to the literary world; I inserted that part in the middle. Admit my crimes? What crimes should I admit to? *(In a loud voice)* I committed no crimes! When you're involved in such an important revolution, what's the big deal if a few people die? These were extreme actions done in the momentary heat of a massive revolutionary movement. Results above all else! Wait, those are Lin Biao's words. I probably shouldn't say them. As for Liu Shaoqi, he was State Chairman, second in charge of the Party Central Committee. If the politburo didn't approve it, if the members of the Standing Committee didn't raise their hands, would he have been ousted? And now you want to blame everything on me, as if I were the arch culprit who created all this anarchy, as if I stirred up the civil war. Am I really that talented? Have I really got that kind of charisma? The Cultural Revolution was initiated and led by Chairman Mao himself. I was only carrying out his directives. What responsibility do I have?

In fact, I was Chairman Mao's dog. When he told me to bite someone, I did it.

(Still stage. The sound of a dog barking gradually approaches, louder and louder, fiercer and fiercer, until finally it seems as if the whole world is filled with the fearful sound of this wild dog.

JIANG QING is also scared of the sound of the dog. In terror, she pulls out the earplug, throws the hearing aid away, and stops up her ears with her hands. The sound of the dog retreats into the distance, gradually fainter and fainter, until at last a deathlike silence is restored.)

JIANG QING: *(Fearfully)* No, no, I am . . . not a dog, no one's dog. I am human, at least I used to be human. . . . Chairman Mao's corpse isn't even cold yet; you shouldn't be trying me like this. This is a loss of face for the Cultural Revolution, a loss of face for the proletarian revolutionary faction! I want to leave! *(She makes as if to leave the confines of the railing.)* I want to leave! *(TANG NA appears to JIANG QING's left.)*

TANG NA: Wait, Miss Lan Ping!

JIANG QING: Who is it?

TANG NA: Tang Na, your second husband.

JIANG QING: Huh, you? What are you doing here?

TANG NA: Court witness.

JIANG QING: Who told you to come?

TANG NA: You!

JIANG QING: Me?

TANG NA: Yes.

(MAO ZEDONG appears on JIANG QING's right.)

MAO ZEDONG: Comrade Jiang Qing!

JIANG QING: *(Drops her head)* Who is it?

MAO ZEDONG: Mao Zedong, your third husband.

JIANG QING: How is it you're here, too?

MAO ZEDONG: Court witness.

JIANG QING: Who would dare ask you to be a court witness?

MAO ZEDONG: You.

JIANG QING: Me, again?

MAO ZEDONG: Yes.

JIANG QING: *(Agitated)* No, I never brought either of you here; only I can give testimony for myself. I want to leave. I want to go! I want to go! I want to go! (JIANG QING *pushes aside the railing and leaves.*)

TANG NA: Where are you going?

JIANG QING: *(Hesitantly)* I . . . want to go to the 1930s . . . to Shanghai . . .

(Blackout. JIANG QING *is playing* NORA, *carrying a small travel bag.* MAO ZEDONG *is playing* HELMER. TANG NA, *sitting to one side, is playing the audience; he watches the following scene with rapt attention.)*

HELMER: Nora, Nora, don't leave now; wait until tomorrow.

NORA: *(Putting on her coat)* I don't want to spend a night in the house of a stranger.

HELMER: Wouldn't it be possible for us to live as brother and sister?

NORA: *(Putting on her hat)* You know very well that wouldn't last long. *(Puts on her shawl)* Good-bye, Torvald. Here—this is your ring; give me back mine.

HELMER: You even want to give back the rings?

NORA: Yes!

HELMER: Here.

NORA: So, it's all over now. I'll just put the keys here. As for running the house, the servants know what to do—in fact they are more familiar with it than I am.

HELMER: It's over, over! Nora, I suppose this means you will never think of me again?

NORA: Oh, I expect I will often think of you, think of the children and this house.

HELMER: May I write to you?

NORA: No, absolutely never write to me.

HELMER: Please, let me at least send you some—

NORA: There's no need to send anything.

HELMER: But I must help you out when you are in need.

NORA: It's not necessary. I don't accept help from strangers.

HELMER: Nora, must I always be only a stranger to you?

NORA: *(Picking up her bag)* Yes, Torvald, unless a miracle of miracles happens.

HELMER: What do you mean by "miracle of miracles"?

NORA: I mean, if we could both change so that— Oh, Torvald, I no longer believe that miracles are possible in this world.

HELMER: But I believe in them. Go on, if we could both change so that what?

NORA: Change so that we could live together like a true husband and wife. Good-bye. (*NORA goes out the hall doorway, exits.*)

HELMER: (*Falls into a chair by the door, with his face in his hands*) Nora! Nora! (*He looks around and rises.*) The room is empty. She's gone. (*A hope sparks from within.*) Oh, a "miracle of miracles." (*From below is heard the bang of a heavy door closing. The lights go down.* HELMER *disappears and exits.* TANG NA *is so excited that he is the first to stand up and applaud. Sound effects: the prolonged applause of the audience. Amidst the applause, blackout.*)

SHANGHAI, 1930S

(*The entrance of the Golden City Theater. The theater is on the corner of Peking Road and Guizhou Road. The space occupied by* TANG NA *in the prologue is now a street scene. The applause has now transformed into the jazz music popular in the 1930s. The neon lights on the theater's marquee and poster board are flashing the following words:* NORA, FIRST PERFORMANCE BY SHANGHAI'S AMATEUR DRAMATISTS. WORLD-RENOWNED PLAY. THE IMMORTAL WORK OF IBSEN. THE BIBLE OF CHINESE WOMEN. A PORTRAIT OF FALSITY AND HYPOCRISY. PERFORMED IN NINETEENTH-CENTURY COSTUME, REALISTIC STAGING ACCORDING TO NORWEGIAN STYLE. DIRECTED BY ZHANG MIN. FEATURING THE STAR OF THE NORTH, LAN PING. *The neon lights gradually diminish. Holding a copy of the program for* A Doll's House, TANG NA *is standing and waiting on the street. He still seems absorbed in the excitement of the performance of* A Doll's House, *which he has just watched.* LAN PING *walks out of the theater. It is early summer (June) weather and she is wearing a blue cheongsam that fits her very nicely and is quite striking. She is excited by the success of the performance, but she is also tired.* TANG NA *goes up to greet her.*)

TANG NA: Miss Lan Ping!

(*Without even looking at* TANG NA *and offering no explanation,* LAN PING *takes the program from* TANG NA's *hand, immediately takes out a pen, and signs her name as if she had done so many times before.* TANG NA *is startled, laughs, but doesn't say anything. There is no ink in* LAN PING's *pen; she gives it a shake, but still no ink.* TANG NA *immediately offers her his pen.* LAN PING *takes it and signs her name on the program.)*

LAN PING: Nice pen.

TANG NA: A Parker.

LAN PING: Here.

TANG NA: Could you inscribe the recipient's name so that people know you signed it for me?

LAN PING: Yes. What is your surname?

TANG NA: Tang, and my given name is the single character Na.

LAN PING: *(Still writing on the program, with her head lowered)* Tang . . . *(Suddenly surprised)* Tang Na? *(Raises her head and looks him over)* Sir, you . . .

TANG NA: That's right, Tang Na.

LAN PING: Oh, Mr. Tang. I am sorry—very, very sorry. I thought it was just some nobody from among the fans in the audience who wanted my autograph. Just now backstage I signed so many, the ink in my pen ran dry. I never thought it would be the famous critic, Tang Na.

TANG NA: I am also one of your fans. And if you mean that I am *not* a "nobody," then perhaps it is because following today's performance of *A Doll's House* I am now more aware of your acting skills and have become your most loyal fan.

LAN PING: Mr. Tang, did you really like my performance of Nora that much?

TANG NA: Far more than *liked* it; I was enthralled by it! Your Nora is a dramatic miracle. From beginning to end, I was drawn in and moved by your performance.

LAN PING: You're exaggerating, but thank you, anyway.

TANG NA: No, I am sincere. Your success lies in the fact that you really live in the role you have created; you and Nora have melded into one. As Stanislavsky said, when you play a part, it is not a matter of transforming the body but transforming the spirit. This is why your performance was so lifelike, so moving. I won't be able to keep from writing a piece about you, praising you.

LAN PING: *(Overjoyed)* Ah, with your review praising me, my status will rise inestimably. Your every word is a priceless jewel. Oh, Mr. Tang, could you first present me with two words in advance.

TANG NA: "Two words"?

LAN PING: That's right.

TANG NA: A two-word review?

LAN PING: But these two words are worth a lot.

TANG NA: Which two?

LAN PING: Tang—Na!

TANG NA: *(Laughing)* Oh, you mean you want my autograph!

LAN PING: Not to reciprocate favors is impolite. Would you mind?

TANG NA: It would be my honor!

LAN PING: *(Takes out her diary and hands it to* TANG NA*)* Would you please inscribe it in my diary?

TANG NA: *(Takes the diary)* So, Miss Lan Ping still writes a diary?

LAN PING: I've been writing it for many years now.

TANG NA: I can see that Miss Lan Ping is a most interesting and ambitious "modern woman."

*(*TANG NA *signs his name on the title page of the diary and then returns it to* LAN PING.*)*

LAN PING: Please, also inscribe the recipient's name; then we will be even.

TANG NA: Oh, so you don't want to go into the red?

*(*TANG NA *takes back the diary.)*

LAN PING: *(Laughing)* If Mr. Tang could add an encouraging remark or two, then I could profit handsomely.

TANG NA: In Miss Lan Ping's presence I am even willing to do business at a loss.

*(*TANG NA *inscribes something in the diary and then hands it back to* LAN PING.*)*

LAN PING: *(Takes it back and reads the inscription)* "Struggle for the freedom and liberation of the nation." Oh, that's wonderful, thank you.

TANG NA: You're quite welcome. *(Hesitates to speak, but finally bucks up his courage to carry through with his assay)* Are you . . . going . . . home now?

LAN PING: Yes.

TANG NA: Is there anyone expecting you?

LAN PING: Oh, no. I live alone. . . . Is anyone expecting you at home?

TANG NA: *(There is an awkward silence between* TANG NA *and* LAN PING. *Each is waiting for the other to take the initiative.)* Hmm . . .

LAN PING: What is it?

TANG NA: May I be so bold as to request the pleasure of your company for a late meal?

LAN PING: *(Happily)* That would be wonderful. Where shall we go?

TANG NA: The DDS Café on Joffre Road.

LAN PING: DDS? Wonderful!

TANG NA: Shall we go!

LAN PING: *(Suddenly puts her arm in TANG NA's)* Is that all right?

TANG NA: *(Surprised)* Oh . . . yes . . . fine.

> *(TANG NA and LAN PING walk arm in arm. The lights go down. Then the scene is the DDS Café on Joffre Road. The waiter leads TANG NA and LAN PING to their table, then brings them a menu.)*

TANG NA: *(In English)* Lady first.

LAN PING: What did you say? I've only been in Shanghai now for less than two years; I don't know English.

TANG NA: Oh, sorry; I asked you to order first.

LAN PING: Borscht, steak, some pudding, and a few pieces of bread.

TANG NA: Anything else?

LAN PING: That's plenty.

TANG NA: Something to drink?

LAN PING: A small vodka . . . No, that's too strong; how about a small glass of white wine.

TANG NA: *(To the waiter)* Borscht, steak, pudding, bread, and white wine for two. *(The waiter leaves.)* You've ordered so little; are you worried I can't afford it?

LAN PING: No, I am not one for false manners. I normally eat even more simply than this—just a bowl of borscht, a few pieces of bread. This is already bourgeois enough!

TANG NA: "Bourgeois enough"?

LAN PING: Naturally.

> *(The waiter brings the borscht, steak, pudding, bread, and white wine, then leaves.)*

TANG NA: *(Stands, raises a glass)* Miss Lan Ping, a toast to congratulate you on this evening's performance. Cheers!

LAN PING: *(Stands, raises a glass)* Thank you! *(They clink glasses and each take a small sip.)*

TANG NA: Please, sit down!

LAN PING: *(Still standing)* Wait, let's drink another.

TANG NA: *(Stands up again)* Okay. *(He fills their glasses with wine.)*

LAN PING: *(Raises her glass)* To . . .

TANG NA: To what?

LAN PING: To express my gratitude.

TANG NA: For this cheap wine and simple fare?

LAN PING: No, I am thanking you for the review you are going to write for me tomorrow.

TANG NA: But I haven't written it yet!

LAN PING: How can you refuse when I am willing to empty glasses with you?

TANG NA: Of course, of course, I'll write it. That's for sure.

LAN PING: *(Clinks glasses with* TANG NA*)* Good; bottoms up. *(They sit down.)*

TANG NA: In order to write the review, allow me to be bold enough to ask you some questions.

LAN PING: Of course.

TANG NA: *(Jotting down notes as he talks)* Miss Lan Ping, I've heard your real surname is Li?

LAN PING: Yes, my real name is Li Yunhe. Lan Ping is my stage name.

TANG NA: And your home is in Shandong?

LAN PING: Zhucheng County in Shandong.

TANG NA: When did you come to Shanghai?

LAN PING: Two years ago, in the summer of 1933.

TANG NA: Why did you come to Shanghai?

LAN PING: As for that—

TANG NA: Look at me, like an interrogator! There's no need to answer if you feel uncomfortable about it.

LAN PING: Oh no, with you I don't feel like concealing anything.

TANG NA: Thank you for your trust in me.

LAN PING: I came to Shanghai because my closest friend was arrested. I left Shandong to hide from the agents who were after me.

TANG NA: Then you are a . . .

LAN PING: I am in the revolutionary party!

TANG NA: *(Surprised)* You?

LAN PING: You don't believe me, or you are surprised?

TANG NA: I believe you, otherwise you wouldn't have joined the left-leaning Amateur Dramatists' Association, and you wouldn't be performing in the progressive play *A Doll's House*. I'm just a little surprised.

LAN PING: About what?

TANG NA: Surprised that you would reveal your political status to someone you've only just met.

LAN PING: It's not really the first time, since I have often met you through the newspapers by reading many of your articles, especially your articles criticizing "soft" entertainment film and promoting the use of film in the service of national salvation against the Japanese.[2] My admiration for you has grown through reading them.

TANG NA: Please, that's too kind of you. On the contrary, it is I who have great admiration for you! And not only do you perform well, you are also a revolutionary.

LAN PING: Mr. Tang is going too far. If it's all right, I wonder if I might ask if Mr. Tang is . . .

TANG NA: (Laughing) Miss Lan Ping, you are too trusting. If I were a member of such an organization, I would never tell somebody else so carelessly the way you do.

LAN PING: Then you—

TANG NA: I am just a writer, an artist; I just use my pen to save the nation. I have no need to join any political organizations. Yet, I also must admit that I have some leftist leanings. Since coming to Shanghai I have seen the imperialists' bullying of our China, seen the inequities between rich and poor, so I have become a little "red" in my thinking.

LAN PING: No wonder when I first saw you I felt a sense of intimacy with you. Oh, I have interrupted your interview!

TANG NA: What is your view of the newly emerging theater?

LAN PING: (Very fluently) I feel that in the context of this difficult but great era, our newly emerging theater should fully develop its social function and shoulder the noble duty of national revolution. If we want to join our dramatic activities with the larger fundamental activities of anti-imperialism and anti-feudalism, then the newly emerging theater will have a healthy development, and only then will beautiful fresh flowers bloom.

TANG NA: Ah, just like you're giving a speech. I have had contact with quite a few actresses before, but I daresay there are very few who are as interesting and opinionated as you. Tomorrow I will definitely write a review to introduce you to the Shanghai audience.

LAN PING: Why tomorrow? Why not write it tonight?

TANG NA: I'd like to chat with you some more.

LAN PING: We'll have time later for chatting. You go on home.

TANG NA: *(Calls to the waiter)* The bill. *(The waiter comes over and hands him the bill.* TANG NA *pays and the waiter leaves.)* I'll take you home.

LAN PING: No, go home directly so you can get going on that review.

TANG NA: Since Miss Lan sets such store by my review, I had better go and get it done.

(TANG NA and LAN PING leave their seats. A young refugee enters and walks up to their table.

There are still some bits of bread on the table.)

LAN PING: Oh, wait, I'll take these bits of bread home with me for my breakfast.

(LAN PING heads back to the table. The young refugee is just about to reach for the bread on the table; he sees LAN PING coming and his hand retracts. As LAN PING takes the bread, she sees the hungry face of the young refugee. LAN PING hesitates for a moment, picks up the bread, and walks away. After going a few steps, she turns around and goes back to the young refugee.)

LAN PING: Are you a refugee from the Northeast? *(The young refugee nods his head.)* Alone? *(He nods his head.)* What about your family? *(He drops his head in silence.)* Did the Japanese . . . *(He lowers his head in despair.* LAN PING *stuffs the bread into his hand.)* Here! *(He looks at* LAN PING *with gratitude, then devours the bread like an animal and leaves.* TANG NA *and* LAN PING *watch the young refugee depart. Blackout.)*

YAN'AN 1938

(A simple hall in the Lu Xun Arts Academy. On the stage is just a broken old table that serves, such as it is, as a lectern. Amidst enthu-siastic applause, MAO ZEDONG *appears behind the lectern. He is dressed simply, the knees on his cotton pants have holes. He is giving a lecture to the audience below—the members of the Lu Xun Arts Academy.)*

MAO ZEDONG: *(Waving his hand so as to stop the applause)* With the armed invasion of our country's three northeastern provinces after the Mukden incident, on September eighteenth, 1931, and since last year's July seventh Marco Polo Bridge incident, the fascist militarists in Japan have carried out a full-scale invasion of the northern, middle, and southern sections of our country. Because of results of the policy of the Nationalist Citizen Government to carry out a national war of resistance, because of the long and persistent struggle of the Communist Party to carry on its national united front, and because the army and the people of the entire nation have risen against the enemy, we have already instigated the great and heroic war of self-defense. This is a great event in the history of the development of our Chinese people. The policies we should now maintain are to uphold the War of Resistance, uphold the united front against Japan, and uphold the protracted war. Seated here today are students from the Lu Xun Arts Academy—those who sing songs, those who sing opera, those who dance, those who paint—all of you are workers in the literary arts. Your sacred duty now is to make large-scale use of all useful forms, carry on artistic creativity, work toward bringing art to the masses, reflect reality, and even more broadly enter into the educational work of the War of Resistance so that our people can be mobilized to guard our sovereign territory.

(Enthusiastic applause below the stage, and from it the long and clear clapping of one person, JIANG QING. She is seated in the first row of students below the stage. When MAO ZEDONG's lecture to the students is finished, so as to attract MAO ZEDONG's attention, JIANG QING stands up on the seat and raises both hands above her head and applauds from this high spot. When the sound of the others' applause has already stopped, she continues clapping as before. This action has attracted MAO ZEDONG's attention. He looks down, sees JIANG QING, and nods his head to show his gratitude.)

JIANG QING: Chairman Mao, please wait! *(JIANG QING walks up onto the stage and says coquettishly)* Chairman, your lecture was marvelous, farsighted, penetrating, profound, and yet explained in simple language. I now understand much, much better the rationale behind national salvation resistance against the Japanese. *(Takes out her diary)* Look, I even took notes for fear that I might lose a single word. Oh, please, Chairman Mao, would it be all right if you signed your autograph? Sign here, here.

MAO ZEDONG: *(Takes the pen and diary JIANG QING has passed to him)* What a lovely pen.

JIANG QING: A friend gave it to me. It's a Parker. If the Chairman likes it, please keep it.

MAO ZEDONG: A gentleman does not take that which is valued by others. *(Signs)* Is that all right?

JIANG QING: *(Takes the diary)* Wonderful, thank you!

MAO ZEDONG: May I inquire as to the female comrade's surname?

JIANG QING: My name is Jiang Qing.

MAO ZEDONG: *(A little pleasantly surprised)* Well, well, so you're Jiang Qing. I have long heard of you.

JIANG QING: The Chairman knows me?

MAO ZEDONG: I saw you perform in *The Fisherman's Revenge*. Your performance of Xiao Guiying was quite good.

JIANG QING: The Chairman enjoys Peking opera?

MAO ZEDONG: Very much. Your name holds a great deal of repute in Yan'an. Jiang Qing. "When the song is over she is no longer seen / By the river *[jiang]* many peaks rise green *[qing]*."[3] What a wonderful name.

JIANG QING: I adopted this name after coming to Yan'an. In Shanghai I was called Lan Ping.

MAO ZEDONG: Jiang Qing? Lan Ping? Green *[qing]* comes from blue *[lan]* and can overcome blue. Does that mean that your life in Yan'an will be more promising than in Shanghai?

JIANG QING: It's just a name I took; no special meaning.

MAO ZEDONG: Such a wonderful name and taken so casually. Just think what you can do when you put your mind to it.

JIANG QING: Chairman, I . . . could I bother you with something?

MAO ZEDONG: What is it? Go ahead!

JIANG QING: After listening to your lecture, there are some things I still don't understand. Could I come to you for some individual instruction?

MAO ZEDONG: The main gate to Yan'an is open to the entire nation's patriotic youth who fight for anti-Japanese resistance. My door is also open to you; please, do come.

JIANG QING: I am very grateful!

(Just before taking his leave, MAO ZEDONG *gives* JIANG QING *a quick look over and somewhat absentmindedly bumps into the table as he turns to leave.)*

JIANG QING: Chairman, be careful!

MAO ZEDONG: Yes, it seems I should be more careful!

JIANG QING: Or, perhaps I could . . . see you home!

MAO ZEDONG: Well . . .

JIANG QING: Didn't you just say that your door was open to me?

MAO ZEDONG: All right, what this Mao person says does indeed count. Let's go; promenade with me, if you will.[4]

JIANG QING: What did you say? I only got through middle school. I don't understand you.

MAO ZEDONG: Oh, it's a line from an old poem. What I mean to say is let us march in unison.

JIANG QING: (Laughing) "March in unison"? Okay (attempting to put her arm in MAO ZEDONG's).

MAO ZEDONG: No need for such politeness; I am not that old yet.

(MAO ZEDONG walks alongside JIANG QING, conscious of maintaining a proper distance.

Blackout. Scene changes to Phoenix Mountain, the site of MAO ZEDONG's cave dwelling, which is very simple in style.)

JIANG QING: (Surprised) Such a great leader lives here?

MAO ZEDONG: The laboring masses throughout the world have yet to be liberated. And when they are, we will still institute the principle of the Paris Commune: my lifestyle will not exceed that of a skilled worker.

JIANG QING: (Looks all around) It's really just four bare walls.

MAO ZEDONG: Not exactly. There are things you cannot see. Over there are all my books. "With the classics one cannot be poor." Indeed, I consider myself very rich.

JIANG QING: No wonder so many young people are rushing to Yan'an. Those who come to Yan'an just to look, if they see no other place than where you live, will never want to leave.

MAO ZEDONG: Why do you say that?

JIANG QING: Because of the air of equality, democracy, and freedom here.

MAO ZEDONG: You shouldn't speak of it as if it were perfect. Yan'an also has its backward side. There are no big Western-style houses, no roads. We are lacking in food and clothing. We have to till our own soil and weave our own cloth. We eat black beans all day, and that makes for poor digestion. The sound of farts can be heard everywhere. Yan'an reeks to high heaven.

JIANG QING: (Laughs) Yet, I like this place. I prefer the farts of the proletariat to the sweet smell of the bourgeoisie.

MAO ZEDONG: You are a determined one, aren't you!

JIANG QING: Otherwise I wouldn't have come to Yan'an. Shanghai *is* bustling, but it is too rotten and dirty.

MAO ZEDONG: Some people have come to Yan'an just for a change of scenery.

JIANG QING: But I came mainly to resist Japan.

MAO ZEDONG: When did you arrive in Yan'an?

JIANG QING: Last year, after the Marco Polo Bridge incident.

MAO ZEDONG: Where were you when you first came?

JIANG QING: At the party training school.

MAO ZEDONG: How did you come to the Arts Academy then?

JIANG QING: I asked to be transferred.

MAO ZEDONG: And your leader agreed?

JIANG QING: I have brought my bags and bedroll to the Arts Academy. How can they not agree? In any case, I'm not leaving. I simply have to get into the Arts Academy. I'll show them how to be unreasonable!

MAO ZEDONG: *(Laughs)* Actually, to accomplish anything, we have to have a little rebellious spirit, this kind of burn-all-your-bridges determination. I approve of your "unreasonableness."

JIANG QING: I am not just fooling around here. I am an actress, and when I was in Shanghai, I was something of a star. If I don't get into the Arts Academy, then who should? Oh—I brought with me some stage photos, programs, and some articles I wrote when I was in Shanghai. I would appreciate your comments. (JIANG QING *takes out from her handbag stage photos, programs, reviews, and her own articles and hands them to* MAO ZEDONG.)

MAO ZEDONG: *(Admiring the photos)* You have quite a few; you really were a star!

JIANG QING: *(Explaining the photos, one by one)* This was when I performed the principal role of Nora in A *Doll's House*. The second is of Katerina, the principal role in Ostrovsky's *The Storm*. And this is the principal role in the Japanese play *Infant Slaughter*.[5] These are all film photos. Yes, I was a female soldier in *God of Freedom*, the wife of a wheelbarrow pusher in *Twenty Cents*, and the wife of the pig farmer, Liu San, in *Bloodbath at Wolf Mountain*. And what must be my most famous role, the wife of Wang Laowu in *Wang Laowu*. As you can see, in film I have excelled in playing wives. How boring!

MAO ZEDONG: Oh, you don't want to perform someone's wife?

JIANG QING: I have played the wives of cart drivers, hunters, and poor wretches.

MAO ZEDONG: Then whose wife would you like to perform?

JIANG QING: How about a general's wife, the wife of a head of state or prime minister, or an empress.

MAO ZEDONG: You are quite ambitious!

JIANG QING: How can an actor survive without ambition?

MAO ZEDONG: So many reviews of your performances?

JIANG QING: They praise especially my performance of Nora. The critics called 1935 the Year of Nora.

MAO ZEDONG: *(Reads)* "The Shanghai audience has gone wild for Miss Lan Ping's performance of Nora—written by Tang Na."

JIANG QING: He is a very well-known critic in Shanghai, a friend of mine, very progressive.

MAO ZEDONG: What a pity I haven't seen any of your many plays and films. I have only seen *The Fisherman's Revenge.*

JIANG QING: The Arts Academy is putting on a performance of a new play in which I have a part. We'll invite you to come and see it when it's ready, okay?

MAO ZEDONG: Of course I will come.

(The BODYGUARD *carries in the meal and puts it on the table. It is a piece of meat cooked in red sauce.)*

JIANG QING: My goodness, I must go. But you haven't given me individual instruction yet! I must be going.

MAO ZEDONG: How can I let a guest leave like this, when it comes time to eat. Shall we eat together? *(To the guard)* Bring another dish. *(To* JIANG QING*)* Why don't you sit! *(The guard leaves.)*

JIANG QING: This is too embarrassing. *(Sits)* Chairman, you also eat so simply? One dish and a soup!

MAO ZEDONG: My stomach is easily taken care of. On the Long March, I ate wild plants and even a leather belt.

(The BODYGUARD *carries in another bowl of rice and a dish and places them before* JIANG QING; *he then stands aside.)*

MAO ZEDONG: Don't be polite, go ahead and eat.

JIANG QING: I'll help myself, don't worry.

MAO ZEDONG: *(Wants to pick up some food with his chopsticks to give to* JIANG QING, *but seeing the* BODYGUARD *to the side, he stops)* Hm, comrade, there's no point you just standing guard there while I eat. Leave. (*The* BODYGUARD *leaves.* MAO ZEDONG *winks at* JIANG QING.) They're keeping an eye on me.

JIANG QING: Keeping an eye out for what?

MAO ZEDONG: For this big piece of fatty meat!

JIANG QING: Why—afraid you won't eat it?

MAO ZEDONG: No, afraid I'll share it with you!

JIANG QING: Share it with me?

MAO ZEDONG: They know I like to eat fatty meat and they went to a lot of trouble today to get me this piece. They're afraid I'll share it with you, so they are keeping an eye on it. They're really stingy. (*He picks up half of the piece of meat and gives it to* JIANG QING.) Go ahead, eat it.

JIANG QING: (*Promptly refuses*) No-no-no. Chairman, they have expressly prepared it for you. How can I eat it? No, I couldn't.

MAO ZEDONG: I'm telling you to eat it, so you should eat it! Good fortune should be enjoyed with others, and good food should be shared.

JIANG QING: I . . . I don't like to eat fatty meat.

MAO ZEDONG: What possible reason can there be for not liking fatty meat? Just eat a little. (*Picks up a piece for* JIANG QING) A larger piece would be hard for me to give up!

JIANG QING: Oh, thank you, thank you!

(MAO ZEDONG *very earnestly picks up with the tips of his fingers the kernels of rice that have fallen on the table, and then puts them into his mouth one by one, just like a peasant.* JIANG QING *is very surprised by this.*)

JIANG QING: Does the Chairman often eat alone?

MAO ZEDONG: Lately it's been that way.

JIANG QING: What about . . . Comrade He Zizhen?

MAO ZEDONG: She . . . she's . . . not here.

JIANG QING: Where has she gone?

(MAO ZEDONG *silently eats his meal.*)

JIANG QING: I've heard . . .

MAO ZEDONG: What have your heard?

JIANG QING: (*Covering up*) Oh, nothing. I heard that Comrade He Zizhen is very pretty, not too tall or too short, neither too skinny nor too fat, the most beautiful woman in Yongxin County.

MAO ZEDONG: Well, let's say she's not ugly!

JIANG QING: I've also heard . . .

MAO ZEDONG: Also heard what?

JIANG QING: That you first met her doing guerrilla work in the Jinggang Mountains, that she fought courageously and can shoot two guns at once.

MAO ZEDONG: She did fight courageously and her shooting is not bad.

JIANG QING: I've also heard . . .

MAO ZEDONG: Also heard what?

JIANG QING: That Comrade He Zizhen has given you four or five children, that your marital feelings have always been good . . .

MAO ZEDONG: Yet, we . . .

JIANG QING: Yes, you . . .

MAO ZEDONG: *(Puts down his bowl and chopsticks)* We haven't been together now for more than half a year. . . . *(For quite a while* MAO ZEDONG *does not speak.)*

JIANG QING: Chairman, it's getting very late; I should go.

MAO ZEDONG: Oh, you're going?

JIANG QING: I came to ask for your individual instruction.

MAO ZEDONG: Yes, that's right, you did.

JIANG QING: Yet I still haven't been instructed on any questions. We only talked about other things.

MAO ZEDONG: Yes, we have strayed rather far from the topic.

JIANG QING: If it is all right with you, I will seek your edification the next time I come?

MAO ZEDONG: My door is open.

JIANG QING: I am only afraid that the guards by your door won't allow me to come in.

MAO ZEDONG: Just tell them that I said you could come.

JIANG QING: Well, then, I will return some other time.

MAO ZEDONG: Thank you.

JIANG QING: Why are you thanking me?

MAO ZEDONG: Thank you for keeping me company for an evening.

JIANG QING: I came to seek your individual instruction.

MAO ZEDONG: That's what you said.

JIANG QING: Good-bye!

MAO ZEDONG: Good-bye!

(JIANG QING *leaves, walking sprightly.* MAO ZEDONG *looks disappointed, as if he has lost something. Blackout.)*

SHANGHAI, 1930S

(*At the front entrance to the Carleton Theater, where the Japanese film* New Earth *is showing, a poster announces the film on the ad board.* TANG NA *is demonstrating to boycott the film, to the pedestrians passing by, to the people buying tickets, and to those entering the theater. Although no pedestrians or spectators actually appear onstage,* TANG NA'S *performance demonstrates their presence.*)

TANG NA: Compatriots, *New Earth* is an anti-Chinese film, a film that insults the Chinese people. Any Chinese who is patriotic or who has a shred of self-respect should not see this film. Compatriots, let us go arm-in-arm to boycott the showing of this reactionary film.

(TANG NA *is looking at his watch and it is evident that he is waiting for* LAN PING. TANG NA *goes up to the ticket booth and continues his demonstration.*)

TANG NA: You, sir, please don't buy a ticket. The Japanese militarists have invaded our northeastern provinces and north China, and they are creating disturbances here in Shanghai. We are irreconcilable enemies, so how at this time can we buy tickets to see their films? Especially since this film insults the Chinese people. Sir, please don't buy a ticket!

(TANG NA *again goes up to the entrance of the theater and looks at his watch, and seeing that* LAN PING *still has not come, he continues his demonstrating to the spectators going into the theater.*)

TANG NA: Ladies, gentlemen, compatriots, *New Earth* is a coproduction of the two fascist nations Japan and Germany. It is a barefaced attempt to justify invasion, it publicly claims our land in the northeast as the "New Earth" of the Japanese Taisho nation, and it incites the Japanese people to set out for this "New Earth." Isn't this the gangster logic of the fascists? Compatriots, yes, return your tickets, resist. That's what it means to be a Chinese with heart.

(LAN PING *rushes up to him.*)

LAN PING: My dear Tang, I am late!

TANG NA: Lan, where were you? You didn't come home *again* last night!

LAN PING: (*Acting like a spoiled child*) I'm rehearsing a new play!

TANG NA: And this morning?

LAN PING: Relaxed and slept!

TANG NA: Where?

LAN PING: In the YWCA dormitory.

TANG NA: I called and they said you weren't there.

LAN PING: *(Hemming and hawing)* Uh, I told them at the front desk to tell anyone who called that I wasn't in. I wanted to sleep.

TANG NA: Really?

LAN PING: Tang, what's with you? I really was sleeping!

TANG NA: With whom?

LAN PING: Oh, my great lover, don't be jealous. I had rehearsed the entire night and was dead tired. How could I still have the energy to sleep with a man?

TANG NA: Then, why didn't you come home to sleep?

LAN PING: I was afraid you would want to sleep with me. It's that time of the month and I am not feeling well.

TANG NA: *(Starting to believe)* Ah. I don't know if this is real or if you are acting.

LAN PING: *(Acting like a spoiled child)* I'm not fooling you. We're not even married, just living together, and already you're so jealous. If we really were married, your eyes would turn bright green from jealousy. Enough of this; someone's coming into the theater. Let's go on with our demonstration! *(Runs over to the entrance)* Attention, compatriots, we must resist the anti-Chinese film *New Earth* . . .

TANG NA: It's already started!

LAN PING: Were there many who went in?

TANG NA: A few returned their tickets after listening to the demonstration. As for others, the more you demonstrate, the more they want to go in.

LAN PING: Traitors!

TANG NA: Don't generalize.

LAN PING: Let's go in.

TANG NA: You want to see this kind of film?

LAN PING: No—to demonstrate.

TANG NA: Go in to demonstrate? But the film has already started!

LAN PING: All the better to stop it.

TANG NA: No, that's not a good method. It's illegal!

LAN PING: What is illegal is showing films on Chinese territory that insult the Chinese. Come on, let's go in.

(LAN PING *and* TANG NA *go into the theater. Blackout. On the screen* New Earth *is showing.*

Hand in hand, LAN PING *and* TANG NA *grope their way in the darkness onto the stage. Then they block the images on the screen.*)

LAN PING: (*Waving both hands and yelling*) We won't allow this film to be shown! Stop the film!

TANG NA: (*Also waving both hands*) Stop the film! Stop! Turn on the lights, turn on the lights!

(*The hall lights brighten. The film stops and the screen goes blank.* LAN PING *and* TANG NA *approach the front of the stage and pass out flyers to the audience below.*)

LAN PING: (*Impassioned*) Compatriots, ladies and gentlemen, one and all, how can you watch this reactionary film? We can't be apathetic anymore, nor can we turn a blind eye to evil. We must rise up and protest, struggle, take up weapons to drive the Japanese invaders out of our land, and drive such reactionary films out of our theaters. Those patriotic Chinese among you, please leave immediately; the traitors and sellouts can stay!

(*A red-turbaned Sikh patrolman blows a whistle and runs immediately onto the stage, using his police club to drive out* LAN PING *and* TANG NA.)

LAN PING: (*Struggling, resisting*) I protest, I protest! You have no right to interfere with us, this is Chinese territory. We have the right to express our ideas and to protest.

(*The Sikh patrolman waves his police club and drives* LAN PING *and* TANG NA *from the stage.*

LAN PING *shouts the slogan "Down with Japanese imperialism" as she makes her way through the audience and heads out of the hall.* TANG NA *maintains with great effort his gentlemanly demeanor. With dignity, he follows* LAN PING *through the audience and out of the hall. Standing on the stage, the Sikh patrolman makes a gesture to the projection room behind the audience to signal that they can turn off the lights and continue showing the film. The hall lights go dim and the film continues. What is showing is no longer* New Earth, *but a scene from the feature film* Wang Laowu *in which* LAN PING *starred in 1937.*)

OFFSTAGE VOICE: Now showing is the 1937 feature film *Wang Laowu* produced by the Lianhua Studio, directed by the famous Chinese film worker Cai Chusheng. It describes the unemployment and poverty suffered by the common people on the eve of the War of Resistance against the Japanese in the squatter area of Shanghai. It belonged to the progressive category of films of that time. It was all the rage after it was shown. In this film Lan Ping plays the wife of the pauper Wang Laowu, a girl who sews clothes for others. Her performance garnered excellent reviews.

(Blackout.)

SHANGHAI 1937, EARLY SUMMER

(The road on which LAN PING *lives and inside her house. It is the middle of the night;* LAN PING *is dead drunk and being helped home by a man. All along the road she is humming and singing the theme song from* Wang Laowu: *"Wang Laowu, a life of pain, clothes all ragged, years lived in vain . . .")*

LAN PING: I'm . . . home. Leave me alone . . . I'm not drunk. Who says . . . I'm drunk? Huh? Who says so? . . . Shit, I'll kill the bastard, ha-ha-ha. Everyone else is drunk . . . I alone am clear. Go away, don't . . . come in. Ha, my great lover. Don't play the sly fox with me. Once you come in, you'll never leave, and I, too, . . . won't bear you to leave. Not . . . today, its too late. I'm . . . too tired. All day long, I perform in *The Storm*, and in the evening we shoot *Wang Laowu*. Just see me to the door, to the door. Go, go, my dear . . . my dear, famous director. Yesterday . . . yesterday we got intimate for the first time. Today, I'm tired, need rest . . . Be good, be good, and I'll give you a big . . . kiss.

*(*LAN PING *hugs the man and kisses him madly.* TANG NA *appears in a corner. Having witnessed the scene, he hides immediately to one side.)*

LAN PING: *(A little more awake)* Satisfied? My famous director! Go and come back tomorrow; I'll wait for you. Being apart can be sweeter than being locked up together day after day!

(The man leaves. LAN PING *opens the door and enters the room. She is so tired, she falls into a chair.* TANG NA *knocks on the door.)*

LAN PING: Go away; I'm exhausted and want to sleep!

*(*TANG NA *still knocks.)*

LAN PING: Go; I won't open the door.

*(*TANG NA *continues to knock without stopping.)*

LAN PING: Shit, I told you to stop, why do you keep knocking? *(Takes off her high heels and throws them savagely at the door)* Okay, go ahead and knock!

(From outside the door TANG NA *hears two thumping sounds and is startled.)*

TANG NA: Lan Ping, it's me!

LAN PING: Who?

TANG NA: Tang Na.

LAN PING: Tang Na? *(Promptly goes barefoot over to the door)* What do you want?

TANG NA: Let me come in to talk.

LAN PING: No; go away!

TANG NA: Open the door!

LAN PING: No.

TANG NA: Open up!

LAN PING: I won't!

TANG NA: This is also my home. We are still husband and wife!

LAN PING: Then come back tomorrow. I want to sleep!

TANG NA: No; I might never come back. You must open the door now.

LAN PING: All right, I'll open it, just to see what you'll do about it!

*(*LAN PING *opens the door.* TANG NA *enters the room.)*

LAN PING: What are you going to do?

TANG NA: Who was that just now kissing you?

LAN PING: Oh, Mr. Tang knows how to shadow people now?

TANG NA: I happened to be passing by.

LAN PING: *(Earnestly)* The great director Zhang, what of it?

TANG NA: Director Zhang? What exactly is your . . . relationship?

LAN PING: Living together, for many months already!

TANG NA: Don't you know he has a wife?

LAN PING: I know, and he also knows that I have a husband!

TANG NA: You . . . You're truly shameless. How can you!

LAN PING: You have no rights binding me. We were never officially married.

TANG NA: But we had that wedding ceremony at the Liuhe Pagoda in Hangzhou. And the lawyer, old Mr. Shen Junru, was our witness.

LAN PING: That was nothing but formalities, and I have never liked being restricted by formalities.

TANG NA: Then, why did you agree to marry me?

LAN PING: First, because you were so persistent, and second, to settle the financial problems we had after we started living together—your parents could then give us some money to help pay off the debts incurred from our unemployment and illness.

TANG NA: Then you *did* plan all along to just throw me aside!

LAN PING: No, that's not true. Marriage should be based on love. If we love each other, it is not because of some marriage license. If we don't love each other, then even if we have a license, it shouldn't be binding. Moreover, I told you straight out long ago that I am a headstrong, petulant, and independent-minded woman who could never be a man's slave, nor a plaything for someone's family. I have my career, my interests. When it comes to love and career, I would prefer to choose career and abandon love. So, when you fell in love with me, I warned you many times that I am not the kind of wife with whom you could grow old, nor a lover with an ever constant heart. If you love me, you will suffer for it. And if you have already suffered for it, you only brought it upon yourself; don't come bothering me about it!

TANG NA: You did this so that your fame would sweep across the land. Don't you know what your friends are saying about you now? They say you just play with men, that you are a rotten apple [*ping*]. Is it possible you are not concerned with the pressure of public opinion?

LAN PING: (*Sneers*) Humph, I am not Ruan Lingyu; I would never kill myself from fear of gossip.[6] I've never been afraid of idle chatter. I, Lan Ping, am a strong woman who would never shrink under the pressure of public opinion. On the contrary, I would look for an opportunity for counterattack.

TANG NA: (*Weeps*) Lan, could it be that you don't love me even a little?

LAN PING: (*Determined*) I don't; I don't love weak men.

TANG NA: Is that great director Zhang stronger than I?

LAN PING: Let me speak from the heart. He is not my ideal man, either. You both lack the kind of fervent willpower needed to subdue me.

TANG NA: Lan . . .

LAN PING: Please leave.

(TANG NA *continues to cry as before.*)

LAN PING: Our love is a thing of the past. Now that we no longer love each other, let's just separate peacefully. How would you have it?

For the past year, you have done nothing but argue with me and berate me. Is that what you want to do now? I'll keep you company if you like. A few days ago we got so crazy we even hit each other. Do you still want to hit me? I have a kitchen knife and a pair of scissors I can let you use. I won't stop you.

(LAN PING *takes out the knife and scissors and throws them in front of* TANG NA. TANG NA *is stunned, and trembles with anger.*)

TANG NA: It's fortunate . . . you're a woman. If you were a man, the whole world would tremble in your presence!

JIANG QING: To reach this goal, I must first get you men to tremble in my presence!

(*Almost as if escaping,* TANG NA *runs out the door. Blackout.*)

YAN'AN 1938, FALL

(*Afternoon, the cave in which* MAO ZEDONG *resides at Phoenix Mountain.* MAO ZEDONG *is at his desk, writing. He writes with abandon, then he smokes and wracks his brain, then he paces the room, and now gazes out the window. The* BODYGUARD *enters quietly. Seeing* MAO ZEDONG *use his forefinger and middle finger to pick some tea leaves out of his teacup and then put them in his mouth to chew, the* BODYGUARD *retreats unnoticed and comes back carrying a kettle of boiled water. He walks lightly up to the edge of* MAO ZEDONG's *desk and makes a gesture to determine if* MAO ZEDONG *wants him to add more water to his teacup.* MAO ZEDONG *indicates that he wants it. So the guard raises the kettle and pours. After adding the water, the guard makes a gesture to determine if* MAO ZEDONG *wants him to comb his hair.* MAO ZEDONG *thinks for a while, nods his head, and puts down his pen to indicate that he does. The* BODYGUARD *then happily puts down the kettle, stands behind* MAO ZEDONG's *chair, pulls* MAO ZEDONG's *shoulders up against the back of the chair and tilts his head back. The guard takes out a wooden comb and lightly combs* MAO ZEDONG's *hair from front to back.* MAO ZEDONG *closes his eyes and his whole body relaxes.*)

BODYGUARD: (*Softly*) Chairman, may I have a word with you?

MAO ZEDONG: Hm.

BODYGUARD: Does that feel good?

MAO ZEDONG: Hm.

BODYGUARD: Should I do it a little harder?

MAO ZEDONG: Hm.

BODYGUARD: Hurt at all?

MAO ZEDONG: Hm.

BODYGUARD: *(Laughs)* I'm trying to get you to talk, Chairman, to relax your mind, but all you can say is "Hm, hm." If you don't open up a little and you keep thinking about your writing, how will you be able to relax?

MAO ZEDONG: Right, right. If I am going to relax, then I should relax. Hm, I'll sing a piece from a Peking opera for you.

BODYGUARD: *(Shows great surprise)* Can the Chairman still sing Peking opera?

MAO ZEDONG: A little. I'll sing the role of a "painted face." *(Closes his eyes and sings "Fen Die'r")* "Battling with heroes, no equal in the world, Ying of Qin destroyed, the Chu emperor gone. Struggle for control of the world." *(In verse)* "Ying of Qin has lost the Way, time has come for us to move. / Six states once consumed now divided again. / Xiang Yu and Liu Bang divide the land at Yuan Gou. / Han occupies the East and I control the West."

BODYGUARD: *(Applauds)* Well sung, well sung!

MAO ZEDONG: Really?

BODYGUARD: As well as anyone I've heard. What opera does that come from?

MAO ZEDONG: *(Laughs)* You don't even know what opera it comes from. How can you tell if I am singing it well? Now I know what you just said was not sincere, only flattery.

BODYGUARD: Well, sometimes it's necessary to flatter a little. If I said it wasn't good, would you be pleased? Chairman, please, what opera *did* it come from?

MAO ZEDONG: *Farewell My Concubine. (Suddenly thinks of something)* Eh, I am also bidding farewell to my concubine!

BODYGUARD: What are you saying?

MAO ZEDONG: I am saying that He Zizhen wants to get divorced . . . (MAO ZEDONG *feels dispirited and becomes silent for quite a while.*)

BODYGUARD: Is there no way to repair things?

MAO ZEDONG: She ran off to Xi'an. I sent her a telegram and urged her to come back, but she refuses. She insists on going to the Soviet Union.

BODYGUARD: Chairman, this matter should be settled once and for all. It has serious repercussions.

MAO ZEDONG: Oh, what have you heard?

BODYGUARD: Don't listen to that stuff.

MAO ZEDONG: Just say it.

BODYGUARD: I'm afraid it'll upset you.

MAO ZEDONG: I will just have to grin and bear it. Tell me!

BODYGUARD: Some people blame Comrade He Zizhen for being petty and jealous, making something out of nothing. They even said she got angry with you and was going to shoot you. How ridiculous! With you gone, who would lead the revolution?

MAO ZEDONG: I can't blame her entirely. Last year, just after completing "On Contradiction," the contradictions in my own home had not been settled. The ancients said that "ordering the state and regulating the family bring peace to the universe," but I have not regulated my family well!

BODYGUARD: And there are also those who say that you are at fault.

MAO ZEDONG: In what way?

BODYGUARD: It is not so much that you are at fault, but that Jiang Qing is mostly to blame.

MAO ZEDONG: What's she go to do with it?

BODYGUARD: They say that she is barging in where she doesn't belong and has made your relations with Comrade He Zizhen even tenser.

MAO ZEDONG: (A *little angry*) My problem with He Zizhen is completely unrelated to Jiang Qing. I had already fallen out with He Zizhen before I knew Jiang Qing. Why do they insist on pulling the two together?

BODYGUARD: People say that Jiang Qing squirmed into the space between you and Comrade He Zizhen.

MAO ZEDONG: Who's squirming into whose space? In these relations between the sexes, both parties are willing.

BODYGUARD: You were willing to get close to Jiang Qing?

MAO ZEDONG: Well, I . . . How should I put it. I . . . It is hard to say exactly!

BODYGUARD: Chairman, I think you should be careful. People say that as a film star, Jiang Qing's past is very checkered and her life promiscuous.

MAO ZEDONG: It's all nonsense. Comrade Kang Sheng has investigated her. (*Impatiently*) All right, all right, I want to write now. Don't comb anymore. The more you comb, the messier things gets!

BODYGUARD: Wait, there's a gray hair! *(He pulls out the hair.)* Huh, look!

MAO ZEDONG: Well, you've got some nerve!

BODYGUARD: What, was I talking nonsense just now?

MAO ZEDONG: No, someone once "dared touch the head of the emperor," and now you dare to pull out hair from the Chairman's head. You'd better watch your step.

BODYGUARD: *(Laughs)* No, I was pulling out some weeds from the Chairman's head.

(BODYGUARD *exits.* MAO ZEDONG *continues to write. The* BODY-GUARD *reenters quietly.)*

BODYGUARD: Chairman . . .

MAO ZEDONG: *(Impatiently)* Don't disturb me!

BODYGUARD: Comrade Agnes Smedley wants to see you.[7]

MAO ZEDONG: *(Without raising his head, he writes and speaks at the same time.)* Not now. I am right at the most crucial point. If you're shitting and only half done, how can you receive guests? Tell Smedley to come back tomorrow. Even if the Old King of Heaven came today, I wouldn't see him.

BODYGUARD: Yes.

(BODYGUARD *exits.* MAO ZEDONG *continues to write, his head buried in his work. From outside comes the sound of a disturbance. Losing his patience, he puts down his pen and is about to explode and hit the table in anger. The* BODYGUARD *enters.)*

MAO ZEDONG: What is it now?

BODYGUARD: Someone else to see you.

MAO ZEDONG: Even if the Old King of Heaven came today, I wouldn't see him.

BODYGUARD: If I don't let her in, she'll make a fuss.

MAO ZEDONG: Let her make a fuss, then.

BODYGUARD: She says she has to come in.

MAO ZEDONG: Who could be so unreasonable?

BODYGUARD: Jiang Qing . . .

(Hearing it is JIANG QING, MAO ZEDONG *immediately stands up and considers leaving his place to go outside to greet her, but on second thought thinks that inappropriate and so sits back down and waves his hand gently to the* BODYGUARD.)

BODYGUARD: Ask her to leave?

MAO ZEDONG: *(Hesitates again)* Wait!

BODYGUARD: What is it?

MAO ZEDONG: Better ask her in!

BODYGUARD: Ask her in?

MAO ZEDONG: If she doesn't stay long, it's all right!

BODYGUARD: It's up to you!

> (MAO ZEDONG *hurriedly arranges the manuscripts on his desk.* JIANG QING *carries a small case in. She puts it down and then rushes right over to* MAO ZEDONG *and kisses him wildly.*)

JIANG QING: I've missed you so much, so much!

MAO ZEDONG: *(Unable to resist)* The bodyguard is still outside; he shouldn't see us!

JIANG QING: *(Still holding him tightly, unwilling to let go)* Let those damn bodyguards see how passionate and loving we are together, and see if next time they dare to refuse me entrance!

MAO ZEDONG: *(Struggles to get out of* JIANG QING's *embrace)* You can't blame them. In fact, at this moment I really am busy with my writing.

JIANG QING: *(Playing the spoiled child)* No, lately you have been avoiding me!

MAO ZEDONG: I have been busy lately.

JIANG QING: If you haven't been avoiding me, then tell me you love me, love me, love me. Go ahead, say it!

> (MAO ZEDONG *impulsively embraces* JIANG QING *and kisses her on the face.*)

MAO ZEDONG: I do like you.

JIANG QING: *(Intoxicated)* Then, why not kiss me on the lips? You always just kiss my face.

MAO ZEDONG: We country folk always just peck on the check. Am I a bumpkin?

JIANG QING: No, you are the most attractive man I've ever met, the only one worthy of idolization. I never would have thought you'd be so affectionate.

MAO ZEDONG: I, too, am a man, with the "seven emotions and six desires."

JIANG QING: In fact, the greater the man, the more affectionate he is. Emperors of old and presidents today, they all fall for women.

MAO ZEDONG: More nonsense!

JIANG QING: Here, come and dance!

(*Out of the case she brought with her* JIANG QING *takes an old phonograph.*)

MAO ZEDONG: Where did you get that?

JIANG QING: Brought it with me from Shanghai.

(JIANG QING *puts on a record, some dance music.*)

JIANG QING: Come on!

MAO ZEDONG: I . . .

JIANG QING: Take a break!

(JIANG QING *and* MAO ZEDONG *dance.* JIANG QING's *dance form is graceful, while* MAO ZEDONG *appears a little clumsy.* JIANG QING *not only dances, she sings at the same time.*)

MAO ZEDONG: Sing a little softer.

JIANG QING: What are you afraid of?

MAO ZEDONG: Don't sing so loud!

JIANG QING: I'm happy!

MAO ZEDONG: You just don't concern yourself with the consequences of your actions, do you!

JIANG QING: I what?

MAO ZEDONG: People have quite a few opinions about you.

JIANG QING: What opinions? In coming to the Communist Party base areas from Shanghai, haven't I participated in the revolution, resisted the Japanese, applied myself in study, and done physical labor? Have I done any worse than anyone else? And yet all I hear is people saying I like the finer things, dressing up, chasing after love. I'm only twenty-four this year. How can I not like the finer things, like dressing up. I'm young; of course I am interested in love. I really don't understand it. I came to Yan'an from Shanghai in search of freedom. How can it not be free here? It's as if I've fled one doll's house only to jump into another more rigid doll's house.

MAO ZEDONG: More nonsense! It's your lifestyle and your lack of discipline that provokes these opinions. This is not Shanghai; how can we be so casual in our lifestyle? You should behave like the country folk so as to avoid idle gossip.

JIANG QING: I have never feared idle gossip!

MAO ZEDONG: (*Displeased*) But I must consider consequences, both in the party and outside it.

(MAO ZEDONG *ceases to dance.* JIANG QING *is uneasy. Awkwardly, neither budge.*)

JIANG QING: Are you angry?

(MAO ZEDONG *still says nothing.*)

JIANG QING: All right, all right, from now on I will concern myself with consequences. I'll do as you say. *(Half serious, half joking)* In everything, everywhere, in my words and actions, I will rigorously demand of myself the standard of the Communist Party member, use the example of Yan'an to reform Shanghai, and your example to reform myself.

MAO ZEDONG: You should know that within the party there are opposing views of the two of us.

JIANG QING: Don't concern yourself with that. As long as the two of us agree, that's all that matters.

MAO ZEDONG: No, we also need the agreement of the Party Central Committee Secretariat.

JIANG QING: Love is our own private affair. What's it got to do with the Party Central Committee Secretariat?

MAO ZEDONG: It's called party discipline!

JIANG QING: So what is the view of the Party Central Committee Secretariat?

MAO ZEDONG: Some oppose us, and some approve, and some don't express a view.

JIANG QING: Then what should we do?

MAO ZEDONG: Unite the majority, isolate the minority, and win over the middle ground.

JIANG QING: The strategy and tactics of the War of Resistance?

MAO ZEDONG: The nature of it is different, but the rationale is the same.

JIANG QING: How long do we have to wait to organize such a "united front"?

MAO ZEDONG: This is not a pressing matter.

JIANG QING: I really wish we could get married today!

MAO ZEDONG: We can't just fool around here; we need to prepare for a long-term, protracted war.

JIANG QING: Eh?

MAO ZEDONG: Even if the Secretariat approves of our getting married, it will be with conditions.

JIANG QING: What conditions?

MAO ZEDONG: There are three. One: before I get officially divorced from He Zizhen, you cannot be called Mao Zedong's wife, only Comrade Jiang Qing.

JIANG QING: What?

MAO ZEDONG: Two: after getting married, your only responsibility is to take care of me.

JIANG QING: That's not a problem.

MAO ZEDONG: Three: for the next twenty years you are not permitted to interfere in politics or meddle in party affairs.

JIANG QING: *(Shaking with anger)* But, that . . . that's completely . . .

MAO ZEDONG: What?

JIANG QING: Completely an unequal treaty.

MAO ZEDONG: An "unequal treaty"?

JIANG QING: That's right. These three conditions restrain me, oppress me, disrespect and distrust me. I am an independent woman who yearns for freedom and democracy. I won't accept it!

MAO ZEDONG: There are only two options open up to us. One: accept the three conditions and begin the nuptials, or two: refuse the three conditions and go our separate ways!

JIANG QING: But we've already . . . how can we separate?

MAO ZEDONG: That leaves only one option, then: we must yield.

JIANG QING: *We* yield? It's I who am yielding; how are you yielding?

MAO ZEDONG: In questions of principle, I have never yielded. Perhaps you should think it over!

JIANG QING: It seems you have already thought it over? You have already agreed to the three conditions? Not only agreed to them, but made them your own conditions for me?

MAO ZEDONG: If that's how you see it.

JIANG QING: *(Firmly, she suddenly makes a decision.)* Fine, I accept them!

MAO ZEDONG: It's for the best. Only in stepping back can there be movement forward. I think I will invite the comrades of the Secretariat for a meal.

JIANG QING: To announce that I have accepted the conditions?

MAO ZEDONG: Don't be so anxious; first make some friendly contacts and enlarge the united front.

JIANG QING: Then, you will invite them today!

MAO ZEDONG: Yes, right now!

(Blackout. Another cave for greeting guests in MAO ZEDONG's *residence. A square table is placed in the middle. At the end turned away*

from the audience are seated a few comrades from the Secretariat. At the end facing the audience are seated MAO ZEDONG *and* JIANG QING.)

MAO ZEDONG: Today Jiang Qing has proposed bringing the comrades from the Secretariat together. You have been invited here today to formally introduce you to Comrade Jiang Qing, to let each of you get to know her, and for her to get to know each of you. There is no other purpose than to establish friendly contact. The few strips of cured meat that General Peng Dehuai had brought here will serve as our main course, and we also have some cheap wine to liven things up. Comrade Jiang Qing, why don't you pour some wine for each of our comrades from the Secretariat?
(With poise, JIANG QING *takes up the wine bottle, leaves her seat, and pours wine for each of the seated guests.)*

MAO ZEDONG: Everyone raise your glasses.
(All stand and raise their glasses.)

MAO ZEDONG: Let us drink to the resistance struggle and to everyone's health. Cheers.

JIANG QING: *(Suddenly)* Wait!
(Everyone listens quietly.)

JIANG QING: And to Comrade Mao Zedong's and my happiness, for the happy news that I am now going to announce: Comrade Mao Zedong and I are marrying today. Cheers.

MAO ZEDONG: *(Shocked)* What? You?
(Everyone is struck dumb. MAO ZEDONG *is at a loss, not knowing what to do. Everyone's glass hangs in midair, not moving a bit.* JIANG QING *takes her glass and raises it to her mouth and empties it in one gulp, then stares at* MAO ZEDONG. *With no way out of this situation,* MAO ZEDONG *can only slowly, very slowly, drink his wine. The others drink their wine at varying speeds and at various times.* JIANG QING *smiles slightly.)*

LUSHAN 1958, SUMMER

("Mei Cottage," No. 180 Hedong Road, formerly the summer home of Song Meiling and Chiang Kai-shek, now the residence of MAO ZEDONG. *There is a meeting room, no longer the simple meeting room of the cave in Yan'an, and the meeting table, chairs, water jars, teacups, et cetera, are also not what they used to be; the only similarity is the position of the meeting table within the meeting room*

[that is, its position on the stage], which is exactly the same as before, not moved at all. Twenty years ago when MAO ZEDONG *invited the members of the Secretariat for a meal, everyone was concerned with the fate of a woman; twenty years later, when* MAO *invites the members of the politburo to attend this meeting, what is being decided is the fate of the entire Chinese nation. The members of the politburo sit upright around the table, their backs to the audience.* MAO ZEDONG's *seat is empty; everyone is waiting for his arrival, as if they had already been waiting a long time.* MAO ZEDONG *rushes into the meeting room.)*

MAO ZEDONG: I'm late because I took a telephone call. Unfortunately, I now need to take some time off and am unable to attend the meeting. Although I called the meeting of the politburo for today, I propose putting off the meeting to another time. The reason for the time off is a personal matter; an old friend of many years—a war comrade, whom I must see—has come to Lushan. It's been twenty years since we've seen each other, so I must go. Please, forgive me!

(The members of the politburo disperse. The BODYGUARD *enters.)*

MAO ZEDONG: *(Can't wait)* Hurry and have her come in!

(The BODYGUARD *exits.* MAO ZEDONG *stands still, staring at the entrance. After a short while,* HE ZIZHEN *enters.)*

MAO ZEDONG: Zizhen!

HE ZIZHEN: *(Greatly surprised; a moment of shock before she dares recognize him)* Runzhi? Is it . . . you?

MAO ZEDONG: It is I, Zizhen!

HE ZIZHEN: How is it possible?

MAO ZEDONG: Yes, yes, I asked Mr. and Mrs. Fang Zhichun to bring you here; didn't they tell you?

HE ZIZHEN: No, they didn't say anything, only that they were bringing me to Lushan to enjoy myself and to escape the heat.

MAO ZEDONG: They couldn't say anything, a public security regulation.

HE ZIZHEN: Still so excessively mysterious.

MAO ZEDONG: Which explains why it's been twenty years. It is so hard to see you. . . .

(HE ZIZHEN weeps.)

MAO ZEDONG: Don't cry, don't cry. Aren't we seeing each other now? Sit down, sit down!

(MAO ZEDONG *pours a cup of tea and hands it to* HE ZIZHEN. HE
ZIZHEN *takes a sip, then feels her pocket.*)

MAO ZEDONG: Looking for cigarettes?

(HE ZIZHEN *nods.* MAO ZEDONG *hands his own cigarettes to her and
she takes one out, lights it, takes a fierce drag on it, then a few more,
then she cries again.*)

MAO ZEDONG: What are you crying for? It's such a rare opportunity
for us to meet. If you cry the whole time, how can we talk?

HE ZIZHEN: I don't know what to say. . . . Twenty years worth of
words all bottled up.

MAO ZEDONG: Zizhen, I'm sorry . . .

(*Tears flow from* MAO ZEDONG's *eyes.* HE ZIZHEN *brings her teacup
over to* MAO ZEDONG's *hands.*)

MAO ZEDONG: Back then, if you had come when I sent the telegram
asking you to return from Xi'an, everything would have been
fine—

HE ZIZHEN: I was too young and too strong-minded. If I had listened
to you, then . . .

(HE ZIZHEN *cries again.*)

MAO ZEDONG: Your health is good?

HE ZIZHEN: Much better. And yours?

MAO ZEDONG: Not as good as when I was young.

HE ZIZHEN: You should take better care of yourself!

MAO ZEDONG: I remember in nineteen thirty-two in the Jiangxi Soviet
areas Wang Ming pushed me right out of power, forcing me to
resign my position so that even the ghosts paid me no heed, and
I passed long days, solitary and alone.[8] Misfortunes never come
singly. I got malaria and was unconscious a lot. I was skin and
bones. If you hadn't kept me company day and night, nursed me,
given me medicine and comfort, then this body of mine might
well have been buried in the Jinggang Mountains . . .

HE ZIZHEN: Had it not been for you, I would have died long ago,
on the Long March. Not far into the march, after reaching Pan
County, in Guizhou, a bomb from an enemy plane dropped on
me. I was badly injured. Blood poured from my whole body. You
got the stretcher bearers to carry me along step by step with the
troops. It went on for a month like that, and I really felt terrible
about being such a burden to everyone. I asked you several times
to leave me behind, but you never agreed to it and said that we

would endure misfortune together, never separate in this life and this world, that you would carry me all the way to northern Shanxi. Then, I was able to go on living . . .

MAO ZEDONG: At that time, we never imagined we would live till now. . . .

HE ZIZHEN: And I'd never have thought I would live in this way. . . . *(Stage falls silent.)*

MAO ZEDONG: Zizhen, don't hate me—

HE ZIZHEN: No, how could I hate you; I hate myself . . .

MAO ZEDONG: Both during the revolution and after the founding of the nation, I was just too busy and didn't take good care of you.

HE ZIZHEN: Don't worry about me. Just take care of yourself. Are you still busy?

MAO ZEDONG: I shouldn't really be very busy, since two years ago I gave up my duties as state chairman. I've given up the day-to-day running of the government and retreated to the background, overseeing only party policy, but I wouldn't have thought . . .

HE ZIZHEN: Wouldn't have thought what?

MAO ZEDONG: That when the reins of power fell into the hands of others, opposition to me would be so strong. At this Lushan meeting, I acknowledged that the Great Leap Forward of the past two years has been a little dizzying and that we should temper the leftist tendency. Who would have thought that as soon you oppose the "left," they'd turn to the "right" and start attacking this and that without looking at the whole picture—and make everything look so bleak. So then you are forced to oppose the right. I know that in doing this I will offend a few friends. In fact, I have offended quite a few over the past few years. I'm really worried that before too long, I will be all alone at the top.

HE ZIZHEN: How is that possible? You would at least still have . . .

MAO ZEDONG: Have what?

HE ZIZHEN: Still have her . . .

MAO ZEDONG: Who?

HE ZIZHEN: Still have Jiang . . . Qing with you . . .

MAO ZEDONG: *(A long sigh)* Ah . . .

HE ZIZHEN: What is it?

MAO ZEDONG: Don't talk about her!

HE ZIZHEN: Doesn't she treat you well?

MAO ZEDONG: We've been living separately now for several years.

HE ZIZHEN: *(Greatly surprised)* Really?

MAO ZEDONG: It's best not to mention this to anyone.

HE ZIZHEN: There's too great an age difference between you . . .

MAO ZEDONG: Yet, it is not because she's bothered by my age, or my earthiness, but that I never let her be in the limelight, that I suppress her.

HE ZIZHEN: She . . . wants to appear in the limelight?

MAO ZEDONG: When I got married to her, the Secretariat stipulated, before the fact, some simple rules—that she could not get involved in politics.

HE ZIZHEN: Oh, but she is still a party member; couldn't you arrange some work for her?

MAO ZEDONG: I have; she's one of my five personal secretaries, but she wants to give orders! She—she is an extremely jealous and vengeful person, and never gets on with anyone. How can I let her grasp real power? I have made quite a few mistakes in my life, and I worry that marrying her was also a mistake. Oh, let's not talk about these things. You a rare guest, and I want to impress you with local delicacies and invite you to eat the famous three "rock" dishes of Lushan: rock hen, rockfish, rock brake. And after eating, we can once again drink tea, and if the moon is out, stroll once more beneath the moon. What do you think?

HE ZIZHEN: *(Moved)* Won't it take you away from state affairs to accompany me like that?

MAO ZEDONG: I've asked for some time off. Today I am neither paying attention to court politics nor concerning myself with any affairs of state. Today I love only a beautiful woman, not my country.

HE ZIZHEN: *(Startled at* MAO ZEDONG's *feelings of nostalgia)* What beautiful woman? I am an old lady now.

MAO ZEDONG: I still can't forget your striking demeanor of that time. You were the most beautiful woman in Yongxin County!

(The BODYGUARD *comes rushing in and whispers to* MAO ZEDONG, *whose expression changes.)*

MAO ZEDONG: What? She found out so quickly?

(The BODYGUARD *withdraws.)*

HE ZIZHEN: What is it?

*(*MAO ZEDONG *doesn't respond, heavy of heart and hesitant.)*

HE ZIZHEN: Tell me, what is it?

*(*MAO ZEDONG *still says nothing.)*

HE ZIZHEN: Is it her . . .

MAO ZEDONG: *(Nodding)* Yes . . .

HE ZIZHEN: She's coming?

MAO ZEDONG: *(Nodding)* Yes . . .

HE ZIZHEN: What is she coming here for?

MAO ZEDONG: She knows I invited you here.

HE ZIZHEN: We've only just got together. How can she keep such a close watch?

MAO ZEDONG: She is a very jealous and vengeful person.

HE ZIZHEN: When is she coming?

MAO ZEDONG: Early tomorrow.

HE ZIZHEN: Early tomorrow?

MAO ZEDONG: I . . .

HE ZIZHEN: Say it; what do you want me to do? *(Stubbornly)* You want me leave?

MAO ZEDONG: *(Hesitates for a long time)* I'll have to . . . have to trouble you.

HE ZIZHEN: Humph, I never should have come!

> (HE ZIZHEN *leaves without a moment's hesitation and slams shut the door. The sound is very like the famous sound of the door slamming as the curtain falls at the end of* A Doll's House. *Blackout.*
>
> *Newsreel. On the screen are scenes showing* MAO ZEDONG *on the wall at Tiananmen, receiving a million Red Guards;* JIANG QING, *in army uniform, waving a copy of Mao's* Little Red Book of Quotations; *and Lin Biao giving a speech atop the wall.)*

OFFSCREEN VOICE: Referred to as Mao Zedong's intimate comrade-in-arms, Lin Biao, Chinese Communist Party vice-chair, once praised Jiang Qing during the Cultural Revolution in the following terms: "Among our women comrades in the party, Comrade Jiang Qing is the most outstanding; and among our party cadres, she is the most outstanding. Her thought is very revolutionary and she has a fervent revolutionary feeling. In the past, due to her years of poor health, we did not have a chance to know her. Now in the midst of the Cultural Revolution we can see the great function she is serving. From the beginning of this movement to the end, Comrade Jiang Qing has been standing at the forefront." *(The images accompanying the offscreen voice continue to show scenes of Cultural Revolution Red Guards "sweeping away the four olds," "struggling against black gangs," "making revolutionary ties,"* "memorizing Mao's quotations," interspersed with frequent scenes of JIANG QING's activities at various occasions during the Cultural Revolution. At the end is a scene of JIANG QING giving a speech. Blackout.

JIANG QING, *wearing a well-pressed army uniform, her head raised and her chest out, holding a copy of Mao's* Little Red Book of Quotations, *is standing center stage, giving a speech.*)

JIANG QING: *(Waving Mao's* Little Red Book*)* Young soldiers of the Red Guards, revolutionary comrades, I have come to see you in the name of Chairman Mao! In the name of Chairman Mao, I greet you, and extend to you the Great Proletarian Cultural Revolution salute. I would like to announce some good news: Chairman Mao is in excellent health!

(A thunder of applause. The sound of cheers and slogans: "Long live Chairman Mao!")

JIANG QING: Revolutionary comrades, young soldiers of the Red Guards, Chairman Mao asked me to come here to learn from the revolutionary left, to become your student, and at the same time to offer you my support. What we support is the revolutionary left. Those who are revolutionary, please come forward. Those who are not, get the hell out of here.

(Another thunderous applause. The sound of slogans: "Learn from the revolutionary left! Long live the Great Proletarian Cultural Revolution!")

JIANG QING: Did you know what this theater in which we are holding our meeting used to be? It used to be a great dye vat for feudalism, capitalism, and revisionism. Every day on this stage, they used to perform the roles of emperors and generals, talented scholars and beauties. How absurd that the socialist stage was ruled by the dead and by foreigners! Our art workers ate the grain grown by the peasants, lived in houses built by the workers; the People's Liberation Army was guarding their national defense lines, and yet we didn't express their interests or extol them. Let me ask you: what is the class stand of artists; where is the oft-stated artists' conscience? *(Suddenly starts crying)*

(A silence throughout the hall. Only the sound of JIANG QING's sobbing is heard, then the sound of a slogan quietly, softly: "Comrade Jiang Qing, don't be sad; we love you!" Then everyone shouts out in unison: "Comrade Jiang Qing, don't be sad; we love you!")

JIANG QING: Thank you, thank you, everyone! I have looked into and thought about this phenomenon for a long time now and have made a report to Chairman Mao. When I became Chairman Mao's loyal mobile sentinel on the cultural front, I began to develop the revolutionary-model theater so that the workers, peasants, and soldiers, and the thought of Mao Zedong, could occupy the stage. Later, Comrade Lin Biao entrusted me to convene an armed forces conference on artwork and only then did I discover that there was a long and thick black line in the arts that started in the 1930s and continued and developed right up to the present. How shocking! So, only then did I propose that we firmly carry out a great socialist revolution on the cultural front. In August, Chairman Mao himself examined, edited, and approved the minutes of this armed-forces conference on artwork, which were distributed to the entire party. On May sixteenth, with great foresight and a strong sense of imperative and urgency, Chairman Mao proposed the national launching of the Great Proletarian Cultural Revolution. So this revolution has been long and hard in coming, and its significance is profound and far-reaching. First was my discovery of problems on the cultural front, then Chairman Mao with his sharp insight into things launched the political and ideological side of the Cultural Revolution! Chairman Mao himself approved my taking on the position of First Assistant Head of the Central Cultural Revolutionary Group. This showed Chairman Mao's great trust in me. He finally understood me and supported me, and it was as if I, a proletarian revolutionary stifled and persecuted for so many years, could finally raise my head proudly! Like the Red Guard soldiers, I want to shout out a thousand times: "Great leader, great teacher, great commander, great helmsman, the reddest red sun in our hearts, to Chairman Mao, long life! Long life! Long life!

(The crowd follows along: "Long life! Long life! Long life!")

JIANG QING: But the struggle is long-term and complex! There are people who are raising the banner of model theater only to destroy model theater, to take it away from its model. Your "spirit engulfs the land," you are "a great river flowing eastward," [9] and yet you are taken as "water flowing under a small bridge," [10] or a frivolous tune. They raise the red flag to oppose the red flag. They have been struggling against us in this way for the past ten years.

How much we have suffered at their hands and been persecuted by them! *(Gradually becoming incoherent, hysterical)* Look! *(Opens her mouth)* These teeth of mine were knocked out by my father! *(Rolls up her pant leg)* And look here, I was bitten by a dog as I was walking along a road when I was young! *(Sobs)* Then there was someone who passed herself off as Chairman Mao's daughter-in-law,[11] but we couldn't accept this, the class struggle struggling right into Chairman Mao's home, with the blade pointed directly at me, out to get me. They blame me for failing to bring credit to Chairman Mao by not giving him a son! In the past it was Wang Ming who wanted to keep me down; now it is Liu Shaoqi. I've always been suppressed, so much so that I could hardly breath, so that my whole body got sick! If not for this Cultural Revolution, I would never have been able to turn myself over! *(Sobs)*

(Sound of slogans: "Learn from Comrade Jiang Qing, the heroic standard-bearer of the Great Proletarian Cultural Revolution! Salute Comrade Jiang Qing, the heroic standard-bearer of the Great Proletarian Cultural Revolution!")

JIANG QING: I am of the proletarian revolutionary faction. I don't shed tears. I am exceptionally firm and strong. I want those people who have suppressed and persecuted me to know who belongs to the true revolutionary faction: Jiang Qing! Now we know that those who are suppressing and attacking me are not part of any revolutionary faction. They are nothing but authorities within the party taking the capitalist road. I can tell you all now that I am in charge of the number-one case in the country against Liu Shaoqi. One day I worked for five or six hours on it, and I told those working on the case, don't veer to the right, struggle fiercely, criticize fiercely, muster up all your firepower. Just a few people is no good. We need ten or twenty people to fiercely struggle. If Liu Shaoqi dies as a result, then so be it, for he is asking for it. Yan Wang in hell has invited him to drink wine. Even those who are near death should not be released. We did surprise-attack interrogations to get him to give up the materials we wanted from him. That's how hard it was—went on for a whole year. Now I can tell you all that Liu Shaoqi is a big traitor, a treasonist, a scab, a spy, a counterrevolutionary; he is the most vile and treacherous, the most heinous, the sliest, most poisonous class enemy. I believe he—he should be cut up with a thousand knives, flayed with ten thousand knives! *(Suddenly changes the subject)* I—I have been put down for twenty years!

(Sound of slogans: "Learn from Comrade Jiang Qing! Salute Comrade Jiang Qing! Whoever opposes Comrade Jiang Qing will have their dog heads smashed in! Swear to die in defense of Comrade Jiang Qing!" Blackout.)

BEIJING 1974

(To one side of the stage, MAO ZEDONG, *ill, his back leaning against the sofa, with his eyes closed, sits listening to his personal secretary,* XIAO FENG, *read to him classical poems.)*

XIAO FENG: *(Reading Xin Qiji's lyric meter to the tune of "Water Dragon Moans")*[12] "The southern skies are vast and clear, / water flows to the horizon and the autumn sky is limitless. / I view from afar the distant peaks, / like jade hairpins and spiral clasps, I present to them my sorrow and bitterness. / The sun sets behind the pavilion, the cry of a solitary goose, a voyager in the south . . ."

MAO ZEDONG: No, that's not right, not "voyager in the south," *traveler* in the south.

XIAO FENG: I misread it. "Traveler in the south, / I take out my precious dagger and look at it, / as I pace along the pavilion's railing and gaze into the distance, / who can know my feelings?"

MAO ZEDONG: The "traveler in the south" is Xin Qiji. He is a traveler in the south, whereas I am a solitary traveling monk, but we have both "taken out our precious daggers and looked at them, / paced along the pavilion's railing and gazed into the distance" with no one to "know our feelings."

XIAO FENG: I understand. You mean no one understands your profound intentions behind the Cultural Revolution.

MAO ZEDONG: *(Sighs)* Ah, "gazing into the distance, / who can know my feelings . . ."

*(*JIANG QING *is now on the other side of the stage.)*

JIANG QING: Xiao Feng!

*(*XIAO FENG *walks from* MAO ZEDONG's *side over to* JIANG QING's.*)*

XIAO FENG: What can I do for you, Comrade Jiang Qing?

JIANG QING: Nothing, really; I want to give you an outfit.

XIAO FENG: Give me an outfit?

JIANG QING: *(Takes a dress out of a bag)* There, an open-collared dress. It was meticulously designed by clothes designers I organized in Beijing, Tianjin, and Shanghai. I synthesized the great achievements in women's clothing styles from the Tang, Song, Yuan, Ming, and Qing dynasties. I want to popularize it so that it becomes the national uniform of Chinese women comrades. This one is for you. Here; try it on. See if it fits and how it looks.

XIAO FENG: Comrade Jiang Qing, I am too ugly to wear such beautiful clothes.

JIANG QING: I am telling you to put it on! Put it on and let Chairman Mao see it. Hopefully he'll say a few words about it and they will be reported to the entire nation.

XIAO FENG: *(Forced)* All right; I'll wear it for him tonight.

JIANG QING: *(Takes out a watch)* Xiao Feng, I also want to give you this watch. It's a Shanghai brand.

XIAO FENG: No-no, I have a watch!

JIANG QING: I'm telling you to take it.

XIAO FENG: *(Forced to take it)* Thank you, Comrade Jiang Qing. Was there something else you wanted to see me about?

JIANG QING: I was wondering if you would . . . would ask Chairman Mao to give me eight thousand yuan.

XIAO FENG: Eight thousand yuan.

JIANG QING: It's money I owe for photography equipment I bought. When you have a moment with the Chairman, just mention it to him.

XIAO FENG: All right.

JIANG QING: Oh, how is the Chairman's health lately?

XIAO FENG: Not the best.

JIANG QING: Does the doctor permit him to see guests?

XIAO FENG: He still permits him to see important guests.

JIANG QING: I want you to notify the Chairman that I would like to see him.

XIAO FENG: Oh, I'm afraid that's not possible.

JIANG QING: What? I have an urgent matter to report. Can't I even see the Chairman?

XIAO FENG: It is the Chairman's directive that if you want to see him, you should first apply through the office.

JIANG QING: *(Angered)* You are misrepresenting an imperial edict!

XIAO FENG: Go and ask the office yourself.

JIANG QING: Have you forgotten who I am? Hm? I am the Chairman's wife! Can it be that I need approval from the office for a visit with my husband?

XIAO FENG: Comrade Jiang Qing, this is the Chairman's wish.

JIANG QING: That's no good. I want you to go right now and notify him.

XIAO FENG: But those in the office will criticize me!

JIANG QING: Do you follow my orders or those of the office? I am a member of the politburo, First Assistant Head of the Central Cultural Revolution Group. What seniority does the office have?

XIAO FENG: Comrade Jiang Qing—

JIANG QING: (*In a thundering rage*) How can you be so evil! The Chairman's wife wants to see the Chairman and you flagrantly obstruct her. Are you a counterrevolutionary? Go, notify him! Tell him it is important!

(*Feeling wronged,* XIAO FENG *goes from* JIANG QING'*s side over to* MAO ZEDONG'*s side.*)

XIAO FENG: Chairman! Comrade Jiang Qing wants to see you.

MAO ZEDONG: Jiang Qing wants to see me? Wants money again?

XIAO FENG: She's asking for another eight thousand.

MAO ZEDONG: Last year I gave thirty thousand when she wanted it, what does she need another eight thousand for?

XIAO FENG: She said it is to repay a debt.

MAO ZEDONG: She knows my health is not good and that I will soon be paying a visit to Marx, so she's preparing an escape route. She's trying to get her hands on my inheritance, my royalties and the like.

(MAO ZEDONG *feels hurt and sheds tears.*)

XIAO FENG: (*Promptly wipes away* MAO ZEDONG'*s tears*) Don't be upset, Chairman.

MAO ZEDONG: Give her the eight thousand and tell her to go away.

XIAO FENG: She still wants to see you, says it is urgent.

MAO ZEDONG: What's so urgent? She's the kind of person who never discusses important things, and trivial matters occupy her time. What could be so goddamn urgent? Over the years, I tried talking with her, but she never paid attention, never carried out what I told her. What good would it do to see her again? She has the works of Marx and Lenin, and my books, but she doesn't even study them. Here I am eighty-one years old, my body in poor health, and she shows no sympathy for me and can only bring me more trouble. Let's see how she fares when I am dead.

XIAO FENG: So, the Chairman won't see her?

MAO ZEDONG: Best not.

XIAO FENG: But she says she must see you.

MAO ZEDONG: How can she be so unreasonable? I guess I'll see her at the politburo meeting. To speak to her alone serves little purpose. I'll say what I have to say publicly, in a party meeting, before the entire membership of the politburo.

XIAO FENG: Yes.

(XIAO FENG *walks from* MAO ZEDONG's *side over to* JIANG QING's *side.*)

XIAO FENG: Comrade Jiang Qing, the Chairman says he will not see you.

JIANG QING: No, I must see him!

XIAO FENG: The Chairman says that he will see you at the politburo meeting.

JIANG QING: (*Laughs aloud*) How can he treat me this way! Am I not still his wife? Any legal wife has the absolute right to see her husband; why can't I? As wife of Chairman of the Chinese Communist Party, I am restrained by the party and restrained by the Chairman? Will I never see him again, then? Is there such a rule in the party regulations? Is there such a law in the marriage code? Would it be acceptable if I wasn't willing to see him? Why don't I have this kind of right? Why can't the office place this kind of restriction on *him*? I . . . want to rebel against him!
(*Blackout*)

Beijing 1976, September

(MAO ZEDONG's *residence. He is now very sick and bedridden. The doctor is giving him a shot; the nurse is to the side, tending to him.* MAO ZEDONG *awakens from a state of unconsciousness; he wants to turn on his back. The doctor shakes his finger at him and advises him to lie quietly.*

MAO ZEDONG *can only obey, but he points a finger to the outside. Neither the doctor nor the nurse understands what he means by it. Later the nurse goes out and brings in his personal secretary,* XIAO FENG, *who stands beside* MAO ZEDONG's *bed, at which point* MAO ZEDONG *nods his head ever so slightly.*)

XIAO FENG: *(To the doctor and the nurse)* The Chairman has called for me.
(The doctor and nurse exit.)

XIAO FENG: *(Bending down over* MAO ZEDONG*)* Chairman, it's me, Xiao Feng. What do you want to say? What is it?
*(*MAO ZEDONG*'s mouth is moving and his voice is extremely low.* XIAO FENG *presses her ear next to* MAO ZEDONG*'s mouth but still cannot hear clearly.* MAO ZEDONG *raises his hand and tries feebly to gesture in the air.* XIAO FENG *supports his arm.* MAO ZEDONG *signs with his hand the character for "Jiang.")*

XIAO FENG: *(Nods her head and says loudly in his ear)* I understand; right away, I'll ask her to come.
(Blackout. Scene changes to Dazhai. JIANG QING *is just answering the telephone.)*

JIANG QING: Yes, it's me, I'm in Dazhai—doing inspection work, organizing the campaign to Criticize Deng Xiaoping and Attack the Rightist Tendency to Reverse the Verdict on him; this is more important than anything! . . . What? You want me to return immediately to Beijing? . . . The Chairman is critically ill? I haven't even been in Dazhai for two days; how can I just throw aside the poor and middle peasants, the village folk, and return to Bejing? . . . What? The Chairman is telling me to return? Why is he suddenly thinking of me? Haven't you misunderstood? The Chairman has said he is unwilling to see me! . . . Was it the Chairman's wish? Let me think it over. What's the rush? . . . I will return to Beijing!
*(*JIANG QING *hangs up the telephone.)*

JIANG QING: He thinks of me only on his deathbed! Am I a plaything at his mercy? At his beck and call? *(Shouts)* Somebody come now!
(A nurse and a guard enter.)

JIANG QING: Come and play poker with me, to relax a bit! *(To the guard)* Today I won't play poker with any men. I hate men. I am a great feminist. Go away and call the other nurse.
(The guard leaves.)

JIANG QING: We women created the world. What use are men? The only contribution men make to the world is that drop of sperm.
(Another nurse comes in and the three begin to play cards.)

JIANG QING: Keep me company while I relax, enjoy myself, and restore my vital energies to prepare to return to Beijing for the next big scene. Humph, the Chairman is critically ill, no reason to get in a panic! The Chairman himself said it many times. Just because the butcher dies doesn't mean you have to eat only bristly pork. Heaven will still stand on high, and China will not collapse! Have I never been through storms before? If the Chairman is no longer with us, I will become a widow. A widow is a widow, but a woman, too, can become emperor; with communism we can also have empresses! To put it rather crudely, I am now the leader of the leftist faction! Deal. Q for Queen.

(*Blackout. In front of* MAO ZEDONG's *deathbed. A deathly silence. The doctor and nurse are to the side, tending to him.* XIAO FENG *is also to one side keeping watch.* JIANG QING *enters and seems almost carefree. The doctor and nurse promptly renew their attentions to* MAO *on the side.*)

JIANG QING: (*Shakes the doctor's hand and appears quite relaxed*) You must be tired; you've been through a lot! But what are you looking so glum for? You should be happy! We are materialists who fear nothing, be happy!

(*The doctor and nurse look dumbfounded.*)

XIAO FENG: Comrade Jiang Qing, the Chairman . . . (*Choked with emotion*) The old man has already fallen unconscious several times . . .

JIANG QING: I don't need you to remind me. The reason I've returned from Dazhai was to see the Chairman.

(JIANG QING *walks up to the side of* MAO ZEDONG's *bed and looks at him coldly, without saying anything for quite a while.* XIAO FENG, *the doctor, and the nurse don't know what* JIANG QING *is thinking or what she might do. They all appear very nervous.*)

JIANG QING: The Chairman hasn't said anything for the past two days?

XIAO FENG: No.

JIANG QING: Did he leave any instructions?

XIAO FENG: No.

JIANG QING: (*Suddenly severe*) Don't you dare think of fooling me!

XIAO FENG: No.

JIANG QING: Are the Chairman's materials here with you?

XIAO FENG: Yes.

JIANG QING: Give them to me.

XIAO FENG: I would need to ask the politburo for instructions about that.

JIANG QING: *(Flies into a rage)* Xiao Feng, do you dare disobey me!

XIAO FENG: I ask you to be quiet; the Chairman is critically ill—

JIANG QING: I'll settle with you later.

(JIANG QING *turns over* MAO ZEDONG's *sheet and pillow and looks to see if there are any documents or materials.*)

XIAO FENG: There isn't a thing there that you would need.

(JIANG QING *goes through* MAO ZEDONG's *pockets and still comes up with nothing.*)

XIAO FENG: Please don't go through his things!

JIANG QING: Look, the Chairman's back is covered with sweat; why don't you wipe it off—are you trying to kill him? Give me a towel!

(*The nurse hands her a towel.* JIANG QING *wants to turn* MAO ZEDONG *over to wipe off the sweat. The doctor becomes anxious and motions to* XIAO FENG *to stop* JIANG QING.)

XIAO FENG: Comrade Jiang Qing, the Chairman has a heart condition and must absolutely not be disturbed. He cannot be moved.

JIANG QING: Who says?

XIAO FENG: The doctor.

JIANG QING: Doctors are all spies. They're all counterrevolutionaries. The Chairman's back is soaking wet. You don't wipe it, and you don't let me wipe it. Isn't this a devious plot to harm the Chairman?

(JIANG QING *turns over* MAO ZEDONG's *body and wipes his back. The doctor, nurse, and* XIAO FENG *weep.*)

JIANG QING: *(Scolding them)* What are you crying for? He hasn't even died and you're crying. Do you want him to die sooner? *(Screams angrily as if gone mad)* Get the hell out of here! All of you! Go outside! Do you hear me! Get the hell out!

(*The doctor, nurse, and* XIAO FENG *tremble with fear, exit.* JIANG QING *forces herself to calm down. She takes a look at* MAO ZEDONG, *sighs and cries an exceptionally grievous cry. She cries for* MAO ZEDONG *and she cries for herself.*)

JIANG QING: Chairman, you have asked me to come, though at first I wasn't really willing. Before coming, I told myself that I should harden my heart, not cry, not shed a single tear for you, suppress my resentment. But now that I see you like this, I cannot bear it anymore. "One night spent together, deep is the sentiment between us." Here I am now, and you can't even speak, can't tell me you love me, or use words of scolding. I have not heard you tell me that you like me for the longest time. You never got used to saying you loved me, only that you liked me. In Yan'an you said it innumerable times, along the Yan River, in the cave, on the bed . . . you told me you liked me. After coming to the city, I rarely heard you say it. At first I thought you no longer said it because you were older and less affectionate and because I had lost the looks of my youth. Later I began to feel that you hated me, which is why you chose to live apart from me. Then, during the Cultural Revolution, we at last reunited to oppose revisionism, to bring down Liu Shaoqi and Lin Biao. But this was demanded by the struggle and there was no feeling between us. So as soon as you had the chance, you criticized me, and even criticized me during a meeting of the politburo and forced me to engage in self-criticism. *(Cries)* Do you know how I have suffered? I really wanted to have a heart-to-heart talk with you, but you would never see me; and now that we meet, that heart-to-heart is impossible—

(MAO ZEDONG *suddenly begins to slowly get up.*)

MAO ZEDONG: You, you're still the same. And you have your ambition, too. You wrote me many letters saying that after the Ninth Plenum you had essentially nothing to do and that you hoped I would arrange some work for you. I advised you to read the letter that Li Gu wrote to Huang Qiong, which in thought and form is an excellent essay. You can't say you had no work—but you wanted to issue orders, form a cabinet, and couldn't wait to replace Zhou Enlai as premier. You'd lost your head. Human value lies in the brilliance of self-knowledge. You were never involved in most of the party's activities in the past. You never participated in the struggles against Chen Duxiu, Qu Qiubai, Li Lisan, Luo Zhanglong, Wang Ming, and Zhang Guotao[13] or marched in the Long March. So I advised you many times not to be too cavalier, to discipline yourself, to be cautious, not to act of your own personal volition, and also not to issue documents or send any materials in your own name. It's just as I said at the Ninth Plenum in those three lines: we want Marxism-Leninism, not revisionism; unity, not division; openness and fairness, not plotting and scheming.

JIANG QING: Can it be that I have no virtues?

MAO ZEDONG: There are two ways of looking at anything. Part good, part bad. Your opposition to Liu Shaoqi and Lin Biao was good and made a contribution. In my life I have done two things. The first was to force Chiang Kai-shek to Taiwan. The second was to light the torch that ignited the Cultural Revolution. To deny your service in this regard would be to deny the Cultural Revolution and to deny myself. I still remember your service; others do not, but I do. Yet, in other regards, all the political labeling, forming the Gang of Four—this was of your own doing and in the final analysis has nothing to do with me. You'd better watch out, for if you don't change your ways, after I die you might suffer serious consequences! Aren't you afraid?

JIANG QING: I am not afraid.

MAO ZEDONG: You're being disingenuous. I can see you are afraid. Afraid that when I die you will lose your patron and will suffer for it. On the outside you show no fear and try to show how at ease you are, but in fact, you are scared to death.

JIANG QING: Chairman . . .

MAO ZEDONG: Afraid?

JIANG QING: Yes, I'm afraid. . . . Chairman, do you still love me—or like me? Please, be honest with me.

MAO ZEDONG: I have never minced words. If back then I had not liked you, I never would have married you, would I? If I had continued to like you, then I would not have lived separately from you after we came to the city.

JIANG QING: Why did you live separately from me?

MAO ZEDONG: Our personalities clashed. You are of steel and I, iron. When we bumped together it made a clanging noise. You always see yourself at the center of things. You're moody, vengeful, and, forgive my directness, a little hysterical. Of course, it takes two hands to clap, and I, too, have my faults. From your perspective, at the least am I not a male chauvinist, a dictator in a family without equality? You should also not mince words. Communist party members should not conceal their views.

JIANG QING: All right, I'll tell you! Our marriage from the beginning was not based on equality. So I . . . (Cries) I . . . How is it that I have felt throughout my life that I am like Nora!

MAO ZEDONG: Nora? Who? Oh, that foreign woman. Humph . . . I'm tired; I don't want to discuss any more questions that should be taken up by others in the future. As for you and me—our participation in the historical turmoil of the last few decades, and our bittersweet marriage of almost forty years—let the future be the judge. I have evaluated myself according to a seventy-to-thirty ratio [*seventy percent good, thirty percent bad*]. What about you? Just let the future be the judge. I am so tired!

(JIANG QING *helps* MAO ZEDONG *walk over to his bed. A poker card falls from* JIANG QING'S *body.*)

MAO ZEDONG: What's that?

JIANG QING: Oh, a poker card.

MAO ZEDONG: Let me see. Oh, Q.

JIANG QING: Right—the queen.

MAO ZEDONG: (*Laughs*) Just like a paper tiger, it's a paper queen.

(MAO ZEDONG *crawls on his own onto the bed and covers himself with the white sheet. He is dead. The nurse, doctor, and* XIAO FENG *enter and cry bitterly.* JIANG QING *stands center stage and faces the audience indifferently and blankly. Blackout.*

A railing from a court of law falls from above and surrounds JIANG QING. *The court is just pronouncing judgment.*)

OFFSTAGE VOICE: Special Procuratorate of the People's Supreme Court of the People's Republic of China now pronounces judgment. We sentence the defendant, Jiang Qing, to death, to be carried out after a two-year reprieve, and stripped of her political rights for the rest of her life.

JIANG QING: (*Waking up from a state of nervousness, waits for a long while, then suddenly shouts out*) Rebellion is just; no crime in revolution! Zhang Chunqiao, Yao Wenyuan, Wang Hongwen, what kind of attitude is this you are taking? What are you doing with your necks drawn in and your heads lowered. You three men don't equal this one woman; fucking men! I'll show you. (*Raises her fist and shouts out loud*) No crime in revolution; rebellion is just!

(*The* BAILIFF *comes to* JIANG QING'S *side, handcuffs her, and takes her away. They walk along slowly for a while and arrive at a prison cell. Inside is a bed and simple utensils.*)

BAILIFF: (*Takes off* JIANG QING'S *handcuffs*) Your prison cell.

(JIANG QING *looks over the whole cell.*)

BAILIFF: Do you need anything else?

(JIANG QING *shakes her head. The* BAILIFF *exits.*)

JIANG QING: (*Suddenly calls out to the* BAILIFF) Wait!

BAILIFF: What is it?

JIANG QING: I want a portrait of Mao Zedong to hang above my bed.

   (BAILIFF *is stunned.*)

NOTES

   The English translation is based on the Chinese text *Jiang Qing he tade zhang-fumen* (Jiang Qing and her husbands), Hong Kong: Fanrong chubanshe, 1991.

   1. The original play has a horse, not a bird.

   2. Soft film (*ruanxing dianying*) was entertainment film criticized by leftist cultural figures in the 1930s. One of its leading supporters was Liu Na'ou.

   3. Couplet from the poem "Xiang ling gu se," by Qian Qi of the Tang.

   4. "*Yu zi xie xing*" comes from "Wuyi" (Without clothes) in the *Book of Odes*. The character Mao Zedong, or Sha Yexin, may be playing here with a line from another poem in the *Book of Odes*, "Ji gu" (Beating the drum), a line of which reads "to grow old with you" (*yu zi xie lao*).

   5. *The Storm* (1860), written by Aleksandr Nikolayevich Ostrovsky (1823–1886). *Eiji Goroshi*, a 1918 play, by Yamamoto Yuzo (1887–1974), is about a widowed factory worker who lives in desperate straits trying to raise her child and support her parents. She is driven to kill her child and is arrested by a sympathetic policeman.

   6. Ruan Lingyu, the most famous film star of the 1930s, killed herself, in 1935, after rumors circulated about her illicit affairs. In her suicide note, she wrote that "gossip is a fearful thing." This line was immortalized by Lu Xun, who used it as a title for an essay condemning gossip.

   7. Agnes Smedley (1890–1950), American journalist sympathetic to the communist cause in China.

   8. With a shift in the revolutionary movement from the urban areas to the countryside, Mao saw his position in the party rise from the late 1920s to 1931. Then Wang Ming's faction emerged to take control of the party apparatus, and Mao's position eroded.

   9. "*Qi tun shan he*" is a reference to the hero Xiang Yu, and "*da jiang dong qu*" comes from Su Shi's famous lyric meter about the Three Kingdoms hero, Zhou Yu, "The Charms of Niannu."

   10. From Ma Zhiyuan's (1260–1325) *sanqu*, "Heaven Pure Sand" ("Tian jing sha").

   11. A reference perhaps to the nurse of Mao's schizophrenic second son, Mao Anying, with whom she fell in love.

   12. Xin Qiji (1140–1207), Song loyalist, frequently wrote lyric meters lamenting the loss of his northern territory to foreign occupiers.

   13. All former heads or high-ranking members of the Chinese Communist Party who were removed from their posts for political or ideological problems.

Green Barracks

Zhang Lili

TRANSLATED BY YUANXI MA

Characters

FANG XIAOSHI   a new soldier, eighteen years old

BAI YU   squad leader, twenty-two years old

JIANG HUA   company commander of the women soldiers'
company, thirty years old

LU XIAOYUN   political instructor of the women soldiers'
company, twenty-eight years old

LIU MEI   an old soldier, twenty years old

YANG NI   a new soldier, sixteen years old

DING DIANDIAN   a new soldier, sixteen years old

TIAN XIANGXIANG   a new soldier, seventeen years old

SIMA CHANGJIANG   the only male in the women soldiers'
     company, technician, twenty-six years old
  BAI LING, BAI YU's sister   staff member of a certain communi-
     cations engineering company in a special economic
     zone, twenty-four years old

*Time: modern times, a period of time flowing past in its natural course
  in the tough barracks*
*Place: Green Barracks, in the midst of a special economic zone, where a
  group of girls in green army uniforms is stationed*

SCENE ONE

*(The empty stage is bathed in green. Green spotlights from all direc-
tions turn the stage into a glistening crystal palace. The green barracks, the green girls, their green lives, are open to interpretation. The
clear, crisp sound of a trumpet rises from afar. Coming closer and
closer, the brittle but pleasant sound resonates in the glittering green
light enwrapping the stage. Singing floats in—a female voice, bright
and childlike, that gradually becomes rich and deep with more and
more feeling . . .)*
"My long, over-shoulder hair cut short, my colorful skirts taken off,
I put on the army uniform and walk into the green barracks.
Standing in front of the mirror, I look so powerful and impressive
     in my wide-brimmed hat.
Hey, am I pretty? You say I am so pretty!
Hey, am I beautiful? You say I am so beautiful!
Green girls in their green years. Oh, I am so lucky.
My ribbons discarded, high-heeled shoes thrown away, I put on
     the army uniform and walk into the green barracks.
Competing on the training ground, I come first as a heroine.
Hey, am I brave? You say I am so brave!
Hey, am I strong? You say I am so strong!
Green girls, green youth. Oh, it's forever hard to forget."
*(The singing gradually fades. The musical trumpet becomes more
and more excited. With baton in hand, a young woman soldier walks
onto the stage with graceful yet vigorous steps. With her back to the
audience, standing at the edge of the stage, she waves the baton,
rhythmically accompanying the trumpet. Suddenly, a crescendo of
music breaks in, covering up the sound of the trumpet with military*

strains. A squad of female soldiers with striking and heroic bearing appears on the glistening green stage. Playing the French horn, trumpet, clarinet, and other instruments, they march in different formations, charging the audience with the vigor and vitality of the green barracks. The silhouetted profiles of these girls seem like sculptures in a green crystal palace. The luxuriant green is intoxicating; its luxuriance suffocates. It is now early morning. The sun emits a tender light, but not enough to drive away the fog in the woods. A breeze shakes the palm-shaped, needle-tipped leaves into a whisper. This expanse of palm woods in white fog seems mystical. Laughter bursts from the woods like a chain of silver bells ringing. At first just tree shadows dancing, female figures in the woods gradually become distinct. Laughing, teasing, and panting, each stands close to a palm tree and stretches herself, all in different postures.

  DING DIANDIAN, *small and slim, hair cut short as a boy's, is jumping about in the thick grass, catching butterflies or grasshoppers.* YANG NI, *not much taller than* DING DIANDIAN, *is picking wildflowers. She has a fair complexion and naturally curly hair. She looks like a doll, with her long eyelashes. Chubby* TIAN XIANGXIANG *is lying on the grass, stretching. She is always sleepy.* FANG XIAOSHI *gives the impression that she is forever squinting at something with her long thin eyes. Leaning on a tree,* BAI YU *is singing an unfamiliar song from a songbook. She is very pretty, a combination of womanliness and heroic spirit. Singing floats in the woods from time to time.* LIU MEI, *a girl with sloping shoulders and slender waist, wanders over and loiters next to* FANG XIAOSHI, *who is playing the trumpet full blast toward the top of a tall tree.*)

LIU MEI: What are you doing, playing like that?

FANG XIAOSHI: Tell me, when will this coconut tree bear coconuts?

LIU MEI: You greedy girl! You think you can reach the coconuts when they come out?

FANG XIAOSHI: Can't we think of some way to reach them? How stupid of you; haven't you ever picked coconuts from this tree?

LIU MEI: Nobody is as greedy as you—like a monkey. (*Laughs*)

FANG XIAOSHI: Are you teasing me? I hear there is a saying: There are eighteen strange things in Guangdong; one is that old ladies climb trees faster than monkeys. Aren't you from Guangdong? Why don't you try it?

LIU MEI: What a sharp tongue you have! See how I'd seal your lips!

(The two chase and tease each other.)

FANG XIAOSHI: *(Laughing and shouting)* See how your slender waist sways. You'd not only move faster than a monkey, but also faster than a serpent. You are a serpent of a beauty!

LIU MEI: *(Grabbing* FANG XIAOSHI *and tickling her)* You dirty mouth! Dare you say that again!

FANG XIAOSHI: *(Beside herself with laughter)* Spare me, Sister Liu Mei. Spare me!

LIU MEI: Still calling me sister! I tell you, this is an army unit. *(Speaking to* YANG NI *and* DING DIANDIAN, *who have come up to them)* You should all call me Old Soldier, do you hear me?

FANG XIAOSHI: Yes, I do. Old Soldier!

LIU MEI: No, add my surname to it; Old Soldier Liu!

YANG NI and DING DIANDIAN: Old Soldier Liu!

FANG XIAOSHI: Yes, Old Soldier Liu! *(Can't help laughing)* Such a vivid image; Old Soldier Liu, the old soldier whose waist sways.

LIU MEI: *(Tickling her again)* Dare you create any new names! *(Speaking to* YANG NI *and* DING DIANDIAN*)* Aren't you going to help me?

*(*YANG NI *and* DING DIANDIAN *join in joyfully.)*

FANG XIAOSHI: Old Soldier Liu, Old Soldier Liu, Old Soldier Liu, please spare me. I'd dare say nothing of the kind. I wouldn't dare anymore.

(A long drawn-out sound of a whistle)

BAI YU: *(Jumping up, shouting)* Fall in, everybody!

(Company Commander JIANG HUA *and Political Instructor* LU XIAO-YUN *appear in the woods. After gathering the squad,* BAI YU *runs to salute and report to the two leaders.)*

BAI YU: Report, Company Commander and Political Instructor! The bare-handed formation drill of the second squad of the third platoon of the first company has been completed. We are now taking a break. Please instruct.

LU XIAOYUN: *(Walking up to the squad, saluting)* At ease. You must be tired.

ALL SOLDIERS: We are not tired.

LU XIAOYUN: That's good if you are not tired. It's all right to complain a little on the first day, but there should be no tears. Now, listen to my command: Attention! Spread out, with a space of one meter between rows!

(The soldiers complete the formation according to the command.)

LU XIAOYUN: No talking! Attention! Remove your caps!

(The soldiers take off their caps. YANG NI*'s curly hair gets entangled with her cap.* FANG XIAOSHI*'s long over-shoulder hair spreads out like a waterfall.* TIAN XIANGXIANG*'s long queue drops to her waistline. Only* DING DIANDIAN*'s short hair looks neat and orderly.* LU XIAOYUN *and the company commander look at each other and laugh.* LU *walks among the women soldiers, looking at their beautiful hair.)*

FANG XIAOSHI: *(Unable to stand it any longer)* What are you doing, Political Instructor?

BAI YU: No talking when you are in formation.

*(*FANG XIAOSHI *sticks out her tongue and makes a face at* YANG NI. *Finally* LU XIAOYUN *goes back to the front of the squad.)*

LU XIAOYUN: I can see that you all love your hair very much. But once you become a soldier, your hair is no longer a personal matter. In the army everything has to be uniform, and there is no exception for hair. Therefore, what we are going to do today is . . . to cut your hair!

NEW SOLDIERS: Cut our hair?!

*(*LU XIAOYUN *takes out a pair of scissors.)*

LU XIAOYUN: Who will be first?

TIAN XIANGXIANG: *(Covering her head)* I don't want to have my hair cut. No, I don't. In my home village, girls all wear long hair. How can I face anyone if my hair is cut short?

YANG NI: I'm not going to have my hair cut, either. I'm just not going to have it cut. With the short hair, I'd look like an old lady. How ugly it'd be!

LU XIAOYUN: *(To* FANG XIAOSHI*)* You'll be the first. You'll take the lead.

FANG XIAOSHI: No, I won't do it if they don't.

LU XIAOYUN: *(Walking up to* TIAN XIANGXIANG*)* Xiangxiang, look around; is there anyone else who still wears long queues like yours? You'll look prettier with short hair. Now, look at us . . . *(taking off her army cap).*

*(*LU XIAOYUN *walks up to* TIAN XIANGXIANG *step by step, and the latter backs off step by step. Suddenly* TIAN XIANGXIANG *screams and runs off to the side, ready to resist, but scared.* LU XIAOYUN *turns to* YANG NI, *who jumps away;* LU *then turns to* FANG XIAOSHI, *who also runs away.)*

FANG XIAOSHI: No, I don't want to have my hair cut. Why should you force us?!

(The squad is now in disorder.)

JIANG HUA: *(Taking a few steps forward)* Now, listen to my command. Attention!

(Startled, the new soldiers fall in.)

JIANG HUA: Routine Service Regulations for Barracks stipulate that women soldiers' hair cannot be longer than to the shoulders. Today we are implementing the regulations by cutting your hair. That is to say, willingly or not willingly, you are going to have your hair cut. Fang Xiaoshi, fall out!

(FANG XIAOSHI falls out very reluctantly.)

JIANG HUA: Very good! *(To LU XIAOYUN)* Now start cutting.

(LU XIAOYUN walks toward FANG XIAOSHI with the scissors. FANG XIAOSHI wants to back off.)

JIANG HUA: Fang Xiaoshi, stand still.

(FANG XIAOSHI caresses her hair, tears rolling down her face. She silently takes out the hairpins and ribbons, surrendering to the mercy of LU XIAOYUN's scissors.)

Scene Two

(The sun is shining, bright and red in the cloudless sky. There is not a breath of wind, and the leaves of the palm trees are utterly still. Cicadas sing one after another as if to stir up the stagnant air. The soldiers look much more spirited with hair just covering their ears. Their army uniforms seem to fit them better, their slender legs wrapped tightly in their army pants.

JIANG HUA is calling out commands. Obviously, the individual drilling is still somewhat sloppy, but they are already out of breath and their cheeks crimson.)

DING DIANDIAN: Report!

JIANG HUA: Yes!

DING DIANDIAN: *(Sounding out)* I . . . I want to go to the bathroom.

YANG NI: *(Timidly)* Report . . . me, too.

JIANG HUA: Didn't you two just go?

DING DIANDIAN: I had too much porridge this morning. . . .

YANG NI: Me, too.

JIANG HUA: So, you're singing the same tune. Don't take so much porridge from now on! Listen to the command and go on with your drilling!

DING DIANDIAN: Company Commander, I have to go—

JIANG HUA: (*Ignoring her*) Attention! Now listen, go on marching! Remember the essential points! March!

(*The company marches on briskly. In the distance the sound of the men soldiers' drilling can be heard. As if deliberately, their shouts rend the air.*)

JIANG HUA: (*Stimulated*) Let's demonstrate the power of the women's company! One, two, one, two, one, two, three, four!

(*The women soldiers stride proudly forward with heads held high, echoing commands in sharp and brisk voices. The men, as if unwilling to be outshone, shout louder than ever. The sun is scorching, heat steaming in the air. The women soldiers persevere with clenched teeth.* JIANG HUA *continues with her commands, persistent and dauntless.* FANG XIAOSHI's *strides become smaller and smaller, her marching sloppy.*)

JIANG HUA: Halt! Fang Xiaoshi, fall out! What's wrong with you?

FANG XIAOSHI: I'm tired!

JIANG HUA: Ask everyone. Who is not tired?

(FANG XIAOSHI *lowers her head without a word.*)

JIANG HUA: All others dismissed. Take a rest. Fang Xiaoshi will go on drilling.

FANG XIAOSHI: Company Commander!

JIANG HUA: Listen to my commands! Attention! Parade step, march!

(*None of the women soldiers leaves. They watch* FANG XIAOSHI *march quietly.*)

JIANG HUA: (*Shouting*) Fang Xiaoshi, focus your attention! Place your arms and legs in the right position. Do your hear? In the right position.

(FANG XIAOSHI *cannot stand it anymore. She simply stops. She stands like a nail fixed to the ground, motionless no matter what command* JIANG HUA *gives.*)

JIANG HUA: (*Furiously*) All right. Now that you don't want to move, just stand there and don't move until I give permission. You must not leave this place. All the others go back to your barracks.

(*The other soldiers, with sympathy in their hearts, dare not say anything. The company is led away in silence. On the big drilling ground, everybody has left except* FANG XIAOSHI, *who stands in the* same place stubbornly. She harshly wipes at tears pouring from her eyes, again and again as if she could never wipe them away. Cicadas in the woods have seemingly become listless in the heat and sound hoarse and exhausted.

A young, bright male officer emerges from the woods carrying a bunch of cables. On his shoulder strap is a bar with two stars. SIMA CHANGJIANG, the technician and lieutenant of the company, looks a head taller than FANG XIAOSHI. Seeing her standing all alone on the drilling ground, he approaches her.

Hearing steps, FANG XIAOSHI lowers her eyes without looking at the person.

SIMA CHANGJIANG walks around her twice, amazed.)

SIMA CHANGJIANG: (Choosing his words) May I ask which company you are in? . . . Are you crying? Why are you standing here all by yourself? . . . You are in the women soldiers' company, aren't you? Did Jiang Hua make you stand here? . . . Please, say something. Hey, to tell you the truth, I'm also in your women soldiers' company.

(FANG XIAOSHI raises her head at last and glances at him, then lowers her eyes again.)

SIMA CHANGJIANG: You don't believe me? Well, I couldn't believe it myself. You don't have a technician in your company. I was asked to work there for a few days. A few days? Who knows how many days are a few days? I'm now going to see your company commander. Look, these are old telephone cables she asked me to bring over for you new soldiers to air your laundry on. Let's go. Follow me.

FANG XIAOSHI: (Finally looking him in the eye) How do you figure I'm in the women soldiers' company?

SIMA CHANGJIANG: Did I need to figure it out? I knew it at first glance. Who would dare to resort to such cruel punishment of a young and beautiful woman soldier except Company Commander Jiang Hua? If you were in my company, once our company commander and political instructor saw your tears, they would perhaps give you some chocolate.

FANG XIAOSHI: So your company commander is a man?

SIMA CHANGJIANG: Where could you find another woman company commander and another women's company in the whole military area?

FANG XIAOSHI: Are there women soldiers in your own company?

SIMA CHANGJIANG: Yes, there are. Half are men and the other half are women.

FANG XIAOSHI: I beg you, please talk to your company commander and political instructor to let me go to your company!

SIMA CHANGJIANG: *(Embarrassed)* I don't think I can do that. . . . If you ask me for help on telephones or communication lines, I can certainly do it. But transferring people . . . *(Shaking his head with a wry smile)*

FANG XIAOSHI: If that's not possible, I'd rather go home.

SIMA CHANGJIANG: That won't do. You're in the army now, you foolish girl. Oh, I'm sorry, I don't know your name yet.

FANG XIAOSHI: Fang Xiaoshi. "Shi" means "poetry."[1] And yours?

SIMA CHANGJIANG: Sima is the same surname as for Sima Qian,[2] and Changjiang are the same characters as those for the Yangtze River. Comrade Fang Xiaoshi, you can never leave the army at will. Actually, your company commander is a good person, one of the most excellent company commanders in the whole army. You'll realize it when you are with her longer.

FANG XIAOSHI: Then why do people call her a witch?

SIMA CHANGJIANG: Wasn't this originated by you women soldiers? She is strict, but she has a good heart. In fact, that's the only way to deal with you girls. If you're treated lightly, you take it with a smile and nothing changes. When you're treated strictly, you cry with bitter tears, and my company commander and political instructor would give in just looking at you girls. Only Company Commander Jiang Hua has a way, severe but effective.

FANG XIAOSHI: It's simply fascism!

SIMA CHANGJIANG: *(Awkwardly)* You're right. It is a little fascist to treat girls like this, a little too severe. . . . Well, you haven't eaten yet, have you? Let's go.

FANG XIAOSHI: It'd be good if I were dead right now. It'd be her doing! *(Starts to cry again)*

SIMA CHANGJIANG: Don't think that way. Life is too short. Now, I'll go and get you something to eat. *(Feeling in his pocket and getting out some chewing gum)* Have this first. I know girls like it.

(FANG XIAOSHI accepts the chewing gum and can't help laughing.)

SIMA CHANGJIANG: All right, hold on! I'll get water and food here right away.

(He turns and runs without taking the telephone cables. FANG XIAO-SHI *watches him disappear. She licks her dry lips and puts the chewing gum in her mouth.*

JIANG HUA *appears with an army canteen and a water bottle, coming up from the other side of the palm woods. She sees the motionless back of* FANG XIAOSHI *and quickens her steps.)*

JIANG HUA: All right now, eat your food.

*(*FANG XIAOSHI *neither speaks nor moves.)*

JIANG HUA: You're young, but you have such a big temper. Come, have some water first. Look at you. I haven't worried so much even about my son.

*(*FANG XIAOSHI's *lips are twitching, tears rolling down.* JIANG HUA *lifts the water bottle up to* FANG XIAOSHI's *lips and feeds her water.* FANG XIAOSHI *looks at her and drinks the water obediently.)*

JIANG HUA: *(Wiping the sweat and tears from* FANG XIAOSHI's *face)* Did you really stand here motionless? I'd admire you. If you kept this perseverance for the training, what an excellent woman soldier you would be! Let's go and sit in the woods.

*(*FANG XIAOSHI *spits out the chewing gum, sees the telephone cables left by* SIMA CHANGJIANG *on the ground, and takes them up.)*

JIANG HUA: Whose cables are they?

*(*FANG XIAOSHI *doesn't answer.)*

JIANG HUA: Has Sima Changjiang been here?

*(*FANG XIAOSHI *nods.)*

JIANG HUA: *(Spying the chewing gum paper on the ground)* Did he give this to you?

*(*FANG XIAOSHI *looks at her as if saying, "So what?")*

JIANG HUA: And you took it?!

*(*FANG XIAOSHI *puts the cables down, deliberately takes out another piece of gum, and puts it in her mouth.)*

JIANG HUA: *(Extremely angry)* What a shame! *(Grabs the chewing gum from her hand and throws it far away)*

FANG XIAOSHI: You! I . . . *(Looking at the canteen in her hand and then looking at the company commander, she throws the canteen away.)*

*(*SIMA CHANGJIANG *shows up with a canteen and water bottle, stunned.)*

JIANG HUA: This is intolerable, utterly intolerable! Come back with me to the company office, both of you.

FANG XIAOSHI: No! I'll never go back! (*She turns and runs away.*)

SIMA CHANGJIANG: Hey, Xiaoshi! (*Wants to chase her but stops, looking at* JIANG HUA)

JIANG HUA: (*Exhausted, waving her hand*) Go! Go and get her back. Be sure to get her back.

(SIMA CHANGJIANG *runs off with the canteen and water bottle.*)

JIANG HUA: (*Hitting her own head in distress*) Oh, this devilish temper of mine! (*She picks up the canteen listlessly, takes up the cables, and walks out haltingly.*)

SCENE THREE

(*In the women soldiers' barracks. It is nap time. Cicadas sing tire-lessly like a band playing forever the same monotonous tune. It is very hot. The women soldiers are lying in bed in the shirts and loose green shorts provided by the army. Nobody is speaking, but almost everybody is tossing and turning in bed. Obviously no one is asleep.*

YANG NI is putting makeup on her doll. She kisses it before she lies down.

DING DIANDIAN quietly gets up from her bed and takes a rod out from under her pillow. She shakes the rod and instantly a lifelike snake emerges, wriggling on the rod. She walks stealthily to YANG NI's *bed and puts the snake close to* YANG NI's *nose.* YANG NI *opens her eyes, frightened, and is about to scream.*)

DING DIANDIAN: Don't scream. It's a phony snake. Let's go to see Xiaoshi.

YANG NI: (*Timidly*) Can we do that?

DING DIANDIAN: Nobody would know. Let's take her some food.

YANG NI: I still have some chocolate and bubble gum. (*Like playing magic,* YANG NI *takes out a lot of nibbles from under her pillow. The two put on their army uniforms quietly.*)

BAI YU: Where are you going?

DING DIANDIAN: We . . . we're going to the bathroom and coming back soon.

YANG NI: Right; we'll be back in just a little while.

BAI YU: (*Sitting up*) Going to the bathroom? (*Laughing*) That was why the company commander told you not to take too much porridge. All right, now take out all the things in your pockets. (DING DIANDIAN *and* YANG NI *slowly take the colorful nibbles out of their pockets.*)

TIAN XIANGXIANG: *(Curling her lips)* Taking so many nibbles to the bathroom. Don't you mind the smell there? As if anybody cares for your nibbles!

BAI YU: All right, now go for as long as you like.

LIU MEI: Squad Leader, they're not going to the bathroom.

DING DIANDIAN: *(Going up to BAI YU's bed slowly)* Er . . . well, Squad Leader, we . . . we want to go and see Xiaoshi. Look, it's scorching hot in the sun. She'll be scorched to death.

YANG NI: I beg you, Squad Leader, please let us go.

LIU MEI: Without the permission of the company commander, she wouldn't dare to move even if you were there. If the company commander knew that she took what you gave her, she would be punished, and you two would not be spared, either.

YANG NI: *(In a sobbing voice)* What shall we do, then?

TIAN XIANGXIANG: She won't be so easily scorched. I was exposed to the sun every day in my home village; the more sunshine I got, the healthier I became.

DING DIANDIAN: You, a fat pig of a woman!

TIAN XIANGXIANG: Squad Leader, she called me a fat pig of a woman!

BAI YU: Diandian! *(To everybody)* The company commander has already brought water and food to Xiaoshi. Now, everybody, go back to bed.

LIU MEI: Oh, Xiaoshi is somebody now. The company commander has to take food to her in person!

TIAN XIANGXIANG: *(Complaining)* Ding Diandian, you are a revolutionary woman soldier now. How could you call people names? If the company commander heard that, you would be told to stand in the sun as a punishment. Then let's see if you dare to call people names!

DING DIANDIAN: *(Mockingly)* Well, the more sunshine you get, the healthier you become! So you've become a fat pig of a woman! *(She can't help laughing herself.)*

TIAN XIANGXIANG: If you call me that name again, I'll report to the company commander. What's wrong with being a little chubby? The company commander has praised me for my working capacity.

LIU MEI: Well, Sister-in-law Tian.[3] *(Pinching her)* You're not fat; you're well-developed. Men will definitely like this well-filled-out figure of our sister-in-law Tian's.

TIAN XIANGXIANG: Is that true? I thought only men in the countryside didn't mind women who were fat. So, men in the city like fat women, too?

LIU MEI: Sure enough! Why don't you ask the commander in chief next time you go to his home? He'd certainly tell you that.

TIAN XIANGXIANG: I wouldn't dare to ask him that. My father said even though my grandfather had saved the commander in chief's life during the Anti-Japanese War,[4] we mustn't always bother him. Last Sunday he invited me to dinner at his house; I didn't even dare to eat much.

LIU MEI: Perhaps the meal wasn't that good?

TIAN XIANGXIANG: Of course it was a good meal, though there weren't any delicacies. But the dishes were so nicely made. The turnip strips were cut as thin as vermicelli. The roots of bean sprouts were trimmed. Actually the roots of bean sprouts wouldn't hurt you. Then, the small and snow-white steamed buns were each as small as an egg. They looked so appealing, not to speak of their taste.

LIU MEI: Indeed! Why didn't you bring some to us?

TIAN XIANGXIANG: I couldn't do such a thing. As I said, I didn't even dare to eat much. I had twelve buns. I heard the commander in chief tell the nanny to go and buy more. I was sure I had already eaten too many.

LIU MEI: Really! Remember to eat more when you go to his house next time.

TIAN XIANGXIANG: I wouldn't dare. Even though the commander in chief said to me, "Xiao Tian, don't be polite," I still didn't dare to eat much.

(*A girl in a T-shirt and miniskirt appears at the door. Her hair is permed in fashionable big waves. She is* BAI LING, BAI YU's *sister.*)

BAI LING: How are you, girls?

(BAI LING's *presence excites the girls. Everything about her strikes them as new and unusual.*)

BAI LING: Actually, all the guards know me, but they still deliberately asked me, "Who do you want to see?" I said, "I've come to see Bai Yu." Then they said, "We know, you're Bai Yu's sister. You look prettier than your sister." I said, "Don't be mistaken. If my sister were in civilian clothes, you would surely say she was much prettier." So, they let me in.

YANG NI: You must have had the perm recently?

BAI LING: Is it nice? To tell you the truth, it's this year's fashion. Damn it! I spent a hundred and twenty yuan for it.

TIAN XIANGXIANG: A hundred twenty yuan, my goodness!

YANG NI: You look very pretty.

TIAN XIANGXIANG: *(Feeling the stiff hair on* BAI LING's *forehead)* What's this? It feels stiff. I don't think this is nice; it looks like the feathers on the head of a pheasant.

BAI LING: *(Doubling up with laughter and tidying the fringe on her forehead)* Sister-in-law Tian! Look at your hair, like that of a mole just coming out of the earth. I'd say it looks nice.

LIU MEI: In my opinion, it doesn't matter whether it's nice or not. Once you're stuck in this green uniform, would you dare to perm your hair? What's more, how many times could you afford a perm with the annual subsidy you get? In any case, I'm definitely going to ask to be demobilized this year.

BAI YU: Stay put and work hard. Revolution needs you. Don't you remember what you said when the company commander came to select new soldiers? You said no clothes were better than the army uniform. The company commander said she wouldn't have accepted you if you weren't so determined to be a soldier.

*(*BAI LING *takes out a photo and walks up to* BAI YU.*)*

BAI LING: What do you think of him, Sis?

BAI YU: *(Looking at the photo)* Who is this?

BAI LING: Tell me whether he is handsome first.

BAI YU: I don't know.

LIU MEI: Let me see it. Oh, he looks like a film star. Very handsome!

DING DIANDIAN: *(Curiously)* But who is it?

BAI LING: My husband!

BAI YU: *(Astonished)* Your husband?

BAI LING: *(Laughing)* Not a formal husband, yet—my boyfriend. But I still like to call him my husband.

BAI YU: That sounds unpleasant!

BAI LING: Unpleasant? How can it be unpleasant? How is it that when I call him that, I feel intimate and moved?

(All laugh heartily.)

LIU MEI: Guangdong people like to call their men that.

TIAN XIANGXIANG: I don't care whether it's unpleasant or not. What husband? You're still a girl. Don't you feel ashamed?

BAI LING: Eh, people have different ideas. What can we do about that? What would you call him? *(In a dramatized tone)* Mr. Husband, your humble wife has come to apologize to you. How's that? Did that sound better?

TIAN XIANGXIANG: *(Nodding)* Yes, much better.

(BAI LING can only laugh and shake her head.)

BAI LING: Girls, I've got you the clothing you wanted.

(The girls swarm around her with cheers of joy.)

BAI LING: Try them on! You try them on too, Sister.

(All the girls become busy with the piles of rich multicolored dresses that seem to fill the room.)

BAI YU: Bai Ling, this . . . this is too low cut!

BAI LING: Too low cut? How about the bikini? This is the new fashion!

TIAN XIANGXIANG: Well, well . . . it's so bare, front and back. I would be terribly ashamed wearing it! What's more, I'm so fat, and this swimming suit is so small . . . it would be so tight on me. . . .

BAI LING: If you stretch it, it'd be bigger, wouldn't it? Come, girls! Let's transform our sister-in-law Tian.

(The girls all lend a hand to put clothes on TIAN XIANGXIANG. The garment is a tight fit.

TIAN XIANGXIANG covers her face with both hands, standing in the middle of the room. BAI LING holds a mirror in front of her.)

BAI LING: Sister-in-law Tian, look at yourself; you surely look so pretty!

(TIAN XIANGXIANG peeks at herself through her fingers. Slowly she moves her hands off her face. She is amazed at her new self in the mirror.)

TIAN XIANGXIANG: So, I look quite nice.

ALL: *(Trying to hold their laughter)* Of course.

TIAN XIANGXIANG: *(Suddenly jumps onto a bed and pulls up a sheet to cover herself)* So, we let men look at us in this manner?!

ALL: *(Bursting out with laughter)* Of course.

TIAN XIANGXIANG: No wonder men would be seduced if they see girls like this. I wouldn't dare to go out dressed in this manner.

LIU MEI: You can set your mind at rest. If you go out in your loose army shorts, nobody will look at you.

(The girls roll on the beds overwhelmed by laughter, except for BAI YU, who has long taken off her fashionable dress and is now watching the girls quietly.

The door opens. Company Commander JIANG HUA *appears in the doorway.*

The laughter suddenly ceases.)

JIANG HUA: Fall in, everybody. Let's go find Fang Xiaoshi.

(All lights go out.)

SCENE FOUR

(A pale crescent moon rises, shedding light over the deep woods. Bull-frogs, the kind that exist only in the south, croon like the sobbing of cows in the night, sending cold shivers down one's spine. The crescent moves into the clouds and the woods become an expanse of darkness. With the grieving sound of a trumpet in the distance, piercing through the palm trees, the dark night seems even more lonesome. FANG XIAOSHI *is sitting under a palm tree, exhausted. The golden trumpet glitters in the pale light from the stars.* SIMA CHANGJIANG *enters, following the sound of the trumpet. Holding his breath, he doesn't want to scare away* FANG XIAOSHI. *Yet, he is attracted by the trumpet and stands there listening for a long time.)*

FANG XIAOSHI: *(Discovering there is someone there)* Who is it?

SIMA CHANGJIANG: *(Startled)* It's me. Don't be afraid. This is Changjiang.

FANG XIAOSHI: Changjiang? *(All kinds of emotions arise in her)* Changjiang!

SIMA CHANGJIANG: Xiaoshi! *(Deliberately light)* So, it's you. What are you doing here?

FANG XIAOSHI: Me? I'm talking to the coconuts.

SIMA CHANGJIANG: Talking? Talking to the coconuts?

FANG XIAOSHI: You don't understand!

SIMA CHANGJIANG: But this is not a coconut tree!

FANG XIAOSHI: Is it not? I think it looks so much like a coconut tree.

SIMA CHANGJIANG: *(Laughing)* It just looks like a coconut tree. Come over and look. Do you see those little fruits on the tips of the branches? Those are not coconuts; palm oil can be squeezed out of those fruits, but you cannot eat them.

FANG XIAOSHI: *(Giving in to his knowledge)* I never knew that!

SIMA CHANGJIANG: You played the trumpet so well, I was fascinated.

FANG XIAOSHI: *(Suddenly on her guard)* Why are you here?

SIMA CHANGJIANG: Looking for you. The company commander asked me to come and look for you.

FANG XIAOSHI: The company commander? She asked you to look for me?

SIMA CHANGJIANG: Come back with me. The company commander is worried to death about you.

FANG XIAOSHI: She? Worried about me? I think she'd be happy if she saw me punished to death.

SIMA CHANGJIANG: The company commander was wrong treating you so severely. But your behavior was even worse.

FANG XIAOSHI: *(Feeling wronged)* So you also think I am wrong? *(Crying sorrowfully)*

SIMA CHANGJIANG: Xiaoshi, don't cry. Xiaoshi, we've just met; forgive me for my frankness. I think though you are wearing the army uniform, you don't look like a soldier.

FANG XIAOSHI: *(In a fit of pique)* Then, what do I look like?

SIMA CHANGJIANG: A high school student, an out-and-out high school student.

FANG XIAOSHI: A high school student? *(Feeling she is looked down upon by him)* What's wrong with a high school student? I'd rather be a high school student than be a soldier. *(She takes off her army jacket and throws it to* SIMA CHANGJIANG.*)*

SIMA CHANGJIANG: *(Suddenly very severely)* Comrade Fang Xiaoshi! *(*FANG XIAOSHI *is shocked.)*

SIMA CHANGJIANG: *(Loosening up)* Don't behave like a child. I can see that you're a smart girl and want to do well. But you'll gradually understand that not everybody can turn out to be a good soldier, especially a good woman soldier.

FANG XIAOSHI: *(Murmuring)* I'm thinking of quitting the army.

SIMA CHANGJIANG: *(Saying every word distinctly)* But I am confident you will turn out to be an excellent soldier.

FANG XIAOSHI: *(Not expecting such a response)* Me?!

SIMA CHANGJIANG: *(Putting the army jacket back on her)* You have the makings of a soldier. You don't believe it now. But let's wait and see. How is that?

FANG XIAOSHI: *(Laughing)* You look like a wizard.

SIMA CHANGJIANG: *(Laughing, too)* No, I am a prophet.

FANG XIAOSHI: *(With a wry smile)* Your prophecy will not come true and you will be disappointed in the end.

SIMA CHANGJIANG: It seems you don't really understand yourself.

FANG XIAOSHI: I dare not say I understand you, but I believe I understand myself better than you do.

SIMA CHANGJIANG: Not necessarily. How can someone who does not have confidence in himself understand himself?

FANG XIAOSHI: Who is it that does not have confidence in himself?

SIMA CHANGJIANG: Well, if he has confidence in himself, where does his confidence lie? In being afraid of hardship and physical exhaustion? In casting away the canteen and running to the woods? In not believing that he can do well in the army? In not believing that he has the makings of a soldier? In thinking himself a good-for-nothing?

FANG XIAOSHI: You . . . it is you who do not have confidence in me *(wiping her tears)*.

SIMA CHANGJIANG: *(Laughing)* All right, now; that's good. It shows that you do have confidence in yourself. You wouldn't let my prophecy fall through and embarrass me, right?

(FANG XIAOSHI nods while wiping away tears.)

SIMA CHANGJIANG: Let's go back.

FANG XIAOSHI: I . . .

SIMA CHANGJIANG: Let's go.

FANG XIAOSHI: Well . . . what do you think the company commander will do to me for my leaving?

SIMA CHANGJIANG: *(Making a face)* That I don't know. She won't eat you up. A true man should have the courage to accept the consequences of his own actions. He should hold the fort even if the sky caves in. Right?

FANG XIAOSHI: *(Looking at him for a long time, nods at last; then suddenly blurts)* You are so nice!

SIMA CHANGJIANG: *(Embarrassed and bewildered, trying to find something to say)* Oh, . . . you're such a good trumpet player!

FANG XIAOSHI: *(Laughing)* You have said that before.

SIMA CHANGJIANG: *(Muttering)* Oh, yes, you're right. I've said that . . .

FANG XIAOSHI: You like it, I'll play it again for you.

(FANG XIAOSHI holds the trumpet close to her lips and starts to play. "Fang Xiaoshi . . ." A thin, sharp voice breaks the silence of the night. The frogs have stopped their crooning.)

FANG XIAOSHI: *(Scared, walking close to SIMA CHANGJIANG)* They're calling me.

SIMA CHANGJIANG: Don't be afraid. It's the company commander and others.

(*The echoes of calls arising one after another resonate through the woods. Sparkling of flashlights sputter in the woods like fireflies. "Come back, Fang Xiaoshi . . ." "Fang Xiaoshi, come back . . ." The sound now gradually comes closer, now drifts away. The woods become silent in the now pitch-black night.*)

SIMA CHANGJIANG: Xiaoshi, let's go back quickly to the company.

(FANG XIAOSHI *looks at him with complete trust and admiration in her eyes.*

The bugle resounds from afar.)

SCENE FIVE

(*The women soldiers' barracks. It is early in the morning. The singing of women soldiers can be heard, full of vitality.* BAI YU *is teaching a song. She sings sentence by sentence and the others sing after her:*

"At eighteen, I join the army and come to the army unit,

My blooming youth shines in the glittering collar insignia,

I hail my choice though no college badge is found on me.

Never will I regret, in my entire life, cherishing the experience of an army woman."

FANG XIAOSHI *is lying in bed, covering her head with a quilt.*

JIANG HUA *enters, holding a bowl of steaming noodles.*)

JIANG HUA: Xiaoshi, eat something.

(FANG XIAOSHI *ignores her.*)

JIANG HUA: I know you hate me. You must be cursing me in your heart, "You witch!" All right, I don't care if you curse me. What could I say when I am the company commander after all? If you were me, some day, perhaps, you would be a worse witch. Well, I'm just like this. I have been so severe, but I am still not able to bring you under control. So you, Fang Xiaoshi, seem to have the upper hand. But, I tell you, don't play these tricks on me. I've seen many like you who can't stand hardship or exhaustion and run away, without scruples. You think you're capable of evading all this? Do you think of yourself as a genius? To use an expression *you* like to say, "You go down in price!"[5] Fang Xiaoshi, you have reduced your own worth. If you think you are somebody, come and show the whole company your skill on the drilling ground. Show everybody you are much stronger than me, the witch. You should understand that once you're a soldier, you're no longer an ordinary person. You can't just act at will. Perhaps you'd say, "Hey, witch, don't you know I'm exhausted?" Yes, I do. Of course I know you're exhausted. Then perhaps you'd say, "Witch, don't you know I have my self-dignity?" Yes, I know that, too. But as a soldier, obedience is your duty. You may think individual drilling involves just a few movements. You may think it was just to punish you that you were told to march under everybody's watchful eye. No, you are wrong. There is only one purpose for telling you to do all that: to cultivate the qualities you must have as a soldier. These qualities are tenacity, indomitability, and dauntlessness. Perhaps you'd say, "I'm a girl, after all." Yes, you're right. Now you're your parents' daughter, and in future you'll be your husband's wife and your children's mother. But once you're in this uniform, you are a soldier first and foremost. To become a qualified soldier, even a man must go through a harsh process. To be worthy of this uniform, a woman has to go through a purgatorial process. It's not an easy process. Fang Xiao-shi, you want to excel in everything. To tell you the truth, I like you a lot. If you really want to fight with me, the witch, you'd better first train yourself to be a real soldier.

(FANG XIAOSHI *lies motionless, but obviously she's moved by* JIANG HUA's *powerful words.*)

JIANG HUA: I have a very bad temper. Yes, I am a witch, an out-and-out witch. I should not have thrown away your chewing gum. *(Taking out some candy)* Here, take it. If you like it, I'll buy more for you.

(FANG XIAOSHI *twitches her lips. Suddenly she cries out loud, hiding her head in her quilt.*)

JIANG HUA: Xiaoshi!

FANG XIAOSHI: Company Commander!

(They hold each other.

LU XIAOYUN *comes up to the bed.)*

LU XIAOYUN: Company Commander!

JIANG HUA: *(Embarrassed, wiping her tears)* So you're back.

LU XIAOYUN: Yes. Company Commander, your husband called long distance saying that your child Jiangjiang is sick. He is busy with a project design and asks you to go home for a few days.

JIANG HUA: What's wrong with Jiangjiang?

LU XIAOYUN: He's been running a fever for a few days already. The doctor said it started with a cold.

JIANG HUA: We are about to have a grand military maneuver in the whole army district. The coordination and liaison between the army, navy, and air force rely solely on the communication network. How can I leave?

LU XIAOYUN: It would be hard without you . . .

JIANG HUA: Let me call home and see what I can do.

LU XIAOYUN: All right.

JIANG HUA: How about you? Did you have a good talk with your husband?

LU XIAOYUN: No, we're through. We quarreled the whole day and night. He insisted on my leaving the army. I refused. In the end he said, "Divorce." I said, "Fine, let's get a divorce." I have moved all my things here.

JIANG HUA: Didn't you tell him you're pregnant?

LU XIAOYUN: (*Wiping her tears*) Yes, I did. You know what he said? "Isn't this a good excuse for you to leave the army? How could you not be taking care of your own child and, instead, leading a group of teenagers, crazily running about like a mother duck!"

JIANG HUA: (*Clenching her teeth*) I can't imagine he could have said that when he was once an army political instructor himself. Let me deal with him. He mustn't think now that he is a crappy manager, he should consider a soldier worthless.

LU XIAOYUN: He always says what I earn a month is not even enough for a bottle of wine and two cartons of cigarettes for him.

JIANG HUA: Don't worry. Stay in the unit and don't go back. See how I'll punish him.

LU XIAOYUN: (*Nodding*) You go and make your call.

(LU XIAOYUN *sits down at the head of* FANG XIAOSHI's *bed. Rubbing her eyes, she manages to calm down.*)

LU XIAOYUN: Xiaoshi, Xiaoshi!

(FANG XIAOSHI *looks at the political instructor for a long time. She finally takes the bowl of noodles and gobbles them down.* LU XIAO-YUN *smiles. Outside, the women soldiers are still singing, "At eighteen . . . ," but they sound much more confident.*)

(*In the women soldiers' company activity room.* SIMA CHANGJIANG *is helping the women soldiers with training in simulated communications.* BAI YU *plays the role of the person on the other end of the line, making all kinds of requests and asking various questions.* SIMA CHANGJIANG *is supervising the training.* TIAN XIANGXIANG *enters, reading something to herself from the notebook in her hand as she walks in. She murmurs to herself until* BAI YU *calls out to her.*)

BAI YU: Tian Xiangxiang, the exam starts now.

TIAN XIANGXIANG: Now? Oh, the exams (*putting away the notebook*).

SIMA CHANGJIANG: Don't be nervous. Listen carefully to the questions before you answer. Understand?

(BAI YU *starts asking questions and* TIAN XIANGXIANG *begins answering. She looks very nervous, with both hands on her chest and eyes staring ahead. She doesn't even hear* BAI YU's *questions clearly.*)

SIMA CHANGJIANG: (*To* BAI YU) Slower, slower. (*To* TIAN XIANGXIANG) These are all simple questions. Relax. Do you want some water?

(SIMA CHANGJIANG *pours a cup of water for* TIAN XIANGXIANG. *She takes it and drinks, giving him a grateful look.* SIMA CHANGJIANG *nods to her. She gradually calms down and answers questions more smoothly. It's clear she is trying her best to speak in good Mandarin.*)

SIMA CHANGJIANG: (*Giving her the test paper*) Quite good. Eighty-nine points, five points more than Diandian's.

TIAN XIANGXIANG: (*Not believing what she hears*) Is that true?

BAI YU: Your hard work has paid off.

TIAN XIANGXIANG: (*Crying*) I thought I would fail. I was so scared that I didn't dare to fall asleep the whole night. I was learning things by heart, under the quilt. I had never expected that I would get five points more than Diandian.

BAI YU: I know. You tossed and tossed, and I kept awake the whole night accompanying you.

TIAN XIANGXIANG: My mind doesn't work fast. Xiaoshi, Diandian, and Ni all do better than me. I was afraid I would be at the bottom of our company in the test. It'd be so disgraceful.

SIMA CHANGJIANG: Now go and have a good sleep. Then write a letter to your grandpa and make him happy, too.

TIAN XIANGXIANG: Yes, I'll do that. (*Going out, pleased*)

BAI YU: (*Shouting*) Next! Fang Xiaoshi.

(FANG XIAOSHI *comes up. It's obvious she is filled with confidence.*)

SIMA CHANGJIANG: Shall we start?

> (FANG XIAOSHI *nods.* BAI YU *begins. One question after another is asked, and the answers come fluently and thoroughly from* FANG XIAOSHI, *like pearls cascading onto a plate of jade.*[6]
>
> *After* BAI YU *finishes her questions,* SIMA CHANGJIANG *continues with his, but not one question baffles* FANG XIAOSHI.)

SIMA CHANGJIANG: *(Excitedly)* You're wonderful, Fang Xiaoshi. You got the highest mark in the whole company, one hundred and twenty points.

BAI YU: *(Holding* FANG XIAOSHI's *hands)* Xiaoshi, you're excellent!

> *(Girls all come up and surround* FANG XIAOSHI.)

SIMA CHANGJIANG: Come, all of you. Here are your test papers. You should be proud of yourselves, girls. *(To* FANG XIAOSHI*)* What did I say? I made the right prophecy, didn't I?

FANG XIAOSHI: *(Sincerely)* It's also because you're a good teacher.

LIU MEI: *(Sourly)* One would rather say we learned well than he taught well. Changjiang, how would you award us?

SIMA CHANGJIANG: Surely I'll reward you. How about chewing gum?

> *(He takes out a bunch of chewing gum packages from his pocket and throws them to them. Girls chew the gum happily.)*

TIAN XIANGXIANG: I don't like chewing gum. Aren't you afraid it'll stick to your teeth?

LIU MEI: *(To* SIMA CHANGJIANG*)* Cut it out. You'd better keep the gum to yourself to help you stop smoking.

DING DIANDIAN: Right! Your reward is always chewing gum. It seems as if you think chewing gum is the only thing we want.

FANG XIAOSHI: I think chewing gum is good enough. Why should you press him?

LIU MEI: We're not pressing *you.* Why should you be worried? Changjiang, it's up to you.

> (SIMA CHANGJIANG *scratches his head and suddenly pats it.)*

LIU MEI: What is it?

SIMA CHANGJIANG: I know what to do. Let me invite you to karaoke. How about that?

ALL: "Karaoke"?

> *(Cheers fill the room.)*

TIAN XIANGXIANG: What is kara . . . k?

LIU MEI: It's singing and listening to music. You'll see when you get there.

FANG XIAOSHI: The company commander won't give permission when so many of us ask for leave.

SIMA CHANGJIANG: Let's sneak. I'll take the responsibility if anything happens.

DING DIANDIAN: That's wonderful. It's a chance we won't get but once in a hundred years.

(BAI YU *comes in with her food.*)

BAI YU: So, you're all here. I was waiting for you in the kitchen. Go quickly to get your food. The cooks ask you to go right away.

(*The girls collect their things and run off.*)

SIMA CHANGJIANG: Bai Yu, I got the books you want.

BAI YU: (*Taking the books and flipping the pages*) Thank you.

BAI LING: Bai Yu, are you really serious about getting into the military academy?

SIMA CHANGJIANG: Do you object to it?

BAI LING: Yes, absolutely. There are so many jobs you can take. Why do you prefer to wear this army uniform? We do the same work; Bai Yu has better skills than I do. But I get more than five hundred yuan a month. How much can you get even if you get promoted to be an officer after you graduate from the military academy? Bai Yu, you're already qualified to be demobilized. Why don't you apply to leave the army?

BAI YU: (*Calmly*) The army unit is good.

SIMA CHANGJIANG: That's right. I'll help you with your preparation. You'll certainly be accepted.

BAI LING: What is good about the army unit? Look at you in this army uniform. A girl of eighteen is like a flower. What are you like? A girl of eighteen like a pine tree—well, a never-aging pine tree (*laughing*).

SIMA CHANGJIANG: It's good to be a never-aging pine tree. Beautiful flowers don't last, but pine trees are evergreen. I . . . I especially like your sister in army uniform.

BAI LING: So, you are the backstage supporter. (*With a glib tongue*) Now, tell me, do you like my sister or do you like my sister in army uniform?

SIMA CHANGJIANG: Didn't I just say that I like your sister in army uniform?

BAI LING: Don't you like my sister? Do you like her if she's not in army uniform?

SIMA CHANGJIANG: I didn't say I didn't like her.

BAI LING: Then, you like her.

SIMA CHANGJIANG: (*Backing out, step-by-step, wiping sweat from his face*) No, no, that's not an appropriate word . . .

BAI LING: All right, if "like" is not an appropriate word, let's use "love." Do you love Bai Yu, or do you love her in army uniform?

SIMA CHANGJIANG: You can't pose such a question. No, you can't . . . what I mean is that your sister is pretty. She's even prettier in army uniform. If she were dressed as you are, she wouldn't be so pretty.

BAI LING: (*Nodding incessantly*) So that's it. So that's it.

SIMA CHANGJIANG: All right, you have a good time. I have to go and get something to eat. (*Hurries off*)

BAI YU: Look, Sister, how you've embarrassed him . . .

BAI LING: Bai Yu, you've made a good choice. He's a nice guy, smart, handsome, and good-tempered. He measures up to the standard. He is at least one-point-eight meters tall, and he is so handsome.

BAI YU: (*Not knowing whether to laugh or cry*) What are you talking about? Sheer nonsense!

BAI LING: So, he is the one who urges you to enter the military academy. He has his schemes.

BAI YU: This has nothing to do with him. It's purely my own business.

BAI LING: What's between you two—

BAI YU: There's nothing between the two of us. He just helps me with my preparation for the exams.

BAI LING: (*Examining* BAI YU) Let me tell you, I am one hundred percent sure that guy is in love with you.

BAI YU: (*Laughing*) How so?

BAI LING: Look at his eyes and listen to his voice, then watch his feelings. It would be inconceivable if he wasn't in love with you.

BAI YU: (*Coldly*) Even if he is, that has nothing to do with me.

BAI LING: Sister, it's worth it trying to get into the military academy, just for him. I know you soldiers are not allowed to be involved in love affairs. You do it secretly now, and when you graduate from the military academy and become an officer, everything will be all right.

BAI YU: You're really an expert in love affairs. You've gone too far in your nonsensical talk. I don't want to get married my whole life.

BAI LING: What?

BAI YU: Look at our father and mother. Don't you feel we have suffered enough? I hate Father.

BAI LING: But I sympathize with him.

BAI YU: I didn't realize until now those women he brought home—

BAI LING: Sister, you are prejudiced against men, and this army life has enhanced your prejudice. Bai Yu, get a boyfriend and try it out. Surely, he'll be good to you, protect and care for you. When you feel wronged, you can cry in his arms. When you're tired, you can lean on his strong shoulders. He can carry you on his motorcycle and run wild. He can hold you up and make you feel you are floating like a cloud. . . .

BAI YU: *(Shaking her head)* No, I don't want that. I really don't want those things. What I want is only to live quietly by myself my whole life.

BAI LING: *(In terror)* Sister, don't you ever think that way. If you don't love him, apply to leave the army. Environment can create competent people. It can change people as well.

BAI YU: No! I have long made up my mind. I will be a professional army woman. I find I am suitable for the role. *(Excited)* Just think if I could be the company commander, I'd be a witch. Who else do I need? I'd be like Jiang Hua, leading a group of big children, and they will be relying on me and trusting me. Isn't that enough?

BAI LING: *(Looking at her sister as if looking at a stranger, near tears)* Bai Yu, what rubbish you are thinking of! Don't you know how pretty you are? Don't you know how smart you are? If only you would walk out of the army barracks and enter any company, you'd be given important work. You are a woman. You should have a woman's career.

BAI YU: *(Unable to comprehend* BAI LING's *pain)* A woman writer from the Soviet Union wrote a book entitled "There Is No Female in the War." Women can take up men's careers. Why can't I?

BAI LING: You . . . you . . . are perverse.

BAI YU: *(With a cold smile)* That's not so bad.

BAI LING: No, Sister, you mustn't be like that. *(Taking up the book from the table and tearing it into pieces)* To hell with your military academy!

("Pia!" BAI YU *slaps* BAI LING *in the face.* BAI LING *raises her head, looks at* BAI YU, *and backs away in horror.)*

BAI YU *eyes her coldly and picks up the pieces of the book from the floor.*

The sound of a bugle is heard, faraway and prolonged.)

SCENE SEVEN

(At the gates of the barracks. For the women soldiers, this is the place where the world divides into two parts. One part is the evergreen palm woods and the other is the ever-bright neon lights glittering with temptation. Girls from the women soldiers' company are festive today. They are beautifully dressed and gorgeously made-up. You'd never know how they could make their hair curly. Colorful hairpins and other ornaments take the place of army caps. The girls stand in a line, in distress, reciting the routine service regulations for barracks in murmurs, like monks saying their prayers. SIMA CHANGJIANG stands to the side, at a loss, holding a bunch of army uniforms in his arms. Obviously the uniforms belong to the women soldiers. BAI YU enters. She looks as distressed as the others.)

SIMA CHANGJIANG: How was it?

BAI YU: The pickets reported everything to the director. I heard the director saying over the phone, "It's outrageous! Tell Jiang Hua to get them back in person." *(Making a face)* It's terrible.

SIMA CHANGJIANG: It was strange. We left separately. Nothing happened when we went out. Why were we caught when we came back?

BAI YU: I can't make it out, either.

SIMA CHANGJIANG: *(Looking over the women soldiers)* Someone must have betrayed us.

BAI YU: How could that happen? There was no reason to do that.

(JIANG HUA hurries in. SIMA CHANGJIANG and BAI YU go up to her.)

BAI YU: Company Commander!

JIANG HUA: *(Looking at her with keen and overbearing eyes)* So, you took the lead?

BAI YU: Yes, it was me.

JIANG HUA: You are so brave! *(Walking around the women soldiers twice)* You are all very pretty! Very fashionable! Why don't you look at each other? Do you still look like soldiers?

BAI YU: Company Commander, it's all my fault. Punish me.

JIANG HUA: I won't let you off easily. I don't understand; what's wrong with wearing this army uniform? Why did you have to change into all this colorful clothing? Where did you change?

FANG XIAOSHI: At the old lady's, who sells groceries.

LIU MEI: At the uncle's,[7] who sells fruit.

YANG NI: I changed in the small store where the little girl sells cold tea.

TIAN XIANGXIANG: I once asked the aunt outside our gate to cut out clothes for me. She called to me when I went out, "Fatty, come and I'll cut out clothes for you at a cheaper price." I said I wasn't going to have anything cut out this time; I wanted to change clothes. She said, "So, you are not allowed to go out in your army uniform?" I said, "No, we are not allowed to go out in colorful clothes." Then she said, "Fatty, come to me again when you want any clothes cut out." I said, "I won't have anything cut out anymore. The clothes you cut out for me last time were all too small, I can't wear them." The aunt said . . .

(FANG XIAOSHI *pulls at the corner of her clothes, hinting at her to be brief.*)

TIAN XIANGXIANG: Don't rush me. I haven't finished yet. Where was I. Oh, yes—

JIANG HUA: *(Interrupting her)* Ding Diandian, how about you?

DING DIANDIAN: At the clothing store, there was a man—

JIANG HUA: Listen to all this! Look at yourselves! What a disgrace! Look how daring you were. You didn't even know those people, and you called them uncle and brother. You had no scruples changing clothes in their places. You weren't afraid something might happen to you, but I was. You take yourselves lightly, but your parents do not. They love you. If anything happened, what could I say to your parents? You did everything furtively and stealthily because you all knew it was wrong to do what you did and you all knew it violated discipline. Then, why did you do it?!

SIMA CHANGJIANG: They did well in the tests, so—

FANG XIAOSHI: Company Commander, we asked Technician Sima to take us there. You can't blame just him—

BAI YU: I am the squad leader. I am also—

JIANG HUA: Shut up, all of you! I will let none of you off easily. How many days have you been in the army uniform? And now do you already dislike it and grow tired of it? Let me tell you, there is still a long way to go. Anyone who doesn't like the army uniform from the bottom of one's heart can never be a real soldier. Now get back to your barracks and take those rubbishy clothes off you.

BAI YU: Yes!

(BAI YU *tries to get her ranks in good order. The girls were left in a whirl by the talking-to and now cannot make out which is a left or right turn. Looking at this squad in multicolored dresses and flowery decorations,* JIANG HUA *heaves a deep sigh.*

The sound of a bugle is heard again spreading throughout the barracks.)

SCENE EIGHT

(*At night, in the switchboard room. Red and green indicator lights flash. Women soldiers' soft, floating voices answering the phone calls carry with them a distinct clarity constituting pleasant and enchanting melodies. It is late. The frequency of flashing is reduced. The women soldiers relax and stretch themselves.*)

LIU MEI: This is really not a job for human beings. I am dead tired.

FANG XIAOSHI: Take off your earphones when you talk.

LIU MEI: That doesn't matter at this time of night.

FANG XIAOSHI: It's not right, anyway.

(LIU MEI *snorts. She takes off her earphones and throws them onto the table. The indicator light goes on.* LIU MEI *puts on her earphones again, roughly.*)

LIU MEI: You're such a bother! (*Angrily*) Hello! Why don't you say something? Are you dead? The line to Changsha has been cut off. No one can get through.

(LIU MEI *does not let the other side go on and pulls out the plug.*)

FANG XIAOSHI: (*Kindly*) You want to get through to Changsha? All right, let me put you through.

LIU MEI: (*Giving her a supercilious look*) You're always the conscientious person!

FANG XIAOSHI: You—

LIU MEI: Who knows who you want to show off to!

FANG XIAOSHI: You! I—

(*A light comes on.* FANG XIAOSHI *takes the call.*)

LIU MEI: (*To* TIAN XIANGXIANG *beside her*) Hey, I told you to talk to Big Wang in the third company. Did you go?

TIAN XIANGXIANG: I feel embarrassed to do so. Though we're from the same village, what would I say to him?

LIU MEI: You can go to the woods and just have a chat. *(Softly)* If Big Wang becomes a voluntary soldier, you can stay in the city, too, right?[8]

TIAN XIANGXIANG: I dare not do such a thing. What if the company commander hears about it . . .

LIU MEI: Well, who would be able to control that kind of thing?

TIAN XIANGXIANG: *(Getting interested)* I . . . I just don't know what Big Wang thinks.

LIU MEI: I can see that he likes you. Don't you remember? That day you couldn't finish your job digging the cables. Didn't he help you with it?

TIAN XIANGXIANG: That's true.

LIU MEI: Another time, when you went to see the doctor and saw him, didn't he take you home on his bike?

TIAN XIANGXIANG: *(A little complacent now, pats her own thigh)* Of course, how could I forget all this? He is good to me.

LIU MEI: If you don't catch him quickly, he will run away.

TIAN XIANGXIANG: I—

(The phone rings and TIAN XIANGXIANG *answers the call.)*

TIAN XIANGXIANG: What's the number? Five-five-four-three-two-three? Here you are. Please begin.

*(*TIAN XIANGXIANG *is about to take off her earphones, then stops. Listening attentively, she laughs.)*

LIU MEI: What is it?

TIAN XIANGXIANG: *(Shaking her hand)* Hush . . .

LIU MEI: *(Understanding now)* Let me listen to it, too.

TIAN XIANGXIANG: The man is unscrupulous, saying things . . .

*(*LIU MEI *puts on her earphones, but takes them off at once.)*

TIAN XIANGXIANG: What's wrong?

LIU MEI: They realized we were listening, so they stopped talking. What did they say just now?

TIAN XIANGXIANG: The man was so unscrupulous . . .

LIU MEI: What did he say?

*(*TIAN XIANGXIANG *whispers something into* LIU MEI's *ears. Both laugh stealthily.)*

FANG XIAOSHI: Don't overdo it. Answer the calls.

LIU MEI: That's none of your business. *(Putting on her earphones)* I am not your "miss." I am your big sister.[9]

(DING DIANDIAN *has been busy for quite a while, now she doesn't have much to do. She can't help stretching herself.*)

DING DIANDIAN: Squad leader, what time is it? It'll soon be daybreak, right?

BAI YU: (*Looking at her watch*) Half past two. There's still a long time to go. Come! Put on some cooling ointment and you won't be sleepy.

(BAI YU *puts some cooling ointment on* DING DIANDIAN. YANG NI *takes some chewing gum out of her pocket and gives it to* DING DIANDIAN, *signaling her to pass it on to others.* LIU MEI *is chewing the gum when* SIMA CHANGJIANG *appears at her back. She stops the movement of her mouth and does her work in a more serious manner.* SIMA CHANGJIANG *takes up the chewing gum, snorts, and throws it to the corner of the wall.* FANG XIAOSHI *is about to explain but, looking at* LIU MEI *at her side, she says nothing.*

SIMA CHANGJIANG *goes along inspecting everyone's work.* YANG NI *knows she is caught. Taking out some chewing gum, she gives it to* SIMA CHANGJIANG.)

YANG NI: Technician Sima Changjiang, do you want some?

(SIMA CHANGJIANG *takes the chewing gum without any expression and softly throws it also to the corner of the wall.*)

SIMA CHANGJIANG: (*Loudly*) Everyone, spit it out! (*Controlling himself, lowers his voice*) Spit it out, everybody! Now I know what's been happening. You go and listen at the supervision station. Who could hear you clearly? It's outrageous. You two, Tian Xiangxiang and Liu Mei, chatting away and eavesdropping. What a mess you have made! If I just warn you nicely, you laugh. If I give you a serious talking-to, you can't stand it. Now this time I won't be scared by your complaints. Starting tomorrow, one more hour is added to vocational training. We will return to the usual time when you have made amends. Comrade Bai Yu, please take up the responsibility seriously.

BAI YU: Yes. But we have too few people in the squad. They are really exhausted.

SIMA CHANGJIANG: Exhausted? You should not relax a bit even though you are exhausted.

(*A red light comes on and* BAI YU *answers the call.*)

BAI YU: (*In a very pleasant voice*) Long Distance Communication Company. . . . You want to talk to your mom? . . . Oh, you're Little

Jiangjiang? Are you all right now? . . . You're still in the hospital? Why, it's so late now; you want to talk to your mom? . . . Me? I'm the aunt who gave you the little panda. Aunt Squirrel aunt, Aunt Donna Duck, Aunt Mickey Mouse, and many other aunts are all here. Your mom is in the lead communication room. Hold on. Aunt Panda is going to transfer your call.

(The girls in the switchboard room fade away. The spotlight is on a corner of the stage with JIANG HUA *and her five-year-old son talking.)*

JIANGJIANG: Mom, why didn't you come home? I'm sick, very sick. Come and see me, if you don't believe it. My buttocks are rotten with shots given me by the aunts here. Mom, don't you love your little Jiangjiang?

JIANG HUA: Oh, yes, I do. My little son, Jiangjiang, is the one I love most.

JIANGJIANG: Then, why didn't you come back and see me? Daddy said he sent you several telegrams. Today Daddy has gone to the work site. I have such a bad headache, so I miss my mom, and I cried. Mom, when are you coming back to see me?

JIANG HUA: My good boy, my dear boy, Mom wants so much to go back to see you, but Mom has so much work to do here. Mom is the company commander. The company commander has to lead many, many soldiers; they are like children. They will miss Mom, too. They will have a headache, too, and they will cry, too. They have to do very important work. Little Jiangjiang, will you blame Mom if I can't go back?

JIANGJIANG: Mom, come back. I miss you so much.

JIANG HUA: Jiangjiang, my darling boy, Mom will go back. Why don't you just go back to bed now?

JIANGJIANG: Mom, Mom, my head aches so much. I miss you so much.

JIANG HUA: *(Choked with sobs)* My sweet Jiangjiang, my dear boy, Mom will ask for leave tomorrow and take the train to go to see my Jiangjiang—

JIANGJIANG: Mom, come quick . . .

(When JIANG HUA *raises her head,* JIANGJIANG *has disappeared. She looks at the red phone receiver in her hand, tears flowing down, soundless. The women soldiers gather around her quietly.)*

WOMEN SOLDIERS: *(Almost in one voice)* Company Commander, go back and see Jiangjiang.

(JIANG HUA *looks at the group of big children in tears and nods with all her might.*)

SCENE NINE

(*In the barracks of the women soldiers' company. The two ends of a very long, used cable are tied to two trees. On the cable hang quilts and clothes.* LIU MEI *enters with a quilt in her arms, wandering in the yard. She observes closely the clothes on the cable.* SIMA CHANG-JIANG *comes up to her face-to-face.* LIU MEI *says nothing. She just stares at him.*)

SIMA CHANGJIANG: *(Stops)* What can I do for you?

LIU MEI: *(Smiles)* Yes. Look, you hung the cable so high. Who could be as tall as you?

(SIMA CHANGJIANG *takes the quilt from* LIU MEI *and throws it on the cable. He turns and leaves.*)

LIU MEI: *(So angry she breaks a branch, but sweetly to him)* Thank you.

SIMA CHANGJIANG: *(Stopping abruptly)* Liu Mei, I have a question for you.

LIU MEI: *(Expecting something, bashfully)* Ask as many questions as you like . . . as long as you—

SIMA CHANGJIANG: *(Interrupting her)* Was it you who called the entrance guard the day we went to the karaoke?

LIU MEI: *(Her face reddens)* How could I have done such a thing? I was with everybody the whole time. You . . . you can go and ask them.

SIMA CHANGJIANG: If you thought what we did was wrong, you didn't have to go with us, and you could have reported on us above-board. Did you feel honored when a notice of criticism of the women soldiers' company was circulated? *(Leaving)*

LIU MEI: How could you . . . How could you make such an unfounded and malicious accusation of me? I . . . I am going to tell the director.

SIMA CHANGJIANG: *(Laughing)* Go ahead. A child who tells lies will be eaten by a wolf. Remember that! *(Exits)*

LIU MEI: *(Clenching her teeth and stamping her foot)* Let's see who is going to be eaten by a wolf.

(*She takes out of her pocket a few tubes of greasepaint and makes marks on the two shirts belonging to* JIANG HUA *and* LU XIAOYUN.

When she sees a man's army jacket, she hesitates, then raises her hand and is about to make marks on it when she sees FANG XIAOSHI *enter with a basin of clothes. She tries to pull the jacket down in a hurry, but it gets caught on a nail on the tree. She gives up the jacket and hides behind the tree.*

As FANG XIAOSHI *is hanging the clothes, she discovers a big hole in the man's jacket. She takes it down and holds it to her face for a long while.)*

FANG XIAOSHI: *(Shouting upstairs)* Yang Ni, throw down my sewing kit.

(FANG XIAOSHI *gets out needle and thread and mends the hole in the man's jacket.*

LIU MEI *comes out from behind the tree.)*

LIU MEI: What are you doing, working so seriously?

(FANG XIAOSHI *gives her a glance and ignores her.)*

LIU MEI: So, you're mending the jacket for Technician Sima. He'll be so pleased if he knows. Let me get him over here.

FANG XIAOSHI: Liu Mei!

LIU MEI: You don't want him here? You, the pitiful one. You wouldn't even dare to let him know that you have mended his jacket for him. Who's going to appreciate your kindness?

(FANG XIAOSHI *looks at* LIU MEI.)

LIU MEI: If I were in love with someone, I would go ahead and show him my love at all cost. At the worst, I'd just give up the army uniform. I don't want to wear it, anyway. The army is really not a place for women. Young girls of eighteen or nineteen are not allowed to fall in love. Can you justify that?

FANG XIAOSHI: This is quite normal.

LIU MEI: To hell with normal! No matter what, I am going to leave the army this year. The company commander asks me to stay for another year. Why should I waste another year of my youth? Only a fool would do that sort of thing.

FANG XIAOSHI: To me, it's quite a good choice to be a soldier. People have different ways of living their lives. Life as a soldier is a very good way of existence.

LIU MEI: *(Sneering)* "Very good"? That's because you have someone here, right? If you feel embarrassed, let me speak to Sima—

FANG XIAOSHI: *(Shaking her head)* No, it's not the right place, nor the right time.

LIU MEI: So, you've really fallen in love with him.

FANG XIAOSHI: Liu Mei, I don't want to talk about it.

LIU MEI: We're just chatting. Don't get serious. *(Taking her quilt, she leaves.)*

(JIANG HUA enters. She looks utterly exhausted.)

FANG XIAOSHI: Company Commander, you're back.

JIANG HUA: Fang Xiaoshi, please find the instructor and ask her to come here.

(FANG XIAOSHI nods and exits. Shortly, LU XIAOYUN enters, with her sleeves and pants rolled up and carrying a shovel, followed by DING DIANDIAN, in rubber boots and a big white apron, carrying two metal pails clinking against each other. LU XIAOYUN hands her spade to DING DIANDIAN.)

LU XIAOYUN: *(To DING DIANDIAN)* Go and ask Big Wang from the third company to come and help us butcher the pig.[10] Tell him that his company can have the pig's tripe and chitterlings as reward.

DING DIANDIAN: All right.

JIANG HUA: Don't go, Diandian. Let me do it later.

LU XIAOYUN: Company Commander, let's get Big Wang. You're too tired.

JIANG HUA: *(Jokingly)* I don't want to give up the pig's tripe and chitterlings. Right, Diandian?

DING DIANDIAN: Yes, you're so right. I love those jumbles in the pig— pig heart, liver, and tripe.

JIANG HUA: All right. Go and make preparations. I'll come in a minute.

DING DIANDIAN: Okay, Company Commander. Teach me how to butcher a pig, so I can do it next time.

JIANG HUA: Aren't you afraid? There'll be a lot of blood . . .

DING DIANDIAN: I'm a soldier now. I'm not afraid of that sort of thing anymore.

JIANG HUA: Very good. I accept you as a little female butcher. Go now. Call me when you are ready.

DING DIANDIAN: Yes, Company Commander. *(Exits)*

JIANG HUA: Were you cleaning the pigsty?

LU XIAOYUN: We've bought another eight piglets, all skipping and jumping about.

JIANG HUA: Don't do such heavy work anymore.

LU XIAOYUN: That's all right. The doctor says I should exercise more.

JIANG HUA: But that's not the way to exercise. Go and wash yourself first.

LU XIAOYUN: *(Expecting something)* What is it? *(Sitting down)*

JIANG HUA: *(Silent for some time, then taking out a piece of paper)* He asked me to give this to you.

LU XIAOYUN: *(Not taking the paper or looking at it, tears pouring down)* I knew long ago that's what he wanted. I knew it long ago.

JIANG HUA: At first I thought if I couldn't come to some kind of agreement with him, you'd better leave the army. A child cannot do without a father. But . . .

LU XIAOYUN: What?

JIANG HUA: But . . . he told me point-blank that he's found another woman. What he wants from you is just your consent to divorce.

LU XIAOYUN: How come . . . it happened so fast.

JIANG HUA: We made a mistake. I shouldn't have had you stay in the army unit. We distanced him from you by doing so. I thought he couldn't stand to be parted from you for several months and would come to get you. We were all wrong. I saw in his office there were so many girls colorfully dressed. He is no longer the big soldier who only had a single woman like you. Now he is an important manager. Xiaoyun, the outside world has changed so much.

LU XIAOYUN: "Changed"?

JIANG HUA: Yes, it's so different from the past. He made me sense the change so acutely. Xiaoyun, we are totally different from him now.

LU XIAOYUN: What you mean is—

JIANG HUA: I also met that woman. He asked her to come over to meet me.

LU XIAOYUN: How could he have done such a thing?

JIANG HUA: Xiaoyun, suddenly I thought of so many things. What have we done to fulfill the tasks of a daughter, wife, and mother? Haven't we done too little? Our parents complain about us, our children blame us, and now our husbands want to leave us. Is it true that this green army uniform is not suitable for women?

LU XIAOYUN: Company Commander!

JIANG HUA: I hadn't been out of the barracks for such a long time. Walking on the street, I felt that even the street was new to me. This was what I wore when I went out. Weren't these just a pair of sneakers on my feet? It seems so natural when we wear them in the barracks every day. In the past we felt we were quite decently dressed walking around in these sneakers in the street. But what's wrong with them now? Your husband looked at my sneakers. Those girls in his company looked at them. Men and women in the street looked at them, too. I couldn't stand their contemptuous looks. Ah . . . we can't blame the girls for changing into civilian clothes stealthily when they went out.

LU XIAOYUN: Company Commander, that's not our fault.

JIANG HUA: You're right, that's not our fault. But can we say it's their fault?

LU XIAOYUN: They don't understand us.

JIANG HUA: Right. But we don't understand them, either. I had a feeling when I came away from your husband's company that it seemed as if I were coming back from the United States. Those people there didn't look like Chinese.

LU XIAOYUN: (*With a bitter smile*) Perhaps they would say we didn't look like people living in the special economic zone when they saw us.

JIANG HUA: I never had the sense that I was living in a special economic zone. The army unit is just the same everywhere. An army unit in a special economic zone should still be an army unit.

LU XIAOYUN: (*With another bitter smile*) But women soldiers in the special economic zone have to be divorced from their husbands, and the divorce should take place smoothly, without anybody being crushed.

JIANG HUA: He and that woman both said that you could all be friends after the divorce. He also said that you could have the child. If you brought up the child, he would give you fifty thousand yuan.

LU XIAOYUN: Fifty thousand yuan? Huazi, can fifty thousand yuan buy me the moon in the sky?[11]

JIANG HUA: "The moon in the sky"?

LU XIAOYUN: (*Sadly*) Company Commander, you know everything between him and me. At first it was he who chased after me. I was still a soldier at that time. Of course, I tried to ignore him. But he made a solemn pledge of love to me, saying he would wait for me. He said, "Xiaoyun, you are the moon in the sky. I'd wait for you even if I should never get you . . ." (*Sobbing*)

JIANG HUA: I know. But who could have imagined things would have turned out like this? I don't believe that anybody cannot live without him. There are so many men in our barracks; you see them everywhere. Let me get you a bunch and you just select from them.

LU XIAOYUN: No, I don't want men anymore, really. Men—
(DING DIANDIAN *enters, with a knife for butchering the pig, followed by* FANG XIAOSHI, TIAN XIANGXIANG, *and* YANG NI.)

GIRLS: Company Commander! Instructor! Everything's prepared. Let's start the job.

JIANG HUA: *(Trying hard to wipe away tears)* Good. Let's go. *(Ready to go)*
(BAI YU *enters. She carries toys, fruit, food, and other things in her hands.)*

BAI YU: Company Commander!
(*The women soldiers surround her, looking at the toys, and each takes one.*)

BAI YU: These are toys the girls asked me to buy for Little Jiangjiang. We want him to know that so many aunts all love him.

JIANG HUA: *(Her eyes brimming with tears)* Thank you, all of you!

ALL SOLDIERS: Company Commander, if there's nobody taking care of Jiangjiang, bring him here. We can take turns looking after him. Company Commander, you just go and don't worry about us. Don't come back before Jiangjiang is fully recovered. Company Commander, we will definitely achieve good results for our women soldiers' company in the grand military maneuver. You trust us, don't you?

JIANG HUA: Yes, I do. Of course I trust you.
(*She and* LU XIAOYUN *look at each other, smiling.* LU XIAOYUN *turns away and wipes tears from her eyes.*)

SCENE TEN

(*In the headquarters of the women soldiers' company. Several award banners are hanging on the walls. The room is empty. A moment later,* LIU MEI *enters and knocks on the door, but there's no response. She pushes the door open and goes in.* LU XIAOYUN *and* SIMA CHANG-JIANG *enter.* LU XIAOYUN *carries a big bunch of prizes in her arms.* SIMA CHANGJIANG *holds an award banner.*)

LIU MEI: Instructor, you're back.

LU XIAOYUN: Did you want to talk to me?

LIU MEI: Yes.

LU XIAOYUN: Good. Actually, I want to talk to you, too.

SIMA CHANGJIANG: Instructor, shall we hang up the banner?

LU XIAOYUN: Yes, of course. The company commander will probably come back today. She'll be happy when she sees it.

SIMA CHANGJIANG: I'll hang it up right now.

LIU MEI: *(Goes up to him)* Technician Sima, I can see the hole in your jacket was well mended. Do you know who did it for you?

SIMA CHANGJIANG: Who?

LIU MEI: *(Sneering)* Didn't she tell you? Fang Xiaoshi.

SIMA CHANGJIANG: How did you know?

LIU MEI: Why, couldn't I have just seen her do it? She held your jacket and kissed it for a long time.

SIMA CHANGJIANG: You . . . you . . . What nonsense you are talking!

LIU MEI: Am I talking nonsense? Why don't you go and ask her yourself? This is surely a sign of some event. Are you going to take care of it?

LU XIAOYUN: Changjiang?

SIMA CHANGJIANG: This is utterly baffling!

LIU MEI: Instructor, you can investigate it. If one word I said were a lie, I would be this *(forming the shape of a turtle with her hand)*.[12] She told me in person that she loved Sima.

SIMA CHANGJIANG: Well . . . I'll go to see her right now. *(Leaves)*

LU XIAOYUN: Now, what's on your mind?

LIU MEI: Instructor, am I on the list of the coming batch of demobilized soldiers?

LU XIAOYUN: It's not decided yet. But you're an old soldier with only three years of service. Very soon there will be the communication competition of the whole army. You have good skills, so be prepared to stay on.

LIU MEI: But I . . . I . . .

LU XIAOYUN: What has happened to you?

LIU MEI: During my home leave not long ago, I . . . with my boyfriend . . .

LU XIAOYUN: *(Anxious to know)* What is it?

LIU MEI: I . . . did that thing with my boyfriend.[13]

LU XIAOYUN: How dare you!

LIU MEI: He forced me.

LU XIAOYUN: You . . . so, you forgot you were a soldier!

LIU MEI: *(Seizing the opportunity)* I know I was wrong. But if you don't let me leave the army, I'm afraid something . . .

LU XIAOYUN: *(Looking at her intently)* You are not telling a lie?

LIU MEI: How can you say such a thing? How could I have told you something like this if I could have helped it?

LU XIAOYUN: *(Totally disappointed)* Liu Mei, why should I have a soldier like you under my command?

LIU MEI: There's nothing wrong with me.

LU XIAOYUN: We will discuss your problem. *(Taking out two shirts with colorful marks on them)* Did you do this?

LIU MEI: *(Giving the shirts a glance)* Yes, I did it.

LU XIAOYUN: Why?

LIU MEI: Why didn't you consider my demobilization?

LU XIAOYUN: So, you thought you could achieve your purpose by doing this?

(LIU MEI *doesn't say anything.*)

LU XIAOYUN: It is because the army needs you that we keep you here. You should feel honored. With your behavior, how can we hand you over to your parents? How can we hand you over to the local unit? People would say you were the kind of person coming from the women soldiers' company. Aren't you ashamed of yourself? I am ashamed.

LIU MEI: Instructor, is there anything else?

LU XIAOYUN: Can't we have a good talk?

LIU MEI: You have got all the information about me. It's for you people to decide what you're going to do with me.
(LU XIAOYUN *is silent for a while. Then, waving her hand, she lets* LIU MEI *go. A moment later she calls her back.*)

LU XIAOYUN: Come back and tell me, is it true what you said about Fang Xiaoshi just now?

LIU MEI: Why don't you go and ask her?

LU XIAOYUN: I'll certainly make an investigation. But don't tell anyone else about it.

LIU MEI: Do people need me to tell them? Perhaps you're the only one who didn't know about it. *(Turns and leaves)*
(The door bangs after her.)

LU XIAOYUN: *(Holding her head with her hands, very much pained)* Oh, good heavens! Please help me.
(LU XIAOYUN *tears the two marked-up shirts with great force and tries*

very hard to hold her tears. The door opens. JIANG HUA *stands in the doorway. For just the short time she's been away, she looks much older, her face wan and sallow.)*

LU XIAOYUN: *(Both surprised and delighted)* Company Commander!

JIANG HUA: Xiaoyun!

LU XIAOYUN: Company Commander, you're finally back. *(Crying on her shoulder, but then laughing)* Company Commander, look; we won a banner.

JIANG HUA: *(Giving a faint smile, her voice trembling)* The walls are filled with banners. *(Counting the banners but in a very, very soft voice)* One, two, three . . . twenty-six, twenty-six banners . . .

LU XIAOYUN: *(Happily)* These twenty-six banners belong to both of us, in only five years . . .

JIANG HUA: Five years, five years. Jiangjiang was just five years old.

LU XIAOYUN: Jiangjiang? How is Jiangjiang?

JIANG HUA: Five years old, a boy of only five . . .

LU XIAOYUN: *(Sensing something wrong)* Company Commander, Jiangjiang . . .

JIANG HUA: *(Silent for a long while)* It was the aftereffect of meningitis.

LU XIAOYUN: Ah!

JIANG HUA: When I rushed to the hospital, he already couldn't tell who I was . . .

LU XIAOYUN: How could that have happened? Just the other day he was talking to all of us over the phone. He still remembered me. Such a smart boy . . .

JIANG HUA: The doctor said it was too late when he was taken to the hospital. Jiangjiang's father regrets so much. *(Tears falling)* But what could he do? He works for a key project of water conservancy; his job is also like fighting a war.

LU XIAOYUN: Company Commander.

JIANG HUA: He said, "Huazi, don't be sad. We're still young, let's have another child." I said, "I don't want another one. I only want Jiangjiang back, just him." I will love him with all my heart. I will love him with all my heart in future . . . I only love him . . .

LU XIAOYUN: Jiangjiang, my poor Jiangjiang . . .

(The two weep silently. They say nothing for a long, long time. Singing of the women soldiers floats in. Hearing the song, JIANG HUA *and* LU XIAOYUN *are deep in thought. "At the age of twenty, I cannot do without the army. I give my youth to my dear company. The*

company has armed me with courage and wisdom. I will fear no more of storms and waves. I will forever hold precious and proud the experience of my life as a soldier.")

Scene Eleven

(Dusk. The remnant rays of sunset spread to the dense palm woods. FANG XIAOSHI walks in from these woods with a tidy backpack on. She puts down the backpack, leaning it against the foot of a tree. Hesitating for a while, she finally takes the elegant trumpet out of its case, puts it to her lips, and tests the sound. Then she plays a few beautiful melodies. The woods grow darker and darker as the sun gradually fades away. The trumpet sings a lonesome tune, floating through the trees. SIMA CHANGJIANG approaches as FANG XIAOSHI steps backward, looking at him for a long time. Lowering his eyes, SIMA CHANGJIANG keeps moving forward slowly. The two almost become one as they reach the edge of the woods. FANG XIAOSHI finally leans against a small palm, powerless.)

FANG XIAOSHI: *(Weakly)* You . . . you came, at last.

SIMA CHANGJIANG: Are you planning to leave like this?

FANG XIAOSHI: *(With a bitter smile)* I thought you wouldn't come . . .

SIMA CHANGJIANG: Come back with me.

FANG XIAOSHI: Don't hate me . . .

SIMA CHANGJIANG: I can understand.

FANG XIAOSHI: It will not be long. . . . I'll graduate in three years.

SIMA CHANGJIANG: No, it won't be long.

FANG XIAOSHI: I'll write to you.

SIMA CHANGJIANG: No, you don't have to.

FANG XIAOSHI: Are you afraid—

SIMA CHANGJIANG: No, Xiaoshi, I . . . *(feeling awkward)*.

FANG XIAOSHI: *(Getting sensitive)* You—

SIMA CHANGJIANG: Let's talk about something else.

FANG XIAOSHI: Changjiang, it's good the way it is. It's only three years. After the three years, I'll have the right, the proper right, don't you think so?

SIMA CHANGJIANG: The company wants to give you a send-off party. Let's go back.

(FANG XIAOSHI, sneering, shakes her head.)

SIMA CHANGJIANG: You shouldn't behave like this . . .

FANG XIAOSHI: What I hate most is a hypocritical display of friendship.

SIMA CHANGJIANG: What the company commander did is for your good—

FANG XIAOSHI: *(Looking at him)* So you are saying the same thing! *(Sobbing sadly)*

SIMA CHANGJIANG: *(At a loss)* Don't cry. Please don't cry. . . . It's true. The company commander did it for your own good.

(FANG XIAOSHI is sobbing. SIMA CHANGJIANG walks round and round the palm tree and FANG XIAOSHI, not knowing what to do. The palm trees block out the last light of the setting sun. It's very dark in the woods.)

SIMA CHANGJIANG: Xiaoshi, Xiaoshi, let's go back. Please let's go . . .

(FANG XIAOSHI gradually stops sobbing. She raises her head and looks at SIMA CHANGJIANG. Suddenly she leans on his shoulder and weeps and weeps.)

SIMA CHANGJIANG: *(Totally bewildered, he wants to push FANG XIAO-SHI away, but feels improper; he is truly confused and losing his wits)* This is not right. Don't behave like this, Xiaoshi. Xiaoshi . . .

(The woods resound with this weeping of a woman and confused words of a man.

A flash of light darts in. SIMA CHANGJIANG is startled.)

SIMA CHANGJIANG: Who is it?

(FANG XIAOSHI is shocked, but holds him even tighter. SIMA CHANG-JIANG pushes her away.)

SIMA CHANGJIANG: You . . . are you really crazy? *(Shouting)* Who is it? Who are you?

(The light is out. For some time . . .)

LU XIAOYUN: It's me.

BOTH OF THEM: *(Surprised)* Instructor!

JIANG HUA: And me, too.

SIMA CHANGJIANG: *(More nervous)* Company Commander!

LU XIAOYUN: *(Trying to make light)* We heard Xiaoshi's trumpet and guessed she must be here. Oh, let's go. Everybody is waiting. We all want to give you a send-off . . .

JIANG HUA: *(Turns the beam on the backpack at the foot of the palm tree)* Did you plan to leave us like this?

SIMA CHANGJIANG: *(Trying to speak for FANG XIAOSHI)* We're just going back to the company . . .

JIANG HUA: You two—

FANG XIAOSHI: No. This has nothing to do with Changjiang. Yes, I'm just leaving.

JIANG HUA: *(With a frosty face)* So, you're leaving, and leaving stealthily, all by yourself.

FANG XIAOSHI: What's the point? It's all a false show of feelings. It makes everybody suffer.

LU XIAOYUN: Xiaoshi, how can you think in this way?

(FANG XIAOSHI doesn't say anything, turns, and picks up the backpack. She looks at SIMA CHANGJIANG with deep feeling.)

FANG XIAOSHI: *(Stretching out her hand)* Let's say good-bye.

SIMA CHANGJIANG: *(Hesitating, finally reaches out and holds her hand)* Xiaoshi, come back with the company commander. *(Tries to pull her)*

FANG XIAOSHI: For what? *(Tossing away his hand in contempt, she turns to leave)*

JIANG HUA: *(Blocking her)* Stop!

(Women soldiers walk out from the woods one after another, BAI YU, YANG NI, LIU MEI, and DING DIANDIAN.)

FANG XIAOSHI: Why? You really want to see me off?

BAI YU: *(Taking out an exquisite toy telephone, she dials, and a series of tinkling rings resound in the woods)* Xiaoshi, do you like it? It's our gift.

(FANG XIAOSHI takes the telephone and wipes away tears.)

LU XIAOYUN: *(Holding FANG XIAOSHI's hand)* All the preparations are done for the party. Let everybody give you a good send-off, all right?

BAI YU: Otherwise, you'll regret it.

ALL: Fang Xiaoshi, come back with us.

(As FANG XIAOSHI hesitates, the girls cluster around her and begin escorting her back.)

JIANG HUA: *(Following closely)* It's outrageous! Go back to the company and write a self-criticism for me. The party branch will reconsider whether we'll send you to school.

FANG XIAOSHI: *(Stands still, clenching her teeth)* Why?

JIANG HUA: Do you have to ask why?

FANG XIAOSHI: *(Tears flowing)* Only for just now—

LU XIAOYUN: *(Trying to stop her)* Company Commander—

FANG XIAOSHI: Despicable! Stupid!

LU XIAOYUN: Xiaoshi, let's go back first.

FANG XIAOSHI: *(Suddenly afraid, retreating)* You . . . Why should you press me like this? I . . . I will never go back! *(Leans on a tree, crying her heart out)*

ALL: Xiaoshi!

(FANG XIAOSHI runs far into the woods, wailing. The moonlight on the leaves of the palms reflects a cold beam like white frost. FANG XIAOSHI's wailing gradually turns to sobbing again. A black shadow wanders about like a specter in the woods.)

FANG XIAOSHI: It's two years now. In the two full years of my life in the barracks, I have experienced so many setbacks and trials. I never imagined that after all this, there would still be such a harsh life awaiting me. . . . Women are perhaps not born to be soldiers. But what about the company commander? I really hate her, the witch of a woman! But I have to admire her. Look at her; when she is in her lieutenant's army uniform, nobody looks more awesome. Damn! She really is an out-and-out woman officer! . . . She has also suffered so much. But why can't she understand us at all? . . . Changjiang, why should I have met you in the barracks? Though I have done nothing yet, I am already a sinful person. Why is it so?

SCENE TWELVE

(In the dense woods. The bright crescent moon looks like a hook. On the ground in the woods a green plastic sheet is spread with all kinds of food and drinks. Joyful women soldiers are sitting around a bright campfire. BAI LING is especially attractive, in her civilian clothes. BAI YU is leading the women soldiers in singing. "Can we hide the longing in our hearts? Can we discard our melancholy feelings? Can we instill more joy into our songs? Can we inspire more heroic spirit to the green we wear? Oh, I do not want to sing, 'My darling, I love you,' because I don't know where you are. Oh, I do not want to sing, 'Mother, I miss you,' because I hate to look like a good-for-nothing if I sing too much of it. Oh, I do not want to sing about parting and death because a good soldier also hopes for good luck . . ." Away from the rest, FANG XIAOSHI sits against a tree all by herself. She is fiddling with the trumpet, playing tunes at will.

BAI LING walks up to SIMA CHANGJIANG, with a bottle of drink.)

BAI LING: Hi, party representative of the women's company; I think you should take a rest.

SIMA CHANGJIANG: Why?

BAI LING: If you finish all the work, you are spoiling the girls.

(SIMA CHANGJIANG *laughs.*)

BAI LING: It seems I should join your company to find a husband.

YANG NI: How can you like army men?

BAI LING: (*Looking at the busy* SIMA CHANGJIANG) Don't you think an army man looks more masculine?

YANG NI: How come you know so much?

BAI LING: Well, the more experience you have, the more knowledgeable you become. I have had a few boyfriends, so I know all about it.

BAI YU: (*Shouting to* FANG XIAOSHI) Xiaoshi, why don't you come over? We're ready to eat grilled chicken wings.

FANG XIAOSHI: You go ahead.

BAI YU: Let me take some for her.

JIANG HUA: Go and talk to her.

(BAI YU *puts two chicken wings on a skewer and walks to* FANG XIAOSHI.)

BAI YU: Come, let's eat together here.

(FANG XIAOSHI *takes the wings and they eat in silence.*)

BAI YU: Delicious, right?

(FANG XIAOSHI *doesn't say anything.*)

BAI YU: Don't you want to go to the military academy?

FANG XIAOSHI: (*Bursts out at last*) Why did you give up taking the entrance exams to the military academy?

BAI YU: The quota is that only one person can go from among us.

FANG XIAOSHI: Humph! You are so kindhearted.

BAI YU: (*Laughing*) No, it's not like that. I have already extended my service time for two years. I was being considered for a promotion to officer last year. But there was no quota then. That was why I thought of getting into the military academy. The headquarters set new regulations this year. There won't be a problem for my promotion now.

FANG XIAOSHI: So you let me go to the military academy.

BAI YU: Of course, it's also the idea of the company commander and instructor.

FANG XIAOSHI: I know they don't trust me . . .

BAI YU: Actually, they did this out of good intention. If it had happened in the past . . .

FANG XIAOSHI: In the past . . . But what have I done after all?

BAI YU: I also believe that you haven't done anything. But it has become the talk of the town. Why don't you just go away for a while to avoid any scandal?

FANG XIAOSHI: *(In embittered grief)* I have done nothing wrong, yet I am the one who is told to hide out!

BAI YU: But you have to admit that you have fallen in love with Sima.

FANG XIAOSHI: . . . Can't I just bury someone deep in my heart?

BAI YU: We live and work together, day in and day out. How can you hide anything?

FANG XIAOSHI: . . . My thoughts are my own business; I haven't affected anyone else.

BAI YU: Xiaoshi, listen to me. If you really have feelings for him, it doesn't matter if you have to be together with him day and night.

FANG XIAOSHI: *(Looking at* BAI YU*)* But he . . . he is very good to you . . . Once you are promoted to be an officer, you will be able to—

BAI YU: You foolish girl. I will live my whole life single.

FANG XIAOSHI: What did you say?

BAI YU: I'm not lying to you.

(JIANG HUA *comes over with two grilled pieces of meat.*)

JIANG HUA: Come, try the squid I grilled. It's delicious.

FANG XIAOSHI: I don't want to eat anything else.

BAI YU: It's really delicious. Try it, Xiaoshi.

JIANG HUA: Still angry with me?

(FANG XIAOSHI *keeps silent.*)

JIANG HUA: What a stubborn girl! Let me tell you, if you don't eat this squid, I will not allow you to go to school.

FANG XIAOSHI: That's just what I want!

JIANG HUA: Look, she doesn't want to go.

FANG XIAOSHI: *(Bursts out)* Who says I don't want to go. . . . I . . . I . . .

JIANG HUA: *(Laughing)* I . . . I now know what's going on in that narrow mind of yours. You think we are driving you out by sending you to school. You think we don't trust you, so we send you to school. You are wrong, Xiaoshi.

FANG XIAOSHI: It's only too clear that you don't trust me.

JIANG HUA: *(Laughing again)* Perhaps I'm a bit old-fashioned. When I was a soldier, we wouldn't even *think* of love affairs between men and women. We were all fools. Soldiers are very different nowadays. They dare think of anything.

FANG XIAOSHI: I don't think there's anything wrong with that.

JIANG HUA: Of course we can't say there's anything wrong. Young people have lively ideas. Yet ideas are, after all, ideas . . .

FANG XIAOSHI: Did I do anything wrong? The only thing I did was mend the jacket for Changjiang. That jacket was caught on a nail and got torn. If it were your shirt, I would have done the same thing.

JIANG HUA: I believe that. But you have to admit that for Changjiang, you—

FANG XIAOSHI: Company Commander, what are the words in the song that was sung just now? "Hide the longing in my heart, discard melancholy feelings." I'm a human being. Can you stop me from thinking? Company Commander, in order to be worthy of this army uniform, you know how hard I have tried to suppress my feelings. If I were not wearing this army uniform, I would have loved him at all cost. That should be my right. *(Tears streaming from her eyes)* But Company Commander, you don't understand any of it. You never stop to think from my point of view. If only you had given me just one understanding glance, one understanding word! You would have seen how strong and firm your soldiers were! I could withstand my emotional storm, even though the storm was the strongest typhoon. But that was not what you did. You don't think I will become a good soldier. You don't trust me. You are even driving me away by sending me to school. Company Commander, I do not understand how on earth I have done wrong! *(Wailing)*

(JIANG HUA is stunned. It seems that she has never realized what her soldiers are thinking and what they need until this moment.)

JIANG HUA: Xiaoshi, thank you for your sincere frankness. Though our age is only some ten years apart, our ideas are so different. But, Xiaoshi, one thing you have to believe, it is not because we don't trust you that we are sending you to school. Do you understand? *(JIANG HUA holds FANG XIAOSHI's hand in hers, waiting for an answer. Looking at JIANG HUA's sincere eyes, FANG XIAOSHI finally nods.)*

JIANG HUA: *(Relieved)* That's good. That's really good. You cannot be on your way to school with such a heavy burden on your back. Work hard at school. The women soldiers' company will wait for you to come back—

FANG XIAOSHI: Company Commander!

(LU XIAOYUN *brings* LIU MEI *in.* LIU MEI *dawdles behind* LU XIAO-YUN.)

JIANG HUA: *(Going up to them)* How did it go?

LU XIAOYUN: When we got to the clinic, she wouldn't go in to have the checkup for better or worse. Finally she told me what she had said was all lies.

JIANG HUA: *(Not knowing whether to be angry or to laugh, but at least relieved)* Oh, Liu Mei, you have such a clever mind, why don't you use it and do something good. *(To* LU XIAOYUN*)* How about you? Did you have a checkup?

LIU MEI: Company Commander, Instructor . . .

JIANG HUA: Something else?

LIU MEI: Company Commander, Instructor . . . I'll listen to you. I don't want to leave now.

(JIANG HUA *and* LU XIAOYUN *are surprised.)*

LIU MEI: Instructor just said to me that the important thing about being a soldier is having aspirations. Compared with the wealthy, we may be poor; compared with those prettily dressed girls, we may own just the army uniform. But we are not inferior to others. First of all, we must not look down upon ourselves.

JIANG HUA: That's right. Liu Mei, you're pretty and clever, and with this army uniform on you, you should walk on the street with full confidence. Even though you are not wearing high heels and you are just in a pair of "liberation shoes," you are still the best.[14]

LIU MEI: I had always considered soldiers poor and that life was hard for soldiers. I looked down on them more and more. That's why I . . . I . . . *(Too embarrassed to go on)* Company Commander, Instructor, I . . . *(Cries)*

JIANG HUA: Liu Mei, is there anything more you want to say? Tell us and we'll all help you.

LU XIAOYUN: Liu Mei, the company commander and myself are more than ten years your elders. Treat us as your big sisters. Is there anything that a big sister would not help a little sister with? (LIU MEI *raises her head and looks at everyone with all kinds of feelings. Then she suddenly bursts out crying bitterly.)*

LIU MEI: Just now I was also telling a lie. Actually he and I, we did that thing. Not long ago I wrote him, telling him that I could leave the army. I said we would get married as soon as I got back home. He sent me a letter back. (*Takes out a letter and gives it to* JIANG HUA. JIANG HUA *and* LU XIAOYUN *read the letter.*)

JIANG HUA: He's gone to Canada?

LIU MEI: (*Sadly*) Yes, he's gone.

LU XIAOYUN: How could he have done that with you when he knew he was going away?

LIU MEI: He promised me that he would take me with him when he went abroad. We would leave as soon as we got married, when I left the army. But he—

JIANG HUA: Such a bastard!

LIU MEI: Company Commander, Instructor, do you still want me in the army? I . . . I did wrong.

JIANG HUA: It isn't easy to be a good soldier. Work hard from now on. Come, stop crying. Let's get the campfire blazing even more brightly. Don't think anymore of the bygones. Come, Xiaoshi, Bai Yu, come over here. Let's eat and drink, sing and dance. Changjiang, why are you standing there? Start some music, music with strong rhythm.

(*Exciting music starts. As if stirred up, the woods seem to dance.* JIANG HUA *takes up a bottle and pours wine into colorful bowls.*)

JIANG HUA: (*Raising a bowl*) Girls, shall we celebrate?

SOLDIERS: (*Cheering*) Let's celebrate!

(*The young women all raise their bowls.*)

JIANG HUA: Girls, I don't know what you are thinking of, but I will forever remember today. I've been in the army for twelve years. So many things have stayed in my memory. However, this is the first time I have ever been drinking and dancing to my heart's content. Yes, I am very, very happy today. (*A little choked up*) . . . Let's drink a toast to Xiaoshi's going to school, and also to Liu Mei's staying in the army . . . Bottoms up!

(*Uninhibited and gallant,* JIANG HUA *finishes her wine in one gulp. The young women soldiers also empty their bowls, then almost throw the bowls skyward. They put more dry branches on the campfire, stirring up bright, warm flames. Following the power of the music, the girls start dancing.*

Among them, tall SIMA CHANGJIANG *looks odd, but he is as excited and joyful as the girls.*

FANG XIAOSHI *and* LIU MEI *hesitate in embarrassment.* JIANG HUA *pushes the two into the cheerful crowd.* FANG XIAOSHI *finally dances* with all her heart. She is an excellent dancer, and surrounded by others, she dances in ecstasy.

BAI YU *stealthily pushes* SIMA CHANGJIANG *to the middle of the group. He stands there looking awkward.*)

JIANG HUA: Changjiang, start dancing. Give us a pas de deux.

(SIMA CHANGJIANG *begins dancing.* FANG XIAOSHI *looks at him gratefully, as she wipes away her falling tears.*

The groups of green moving here and there create quite a commotion in the woods.

The fire gradually dies out.)

SCENE THIRTEEN

(*A few years later, at the drilling ground by the woods. It is dusk.* BAI YU, *who is now the company commander, is training a group of new soldiers. She is no less harsh than the previous company commander,* JIANG HUA. *The formation marches up and down. One corner of the drilling ground quiets down. Someone is playing the trumpet in the distance. It is jarring to the ear as there is no real tune.*

SIMA CHANGJIANG, *who is now a major, enters with* FANG XIAO-SHI *carrying a backpack.*

She is in officer uniform and obviously much more mature. The two of them walk to the edge of the woods, without words. It seems they are both listening to the trumpet, yet both look lost in reminiscence.)

SIMA CHANGJIANG: It's a new soldier; obviously she doesn't know how to play it yet.

FANG XIAOSHI: You're right. She is at the same level as when I was a soldier.

(FANG XIAOSHI *walks over to the palm tree to which she had once played her trumpet wildly, and feels its trunk.*)

FANG XIAOSHI: I was so stupid at that time. I thought this palm tree was a coconut tree. I even dreamed of eating coconuts. For a long time I couldn't make out why this tree did not blossom and bear fruit.

SIMA CHANGJIANG: Didn't you ever think of asking others about it?

FANG XIAOSHI: (*Laughing*) At that time I thought I knew so many things. You told me that this was not a coconut tree. I didn't believe you.

(*Both laugh. Silence.*)

FANG XIAOSHI: (*Getting out the trumpet*) That girl is too much out of tune. I have to teach her. See how I do it . . .

(FANG XIAOSHI *starts to play the trumpet. It sounds so smooth and pleasant. The out-of-tune trumpet follows* FANG XIAOSHI's *and gradually it picks up the tune.*)

SIMA CHANGJIANG: You are still so good.

FANG XIAOSHI: I am still good in many things. Don't you belittle me.

SIMA CHANGJIANG: How dare I? What great efforts I have made in getting you, an excellent instructor, back to us. How dare I belittle you.

FANG XIAOSHI: You have a glib tongue. I was afraid you might want to avoid me as much as possible. How could you want me back?

SIMA CHANGJIANG: Xiaoshi, how could I . . .

FANG XIAOSHI: (*With a bitter smile*) You should have told me then . . .

SIMA CHANGJIANG: I . . . I just didn't have the courage. I didn't want to hurt you—

FANG XIAOSHI: Yes, I know. I shouldn't blame you. If I had been more rational and calmer, I would have detected it. Actually, I already sensed it, but I just didn't want to believe it in my heart. (*Tears fill her eyes.*) I can't blame you. Anyway, during the three years at the military academy, you had made me suffer a great deal, yet you also filled me with fantasies. Your existence had enriched my monotonous life.

SIMA CHANGJIANG: After you went to school, I thought of telling you everything, but I still didn't have the courage, not until you graduated . . .

FANG XIAOSHI: (*Heaving a long sigh*) Well, it's all over now. . . . Perhaps this is better. What do you think?

SIMA CHANGJIANG: Perhaps. Well, how is everything with you?

FANG XIAOSHI: What do you mean?

SIMA CHANGJIANG: Are you . . . are you still single?

FANG XIAOSHI: Is there anything wrong with being single?

(SIMA CHANGJIANG *doesn't know what to say.*)

FANG XIAOSHI: (*Changing the subject*) I know it's Bai Yu who insisted so strongly that I come work with her. Why should she want me and nobody else?

SIMA CHANGJIANG: You are . . . you two are old comrades-in-arms.

FANG XIAOSHI: (*Understandingly*) Tell me, what can I do for you?

SIMA CHANGJIANG: No, I can no longer . . .

FANG XIAOSHI: Look at you; is this the behavior of a real man? Bai Yu thinks if I am here, you'll stop chasing after her, right?
(SIMA CHANGJIANG *nods.*)

FANG XIAOSHI: I'm quite certain she wants me here because she finds it hard to resist you. Is that right?

SIMA CHANGJIANG: How do you know?

FANG XIAOSHI: Do you forget that I am an instructor? I specialize in working with people. This problem of yours is so obvious.

SIMA CHANGJIANG: I think she accepts me, in her feelings, but for that groundless concept growing in her, she always . . .

FANG XIAOSHI: Yes, besides, she once promised me. Even though it's up to you to decide, she'll always think of me.

SIMA CHANGJIANG: (*Smiling bitterly*) How did it happen that I just love her?

FANG XIAOSHI: (*Jokingly*) She is prettier than me.

SIMA CHANGJIANG: If anyone could explain feelings clearly and logically, he would deserve the Nobel Prize.

FANG XIAOSHI: Look, they are coming.
(BAI YU *enters, leading the women soldiers, who are marching in orderly strides.* BAI YU *stops in front of* FANG XIAOSHI, *and Platoon Leader* LIU MEI *leads the soldiers away. The two women slowly walk toward each other, gazing intently for a long time. Then, with a solemn army salute, they embrace each other.*)

BAI YU: So, you are back, after all.

FANG XIAOSHI: I hear you requested it again and again.

BAI YU: Really? (*Glancing at* SIMA CHANGJIANG) It was Changjiang who spared no effort in getting you here. He is now the section chief in charge of training.

SIMA CHANGJIANG: (*Laughing*) I don't know for whom I am preparing the wedding gown.

FANG XIAOSHI: I want you . . . two . . .

BAI YU: No, no! Xiaoshi, I really want you and—

FANG XIAOSHI: (*Interrupting*) Oh, I forgot to tell you guys I have a boyfriend.

BAI YU: (*Unexpected*) What?

FANG XIAOSHI: Yes, he is a very good fellow, a schoolmate from the military academy.

SIMA CHANGJIANG: Xiaoshi—

FANG XIAOSHI: Next time I'll show you his picture. *(Changing the subject)* Bai Yu, I also want . . . very much for us to work together.

BAI YU: Me, too. By the way, our old company commander is now a battalion political instructor, and our old instructor is working in the political section.

FANG XIAOSHI: I saw them just now. Changjiang took me to them. The company commander said the moment she saw me, "Xiaoshi, do you still hate me? Would you blame me?" I said to her, "I blame nobody." It's true; I don't blame anybody now. We were all so young then. *(Looking at the new soldiers practicing on the drilling ground)* I was as young as them.

BAI YU: You are not old—not even twenty-five yet.

FANG XIAOSHI: *(Laughing)* After all, I am different now, right?

SIMA CHANGJIANG: Of course you're different. You are the political instructor and she is the company commander.

FANG XIAOSHI: *(Naughtily)* Why don't we try out our cooperation now?

BAI YU: That's just what I was thinking of.

(BAI YU gives a command and gathers her ranks.)

BAI YU: Let me introduce to you our new political instructor, Fang Xiaoshi.

(All clap. FANG XIAOSHI salutes them, solemn and dignified.)

FANG XIAOSHI: How are you? When I was a new soldier, I also practiced parade steps here. I was afraid of hardship and difficulty. I cried and flew into a temper. The company commander knew it, and all the old soldiers knew it.

(DING DIANDIAN, YANG NI, and TIAN XIANGXIANG are laughing among the ranks.)

FANG XIAOSHI: At that time we were silly, yet so lovely. Many years have passed, but the trees here are still so green and the women soldiers still so pretty. I love the green barracks. How about you?

ALL: We love the green barracks.

FANG XIAOSHI: That's wonderful! I want to do the drilling with you today once more. Am I welcome?

(Everybody claps. FANG XIAOSHI and BAI YU join the ranks briskly, standing at the head. SIMA CHANGJIANG gives commands loudly. The women soldiers march in orderly steps.

The sun shines warmly. The women soldiers in green formation march in the sunshine with rhythmic and forceful strides, march with purpose as if heading for the sun.)

NOTES

Green Barracks (Lüse yingdi) was written in April 1990 and first published in the third issue of *Xin juben* (New drama script) in 1992. The English translation was based on *Lüse yingdi*, in Zhang Lili, *Zhang Lili juzhuo xuan* (Selected plays of Zhang Lili), Beijing: Zhongguo xiju chubanshe, 1992, 263–327.

1. The Chinese character for "shi" means "poetry."

2. Sima Qian, the famous historian and writer in ancient China.

3. "Sister-in-law" is a way of generally addressing a married woman in the countryside. Here, it is used in a mocking tone.

4. The Anti-Japanese War is also called the War of Resistance to Japan, which lasted eight years, from 1937 to 1945.

5. "You go down in price" is a literal translation of a colloquial Chinese expression that means one reduces one's worth by a certain behavior or action.

6. "Pearls cascading onto a plate of jade" is a Chinese expression meaning something falling out fast and smooth.

7. "Uncle" here does not mean a relative. In China people often address those who are a generation older than themselves as "uncle" or "aunt" to show respect.

8. Many Chinese people who live in the countryside would like to get a residence permit and live in the city as, on the whole, urban life is still better and more comfortable than rural life. There are several ways to achieve the goal: by finding a job in the city, by marrying someone who has already received a city residence permit, and by other connections.

9. The Chinese words for "miss" literally mean "small sister," so this "big sister" is a retort.

10. In the army units in China, the soldiers usually raise pigs themselves. Now and then they butcher a pig to improve their diet.

11. "Huazi" is Jiang Hua's nickname used between intimate friends.

12. In China the image of "turtle" has a derogatory implication for certain occasions. It is used most commonly for a man when his wife is adulterous. Here Liu Mei means that if she had lied, she would be a contemptible person.

13. "That thing" here means "making love." In China, most people, especially in the army, feel embarrassed to use the term "making love" directly. They use all kinds of euphemisms, and here "that thing" is one.

14. "Liberation shoes" is a term the Chinese use for shoes worn by soldiers, issued to them by the army, called the People's Liberation Army, hence the word "liberation."

Wild Grass

Zhang Mingyuan

TRANSLATED BY PHILIP F. WILLIAMS

(A modern-style play, without divisions into acts)

Characters

FOURTH	ROOTSY
ERQIN ("Second Celery")	SIXTH BROTHER
QIUZI ("Autumn Son")	FOREMAN WU
SEVENTH UNCLE	SALESWOMAN
RICHIE	VARIOUS TOWNSFOLK
ELDEST BROTHER	

Time: contemporary (late-twentieth-century Deng era)
Place: Heilongjiang Province in China's frontier in the far Northeast,
also still known as Manchuria in spite of the Han Chinese assimi-
lation of the Manchus

(In the wake of a swashbuckling melody played on a suona *horn, a*
rasping male voice begins to sing a Shandong ditty:
"It's March, and it's off to the Northeast we go,
With a pair of reed hampers and three lengths of rope.
Our toddlers ride ahead 'neath the tip of the shoulder pole,
While dangling back behind—woks, ladles, gourds, and bowls;
Yet our old yellow dog we abandoned back home.
Aiyoyo—moving northeast with all you own,
Bringing all the family, out to find a new home."
The curtain rises while the song is being sung. The setting is a
train station platform, where small groups of travelers are waiting for
a train. A group bound for the Northeast is crowded together at one
corner of the platform. The group's leader is SEVENTH UNCLE. *This*
is the first time they've gone to the Northeast in search of work; they
are quietly waiting for their train to reach the station. While they are
drawn to the mystery of a faraway place, they are also troubled by
wistful longings for their old homeland.)

SEVENTH UNCLE: Qiqihar's a place where there are two windy seasons
each year.[1] As soon as the season arrives, the wind blows hard for
six months.

ROOTSY: So, it blows hard every day?

SEVENTH UNCLE: When the wind starts blowing, sand flies through
the air and pebbles scoot along the ground. The skies above are
murky, and the ground below is dim and hard to make out.
People scurry about on the ground while their hats fly through
the air.

ROOTSY: Then, how do they manage to work?

SEVENTH UNCLE: They can handle it. They fasten a rope around
their waists and tie the loose ends to a big tree.

ROOTSY: How would they manage, all tied together like that?

RICHIE: To heck with these silly tall tales!

(Everybody laughs. FOURTH, *as motionless as the torso of a statue,*
sits at one side of the stage, with his back to the audience.)

SEVENTH UNCLE: Now, Fourth, don't make things hard for yourself. Seventh Uncle's going to take you pioneering to the Northeast for a few years. You'll have the best to eat and drink there, then come back home with your pockets stuffed with cash; that's what's known as "returning to your hometown clad in silk brocade." Everybody'll look up to you—

RICHIE: Don't take those double-talking wenches seriously! They're all in a headlong rush for money and fun, but when your money runs out—

SEVENTH UNCLE: (Gives RICHIE a kick) If you can't say anything worthwhile, just stand aside and try dozing off for awhile; nobody'd write you off as a mute!

RICHIE: What did I do wrong, anyway? You twisted my good intentions into the beastliness of an ass, and—

SEVENTH UNCLE: (Interrupting RICHIE) Fourth, a real man's ambitions stretch as far as you can see in all four directions; you can't be sentimental and gushy like a woman! Take it from me—I've been through all this before. There isn't anything so earthshaking about a woman. (SEVENTH UNCLE suddenly falls silent, staring at someone in front of him for a moment.) Fourth, she's . . . she's come. (ERQIN hurries up onto the platform. About twenty years old, she's both intelligent-looking and pretty. Wearing a short red jacket and carrying a parcel, she moves through the crowd, anxiously searching for someone. When she makes out where FOURTH is, her anxiety gives way to sorrow as she comes to a halt. SEVENTH UNCLE nudges FOURTH, who silently walks over to ERQIN. The two of them stare at each other for a moment, then avert their eyes.)

RICHIE: It's really a case of "old love affairs are hard to break off"— (RICHIE falls silent once he notices SEVENTH UNCLE glaring at him.)

FOURTH: Erqin—(becoming sarcastic) whoops, since there's a relation to my mother involved, I ought to call you "sister-in-law" now, instead—

ERQIN: (In anguish) Fourth—

FOURTH: Instead of entertaining those wedding guests back home, you run over here. You could explain your visit to other people, but it would sound awkward. (ERQIN hands the parcel to FOURTH, who comes out with an odd chuckle once he's opened it.) So you've sent me a batch of wedding candy?

ERQIN: *(Hastily)* No, it isn't.

FOURTH: *(Hurls the box of candy down on the pavement)* I'm not a three-year-old child that you can tread on and then soothe with a few pieces of candy. . . .

ERQIN: *(Woodenly bends down to pick up the candy)* It's what I just got through buying at our co-op store. The year that my grandfather went over the Pass to the Northeast, my grandmother brought him a bottle of honey so that he'd often remember sweet things about home and come back a bit earlier than expected. . . .

FOURTH: *(Dumbfounded, as if lost in thought)* Come back?

ERQIN: *(Guilelessly)* I'll be in service at their household for a few years—as soon as I've fully repaid the debt, I'll leave them behind. Fourth, I'll be waiting for you to come back.

FOURTH: Waiting for me? If I die, what then?

ERQIN: Don't say unlucky things when you're leaving home on a long journey. My father owes them, and he's using me to pay the debt back. If I didn't go to them, they could zero in on my family, and . . . I'll be waiting for you; I'll always be yours.

FOURTH: Once you marry into their family, you'll be theirs.

ERQIN: *(With melancholy)* You know what sort of person he is, yet still say—

FOURTH: He's your husband!

ERQIN: *(In a daze)* "Husband"? He's a lunatic . . . a lunatic . . . *(She makes ready to leave the platform.)*

FOURTH: *(Realizing he had inadvertently said something he should have kept to himself)* Erqin—*(reaching out to accept the box of candy)* Seventh Uncle says that on the other side of the Pass, it's a land of riches—gold, silver, and other precious things roll around all over the place. Wait for me—wait till I earn a fortune and come back . . .

ERQIN: *(With sincerity)* I'll be waiting for you. . . .

FOURTH: *(With fierce determination)* If they've spent five hundred yuan for you, I'll spend five thousand—no, fifty thousand! With head held high and not budging an inch, I'll take you back from them. Wait for me!

ERQIN: I'll be waiting. No matter what fate has in store for me, I'll wait for you.

(With a series of whistles, the long train rumbles into the station. Just as the train is slowly grinding to a halt, the train station announcer heralds its arrival: "Train number five sixty-five from Jinan to Qiqihar has entered the station. The train will stop here for three minutes, and we request passengers to please not shove or crowd on or off." Before the announcement is over, crowds of people are crazily piling their way off the train. Various voices from the crowd on the platform [Boorishly]: "Hurry and get on!" "Hurry and push your way on!" "Take a seat!" "Pull me up, pull me up!" "Hey, you're trampling all over my feet—are you blind?")

ERQIN: Fourth!

FOURTH: *(Roughly)* Go on back! *(He runs off.)*

ERQIN: Fourth!

(After the steam whistle blows a long note, the train lurches into motion. The emptied platform is now a desolate expanse. ERQIN *listlessly stares at the departing train as it lumbers off into the distance. A female vocalist starts singing plaintively, as if sobbing:*
"March brings red to the blossoms of the peach,
As my man goes after gold in the distant Northeast.
I saw you off there at the Yellow River delta,
Urging you to drink before your distant trek.
Don't forget your maiden, who at home must e'er await
Greetings from your bridal chair in front of her gate.
Aiyoyo, not to know which year
Shandong will finally welcome back her long-lost mate."

The lights gradually dim during the song. From the now darkened stage emerges the rumble and clatter of an accelerating train.

A spotlight suddenly shines upon the left side of the stage to reveal FOURTH. *Alone, he squats hunched over the ground while counting the money he's earned. Hearing cries from a formation of wild geese flying overhead, he raises his head to take a look, and whistles at the birds passing high above him. Dumping the money from his hands onto a spread-out cloth, he heaves a sigh before wrapping his earnings up into a small bundle.)*

FOURTH: That's three years and six months . . . and twenty-one days, too. I once thought that by this time I'd have struck it rich already. Instead, after all that fuss about how rich we'd get, I've had to scrape money together—a little here, a little there. How could one lifetime be long enough to scrape together all of five thousand yuan? "Gold, silver, and other precious things roll around all over the place." (FOURTH *laughs derisively.*) What a bunch of crap he fed us!

(The setting shifts to a workers' shack. A washbasin rests atop an adobe platform bed. A square piece of plywood lies atop the wash-basin, and several items of ordinary food and drink have been placed upon the plywood. ELDEST BROTHER *is reclining in the space near-est this makeshift dining table. In his hand he holds a slender bam-boo rod. Among the others there, some slump against the wall, oth-ers are lying down, while still others sit and smoke quietly. Nobody is talking.* FOURTH *walks from center stage to the shack. Tying the string of an apron around his waist, he picks up a kitchen knife and starts peeling turnips.*

RICHIE *is practicing the ring toss indoors. After missing his tar-get bottle every time for a few tosses,* RICHIE *kicks the bottle away in exasperation. Whirling around a couple of times,* RICHIE *then rushes to the doorway, where he takes a long look at the street in front of the shack. Only afterward does he dejectedly return to the old shack. Noticing that* ELDEST BROTHER *has turned his back to the dining table,* RICHIE *slips over to it. He is on the verge of grabbing some meat in one of the dishes when* ELDEST BROTHER*'s bamboo rod slams onto the back of* RICHIE*'s hand. Yelping "ouch" a couple of times,* RICHIE *takes a seat on the edge of the platform bed.)*

RICHIE: You're really mean! I was just testing to see how vigilant you were.

ELDEST BROTHER: But weren't you afraid of getting grease on your paws?

RICHIE: *(Crossly)* You mean it's for him to eat, but there's nothing for us to eat? So, he's the only one who's grown a proper set of teeth?

ELDEST BROTHER: When he's eaten, he can spit out money. When you've eaten, there's nothing but dung that can pour out of you.

RICHIE: *(As if consulting with* ELDEST BROTHER*)* I'll just taste a slice of meat, that thin slice there.

ELDEST BROTHER: Okay. (RICHIE *gleefully reaches out to grab some meat, but again gets a whack on the hand instead.)*

RICHIE: Foreman Wu is your own father!

ELDEST BROTHER: "Father"? He's more like an honored ancestor!

RICHIE: In that case, why don't you just hack off a piece of board and make an altar for worshipping him?

ELDEST BROTHER: (*Whacks* RICHIE *once more*) That's for you spinning your wild tales!

(ROOTSY *is moaning on the platform bed; everybody turns a deaf ear to him.*)

ROOTSY: I'm dying from pain—

RICHIE: If you died from pain, we'd be spared a chump whose work doesn't even cover what his food costs.

SIXTH BROTHER: My mother . . . she wrote a letter. She's . . . she's asking for money . . . (*He chokes back a couple of sobs.*)

RICHIE: Whatever little thing happens, you're always dripping your stinking tears on the floor—just like a woman! (ROOTSY *continues to moan.*) Just look at you! They let you take a few days off, and you complain about this-and-that place hurting, just like a braying donkey! Let's have it a little louder; best thing would be for you to shout till the roof caves in—we could all be crushed to death together. (ROOTSY *falls silent.*) If you stay cooped up in here for another couple of days, you're bound to come down with cholera. Go do the ring toss and win a couple packs of cigarettes to smoke. Who's going? (*Everyone remains silent.*) Well, what are you waiting for—death? Isn't it true that you still have corn-flour gruel to eat? If things here get really bad, you can always go out to beg for food. Anybody who caught sight of that hangdog look of yours would think your father had just died!

ELDEST BROTHER: (*Lifts* RICHIE *up in midair while addressing* SIXTH BROTHER) Take off your holey socks and stuff them in his mouth.

RICHIE: Don't do it; don't. I'll pretend I'm deaf and dumb.

ELDEST BROTHER: Why don't you go die in place of a good person?

RICHIE: A good person doesn't have a long life, and a bad person doesn't live long enough. (*Suddenly*) Seventh Uncle has come back!

(*An uproar breaks out as everybody pushes and shoves toward the doorway.* RICHIE *takes this opportunity to grab a piece of meat and shove it in his mouth. Once the others realize they've been tricked, they begin to scold him: "Greedy gut—you got consumption or something?" "Spit it out!" "A reincarnated hungry ghost!"*)

RICHIE: I've already taken money out of my pocket. I have a share in the food and drink on the table.

ELDEST BROTHER: All of the guys here have a share; not just you. If everybody ate it up, could we ask for our money back?

(As soon as ELDEST BROTHER *mentions money, everyone becomes discouraged.)*

RICHIE: Let's bring an action against him.

ELDEST BROTHER: Bring an action? Against who?

RICHIE: Foreman Wu! He hasn't given us the money he owes us.

ELDEST BROTHER: You mean outsiders from another province would bring a lawsuit against an insider with good local connections— and still expect to win?

SIXTH BROTHER: My mother sent a letter asking for money . . .

ELDEST BROTHER: Before anybody else could knock him down with a lawsuit, he'd have long since run us out of town. *(*ROOTSY *again starts moaning.)* You'd better go see a doctor.

ROOTSY: As long as I bear with it, things . . . should be all right.

(A few people come in from the outside and listlessly lie down on the adobe platform bed. Everyone is silent.)

RICHIE: Who has wine? Let's borrow some. *(Noticing that nobody has responded, he leaps onto the bed, where he starts rummaging through various things piled all over it. From somebody else's baggage he pulls out an empty wine bottle. He turns the bottle upside down for a long time, but there's not even a drop of wine in it. He flings the bottle out the door.)* Fourth, do you have any? *(*FOURTH *says nothing.)* You gone deaf and dumb? How come you're so stubborn? Other people have good reason to be stubborn, but you don't! You bastard, you grabbed a handful—

SIXTH BROTHER: *(Interrupting* RICHIE*)* My . . . my mother—

RICHIE: Damn it. If Foreman Wu gives out the money that's due, the first thing I'll do is order a shot of liquor, the second thing I'll do is order a shot of liquor, and the third thing I'll do is order still another—

*(*SEVENTH UNCLE *and* FOREMAN WU *have drunk so much wine that their faces are flushed and they are unsteady on their feet. The workers all suddenly sit up and stare at the two men who've just arrived.)*

FOREMAN WU: *(With a casual air)* So, everybody's at home? *(Nobody utters a sound.)* How come you didn't go out for a stroll? *(Hiccoughs)* All shut up at home like this, aren't you afraid you'll give some maggots a place to hatch out?

ELDEST BROTHER: Have you been drinking?

FOREMAN WU: We had—uhh, we were just snacking. Ol' Seventh's just about done for—can't handle more than a few cups!

ELDEST BROTHER: Seventh Uncle, everything's all ready.

SEVENTH UNCLE: *(Embarrassed)* Let's everybody eat!

ELDEST BROTHER: This is what we prepared for Master Wu.

FOREMAN WU: I'm very grateful.

ELDEST BROTHER: In that case, how about passing out the wages? We've all been waiting desperately for the money!

SEVENTH UNCLE: *(Stopping* ELDEST BROTHER *from continuing)* How could you say a thing like that? Er—Master Wu stands by what he says to us. And for the sake of this little bit of money of ours, he ran around for several days. You think he'd welsh on us?

RICHIE: *(Leaping for joy)* I feel he can't help but give it to us, and there'll be wine, too.

SIXTH BROTHER: Here comes the money.

(Everyone's expression becomes animated. One laborer gives his seat to FOREMAN WU; *another pours him some water; a third lights the foreman's cigarette.* SEVENTH UNCLE *retreats to the other end of the table and begins smoking.)*

RICHIE: Hurry and give out the money. Our throats are all hoarse from talking.

FOREMAN WU: What's the hurry? I've got something to tell you. I've long heard that our brothers from Shandong are fine, straight-forward fellows who stand up for what's right. As soon as we worked together on this project, I sure enough realized it's true. But I'm not any worse than you fellows; for the sake of friends, I could put up with knives piercing my ribs from both left and right and not begrudge the pain. If you don't believe me, just go ask around town—just see if there's anyone who doesn't know about Old Wu . . .

(The others have started whispering to one another.)

ELDEST BROTHER: We all know you're a swell guy. Now how about getting out the money?

FOREMAN WU: *(Sighs)* I'm not afraid of your laughing at me. This time I was really taken to the cleaners. Look here, I've been running around for over ten days and only came up with a few dollars. Subtracting what I spent on wining and dining, giving presents, and paying pledges to a temple, there weren't more than a few coppers left in the end. In working together this time, we haven't emphasized money and property, but friendship and fellow feeling instead—

RICHIE: Are you beating around the bush with us?

ELDEST BROTHER: Have you got the money or not?

FOREMAN WU: Old Seventh, tell them. (SEVENTH UNCLE *declines with a wave of his hand.*) I'm someone who stands up for what's right. I can't just look on while you're holed up here without work. (WU *pulls out a wad of cash.*) This money is the exact amount you'll need for your traveling expenses back home. (*Noticing that nobody has made a move toward the money,* WU *chuckles.*) Okay, as far as I'm concerned, I've treated you right all along. I've done all I can to do my duty by you. This evening I'll have two dining tables set up for you at the Hundred Flowers Garden and give you a farewell banquet. We can chalk it up to the experience of having gotten acquainted. Even if I have to sell all my pots and pans for scrap, I'll make sure I send you off with enough money to have a happy trip back. Okay, now that we've agreed, I'll go and arrange things.

ELDEST BROTHER: (*Presses forward till he's nose to nose with* FOREMAN WU) You're not giving out our wages, but you still want to get out of this door?

FOREMAN WU: What do you think you're doing? What're you doing?

ELDEST BROTHER: Take out the money!

FOREMAN WU: There isn't any more to take out! All that's left here is this one life of mine.

ELDEST BROTHER: How many yuan is that dog's life of yours worth? (*The men begin shouting: "Pleading empty pockets won't cut it!" "Beat him to death!" "Don't let him go!" While lying on the platform bed,* ROOTSY *is smashing his head against the edge, and starts to cry.* ELDEST BROTHER *grabs* FOREMAN WU *around the collar.*)

FOREMAN WU: What're you doing? What're you doing! If you so much as bump me a little off balance, you'll have to kneel down and help me stand up straight again. What haven't I been through in my life, anyway? Don't go ignoring your conscience. If it weren't for me, other people would come over and carry off your shack— you wouldn't even have a place to stay. Old Seventh, you're clear about this, aren't you?

SEVENTH UNCLE: You fellows hold it right there!

FOREMAN WU: You may not know when a storm might blow through outdoors. But don't you even realize it when your shoes are pinching your own feet? The higher-ups have again started investigating the registration papers of migrants. Now, who have you been relying on to have a peaceful life free of trouble? If it hadn't been for me handling things, you would have been driven out of here long ago! You don't believe me? Then, just give it a try. If you can stay here without incident tonight, then I don't mind having my head cut off.

ELDEST BROTHER: The money that over twenty guys have earned with their blood and sweat can't be tossed away with nothing to show for it!

FOREMAN WU: I've explained it clearly to you—the money amounts to exactly this much. Demand more if you will, but there's nothing I can do about it. You can go to my house at Eight Sunnyside Lane and take away whatever you can find of value; I won't count it against you as robbery.

(A voice in the crowd calls out: "Death to him!")

ELDEST BROTHER: (Restraining the others) This tableful of food and drink is what we've put together by pooling our money; let's have him eat the whole spread now. (The crowd rushes up to grab FOREMAN WU and force him over to the edge of the platform bed.)

FOREMAN WU: Zhang Seventh! Zhang Seventh! Damn it, don't just sit there on your hands!

SEVENTH UNCLE: (Pushing the crowd away from WU, and laying down the law to them) So, you want to beat up somebody, do you? Every last one of you's still wet behind the ears and reeking of mother's milk—but you imagine you're about to be carried into a temple and worshipped as a god! Start flailing away—let's see who's got the best knack for it! (The commotion stops and the crowd falls silent.) Seniority's not something to consider here? We have to treat a guest I invite like a human being. Just look at you, trying to pull off some kind of hooligan shenanigans!

ELDEST BROTHER: Seventh Uncle, he—

SEVENTH UNCLE: I haven't died yet; are you trying to steal my authority or something? (Thumps his own chest once) In this shack, what I say goes!

FOREMAN WU: (Unctuously) Old Seventh, what's that you're saying? I know how sick at heart all the fellows feel. Just let them blow off some steam. Eldest Brother, I apologize to you all. Go ahead and hit me, you'll feel a little better for it. Men from Shandong are all stout fellows I'm happy to work with. Go ahead and hit me— it'll count as my apology to you.

SEVENTH UNCLE: Brother Wu, for you to have said all that is already enough of an apology. I'm the one who has the final say in this matter; it doesn't concern you. I led them to come way up here to work, and have the final say in decisions made in this shack. Give me the money. (WU *tosses the money onto the platform bed*). Whoever wants it, come get it—just don't throng up here like a bunch of hungry whelps! Let's see who'll make trouble right here in front of my eyes. It's okay if we don't ask for the money, but losing our reputation just won't do! (*All the young men are standing around disconsolately.*)

FOREMAN WU: Migrant workers are all clear about one rule of thumb: if there's money to make, then there's money to lose. Fortunately, we have plenty of time left to do better. Gentlemen, if you have any future problems, just look me up; I'll be happy to serve you with the diligence of a horse or dog. As for tonight, I won't leave the Hundred Flowers Garden till I've seen you all there. (*Exits*) (FOURTH *has been staying just outside the doorway all along, but when he sees* WU *about to come out, he jumps aside.*)

ELDEST BROTHER: (*Harboring a grievance*) Seventh Uncle—

SEVENTH UNCLE: Just hold it right there! Better not try to kill a skunk for its pelt and wind up all stinking from head to toe!

RICHIE: Since he's not eating it, let's eat it. (*He hops onto the platform bed, grabbing food and shoving it into his mouth. Everybody else also rushes forward to start eating.*)

FOURTH: (*Holding a kitchen cleaver in his hand, he walks over to where* ELDEST BROTHER *is standing.*) So, you just let him leave? (SEVENTH UNCLE *lies down on the platform bed, stretching out comfortably.* ELDEST BROTHER *remains silent.*)

FOURTH: So, we're not demanding our money anymore? (*The others keep eating as before.*) We gave him two months of our work for free?

RICHIE: (*Talks while chewing*) As far as demanding our money goes, just now you didn't even make a move in that direction, did you? You looked like a mouse keeping its distance from a cat.

FOURTH: Seventh Uncle, we've got no choice but to demand this money of ours!

SEVENTH UNCLE: *(Kicking* FOURTH*)* Stay over at the other side.

FOURTH: Skittish Shandong bears—a whole shackful of them[2]—

ELDEST BROTHER: Who are you talking about?

FOURTH: The whole bunch.

RICHIE: This dish is too bland. Fourth, didn't you put any salt in it?

FOURTH: Your hands haven't touched any of the money you're owed, but you're a nitpicker when it comes to eating. None of you seems to mind us losing our reputation. We've been bluffed by one man alone—

ELDEST BROTHER: If you can get the money, go get it.

RICHIE: If he can bring the money back, I can stuff it in my ears and then pull it back out from my nostrils. *(Venting their pent-up frustrations, the others break out in uproarious laughter.)*

FOURTH: I'll let you all eat! *(He flips the dining table over on the platform bed, and the others yell in surprise. A tense silence follows.)*

ELDEST BROTHER: Is your hide ready for tanning?

RICHIE: Let's whip his hide into shape!

(The others slowly close in on FOURTH, *who edges his way backward step-by-step. He backs off as far as the doorway, where he trips and falls down. As the others angrily swarm over him, the stage lights go dark.*

Several days later in a narrow lane, FOURTH *is leaning against a utility pole. There is a magazine tucked under his arm. He clumsily lights a cigarette; his anxiety is clearly apparent. Now that the cigarette is lit, his nervous gaze is directed at the corner of the lane and an adjoining street.*

FOREMAN WU *walks up, carrying a small leather satchel.)*

FOURTH: Hello, Mr. Wu.

FOREMAN WU: Hi. Trying to pick up a girl?

FOURTH: No, my mood isn't as carefree as yours. Have a cigarette.

FOREMAN WU: Nope, not for me.

FOURTH: Come on, have one.

FOREMAN WU: Damn it, I'm not smoking!

FOURTH: *(Extremely aggressively)* I'll damn well make you smoke one!

FOREMAN WU: *(Realizing that something is up,* WU *decides to take a softer line, and accepts a cigarette.)* So, the brand is "Great Front Gate"?[3] *(Now smoking the cigarette)* You haven't left town yet, then?

FOURTH: My accounts haven't been settled yet.

FOREMAN WU: Accounts? What accounts?

FOURTH: You said your home is at Eight Sunnyside Lane. I suppose you didn't remember it right, did you?

FOREMAN WU: *(His attitude changing)* What do you mean?

FOURTH: I was going to pay you a visit.

FOREMAN WU: I'll take you there some other day.

FOURTH: I've found it already—it's at Sixteen Riverside Lane.

FOREMAN WU: What're you after?

FOURTH: *(Exhaling a cloud of smoke)* Give me back the money I earned with my blood and sweat.

FOREMAN WU: Old Seventh and I have already clearly accounted for everything.

FOURTH: *(Sneering)* You went wining and dining with Old Zhang Seventh; he's peddled your side of the story. I'm not the same kettle of fish!

FOREMAN WU: Our business venture lost money this time.

FOURTH: Not everybody in my work group is a dimwit.

FOREMAN WU: I'm not going to discuss this with you. *(Makes ready to leave)*

FOURTH: *(Holding* WU *back)* I'm going to discuss it with you.

FOREMAN WU: Now listen, kid—

FOURTH: I'm a man of twenty-three!

FOREMAN WU: Let's go look for a place to talk this over.

FOURTH: I'll use this gadget to talk things over with! *(Flings down his magazine to reveal a kitchen cleaver he had hidden in its pages)*

FOREMAN WU: What do you . . . you want, anyway?

FOURTH: There sure as hell isn't any Old Zhang Seventh here!

FOREMAN WU: A murderer pays with his life!

FOURTH: Once I've killed you, I'll hightail it to distant provinces. Where would they go to look for a migrant laborer, anyway?

FOREMAN WU: Fourth, we've come to know each other during this past job, and gotten along pretty well—

FOURTH: We've gotten along pretty well, all right, but money is still money!

FOREMAN WU: I really did lose money—

FOURTH: *(Fingering the cleaver blade)* It's newly sharpened.

FOREMAN WU: Help, somebody!

FOURTH: This is a dead-end alley.

FOREMAN WU: Police!

FOURTH: Even if the police happened to see us, they'd make a detour around us. Now, let's have it.

(FOURTH *closes in on* WU. WU *knocks the cleaver out of* FOURTH's *hand with a violent kick.*

WU *reaches out to pick up the cleaver from the pavement, but* FOURTH's *foot clomps down on the back of* WU's *hand, pinning it to the ground.*)

FOURTH: Let's handle the situation like this: you give me a hack, then I'll give you a hack. If you kill me with your hack, then you'll have gotten the better part of the deal. But if you can't hack me to death, I surely won't let you off so easily. Let's go, the first hack is yours.

FOREMAN WU: But look at me: I've got a family to support!

FOURTH: So what?! Outside of fairy tales, nobody hops out of a mass of rock to enter the world of the living.[4]

FOREMAN WU: If I had the money, how could I not have taken it out for you by now?

FOURTH: No more nonsense—go ahead and hack.

FOREMAN WU: I—I don't condone killing!

FOURTH: Not a bad heart you've got there!

FOREMAN WU: (*In a pleading manner*) Forget it—for this hack I'll pass.

FOURTH: Go ahead and pass up your turn, but I won't pass up mine! (FOURTH *reaches down to pick up the cleaver, but* WU *lunges to snatch it up first.*) Go ahead and hack—don't keep jabbering on and on. (FOURTH *presses up close to* FOREMAN WU, *who muddle-headedly hacks him once. Blood starts to seep out from somewhere on* FOURTH's *shoulder.*)

FOREMAN WU: (*Throws down the cleaver in a panic*) Blood's coming out! Blood's coming out!

FOURTH: (*Picks up the cleaver*) Now it's my turn!

FOREMAN WU: (*Imploringly*) Good brother, don't hack me—

FOURTH: Take out the money!

FOREMAN WU: Let me off, would you? I'll kneel down to you. (WU *kneels down on the pavement.*)

FOURTH: (*Sneering*) You really won't take the money out, eh?

FOREMAN WU: Let me go, would you?

FOURTH: Go? (*Thinks for a moment*) Then go—but watch out.

FOREMAN WU: (*Getting up from the ground*) Thanks. (*He makes ready to leave.*)

FOURTH: Your son Wu Xiaolong is in the fifth class of the fourth grade at Riverbank Elementary School. Tomorrow evening, you'd best wait to go claim his corpse for disposal. Go on, go on, you'd better leave now.

FOREMAN WU: Why, you're—you're really low-down in the gutter!

FOURTH: You flatter me.

FOREMAN WU: Damn it! (*Unzipping his satchel, he takes out some bills.*) There you go.

FOURTH: Take out some more!

FOREMAN WU: Can't you recognize the genuine item when you see it? That's five hundred yuan!

FOURTH: I need my whole group's wages.

FOREMAN WU: You criminal vagrant, you!

FOURTH: Nope, I'm a shiftless migrant.[5]

FOREMAN WU: There you go! (WU *takes several small bundles of currency out of his money purse. He flings them down one by one at* FOURTH's *feet, letting out a curse each time he flings down a bundle.*) You damned well won't have a peaceful death. Hope you choke to death when you're drinking wine. Hope you get crushed to death by a car when you're walking the streets. Hope you slip and fall to your death when you're at work. Damn! Fifty-three hundred yuan. (WU *grabs back one of the bundles from where* FOURTH *had stuck it in his shirt.*) This is the money I spent on our restaurant meal, plus the money I already gave out to everybody, along with the extra three hundred yuan I gave Old Seventh—

FOURTH: You gave Old Seventh an extra three hundred yuan?

FOREMAN WU: It's none of your damned business.

FOURTH: To think that he sold out our whole group for only three hundred—

FOREMAN WU: Fourth! You won't have a peaceful death! (*Exits*) (FOURTH *woodenly strips off his shirt. He picks up the money on the pavement and places it in his shirt, which he wraps into a bundle. As he stares at all this money, he is frozen in indecision.*

Quite a while passes before he starts to weep. The stage lights darken.)

The workers' shack now exudes the spirit of a defeated army, with its banners fallen and its soldiers dispersed. Packed and tied up, the workers' luggage is piled on the platform bed. SEVENTH UNCLE *has been over-enthusiastically helping the others pack for the journey.)*

SEVENTH UNCLE: Take care of each other on your trip back. Rootsy tends to come down with motion sickness; be sure to stick a big piece of adhesive tape on his navel. Richie, give your mouth a little more rest once you're on the train; don't stir up trouble. Eldest Brother, once you've gotten back home, tell the folks in the family that your Seventh Uncle has suffered a setback. By the time the weather warms up, I'll return to Shandong to bring all of you back for another round of work here. . . . Go on back to our old village now, and send some letters to your Seventh Uncle whether or not there's any news to report.

ELDEST BROTHER: Where has Fourth gone?

RICHIE: "Once the father dies, the mother marries somebody else." Let each of us mind his own business.

ROOTSY: For several days now, Fourth has been going out early in the morning, and not coming back till late in the evening.

SIXTH BROTHER: Let each of us—

RICHIE: Your tongue is a blot on decency. Step aside and take a rest.

ROOTSY: Seventh Uncle, will you be all right staying here by yourself?

SEVENTH UNCLE: Your Seventh Uncle has been leaving the old home village to go to work since the age of sixteen. I'm used to living alone.

ELDEST BROTHER: That rascal Fourth!

SEVENTH UNCLE: Don't wait any longer for him. It's better to leave a bit early.

RICHIE: Seventh Uncle, keep going out to find some work!

SEVENTH UNCLE: *(Sighing)* I've run myself ragged doing that these past few days!

RICHIE: How about if I stay here to keep you company?

SEVENTH UNCLE: Better you go on back. It'll be simpler to get by if I'm on my own. With any more of you here, I wouldn't have the wherewithal.

ELDEST BROTHER: *(Picking up his baggage)* Feeling dizzy can't be likened to dying, anyway. Let's go.

(With lowered heads and in a dispirited mood, the young men all walk out the door. FOURTH *suddenly arrives at the shack.)*

ELDEST BROTHER: Where did you run off to? I've hardly caught a glimpse of you the past several days!

FOURTH: You're going to leave?

ELDEST BROTHER: Hurry and go pack up your bags—we're waiting for you.

FOURTH: So, you're going to leave just like that?

RICHIE: You wouldn't have us leave, but wait here for death instead?

FOURTH: Sixth Brother, there's work now. *(The others all look at* FOURTH *in disbelief.)*

ELDEST BROTHER: There's work?

FOURTH: At the Number Three Mart—

RICHIE: So a little rabbit can pull a big cart[6]—

FOURTH: At the Number Three Mart, they're building a warehouse. They need us to complete the job in thirty days. They can pay us six yuan per day for each workman.

SEVENTH UNCLE: Who's doing the contracting?

FOURTH: I am.

SEVENTH UNCLE: Who's your contact for this?

FOURTH: *(Evasively)* An acquaintance.

SEVENTH UNCLE: *(Insistently)* So who's your contact?

FOURTH: *(Vehemently)* I'm not saying!

SEVENTH UNCLE: *(Feeling insulted)* Playing games with me, eh?

FOURTH: *(Turning away from* SEVENTH UNCLE *to address the others)* Are you joining up? *(They all remain silent.)* You left our village empty-handed; you still want to be that way when you go back?

ELDEST BROTHER: You've never been out front arranging jobs before—

FOURTH: But isn't this job already settled? I've settled it!

RICHIE: Let's hurry up and leave. He's monkeying around with us!

FOURTH: Are you joining up or not?

(All the others look at SEVENTH UNCLE. *He picks up one bundle of baggage after another from the platform bed and tosses each bundle to its owner.)*

SEVENTH UNCLE: Let's go. It won't be long before tonight's last train pulls out. *(The others reluctantly start to shuffle away.)*

FOURTH: This job pays in advance. Are you joining up? *(Everybody stops in their tracks.)* Each man gets fifty yuan in advance pay. *(Unhooking a money belt from around his waist, he pulls out a wad of currency.)*

RICHIE: You really are the papa!

ROOTSY: We've got work now! There's work! *(The atmosphere grows lively.)*

SEVENTH UNCLE: *(As if hammering on a mountain to startle a tiger out of its den)* Where'd that money come from?

FOURTH: This money's not stolen!

SEVENTH UNCLE: I've been in this trade for over thirty years; workers always get paid after the job's been completed.

FOURTH: The guys' pockets are all empty—you can't expect them to keep body and soul together by sipping the northwestern breeze!

SEVENTH UNCLE: We're known for coping with hardship. *(Addressing the others)* Time for you all to leave! *(Nobody moves)*

FOURTH: How come you're driving us all out?

SEVENTH UNCLE: I feel bad seeing everybody stretched out as still as corpses on the platform bed every day.

FOURTH: Can't you see there's work for us here now?

SEVENTH UNCLE: If work was really so easy to come by in this area, would I be sending everybody away? *(Threateningly)* There's something fishy about where that money of yours came from; don't get everybody mixed up in your shady schemes.

FOURTH: This is advance pay from the work project. The only thing you fellows need to bother with is doing the work. I'll fully accept the consequences if any problems crop up. Do you want money? *(Nobody moves.)* You want money? *(They remain silent.)* Then get out! Get out! *(Fiercely)* You bastards are really a bunch of little Shandong bears! As soon as I raise high the army recruitment banner, there'll be soldiers ready to join up. I've got the money; I'll go somewhere else to find workers—

ELDEST BROTHER: Fourth, I'm joining up.

ROOTSY: Same here.

SEVENTH UNCLE: Who are you all following, anyway? *(The other young men hesitate;* SEVENTH UNCLE *then addresses* FOURTH.*)* Fourth, explain about all these job arrangements; your Seventh Uncle will help you weigh all the pros and cons—

FOURTH: *(Vehemently)* I'm deciding things on my own!

*(*SEVENTH UNCLE *slaps* FOURTH *in the face; a hush falls over the whole group. As if totally unaware of what has just happened,* FOURTH *passes out advance-pay packets to all the other young men.)*

FOURTH: Eldest Brother, I'm giving you twenty yuan extra. You'll be leading the work group starting tomorrow. (*Glancing at* SEVENTH UNCLE, ELDEST BROTHER *hesitates to assent.*) Go on and take it! (ELDEST BROTHER *accepts the money. The others soundlessly crowd around* FOURTH, *from whom each receives his pay before quietly stepping aside to unpack his baggage.*)

RICHIE: (*Suddenly*) I'm gonna go cash in my train ticket. If any of you want me to take yours along for cashing in, then give me thirty cents in advance. (*The others grow animated again, except for* SEVENTH UNCLE. *He gloomily stares at the others for a while, then suddenly hops onto the bed, gathers his baggage together under one arm, and leaves the shack.* FOURTH *follows him outside the shack.*)

FOURTH: Seventh Uncle, don't leave.

SEVENTH UNCLE: If this place doesn't provide for me, I've got a place that does.

FOURTH: We can't let you go off all alone—

SEVENTH UNCLE: You're really a stickler for the old formalities.

FOURTH: I can't just sit by and watch everybody fold up and go back—and you're my elder . . .

SEVENTH UNCLE: Your elder, am I? Then tell me about this job and this money you came up with—how did it all happen?

FOURTH: (*Hesitating momentarily before replying*) Seventh Uncle, if you want to get away and relieve yourself of your worries for a while, then please go right on ahead. Whenever you'd like to come back—

SEVENTH UNCLE: (*Interrupting* FOURTH) I'll come back to watch you all carrying out the cooking stove!7 (*Exits*)

(FOURTH *remains wearily standing in the courtyard for a while. As the moonlight shines upon him, he appears all the more solitary a figure. The stage lights gradually darken.*)

(*Two years later, one corner of the workers' shack contains two new walls that form the boundary between the new, separate room and the rest of the shack. The separate room contains a wooden bed over-hung with mosquito netting, and several portraits of famous movie starlets have been stuck on the wall.* FOURTH *sits behind the desk, distributing pay packets to everybody in the work group. Judging from his dress, there have been obvious changes in his life. By this time he* is more shrewd, capable, and experienced, though traces of his old countrified airs still remain.)

FOURTH: Next!

RICHIE: (Crowding his way in) My turn—my turn! Don't crowd around; it's not as if we're grappling over who gets a funeral cap to wear at a rich guy's funeral![8] (Now standing in front of FOURTH's desk) I've damned well got wine to drink again!

FOURTH: (Handing RICHIE his pay, and having him circle his name in the account book) Richie, don't use so much of your money for filling up your stomach. Learn to put some aside so you can someday afford to take a wife; otherwise, your family line will be cut off.

RICHIE: My family line cut off? I've been sowing my wild oats all over the damned place—leaving future descendants behind right and left!

FOURTH: Next! (ELDEST BROTHER accepts his pay packet and draws a circle around his name.) Eldest Brother, you've earned the most of all—maybe it's time you treat us to some good food and drink.

ELDEST BROTHER: You mean you'd need me to treat you to a drink?

SIXTH BROTHER: Fourth . . . Fourth Brother. There isn't any . . . isn't any . . .

FOURTH: There isn't anything the matter anymore.

RICHIE: (Watches FOURTH count out the rest of the money, and then begins to fuss) What's the deal with this shack? Everybody here does the same work, but the pay comes out at different levels. This piddling amount of pay I got wouldn't even be enough to satisfy the mourner responsible for buying spirit money to burn![9]

ELDEST BROTHER: If you were as methodical at work as you are in scolding people, there's no way Fourth would give you less wages than anybody else.

RICHIE: Don't show off what a goody-goody you are just because you got a bigger share than your mates! Aren't you afraid of dying from the stench when you hug his stinking feet in front of your face?

ROOTSY: A little louder, would you? Now we have a play to watch. Make him supplement your pay.

SIXTH BROTHER: Up to—up to monkey business . . . monkey business . . .

ELDEST BROTHER: You keep egging Richie on, and he'll pester
Fourth into losing his temper. All you bastards behave yourselves!

RICHIE: What've we got to fear from him losing his temper? Would
he dare grab anybody's head and trample it into a bubbly mush?
Sixth Brother, what did your pay come to?

SIXTH BROTHER: Two—two hundred and ten.

RICHIE: Rootsy, how about yours?

ROOTSY: Two hundred and thirty.

RICHIE: (*Asks some others how much they were paid, and then flies into
a rage*) Fourth, the way you dish out servings depends on how
much you like each guy at the table! Among everybody here,
young and old, you pay me the least! If you were my papa, I'd
whack you a couple of times to show my respect. Give me a pay
supplement! If you don't, I'll chop your desk to pieces! I'll—

FOURTH: (*Once he steps over to stand in the doorway,* RICHIE *suddenly
stops quarreling with him. He speaks in an affable manner.*) How
much do I owe you?

RICHIE: Eldest Brother got three hundred thirty yuan, but I only got
a hundred and fifty.

FOURTH: Is that so?

RICHIE: I didn't throw your kid down into a well or anything. Why're
you staring at me with such a steely gaze?

FOURTH: How much would you like as a supplement?

RICHIE: Whatever you care to award me with.

FOURTH: Come over here. Come on! (RICHIE *steps over in front of*
FOURTH, *who uses his third finger to give* RICHIE *a loud thump on
the chin. The others all laugh.*)

FOURTH: You have the gall to compare yourself with Eldest Brother?

RICHIE: I didn't work any less than he did!

FOURTH: Come over here—I'll give you a few more as a supplement.

RICHIE: (*Backing away while rubbing his chin*) Back when Seventh
Uncle was in charge, he'd always ladle us out equal shares. If
there was even a dime left over, he'd buy some candy and have
everybody share it—

FOURTH: Then go look up Seventh Uncle. In a magistrate's office,
the magistrate gives the orders. Here at my place, you have to
recognize that I'm in charge. (*Taking out a small notebook*) On
the afternoon of the sixth, you said you had an ache in your gut.
The upshot was that you went to a bar and got roaring drunk. On

the afternoon of the thirteenth, you went off on the sly to watch a martial arts movie—

RICHIE: (*Stopping up his ears*) I'm not listening to all this, I tell you! Just supplement my pay!

FOURTH: Wait a bit, would you?

RICHIE: I'll smash up your desk! (*He picks up a bricklayer's cleaver and rushes into* FOURTH's *private room, but* ELDEST BROTHER *and some others hold him back. The more they hold him back, the more happily* RICHIE *lunges toward the desk.*) This won't do! I'd rather beat him silly than let him run roughshod over me. Do you wanna trample me? Aren't you afraid your toes will get crushed? I'll smash his desk!

FOURTH: (*Mockingly*) Don't grab him; let him smash it up.

ROOTSY: Brother Richie, if you smash his desk, he'll dock your wages.

RICHIE: Let him dock them! Let him dock them! (ELDEST BROTHER *has not relaxed his grip on* RICHIE. SIXTH BROTHER *sneaks up and gives* ELDEST BROTHER *a yank, signaling him to loosen his hold on* RICHIE, *who takes advantage of the situation to throw down the bricklayer's cleaver.*) So he'd dock my wages? How come he doesn't dock his own? Every day you stay home from work, but you get more money than everybody else. All of us in this shack have been keeping you fed and housed for nothing.

ELDEST BROTHER: Richie, what's with all this nonsense? Fourth, go on with your business.

FOURTH: (FOURTH *steps forward, pressing close to* RICHIE, *who defiantly stands up to him.* FOURTH *sneers.*) Coward, I'd rather fight a lion bare-handed than be measured up against a toad. Better go off and amuse yourself.

RICHIE: Who's a toad? Who's a toad? (*He rancorously throws himself at* FOURTH. FOURTH *gives him a backhanded shove, and he falls down on the floor.*)

FOURTH: If you won't work, then get the hell out! We won't miss you here!

RICHIE: (*Kicking up a row*) He injured me! I've gotta have time off to recover from an injury on the job—an injury on the job! (*The sound of the eyeglasses saleswoman hawking her wares on the street reaches the shack. The workers exchange knowing glances and smile. The eyeglasses saleswoman enters the stage.*)

SALESWOMAN: (*In a tone of familiarity*) So, everybody's off work today?

RICHIE: *(As if a supporter has arrived)* Fourth, do you dare hit one of my fingers?

SALESWOMAN: Richie, what's been going on here?

RICHIE: Fourth's been hitting us. *Aiyo,* my collarbone's broken!

SALESWOMAN: Come here; Sister will take a look at it for you.

FOURTH: Don't pay any attention to him.

SALESWOMAN: "When working far from home, you'll earn money if you get along . . . If the elders take advantage of the younger ones, wouldn't you become a laughingstock?"

ROOTSY: Sister, Richie's a year older than he is. *(Everyone laughs.)*

SALESWOMAN: You can't tell whether someone's older or younger just from his age. Some establish themselves in the world earlier, and some later. Old Naughty Boy in *Tale of the Vulture-Shooting Heroes* was over sixty years old and still hadn't established himself in the world, had he?[10] *(Everyone laughs uproariously.)*

RICHIE: Who are you partial to? *Aiyo*—

SALESWOMAN: I'm partial to you, brother. Lie down and straighten out. *(She stretches out RICHIE's legs and starts to knead his lower back.)* Bear with it, now; I'm going to be rubbing hard. *(RICHIE suddenly laughs so hard that he starts rolling all over the floor.)*

RICHIE: You poked my funny bone!

SALESWOMAN: Better get up.

RICHIE: *(Getting up, he speaks obsequiously.)* You've really got a lot of strength in your hands.

SALESWOMAN: Curing this kind of illness is my specialty. *(She turns to address the other workers.)* Don't just stand there watching the fun; buy some eyeglasses. These are the newest goods on the market: tinted glasses, sunglasses, horn-rimmed glasses, and folding glasses. Old people who wear them look young, and young people who wear them are attractive. Go ahead and buy some— are you saving up money to take a mistress or something?
(All the workers gather around her in a circle. Some play with the glasses, while others try them on and start to walk away, prompting the SALESWOMAN to chase after the culprits and playfully whack them into giving the glasses back to her. After engaging in these antics for a while, the workers tactfully slip away one by one.)

RICHIE: *(Lies down on the bed)* I'm not leaving this place; we'll see what he can do about it.

ELDEST BROTHER: There's no advantage to you in getting angry at him. I'm going off to the post office. *(Exit)*

RICHIE: You're damned well the best, and other guys are all riffraff. Your pockets are bulging, and there's a woman in your embrace—you're almost as well off as an American president.

SALESWOMAN: Richie, several more girls have come here from my village—they've got vendors' stands at the Xinkai Road Market. There're a variety of eyeglasses that're sharp-looking and cheap to boot, and with a face shaped like yours, you'll look mighty handsome wearing them.

RICHIE: Quit bluffing me.

FOURTH: *(Gives RICHIE a few small bills)* Go buy some roasted chicken.

RICHIE: Don't go buying people off with roasted chicken.

FOURTH: This isn't a matter involving you alone. If I want you here, I'll keep you on. There are more and more men to choose from; if everyone acted like you, our shop would have gone out of business long ago. Now get going—go off and have a meal at a restaurant.

RICHIE: *(Taking the money)* You can't stop up my mouth with roasted chicken. *(Rancorously)* Whatever you deduct, I'll eat up and spend! If you give me too little, I'll make you give me back piecemeal what you owe me! *(Exits)*

FOURTH: I told you today is payday. Why did you still come?

SALESWOMAN: *(Sweetly)* Don't other people ever miss you? Once you're married off to somebody else, even if I wanted to come, I couldn't anymore. Besides, right when you were giving out their pay, I was doing business. Hey, Foreman, when you've got an old friend who's hurried here from afar, wouldn't you even give her a drink of water to soothe her throat?

FOURTH: Would a drink of water satisfy you?

SALESWOMAN: Then could you buy me some ice cream?

FOURTH: I've got a bottle of soda in my desk. *(He enters the private room to get the soda.)* Here you go!

SALESWOMAN: *(Also entering the room)* Did you save it for me?

FOURTH: Since I'm having you drink it, just drink it.

SALESWOMAN: *(Once she's finished the soda, she hugs FOURTH around the neck.)* I was really fortunate to meet you in the Northeast. *(She burps.* FOURTH *repeatedly tries to push her arms aside, hoping to get away.)* That soda really packs a punch. . . . Are you really going to marry that lame girl?

FOURTH: What do you think?

SALESWOMAN: *(Sighs)* As soon as I think about that, I get terribly upset. Oh well, you win some and you lose some.

FOURTH: I'll set you up with a place.

SALESWOMAN: *(Her lip curling in disappointment)* A man is always chewing the one in his mouth, eyeing the one in his bowl, and thinking fondly of the one on his plate.

FOURTH: It's boring to always be shoveling down the same old bowl of rice.

SALESWOMAN: Seriously, when it comes to you and her . . . you're really blind.

FOURTH: If it were the two of us, would you go through with it?

SALESWOMAN: Would you dare go back on your word to her? If you dare, I'll move my bedroll over here right away! Regardless of who's better looking, there's nothing at all wrong with me—I'm not a cripple like her. She's also three years older than you.

FOURTH: A good man doesn't have a good wife, but a rascally guy has a pretty wife. Don't underestimate her—what she already has is beyond what you could get over a lifetime.

SALESWOMAN: Isn't it just that she's a city resident? What's so great about that?

FOURTH: There's actually nothing great about her. Still, her uncle's on the local party construction committee; he can move mountains. That's what's known as a "universal entry permit." With her, I can advance higher and higher with every step. Without her, I'll always be just a migrant. In a place like this, I'd have a hard time even taking a normal breath.

SALESWOMAN: So, the manly guy will be hanging on to his wife's loins from behind. Aren't you afraid of the urine stench?

FOURTH: What do you know about it? Hanging on to my wife's loins is nothing; if hanging on to a dog's backside worked, I'd do that.

SALESWOMAN: You always come out with lots of crazy ideas!

FOURTH: Han Xin was able to bear the humiliation of crawling underneath the legs of ruffians, and only later became a great general. I can bear humiliation, too. Just wait, there'll be a time when I'll be awesome in every way.

SALESWOMAN: Don't get carried away by all the fun you're having now. Be careful, or you'll run afoul of the authorities.

FOURTH: You're cursing me, you vixen!

SALESWOMAN: If others curse you, they tack ten extra years onto your lifespan.

FOURTH: I'll let you curse me, I'll let you curse . . . (*Throwing off all restraints, the two of them passionately embrace.*)

SALESWOMAN: Just look what a hurry you're in; you haven't yet latched the door.

FOURTH: (FOURTH *gets up to latch the door, then returns to unbutton the saleswoman's clothes.*) You aren't undressing yourself; what are you waiting for?

SALESWOMAN: It's always a cat that carries off a fish, never a fish that carries off a cat.

(ERQIN *enters the stage. Her complexion is wan and sallow. She hesitatingly knocks on the door.*)

FOURTH: There's somebody knocking on the door.

SALESWOMAN: No, there isn't.

FOURTH: Listen—

SALESWOMAN: Your ears are bewitched.

FOURTH: As soon as it's time for this, your ears aren't of any more use.

(ERQIN *again knocks on the door.*)

SALESWOMAN: It's really—

FOURTH: Have they come back?

SALESWOMAN: Are you afraid of them? You coward—

FOURTH: Oh no, eight chances out of ten it's—

SALESWOMAN: The cripple?

FOURTH: Don't make a sound.

SALESWOMAN: (*Intentionally*) I'll open the door and see who it is.

FOURTH: Don't open it!

SALESWOMAN: I've got to make her take a look at us. I'll take off my clothes and go open the door.

FOURTH: Please, Auntie[11] . . .

SALESWOMAN: I'll let her know she's getting leftovers.

FOURTH: You wouldn't dare! (ERQIN *again knocks.*) I'll go take a look. (*Peeking out from the crack between the door and its frame,* FOURTH *sees* ERQIN, *whose back faces him. He then slips back into the room.*)

SALESWOMAN: Is it her?

FOURTH: *(Breathing a sigh of relief)* Damn it, I don't know who it is, just that she's a woman.

SALESWOMAN: It must be that cleaver seller.

FOURTH: That'd be unlucky. *(Everyone falls silent. Exhausted from her trip, ERQIN leans against the door.)* She's left.

SALESWOMAN: Look how frightened you were, you worthless thing.

FOURTH: If we'd let her crowd her way in here, it would've been a mess.

SALESWOMAN: I'd be happy to let her see us. If she wouldn't want you, I'd still want you. *(She lets the mosquito net down over the bed again.)*

FOURTH: Want, want, want. I'll give you— *(Having all but abandoned her hopes, ERQIN knocks twice more.)* She hasn't left—

SALESWOMAN: *(Hopping down from the bed, she walks to the door while buttoning up her shirt.)* We've met up with a ghoul today. *(She yanks open the door, where ERQIN was leaning, catching the visitor unprepared. ERQIN lurches a few steps inside before regaining her balance and coming to a halt.)* Nobody here's buying cleavers. Hurry up and be on your way!

ERQIN: Cleavers? I'm not buying a cleaver.

SALESWOMAN: I'm telling you to leave!

ERQIN: I'm looking for somebody.

SALESWOMAN: Go back on the street if you're looking for somebody. The folks here are well settled and have their own connections.

ERQIN: I'm looking for Fourth Brother. *(FOURTH is standing dumb-founded in the private room.)*

SALESWOMAN: *(Squinting)* Fourth Brother? There's no Fourth Sister, either.

ERQIN: How come your tongue's so sharp?

SALESWOMAN: If you don't care for my sharp tongue, don't listen to it. Better just leave.

ERQIN: You mean Fourth isn't here?

SALESWOMAN: He's left.

ERQIN: Where'd he go?

SALESWOMAN: America.

(The SALESWOMAN slams the door shut. As a despondent ERQIN is about to leave, FOURTH breaks free of the firm restraining hold the SALESWOMAN had on him, and bursts out of the shack.)

FOURTH: Erqin!

(Struck speechless with surprise at the sight of FOURTH, ERQIN *merely stares at him.)*

FOURTH: Erqin—

ERQIN: *(Happily)* I've found you after all.

(Noticing that ERQIN *is leaning weakly against the door frame,* FOURTH *puts an arm around her and helps her into the shack.)*

SALESWOMAN: *(Brimming with jealousy)* You've surely got a sweet young thing here!

FOURTH: *(Finding it inconvenient to let his anger ignite)* Hmmm, you'd better go hawk your wares. *(To* ERQIN*)* I'll get you some water to wash your face with—

ERQIN: There's no need—

FOURTH: *(Picking up a washbasin and walking to the front door, he pauses for a moment next to the* SALESWOMAN.*)* Hurry up and leave! *(Exits)*

ERQIN: Fourth—

SALESWOMAN: Where are you from?

ERQIN: Our old home.

SALESWOMAN: Is Fourth your own brother?

ERQIN: *(Weakly)* No—

SALESWOMAN: *(Mysteriously)* Lemme tell you, he's quite attractive for a man hereabouts—

ERQIN: "Attractive"?

SALESWOMAN: Sure enough! Not only is he capable, but when it comes to looks, he's—

FOURTH: *(Having just returned, he glares at the* SALESWOMAN.*)* I'm not buying glasses. *(Turning to* ERQIN*)* You can wash your face.

SALESWOMAN: *(Straightening up her eyeglasses sales case)* What's this crap about not buying glasses? You've wasted so much of my time! Before you call me over next time, first decide whether or not you can afford it. *(*SALESWOMAN *leaves the stage in a huff.)*

ERQIN: Fourth—

FOURTH: *(Explaining)* She's an eyeglasses saleswoman. . . . How did you get here?

ERQIN: I came by train.

FOURTH: How many days did it take?

ERQIN: It's been seven days since I left.

FOURTH: *(With amazement)* Seven days?

ERQIN: *(With fatigue)* Looking for you was really difficult. . . . At any rate, I've finally found you.

FOURTH: Where did you stay these past several days?

ERQIN: *(Sluggishly)* Stay?

FOURTH: Where did you stay at night?

ERQIN: *(Pausing momentarily)* The train station.

FOURTH: The train station?!

ERQIN: *(Weakly)* They wouldn't let me stay there, and were always driving me out. Twice they even made me go to the office where the railway police are. They asked me—oh, the people here, they're really wicked.

FOURTH: You've been through hardship—

ERQIN: It wasn't till this morning that I found out you were here.

FOURTH: Why didn't you send me a telegram?

ERQIN: I just guessed I could find you. *(Proudly)* And I did!

FOURTH: *(Taking* ERQIN *by the hand)* You should've sent a telegram!

ERQIN: *(Letting herself go, she strokes* FOURTH) Fourth—

FOURTH: Just look how gaunt you've become. . . . If only you'd written a letter—

ERQIN: I . . . I rushed here without letting anybody know about it.

FOURTH: *(Struck dumb momentarily)* Without letting anybody know?

ERQIN: I missed you . . . a lot. It was five years already—

FOURTH: Five years . . .

ERQIN: For five years I was waiting on them all hand and foot. I'd long since paid back the debt my father'd owed them. I didn't need you to come spend a lot of money to redeem me from service; I've come here on my own—

FOURTH: *(With trepidation)* Do—do they know about this?

ERQIN: No. *(Happily)* It's wonderful we're together. *(Brimming with hope)* Nobody can interfere; it's just the two of us now, free and at our ease.

FOURTH: Did you get divorced?

ERQIN: *(Dispiritedly)* They wouldn't let me go through the formalities.

FOURTH: Does anyone know that you've come here on the sly?

ERQIN: No, I never revealed this to anybody.

FOURTH: Oh, great . . .

ERQIN: What?

FOURTH: *(Concealing his alarm)* Rest here a couple of days first.

ERQIN: *(Coquettishly pretending to be displeased)* I'm not tired; now that I've seen you, I'm not at all tired. Fourth, do you think I look any different?

FOURTH: You're even prettier than before.

ERQIN: Really? I'm like any other adult now, but when we were young, you always carried me around on your shoulders.

FOURTH: I'd take you outside the village to play . . .

ERQIN: It's better this time . . .

FOURTH: *(At odds with himself)* This time . . . over a span of five years, it seems that anything could happen.

ERQIN: Of course. You didn't realize I'd be able to come, did you?

FOURTH: *(With trepidation)* If they come looking for us, what'll we do?

ERQIN: Nobody knows I've come here.

FOURTH: There's a lot of people and plenty of loose tongues here. The news about you is bound to make its way back to the village.

ERQIN: It couldn't!

FOURTH: If they come looking for us, we'll both be done for.

ERQIN: Nobody knows!

FOURTH: The news'll get back there soon! *(ERQIN is speechless with dismay.)* Rest up for a couple of days—then you'd better go back!

ERQIN: *(Shocked)* I'm not going back!

FOURTH: I'll give you traveling expenses!

(A moment of silence follows.)

ERQIN: Have . . . have you got someone else?

FOURTH: What kind of thing is that to say?

ERQIN: Well, then—

FOURTH: You're hungry, aren't you? I'll go buy you some steamed buns with stuffing—

ERQIN: Fourth, I'm not going back!

FOURTH: Wait here, and in just a little while I'll—

ERQIN: *(Interrupting FOURTH again)* Tell me, have you got someone else?

FOURTH: You're hungry.

ERQIN: Tell me.

FOURTH: I've missed you all along.

ERQIN: There's nobody else?

FOURTH: You've just been making wild guesses.

ERQIN: *(Heaves a drawn-out sigh)* I'm really hungry.

> *(FOURTH departs. ERQIN looks all around the room. Extremely fatigued, she leans against the wall at the edge of the platform bed and falls asleep. A short while later, FOURTH returns carrying an order of steamed buns, which he puts down.)*

FOURTH: *(Softly)* Erqin, it's better you sleep on the bed.

> *(ERQIN has not stirred, so FOURTH picks her up and lays her down upon the bed. He starts to pull over the quilt with the idea of covering her with it, but notices that it's too filthy. Throwing the quilt aside, FOURTH takes off the suit coat he'd been wearing and covers ERQIN with it.)*

SALESWOMAN: *(Returning onstage, she walks up behind FOURTH.)* She's your mistress, eh?

FOURTH: *(Greatly startled)* Get out!

SALESWOMAN: You no longer know who I am?

FOURTH: What are you up to?

SALESWOMAN: I'm still as famished as ever.

FOURTH: You despicable thing.

SALESWOMAN: In an affair between two people, if one's despicable, then they're both despicable. *(Gazing at ERQIN)* She's quite pretty. *(Licentiously gives FOURTH a pinch)* You've really got what it takes!

FOURTH: What are you after?

SALESWOMAN: I left something here! *(Pulls out a brassiere that had been underneath ERQIN on the platform bed)* Just look!

FOURTH: If you still won't leave, I'll strangle you!

SALESWOMAN: You've turned hostile mighty fast! When I came over it was all "sweet big sister" and "darling little sister," but when it's time to leave, I've turned into a damned White Bone Demon.[12] Today I'll let her rush in for hers, but I'll be back again tomorrow.

FOURTH: *(Throwing two ten-yuan bills over in her direction)* Don't come back tomorrow.

SALESWOMAN: *(Picking up the bills from the floor)* Such a pity just to throw them away! I'll keep the money to buy some tonic for you. See you tomorrow! *(She exits, but after FOURTH shuts the door, she again barges in.)* How about buying her a pair of glasses? I'll give you two a discount—

FOURTH: *(Shoving the saleswoman back)* Get out of here!

SALESWOMAN: What are you shoving for? If you twist my spine out of alignment, you'll have to wait on me hand and foot! *(Resumes loudly hawking her wares)* Eyeglasses! *(Exits)*

(FOURTH dejectedly leans against the door, listening to the sound of hawking as it fades in the distance. He goes back into the room, where he quietly gazes at ERQIN. He wants to kiss her, but just as their lips are about to meet, he suddenly stands up and guiltily backs away. Opening the door, he steps outside and shuts the door behind him. He is sunk in misery as he leans against the door frame. The stage lights are extinguished.

Music starts: the stirring measures of a wedding march are punctuated by firecracker explosions. The master of ceremonies shouts: "Bow to your parents! Bow to your guests! Newlyweds bow to each other!" A chorus of clapping and cheers suddenly rises, then gradually fades into the distance. A soft and delicate dance tune begins. It is now evening at the work site.

A new building that has not yet been completed stands desolate in the night. The dance tune fades in and out of earshot, and as if by chance, metamorphoses into the familiar folk song about striking out into the Northeast frontier. It seems as though the delicately melancholy voice of the female vocalist emerges from a very faraway place:

"March brings red to the blossoms of the peach,
As my man goes after gold in the distant Northeast.
I saw you off there at the Yellow River delta,
Urging you to drink before your distant trek.
Don't forget your maiden, who at home must e'er await
Greetings from your bridal chair in front of her gate.
Aiyoyo, not to know which year
Shandong will finally welcome back her long-lost mate."

Carrying a pack on her back, ERQIN walks forward from the back of the stage. She walks mechanically, stopping only when she reaches the front of the scaffolding. She blankly looks out into the vast and hazy night sky.)

ERQIN: *(Mumbling to herself)* The sky is really lofty, and the stars truly far away. A star is nothing but a piece of gold. If I go up, I can pluck it from the sky; surely it's there for the plucking. . . . *(She absentmindedly climbs up the scaffolding.)* The sky's getting closer to me, and so are the stars. But why can't I touch the sky? I can't pluck the stars from the sky, either. The sky must be soft, and the stars must be burning hot to the touch. . . . Old Man Heaven, you shouldn't deceive me! A man comes to the Northeast to look for gold and make lots of money; that's a man's business. What would I come here for? I can't find gold, and I can't make big money. Even less can I redeem that heart. It's been bought off by this city. . . . (*Chuckles bitterly*) I rushed here from a faraway place a thousand miles distant to look for him. But my main backer in life had gone back on his word, and the waters that had buoyed me up all drained away.[13] The fate of mine informed by that one sentence couldn't be changed even if I wanted to change it; it couldn't be exchanged for some other fate even if I wanted to exchange it. What am I seeking? What can I seek?

(*A gust of wind tousles* ERQIN's *hair. She looks downward; her backpack has fallen to the ground. She tightly holds on to a scaffolding pole, and fearfully gazes down at the ground. Her instinct to live on has gotten the upper hand. Miserable, she sits immobile on the scaffold.*)

FOURTH: (*Hurrying onstage*) Erqin! Erqin! (*He trips over her backpack. Fearfully picking it up from the ground, he frantically peers about on all sides.*) Erqin! Erqin!

ERQIN: (*Dazedly raises her head and speaks as if unconscious*) Who's calling out for me? Someone with a voodoo curse?

FOURTH: (*Pleasantly surprised*) Erqin, hurry and come down, it's dangerous up there!

ERQIN: (*Mechanically repeating after* FOURTH) "Dangerous"?

FOURTH: Hurry on down!

ERQIN: Who are you?

FOURTH: Your Fourth! I'm your Fourth!

ERQIN: Fourth . . .

FOURTH: Don't frighten me now, good Erqin. I've been worried to death about you.

ERQIN: It's really nice up here.

FOURTH: Don't take leave of your senses!

ERQIN: The stars are scorching to the touch; I'll give you one.

FOURTH: Do you want to drive me mad? I'm sorry for what I did to you; I apologize. . . . Come on down; it's okay even if you hit me or scold me. Just come on down.

ERQIN: It's too stifling down there; it's refreshing up here.

FOURTH: You need to pull yourself together a bit.

ERQIN: I've pulled myself together.

FOURTH: It's all my fault. Do you have to make me die in front of you to atone for it?

ERQIN: Your life's worth more money than mine. Don't waste it.

FOURTH: Erqin—

ERQIN: *(Despondently)* You'd better hurry on back. Whether I live or die doesn't have anything to do with you.

FOURTH: You came to me for help—I have to take responsibility for you.

ERQIN: If you'd taken responsibility for me, you surely would have gone back earlier to redeem me from service. Once you got money, you long since forgot about me. You blame me for not working my own way out of that fix, and for running up here to annoy you—

FOURTH: What kind of thing is that to say? I'm begging you to come down! Come down. *(Kneels on the ground)* Even if I've committed a thousand wrongs, or done ten thousand things I shouldn't have, now that you're seeing me kneel to you like this, you've got to go on living. If you were to meet with some terrible misfortune, how could I bear to face other people? How could I go on living? Erqin, you don't know how hard I've had it just to try staying human—or how hard a struggle it's been to have gotten as far I've come. In a city as big as this, there's nowhere we could get a footing. Other people would curse us as migrant rovers, darkies, or third-class citizens. We'd work so long and hard we nearly keeled over, but we couldn't get so much as a word of thanks for our labors. When we'd go into a store or stroll through an open market, other people would give us a wide berth. If we wanted to establish our position, we had to work; if there was no work to do, we'd just have to starve to death! We had no backer to help us; if we got too poor, the only thing we could count on would be a swift kick out of the place! I had my fill of poverty. When I got hold of some money, I wanted to go back to redeem you from service. But if I'd redeemed you, we'd still be paupers. If I wasn't able to give you a good life, I'd rather just suffer on my own. So I used that stash of money to find work for all the fellows from back home. That's what I spent a lot of money buying. Ever since that time, all the fellows have trusted me, and I've smoothed out a path for them to follow. The more I pursued this line of work, the more wrapped up I got in it—and the more addicted I got to it. Without knowing what was happening, I let other people impose on me. Once they'd done that, I couldn't disentangle myself. I was walking forward with my eyes shut. Erqin, nobody makes allowances for me, or understands all this.

(In the midst of FOURTH's *long explanation,* ERQIN *has climbed down from the scaffolding, in spite of being very much of two minds about the whole thing. She quietly stands in front of* FOURTH. *Still on his knees,* FOURTH *lurches forward and throws his arms around her legs.)*

ERQIN: Get up; if you let other people see—

FOURTH: You're going to live on right and proper, live on right and proper—

ERQIN: I shouldn't have come looking for you. I had a family; though it wasn't so heartwarming, it still could be called a family, after all. I had a husband; though he was a lunatic, he still was a bona fide husband. *(Forces herself to seem relaxed)* I haven't yet told you that my mother-in-law treated me quite well. They didn't hit me that year I saw you off at the train station. My younger brother-in-law would always carry water for me; he . . . he wouldn't often flip his lid—

FOURTH: Complaining's not enough to soothe hatred. Hit me!

ERQIN: *(Stroking* FOURTH's *hair)* Your hair's so long . . . When you betrothed yourself to her, the other fellows from back home said you were going off to be somebody else's cur, to be a good little "grandson" of the city folk. Listening to what they said, my heart felt out of sorts. It was only to keep from being somebody else's cur that you ran way out here in the first place. You've sold yourself too cheaply. Maybe it's all right that you didn't consider things on my behalf, but you can't but consider things on your own behalf. If you have to spend your life with her and always depend on others, then you'd be violating your own sense of what's right and proper—

FOURTH: If I don't first become a grandson, then I couldn't later become a patriarch. If I don't damned well sell myself a bit cheaply, then I'll have to end up as rotten as I've been up till now! Today I'll become a cur, but tomorrow I'll be nothing other than a tiger, a lion! They'll be able to see what sort of moves I can make on this chessboard!

ERQIN: You've already managed quite well for yourself up to now. Why must you—

FOURTH: *(Coldly)* To do even better than this!

ERQIN: And for the sake of this, you're going to treat the "major affair of your whole life" as a mere game? [14]

FOURTH: The "major affair of your whole life," is it? The major affair of my whole life is to become a man of high status! My entire life's revolved around keeping others from getting the upper hand over me.

ERQIN: There's always going to be someone who gets the upper hand over you.

FOURTH: That's another thing altogether. You see, there are more and more construction crews entering the city nowadays, and some can't even earn back what they spent on traveling expenses. All sorts of lines of work here haven't got any openings. There are more and more of our own fellows here—they've all rushed up here to join me. None of them complains, even if we work straight through to midnight. But if I let them sit idly by for just three days in a row, then there's no end to their wails of complaint. If I fall by the wayside, all of these fellows will, too.

ERQIN: Fourth—

FOURTH: Our last few work projects were all dug up for us by Section Chief Tao of the Municipal Construction Committee. He's got a crippled niece who hasn't been able to get a husband. Foreman Wu's served as the go-between in arranging the marriage. She needs a husband, and I need a backer.

ERQIN: If I were you, I'd have to handle things the same way. But you're paying too high a price—

FOURTH: "A price" . . . (ERQIN *reaches across and takes her backpack out of* FOURTH's *grasp.*) Where're you going?

ERQIN: Back home.

FOURTH: You're going back?

ERQIN: You're going to spend your life here with the cripple, and I'll go back and spend my life with the lunatic. As for the feelings we've had for each other since childhood . . . well, it's at least fair this way.

FOURTH: You can't go back! Now that you've come out here, you can't just go back!

ERQIN: You've been driving me away, haven't you?

FOURTH: Don't leave; I'll support you here.

ERQIN: How? As your concubine?

FOURTH: Any more talk like that, and I'll slap you! *(Pleading)* Don't talk that way; you don't know how lonely I've been. . . .

ERQIN: *(Sighs)* Ahh, you . . . you better find me a job, then.

FOURTH: Fine. Stay on here and wait for me.

ERQIN: How many years?

FOURTH: *(Embracing* ERQIN*)* Wait till she's no longer of use to me.

ERQIN: When she's no longer of use to you, I won't be, either.

FOURTH: I can't do without you. *(Both fall silent for a while.)*

ERQIN: If you could do without me, I wouldn't have come up here.

FOURTH: Erqin!

ERQIN: Fourth!

(Tightly embracing each other, both sob loudly. The stage lights are extinguished.

As the music begins, there is a bout of crying from a baby. A woman's gentle voice starts to sing "Rock-a-bye, Baby."

Several months later, in the work shed, the men there ring a makeshift table built of surplus planks. They are drinking wine. FOREMAN WU *is sitting next to* FOURTH; *wearing an apron,* ERQIN *is pouring the men wine and serving them dishes. She is masking her deep agony with an air of self-indulgence, and hiding her giant disappointment with a smiling face.)*

FOURTH: Let's everybody hold it right there for a minute! Let me say a few words. What we're drinking today is the wine of celebration —the wine for celebrating our son's first year! Our son belongs to the generation begotten by the pathbreakers to the Northeast. Once he's grown up, he's bound to become a hale fellow among the city folk. There's another thing to celebrate: I've bought an urban household registration permit for four thousand yuan. We're perfectly valid city folk, now—not shiftless migrants anymore.

RICHIE: I swear I'm the honored ancestor of any damned good-for-nothing who calls me a shiftless migrant!

ELDEST BROTHER: Better drink up your glassful.

FOURTH: Let's everybody drink! Whoever doesn't get drunk is as puny as this!

FOREMAN WU: Drink up! I'll damn well give up my long life to keep you company. (*He pours eight tiny shot glasses of wine, lining them up on the table. With his palms flat against the table and his ten fingers stretched out, all at once he grabs up the eight shot glasses in the crooks between his ten fingers. Beginning with the shot glass between the thumb and forefinger of his left hand, he downs each of the shot glasses in that hand, and then continues by finishing off the remaining four shot glasses in his right hand.*) This is what is known as "each floor of the tower higher than the last, and climbing higher with every step."

FOURTH: For my turn, it's "the Buddha lighting his lamp." (*He pours wine into nine shot glasses, which he arrays in the shape of a pagoda right in the center of his upturned palm. He thereupon drinks them all down in a single draught.*) How was that? (*The others all cheer.*)

ELDER BROTHER: This one of mine's called "ever-flowing waters." Richie, pour more in. (RICHIE *fills two bowls with wine.* ELDER BROTHER *lifts the bowl to his lips, tilting it up slightly, and keeps drinking continuously as* RICHIE *gradually pours the contents of the second bowl into the first. The wine is soon all drunk.*) We guys really haven't ever been afraid of anybody.

FOREMAN WU: You can really hold your liquor! Niece Erqin, come over and have a couple drinks with your uncle.

ERQIN: Have a drink with you? You're not up to snuff—

FOREMAN WU: You write me off as too old? You wouldn't give me a little face?

ERQIN: Face isn't something I can give to everyone.

FOREMAN WU: You look down on your uncle.

ERQIN: If I looked up to you, what difference could that make?

FOREMAN WU: Have a drink. If you don't have a drink, then I'll raise my glass and have one.

ERQIN: Go ahead and raise your glass.

FOREMAN WU: If I kneel down to you, will you have a drink?

ERQIN: Kneel down!

(*Voices from the group call out: "Make him kneel down!" "Kneel down!" "He's a bastard if he doesn't kneel."*)

FOREMAN WU: What in hell wouldn't I dare do? (*He kneels down and lifts his drink in a toast.*) Do me the honor of your esteemed companionship. (*The others all roar with cathartic laughter.*)

ERQIN: Just keep kneeling there.

FOURTH: (*Helping* WU *extricate himself from an embarrassing situation*) Erqin, drink a little. Just for good luck's sake.

ELDER BROTHER: (*Puts a restraining hand on* FOURTH) Fourth . . .

ERQIN: (*To* FOURTH) So you're urging me on, too?

FOURTH: Just drink a little; it doesn't matter.

ELDER BROTHER: Have you had one too many?

FOURTH: This is my wine! Erqin—

ERQIN: Don't they say that a person who's drinking can't die?

FOREMAN WU: Can't die . . .

ERQIN: Fourth's urged me on—I'll drink it! (*She drains it in one draught.*)

FOREMAN WU: That's the stuff! A real hero! (*He gets up from the floor.*)

RICHIE: What sort of a hero is she? Fourth's the only one you could call a hero. He'd been married only four months and already had a baby boy to carry around. He wasted no more time about it than a dog or a cat; which one is he, anyway? A dog or a cat?

FOURTH: Hell, I'm a dragon! As for all that stuff about the four months, in conceiving our son, we did it out of love for each other; neither of us dallied around.

ELDEST BROTHER: Just like a cat holding a mouse in its mouth—both happy and worried at the same time.

RICHIE: You were so busy conceiving your son that you just tossed everybody else off to one side. How damned filthy jealous we were!

FOURTH: If you don't want to drink, get out of here.

RICHIE: Okay, I'm paying up!

FOREMAN WU: Have a drink. What's the use of taking Sesame Chen's rotten grain to task?

RICHIE: Hold off, would you? I can't even take a step forward without you popping up out of the woodwork somewhere.

FOREMAN WU: I came here on Fourth's behalf, not on yours. I don't care what you do with your wine; it's up to you.

RICHIE: I'd dump my wine into the privy before letting you drink any of it.

FOURTH: Have a drink. What the hell is this drunken raving about?

RICHIE: He's your papa; go side with him.

FOURTH: You little son of a bitch!

(ERQIN *brings out the dishes.*)

RICHIE: Erqin, fill up my elder cousin's cup. If you don't want to drink, that's your problem. I'm paying for my own damned portion here.

FOURTH: If you have any regrets, then take back your money. Two and a half yuan isn't enough to get yourself riled up over.

FOREMAN WU: To heck with it, we're here to drink, not to lose our temper. Let's take the celebration to its climax, not get down in our cups.

FOURTH: Let's everybody enjoy ourselves!

RICHIE: *(Singing as if in a drunken delirium)*
"It's March, and it's off to the Northeast we go,
With a pair of reed hampers and three lengths of rope . . ."

VOICES FROM THE GROUP:
"Our toddlers ride ahead 'neath the tip of our shoulder pole,
While dangling back behind—woks, ladles, gourds, and bowls . . ."
(The assembled men stir up a raucous din as they sing.)

FOREMAN WU: Erqin, come sit over here by your uncle. (ERQIN *takes a seat.)* Niece, your uncle here's going to match you up with a husband—

FOURTH: Better keep on with your drinking. What's the use of talking nonsense?

FOREMAN WU: This is a proper matter to discuss.

ERQIN: You found Fourth a good father-in-law; what kind of fellow could you find for me?

FOREMAN WU: That depends on what kind you want.

ERQIN: I want somebody who's wealthy.

FOREMAN WU: *(With an impassive expression on his face)* I'm surely wealthy. How about it?

ERQIN: You? *(She laughs uproariously.)*

FOREMAN WU: Don't just laugh—say something.

ERQIN: Are you serious or joking?

FOREMAN WU: If I'd been joking, I wouldn't have said anything more about it.

ERQIN: I'd go along with your idea, all right—it's just that I wouldn't dare appear in public afterward.

FOREMAN WU: What would you be afraid of?

ERQIN: All the guys here would look at us and wonder if that old fellow looks more like my father or my grandfather.

ROOTSY: Naw, he looks more like your great uncle! (*All the workers break out in noisy laughter.*)

FOREMAN WU: With couples abroad, there's often an older husband with a younger wife. I didn't spruce myself up today; if I'd dressed up and groomed myself better, I'd have looked over ten years younger. Men don't look as old as they really are.

SIXTH BROTHER: He . . . he doesn't yet look old?

ERQIN: That really doesn't bother me. (*Peering at* WU) From far away you look like a white-haired Lü Dongbin, but closer up you resemble the graybeard Zhang Gelao.[15] (*General laughter.*)

FOREMAN WU: (*Pretending to be angry*) If the couple didn't have an older one, then there wouldn't be a younger one, either.

ERQIN: A younger one? I wouldn't be your younger wife—no way![16]

FOURTH: You've drunk too much.

ERQIN: Isn't this the wine of celebration?

FOURTH: Erqin!

ERQIN: Isn't this the wine for celebrating your son's birthday?

FOURTH: Go back to your room and take a rest for a while.

ERQIN: What makes you think you can ride herd on me? Nobody's written my name in your household registration booklet.[17]

FOREMAN WU: Right, tonight we're just letting everybody enjoy themselves.

ERQIN: You're really a kindhearted one.

FOREMAN WU: Yep.

ERQIN: No matter when it might be in this world, the good out-number the wicked.

FOREMAN WU: Yep.

ERQIN: Come on, let's drink a toast to all the good people under Heaven!

ELDEST BROTHER: Erqin, don't drink anymore.

ERQIN: (*Ignoring him*) Come on, let's everybody drink up! (*The others join her in drinking a toast.*)

ERQIN: Let's drink a toast to all of the wicked under Heaven.

RICHIE: Long live the wicked! (*The others join in her toast.*)

ERQIN: Let's drink a toast to all those under Heaven who aren't human but still manage to keep breathing between gasps. (*The group shouts in approval and joins her in drinking a toast.*)

FOURTH: Erqin, don't drink anymore.

ERQIN: It's your wine I'm drinking; don't be so stingy.

FOURTH: I'm afraid you've gotten drunk.

ERQIN: I'm just happy—I couldn't have gotten drunk. The wine in a celebration can't make you drunk.

FOURTH: Don't become a laughingstock for others.

ERQIN: Who in the hell would dare laugh at me? (*Pointing at a couple of individuals in the group*) Would you? Or you? Anyone who laughs at me won't have any descendants!

FOURTH: Erqin!

ERQIN: Don't keep whining, "Erqin, Erqin"—I'm sick of listening to it! Come on, let's the two of us drink!

FOURTH: I'm not drinking with you!

ERQIN: Too fond of the wine to let me drink it? Isn't it just sorghum wine? Richie, go buy me some wine, and keep the change.

RICHIE: (*Sways back and forth as he takes a few steps*) How come the floor's moving around?

ERQIN: Rootsy, you go instead.

RICHIE: Who in the hell'd dare go in my place? I—

ELDEST BROTHER: Hold it right there. (*He leans a bit on* RICHIE, *who falls flat on the floor.*)

ERQIN: Not a single one of them of any use. I'll go myself—

FOURTH: Erqin—

ERQIN: It's your day of celebration; you at least have to let me enjoy myself!

RICHIE: (*Staggers back to a standing position*) Erqin, I—I'll go there with you. As for that guy who isn't human . . . don't bother with him.

ERQIN: Don't cotton up to me.

RICHIE: I—I know how you're suffering inside. Real men—two-legged men who're alive—are all over the street, strolling here and there. . . . They're easy to find.

ERQIN: Easy to find? Go get one tomorrow.

RICHIE: Get one? Get one what?

ERQIN: A man, of course.

RICHIE: Ah yes, that's right! Whoops, there's a bit of vegetable right here. (*Strokes* ERQIN's *neck*)

ERQIN: (*Slaps* RICHIE *in the face*) What do you think you're pawing?

RICHIE: How—how come you did that?

ERQIN: (*Suddenly laughs*) A parent's slap means she cherishes a naughty child, and a scolding means she loves him. If there's neither a slap nor a scolding, then it's a calamity in the making for the child.[18] *(She laughs uproariously as she walks out the door.)*

RICHIE: *(Stroking his face)* Damn it to hell . . .

(The others burst out laughing. Once ERQIN is outside the front door, an alcoholic soup starts welling up from her stomach to her throat. Feeling nauseous, she tugs her collar snugly around her neck, but finally can't hold it down any longer, and throws up. Afterwards, she shuffles next to the wall, on which she is listlessly leaning as the lights indoors are extinguished. A shaft of light illuminates her face, revealing the visage of a person seemingly lost in thought.

From a distance, the melody of "Off to the Northeast" becomes audible and gradually gets nearer and louder. QIUZI enters the stage. He is an optimistic young fellow. His bedroll and other baggage are slung diagonally over his back. He is playing a harmonica while walking along. When he reaches the place where ERQIN is leaning, he stops in his tracks.)

QIUZI: Excuse me, Miss, is Fourth here?

ERQIN: *(Drunkenly)* Who—who're you looking for?

QIUZI: Fourth, the big foreman.

ERQIN: Who're you?

QIUZI: My name's Qiuzi.

ERQIN: You've come late.

QIUZI: "Late"?

ERQIN: He's dead.

QIUZI: "Dead"? I saw him just day before yesterday!

ERQIN: He just now died.

QIUZI: *(Despondently)* A fellow wants to rush into a bright future, only to find it's all gone dark around him. *(He sits down on the doorstep, mute in the face of his own worries. After a while, he breaks the silence.)* What did he die from?

ERQIN: Cancer!

QIUZI: What was the cancer of?

ERQIN: Just go ask him yourself!

QIUZI: *(Suspiciously)* Seems you're drunk, aren't you?

ERQIN: And the odds are five to one you're fond of hitting the bottle.

(Sounds of laughter and drinking games indoors reach them both.)

QIUZI: Something here doesn't add up. You've been pulling a trick on me, haven't you?

ERQIN: *(Talking to herself instead of responding)* Dead—died long ago.

QIUZI: Listen to all the hubbub indoors—they're all laughing.

ERQIN: They're all crying. . . .

QIUZI: You can't even distinguish laughter from crying. If you aren't a mental case, then you're raving mad.

ERQIN: *(Enraged)* Get out of here! Get away from me!

QIUZI: *(Jokingly)* You couldn't really drive me away from here. To get me to come work here, Fourth had to pull the rug from under my old work unit. He'd abandon you before he'd abandon me.

ERQIN: *(To herself)* He's always gone off and abandoned me.

QIUZI: *(Rushing indoors)* Fourth! Fourth, I'm here!

FOURTH: *(Indoors)* Hey, get your ass in here! What in the hell took you so long to get here, little rascal?

QIUZI: *(Winking at* ERQIN*)* Did you hear that? "Get your ass in here"—that's an expression of friendliness. You'd better go learn something about that!

(He goes inside. ERQIN *remains standing forlornly in the courtyard. The stage lights go dark.*

Later, the lights come back on to reveal a table placed in the middle of the stage. Leaning over the table and propping himself up with both hands, FOURTH *is addressing the audience below the stage.)*

FOURTH: You'd have me state my position? Well, then, here goes. I've eaten and drunk here as your guest, and it wouldn't be right if I didn't state my position. Isn't the meeting here all about making donations? What's all this talk about making donations? Isn't the problem just that there's a shortage of money to spend? I've also had times when I was short of money. I've been there, and know how bad it feels to have to keep a wary eye on your boss's facial expression while you're eating the food he's provided. Being short a mere penny can lead to difficulties for even a hero; I've experienced this. For over ten years I've had the clearest understanding of poverty's bitterness and wealth's sweetness. I know exactly what you're going through; we're a case of eight ounces being no different than half a pound—

ANONYMOUS VOICE: Hey, don't make a long speech and then come up short when it's time to spend money. How much are you donating?

FOURTH: Come up short in spending money? What damned sort of guy do you think I am? I'm pulling out the money! On behalf of the Mount Tai United Construction Company, I'm donating forty thousand yuan to your television station—*(the hall is so hushed that one could hear a pin drop)*—and am adding another thirty thousand yuan on top of that![19] *(More silence, followed by a round of thunderous applause)* I, Four—er, Zhang Tianxing— couldn't have gotten the title of peasant entrepreneur for nothing; I can deliver the real goods. Even a lone commoner has a responsibility to society. *(During a round of applause, he quietly makes a comment to himself.)* Damn! If you're rich, then you're the granddaddy.

ANONYMOUS VOICE: May I ask Chief Manager Zhang how many workers are under your leadership?

FOURTH: You're asking about my soldiers and armaments? Hmm, it's very fluid. During the busy season, there are over a thousand, but when business is slack, there're only a few around.

ANONYMOUS VOICE: Chief Manager Zhang, I'd like to ask you a bit about your private life. I've heard that your wife is from the city. How do the two of you get along emotionally?

FOURTH: My family is the same as yours—no better and no worse than any of yours.

ANONYMOUS VOICE: Do you have a woman on the side? It's very fashionable.

FOURTH: Yep, half the human race does.

ANONYMOUS VOICE: Some people say you give bribes—is it true?

FOURTH: If today's donation is also considered bribery, then I wouldn't deny it.

ANONYMOUS VOICE: Are you a Communist Party member?

FOURTH: I'm preparing to join.

(Everyone laughs. Now and then, camera flashbulbs shed a momentary glare on the scene. The sounds of laughter and applause continue for quite some time. FOURTH *continually says thanks, and nods in appreciation to the audience. The hubbub gradually dies down; all fall silent.*

FOURTH's *smile has disappeared. Sitting on the table, he is now lackadaisically fiddling with a pile of business cards. A young woman assistant walks onstage.)*

YOUNG WOMAN: Fourth . . . *(She notices he's glaring at her, and hurries to adopt a different tone.)* Chief Manager Zhang, Manager Wu is looking for you.

FOURTH: *(Disapprovingly)* Tell him I'm not in!

YOUNG WOMAN: Uhh, you can't afford to offend a man like him. . . . *(FOREMAN WU comes onstage. He is much older and plumper than before.)*

FOREMAN WU: Fourth, don't burn your bridges once you've crossed them.

FOURTH: *(Pretending to be happy to see WU)* Please, have a seat, Old Wu. *(To his young woman assistant)* Brew Manager Wu a cup of coffee.

FOREMAN WU: I'm not used to drinking that stuff.

(The young woman leaves the stage.)

FOREMAN WU: So you've had your own business card printed? It's quite the fashion these days!

FOURTH: It's also just convenient.

FOREMAN WU: You're a chap who really keeps up with fashion.

FOURTH: No better than you.

FOREMAN WU: You shell out seventy or eighty thousand yuan and get two or three hundred thousand back; you're pretty good at settling these little accounts.[20]

FOURTH: How could I get that much? You've overpraised me.

FOREMAN WU: Don't be modest. However, this latest trick is a bit too mean. How could you snatch the meat out of my bowl like that?

FOURTH: *(Pretending to be shocked)* Is that so?

FOREMAN WU: You know all about it.

FOURTH: There's nothing out of line in this deal—

FOREMAN WU: We higher-ups don't bear grudges against underlings for their mistakes. As for me, I can retreat a step. Let's also get a merger going that links our two firms together—

FOURTH: A merger?

FOREMAN WU: A merger.

FOURTH: Let's handle things this way: I've got another job in my hands now—I'll give it to you.

FOREMAN WU: What job?

FOURTH: The Xinlitun Brick Kiln. Lots of money to rake in there.

FOREMAN WU: *(Cunningly)* That's mighty kindhearted of you. But it'd be better if you'd just hold on to that job for yourself. Let's merge; there's lots of room for negotiating the details.

FOURTH: (*Changing the subject*) Have you set the date for your daughter's marriage? I've already gotten together a lot of wedding presents—don't drop me off your list.

FOREMAN WU: Don't be uncompromising.

FOURTH: (*Speaking in the direction of the curtain at side stage*) Miss Qi, call a taxi for Manager Wu.

FOREMAN WU: (*With a cold smile*) All right, young fellow, all right.

FOURTH: When we start work on the big television station building tomorrow, please, do stop by to enjoy the hustle and bustle.

FOREMAN WU: (*Pityingly, with sinister overtones*) Such good things couldn't descend on me.

(*The stage lights go dark.*

The rhythmic chirps of a cricket emerge from the darkness. The lights come on inside a new building that is not quite completed.)

ERQIN: A cricket.

QIUZI: Where is it?

ERQIN: Here, here—

QIUZI: I've caught it.

ERQIN: Put it in the little box.

QIUZI: Take a guess—is this little cricket male or female?

ERQIN: I don't know.

QIUZI: I know. It's a female.

ERQIN: How do you know?

QIUZI: Because it was chirping. Do you know why it was chirping?

ERQIN: It got hungry.

QIUZI: No, it was looking for a mate.

ERQIN: (*Jokingly*) That's just your wickedness coming out.

QIUZI: (*Seriously*) It's what my mother told me: whenever crickets chirp, they're looking for a mate.

ERQIN: (*Letting the cricket go*) Better go look for your mate. (*Sighing*) It's freer than people are. (*She walks onto the balcony, and looks far out into the distance.*)

QIUZI: Actually, people are freer than it is. Snatched up in our hand, it dies if we make it die, and lives if we let it live. Right? (*Noticing that* ERQIN *didn't reply, he follows her out to the balcony.*) What are you looking at?

ERQIN: The little two-story house where Fourth's family lives.

QIUZI: Next week, somebody else will be moving in there. His wife is lucky.

ERQIN: One person more dead than the next—

QIUZI: One person more alive than the next. *(Brimming with a manly air)* On the very day I strike it rich, I'll buy you a big apartment building. We'll live in a suite on the top floor, just right for gazing out over the entire world.

ERQIN: *(Sighing)* If I found my match for life, I'd be just as happy living with him in a cold and broken-down hovel.

QIUZI: How could I make you live in a cold, broken-down hovel? We're surely going to have a big house of our own.

ERQIN: All right, just don't get carried away with those promises of yours. I don't care about size. Living in a little bungalow would be even better.

QIUZI: Right, a bungalow would actually be better. We'd be spared the trouble of going up and down the stairs everyday. We'll buy a piece of land and build a spacious bungalow on it.

ERQIN: Can land be bought that easily?

QIUZI: We'll look up Fourth; he'll know a way to do it.

ERQIN: *(In an unnatural tone)* Don't go looking him up . . .

QIUZI: He's been quite nice to you, and could show a little respect for our feelings.

ERQIN: If you dare go behind my back to ask him for a favor—

QIUZI: Don't get angry—

ERQIN: Listen to me: don't ask him for a favor.

QIUZI: He's got broader experience in handling matters than we do—

ERQIN: *(Uncompromisingly)* If we can't afford to do things on our own, let's just not do anything.

QIUZI: Okay, okay, we won't rely on the gods and the emperor, we'll only rely on ourselves to care of ourselves.

ERQIN: *(Her mind now at ease)* Now you're on the right track.

QIUZI: Let's go back home during winter this year and handle the arrangements for our marriage first.

ERQIN: *(Intentionally changing the subject)* Let's first get our house set up; it needn't be too large. We'll plant some vegetables and flowers in the courtyard.

QIUZI: Fine with me . . . *(Taking up the thread of the conversation where he'd left it)* My mother's long yearned for me to get married. She's bound to be happy when she sees you.

ERQIN: We'll raise a few chickens, and once we've fattened up a rooster, we'll have fresh meat on our table—

QIUZI: My mother's saved several bolts of fine cloth for my wedding, and whenever she recalls it, she takes them out and looks them over. Once this job's completed, let's go. We can first register our marriage with the government—

ERQIN: I like bunny rabbits; I'll raise a few of the kind with thick fur—

QIUZI: I'm talking with you about the arrangements for our marriage! Don't interrupt me.

ERQIN: *(Uneasy once again)* Why must we go back?

QIUZI: Of course we have to go back; this is an important matter.

ERQIN: If we didn't register with the government, we'd still be married all the same.

QIUZI: That'd be illegal.

ERQIN: When you came pioneering out here, where were all those rules you're talking about?

QIUZI: You don't want to go back home? (ERQIN *remains silent.*) Why's that? You don't get letters from back home, either.

ERQIN: *(Disapprovingly)* Do I have to tell you whenever I get a letter?

QIUZI: Marriage is an important thing you always have to tell your relatives about.

ERQIN: As soon as youths reach the age of eighteen, they gain the full rights of citizenship and the right to make decisions on their own. What's the need for talking things over with the family?

QIUZI: The important matter of marriage—

ERQIN: This is one's own important matter, not the parents' important matter. If you're afraid that doing things this way would mean our marriage isn't a sure thing, then go back home and find someone who can give that to you. Find a young woman whose family has all the works: father and mother, lots of sisters elder and younger, family rules, a family genealogy, along with three go-betweens and six official certificates. . . . And on top of that, get an insurance company to insure your marriage for a fifty-year term—

QIUZI: Egad, you're making it seem as though I can't make any decisions on my own. I've ventured all over the country on my own, and there hasn't been anything that I couldn't pick up or put back down. It's just that I'm left following your wishes on everything—

ERQIN: If we can make decisions on our own, then let's not always be going back home to ask for permission.

QIUZI: Of course we can decide things on our own, but—

ERQIN: Later—let's talk about this later on.

QIUZI: If you really are unwilling—

ERQIN: Let's first get set up in a house—

QIUZI: Okay, I'll ask Fourth—

ERQIN: *(Flaring with indignation)* If you look him up, I'll leave you and go far away!

QIUZI: Why is it that as soon as I mention Fourth, you—

ERQIN: *(Apologetically)* Don't take it to heart; it's just that I don't want to ask favors of other people.

QIUZI: When it comes to falling out with somebody, you fall out right away, just like a child. You blow cold one moment, hot the next. When cold, you're like a chunk of ice; when hot, you're like a red-hot stove.

ERQIN: Qiuzi, don't take me to task. I don't know why, but when I'm with the rest of the group, I defer to them on everything. Whether they're old or young, I neither argue with them nor question something they've done. When I'm with you, I always want to vent some of my anger; but once I've finished blowing off some steam, I also regret having done it in the first place.

QIUZI: *(With sincerity)* I'm willing to see you lose your temper like a spoiled little sister. I'm willing to provoke you to tears, and then cajole you back to laughter. Ever since I first saw you, I've felt that to go on living was meaningful after all. I wish we would now both become children again. *(He becomes intoxicated with his own fantasies.)* I'd lead you outside of the village to play, and when you'd get tired, I'd carry you on my back. When you'd cry, I'd humor you. We'd make ourselves a bed on the ground out of flowers and weeds, and play house. You'd be the mama, and I'd be the papa—but who'd be our child?

ERQIN: *(Recalling those long-lost years, and speaking as if in a dream)* A little white rabbit. I'd swaddle him in colorful clothing. You'd say he's gotten sick, and has to be given a shot. He'd die, and I'd cry. I'd scold you on that occasion—

QIUZI: I wouldn't get angry, but humor you instead.

ERQIN: You'd humor me. You'd steal one of your family's rabbits and give it to me. Your father would give you a spanking for that. You'd tell him that you'd lost the rabbit.

QIUZI: My mother'd never give me a spanking—

ERQIN: Those days were really fine—we were happy and free, without a care in the world. *(Impulsively)* Let's get married! I'll spend my life managing our household. I won't become a burden to you, or slow you down in your career. I'll take good care of you, and make you happy as can be. We'll get along fine, and I'll also bear a little son—a smart son, a healthy and sturdy son. Fourth—

QIUZI: *(Quizzically)* Erqin?

ERQIN: *(Awakening to her gaffe)* I'll bear—I'll bear you four children, no fewer than in a family headed by an official. *(Before she realizes it, tears have begun to roll down her cheeks.)*

QIUZI: *(Heaving a long sigh)* She still longs for him.

> *(The stage lights go dark.*
>
> On a street. FOURTH *is leaning against a utility pole while smoking.* QIUZI *and* ERQIN *are walking by, when they notice* FOURTH *standing there. They awkwardly come to a halt in front of* FOURTH.*)*

QIUZI: Oh—it's Fourth.

FOURTH: I was just saying I couldn't find you.

QIUZI: This is a day off—

FOURTH: Tomorrow, take thirty workers to the Huaxing Store for indoor construction work.

QIUZI: Okay. *(Turning to* ERQIN*)* Let's go.

FOURTH: Erqin—wait a minute.

> *(*QIUZI *looks at* ERQIN *with a hesitant expression on his face.)*

ERQIN: You'd better go on ahead.

> *(*QIUZI *reluctantly leaves.)*

ERQIN: *(Turns back to* FOURTH*)* So what's up? *(*FOURTH *is staring at* ERQIN, *and during an awkward silence shows no sign of replying. Afraid of being found out,* ERQIN *continues talking.)* You got featured in the newspaper again. There was even a photo of you this time.

FOURTH: What have you two been getting up to?

ERQIN: We were taking a stroll.

FOURTH: You run up seven flights of stairs when taking a stroll?

ERQIN: *(In a confrontational tone)* You mean you don't permit it?

> *(Both are silent for a while.)*

FOURTH: If he dares lay a hand on you, I'll butcher him!

ERQIN: *(Sarcastically)* Are you jealous?

FOURTH: Me? Jealous of him? He's not even in my league!

ERQIN: Well, I got jealous a long time ago. *(She turns to walk away.)*

FOURTH: Don't leave.

ERQIN: Is something up?

FOURTH: I'd like to talk for a while.

ERQIN: What's there to say? *(Both fall silent again.)*

FOURTH: *(Choked up with emotion)* Is he really . . . behaving himself properly?

ERQIN: What would you like to know?

FOURTH: I'd like to know everything.

ERQIN: Then I'll tell you. He now does everything that a man can do. He likes me, loves me, kisses me, and hugs me. We watch movies and go to the park together.

FOURTH: *(Anxiously pressing for more)* And what else?

ERQIN: *(Intentionally hardening her features into an expression of contempt)* We sleep together.

FOURTH: *(Raises his hand and slaps* ERQIN *across the face)* That bastard! How could you hitch up with him?

ERQIN: What gives you the right to slap me?

FOURTH: It's because of my feelings!

ERQIN: Your feelings! Did you ever stop to think for a moment about *my* feelings? *(With indifference, as if discussing someone else's affairs)* A woman can't always be left solitary and alone. She needs someone to listen to what she says. She needs a broad chest to lean on. She needs a little house that keeps out rain in summer and blocks the wind in winter. She needs a warm family life. She needs to be a wife and a mother. . . . You could have given me all of these things, but you haven't given me any of them at all. You tossed me aside to slowly wither away. If I had died, then that would have solved a lot of your problems. But I just wouldn't die, and kept living on this way, muddling along halfway between life and death. What was the use of all this, anyway? I'm already twenty-eight. When a person passes the age of thirty, it's like the sun advancing beyond its noon apogee. I couldn't throw away this precious time on mere waiting. But you had your wife and your son, and would be interviewed on the radio and be written about in the newspaper. Did you ever consider things on my behalf? I spent five years with the lunatic, and yearned each and every day for you to come back and redeem me from service. When I got pregnant, I secretly arranged for it to end in a miscarriage, all for the sake of my coming marriage to you. Their whole family beat me for it, and really harshly. I tried to run away again and again before finally succeeding on the fifth attempt. But you went and got yourself married to someone else. If you could have given me your child from another marriage, I'd have still brought him up like a child of my own, and could have taken care of him for the rest of my life. It would've been best if he had been a son, especially a son who looked like you. I would have raised him properly, seeing to it that someday his prospects would have been as bright as his father's. It's too bad I'd been waiting all for nothing—all for nothing.

FOURTH: *(Embraces* ERQIN*)* Erqin—

ERQIN: You were afraid I'd ruin your great enterprise. You feared that I'd cling to you so tightly that you wouldn't be able to shake me off afterward—

FOURTH: No! No—

ERQIN: If only I'd been her, how good things would have been.

FOURTH: *(With sincerity)* I've been too selfish. But if I hadn't been that way, how could I have managed to be where I am now? I wanted to succeed, and that meant I had to exert myself ten times harder than other people. The only way I could move forward a bit faster was to borrow some authority from others. I didn't dare overlook the slightest thing that might help, and was always extremely careful, to the point of often trembling with fear and anxiety. I was groping my way along submerged rocks to cross the river.[21] I couldn't just do whatever I felt like; if I had, all I'd worked for would have come to nothing. Instead, I've now got what I've worked for. What others don't have, I've got.

ERQIN: You could also have even more. I know you're fond of me— that I've still got a place in your heart. I wish I hated you, but I can't. Each day, I dreamed of you and you alone. You were so far away, and no matter how I tried, I couldn't reach you. . . . I had the same dream every day. . . . Let's go away! Let's go to another city, just the two of us. What's between Qiuzi and me really amounts to nothing at all. Living by yourself is too lonely; I'm afraid of loneliness. I don't want to feel all empty inside; there has to be somebody in my heart before I can feel there's an anchor in my life. Even though you don't much like him, I brought him into the act. . . . Let's go away! As long as we're together, I can endure any hardship we might face. Let's start a family, a warm and loving family. . . .

(Having been touched by the feelings ERQIN *has expressed,* FOURTH *embraces her tightly. After the heat of passion ebbs, he again sobers up.)*

FOURTH: You've gotten cold. You've been shivering constantly.

ERQIN: I'm not cold.

FOURTH: *(Taking off his jacket)* Here, put this on.

ERQIN: Are we leaving?

FOURTH: I'll see you off.

ERQIN: So, you're unwilling?

FOURTH: Your ideas for handling all this are too simple.

ERQIN: *(With disappointment)* You just can't do without those new buildings.

FOURTH: There are over a hundred workers involved!

ERQIN: *(Sarcastically)* Over a hundred workers—what a kindhearted fellow you are! You can't do without anybody you know except for me. The way things look, I should get married.

FOURTH: You didn't get divorced. If you get married again, you'll be committing bigamy.

ERQIN: It's been several years since I've been with the lunatic. Could we still be considered husband and wife after all that time has passed?

FOURTH: You'd better think it over carefully—

ERQIN: Seeking you out was hopeless from the start—

FOURTH: I'll set you up with a guy from the city—

ERQIN: Qiuzi loves me—that's enough. I can love him—I can. . . .
    (She prepares to depart.)

FOURTH: I'll see you off.

ERQIN: No, I'll go by myself. *(Exits)*

FOURTH: *(Dumbfounded,* FOURTH *watches as* ERQIN *leaves.)* She's gone away. She's gone away to be with Qiuzi. *(He looks around in a circle.)* That—that year, it was right here where I took back the money I'd earned with my sweat and toil. And today it's again here where I've been robbed by somebody else—
    (A car horn honks, and the young woman assistant comes onstage.)

YOUNG WOMAN: Chief Manager Zhang—

FOURTH: *(Dementedly)* Don't keep following me around all the time!

YOUNG WOMAN: Your relative is looking for you. *(Feeling wronged)* If he hadn't said he was your relative, I wouldn't have bothered. . . .

FOURTH: My relative?

YOUNG WOMAN: (*Speaking in the direction of the curtain at one side of the stage*) Come on over!

(SEVENTH UNCLE *hobbles onstage carrying his baggage. By this time, he has become very old and decrepit.*)

FOURTH: Seventh Uncle?

SEVENTH UNCLE: Fourth . . .

(*The stage lights go dark.*

In a room, FOURTH *dumps all of the contents of his desk drawer onto the desk, and starts copying information from various slips of paper into his little notebook.* FOREMAN WU *comes onstage; he is grinning to himself, and quietly chuckling with an air of schadenfreude. Coming up behind* FOURTH, *he grabs the latter's notebook and starts to read it.* FOURTH *is greatly startled and grabs the notebook back.*)

FOURTH: Why, you cat, you! I didn't hear a peep out of you just now!

FOREMAN WU: I was afraid I'd startle you.

FOURTH: Don't give me that crap.

FOREMAN WU: (*Flipping through the newspapers on* FOURTH's *desk*) "Young Farmer Turned Entrepreneur" . . . So, you've kept all these newspapers that mention you, eh? That's fine; keep all of them. Looking them over now and then can banish your worries and cares. Better yet, hire somebody to write some reportage fiction about you. That gimmick'll give you more of a thrill than just some newspaper article—

FOURTH: Shut up!

FOREMAN WU: Your salad days are over, as it turns out. In return for what you've done, getting sent to prison or the execution ground wouldn't be too severe.

FOURTH: Get the hell out of here!

FOREMAN WU: Don't be blind to a favor when someone's dangling it right in front of your nose. I've taken advantage of the circumstance of your still being here to come pay you a visit. Once you've reached the place where you're headed, if I were going to see you again, it'd have to be a prison visit.

FOURTH: So you've come to visit me just for the fun of it? I haven't done a damned thing that's a capital offense!

FOREMAN WU: There's more than one way of looking at that. Everything depends on whether your case is in sync with the rhythm of a government crackdown. If it is, then I suppose you'll take that death-row paddy wagon to your final destination.[22]

FOURTH: *(With a sneering chuckle)* From the looks of all this, you've gone to a lot of trouble on my behalf!

FOREMAN WU: Don't mention it. After all, the two of us have been friends for over ten years now. When thinking back over the long spell when we were in cahoots with each other, you could say that we cooperated pretty well. *(Discovering that there is half a bottle of wine on the table, WU takes out two glasses and divvies up the remaining wine.)* Come on, let me help you get over the shock.

FOURTH: *(Takes a swig of the wine)* Why've you come here?

FOREMAN WU: How could I be fooled by any of this? *(He pulls a newspaper out of his pocket and reads a headline.)* "Take Severe Action against All Who Give or Take Bribes; Rectify Party Discipline and National Law." This is the beginning of the big squeeze. Say, when'll you appear on the witness stand?

FOURTH: You're really in the know about the latest news.

FOREMAN WU: This isn't out of concern for you.

FOURTH: Uhh, it's at one o'clock tomorrow afternoon.

FOREMAN WU: I long ago urged you to take a bit lower profile. And suppose you got mixed up in a big wrangle at some point? You could suddenly worm your way out of the problem on the sly without anybody being the wiser for it, and keep it a secret from all and sundry. But a great one you were, never knowing when enough was enough. What was the use of all that chasing after empty fame? You got in the papers and in the news broadcasts, not even bothering to calculate how a migrant rover would be expected to—

FOURTH: *(Douses WU's face with the wine left in his glass)* Your ancestors were migrant rovers!

FOREMAN WU: *(Wiping his face dry)* I know how bad you feel.

FOURTH: I've got a city household registration card.

FOREMAN WU: That's just something you bought. As soon as it comes under investigation, it won't be of any more use to you. Even paper can feel too rough when you're wiping your arse with it.

FOURTH: Really?

FOREMAN WU: Who knows? The government's policies are always changing. And I really sympathize with you, regardless of how you almost killed me that year.

FOURTH: It was you who almost killed me!

FOREMAN WU: You've still got my sympathy. Where's the guy who doesn't vie with others for a better future? Who doesn't compete to rise head and shoulders above the others? To tell you the truth, it doesn't matter that I earn even more than a provincial governor; if one of them would trade places with me and let me be a cadre for a few days, I wouldn't hesitate switching with him. This is what's known as social position. But when it comes to people like us, we're at best referred to as engineering project tradesmen, and at worst called evil work-gang foremen. Fourth, you could be considered pretty good in our line of work, and your prospects were brighter than mine. Naturally, I still sympathize with you—

FOURTH: What did you come here for, anyway?

FOREMAN WU: What have you got written down in that little notebook?

FOURTH: You meddle too much in other people's business.

FOREMAN WU: Is all that going to be revealed tomorrow?

FOURTH: It doesn't have anything to do with you.

FOREMAN WU: Why bother with all that? The credit for what you've achieved up to now should go to others.

FOURTH: Bullshit! Back when I was a pauper, who knew who I was? Didn't they also call me a migrant rover? And what's this about "credit"? I bought that with my own money. If I go to prison, nobody else who's involved should imagine he'll get out of it; everybody can join me in sampling the flavor of squatting in a prison cell.

FOREMAN WU: Do you know who told me to come here?

FOURTH: Even if the national leader himself told you to come, I wouldn't defer to him.

FOREMAN WU: Shouldn't you consider the future? There'll be time to recoup your losses; why make a show of reckless courage? Director Zhao has a message for you: if you're careful about what you say in the docket, he'll find someone to come up with a way of turning your major problems into minor difficulties, and then make the minor difficulties come to naught. If you want this to happen someday, you've got to depend on others.

FOURTH: You came here to intimidate me!

FOREMAN WU: Don't put it like that. Lashing out wildly won't be of any help to you.

FOURTH: Don't play the part of my good private counselor. I'm not at all some damned official or party member. I can't rise up to those heights, just as I couldn't that year I came here bare-handed and broke. To hell with those "master" officials all sitting together! I won't swallow the crap they throw my way! Let me tell you, I'm writing everything down, one stroke at a time!

FOREMAN WU: The public security organs are run by people. Don't forget that officials protect one another.

FOURTH: If they've committed an offense, it's hard to imagine how they'd get off just like that.

FOREMAN WU: I'm doing this for your own good.

FOURTH: I should have killed you at the very beginning!

FOREMAN WU: If you'd done that, you wouldn't have come so far as you are today. Don't forget that I was the one who helped you take your first big step on your upward path.

FOURTH: And you're also the one who's buried me!

FOREMAN WU: Don't blame the kitchen god whenever you have a little stomachache. Remember: say what has to be said, but be careful not to say what shouldn't be said. Keep your future options open.

FOURTH: Get out!

FOREMAN WU: Good-bye. Don't forget to appear in court tomorrow. *(Exits)*

(FOURTH stands blankly in the middle of the stage. ROOTSY comes onstage and walks up to him.)

ROOTSY: Fourth—

FOURTH: What is it?

ROOTSY: Erqin's getting married to Qiuzi tomorrow; Seventh Uncle's asking whether you're going or not.

FOURTH: "Getting married"?

(The stage lights go dark.

It's morning in the work shed, which is imbued with an atmosphere of celebration and joy. Candy and melon seeds have been placed on the tables. People are laughing and boisterous. The only one who isn't is the apron-clad SEVENTH UNCLE, who's sitting by the doorway peeling radishes with a knife. ERQIN grabs a piece of candy and brings it over to SEVENTH UNCLE.)

ERQIN: Seventh Uncle, have a piece of candy.

SEVENTH UNCLE: I'm—I'm afraid it's not quite proper for me to eat any of this wedding candy. From your family's standpoint, I'm your father's brother; and from his family's perspective, he should also consider me his uncle. If I'm called on to serve as the elder in this ceremony, then—

ERQIN: Seventh Uncle, are you saying that I'm doing the wrong thing in getting married? If I'd been your daughter, could you have been hardhearted enough to marry me off to the lunatic?

SEVENTH UNCLE: Fate is something everybody has to consider—

ERQIN: I don't believe it! Besides, Qiuzi's a good man—

SEVENTH UNCLE: True enough. However, Fourth—

ERQIN: Don't bring him into this!

SEVENTH UNCLE: Well, you still have to tell the elders in both families about this first—

ERQIN: They long ago made all the arrangements for the rest of my life. If I'd followed everything they said, I wouldn't be where I am today.

SEVENTH UNCLE: Does Qiuzi know about that situation?

ERQIN: I've told him.

SEVENTH UNCLE: (*Pauses for a moment*) Actually, I don't observe any taboos at all, it's just that I'm afraid you'll lose out in the end. Qiuzi, come over here. (QIUZI *walks over to them.*) Now listen, I'm putting Erqin under your care. If she suffers any mishaps, I won't show you any mercy.

QIUZI: I'll take good care of her for sure.

SEVENTH UNCLE: How'll you handle that problem with the family back home?

QIUZI: As soon as time permits, I'll take Erqin back there and haul them into court with a lawsuit based on the Marriage Law.[23]

SEVENTH UNCLE: Good heavens, you've left your Seventh Uncle speechless!

RICHIE: Erqin, listen to what your elder cousin has to tell you: I want you to come back often and visit us! What's more, if Qiuzi bullies you—

ROOTSY: Then we'll all give him a thrashing!
(*Everybody laughs.*)

RICHIE: Time for the two of you to sing a song. Bad enough that there's no wine—can we do without a song?

ERQIN: I can't sing well.

QIUZI: This isn't any contest between celebrity singers. Let's just sing.
(QIUZI *starts playing a harmonica.*)
ERQIN: In that case, let's sing "Off to the Northeast."
(*The song begins:*)
"March brings red to the blossoms of the peach,
As Sister follows Brother to the far Northeast.
Sip the local brew before you start on your route,
For a myriad *li* we'll be traveling as a group.
There's dusty windstorms, rain north of the Pass,[24]
The path there's merciless, yet somehow there's mercy.
Aiyoyo—It's all for the sake of a better day to come."
(*Everybody joins in with a refrain of the last two lines:*
"Aiyoyo—It's all for the sake of a better day to come."
        FOURTH *comes onstage. The others all stand up, and the atmosphere turns tense at once.*)
ROOTSY: (*Pulling a bench over and wiping it clean with his sleeve*)
Have a seat, Fourth.
FOURTH: (*Lighting a cigarette, standing with one foot propped on the bench*) You'd hold an important event like this, and not even prepare a couple of banquet tables?
ELDEST BROTHER: (*With an air of authority as the elder*) Qiuzi wanted to set up tables for a banquet, but the rest of us wouldn't let him. By being a little more thrifty, they'll have more money to spend on family things.
FOURTH: Erqin, did you after all—
RICHIE: (*Breaking through the circle of men around* FOURTH *and holding out a few newspapers for* FOURTH *to see*) Fourth, these papers have written all about what you've done; I've read them several times over already. I bought more than ten of them! Once we mail them back to the old village for all the guys there to read—
FOURTH: (*Grabs the newspapers and rips them to shreds*) If anybody else mentions this goddamn crap again— (*Everyone is shocked*)
FOURTH: (*In a warm manner*) Where are they living now?
ELDEST BROTHER: They've rented a little house; all of us have been fixing it up.
FOURTH: (*Indignantly*) What's the matter, Qiuzi—cat got your tongue?

QIUZI: *(Calmly)* Today is my special day, and I want all the guys to have a good time. I don't intend to offend anyone, but if someone offends me—

ERQIN: *(Cutting him off)* Qiuzi. *(Turning to* FOURTH*)* Fourth, it's been five years since I've come out here, and you haven't skimped in helping me all that time. Qiuzi and I would like to thank you for all you've done. I actually should have gone in person to invite you here, but I was afraid I'd delay your important business. If you're not cold-shouldering us, then have a piece of candy, and we can just consider this . . . a reunion of old hometown friends.

FOURTH: *(With a wry smile)* I should have told you sooner that I'd prepared you some wedding presents, and didn't want outsiders to laugh at my old family for not having attended your ceremony. . . . Qiuzi, do treat this sister of mine properly.

QIUZI: I will.

(Everybody lets out a sigh of relief. FOURTH *then takes a wad of bills out of his money purse.)*

FOURTH: Here are the wages for this job. *(He divvies up the money for everybody. As they all count their pay, they become dumbfounded with surprise.)*

ELDEST BROTHER: Fourth, our pay's too much this time.

RICHIE: He's given us our bonuses.

QIUZI: My pay's two hundred more than it's supposed to be! What's going on?

FOURTH: Just take however much I've given you.

QIUZI: If our pay's a penny short, we'll stop working; but if it's a dime too high, we need to ask for an explanation.

FOURTH: For your next job . . . you'll be merged with the Sixth Construction Brigade of the Number Five Municipal Construction Company, and will go to Guangzhou to build a hotel.

ELDEST BROTHER: Guangzhou?

FOURTH: The job'll take a year to complete.

(The workers first whisper to one another, and then start shouting and jumping for joy.)

FOURTH: Seventh Uncle, I've found you a place in the city where you can work as a gatekeeper, so you needn't go with them.

(Turning to QIUZI*)* Qiuzi, you'll be the group leader.

QIUZI: Me? Then how about you?

FOURTH: What did I go hire you for, anyway?!
(Everyone falls silent for a moment.)
SEVENTH UNCLE: Four chances out of five it's because—
FOURTH: This group has stayed together for ten years; we couldn't be
subdued, and we couldn't be split up. Eldest Brother's skilled at
staying on good terms with everybody, but he's a bit naïve, and
will eventually be too timid to venture where the group needs to
go. . . . Qiuzi—you're better at strategizing than the others. I'm
just asking you to do it this one time. . . .
QIUZI: What's gone wrong?
FOURTH: *(Glancing at his watch)* I've been summoned for trial. I'm
appearing in court at one in the afternoon.
(Everyone is stunned by the news.)
SEVENTH UNCLE: *(After a pause)* I told you there was something not
quite right about all this!
ELDEST BROTHER: Have you been accused by somebody?
SEVENTH UNCLE: Better think of some trick to have up your sleeve!
Any good move you might make?
RICHIE: Could they sentence you to jail?
FOURTH: It's not certain.
ERQIN: It won't be anything major. Maybe they made a mistake—
FOURTH: I'll be okay. I'm just afraid that our group won't have a
backbone anymore, and will have to roll on back where we came
from. . . . Qiuzi . . .
(Everyone stares at QIUZI.)
QIUZI: Erqin—will you wait for me?
ERQIN: *(Pauses for a moment)* Here I go again with waiting.
QIUZI: It's only one year. . . .
ERQIN: Well . . . go on, then.
QIUZI: As long as the group has faith in me!
(Voices in the crowd: "We've got faith in you!" "Just handle things!")
QIUZI: When do we leave?
FOURTH: Three days from now. The train tickets have already been
reserved. *(Hands QIUZI a slip of paper)* Go to the company and
ask for Manager Li.
QIUZI: Okay, it's all clear.
FOURTH: *(Takes out a wad of money)* Originally, I should have bought
you some wedding presents, but I didn't have the time. Take this
and buy her something rare and fine for me.

QIUZI: That wouldn't do! You'll still need money to handle your
   problems—
FOURTH: *(Fiercely)* You looking down on me already? You don't dare
   spend it? I haven't been executed yet!
QIUZI: Fourth—
ERQIN: *(To QIUZI)* Better take it. *(Turning to FOURTH)* Fourth, when
   you're thrashing through your problems, don't lose your temper.
   When you're in the courtroom, just say whatever you're supposed
   to say. Whether the criminal charges are major or minor, we'll
   all be waiting for you after it's all over. Even if the charges are
   true—once you get out of jail, you'll still be the same person
   we've always known.
ELDEST BROTHER: If you need money, we'll all scrape it together
   somehow. If you need witnesses, we're ready to go testify!
RICHIE: Who caused this trouble for you? I'll ransack his house!
SEVENTH UNCLE: As the saying goes, "As long as the green mountains
   remain, there's no need to worry about firewood." Fourth, keep
   your head up and your back straight; don't lose your courage!
FOURTH: *(With tears falling)* I apologize to you all. That year when
   we came up here, Seventh Uncle said that north of the Great
   Pass, there was treasure. I threw my life to the winds in search of
   treasure. Actually, I'd long had a treasure without knowing it. . . .
   I don't know when I lost it. . . . It's lost now, and I won't ever get
   it back again. . . .
   *(The others silently listen to him, and at this point the sound of
   twelve chimes of the clock reaches them from afar. The stage lights
   go dark.*
      A male vocalist sings:
   "In the year's first month and the month's first day,
   I ride up through the Pass on the Northeast railway,
   With a bundle of baggage and a pair of hands.
   The train's metal bones clang onward all the way.
   There's dusty windstorms, rain north of the Pass,
   But let me travel through this broad northern land.
   Aiyoyo—It's all for the sake of a better day to come."
   During the singing, FOURTH *stands at the front of the stage. He
   raises his head, as if he has entered some kind of fantasy realm. In a
   remote part of the stage, far to the back, a red sun begins to ascend.*

Joining in with the refrain at the end of the song, the group of migrants walks toward the back of the stage in the direction of the sun. The curtain slowly descends, marking the end of the play.)

NOTES

This translation is based on *Duoyu de xiatian* (A rainy summer), first published in *Juzuo jia* (Playwright) 3 (1989): 4–27.

1. Qiqihar is a couple of hundred kilometers northwest of Harbin, the largest city and provincial capital of the far northern Heilongjiang province. One of the northernmost stops of Heilongjiang's major trunk railway line to the south, Qiqihar is something of a gateway to the Great Northern Wilderness (*Beidahuang*) that spreads for a vast expanse up to the border with Russia. While there are many towns and villages north of Qiqihar, it could be considered China's northernmost bona fide city.

2. Like its North American counterpart, the Asiatic black bear is surprisingly timid and easily frightened for such a large and powerful animal. Calling someone a "bear" is equivalent to scorning him as a coward.

3. *Da Qian Men*, the brand name of an above-average PRC cigarette, refers to the ornamental front city gate in central Beijing—one of the very few portions of the old Beijing city wall that was not torn down under Mao Zedong.

4. Fourth is referring to mythic literary characters like Sun Wukong, the Monkey King of Wu Cheng'en's great Ming novel *Journey to the West*. Sun Wukong has no parents or other family members, but emerges from a rock mass fully formed and energized.

5. The playwright uses a clever pun here. Wu curses Fourth as a *liumang*—a criminal vagrant or "hooligan." Fourth wittily replies that he's actually a *mangliu*—an illegal migrant or "roamer." The characters for *liu* are identical, while the characters for *mang* are different. See also Philip F. Williams, "Migrant Laborer Subcultures in Recent Chinese Literature: A Communicative Perspective," *Intercultural Communication Studies* 8, 2 (1998–1999): 153–161.

6. Richie expresses his sarcasm through a fairy-tale nursery rhyme.

7. "Carrying out the cooking stove" refers to one of two possible situations: (a) carrying the most essential household item out of a house, i.e., moving out of a residence once and for all; or (b) getting embroiled in a fierce argument (*qihong*). The second usage is an idiom common in Shandong and thus more likely; but in either case, Seventh Uncle is angrily predicting failure for the work group under Fourth's new leadership.

8. "Grappling over who gets a funeral cap" refers to an unscrupulous person who tries to curry favor with someone whose relative has died by vying with others to put on the best possible show of mourning for the deceased. Because a very limited number of mourning caps are provided at the typical funeral, they can easily become bones of contention among the hangers-on and hustlers in attendance.

9. Among the various expenditures associated with traditional funerals, "spirit money" (*huang zhi*) is one of the least expensive.

10. *Tale of the Vulture-Shooting Heroes (She diao yingxiong zhuan)* is a *wuxia xiaoshuo* (knight errantry novel).

11. Fourth uses a term of respect for an older woman, *Gu nainai* or "Auntie," when beseeching the saleswoman not to reveal herself, and thus their sexual relationship, to the person knocking on the door.

12. The White Bone Demon is an evil female spirit that preys upon unsuspecting men like the monk Tripitaka of the classic Ming novel *Xi you ji* [Journey to the West]. It is still current as a term of vilification, for Jiang Qing was often openly likened to the White Bone Demon after the palace coup that swept her from power subsequent to Mao Zedong's death in 1976.

13. Literally, *kaoshan shan dao, kao shui shui liu* (I depended on the mountain, but the mountain collapsed; I depended on the waters, but the waters flowed away). *Kaoshan* here refers to Erqin's key backer or supporter (i.e., Fourth), a point that could be missed by an overly literal rendering into English.

14. The "major affair of your whole life" *(zhongsheng dashi)* refers to arranging a marriage of permanence.

15. A ninth-century scholar-recluse, Lü Dongbin has been portrayed for centuries in Chinese art and literature as the quintessential old white-haired hermit. Zhang Gelao also represents an elderly man of the type to which Erqin likens the crestfallen Foreman Wu.

16. In premodern China, men wealthy enough to take a second wife or a concubine would commonly refer to this junior member within the family hierarchy as their *xiao laopo* or *yi taitai*, respectively. Though polygamy became illegal in twentieth-century China, some men have maintained this old practice in an informal way with a kept woman. Erqin resents even the jocular suggestion that she might be willing to share a husband with his senior or legal wife. Even though her comment is in reply to Foreman Wu's banter, she has implicitly directed her resentment at Fourth.

17. Urban residents especially prize their government-mandated household registration booklets, which give them many privileges denied rural Chinese residents, such as legal urban residence and subsidized prices for housing and various commodities.

18. This rhymed old saw roughly approximates the English saying, "Spare the rod and spoil the child." The suggestion is that if parents spoil a naughty child by neglecting to apply even mild disciplinary actions like scolding and spanking, then society as a whole will eventually apply much harsher punishments to that poorly socialized individual who has reached adulthood.

19. The sum of seventy thousand yuan was roughly equivalent to ten thousand dollars at the time of publication (1989).

20. *Suan zhang* or "settle accounts" can also mean "get revenge," and the obviously displeased Foreman Wu seems to have wanted to generate a double entendre with this term.

21. The phrase *mo shitou guo he*, or "groping one's way along submerged rocks to cross the river," has strong political overtones. Deng Xiaoping often used this phrase to justify the seemingly "experimental" use of market incentives in a one-party Leninist state that had long been hostile to capitalism in almost any form.

22. The original Chinese version is less explicit than the English rendering, but Foreman Wu implicitly makes the point that white-collar crimes can result in the most severe sentence of execution if a government crackdown coincides with the sentencing of a convict. The police vehicle alluded to is the one that conveys death-row inmates to the execution grounds on the outskirts of a city.

23. The Marriage Law, enacted soon after the Communist victory in the civil war of the late 1940s, stipulates that marriage is a consensual act for both parties; it thus rules out marital unions based on indentured servitude, as in Erqin's first marriage.

24. The Pass refers to the mountain passes separating China proper from the vast Manchurian Northeast. Shanhaiguan, where the Great Wall meets the seacoast, is a major landmark of this boundary.

NOTES ON PLAYWRIGHTS

He Jiping

Born in Beijing, in 1951, He Jiping was employed as a playwright in Beijing People's Art Theater after graduating from the department of dramatic literature at Central Drama College, in 1982. Her first play, entitled *Good Fortune Building (Haoyun dasha)*, completed in 1984, depicts the life experience and struggles of Hong Kong residents from different social classes and their search for happiness in a materialist society. Influenced by Lao She's *Teahouse*, she believes in delving into life to create realistic drama for common people. While writing *The World's Top Restaurant*, not only did she work with chefs and waiters in a Beijing duck restaurant to learn about their lifestyle and their stories, she also researched the history of Chinese cuisine to find inspiration from traditional Chinese culture. Her play belongs to the literary trend of the 1980s known as "seeking for roots" in the traditional and local cultures, for a rejuvenation of new culture—culinary art in old Beijing became for her a reservoir of aesthetic, philosophical, and psychological themes. It also addresses contemporary audiences' interest in the entrepreneurial spirit. Together with Lao She's *Teahouse*, He Jiping's *The World's Top Restaurant* holds an important place in the history of modern Chinese drama, with its depictions of people in the restaurant business, who were looked down on in traditional society. In 1989 He Jiping moved to Hong Kong, where she writes television drama scripts for the local audiences.

Liu Shugang

Born in Cixian, Hebei Province, in 1940, Liu Shugang developed a passion for literature and art in middle school, when he began to write drama scripts and edited school journals. He graduated from the acting department at Central Drama College and became an actor in Central Experimental Theater in 1962. He started writing drama scripts in 1965. He served as the president of Central Experimental Theater from 1988 to 1989. His training as an actor aided him in his later, more successful career as a playwright. Starting in the 1980s, he won recognition for his more than twenty film, stage drama, and television drama scripts. Among the best known is his play entitled *Investigations of Fifteen Cases of Divorce (Shiwuzhuang lihun'an de diaocha pooxi)*, premiered by Central Experimental Theater, in 1983. Combining a Brechtian technique of two narrators with a play-within-a-play structure, his script explored moral dilemmas of divorce in contemporary China, its social and ideological contexts, and its impact on children and family. After one hundred and fifty shows in Beijing, *Investigations of Fifteen Cases of Divorce* was performed by theaters in different cities in China and in Columbus, Ohio, in 1987. Its script won the Zhongshan Literature Award *(Zhongshan wenxue jiang)* in 1988. Similarly, *The Dead Visiting the Living* won the award for Best Drama Script in its third national competition (Disanjie quanguo youxiu juben chuangzuo jiang) and was performed in the Soviet Union in 1988 and in Singapore in 1991. In 1988 China Dramatic Art Research Association selected Liu Shugang as one of the ten best playwrights in contemporary China.

Sha Yexin

Born in 1939, into a Moslem family, Sha Yexin graduated from the Chinese department at Eastern China Teacher's College (Huadong Shifan Daxue), in 1961. After further studies in the training class of operatic script writing in Shanghai Opera School (Shanghai Xiqu Xueyuan), Sha became a professional scriptwriter in Shanghai People's Art Theater in 1963. Sha was appointed president of Shanghai People's Art Theater in 1985. Having published his first one-act play in 1965, Sha became one of the most important playwrights with the controversial performance of his play *If I Were for Real* (coauthored with Li Shoucheng and Yao Mingde) in 1979, a sophisticated, Brechtian play that critiques CCP corruption and the loss of idealism in early post-Maoist China. His 1983 play, *The Secret History of Marx (Makesi mishi)*, caused another critical debate on how to evaluate the life stories of Karl Marx, who was portrayed as an ordinary man with his own sorrows and unhappiness rather than an unwavering revolutionary leader of the Communist movement. His 1986 play, *In Search of a Good Man (Xunzhao nanzihan)*, staged the comic experience of a woman's quest for an ideal mate in contemporary China and her disappointment in several men lacking either masculine or spiritual qualities. The 1988 performance of his *Jesus, Confucius and the Beatle Lennon (Yesu, Kongzi, pitoushi Lienong)* presented another dimension of

Sha's dramatic talent. With a time span of thousands of years and an infinite space that transcends the boundaries of heaven and earth, Jesus, Confucius, and Lennon, dispatched by God to investigate problematic kingdoms on earth, engaged themselves in philosophical dialogues on Christianity, Confucianism, and modernist culture.

Yang Limin

Born in 1947, in Qiqihar, Heilongjiang Province, Yang Limin became an oil worker in Daqing oilfield after graduating from high school. He studied in the drama training class at Central Drama College in Beijing in 1974, and upon graduation, returned to Daqing to continue his creative writing. From 1987 to 1990 he was enrolled in the M.A. program of dramatic literature at Central Drama College. After completion of his M.A. degree, he was appointed deputy chief of the Cultural Bureau of Daqing City and began his professional drama writing career. His best-known plays include *Grand Snowy Land (Da xuedi)*, *Black Rose (Heise de meigui)*, *Grand Wilderness (Da huangyuan)*, and *A Couple in Crisis (Weiqing fufu)*. Having benefited from years of hardship as an ordinary worker in the Northeast, Yang's plays stand out with their unique local color and penetrating vision of life in the remote wilderness. Together with other playwrights from the same region, he helped pioneer a new genre known as the "Northeast drama" *(Dongbei xiju)*. He was selected by the China Dramatic Art Research Association as one of the ten best dramatists in contemporary China.

Zhang Lili

Born in 1956, in Sichuan Province, Zhang Lili joined the Singing and Dancing Ensemble of Guangzhou at age fourteen, first as a dancer, then as a typist, a librarian, and finally, as a scriptwriter. She started publishing drama scripts, short stories, prose, and reportage works in 1976. From 1984 to 1992 she completed five plays, including such well-received dramas as *Unequal Formula of Life (Rensheng budengshi); Mother, You Were Young Once Before (Mama, ni ye ceng nianqing); Homecoming (Gui qu lai)*; and *Green Barracks (Lüse yingdi)*. As a woman playwright Zhang Lili holds an important place in the history of contemporary Chinese drama for her sensitive and timely portrayals of the soldier's life. *Homecoming*, for instance, depicts the 1979 China-Vietnam border war, when both men and women were called on to sacrifice for the nation. Unlike the Maoist soldier plays, however, *Homecoming* does not present one-dimensional heroic soldiers, but their dreams and desires for personal happiness. It also bitterly criticizes the post-Maoist pursuit of economic success without spiritual fulfillment. Zhang's women's plays also won her national acclaim, as seen in her *Unequal Formula of Life*, which resulted in a national debate on love and marriage, spearheaded by *Women's Magazine (Funü zazhi)*, after its Beijing performances in 1985.

Zhang Mingyuan

Born in 1954, into a family of teachers in Heilongjiang Province, Zhang developed a passion for literature and art at an early age and published several pieces during the Cultural Revolution when she was a sent-down youth in the countryside. After graduating from the drama writing program at Art Academy of Heilongjiang Province, she was appointed as a professional playwright in Qiqihar City. Her first play, *Wild Grass*, won her immediate recognition in 1989, both in the Northeast and in Beijing. With her sensibility as a woman playwright, Zhang depicted, for the first time in the history of Chinese drama, the struggling lives of migrant workers, from the rural areas to the city, losing their traditional values when confronted with the challenges of modernity. Her second play, *Warm Winter (Nuandong)*, written in 1990, combined realist and expressionist traditions in depicting a family tragedy. It depicts the lonely life of a widow who runs a funeral shop to support her children. As the results of her obsessive love and suppression, her three children end up in unsuccessful marriages, quit college right before graduation, or carry out the tedious work of running the funeral shop after her death. *Warm Winter* won praise from drama critics and audiences for its psychological portrayals of everyday life. Some of her similar television dramas and radio plays won national prizes for their popular appeal.

NOTES ON EDITOR AND TRANSLATORS

Xiaomei Chen is associate professor of Chinese and comparative literature at Ohio State University. She received her Ph.D. in comparative literature at Indiana University, in 1989. She is author of *Occidentalism: A Theory of Counter-Discourse in Post-Mao China* (Oxford University Press, 1995; second, revised and expanded edition, Rowman and Littlefield, 2002) and *Acting the Right Part: Political Theater and Popular Drama in Contemporary China* (University of Hawai'i Press, 2002). She is coeditor, with Claire Sponsler, of *East of West: Cross-cultural Performance and the Staging of Differences* (Palgrave, 2000). She is currently working on a history of the dramatic culture from the late Qing to the Republican period and on a study of everyday life in Maoist China.

Kirk A. Denton is associate professor of modern Chinese literature at Ohio State University. He is author of *The Problematic of Self in Modern Chinese Literature: Hu Feng and Lu Ling* (Stanford University Press, 1998) and editor of *Modern Chinese Literary Thought: Writings on Literature, 1893–1945* (Stanford University Press, 1996). Denton is editor of the journal *Modern Chinese Literature and Culture* and manages the online MCLC (Modern Chinese Literature and Culture) Resource Center.

Edward M. Gunn is professor of Chinese literature and current chair of the department of Asian studies at Cornell University. He is the author of *Unwelcome Muse: Chinese Literature in Shanghai and Peking, 1937–1945* (Columbia University Press, 1981) and *Rewriting Chinese: Style and Innovation in*

Twentieth-Century Chinese Prose (Stanford University Press, 1991). He edited a volume of modern Chinese plays in translation, *Twentieth-Century Chinese Drama: An Anthology* (Indiana University Press, 1983), and has published translations, among them the novel *Backed against the Sea*, by Wang Wen-xing (Ithaca, N.Y.: East Asian Program, Cornell University, 1993). His more recent research focuses on the use of local, subnational languages in contemporary Chinese literature and media.

Yuanxi Ma is director of translation at China Practice Group of Baker & McKenzie International Law Firm, Chicago Office. She received her Ph.D. in American literature and comparative literature at State University of New York at Buffalo, in 1992. She has taught modern Chinese literature and Chinese women's studies at New York University, New School for Social Studies, and SUNY at Buffalo. Her research area is modern and contemporary Chinese women writers and various women's magazines in China. Publications include articles in both books and journals, such as "Self-Reinstating and Coming to 'Conscious Aloneness,'" in Sharon K. Hom, ed., *Chinese Women Traversing Diaspora: Memoirs, Essays, and Poetry* (Garland Publishing, 1999).

Charles Qianzhi Wu is professor of Chinese and humanities at Reed College, with a focus on twentieth-century literature and film.

Philip F. Williams is professor of Chinese literature and interdisciplinary studies at Arizona State University, where he teaches upper-level Chinese language and culture courses. He has published translations of Shen Congwen, Zhang Xianliang, Qian Zhongshu, Wang Meng, and Han Yu. His books include *Village Echoes: The Fiction of Wu Zuxiang* (Westview, 1993) and *Critical Essays on Chinese Women and Literature*, volumes 1–2 (Daw Shiang Publishing, 1999/2001).

Timothy C. Wong is professor of Chinese and director of the Center for Asian Studies at Arizona State University, where he has taught Chinese language and literature from 1974 to 1984, and since 1995. Wong publishes generally on traditional Chinese fiction and narratology. He has also published a number of translations of traditional Chinese fiction and poetry, as well as essays on twentieth-century Chinese literature.